Site Design and Construction Detailing

Site Design and Construction Detailing

SECOND EDITION

Theodore D. Walker

PDA PUBLISHERS CORPORATION

Library of Congress Catalog Card Number: 77-18668

ISBN 0-914886-32-0

PDA Publishers Corporation
1725 E. Fountain
Mesa, Arizona 85203

Contents

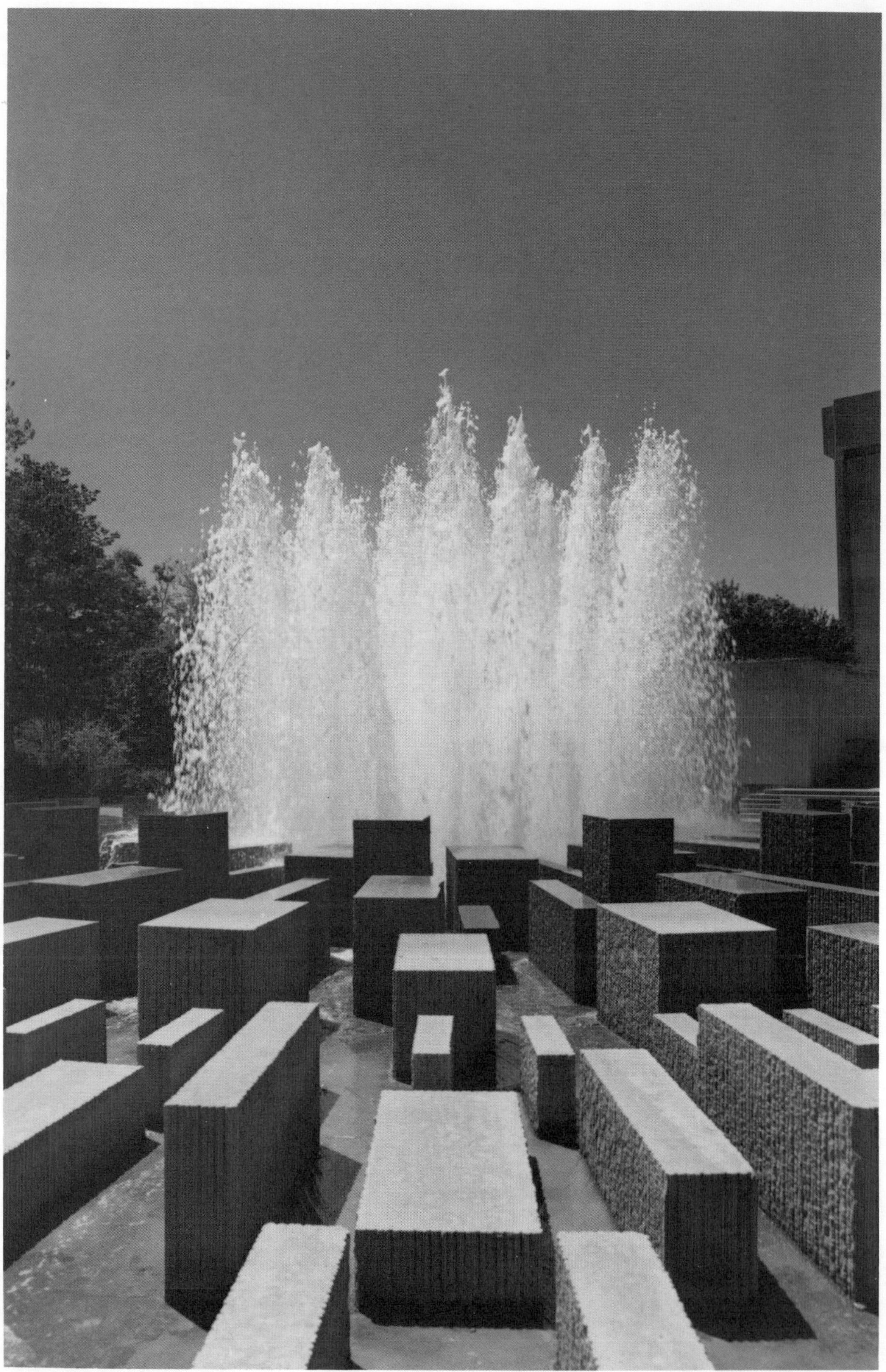

1

Site Design and Construction Detailing

ABOUT THIS BOOK

This is an introduction to, rather than a comprehensive reference of, the subject of site design and construction detailing. It is assumed that the reader is familiar with the basic principles of design and these will not be discussed. Design is illustrated in the drawings and photographs, and the focus of this book is on design implementation. It is intended that the material, facts, and concepts presented herein will generate greater creativity and innovation in the use of various construction materials.

Design is of little value, as far as a site is concerned, unless that design can be implemented. A concept is of little use to anyone until it is constructed and becomes functional. The designer needs to be familiar with construction materials, how they can be used, and how to prepare the necessary drawings for implementation, in order to effectively bring a design concept to fruition.

To serve as a base for the rest of the book, Chapter 2 discusses the nature of construction drawings, including their place in design and implementation, and Chapter 3 presents the characteristics, origin, and nature of construction materials. The remaining chapters briefly describe and illustrate design possibilities and construction details of paving, curbs, edging, steps, ramps, walls, fences, structures, play equipment, site furniture and fixtures, pools and fountains, and site utilities. Additional reading references and sources of information have been placed at the end of each chapter for those who wish to do additional research, and an appendix at the end of the book contains data of a miscellaneous nature.

Because this book is not complete, the reader is encouraged to research beyond these pages and generate new facts and ideas. New materials periodically appear on the market along with new ways and methods of using them. Much can be learned from observation, manufacturer's literature, suppliers, and knowledgeable and experienced contractors.

CAUTION

It is not intended that any drawings or ideas in this book be copied. Some designs, products, or processes may be patented or copyrighted, and copying will incur risks of violating the law. Techniques and processes illustrated may be applicable or limited to certain areas of this country and not practical, durable, or available elsewhere.

2

Preparation of Construction Drawings

WHY DRAWINGS?

Drawings typically provide a very essential portion, of the information which a contractor needs to construct a project. They are the visual means for showing the layout of the various elements which fit onto a site and their sizes and shapes. Combined with such other information on the drawings as elevations and detail sections (a visual representation of the vertical sizes) and shapes, the character and relationships of the materials being specified can be shown. It is not practical to include on the drawings all of the notes and information which determine the quality of materials and workmanship that must be a part of the projects. These, in general, become part of the written specifications which will accompany most drawings. Also included in written specifications are such items as bidding procedures, guarantees, and many other items of a descriptive nature which can only be covered in written form. The methods and techniques of writing specifications are not covered in this book but can be reviewed by reading the references at the end of this chapter.

It is important that all of the graphic representation be complete. All details should clearly show the contractor how the work is to be performed in terms of material, size and relationships. Identifying notes and other brief information not included in the specifications should be concise, clear, simple, easily understood, and free from any vagueness or chance of misunderstanding. It becomes quite easy for a site designer to assume that all contractors will be as familiar with the materials and their use as he is, but while some contractors will be extremely knowledgeable, not all of them will be. In order to secure uniform bidding and to ensure that the client or owner receives the maximum value for his dollar, extreme care should be taken to include every necessary item of information either on the drawings or in the written specifications.

DRAFTING TECHNIQUES

For the purposes of this book it is assumed that the user is familiar with drafting tools and equipment; therefore, the different types and their use will not be discussed here. It is also assumed that the user is familiar with freehand lettering. Several styles and techniques can be found as examples in the illustrations throughout this book. The use of mechanical lettering devices or transfer lettering is generally not considered practical or economical for most construction drawings; however, in some instances where details are standardized and sheets are prepared for long term use, mechanical lettering with ink may be considered practical. Transfer letters also fit into this category. A number of offices quite frequently use transfer letters for the preparation of a standardized title block which may be reproduced in large quantities as stock sheets or attached to the end of the drawing with transparent tape.

Machine generated lettering (such as "Kroytype"), which is applied to an adhesive backed transparent strip, will save considerable time over several other methods for titles and the major lettering for most drawings. The transparent tape can be easily pressed into place on a drawing, repositioned when necessary, or removed and replaced when corrections are required. It reduces the messiness caused by having to remove ink or erasing pencil and then redrafting over the altered area.

Drawings are nearly always prepared on transparent paper or polyester film, from which prints can be made for use by contractors, owners, and others involved in a project. Because the process of making prints involves the use of photo sensitive paper it is essential that the lines on the original drawings be crisp, sharp, and dark enough to produce a good image on the photo sensitive paper. If the lines are too light or too fuzzy the print will not be readable and the contractor will not be able to bid a project effectively or perform the work.

There is a hierarchy of line quality which aids in the readability of drawings. Those items which are most important should be drafted with the darkest lines, the lighter lines for those items which are less important. There can be a hierarchy of three or more line weights. For instance, building lines can be drawn with the darkest, sidewalks with medium line weight, and dimension lines with the lightest line weight.

In some situations it may be necessary to differentiate between existing materials and those which are proposed. The use of shading techniques can assist the draftsman in differentiating between the two. For crisp shading techniques, preprinted fine dot patterns on sheets with adhesive backing can be used. The sheets can be cut to the desired shape and applied directly to the drawing. Similar patterns in cross matching and textural patterns can also be secured in sheets with adhesive backing. Be careful not to become too artistic or place too much graphic symbolism on drawings, as it may detract from the purpose of the drawings — construct a project.

Most drawings will be prepared with pencils or ink. Pencil lines are much faster to draw and easier to erase, though they are also easier to smudge, except when plastic lead is used on polyester film. Ink is more difficult to use, even though it provides a much cleaner, crisper line that will not smudge, and it is difficult to erase, except on polyester film. With practice a draftsman or designer can easily acquire the skills for preparing excellent drawings using pencil or ink.

Color on original drawings will not reproduce as color on prints. Most photo sensitive papers will reproduce red much the same as black. Most print papers are not sensitive to light blue and this color can be used for guidelines and notes of a temporary nature which are not to be reproduced on prints to be given to the contractor. Other colors may or may not reproduce well depending upon the intensity of the pigment and the sensitivity of the print paper to that particular color.

Using a computer will speed up drafting time and reduce the drudgery of repetitive drawing especially when the same base drawing of a site is used several times such as for site layout, grading, drainage, other utilities, irrigation and planting plans. The computer is especially useful and time saving when it comes to revisions. New drawings without erasure marks can be prepared quickly and easily.

SCALE

Whether an engineer's or an architect's scale is used on a project depends upon the circumstances. Quite frequently an engineer's scale is used for large scale layout drawings where the scale may be one inch to ten feet or larger, such as one inch equaling fifty feet. Most drawings on which small scale plans, elevations, and sections are prepared may utilize a scale of ⅛-inch or smaller. It will not be unusual on sheets containing several construction details to utilize several different scales, such as ¾-inch equals 1 foot and 1½ inches equal 1 foot. Occasionally a detail may be drawn to full scale or actual size. The architect's scale with its fractions, inches, and feet lends itself for use with most construction materials, which are also dimensioned in the same units of measurement.

Some site work may require conversion from architect's scale to an engineer's scale, where changes of vertical elevation are involved. A set of steps may be dimensioned in details with inches and fractions for the convenience of the carpenter and other tradesmen who may be building the set of steps. However, for the use of the engineer who will be establishing the grades on the site, the top and bottom of the steps may be expressed in feet and decimals in order to be compatible with the rest of the grading on the site.

DECIMAL AND METRIC EQUIVALENTS OF INCHES

Inches	Decimals of a foot	Centimeters	Inches	Decimals of a foot	Centimeters
1	.0833	2.54	7	.5833	17.78
2	.1667	5.08	8	.6667	20.32
3	.2500	7.62	9	.7500	22.86
4	.3333	10.16	10	.8333	25.40
5	.4167	12.17	11	.9167	27.94
6	.5000	15.24	12	1.0000	30.48

DECIMAL AND METRIC EQUIVALENTS OF FRACTIONS

Fractions of an inch	Decimals of an inch	Millimeters	Fractions of an inch	Decimals of an inch	Millimeters
1/16	0.0625	1.588	9/16	0.5625	14.288
1/8	0.1250	3.175	5/8	0.6250	15.875
3/16	0.1875	4.763	11/16	0.6875	17.463
1/4	0.2500	6.350	3/4	0.7500	19.050
5/16	0.3125	7.938	13/16	0.8125	20.638
3/8	0.3750	9.525	7/8	0.8750	22.225
7/16	0.4375	11.113	15/16	0.9375	23.813
1/2	0.5000	12.700	1.0	1.0000	25.400

ORGANIZATION OF THE DRAWINGS

Many drawings will be complex enough that a cover sheet may be desirable, on which may be placed a map showing the location of the project and an index to the drawings within the set. Generally the layout sheets are placed first in a set, with plan, elevations, and construction details following, but this depends upon the nature of the project. Where several detail plans for different site elements are included, it is generally best to take a particular plan with its elevations, sections, and details and place them together, with the next site element plan, section, and details following. Most of the time, it is quite desirable that all of those drawings and details which are related be grouped together. This will reduce the chances of errors and omissions by the contractor, which would be present if he were forced to hunt back and forth through the drawings to find every detail.

From the standpoint of cost of printing, handling, and visual appearance, the drawings should all be on the same size original sheet. It is also recommended that uniform borders and title blocks be used on all drawings, though placement and size of title block can vary according to personal taste. The title block may be a simple rectangle located in the lower right-hand corner of a sheet, or it may extend the full length of the bottom of the sheet or the full width of the sheet end opposite the binding. It is desirable that all drawings be bound along the left-hand side and that sheet numbers be placed in the lower right-hand corner for convenience of all parties — site designer, owners, and contractors. Allow extra border space along the left-hand side for binding. Generally 1½ inches should be considered a minimum.

Besides an index of drawings on the cover sheet, other techniques of cross-referencing are desirable. Cross-references may be in the form of notes here and there among the drawings and layout plans or the various types of graphic symbols with a numbering system that identifies the detail number and the page on which it appears. Some of these techniques can be observed among the illustrations within this book and among the sample legends provided.

DIMENSIONS AND DIMENSIONING

Even though a detail may provide a good visual representation of how the finished site element might be constructed and the graphic

SCHEDULE OF DRAWINGS

1	SITE PLAN
2	GRADING PLAN
3	TEALTOWN ENTRY FEATURE
4	BROOKVIEW ENTRY FEATURE
5	PLAYLOT PLAN
6	PLAYLOT DETAILS
7	PLAYLOT DETAILS
8	SIGNS
9	LIGHTS & SIGNS
10	RECREATION AREA PLAN
11	RECREATION AREA DETAILS
12	TENNIS / MODELS PLAZA
13	PATIO / STAGE
14	ENTRANCE PLAZA
15	BOAT DOCK
16	PLANTING PLAN REFERENCE SHEET
17	PLANTING PLAN
18	RECREATION AREA PLANTING PLAN
19	PLANTING PLAN
20	ENTRY PLANTING PLAN
21	PLANTING PLAN
22	PLANTING PLAN

WILLOWBROOK PHASE I

RYAN HOMES INC · CINCINNATI

THE DESIGNERS FORUM INC.
1200 WEST HENDERSON ROAD
COLUMBUS · OHIO · 43220

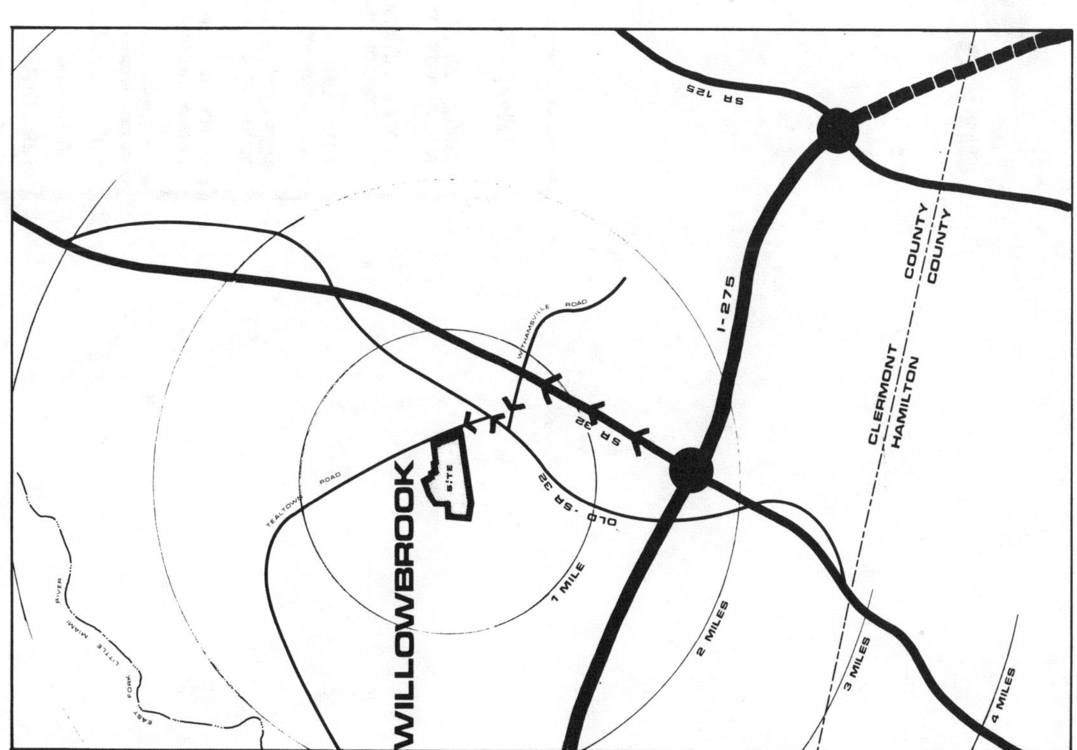

WILLOWBROOK
SITE
TEALTOWN ROAD
WITHAMSVILLE ROAD
SR 32
OLD SR 32
I-275
SR 125
CLERMONT COUNTY
HAMILTON COUNTY
EAST FORK LITTLE MIAMI RIVER
1 MILE
2 MILES
3 MILES
4 MILES

Figure 2.1 *Title sheet.*

The Designers Forum, Inc.

suddeth park

CITY OF AKRON
OHIO

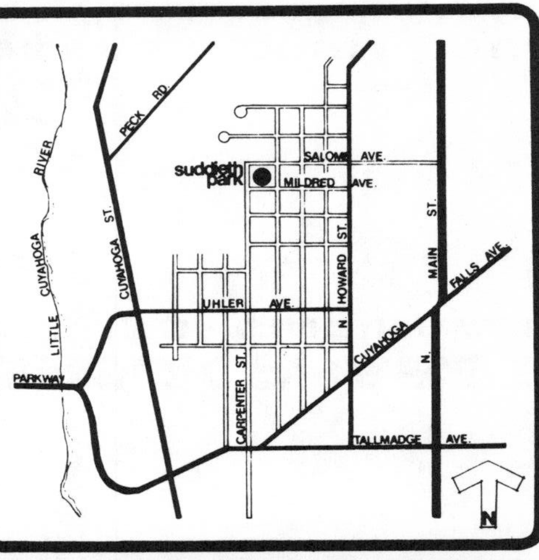

PECK RD.
RIVER
CUYAHOGA
LITTLE
PARKWAY
CUYAHOGA ST.
suddeth park
SALOME AVE.
MILDRED AVE.
UHLER AVE.
CARPENTER ST.
N HOWARD ST.
MAIN ST.
N.
FALLS AVE.
CUYAHOGA
TALLMADGE AVE.
N

JOHN S. BALLARD	**MAYOR**
DAVID W. ZIMMER DIRECTOR OF PUBLIC SERVICE	DATE
JAMES A. ALKIRE DIRECTOR OF PLANNING & URBAN RENEWAL	DATE
CHARLES E. SUSONG CITY ENGINEER	DATE
ROBERT D. ANDERSON MANAGER OF PARKS & RECREATION	DATE
GARY W. MEISNER DESIGN ADMINISTRATOR	DATE

TITLE SHEET	□
SURVEY	□
LAYOUT	1
GRADING	2
UTILITIES	3
PLANTING	4
DETAILS:	
STORAGE BUILDING	5,6
TRELLIS	7
TIMBER WALLS	8
PLAY EQUIPMENT	9,10
MISCELLANEOUS	11,12
UTILITIES	12

BONNELL AND ASSOCIATES
LANDSCAPE ARCHITECTS
129 SOUTH MAIN STREET
N. CANTON, OHIO 44720
TEL. 499-9944

MICHAEL D. YEAGLEY — ARCHITECT
234 DOGWOOD AVE.
LOUISVILLE, OHIO 44641 — TEL 875-8222

VICTOR MAYFIELD & ASSOCS. INC. — CONSULTING ENGINEERS
2556 CLEARVIEW AVE. N.W.
CANTON, OHIO 47718 — TEL. 452-4061

Figure 2.2 *Title sheet.*

Bonnell and Associates

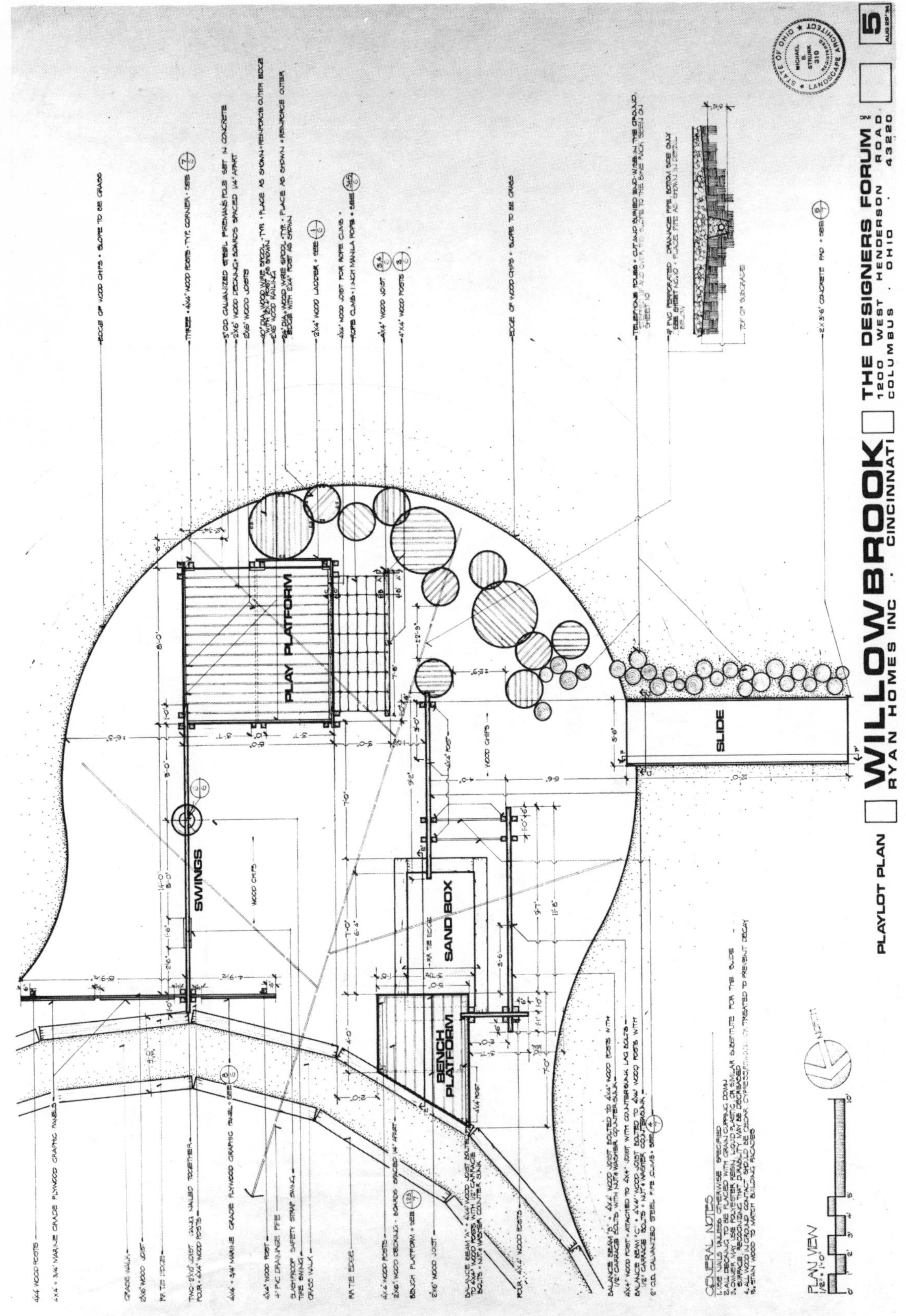
PLAYLOT PLAN
WILLOWBROOK
RYAN HOMES INC · CINCINNATI
THE DESIGNERS FORUM
1200 WEST HENDERSON ROAD
COLUMBUS · OHIO · 43220
SWINGS
PLAY PLATFORM
SAND BOX
BENCH PLATFORM
SLIDE
GENERAL NOTES
PLAN VIEW

Figure 2.3 *Layout plan.*

The Designers Forum, Inc.

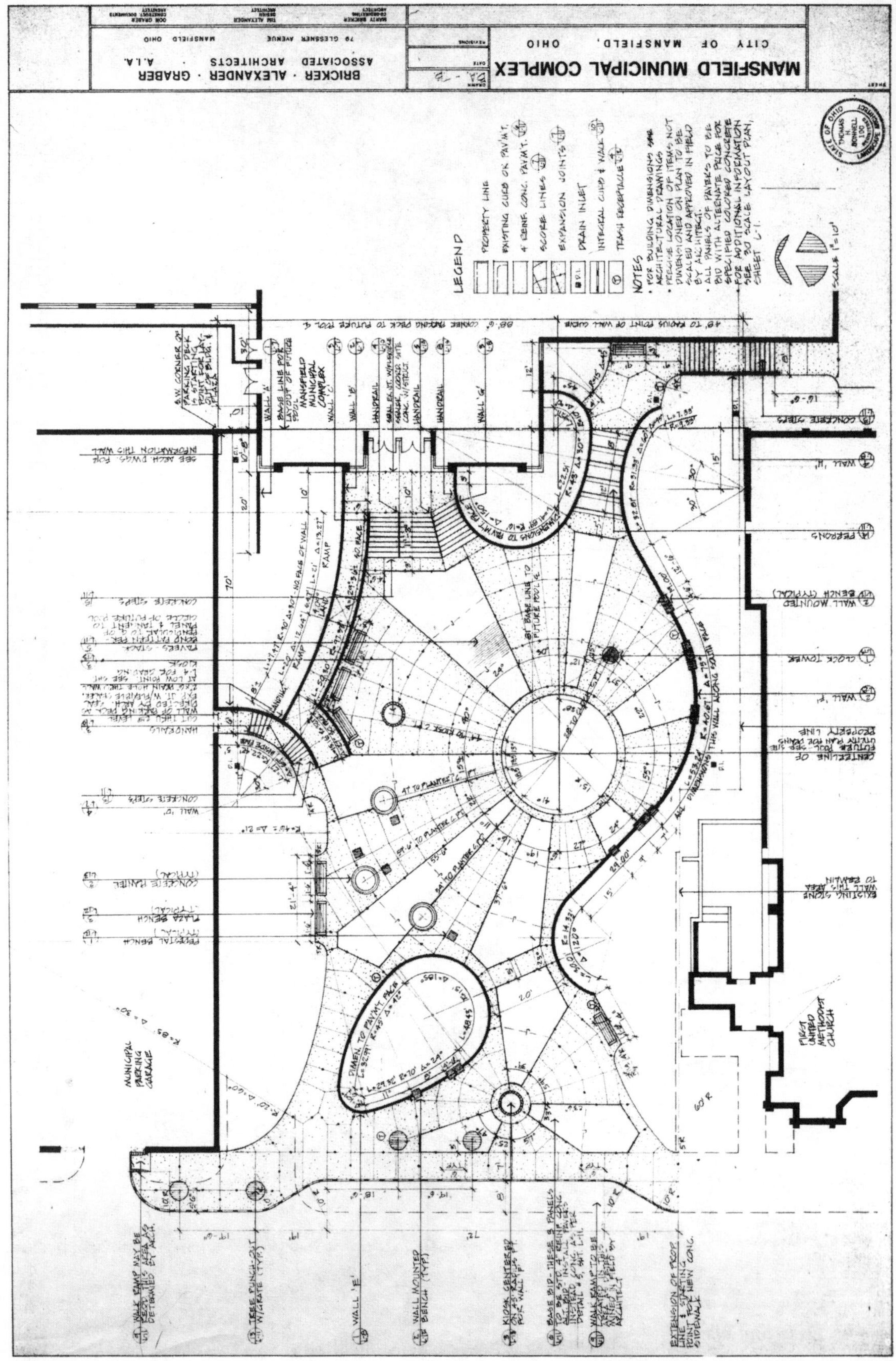

Figure 2.4 *Layout plan.* Bonnell and Associates

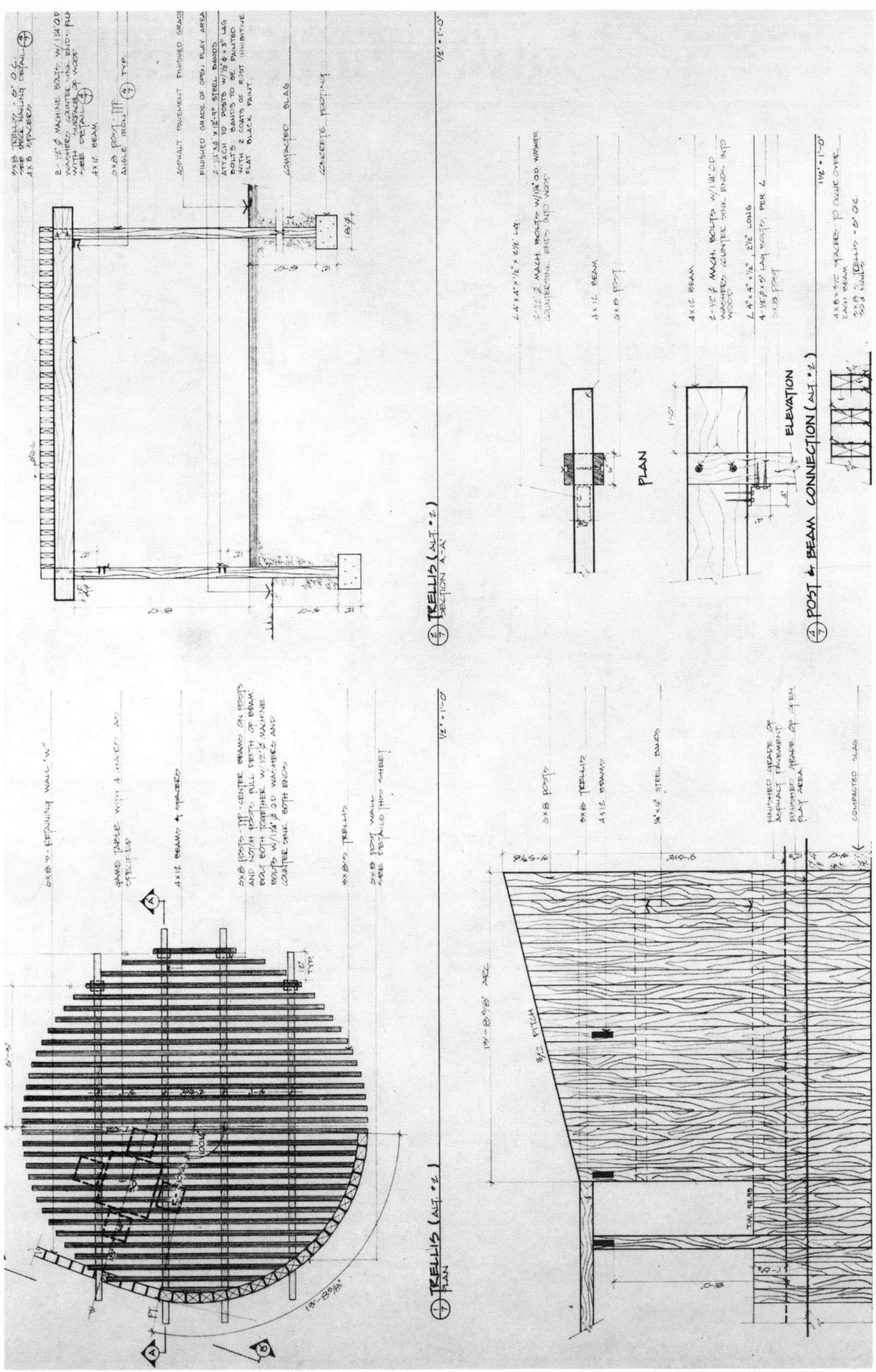

TRELLIS (ALT. 2)
PLAN
TRELLIS (ALT. 2)
SECTION A-A'
POST & BEAM CONNECTION (ALT. 2)
PLAN
ELEVATION

Figure 2.5 *Plan, elevations, sections and details on same sheet.*

Bonnell and Associates

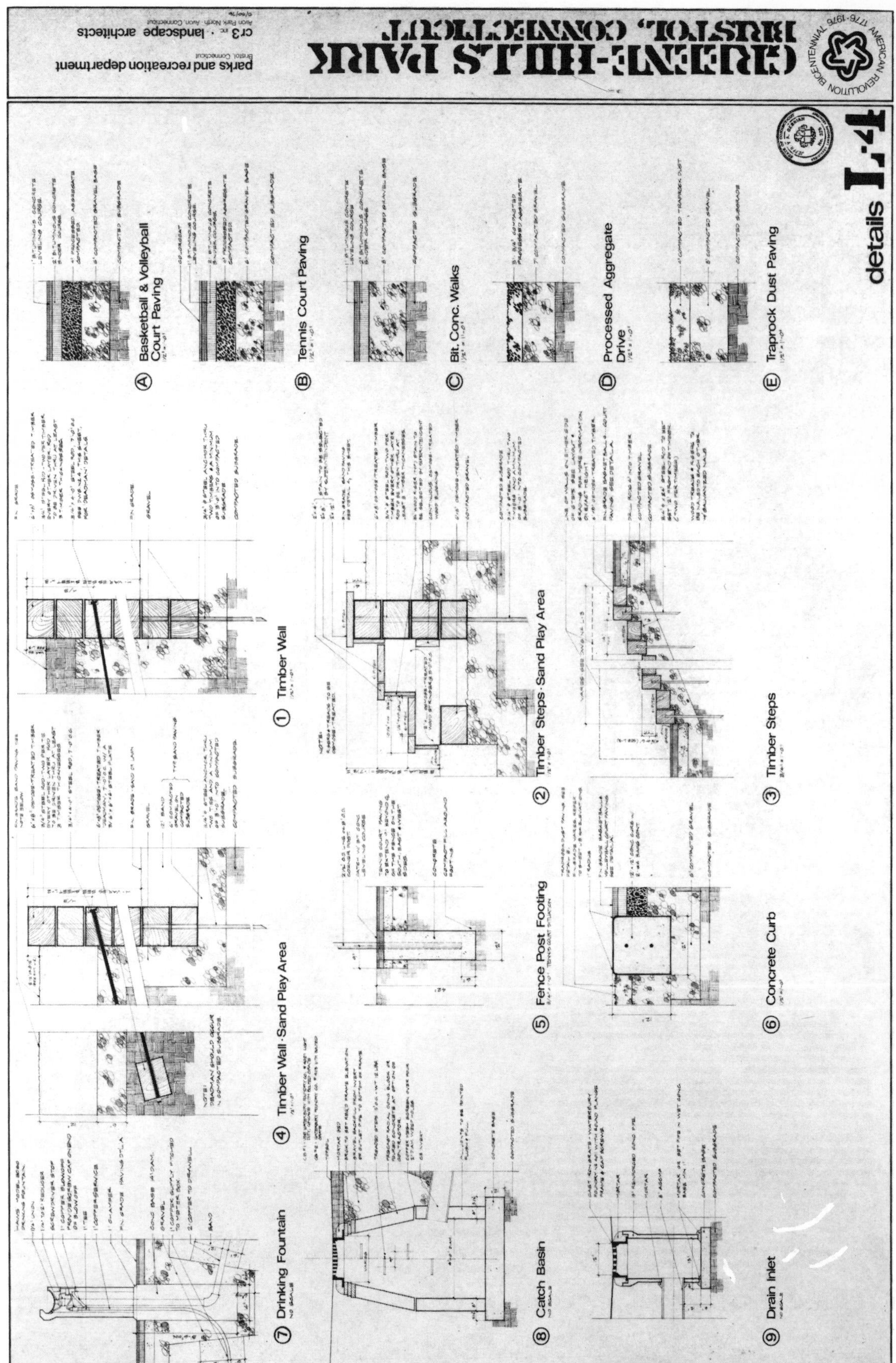

GREENE-HILLS PARK
BRISTOL, CONNECTICUT
parks and recreation department
Bristol, Connecticut
cr3 inc · landscape architects
AMERICAN REVOLUTION BICENTENNIAL 1776-1976
details
L-4
Ⓐ Basketball & Volleyball Court Paving
Ⓑ Tennis Court Paving
Ⓒ Bit. Conc. Walks
Ⓓ Processed Aggregate Drive
Ⓔ Traprock Dust Paving
① Timber Wall
② Timber Steps · Sand Play Area
③ Timber Steps
④ Timber Wall · Sand Play Area
⑤ Fence Post Footing
⑥ Concrete Curb
⑦ Drinking Fountain
⑧ Catch Basin
⑨ Drain Inlet

Figure 2.6 *Detail sheet.*

CR3, inc.

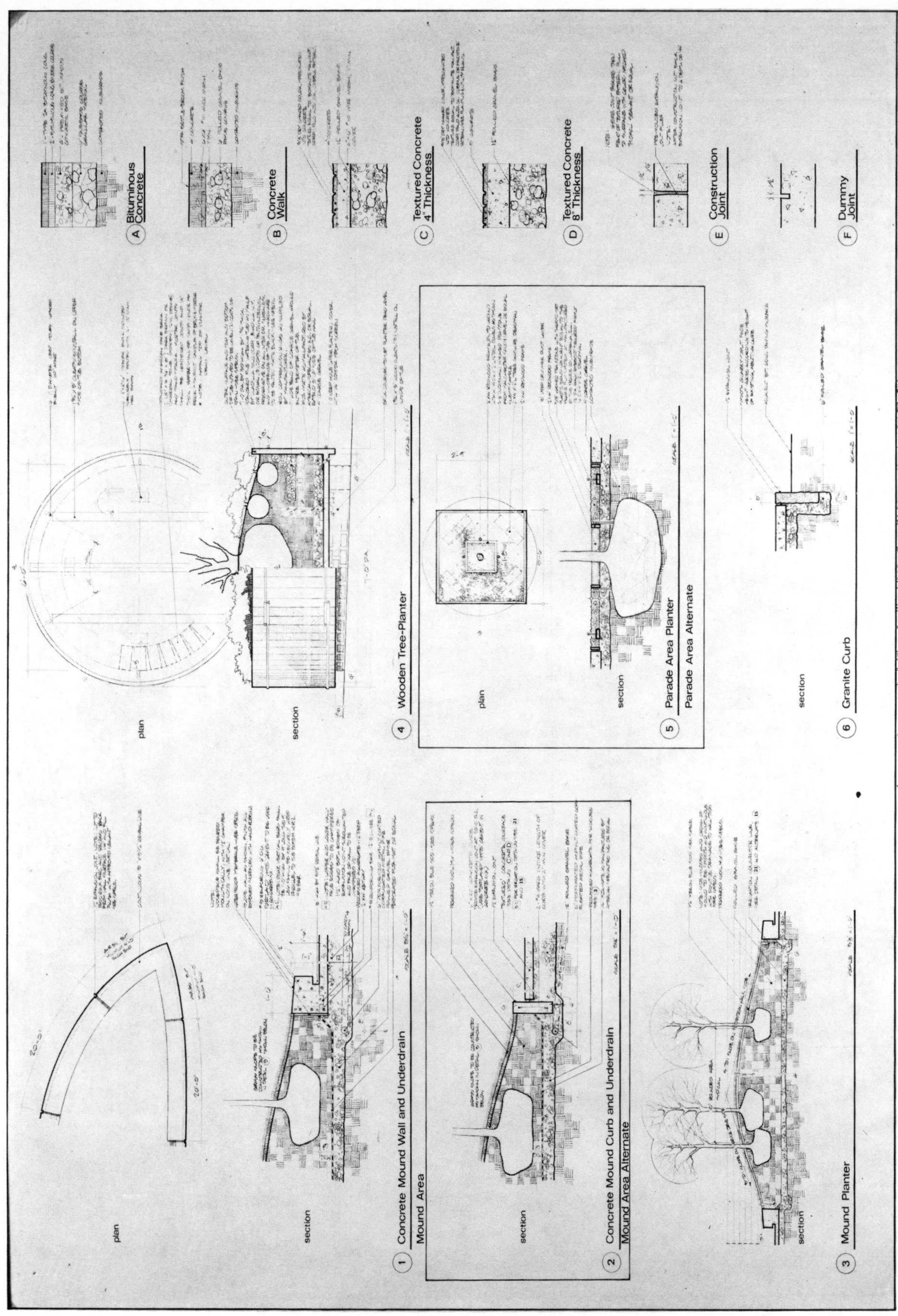
plan
section
1 Concrete Mound Wall and Underdrain
Mound Area
section
2 Concrete Mound Curb and Underdrain
Mound Area Alternate
section
3 Mound Planter
plan
section
4 Wooden Tree-Planter
plan
section
5 Parade Area Planter
Parade Area Alternate
section
6 Granite Curb
A Bituminous Concrete
B Concrete Walk
C Textured Concrete 4" Thickness
D Textured Concrete 8" Thickness
E Construction Joint
F Dummy Joint

Figure 2.7 *Detail sheet.*

Johnson and Dee

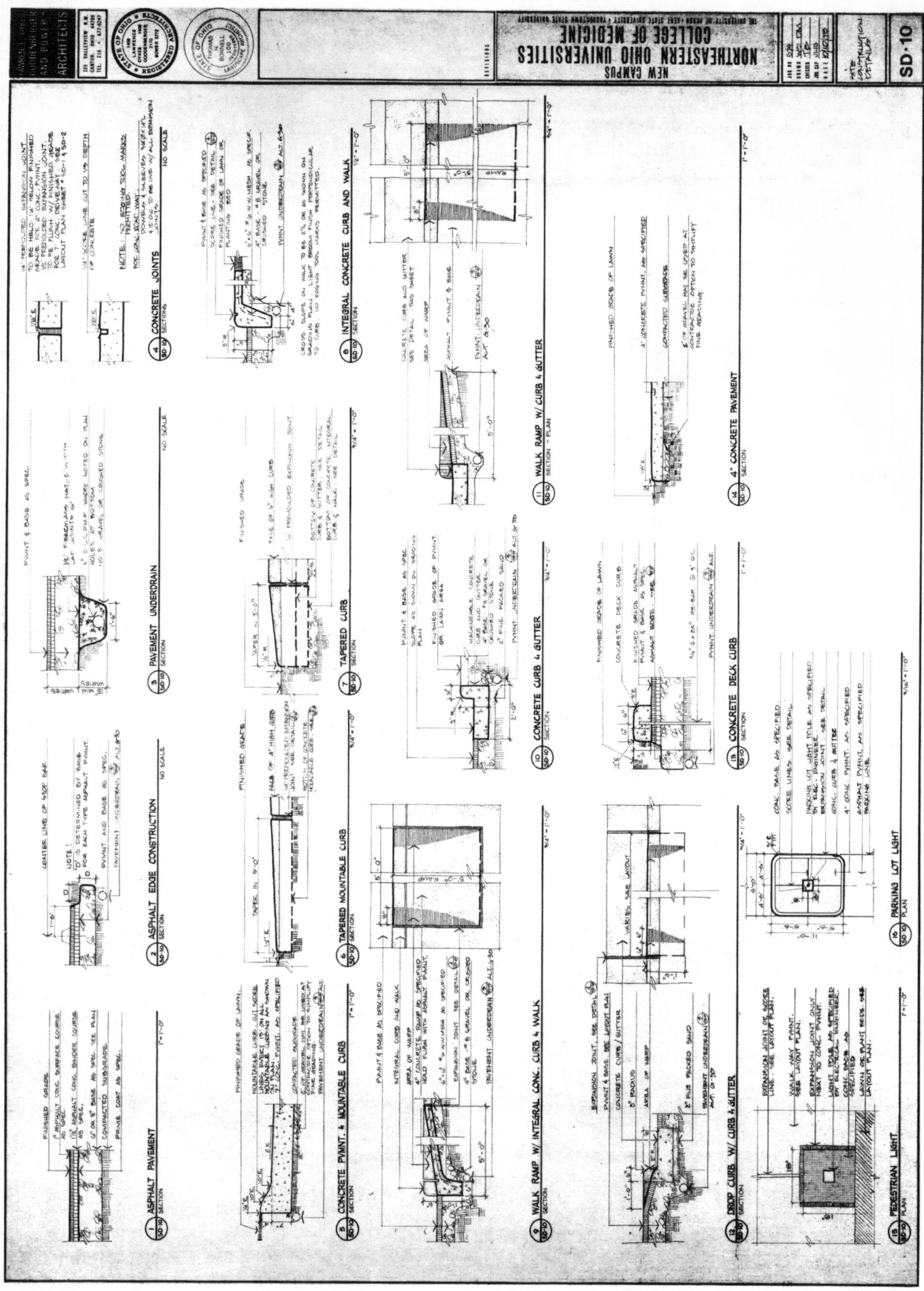
NEW CAMPUS
NORTHEASTERN OHIO UNIVERSITIES
COLLEGE OF MEDICINE
SD·10
ASPHALT PAVEMENT
ASPHALT EDGE CONSTRUCTION
PAVEMENT UNDERDRAIN
CONCRETE JOINTS
CONCRETE PVMNT. & MOUNTABLE CURB
TAPERED MOUNTABLE CURB
TAPERED CURB
INTEGRAL CONCRETE CURB AND WALK
WALK RAMP W/ INTEGRAL CONC. CURB & WALK
CONCRETE CURB & GUTTER
WALK RAMP W/ CURB & GUTTER
DROP CURB W/ CURB & GUTTER
CONCRETE DECK CURB
4" CONCRETE PAVEMENT
PEDESTRIAN LIGHT
PARKING LOT LIGHT

Figure 2.8 *Detail sheet.*

Bonnell and Associates

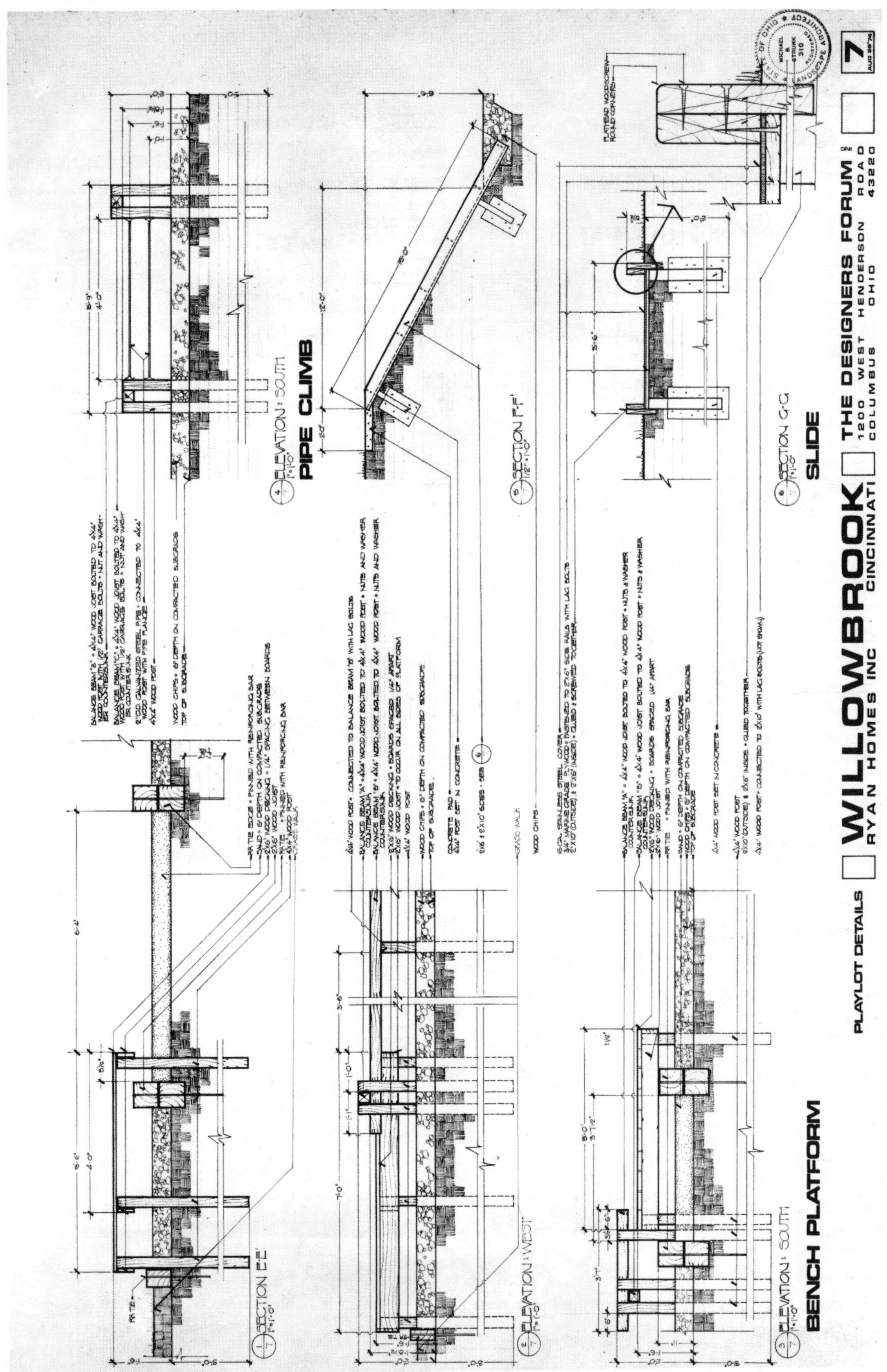
BENCH PLATFORM
PIPE CLIMB
SLIDE
PLAYLOT DETAILS
WILLOWBROOK
RYAN HOMES INC
CINCINNATI
THE DESIGNERS FORUM
1200 WEST HENDERSON ROAD
COLUMBUS OHIO 43220
7

Figure 2.9 *Detail sheet.*

The Designers Forum, Inc.

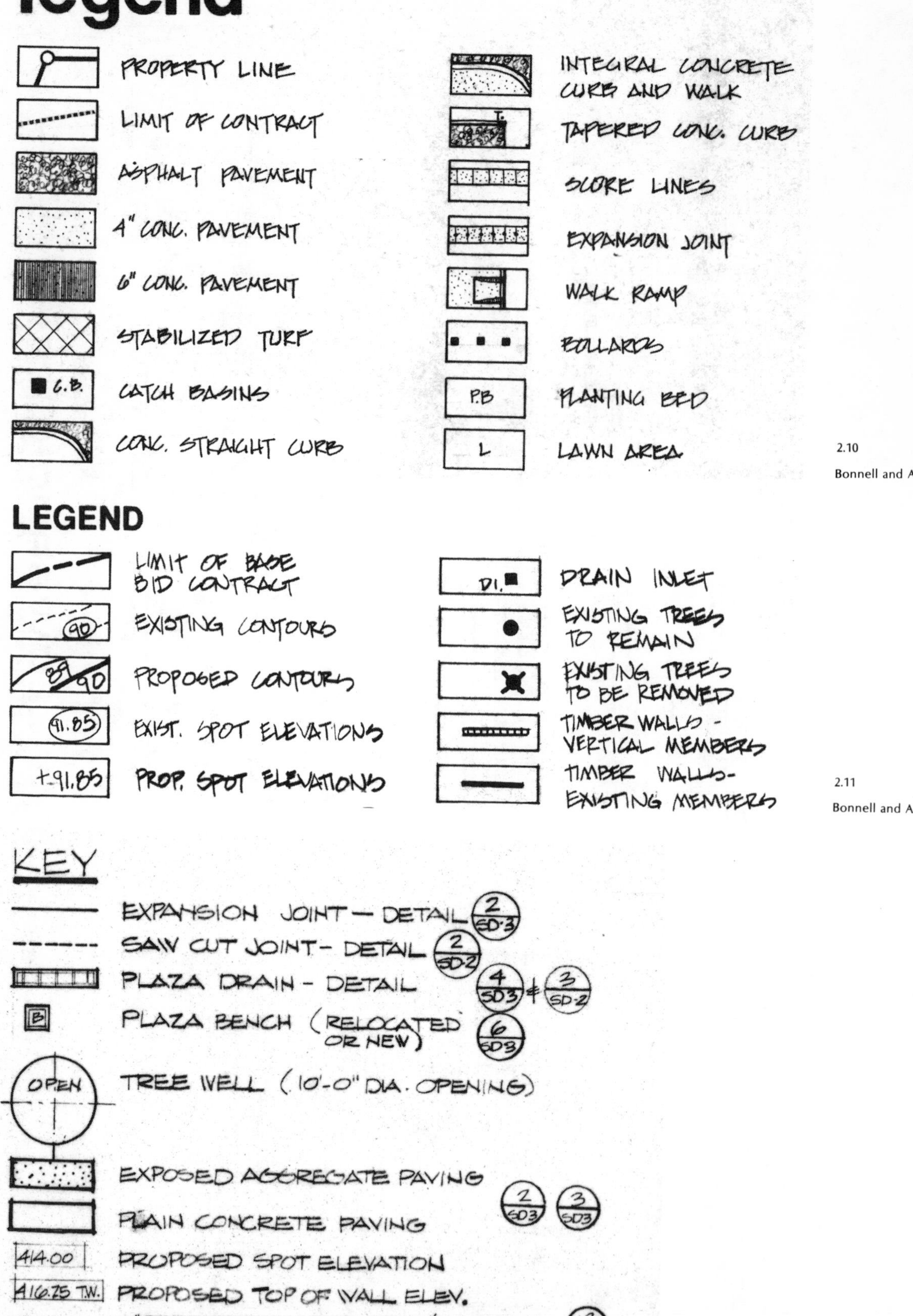
legend
PROPERTY LINE
LIMIT OF CONTRACT
ASPHALT PAVEMENT
4" CONC. PAVEMENT
6" CONC. PAVEMENT
STABILIZED TURF
C.B.
CATCH BASINS
CONC. STRAIGHT CURB
INTEGRAL CONCRETE CURB AND WALK
T.
TAPERED CONC. CURB
SCORE LINES
EXPANSION JOINT
WALK RAMP
BOLLARDS
P.B
PLANTING BED
L
LAWN AREA
LEGEND
LIMIT OF BASE BID CONTRACT
90
EXISTING CONTOURS
89
90
PROPOSED CONTOURS
91.85
EXIST. SPOT ELEVATIONS
+91.85
PROP. SPOT ELEVATIONS
DI.
DRAIN INLET
EXISTING TREES TO REMAIN
EXISTING TREES TO BE REMOVED
TIMBER WALLS - VERTICAL MEMBERS
TIMBER WALLS - EXISTING MEMBERS
KEY
EXPANSION JOINT — DETAIL 2/SD-3
SAW CUT JOINT - DETAIL 2/SD-2
PLAZA DRAIN - DETAIL 4/SD3 & 3/SD-2
B
PLAZA BENCH (RELOCATED OR NEW) 6/SD3
OPEN
TREE WELL (10'-0" DIA. OPENING)
EXPOSED AGGREGATE PAVING
PLAIN CONCRETE PAVING
2/SD3
3/SD3
414.00
PROPOSED SPOT ELEVATION
416.75 T.W.
PROPOSED TOP OF WALL ELEV.
6" PERFORATED DRAINTILE W/CLEANOUTS 12/SD4
DRAINAGE SWALE & DIRECTION OF FLOW

2.10
Bonnell and Associates

2.11
Bonnell and Associates

2.12
Johnson, Johnson and Roy

Figure 2.10 - 2.12 *Sample legends and symbols.*

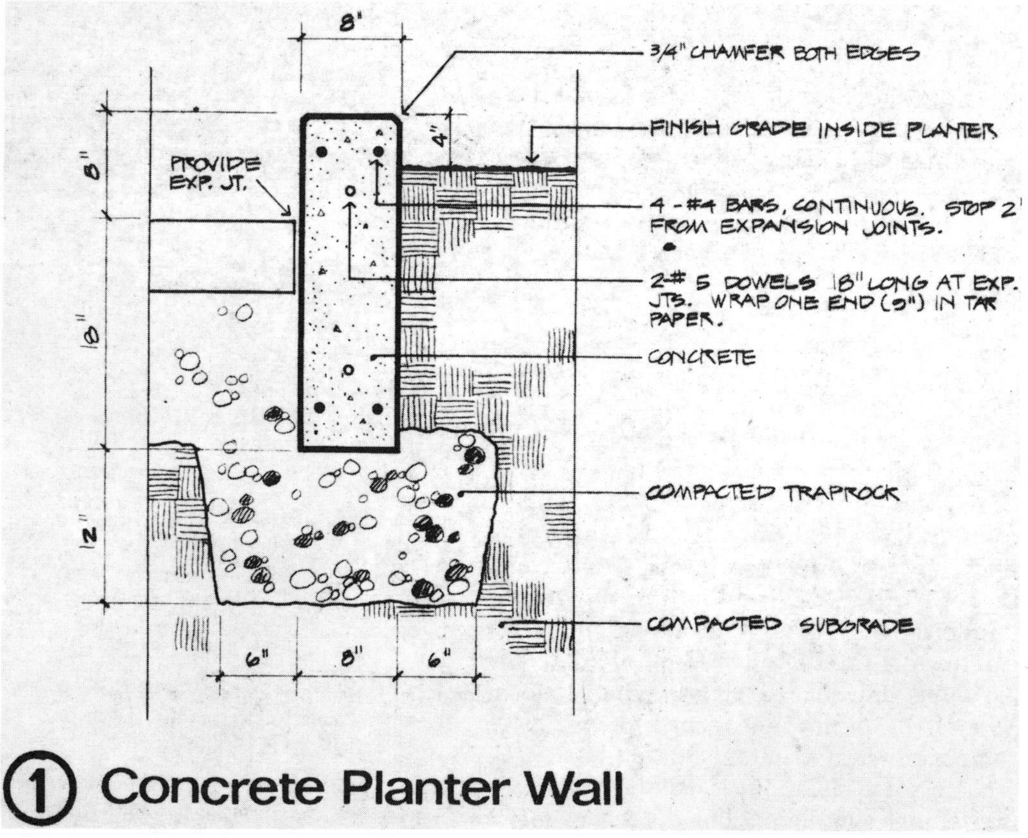
8'
3/4" CHAMFER BOTH EDGES
FINISH GRADE INSIDE PLANTER
PROVIDE EXP. JT.
4"
8"
4 - #4 BARS, CONTINUOUS. STOP 2' FROM EXPANSION JOINTS.
2-# 5 DOWELS 18" LONG AT EXP. JTS. WRAP ONE END (9") IN TAR PAPER.
18"
CONCRETE
COMPACTED TRAPROCK
12"
COMPACTED SUBGRADE
6"
8"
6"
1 Concrete Planter Wall

Figure 2.13 *Dimensioning of a detail.* CR3, inc.

symbols identify the materials, some additional assistance for the contractor is necessary. Dimension lines and figures can provide immediate information on the distances and sizes involved without the contractor's relying on a scale to obtain the same information. Print paper changes size with the moisture content of the air, leading to errors when a scale is used. Accurate dimensions provide a uniform base for bidding by all the contractors in the initial bidding process.

Dimension lines are best when they are solid lines placed parallel to the object being dimensioned. They should terminate at a similar weight line which projects at a 90-degree angle or perpendicular to the object being dimensioned. These light perpendicular lines should not touch the object but be separated by 1/16 of an inch. There are three different ways in which dimension lines may be drafted: 1) terminated by arrows at the project line, 2) terminated by intersecting the projection line, and use of a slash or dot at the intersection. The use of the slash is probably the fastest technique and is rather handy for tight situations where the arrows may become crowded or where the arrows, if they are too bold, may appear to be x's rather than arrows.

Dimension lines should never be criss-crossed or cross one another unless that is the only way that a particular object can be dimensioned. If this is the case, it is desirable to break one of the dimension lines as if it were crossing over or under the other dimension lines.

Dimension lines can be organized so that they are neat in appearance. If possible, organize them in groups on two sides of the object, such as the left side and the top. Dimension lines may appear in a series with one to three sets along the side of an object. The first group may be identifying small objects close to each other, the second set may identify some center lines occurring along the object being dimensioned, and the last will be an overall dimension from end to end. When sets are used, it is essential that some double checking be done to be sure that the total of all of the small dimensions equals the overall dimension. Through additional checking it is possible to avoid some serious errors.

Dimensions for layout drawings, particularly site plans, may be shown by utilizing one of several different methods. One approach is to develop reference or base lines from a known point on the site that is stable and will always be there regardless of the construction scheduled to occur on the site. The base lines may run in one, two, or more directions and all additional dimension lines may be referred back to these base lines.

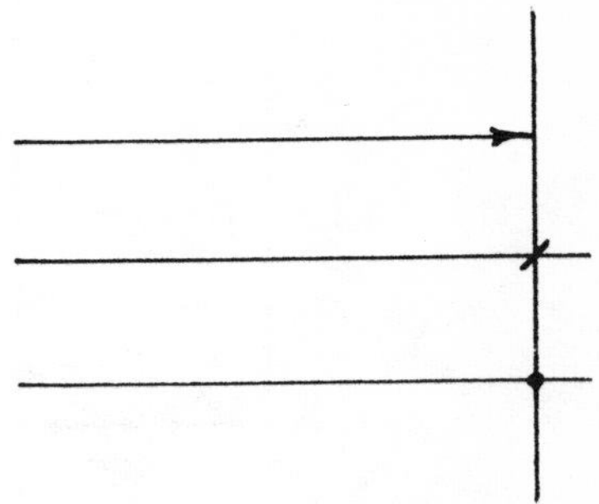

Figure 2.14 *Three techniques for terminating a dimension line.*

Another technique is the grid system. The grids may be in 100-foot squares (or another module), beginning again at some known point. Some type of monument can be installed to ensure long term stability. Grid systems may be desirable for large scale projects such as campuses, where the grids may be a permanent dimensioning system to which all future work is referenced, including the identification of underground utilities, renovations, and repairs. Contractors can be required to reference their "as-built" drawings to this grid system to form a part of the permanent record for use by the campus physical plant department.

In some situations it may be desirable to utilize angles in dimensioning. Angles may be especially useful in the layout of sidewalks and any other angled design lines. Angles are identified by degrees, minutes, and seconds and may be combined with some of the other layout dimensioning techniques. Circles or parts thereof may be identified by the use of a radius point which is tied into some other dimensioning system. A radius may be abbreviated to a simple capital "R" preceding the dimension figure or a capital "D" for diameter.

A fourth dimensioning system useful for irregular curving lines that cannot be identified with radii is offsets. Offsets can be used with base lines spaced at regular intervals for ease in staking on the ground. If they are uniformly developed and not too far apart, the same lines can be created on the ground as was created on the drawing.

It is important when dimensioning wood that the figures reflect finished dimensions rather than nominal dimensions. For instance, a note on a detail may identify a piece of wood as a 2 x 4 but the actual dimensions would reflect the finished dimensions of 1½ inches x 3½ inches. If the drawing is not drafted to the finished dimensions, it is possible that serious errors might result and the project will not be the same as the designer intended.

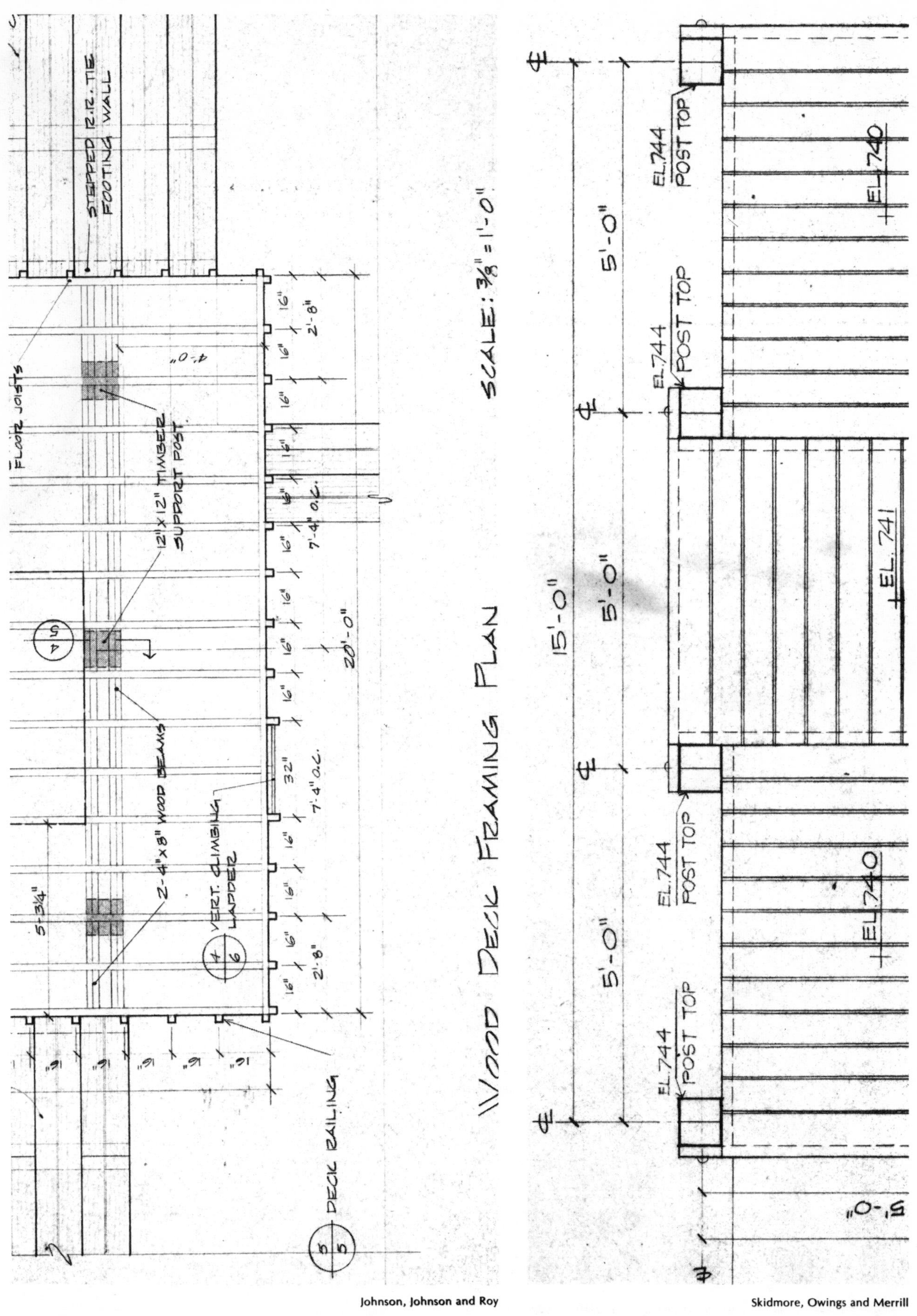
STEPPED R.R. TIE FOOTING WALL
FLOOR JOISTS
12" X 12" TIMBER SUPPORT POST
2-4"x8" WOOD BEAMS
VERT. CLIMBING LADDER
DECK RAILING
4'-0"
2'-8"
7'-4" O.C.
20'-0"
32"
5-3¼"
16"
WOOD DECK FRAMING PLAN
SCALE: 3/8" = 1'-0"
15'-0"
5'-0"
EL.744
POST TOP
EL.740
EL.741

Johnson, Johnson and Roy

Skidmore, Owings and Merrill

Figure 2.15 *Dimensioning techniques.*

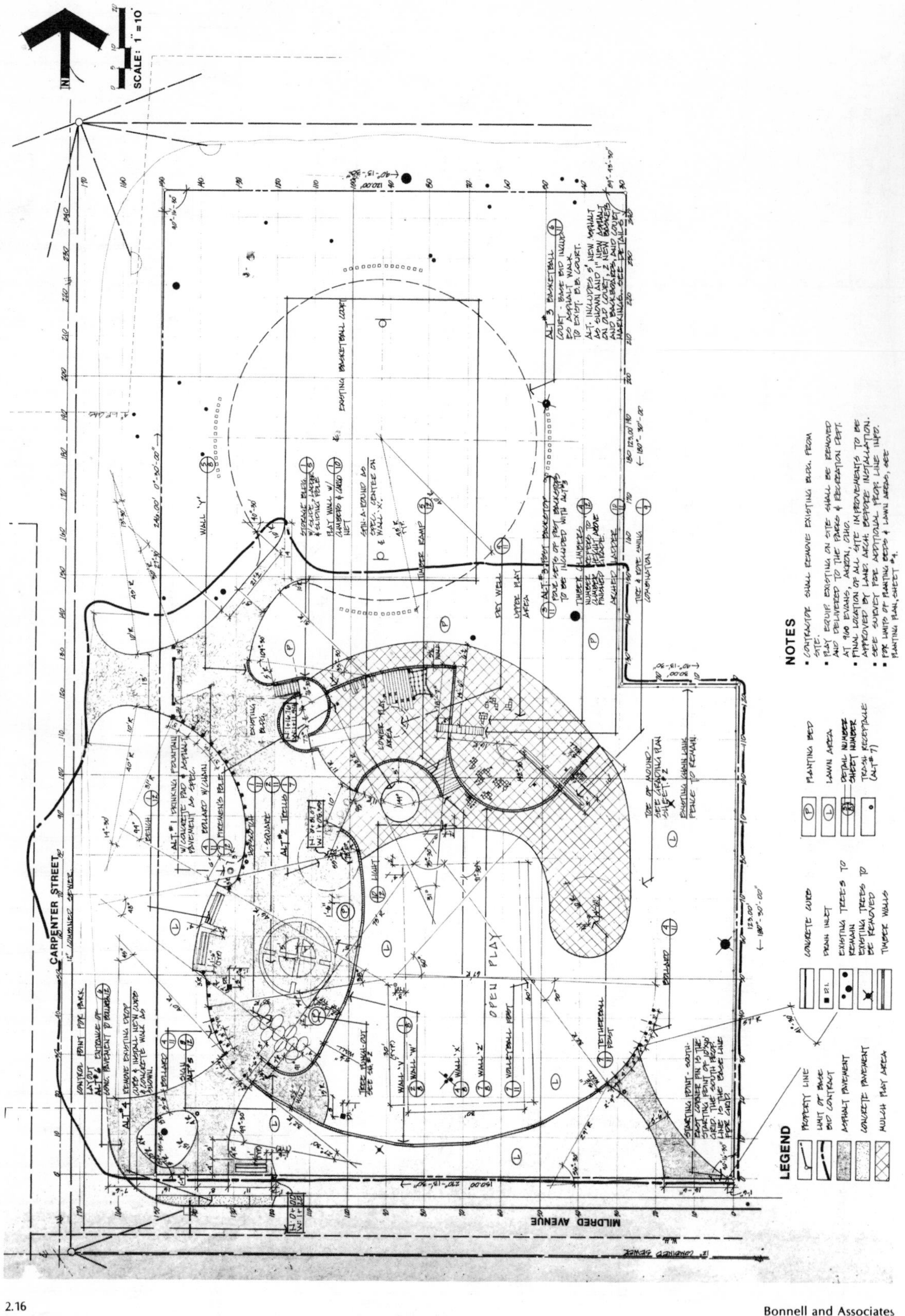

2.16

Bonnell and Associates

Figures 2.16 - 2.17 *Dimensioning using grid system, angles, radii, etc.*

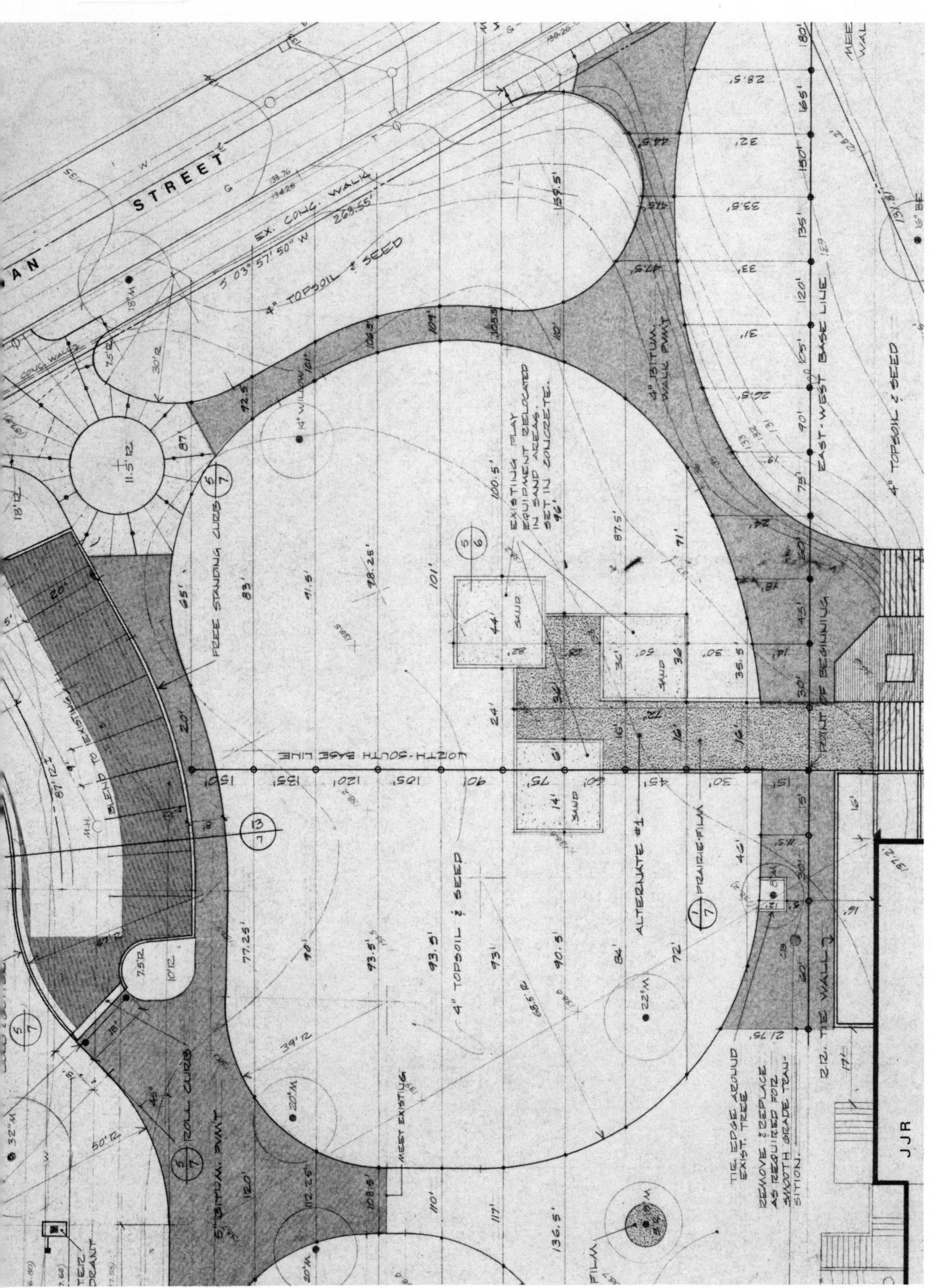
STREET
EX. CONC. WALK
S 03° 57' 50" W 263.55'
4" TOPSOIL & SEED
4" BITUM. WALK PVMT
EXISTING PLAY EQUIPMENT RELOCATED IN SAND AREAS. SET IN CONCRETE.
FREE STANDING CURB
EAST-WEST BASE LINE
NORTH-SOUTH BASE LINE
POINT OF BEGINNING
SAND
BLEND TO EXISTING
ALTERNATE #1
PRAIRIE FILM
4" TOPSOIL & SEED
ROLL CURB
5" BITUM. PVMT
MEET EXISTING
TIE EDGE AROUND EXIST. TREE
REMOVE & REPLACE AS REQUIRED FOR SMOOTH GRADE TRANSITION.
R.R. TIE WALL
JJR
Johnson, Johnson and Roy

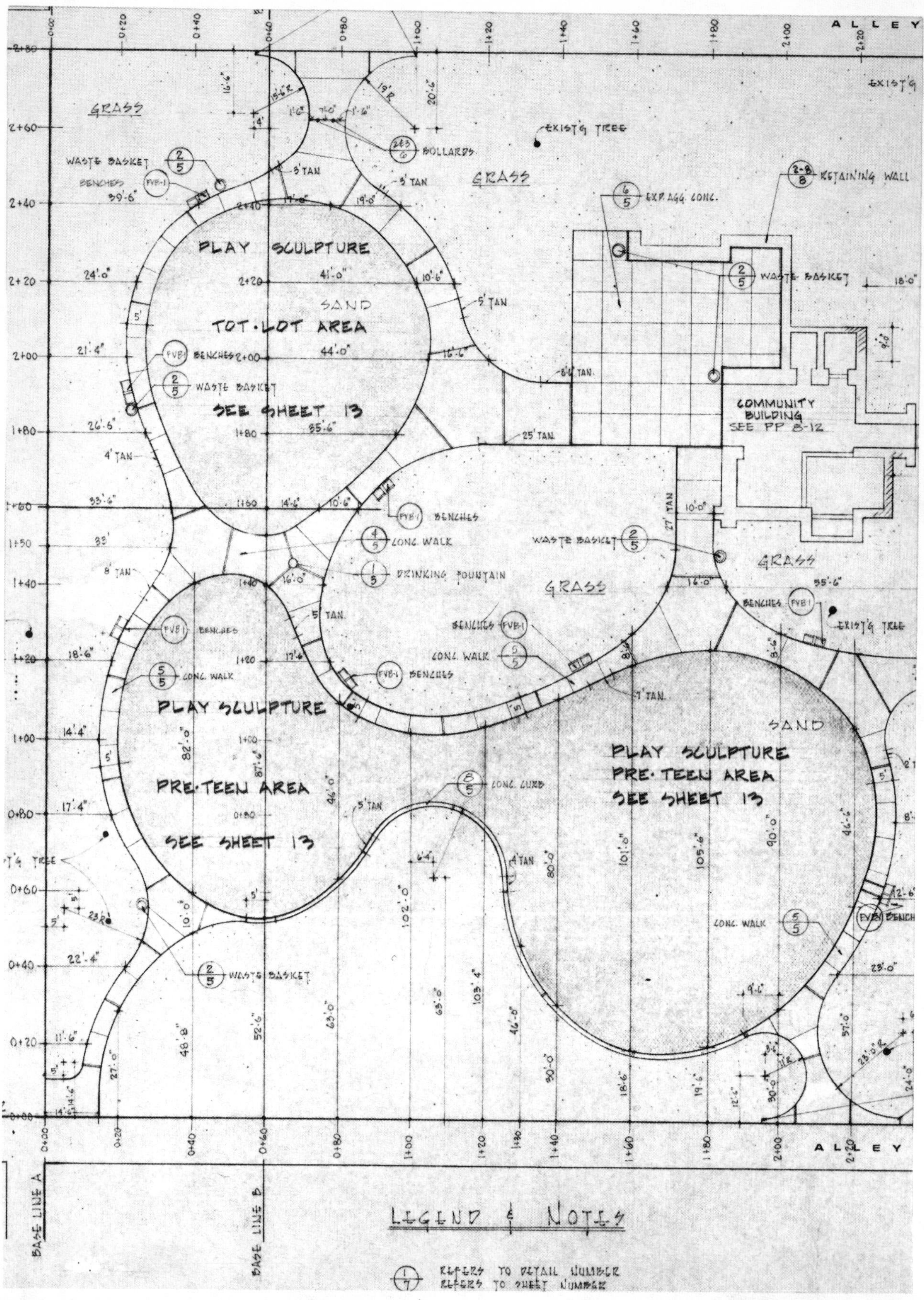
ALLEY
GRASS
WASTE BASKET
BENCHES
BOLLARDS
EXIST'G TREE
PLAY SCULPTURE
SAND
TOT·LOT AREA
SEE SHEET 13
EXP. AGG. CONC.
RETAINING WALL
WASTE BASKET
COMMUNITY BUILDING
SEE PP 8-12
CONC. WALK
DRINKING FOUNTAIN
PRE·TEEN AREA
CONC. CURB
BASE LINE A
BASE LINE B
LEGEND & NOTES
REFERS TO DETAIL NUMBER
REFERS TO SHEET NUMBER

Figure 2.18 *Dimensioning using base lines and offsets.*

Browning-Day-Pollak-Associates-Inc.

DETAILING AND SYMBOLS

A construction detail may be an enlarged portion of the plan, an elevation view, or a section through part or all of the same site element. Under some circumstances, though more time consuming to draw, an isometric may provide a better explanation of how an object or site element is to appear when constructed.

In order to provide a systematic layout of details on the sheets, it is best to rough them out individually and place the rough sketches underneath the tracing for the final draft.

The drafting of details also requires a hierarchy of line values, with the heaviest lines used for the object, lighter lines for material symbols, and lightest for dimension lines.

Most materials used in construction details can be identified readily with certain symbols. Symbols, while varying somewhat in their graphic character, still have a general appearance which can be readily identified by most contractors, and these symbols generally are standardized. However, to be sure that each symbol is adequately understood by those who are using the drawings it is desirable to reproduce the symbols in a legend.

Some details may be used over and over again for several different projects. These may include standard curb, walk, and catch basin details required by local governmental units. Drafting time can be saved by preparing a master detail with ink, reproducing it onto an adhesive backed transparent polyester film (such as "Stikybak") in an office photocopier, and applying it to a drawing. Notes and lists of materials can be prepared by a word processor or typewriter onto this same film and applied to a drawing thus saving much time in comparison to hand lettering. When changes occur it is very easy to remove the film, prepare a new film in the word processor and reapply.

To reduce the amount of space required for notes on drawings and to minimize the tediousness of lettering, some abbreviations for certain words can be used. Not all of these abbreviations may be readily understood, however, and some may need to be identified in the legend in order to avoid misunderstanding.

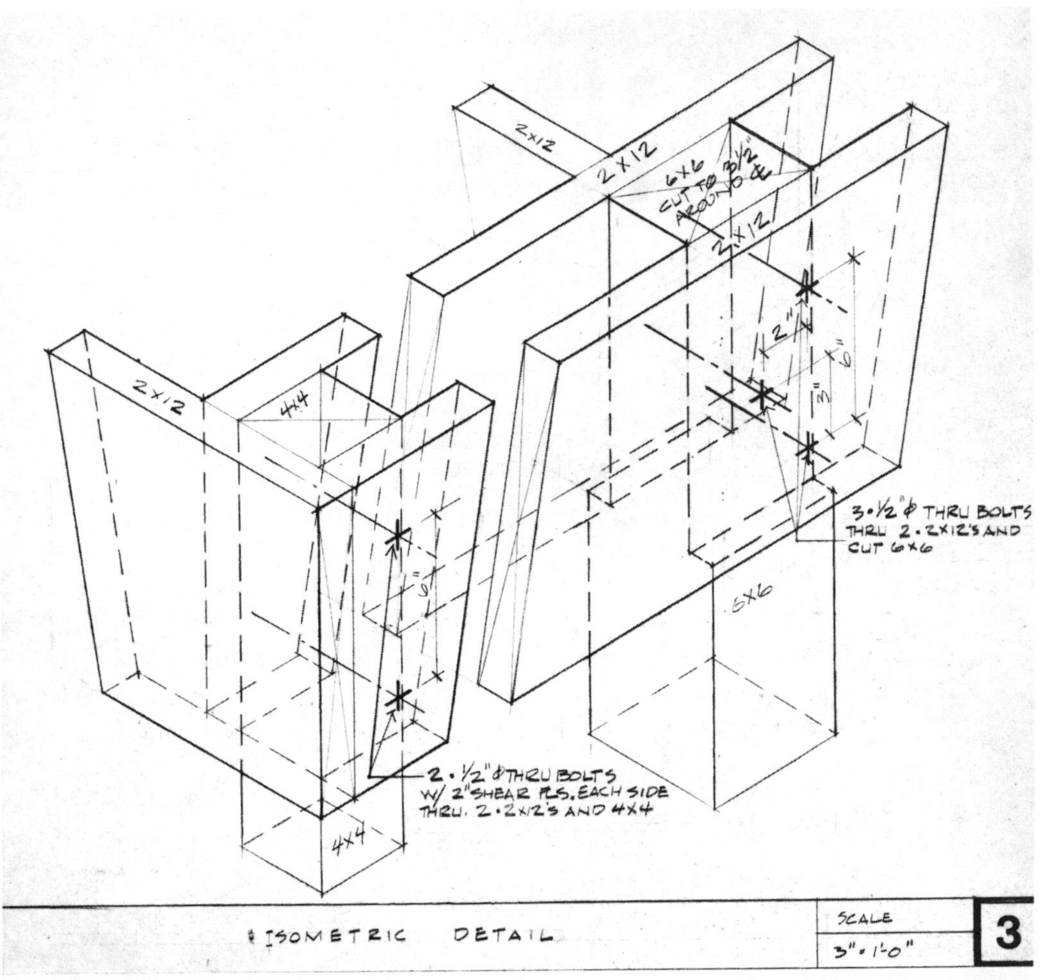

2x12
2x12
2x12
2x12
4x4
4x4
6x6
3 • 1/2" ϕ THRU BOLTS THRU 2 • 2X12'S AND CUT 6X6
2 • 1/2" ϕ THRU BOLTS W/ 2" SHEAR PLS. EACH SIDE THRU. 2 • 2X12'S AND 4X4
ISOMETRIC DETAIL
SCALE
3" = 1'-0"
3

Figure 2.19 *Isometric Detail.*

Skidmore, Owings and Merrill

SYMBOLS FOR MATERIALS

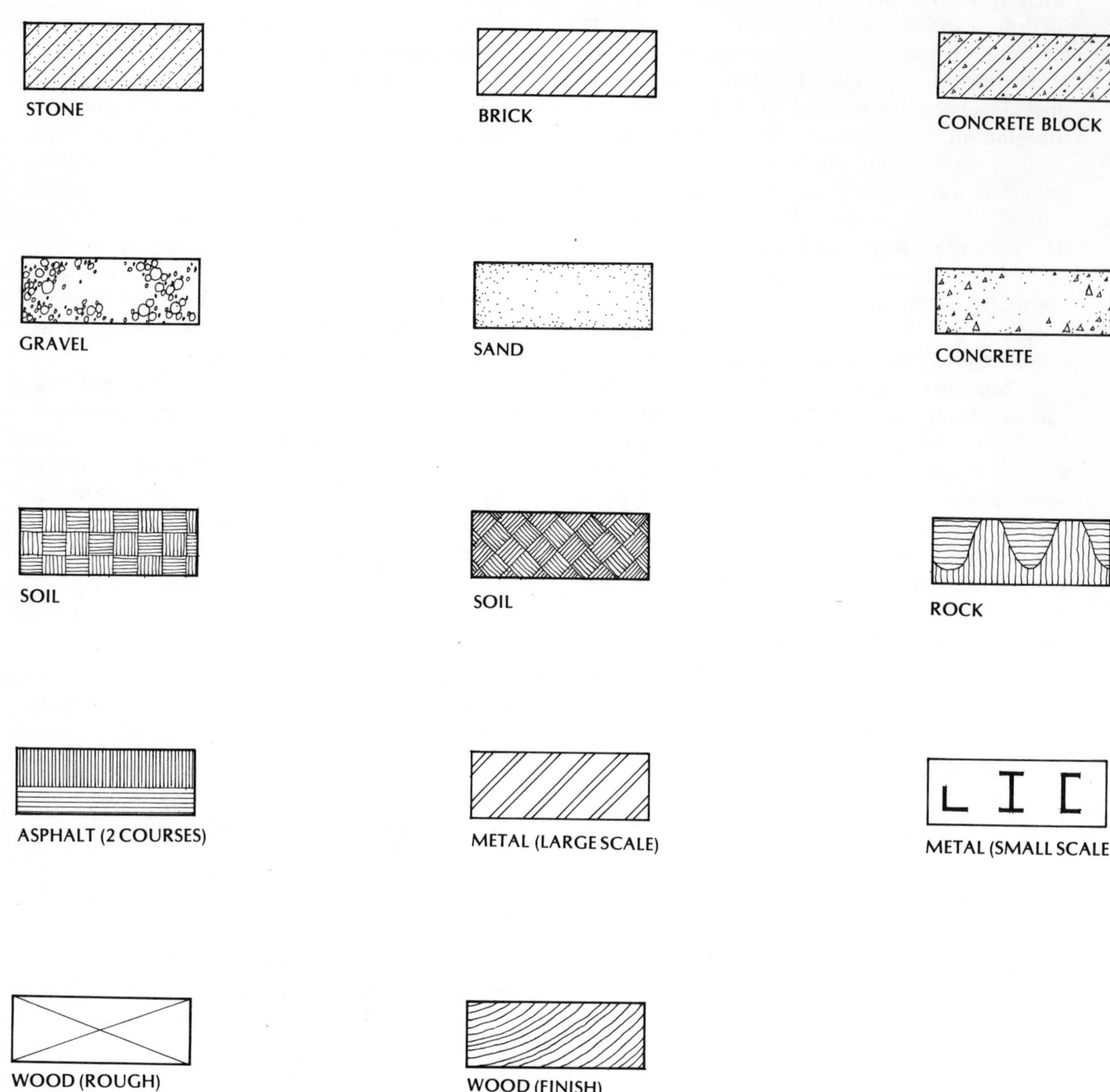
STONE
BRICK
CONCRETE BLOCK
GRAVEL
SAND
CONCRETE
SOIL
SOIL
ROCK
ASPHALT (2 COURSES)
METAL (LARGE SCALE)
METAL (SMALL SCALE)
WOOD (ROUGH)
WOOD (FINISH)

LIST OF ABBREVIATIONS

ABV	*above*
ADD	*addendum*
ADH	*adhesive*
ADJ	*adjacent*
ADJT	*adjustable*
AGG	*aggregate*
ALT	*alternate*
AL	*aluminum*
ANC	*anchor, anchorage*
ANOD	*anodized*
APX	*approximate*
ARCH	*architect (ural)*
AD	*area drain*
ASPH	*asphalt*
BIT	*bituminous*
BLK	*block*
BD	*board*
BS	*both sides*
BW	*both ways*
BOT	*bottom*
BRK	*brick*
BBZ	*bronze*
BLDG	*building*
BUR	*built up roofing*
BBD	*bulletin board*
CAD	*cadmium*
CI	*cast iron*
CIPC	*cast-in-place concrete*
CST	*cast stone*
CB	*catch basin*
CK	*calk(ing) caulk(ing)*
CEM	*cement*
PCPL	*cement plaster (portland)*
CM	*centimeter(s)*
CER	*ceramic*
CT	*ceramic tile*
CMT	*ceramic mosaic (tile)*
CHAM	*chamfer*
CR	*chromium (plated)*
CIR	*circle*
CIRC	*circumference*
CLR	*clear (ance)*
COMB	*combination*
COMPO	*composition (composite)*
COMP	*compress (ed), (ion), (ible)*
CONC	*concrete*
CMU	*concrete masonry unit*
CX	*connection*
CONST	*construction*
CONT	*continuous or continue*
CONTR	*contract (or)*
CLL	*contract limit line*
CJT	*control joint*
CPR	*copper*
CORR	*corrugated*
CS	*countersink*
CTSK	*countersunk screw*
CRS	*course(s)*
CRG	*cross grain*
CFT	*cubic foot*
CYD	*cubic yard*
DP	*dampproofing*
DL	*dead load*
DEM	*demolish, demotion*
DEP	*depressed*
DTL	*detail*
DIAG	*diagonal*
DIAM	*diameter*
DIM	*dimension*
DIV	*division*
DS	*downspout*
D	*drain*
DT	*drain tile*
DWG	*drawing*
DF	*drinking fountain*
EF	*each face*
E	*east*
ELEC	*electric(al)*
EL	*elevation*
ENC	*enclosure(ure)*
EQ	*equal*
EQP	*equipment*
EST	*estimate*
EXCA	*excavate*
EXG	*existing*
EB	*expansion bolt*
EXP	*exposed*
EXT	*exterior*
EXS	*extra strong*
FB	*face brick*
FOC	*face of concrete*
FOF	*face of finish*
FOM	*face of masonry*
FAS	*fasten, fastener*
FN	*fence*
FIN	*finish(ed)*
FFL	*finished floor line*
FBRK	*fire brick*
FPL	*fireplace*
FLG	*flashing*
FHMS	*flathead machine screw*
FHWS	*flathead wood screw*
FLX	*flexible*
FLR	*floor(ing)*
FD	*floor drain*
FJT	*flush joint*
FTG	*footing*
FND	*foundation*
FR	*frame(d), (ing)*
FS	*full size*
FBO	*furnished by others*
FUT	*future*
GA	*gage, gauge*
GV	*galvanized*
GI	*galvanized iron*
GP	*galvanized pipe*
GSS	*galvanized steel sheet*
GC	*general contract(or)*
GD	*grade, grading*
GRN	*granite*
GVL	*gravel*
GT	*grout*
HDW	*hardware*
HWD	*hardwood*
HDR	*header*
HD	*heavy duty*
HT	*height*
HX	*hexagonal*
HES	*high early-strength cement*
HK	*hook(s)*
HOR	*horizontal*
HB	*hose bibb*
INCL	*include(d), (ing)*
ID	*inside diameter*
INT	*interior*
INV	*invert*
IPS	*iron pipe size*
JT	*joint filler*
J	*joist*
KO	*knockout*
LAD	*ladder*
LB	*lag bolt*
LH	*left hand*
L	*length*
LT	*light*
LC	*light control*
LW	*lightweight*
LWC	*lightweight concrete*
LMS	*limestone*
LL	*live load*
LVR	*louver*
LPT	*low point*
MB	*machine bolt*
MI	*malleable iron*
MH	*manhole*
MFR	*manufacture(er)*
MRB	*marble*
MAS	*masonry*
MO	*masonry opening*
MTL	*mateial(s)*
MAX	*maximum*
MECH	*mechanic(al)*
MED	*medium*
MBR	*member*
MMB	*membrane*
MET	*metal*
M	*meter(s)*
MM	*millimeter(s)*
MIN	*minimum*
MISC	*miscellaneous*

ABBREVIATIONS (continued)

MOD	*modular*
MOV	*movable*
NL	*nailable*
NAT	*natural*
NI	*nickel*
NOM	*nominal*
N	*north*
NIC	*not in contact*
NTS	*not to scale*
OBS	*obscure*
OC	*on center(s)*
OP	*opaque*
OPG	*opening*
OPP	*opposite*
OPH	*opposite hand*
OPS	*opposite surface*
OD	*outside diameter*
OA	*overall*
OH	*overhead*
PNT	*paint(ed)*
PAR	*parallel*
PK	*parking*
PV	*pave(d), (ing)*
PVMT	*pavement*
PED	*pedestal*
PERF	*perforate(d)*
PERI	*perimeter*
PL	*plate*
PG	*plate glass*
PWD	*plywood*
PT	*point*
PVC	*polyvinyl chloride*
PTC	*post-tensioned concrete*
PCF	*pounds per cubic foot*
PFL	*pounds per linear foot*
PSF	*pounds per square foot*
PSI	*pounds per square inch*
PCC	*precast concrete*
PFB	*prefabricate(d)*
PFN	*prefinished*
PRF	*performed*
PCS	*prestressed concrete*
PL	*property line*
QT	*quarry tile*
RAD	*radius*
RL	*rail(ing)*
RWC	*rainwater conductor*
REF	*reference*
RFL	*reflect(ed), (ive), (or)*
REG	*register*
RE	*reinforce(d), (ing)*
RCP	*reinforced concrete pipe*
RET	*return*
RVS	*reverse (side)*
REV	*revision(s), revised*
RH	*right hand*
ROW	*right of way*
R	*riser*
RD	*roof drain*
RM	*room*
RO	*rough opening*
RBL	*rubble stone*
SCH	*schedule*
SCN	*screen*
SNT	*sealant*
STG	*seating*
SEC	*section*
SHT	*sheet*
SHO	*shore(d), (ing)*
SIM	*similar*
SL	*sleeve*
SP	*soundproof*
S	*south*
SPC	*spacer*
SPL	*special*
SPEC	*specification(s)*
SQ	*square*
SST	*stainless steel*
STD	*standard*
STA	*station*
ST	*steel*
STO	*storage*
SD	*storm drain*
STR	*structural*
SCT	*structural clay tile*
SYM	*symmetry(ical)*
SYN	*synthetic*
SYS	*system*
TEL	*telephone*
TV	*television*
TC	*terra cotta*
TZ	*terrazzo*
THK	*thick(ness)*
THR	*threshold*
TOL	*tolerance*
T&G	*tongue and groove*
TSL	*top of slab*
TST	*top of steel*
TW	*top of wall*
T	*tread*
TYP	*typical*
UC	*undercut*
UNF	*unfinished*
VJ	*v-joint(ed)*
VB	*vapor barrier*
VERT	*vertical*
VG	*vertical grain*
WTW	*wall to wall*
WP	*waterproofing*
WS	*waterstop*
W	*west*
WHB	*wheel bumper*
W	*width, wide*
WM	*wire mesh*
WO	*without*
WD	*wood*
WB	*wood base*
WI	*wrought iron*

SYMBOLS AS ABBREVIATIONS

∠	angle
ϕ	round
℄	centerline
d	penny

REFERENCES FOR FURTHER READING

ASTM Standards in Building Codes. Philadelphia: American Society for Testing and Materials, (updated periodically).

Callendar, J.J. *Time Savers Standards for Architectural Design Data.* 6th Edition. New York: McGraw-Hill, 1982.

Day, D. "Layout of Landscape Elements," *Handbook of Landscape Architectural Construction.* Washington, DC: Landscape Architecture Foundation, 1973.

deChira, J., and Callendar, J.J., Editors. *Time Savers Standards for Building Types.* 2nd Edition. New York: McGraw-Hill, 1980.

Hepler, D.E., and Wallach, P.I. *Architecture: Drafting and Design.* 3rd Edition. New York: McGraw-Hill, 1976.

Lane, K.F., and Roberts, J.M. *Fundamental Land.* Ames, Iowa: Iowa State University, 1979.

Meier, H.W. *Construction Specifications Handbook.* 3rd Edition. New York: Prentice-Hall, 1983.

Ramsey, C.G., and Sleeper, H.R. *Architectural Graphics Standards.* 7th Edition. New York: Wiley, 1981.

Seelye, E.E. *Data Book for Civil Engineers: Design.* Vol. 1, 3rd Edition. New York: Wiley, 1960.

Untermann, R.K. *Principles and Practices of Grading, Drainage and Road Alignment: An Ecologic Approach.* Reston, VA: Reston, 1978.

VanDyke, S. *From Line to Design.* 2nd Edition. Mesa, Arizona: PDA Publishers, 1985.

Walker, T.D., *Perspective Sketches.* 4th Edition. Mesa, Arizona: PDA Publishers, 1982.

Walker, T.D. *Plan Graphics.* 3rd Edition. Mesa, Arizona; PDA Publishers, 1985.

Young, D.L. "Preparation of Construction Plans," *Handbook of Landscape Architectural Construction.* Washington, DC: Landscape Architecture Foundation, 1973.

3

Construction Materials

In order to effectively design the various elements which may be placed on a site, whether it be paving, walls, steps, or a bench, some familiarity with materials used in construction is essential. This chapter briefly describes the history and origin of such materials as asphalt, concrete, brick, stone, metals, paints, plastics, and wood. It also serves as an introduction to characteristics, such as strengths and sizes, which affect their use in site design.

ASPHALT

Asphalt is derived from petroleum as part of a process for preparing such products as gasoline, fuel oil, diesel oil, and lubricating oils. A similar refining process occurs in nature as well, resulting in such natural deposits as the asphalt lake in Trinidad and outcroppings of rock asphalt or the formation of asphalt in porous rock structures.

In color, asphalt varies from dark brown to black. It is composed principally of bitumens which result from petroleum processing. It is an adhesive which is waterproof, durable, and resistant to the action of acids, alkalis, and salts. When mixed with mineral aggregates it forms a controllable plastic substance.

The use of asphalt has its disadvantages because it moves under some situations of heat, it sticks to shoes and tires, and it will dissolve when gasoline or similar fluids are spilled on it.

The asphalt refined from petroleum comes in a variety of grades and types which vary in character from solids to almost water-thin liquids. The basic semi-solid form is known as asphalt cement.

In general, there are four types of asphalt cement, three of which are further liquified by cutting back (thinning) with petroleum distillates:

1. Slow curing — Cut back with slowly volatile oils which make the cement slow to harden.
2. Medium curing — Cut back with kerosene.
3. Rapid curing — Cut back with gasoline.
4. Asphalt emulsion — Asphalt cement mixed with water and an emulsifier.

The first three are used in a variety of ways depending on conditions and needs. These uses extend from tack coats, for bonding an asphalt surface to a concrete surface, to patching mixes.

Asphalt emulsion is used for sealing established asphalt paving, waterproofing basements and retaining walls, and mulching (generally mixed with straw or other similar material).

Asphalt concrete (also called "blacktop") is the paving mix composed of asphalt cement, coarse and fine aggregate, and mineral filler and dust. The amount of each depends on the design mix. The base course will contain a larger proportion of coarse aggregates, in contrast to the wearing course (applied above the base course) where a denser, tighter

Figure 3.1 *Hexagonal pre-cast asphalt pavers.*

Figure 3.2 *Rectangular pre-cast asphalt pavers.*

material is needed. The larger aggregate provides the mix with strength needed for the base course, while the fine aggregate of the wearing course provides a smoother surface and resists water penetration. For tennis courts and similar paved surfaces where a precision slope is required, an additional leveling course of asphalt cement and fine aggregate such as sand may be applied.

Aggregates used in asphalt paving should be crushed stone, slag, or gravel with angular, pitted, or rough surface textures. Polished aggregates should not be used, as they do not bind together well. All aggregates must be free from clay, silt, and organic matter.

Most asphalt is laid on a gravel base varying in depth depending on local soil conditions; "full-depth" asphalt concrete pavement, however, is laid directly on the sub-grade without a gravel base. Full-depth asphalt concrete varies from four to twelve inches in depth depending on the weight of vehicles to use the pavement and on subgrade conditions. Consult the Asphalt Institute for local recommendations. The subgrade should be free from debris and the soil thoroughly compacted. Otherwise, settling and cracking of the pavement will result.

The surface drainage for asphalt pavement should never be less than one percent or one-foot drop in every 100 feet. A two percent or ¼ inch per foot slope is generally considered ideal.

Usage

About 90 percent of the roads and parking lots in the United States are composed of asphalt concrete pavement. Besides these, asphalt concrete is also utilized for curbs and recreational areas including tennis and basketball courts, tracks, bicycle and golf cart paths, and sidewalks.

Asphalt concrete curbs can be constructed by a machine which extrudes the hot mix on top of the edge of asphalt paving. Though less expensive than poured-in-place concrete, asphalt curbs are easily damaged by tires and snowplows.

When thin applications of asphalt concrete paving are used, such as for sidewalks, an edging material of steel or treated wood is desirable to provide a stable finished edge. Design lines can be established and more readily controlled with the use of edging.

In general, asphalt paving can be used as soon as it is laid; however, it can easily be punctured by sharp objects on hot days, such as a chair with a person sitting on it placed on an asphalt walk.

Other uses of asphalt include asphalt impregnated fiber strips for expansion joints, insulated sheathing for building construction, roofing paper, shingles, and paving blocks.

In a number of applications utilizing asphalt pavement the addition of color coatings becomes desirable. This might include line striping for parking lots and basketball and tennis courts, or the complete covering of the paving surface with color sometimes requested for play areas, tennis courts, etc. There are a number of brand name products available in a wide range of colors, which are based either on asphalt emulsion or synthetic resins compatible with asphalts, that should be applied according to the manufacturers recommendations. Newly laid asphalt should cure 30 days before the application of sealers or color coating.

Because of varying local conditions such as soils, temperature ranges, etc., consult representatives of the Asphalt Institute for recommendations of mix design and specifications applicable to your site problem.

CONCRETE

Concrete is one of the most popular major construction materials. Almost any shape can be created with it, and it is readily available for use by designers in nearly every community.

Concrete is composed of four ingredients: sand, gravel or crushed stone, water, and cement. Cement is the agent which binds the aggregates (sand and gravel) together in permanent form. It is thus incorrect to refer to a sidewalk as a "cement sidewalk" when it is actually a "concrete sidewalk."

History of Cement

Cement occurs in nature in the form of calcium carbonate, which is the basic material found in cave and ocean formations.

The first manufacture of cement began during the Roman Empire when the Romans used slake lime and volcanic ash to produce a hydraulic cement that hardened under water. This process was lost, due to the fall of the Empire in the 400's A.D., until the British discovered the process for making cement in the 18th century. In the United States, natural hydraulic cements were discovered in New York in 1818 and were used to construct the Erie Canal.

Portland cement, the type of cement used today, was invented by the British in 1824. This cement is so named because the fine gray powder was the same color as the natural stone quarried on the Isle of Portland in Southern Great Britain. The manufacture of portland cement in the United States began in the late 19th century. Confusion resulted from the use of many different formulas in this period of time, and in 1917 a standard formula was established and adopted. At about the same time, the Portland Cement Association was formed and it became the coordinating organization for all of the manufacturers. Air entrained concrete was perfected in the early 1940's.

Cement Processing

The basic ingredients of portland cement include approximately 60 percent lime, 25 percent silica, and 10 percent alumina. The remainder is composed of iron oxide and gypsum.

Lime, the principal ingredient, may be derived from such materials as limestone, oyster shells, chalk, and "marl" clay. Silica and alumina can be found in shale, clay, silica sand, slate, and blast furnace slag. Iron oxide comes from iron ore. Gypsum (derived from natural deposits of calcium sulfate) regulates the time of setting or hardening of the cement.

To make cement, quarried limestone and raw materials are crushed into fine particles which are then heated to 2,600 to 3,000°F. in a large rotating kiln (a cylindrical type in an almost horizontal position). Raw materials are placed in the upper opening, and at the end of about four hours the particles emerge from the lower end of the kiln as clinkers about the size of marbles. A small amount of gypsum is added to the clinkers which are reground into the fine gray powder which is the final cement product. It is stored in silos for future bulk shipment or sacked. Each sack contains 94 pounds or one cubic foot of cement.

There are five types of portland cement, as follows:

Type 1. General Purpose Portland Cement - a gray cement which is the most commonly used type in normal construction.

Type 2. Modified Portland Cement - a cement designed for use where the heat of hydration must be controlled such as in very large, massive pours (dams, piers, heavy abutments, etc.). It must also be used where resistance against sulfate attack is needed; such as in sewage drainage structures or applications in contact with high sulfate soils.

Type 3. High Early Strength Portland Cement - provides an earlier and higher strength gain for use in projects where forms must be removed quickly or concrete must be put into use early or for minimizing the cost of protection required in cold weather construction.

Type 4. Low Heat of Hydration Portland Cement - less heat of hydration than Type 2. Achieves greatest strength very slowly and requires prolonged curing.

Type 5. Sulfate Resistant Portland Cement - a cement which provides the greatest resistance to alkali attack. It is most commonly used for projects in contact with soil and water containing large concentrations of sulfates.

Type 1 is also available as a white portland cement with the same characteristics of strength and quality. It is substituted for the gray portland cement where the distinctive white character is needed, such as in paving strips, precast panels with colored exposed aggregates, sculpture, and mixes in which color pigments are added.

For most site design uses which are exposed to freezing and thawing, an air entraining agent should be added to the Type 1 cement, whether gray or white, to increase the resistance of the concrete to frost damage and scaling action caused by salt and de-icing compounds. The air entraining agent is a soapy or fat-like compound which causes microscopic air bubbles to form during mixing of the concrete. Billions of bubbles occur in each cubic foot of concrete mix. The amount of air to be trapped in the mix is a percentage by volume and recommendations vary according to the maximum size of aggregate being used in the mix. This variation is from five percent at 2½ inches maximum aggregate size up to seven percent at ½ inch maximum aggregate size. These figures can each vary plus or minus one percent. Water repelling agents can be added to reduce water absorption and staining.

When faster setting is desired in cold weather (in order to complete a project), about one pound of calcium chloride per sack can be used. Chemical retardants can be added in hot weather to slow down the setting action. They can also be sprayed on the surface of paving or forms of walls to permit exposing the aggregate.

Characteristics

Soon after the moment that water is added to cement, a chemical reaction takes place and heat of hydration occurs in the resulting paste. The setting or hardening process has begun.

When the water and cement are mixed with the aggregates, a plastic mass is transformed into a solid glomeration as the hardening is completed. This chemical change is irreversible.

Even though hard a few hours after placement, concrete requires a curing period to achieve full strength. Concrete is rated according to its compressive strength, with a range of 3,000 to 3,500 pounds per square inch (p.s.i.) considered normal or average. A range of 4,500 to 5,000 p.s.i. is used for precasting concrete and other uses where greater strength is needed.

Whether or not concrete achieves its rated strength depends on the curing period and how it is treated. Half of its rate of strength occurs in the first seven days, providing the concrete does not dry too rapidly. It must be kept moist by plastic coverings, chemical compounds, puddling with water, or some other technique. The remainder of its rated strength will occur in 28 days, though the curing process or chemical activity does not completely stop until two years have elapsed.

The key to concrete strength is the amount of water and cement used. More cement is used for the stronger mixes. Too much water can negate strength to be achieved by using the extra cement. The mix needs to be "stiff" rather than "soupy." A mix for paving will be stiffer than one for retaining walls where placement in the forms becomes important. Stiffness of the mix is measured in a "slump" test. In this test, concrete is poured into a cone, the cone is removed and set next to the pile of concrete, and the resulting sag or slump of the plastic concrete is measured in relation to the adjacent cone top. A four-inch slump is considered good for pavement and six inches for walls and other projects involving complex forming and reinforcing patterns.

Concrete quality is also determined by the gradation of aggregates, and a mix of sizes is desirable to ensure greatest surface exposure of aggregates to the paste and the filling of spaces between aggregate particles. Crushed stone provides better contact and binding with the cement paste than smooth gravel.

Concrete shrinks as it cures, thus creating a need for joints. It also expands during warm weather periods and contracts during cold weather. The amount of expansion is approximately ⅝ inch per 100 feet for 100 degrees of temperature change.

Concrete is good under compression but poor under tension. Compression occurs when particles are pushed together. Tension occurs when a force pulls the particles apart. By adding reinforcing, the tension problem can be resolved, as steel has good tensile strength.

Welded wire fabric or mesh is commonly used in flat work (paving) and deformed steel bars or rods in walls, piers, columns, etc.

Besides concrete, portland cement is also used in making mortar for masonry work and in mixes for grouting, parging, and stucco.

Finishes

The plastic character of concrete allows a variety of finishes. For paving, it may range from glassy smooth to very coarse. Smooth pavement can be achieved by careful trowelling with a steel trowel, but this surface is slick and slippery when used out-of-doors. A wood float will provide a coarser finish, and many walks and ramps can be effectively roughened in a uniform pattern with a stiff broom, a technique in common use.

Another pavement finish consists of exposing the surface aggregates either by using chemical retardants, brushing with water when the mix is almost set, or sandblasting the surface after set.

A number of patterns may be stamped, scored, or sawed into the surface of paving. Metal stamps which imitate stone, brick, or tile patterns can be stamped in the concrete surface before it completely hardens. Random surface patterns can be achieved by embedding strips of wood or plastic into the surface during finishing or tooling with a ½ inch or ¾ inch piece of bent electrical conduit or copper pipe.

Square or rectangular patterns may be achieved by using dividers. Such decay-resistant wood as redwoods, cedar, or cypress are most commonly used. Uniform squares or rectangles of any size can be created (or random patterns of varying sizes), depending upon the designers intent and effect desired. The wood dividers can double as expansion and contraction joints, but the wood strips will heave under some freeze-thaw conditions and will need to be held in place with galvanized nails as illustrated in Chapter 4.

Additional patterns can be created by using strips of masonry units such as brick as dividers. Varying techniques are illustrated in Chapter 4. Where foot traffic will wear down a broom finish, the use of abrasive grains may provide a longer lasting non-slip finish. Silican carbide and aluminum oxide are the most common. The former has a sparkle which may or may not be desirable. The grains are spread over the surface during the final finish in the quantity of ¼ to ½ pound per square foot and lightly trowelled into the final surface.

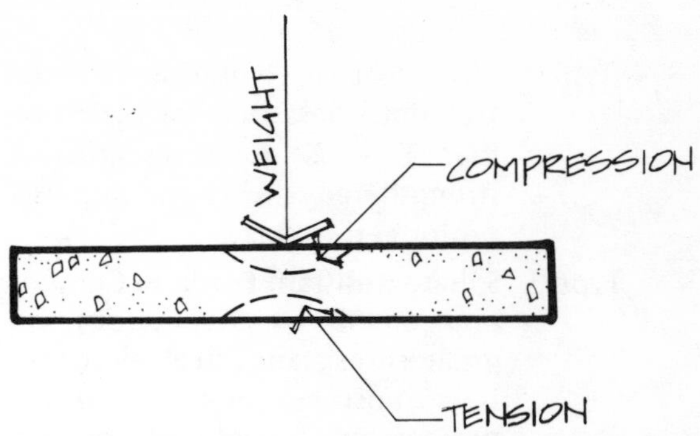
WEIGHT
COMPRESSION
TENSION

Figure 3.3 *Areas of compression and tension in concrete relative to the application of weight.*

Many techniques can be used for walls, from a simple form finish with its plainness to complex patterns. Rubber mats or specific designed patterns formed with fiber glass can be inserted inside the usual forms to obtain any number of creative finishes with very smooth surfaces. Corrugated or irregular rough patterns can be achieved by placing various sizes of wood strips inside the forms. The wood grains can be accentuated by sand blasting to bring out the grain before pouring the concrete against it. After a wall is cured the surface can be sand blasted or bush hammered to create a uniform surface texture or expose the aggregate.

Another way to finish concrete walls is to cover the surface with brick, stone, or precast veneer. Precast concrete offers the advantage of high quality and carefully controlled exposure of aggregates. These techniques are much more expensive than a conventional wall but can be especially attractive and useful in site design.

Precast Concrete

This method of handling concrete enables much greater control over quality when compared to cast-in-place concrete. All the conditions of mixing, handling, and curing can be very carefully controlled to ensure a superior product. Products in this category include standard sized concrete masonry units, custom precast or cast stone, utilty structures, and pipe.

Besides the usual ingredients of concrete, such other aggregates as cinders, expanded slag, expanded shale, clay or slate, or volcanic materials may be used depending upon local conditions. Expanded shale is much lighter in weight and can reduce the weight of precast units by approximately 35 percent.

Concrete masonry units are produced in many sizes, shapes, and patterns, but there are a few standard units in wide use which are

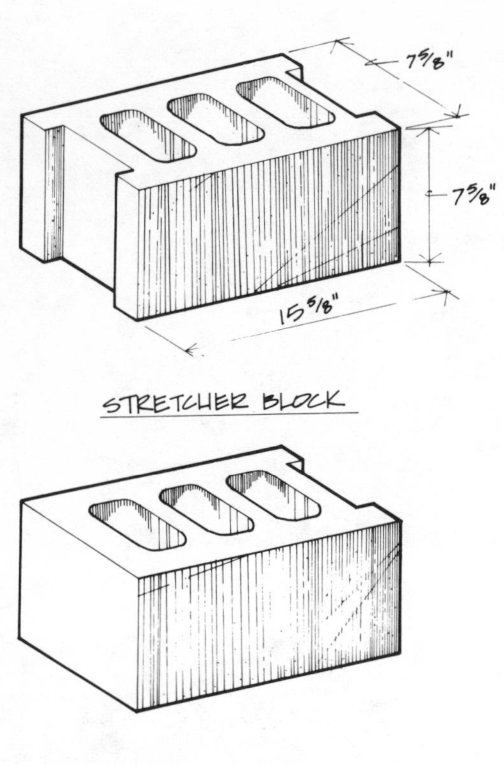
7⅝"
7⅝"
15⅝"
STRETCHER BLOCK
CORNER BLOCK
Figure 3.4 *Pre-cast concrete block.*

available nearly everywhere. These units are commonly used for walls and partitions of buildings as backups for brick or stone, for masonry in planters and retaining walls, and for foundations. There are stretcher blocks, corner blocks, etc., in four-, six- and eight-inch widths with heights of eight inches and lengths of sixteen inches. The actual size of all of these units is ⅜-inch less to allow for mortar. These modules relate to other modules of building materials. Three courses of standard face brick can be laid to equal one course of concrete block.

Many different types and sizes of pavers are constructed of precast concrete. Squares, rectangles, geometric shapes, and interlocking patterns are available.

Custom precast units are used for such things as veneer slabs of exposed aggregates for walls, stair trends, benches or seating, fountains, planters, bollards, and screens.

Manholes, catch basins, septic tanks, burial vaults, light poles, riprap, cribbing, tree grates, and wheel stops are additional examples of precast concrete units of a utility nature. Sewer and culvert pipes are precast. Sewer pipe in the smaller sizes of four to twelve inches in diameter are not reinforced, but the larger sizes are reinforced. Pipe diameter increases in two-inch increments from four to twelve inches, then in three-inch increments to 24 inches, and in six-inch increments above 24 inches. Culvert pipe requires higher compressive values because of its exposure to greater weight. It is always reinforced and the walls are thicker. When asbestos is added to cement to form a pipe of lighter weight, a smoother and lower friction (less resistance to flow of water) pipe is also produced.

Prestressed Concrete

This is another form of precast concrete. As was discussed earlier, concrete is good under compression but poor in tension. Prestressing has made possible the production of bridge and roof beams of varying shapes which are light in weight yet can carry significant loads without failure.

In regular reinforced concrete some tension occurs in the concrete before the steel reinforcing begins to absorb the tensile forces and some cracking results under loading. In prestressed concrete, cables are used, rather than deformed bars, for the reinforcing. The cables are pulled into tension in the forms before the concrete is poured. After initial curing the cables are released and the beam is removed from the forms. When a load is applied, the tension is immediately absorbed and no cracking or failure of the concrete occurs. Sizing of prestressed beams in relation to expected loads is an area of specialized engineering design. Shapes of beams are described by the following terms: I-beam, double tee, single-tee, channel, and single-wing tee.

Color

Color can be added to concrete through the use of pigments in the mix before pouring or stains and paints can be applied afterward. Uniformity and consistency of color when using pigments and stains is difficult to achieve. Certain paints and coatings may peel or flake off.

High quality mineral pigments only should be mixed into concrete. Impurities will reduce the strength of the mixes. Even pure pigment should not exceed ten percent of the weight of the cement, or 9.4 pounds per sack, in order to preserve the rated strength of the concrete mix.

Gray colors slightly to much darker than normal concrete can be achieved by using black iron oxide. Other color and pigments include: red — red oxide of iron, brown — brown oxide of iron, buff — yellow oxide of iron, blue — cobalt oxide, and green — chromium oxide.

MASONRY

In this section several materials will be discussed, including brick, other related clay products, and stone. Though brick and stone are not necessarily very related in their characteristics as materials, the way they are used on the site can be quite similar.

Brick

Brick is of ancient origin, having been used since early recorded history. It is manufactured from clay or shale which has been mined, pulverized, mixed, formed, cut to size, dried, and fired in a kiln for several hours or days at 1600-2000° F.

The quality of the raw materials and the length of the firing process influences the durability of the brick. The inherent or added minerals determine the color characteristics, which can vary according to the length of time, temperature, and oxidation occurring in the firing process.

Dark-colored bricks which ring when hit together generally are dense, well-fired units and can be considered quite durable. Salmon colored units which sound dull are generally soft and subject to early deterioration when exposed to the weather. The softer brick absorbs water more readily and thus will be subject to considerable stress in freeze-thaw cycles. High quality units will have little, if any, absorption characteristics and they will not be so subject to freeze-thaw damage. Bricks which absorb water too rapidly will rob the mortar of moisture needed to ensure the complete chemistry of set and arrival at full strength.

There is available for designers a wide range of shapes, sizes, color (including flashing and glazes), and surface textures. This includes both pavers and building brick. The former are generally solid units, while the latter contain cores of varying size and number. Units vary enough from batch to batch in the manufacturing process so that matching is difficult where continuity of color is required. All brick needed to complete a project should be selected from the same batch in the total quantity needed. Not all sizes, shapes, colors, and textures are available in any one locality. Some suppliers ship regularly to various parts of the country, but shipping costs will be one of the major factors in determining feasibility of use.

Standard bricks are 2¼ inches thick by 3¾ inches wide by 8 inches long. Check local suppliers for variability from standard and other sizes available.

Figure 3.5 *Rectangular and square brick pavers.*

Figure 3.6 *Hexagonal brick pavers.*

Other Clay Units

Patio and quarry tile come in several different forms. Quarry tile is generally square, thin, and quite hard. Some of the other clay patio tiles are soft and come in a variety of shapes. The soft tile units are best where freeze-thaw cycles are not a problem. Because quarry tile is thin, it is usually used over a concrete base and mortared in place.

Ceramic tile or glazed units are highly colorful, and mosaic patterns can be created. Out-of-doors, they are sometimes used in pools and fountains or on building walls. Squares in ½-inch and 4-inch sizes are quite common, and some other sizes are available. They are quite thin and are always used as a veneer over another solid surface material.

Vitrified clay pipe is used frequently for sanitary sewage systems and some other uses. It has superior durability. Pipes come in varying diameters and lengths with bell and spigot ends. Agricultural tiles are also round but unglazed, vary in diameter from 4 to 8 inches, and are 2 feet in length with straight ends. Chimney flue tiles are square or rectangular and a variety of uses can be found for them, depending upon the creativity of the designer.

Stone

This material is as old as the earth itself and is available in an infinite variety of sizes, shapes, colors, and textures. As a natural material it can be an excellent asset in site design where a natural character and richness are desired. Local availability of certain types and transportation costs are limiting factors in using stone in design.

The most common kinds of stone are as follows:

1. Sedimentary types such as sandstone, brownstone, bluestone, and limestone. These are somewhat soft, thus easy to cut and work, but they are subject to staining and weathering because of their porous character.
2. A metamorphic form of limestone is marble, which is harder, more durable, easy to carve and polish, and popular because of its patterns and beauty.
3. A metamorphic form of shale is slate, which is a hard and durable stone which varies from blue to gray to black with some types occurring as red.
4. An igneous rock is granite, which is quite hard and thus very durable. Its colors range from almost white to dark gray, with some pink forms occurring. It can be carved and cut into many shapes and sizes. It resists staining and weathers well.
5. Volcanic rock is dark in character and is limited in use to lump sizes. It is not practical to carve, cut, and use like the types of stone previously mentioned. It is coarse, sharp, and harsh to bare skin.
6. A fine-grained, hard stone is traprock. It fractures easily and is most useful as an aggregate for concrete, base course for paving, mulches, etc.

Mining and Processing

Stone is quarried wherever it occurs in nature or is in such a state that it can be mined economically. Using drills and wedges, stone is broken into blocks and then split or sawn into the desired shapes. The surface textures of stone can be varied considerably. The roughest is the split-face caused when one piece of stone is split from another. Stone which is sawn can vary according to the type of saw. Using steel shot produces a surface texture with random scoring of varying depths. Chat sawing produces a fairly fine-pebbled finish, and the smoothest sawing is done by a diamond saw. A moderately granular finish can be produced by using a sand saw, and more texture can be achieved by bush hammering the surface.

A fine textured surface called "honed face" results when using a grinding wheel to remove saw marks. The surface can also be tooled to create a grooved or corrugated surface with four, six, or eight grooves per inch. Denser and harder stone can be buffed by a carborundum wheel to produce a polished or glass-like surface. Letters and patterns can be incised into the surface of the stone by using chisels or sandblasting.

Processing varies somewhat from one kind of stone to another and the above description may not be applicable to all varieties of stone. Check with local suppliers for the availability of particular textures and review their samples.

Strength and Hardness

As a comparison of compressive strength, granite ranges from 26,000 to 30,000 p.s.i., while white marble is around 10,500 p.s.i. (ASTM C170-65). The Bureau of Standards Abrasive Tests rate limestone from 1 to 24, slate from 6 to 12, and granite from 37 to 88.

METALS

Iron and Steel

The manufacture of iron is of a very ancient origin and no one knows just exactly when man learned how to make and use it.

About six hundred years ago the process of manufacturing iron in quantities through the use of a blast furnace was originated. The first successful blast furnace on the American continent was built in 1644 in Massachusetts and in 1646 the first sustained production began. During the 1700's, with the development of the industrial revolution, the demand for steel and iron began to encourage the development of methods for producing large quantities of iron.

By the mid-19th century the technology was developed for refining iron into steel through the use of the open hearth furnace, and steel began to take the place of wrought iron and quickly found many other uses. By 1874 structural steel for the construction of bridges began to be manufactured, and by the late 1890's steel tubing was available in large quantities.

Iron makes up about five percent of the surface crust of the earth and is derived from minerals typically called iron ores. Two principal ores which contain large concentrations of iron include hematite and magnetite. These minerals are found in several locations throughout the United States, but mining is currently limited to the richest concentrations. The ore is mined either by the open pit method or shaft mining, with open pit mining the most common and economical.

The iron ore is combined with other ingredients in order to produce iron from the blast furnace. Approximately one ton of iron can be manufactured from one and three-quarters ton of ore, three-fourths ton of coke, one-fourth ton of limestone, and four tons of air. The coke is used in the heating process to melt the iron ore, the limestone helps to separate impurities from the ore, and the air provides oxygen which combines with the carbon from the burning coke to form carbon monoxide, which combines with the oxygen in the ore to form carbon dioxide. This frees the iron from its imprisonment in the iron ore and causes it to separate.

The iron from the blast furnace is typically called pig iron and is about 95 percent pure. The remaining five percent is made up largely of carbon with small amounts of manganese, phosphorous, sulfur, and a few other elements. This pig iron can be cast in a foundry into various shapes and forms typically called cast iron.

When the pig iron is mixed with some glass-like slag it becomes wrought iron. A piece of wrought iron one inch square will contain about 250,000 tiny iron silicate particles which are like black glass. This iron silicate makes the wrought iron more malleable, which means it is easier to work, and more resistant to corrosion than other kinds of iron.

The iron may also be processed further into steel. Steel is an alloy or mixture of iron and small amounts of carbon and other materials. It is stronger than iron and can be shaped into many more products. There are many different combinations of ingredients and the manufacture of steel alloys may vary from company to company.

Stainless steel is one of those special alloys which has a special quality for resisting corrosion and rust. Chromium is the chief ingredient used in making stainless steel and some high quality stainless steel also incorporates the use of nickel as an ingredient.

To prevent iron and steel products from rusting they can be coated with zinc, which is also known as galvanized iron. The products are cleaned with acid and then dipped into a bath of melted zinc, a process which is called "hot dip galvanizing." It is used to coat steel sheets, nails, wire, pipes, and similar products. The crystals which are deposited upon the surface of the iron or steel give the surface appearance a spotted or mottled look. The rustproof finish of galvanized iron can be destroyed through exposure to sulfurous compounds.

Such steel products as bolts, screws, etc., are typically electroplated with cadmium to prevent rusting.

Aluminum

This silvery white metal is popular because of its lightweight and rustproof characteristics. Its popularity parallels that of the airplane, as it is the principal metal used in the manufacture of aircraft. However, aluminum is quite soft and it must be combined with other metals to create alloys in order to make it as strong as steel.

In contrast to the other metals, aluminum does not occur as a metal in nature. It is necessary to manufacture it from "bauxite."

Aluminum is a material of recent discovery. It was first found as part of a compound in 1807 but was not separated as a separate entity until 1825. From that time until 1866 several individuals attempted to find inexpensive ways to extract aluminum but were not successful. In

1886, the process of making aluminum with the use of electricity was developed and the aluminum industry was born. Large-scale production, however, did not occur until the beginning of World War I when the need for aluminum greatly expanded.

In nature, aluminum exists only in chemical compounds with oxygen, silicon, and other elements. These compounds make up more than 15 percent of the earth's crust. Aluminum can be made inexpensively from an ore called bauxite, which occurs in hard, rock-like formations but also in some places may be as soft as mud.

To separate the aluminum from the bauxite ore, the ore is first crushed and then mixed with lime, soy ash, and hot water, which is then mixed in a digester under steam pressure to form a caustic soda which dissolves the aluminum from the ore and leaves the other impurities as solids. A filter separates the solids from the alumina solution. The alumina is then precipitated out in the form of crystals and is run through a kiln to remove the water. The pure alumina is further processed to make molten aluminum. Two pounds of alumina with a half pound of carbon anode and eight to ten kilowatts of electricity will produce one pound of aluminum.

The molten metal of aluminum can be combined with such other metals as copper, magnesium, silicon, or zinc to form alloys which are cast into ingots. The ingots can be processed further into a number of products. One of these is plate or sheet metal which might be rolled down further into various thicknesses of foil. Ingots can also be processed into bars and rods or extruded into a number of products such as angles, T-sections, and combinations of similar shapes. Extrusions can also be made into square, round, or rectangular tubing for a multitude of uses. Wire can also be manufactured from aluminum of various gages.

Because of its rustproof characteristics, aluminum is oft times used in its natural state without any additional finish or coating added. Exposed aluminum forms a thin coating of aluminum oxide that protects the metal against any additional injury. This keeps the surface of the aluminum from deteriorating. For some particular uses, sheet aluminum can be coated with chemicals, other metals, plastics, or porcelain enamel to give it particular colors and finishes.

Aluminum can also be anodized by an electrochemical process that thickens the aluminum's natural oxide coating. The coating can be clear and colorless or it can be combined with certain types of dyes to create any number of color variations. In color anodizing, the aluminum article is dipped into an acid electrolyte. Electrical current is passed through the electrolyte and the aluminum serves as the anode. The acid is washed off the aluminum and the article is dipped into a hot dye bath, after which the dyed surface is sealed by dipping the aluminum in a hot nickel acetate solution.

Lead

Before the development of plastics, this soft, very heavy metal had a number of uses in site design. Sheet lead was frequently used as flashing and as a waterproofing layer for roof top pools and fountains. As a hot liquid, it was used to seal expansion and other joints. Lead is still popular in electronics and in the manufacture of automobile batteries, and it is alloyed with tin to make solder and used as a binding agent for uniting several other metals.

Copper

Copper was one of the first metals known to man. He was able to use it as he found it and manufactured ornaments, tools, and weapons. It was probably used around 8000 BC, but by 3800 BC men had discovered how to melt and alloy copper with tin and make bronze. The process of making brass by combining zinc and copper was discovered somewhere between 1000 BC and 600 BC.

Until the 1800's the demand for copper was not too great, and existing supplies of high grade ore satisfied that demand. The rapid growth of electric lighting and communication systems by the late 1800's greatly increased the demand for copper and new supplies of copper ore were required. Only low grade ores were found and mass production techniques evolved in order to economically produce copper. These low grade ores contain somewhere around four percent or less copper. Five tons may yield as little as 20 pounds of refined copper.

The copper ore is mined from open pits and shipped to the mills, where it is crushed into small particles and placed in the "ball mill" (a rotating drum containing iron balls that grind the ore into fine, dust-like particles), and a souplike mixture called a slurry is created. The slurry is moved to floatation cells to concentrate the copper by mixing it with oil, air, water and some other chemicals. The chemicals bring the copper minerals to the top to be scraped off and dried. The waste settles to the bottom and is discarded. The copper concentrate is placed in a furnace and heated, and the impurities raise to the top and form a slag which is drained off. The copper is then moved into a converter where blister copper, which is about 97 percent pure, is drawn off and cast into anodes to be used in electrolytic refining, where electric current causes the copper to deposit on the cathodes from the anodes and becomes 99.9 percent pure.

This pure copper is further processed into a multitude of uses. Some of these products which apply to site design include copper wire for conducting electrical current, copper sheets for roofing and flashing, pipe, and copper combined in alloys to make hardware, art work, sculpture, bronze plaques, etc.

Copper is an ideal conductor of electricity. Only silver is a better conductor, but it is too expensive for common use. It is also an excellent conductor of heat and thus it is used in many heating and refrigeration systems.

Pure copper is malleable. It does not break apart when hammered or forged, and thus can be easily worked or shaped in any direction. Copper has the ability to be drawn into very thin wires without breaking. Many electrical cables are wound from a large number of small copper wires for better conduction of electricity.

Copper will not rust and is very resistant to corrosion. When it is exposed to damp air the surface changes from a reddish-orange to a reddish-brown color and after long exposure becomes coated with a green film called "patina," which in turn protects the copper from further corrosion.

There are two alloys of copper which are rather widely used. The first is bronze, an alloy of copper and tin, with the amount of tin used varying from a small amount to 25 percent. Occasionally other metals are used for special purposes. Phosphorus, in particular, hardens and strengthens bronze. Like copper, bronze resists corrosion and has an indefinite life span. Bronze is used in many products including sculpture, statuary, bells, hardware, light fixtures, ornaments, etc.

The other alloy of copper is brass, which is a mixture of copper and zinc. The amount of copper that is used in this alloy varies anywhere from 55 to more than 95 percent. The color of the brass varies with the composition of the ingredients. When it contains approximately 70 percent copper the alloy is a clear, golden yellow metal sometimes referred to as yellow brass. When 80 percent or more copper is used it begins to turn red in color and would be called red brass. With the higher zinc content the brass is at its strongest and toughest quality. At 55 percent copper the alloy can become rather hard and somewhat brittle. Brass is widely used in the manufacture of hardware, electrical and plumbing fixtures, and metal decorations.

PAINT AND RELATED PROTECTIVE COATINGS

Paints and other coatings provide protection against corrosion and deterioration and with their inherent color can compliment the design of the site, creating harmony with other materials, or be used as accents.

History

Use of paint dates back to pre-historic men who used colored material such as plants or clay ground into powder with water added. The Egyptians, dating back approximately 8000 years ago, were apparently the first group of people to use extensively a wide variety of colors. By 1500 BC they had begun to import a wide range of plants providing the entire spectrum of colors. By this same time the Greeks were aware of the process of making paint.

The Romans acquired the knowledge of making paint from the Egyptians and used it until approximately AD400 when the art of making paint was lost after the collapse of the Roman Empire. Not until the end of the middle ages was the process of making paint again discovered by the English who first restricted its use to churches. Later use included public buildings and the homes of wealthy persons.

The commercial manufacture of paint began in the 1700's in the United States and Europe. In these early efforts, only the individual ingredients of paint were prepared and it was up to the painter himself to do the mixing. In 1867 the first prepared paints completely mixed were placed on the market.

Many new pigments and synthetic resins were developed during World War I and II. As a result of this development many new types of paints have evolved to satisfy a variety of situations and problems, and considerable improvements have resulted in paint quality and durability.

Components and Ingredients

There are three basic categories of coatings which are related to each other. These are paints, varnishes, and lacquers. It is rare that lacquers are used in any kind of site design situations and they will not be considered here.

Paint is a combination of pigment and a liquid which is sometimes referred to as a vehicle or binder. The pigment imparts color and serves to hide the surface over which it is being placed and also influences such other paint characteristics as workability and stability after exposure. The binder may be either a vegetable oil or a synthetic resin; the first is thinned in an organic solvent and the second is usually dispersed in water. The solvent-thinned paints dry and harden when their components are exposed to atmospheric oxygen. The water-thinned paints harden when the moisture evaporates from among the resin particles.

Varnish is different from paint in that it consists only of the binder and thus is transparent. Its single purpose is to provide a protective film over some kind of surface.

Stains for exterior use are principally a hybrid between paint and varnish. They contain a small amount of coloring material to alter the basic color of the surface being stained, but the principal ingredient is the binder or vehicle, which is transparent. The texture and surface characteristics of the material being covered are allowed to show through. Some heavy-bodied stains contain more pigment and come closer to approaching regular paint.

Pigments

Such compounds as lead oxide, lead carbonate, lead sulfate, zinc oxide, zinc sulfate, and titanium dioxide have been used as pigments. The use of lead is decreasing due to pollution problems and its toxicity. As a result, titanium dioxide is being used as a replacement and has good hiding power as a pigment. Red lead has been popular for metal primers because of its rust inhibiting characteristics. All of the above pigments are considered to be organic.

Some synthetic organic pigments include phthalocyanines in blues and greens, and toluidines in reds and yellows. Organic and inorganic pigments each have their strengths and weaknesses, and there is a place for each in certain paint formations.

Extenders

These materials are related to pigments in that they have very similar characteristics, but they serve other particular functions in the paint formulation in that they, depending upon the kinds, add to tint retention, mildew resistance, dispersion characteristics, cracking retardation, gloss reduction, etc. Some of these extenders include calcium carbonate, aluminum silicate, magnesium silicate, silica barium sulfate and calcium sulfate.

Solvents

Many binders are so thick that they require some sort of thinning or dissolving to make them spreadable or sprayable. Mineral spirits, a petroleum distillate, along with turpentine are common solvents used in oil base paints. For synthetic resins the higher solvent power of chlorinated hydrocarbons, naptha, toluene, and xylene are required. Water is a thinner used commonly in emulsion paints such as latex. The use of the wrong solvent as a thinner can seriously impair the quality of the paint. Solvents perform more than the functions of just thinning the coatings. They wet the surface and contribute to adhesion by penetrating into the porous openings of the surface being painted and taking the paint with them. They also aid in "leveling," helping the paint to spread uniformly as it is being applied. Solvents cannot dry too rapidly or too slowly. The timing must be just right in order to achieve the uniform thickness of the paint film without it's sagging from being too wet or crusting from evaporating too quickly.

Because of toxicity and strong odor problems turpentine is losing out in favor as a solvent, and mineral spirits is being produced as an odorless solvent for those situations where air pollution regulations require it.

Additives

With the technological advances which have occurred in recent years the quality of paint has increased dramatically. Whereas at one time the old lead linseed oil paint would last only about three years on the surface of buildings, it is now possible to secure a five to ten year life span on most painted surfaces and in some cases up to 20 years.

Some of the additives include the following:

1. Anti-flooding Agents: These are silicon oils or fatty acid esters which help to keep the white hiding pigment and the color particles from separating from each other.
2. Anti-skinning Agents: These are chemicals which prevent the formulation from forming a skin while it is in storage in the can. They are designed, however, to quickly dissipate when applied.

3. Coalescing Agents: These are chemicals which cause the latex particles in water-thinned paints to pack together to form a uniform film during the time that the water is evaporating away from the surface.
4. Dryers: These are catalysts that play a definite role in the chemical reaction and speed up the oxidation in such binders as alkyds and vegetable oils so that they will dry in a reasonable amount of time. Without this additive some paints would require a week to dry, but with it they can dry overnight. Cobalt is an effective dryer with calcium and zirconium as auxilliary dryers.
5. Defoamers: These are used to prevent the formation of foam during the manufacture of latex paints and also to prevent the formation of bubbly surfaces during applications. Such defoamers include mineral spirits, pine oil, octyl alcohol, and some esters of fatty acids.
6. Emulsifiers: Latex paints are emulsions. When pigment is added to the latex emulsions, an additional emulsifier is needed to prevent the pigment from breaking down the emulsion into which it is being inserted. Some of these emulsifiers are amine soaps and anionic surface active agents.
7. Stabilizers: These lower the freezing point of paint to avoid the possibility of the paint freezing in storage. Ethylene, diethylene or propylene glycols are the most frequently used stabilizers.
8. Pigment Suspension Aid: This chemical aids in the suspension of the pigment in the vehicle and prevents it from settling or caking at the bottom of the container.
9. Pigment Wetting Agents: This chemical ensures that each particle of pigment is coated with binder, thus replacing any air pockets between particles of pigments, and speeds the dispersion of the pigment in the vehicle. Without this wetting agent, the pigment would not be uniformly dispersed through the entire vehicle and there would be inconsistencies in gloss, color, and texture. In water-based or water-thinned paints potassium tripolyphosphate and tetrapotassium pyrophosphate are used. Lecithin and esters of fatty acids are used in solvent paints.
10. Preservatives: These are added to eliminate bacteria contamination. They also inhibit the growth of mildew and other types of bacteria growth on the finished surface of paint.
11. Viscosity Control Agents: These are agents which help create a uniform, creamy, easy-to-spread consistency in paint. They are related to thixotropic agents which control the thick-thin ability. Viscosity control agents for solvent-thinned paints include bentonite or hydrogenated caster oil. Latex paints use cellulose thickeners and require the use of preservatives.

Paint Formulations:

1. Linseed Oil Paints: Until the technological advances of manufacturing paint in recent years, linseed oil-based paints were the most popular. Linseed oil is derived from flax seed.
2. Alkyd Resins: These resins are made from treated vegetable oil such as soybean, safflower, tung, or caster oils. The alkyd resins have largely replaced linseed oil in paint formulation. Generally they are lower in cost, quite durable, flexible, and they have good gloss retention. They dry by oxidation and are able to harden fairly rapidly. They can be purchased as either flats or enamels and are compatible with other resins and oils.
3. Epoxy: This formulation is more expensive than others but extremely tough. Generally epoxy resins are combined with other resins to provide a number of different combinations for various uses. Coal tar epoxies withstand both fresh and salt water exposure and can resist a number of chemicals.
4. Rubber-Based Resins: These solvent, thinnable binders include two types, which are commonly used for masonry and surfaces exposed to moisture. They are chlorinated rubber and styrene acrylate. Chlorinated rubber is very resistant to corrosion and is quite flexible since it is 35 percent rubber.
5. Urethanes: There are a number of formulations which fit into this category of synthetic resins. In general this product cures faster and produces a

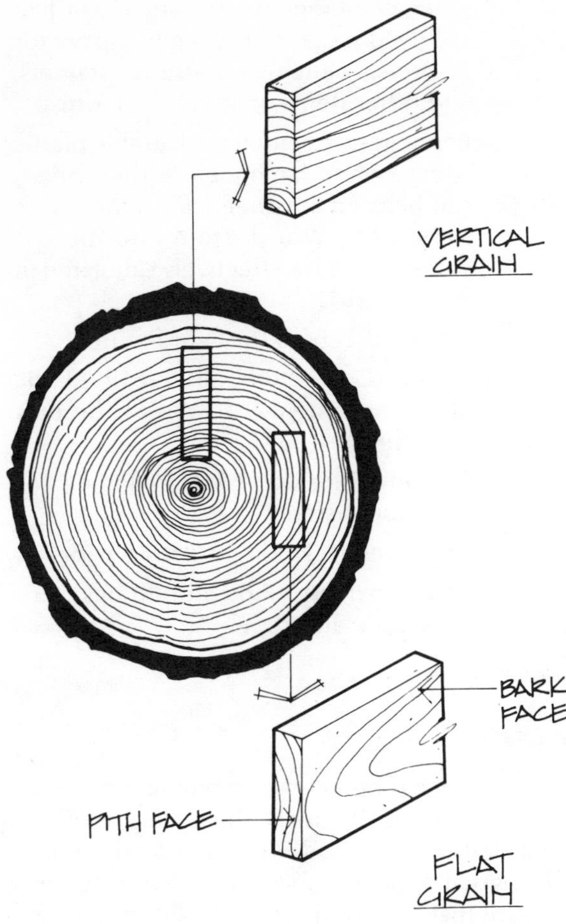
VERTICAL GRAIN
BARK FACE
PITH FACE
FLAT GRAIN

Figure 3.7 *Characteristics of wood affecting paint adhesion.*

harder, more flexible film than does alkyd. It also has better abrasion, solvent, and chemical resistance. However, urethane compounds or formulations do not hold their gloss as well during exterior exposure as the alkyds and are generally more expensive. As a varnish, urethane generally is superior to other varnishes used as a clear sealer for exterior use.

6. Vinyls: There are also a number of formulations in this category much like urethane. Two of the more common are vinyl chloride and vinyl acetate copolymer which have been modified to improve adhesion to metal and are commonly used in plasticized solutions for aluminum siding and galvanized cold rolled steel.
7. Latex: Paints which fit into this category must be stored where they will not freeze during the winter time because of the amount of water which is present in the formulations. They must be applied when the temperature is above 40°F. Some formulations specify 50°F. as a minimum.
8. Acrylics: There are a number of different combinations of chemicals which make up this particular group and relate to the family of latex paints. Some are used for exterior painting, others for interiors; some are called flats, others semi-gloss, some high-gloss. In general, this formulation provides good color stability and resistance to heat, light and weathering and imparts good flexibility and strength. The principal components of acrylic latex paints are ethylacrylate and methylmethacrylate. The former is somewhat soft and has little abrasion and scrub resistance, while the latter is a hard, tough compound which, when combined with the former, makes an excellent paint. Tests have shown that this paint provides a more trouble-free coating over Southern Yellow Pine because it is able to expand and contract in several different directions as the wood does.

Paint formulations one through six are solvent-thinned while the last two groups are water-thinned.

Quality

High quality paint requires the proper formulation of ingredients which are compatible with each other and properly balanced. Because of varying environmental conditions across country and different kinds of surfaces to which paints are applied, careful research must be conducted to select the paint which will be most durable and most compatible with the particular situation involved.

Primers

This is the first coat which is applied to new surfaces such as wood and metal. It acts as an adhesive between the material to which it is applied and the finished coating applied on top. The finish coat provides a thick or continuous film as a protection. It will not adhere to the new surface by itself. The primer, in contrast, will not provide a film of protective material as a final coating. Its sole purpose is to adhere to the surface to which it is applied and act as the adhesive for the finished coat.

Besides serving as an adhesive, primers, in the case of metals, also serve as anti-corrosive systems and thus serve another extremely important function.

In some cases, primers also perform as sealers on such surfaces as porous or fibrous wood or the paper facing of gypsum wallboard. They prevent subsequent coats from being unnecessarily soaked up by the absorbant surface.

Finish Coats or Top Coats

This is the layer which forms the final protective system in the painting process and is the decorative or asthetic coating which provides the color and final texture. This is the coat which also provides resistance to weather, chemicals, dirt, scrubbing, and staining.

As a basis of comparison, flat paint contains a higher percentage of pigment and extender than do the glossy enamels. The glossy paints tend to be harder than those that are flat and are usually more resistant to dirts, stains, and abrasions.

PLASTICS

Plastics are synthetic chemical compounds derived from such sources as coal and petroleum with some limestone, salt, and water also used. Hundreds of different formulas and characteristics have been developed in plastics. Some plastics are soft and pliable while others are hard. There are opaque plastics and others that are transparent.

Some development of plastics began as early as the mid-1800's but the first major invention was celluloid in 1869. Cellophane came along in 1908. World War II accelerated the development of plastic, and the rapid pace has continued ever since, as plastic continues to replace many other traditional materials.

The following list is a tabulation of a few of the many kinds of plastics, along with some of their uses applicable to site design:

1. Vinyl (vinylidene chloride): Water stops, membrane waterproofing, and color coating for chainlink fences.
2. Polyethylene: Sheet plastic for waterproofing, flexible pipe for irrigation systems, corrugated drainage pipe, and insulation for electrical wire.
3. Urethane: Flexible sealant for expansion joints.
4. Epoxy: Applied like paint to seal the insides of pools and fountains, used as glues, combined with fiberglass cloth to be used as a reinforced plastic for planters, benches, waste containers, and other items of street furniture.
5. Phenolics: A very hard, durable plastic which, when laminated in thin sheets, can be used as veneers for doors, table tops, etc. Wood grain and marble patterns can be effectively simulated in this material.
6. Acrylics: Lenses for light fixtures.
7. Nylon: Gears; tees, ells, etc. in plastic plumbing systems; bristles for brooms and paint brushes.
8. Polyvinylchloride (P.V.C.): Piping for irrigation systems.
9. Polystyrene: Foam insulation panels.
10. Polypropylene: Pipe and fittings, wire insulation, and rope.

WOOD

Wood has been used as building material, fuel, and tools by man since very early in recorded history. Today it is a material which has a great appeal to man as evidenced by the amount that is used within man's living environment. This appeal has carried over into the use of other materials, such as plastics where imitation wood-grain patterns are used to provide the effect of wood at a lower cost.

Physical Properties

Wood is made up of cells which are bonded together by natural cement called lignin. These cells are essentially cellulose in character and vary in size and shape according to their function. Most are elongated and in a vertical position within the tree. These cells are known as fibers in hardwoods and tracheids in softwoods. In size, wood cells vary from about 1/25- to 1/3-inch in length, and their width is approximately one hundredth of their length.

Native trees are divided and classified in two groups, "hardwoods" and "softwoods." These terms have nothing to do with the hardness or softness of the wood itself. In fact, some species of softwoods will be harder than some of the species of the hardwoods. Hardwoods are identified as those trees having broad leaves and the softwoods are conifers with needle-like or scale-like leaves. Whereas most of the hardwoods will shed their leaves at the end of each growing season (deciduous) the softwoods are evergreens with the exception of Cypress and Larch. A large proportion of lumber used in the construction industry is derived from the softwoods because they are structurally superior and easier to handle. Southern Pine and Douglas Fir are two major species in current use.

A cross section of a tree shows three distinct layers. The outer layer is the bark, followed by a lighter colored layer just beneath it called sapwood and the inner layer called heartwood. Between the bark and sapwood is a thin band of tissue called the cambium which lays down each annual ring of new growth. The annual rings of the tree occur in two portions. The light-colored portion is called springwood and the darker portion is called summerwood. Large, thin walled cells with large cavities are formed during the early part of the growing season and thus are called "springwood." Thicker walled cells with smaller cavities are formed later in the year and are called the "summerwood" portion. Because of the thicker cells, the summerwood is usually darker in color and creates the distinctive ring which can be noticed in the typical wood cross section. The spacing of the rings and the proportion of springwood versus summerwood have an effect upon the strength properties of a particular species. Generally those species which have narrow growth rings have higher strength properties than those with wide rings.

The sapwood functions in conducting sap from the leaves to the roots and also serves as food storage for the tree. As the tree grows, the inner sapwood cells cease their function of conducting sap and become part of the inactive heartwood. Some species will have a distinctive darker color in their heartwood as contrasted to the sapwood. One of these dramatic contrasts occurs in redwood, where the heartwood has a dark distinctive red color in contrast to the almost cream color of the sapwood. Heartwood is generally more durable because of its inherent chemical properties that resist decay, but the sapwood more readily accepts chemical preservatives.

The weight of wood varies according to moisture content, density, and sapwood thickness. At about 15 percent moisture content the following weights per cubic foot of lumber indicate some of the variation between species: Western Red Cedar, 23.4 pounds; Douglas Fir, 34.3 pounds; White Oak, 46.8 pounds.

Greenwood contains moisture both in the cells and in the voids between the cells. This liquid in the wood is titled "moisture content" (MC). In the seasoning process, moisture is lost first in the voids between the cells and the cells themselves remain saturated until all of this free water between the cells has been evaporated; this is called the fiber saturation point. Depending upon the species, the fiber saturation point is between 25 and 35 percent of the moisture content.

The loss of liquid or moisture from the voids between the cells does not affect the physical dimensions of the wood, but as moisture is lost below the fiber saturation point, shrinkage begins to occur. To ensure a uniform shrinkage and make sure sufficient moisture is lost, wood is dried in ovens or kilns. To reduce susceptibility to decay, wood must either have an MC of 100 percent (that is, totally submerged in water) or be continuously dry (an MC of 20 percent or less). As wood dries, the shrinkage occurs perpendicularly to the grain and very little shrinkage occurs parallel to the grain. In general, the shrinkage amounts to approximately one percent for each four percent change in moisture content for softwoods. Over a period of time, wood obtains an equilibrium in its moisture content corresponding to the humidity and temperature of the surrounding environment. This then will vary from season to season as atmospheric changes occur.

As the MC is reduced below the fiber saturation point and the cells decrease in size, there is a corresponding increase in strength in most species.

Mechanical Properties

The structural characteristics vary somewhat from species to species but many of the characteristics are shared in common by different species.

In comparison to many other materials, wood is soft and thus rather resilient. It can be easily cut and nailed. It is easier to carve and shape. Wood has a certain warmth and comfort when in contact with the skin and can be considered an ideal material for human contact. Because of its internal characteristics and voids between the cells it does not readily conduct heat and thus becomes an insulator. This is one of the reasons for its warmth during skin contact.

When exposed to the weather, wood surfaces gradually bleach and become light to dark gray in color. If exposed to cycles of wetting and drying, the surface will begin to crack and deteriorate. Because of its porosity, wood readily accepts paints, stains and preservatives. Wood beams, when used in structures, are more resistant to failure during a fire than steel beams. Steel readily fails when heated, whereas a wood beam will have to burn for a while before it will fail.

Wood is strongest when the loads or stresses are parallel to the grain rather than perpendicular to the grain, whether in tension or in compression. It is not possible, however, in every situation to design with the loads parallel to the grain. With an understanding of the physical characteristics and mechanical properties of wood, the designer can use wood satisfactorily even when the loads and stresses are perpendicular to the grain.

In tension the stresses create a tendency for the wood fibers to elongate and cause them to slip by each other when the forces are parallel to the grain. When the grain is at an angle or the piece of wood contains knots or holes, this resistance to tension is substantially reduced. When weight is applied perpendicular to a wood beam, such as illustrated, compression is created in the wood fibers adjacent to the area where the force or weight is applied and tension is created in the wood fibers on the opposite side. This is called fiber stress in bending.

When wood fails or slippage occurs among the wood fibers, the resulting action is called shear. There are two kinds of shear which can occur; shear parallel to the grain and shear perpendicular to the grain. An example of shear parallel to the grain would be in the process of driving a stake into the ground with a hammer hitting one-half of the stake and the wood slipping and separating parallel to the grain. Shear perpendicular to the grain would occur by taking hold of the ends of the small stake and breaking it in half across the knee.

To aid the designer, tables have been developed which take into account all the structural and mechanical characteristics of wood so that beams can be selected without the extensive use of mathematical computations to determine sizes needed. Such factors as modulus of elasticity, maximum fiber in bending, maximum allowable compression (psi), and maximum tension, have all been taken into account in the calculations for the tables.

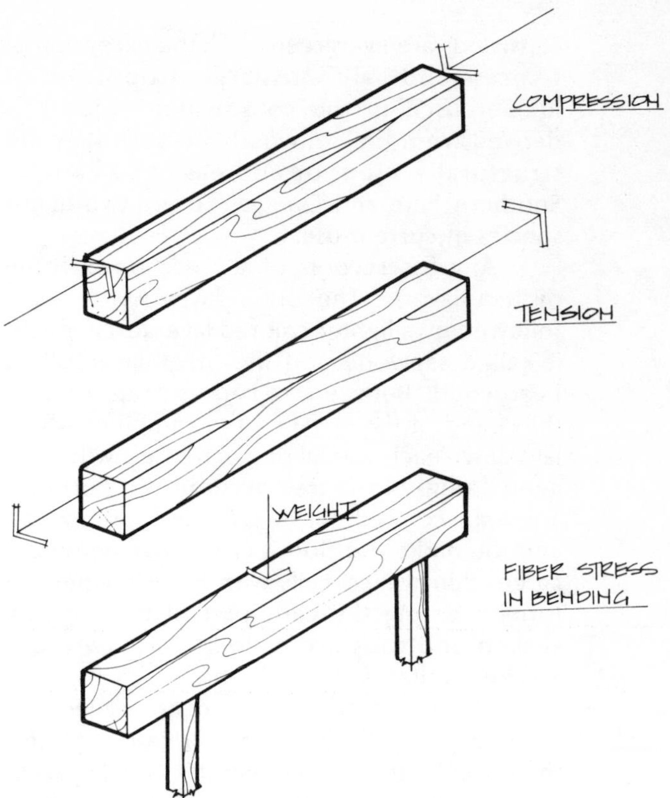
COMPRESSION
TENSION
WEIGHT
FIBER STRESS
IN BENDING

Figure 3.8 *Stress factors in wood.*

Wood Products

Lumber is sold in one of two ways; either by lineal feet or by board feet. The standard unit of measurement used by the lumber industry is the board foot, but for buyers' convenience most lumber yards will sell on the basis of lineal feet, and they have converted their prices to that measure. Lumber is sold in 2-foot increments ranging in general from 8 to 18 feet, though other lengths are available on special order or at extra cost. Thicknesses begin at 1 inch for most stuctural lumber and then are in 2-inch increments up to 12 inches.

One board foot consists of 1 inch x 12 inches x 12 inches or a square foot 1 inch thick. Any timber or board can easily be converted to board feet by multiplying the thickness in inches x the width in feet x the length in feet. To determine the number of board feet in an 8 foot length of a 2 x 4 you would multiply 2 x .33 x 8 and this would yield 5.333 board feet.

When we refer to a 2 x 4 x 8 we are referring to the thickness and width in nominal dimensions. The dressed or actual dimensions are less. One-inch-thick lumber has actual dimensions ¼-inch less, or the lumber is ¾-inch thick. Two-inch and larger boards are dressed ½-inch less up to 6 inches. Timbers above 6 inches in size are dressed ¾-inch less. A 4 x 4 is actually then 3½ x 3½ inches. A 2 x 12 actually measures 1½ x 11¼ inches. The dimensions for length is actual. If it is listed as 8 feet, this is what it measures.

When it comes to detailing lumber materials on drawings, it is necessary to remember the actual dimensions and use them to scale as a basis for the detailing. When it is time to label the materials, it is standard practice to label the nominal dimension rather than the actual dimension.

Wood shingles are sold by the square. A square is equal to 100 square feet. Four bundles are required to cover one square. (Three bundles of asphalt shingles cover one square.)

Sheet lumber includes insulation board, hardboard, particleboard and plywood; which is the reassembly of wood in various forms combined with glue to create usable panels. The standard size of these panels is 4 feet by 8 feet, though other sizes are available in some types or by special order. Thickness, in general, starts at ⅛-inch and increases in ⅛-inch increments up to 1⅛ inches thick.

Insulation board is a very light material used as sheathing on the exterior of the stud framework for homes and other small buildings. The outside surface generally is impregnated with asphalt emulsion which gives it its black appearance.

Hardboard comes in a standard density or tempered (high density). The former is used for interior work and the latter is capable of being used for exterior exposures.

Particleboard is manufactured in various densities and consists of wood chips or shavings and glue pressed into various densities depending upon intended use. Sheets of particleboard are used for subflooring, as cores for hardwood veneers, and in the manufacture of furniture and cabinets.

Plywood consists of an odd number of thin sheets of wood which have been glued together. The grain of each layer is perpendicular to the adjacent layer. However, the grain on the outside layers or plies are parallel to each other to provide stability. This technique of alternating layers provides equalized strength and minimizes any dimensional changes.

There are two kinds of plywood, softwood plywood and hardwood plywood. Softwood plywood is manufactured principally from Douglas Fir but several other species of wood are used. Hardwood plywood contains much thinner quality and sometimes prefinished layers. The veneers may be any one of several hardwood species such as black walnut, cherry, oak, birch, maple, mahogany, and teak.

There are three basic kinds of softwood plywood: interior, exterior and marine. The interior type of plywood utilizes non-water proof adhesives and should be restricted to indoor use. The exterior utilizes water-proof adhesives and can be used in most exterior exposures. Marine plywood is designed for use on the hulls of racing boats and larger boats and is designed for contact with water, and it is good for many exterior uses.

Plywood is graded on the basis of the presence or absence of defects on the face or surface plies of the sheets or panels. These grades range from A, which is best, through B and C, down to D, which is poorest. An A-A grade then would apply to a grading of both sides of a sheet, and a sheet thus graded would have only minor surface defects and the faces rated A would have been sanded. A-A grade plywood is used for partitions, cabinets, furniture and other high quality finished woodwork. Another common plywood combination would be A-D where the A side is exposed and the D side is hidden. The D side would contain knot holes, large splits, and other unsightly defects. For some flooring and roof sheathing C-D grades of plywood quite frequently are used. The grade C side has smaller knot holes and splits than the D side.

Even though the exterior grades of plywood contain waterproof adhesives, the surface of the wood will gradually break down when exposed to the weather, thus requiring some sort of protective coating, such as paint, to prevent this deterioration.

Some specialized types of plywood with veneers of redwood or cedar, intended for exterior exposure, are available. In many areas (especially where rainfall is low), these can be left unpainted much as solid redwood or cedar can be left exposed to the weather. These plywood sheets come grooved or striated, brushed, rough sawn or embossed to create a variety of shadow patterns and textures.

Strips of lumber can be glued or laminated together to create beams, girders, or structural members in a variety of sizes and shapes. Some of the more common structures in which laminated beams have been used are bridges and the insides of churches and auditoriums.

The wood used in laminations is generally from the softwood species and inclues Douglas Fir, Larch, Southern Pine and Redwood. The quality of laminated timber should conform to American Institute of Timber Construction (AITC) Standards.

Wood Preservatives

There are three principal types of preservatives: 1) creosote, 2) pentachlorophenol, and 3) metallic salts of which the two most common are ammoniacal copper arsenate and chromated copper arsenate.

Creosote has been used to treat marine piling, utility poles, and railroad ties for many years and is a widely known preservative.

Pentachlorophenol has risen in popularity in recent years and is widely used to treat fence posts, utitlity poles, and timbers used for pole barns and retaining walls. This particular chemical is dissolved in petroleum distillates ranging from heavy solvents to very light mineral spirits. The heavy oils have the advantage of making the wood very stable relative to moisture absorption and drying, and thus it is more resistant to surface deterioration. However, a disadvantage is the continuous bleeding of the oil for several years, preventing this wood from being painted or stained. With the use of very light distillates the wood can be painted.

The metallic salts (copper compounds) use water as a carrier. Wood which is treated with these chemicals will have a greenish cast which dissipates with age after it is exposed to the out-of-doors. However, the wood will not become as dark a silver gray as untreated wood. (In contrast, the penta-treated woods range from light to dark browns in color.) When water is used as a carrier the treated wood can easily be painted or stained.

Timbers treated with creote or metallic salts are unharmed by sea water, but penta-treated wood should not be exposed to a salt-water environment.

Over-the-counter preservative preparations are usually light petroleum distillates with an approximate five percent solution of the pentachlorophenol. Wood can be dipped, painted, or sprayed with the solution for temporary protection, but long range protection requires that wood be treated commercially in pressure tanks where the preservative can be forced into the cells and into the very interior of each timber. Thus, long range protection against insect and fungus attack and decay is assured. Treatments for long-lasting protection should conform to the standards of the American Wood Preservers Association.

REFERENCES FOR FURTHER READING

Asphalt Institute. "Asphalt," *Handbook of Landscape Architectural Construction.* Washington, DC: Landscape Architecture Foundation, 1973.

Banov, A. *Paints and Coatings Handbook.* 2nd Edition. New York: McGraw-Hill, 1981.

Brady, G.S. *Materials Handbook.* 11th Edition. New York: McGraw-Hill, 1977.

Brick Institute. "Masonry," *Handbook of Landscape Architectural Construction.* Washington, DC: Landscape Architecture Foundation, 1973.

California Redwood Association. "Redwood," *Handbook of Landscape Architectural Construction.* Washington, DC: Landscape Architecture Foundation, 1973.

Ramsey, C.G., and Sleeper, H.R. *Architectural Graphics Standards.* 7th Edition. New York: Wiley, 1981.

Associations and Organizations

Aluminum Association
818 Connecticut Ave., N.W.
Washington, DC 20006

American Concrete Institute
P.O. Box 19150
Redford Station
Detroit, Michigan 48219

American Institute of Timber Construction
333 West Hampden Ave.
Englewood, Colorado 80110

American Iron and Steel Institute
1000 16th Street Northwest
Washington, DC 20036

American Plywood Association
P.O. Box 11700
Tacoma, Washington 98411

American Society for Testing and Materials
1916 Race Street
Philadelphia, Pennsylvania 19103

American Wood Preservers Institute
1651 Old Meadow Road
McLean, Virginia 22102

Asphalt Institute
College Park, Maryland 20740

Brick Institute of America
1750 Old Meadow Road
McLean, Virginia 22102

Building Stone Institute
420 Lexington Ave.
New York, New York 10170

California Redwood Association
591 Redwood Highway #3100
Mill Valley, California 94941

Construction Specifications Institute
601 Madison Street
Alexandria, Virginia 22314

Illuminating Engineering Society of
North America
c/o United Engineering Center
345 E. 47th Street
New York, New York 10017

National Crushed Stone Association
1415 Elliot Place, N.W.
Washington, DC 20007

Portland Cement Association
5420 Old Orchard Road
Skokie, Illinois 60077

Red Cedar Shingle and Handsplit Shake Bureau
515 116th Avenue N.E. Suite 275
Bellevue, Washington 98004

Southern Forest Products Association
P.O. Box 52468
New Orleans, Louisiana 70152

Western Wood Products Association
Yeon Building
Portland, Oregon 97204

Figure 4.1 *Old worn and weathered brick.* A. E. Bye and Associates

4

Paving

With a basic understanding of materials and how they work together, the site designer can create many aesthetic and interesting patterns with paving. Limitations other than the material itself might be the function of the paving, cost factors, and the physical environment (frost, temperature fluctuation, etc.).

As soon as new land is developed paving is installed. It provides a solid surface under foot and covers up mud, making all-season travel possible. It can probably be considered one of the standard amenities of civilization. Everywhere around us roads, walks, driveways, patios, parking lots, are paved. Too much paving is drab looking, and it is the function of the trained designer to improve the appearance of new paving. It seems essential that the general public be educated as to the variables and increased beauty that can be incorporated into paving surfaces by a little forethought and planning.

One of the disadvantages occurring with increased paving has been increased water runoff. This has reduced the amount of water sinking into the subsurface aquifers and water tables which recharge culinary water sources. Experiments are being conducted in the use of porous paving surfaces which will allow the water to percolate into the soil below instead of draining the water into rivers and oceans where it is of little value. Some of these include asphaltic concrete, gravel held together with epoxy, and pre-cast concrete grids.

COST FACTORS

Because the aggregates used are available locally and only the portland cement and asphalt cement need be transported, concrete and asphalt concrete are generally the least expensive paving. They also can be installed with a great deal of ease requiring a minimum amount of hand labor.

A great deal of hand labor is required for the installation of brick, stone, and precast pavers, thus greatly increasing the cost of these kinds of pavements. The use of complex patterns and the inavailability of skilled workers may complicate the cast problem even further.

PHYSICAL CHARACTERISTICS

Concrete reflects light. This has the disadvantage of causing glare and uncomfortable light levels. It has the advantage of not absorbing a great deal of heat and being comfortable to bare feet. The opposite is true for asphalt which reflects little but readily absorbs the sun, increasing the surface temperature and making it unbearable for bare feet.

Concrete expands and contracts with temperature changes; thus expansion and contraction joints must be provided to allow for this movement. Asphaltic concrete is more flexible and joints need not be provided.

Paving may be affected by freeze-thaw cycles in those portions of the country where temperatures go below 32°F. or 0° C. The effects may occur in one or several different areas of paving. The surface of the paving, in the case of concrete, might be damaged by the freezing of absorbed water, or deterioration from de-icing salts. Moisture may also creep into the mortar joints of paving units or into the expansion joints of poured concrete. Even the base may be affected when water gets underneath the paving and causes it to heave and break apart during freezing. Pavers such as stone or brick may also absorb moisture and break apart because of freezing within the structure of the paver.

Quality of materials and workmanship will play a large part in alleviating some of the problems previously discussed. Air entrainment will minimize surface damage to concrete. High quality severe weather (SW) rated brick will minimize damage to that particular type of paving unit. In the case of stone, the use of porous types, such as limestone, should not be used where the paving is subjected to rapid temperature changes and freeze-thaw cycles.

By using urethane sealants to close off expansion joints, water can be kept out of them and from accumulating below to create frost damage. High quality mortar can be used for brick and stone pavers. The joints should be tight and their surfaces sealed with a good tool to prevent moisture from penetrating the mortar and joint. A sealer applied to the entire paving surface may be desirable to prevent freeze damage.

A good porous base under most paving will prevent the accumulation of moisture and in some cases should be thicker than would normally be used to allow greater capacity for moisture flow, especially if water tables are high or the soil below the base has little moisture-absorbing capability. In some cases drain tile may be required to carry off the excess moisture.

Because paving materials will crack and break up from any vertical movement, it is important that the soil underneath be stable. Preferably, the soil should be original and undisturbed. If, however, this is not practical and fill has been used, the fill must be compacted thoroughly to prevent any further settling. There are certain standards used by State Highway Departments for achieving this high quality of compaction, and these standards can be referred to on any particular design project as a specification.

Certain soils are more troublesome than others. Any soil containing organic matter will be especially difficult as a base or subbase material. The decomposition of the organic matter ultimately creates a softness in the soil and makes it unstable. Gravelly and sandy soils generally make excellent base material if they are free from organic matter. Falling somewhere in between are the clay soils, which when free from organic matter are relatively stable but still subject to some expansion during water accumulation and frost penetration.

For unstable soils it may be necessary in some instances to provide a soil cement subbase. A foot or more of soil can be dug up, mixed with portland cement and rolled back into place to achieve a subbase of about 700 p.s.i.

Because a uniform base and/or subbase are difficult to achieve, it is essential to reinforce concrete paving. For light duty areas such as sidewalks and patios, welded wire reinforcing mesh (or welded wire fabric) can be installed. Commonly used mesh is a 6 inch by 6 inch square with 10 gauge wire in each direction (6 x 6 10/10). For heavier duty applications such as driveways, sidewalks in public areas, etc., a 6 gauge mesh (6 x 6 6/6) is used.

PAVING THICKNESSES AND COMBINATIONS

As a general rule, concrete can be laid 4 inches in depth for residential walks, patios, and driveways. For roads, public sidewalks, and areas where there is a possibility of heavy vehicular traffic, the depth should be 5 to 6 inches. The base underneath may be gravel ranging from 4 to 8 inches, varying with the thickness of the concrete and the nature of the soil.

There are several combinations in the use of asphaltic concrete. Two of the possibilities are as follows: "Full-depth" asphaltic concrete does not require the use of a gravel base and can be placed directly on the soil. It would include a 4½ inch asphaltic concrete base course with 1½ inch wearing course. For tennis courts or any other surface where careful attention to slope is required, a ¾ inch leveling course is added on top. The thickness of the base course would be increased for poor soils and heavy traffic. The second possibility for asphaltic concrete is for parking lots and driveways where medium traffic occurs. This involves the placement of 6 to 8 inches of gravel fill as a base over the soil followed by 2 to 3 inches of asphaltic concrete base course and 1½ inches of wearing course.

Occasionally inexpensive sidewalks and bicycle trails are constructed of 5 inches of asphaltic concrete over 4 inches of gravel. While this makes an inexpensive paving material it is subject to early deterioration in frost prone areas and will require replacement as a result.

SCHEDULE OF SURFACE MATERIALS

SYMBOL	LOCATION	MATERIALS & DEPTHS
(A)	DRIVES & PARKING	1½" CLASS 2 BIT. CONC. 2" CL. 1 BIT. CONC. 4" PROCESSED AGG. 6" BANK RUN GRAVEL COMPACTED SUBGRADE
(B)	WALKS	2" CLASS 2 BIT. CONC. 4" PROCESSED AGG. 4" BANK RUN GRAVEL COMPACTED SUBGRADE
(C)	WALKS	4" CONCRETE 6" BANK RUN GRAVEL COMPACTED SUBGRADE
(D)	DRIVES & WALKS	INTERLOCKING CONC. PAVERS - SAND FILLED JOINTS 1¼" SAND 8" BANK RUN GRAVEL 2 COURSES COMPACTED SUBGRADE
(E)	CRUSHER DUST DRIVE	3" CRUSHER DUST 12" BANK RUN GRAVEL COMPACTED SUBGRADE
(F)	TENNIS & TRACK	1" RUB KOR 2" BIT. CONC. BINDER 4" PROCESSED AGG. 6" BANK RUN GRAVEL COMPACTED SUBGRADE

Figure 4.2 *Paving combinations.*

CR3, inc.

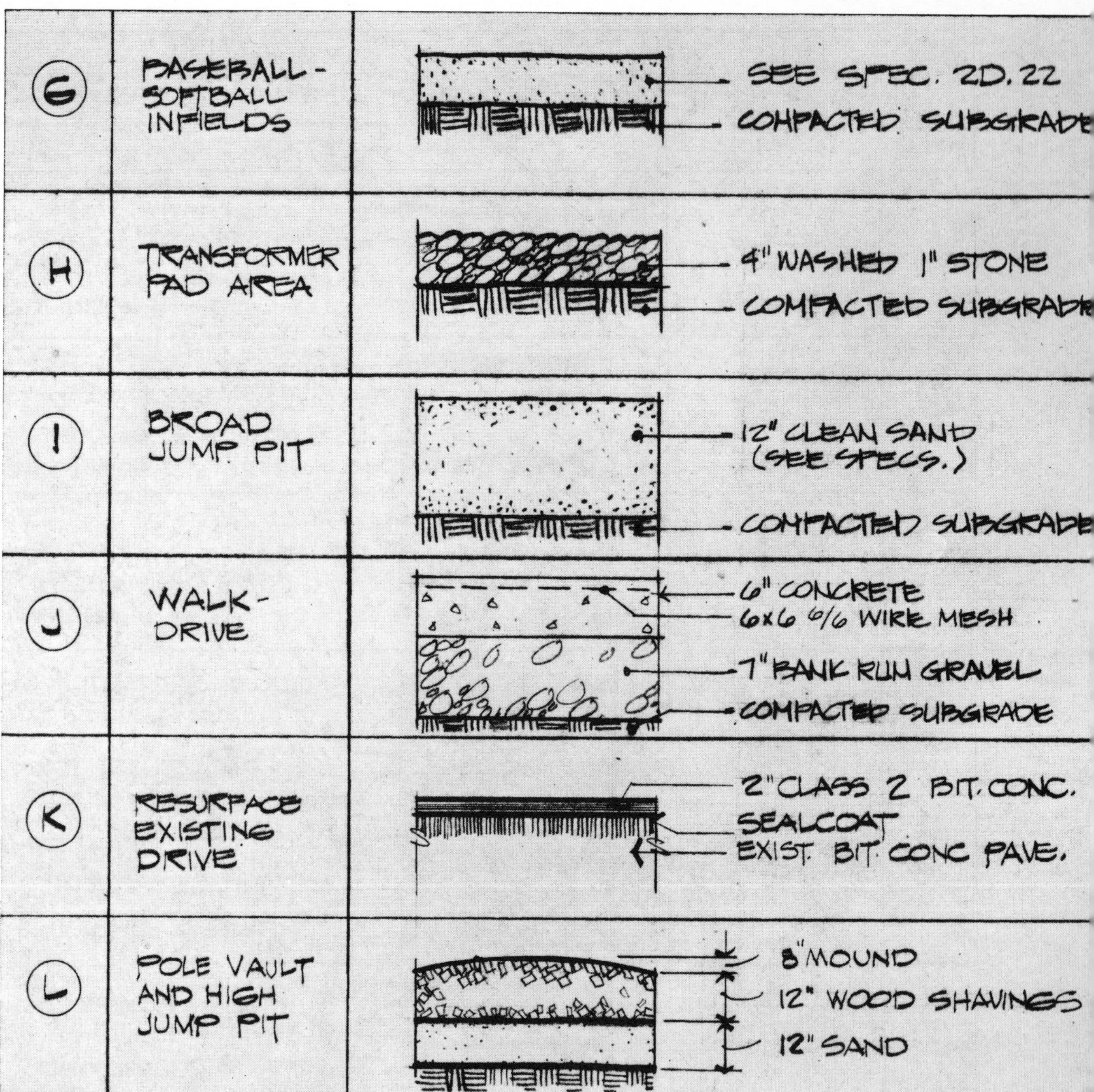
G
BASEBALL-
SOFTBALL
INFIELDS
SEE SPEC. 2D.22
COMPACTED SUBGRADE
H
TRANSFORMER
PAD AREA
4" WASHED 1" STONE
COMPACTED SUBGRADE
I
BROAD
JUMP PIT
12" CLEAN SAND
(SEE SPECS.)
COMPACTED SUBGRADE
J
WALK-
DRIVE
6" CONCRETE
6x6 6/6 WIRE MESH
7" BANK RUN GRAVEL
COMPACTED SUBGRADE
K
RESURFACE
EXISTING
DRIVE
2" CLASS 2 BIT. CONC.
SEALCOAT
EXIST. BIT. CONC PAVE.
L
POLE VAULT
AND HIGH
JUMP PIT
8" MOUND
12" WOOD SHAVINGS
12" SAND

Figure 4.3 *Paving combinations.*

CR3, inc.

PAVING SCHEDULE

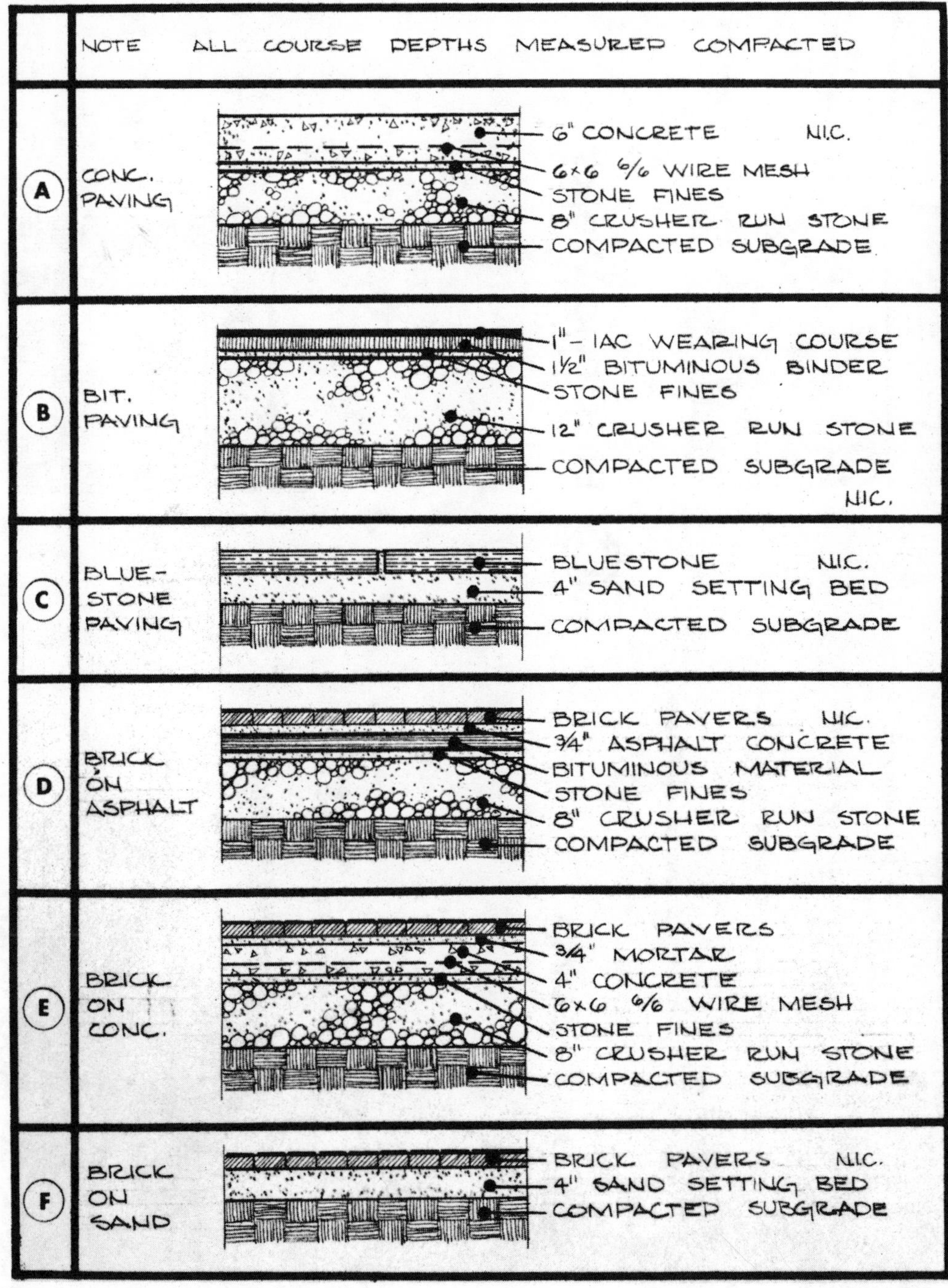
NOTE ALL COURSE DEPTHS MEASURED COMPACTED
A
CONC. PAVING
6" CONCRETE N.I.C.
6×6 6/6 WIRE MESH
STONE FINES
8" CRUSHER RUN STONE
COMPACTED SUBGRADE
B
BIT. PAVING
1"- IAC WEARING COURSE
1½" BITUMINOUS BINDER
STONE FINES
12" CRUSHER RUN STONE
COMPACTED SUBGRADE
N.I.C.
C
BLUE-STONE PAVING
BLUESTONE N.I.C.
4" SAND SETTING BED
COMPACTED SUBGRADE
D
BRICK ON ASPHALT
BRICK PAVERS N.I.C.
¾" ASPHALT CONCRETE
BITUMINOUS MATERIAL
STONE FINES
8" CRUSHER RUN STONE
COMPACTED SUBGRADE
E
BRICK ON CONC.
BRICK PAVERS
¾" MORTAR
4" CONCRETE
6×6 6/6 WIRE MESH
STONE FINES
8" CRUSHER RUN STONE
COMPACTED SUBGRADE
F
BRICK ON SAND
BRICK PAVERS N.I.C.
4" SAND SETTING BED
COMPACTED SUBGRADE

Figure 4.4 *Paving combinations.*

Saratoga Associates

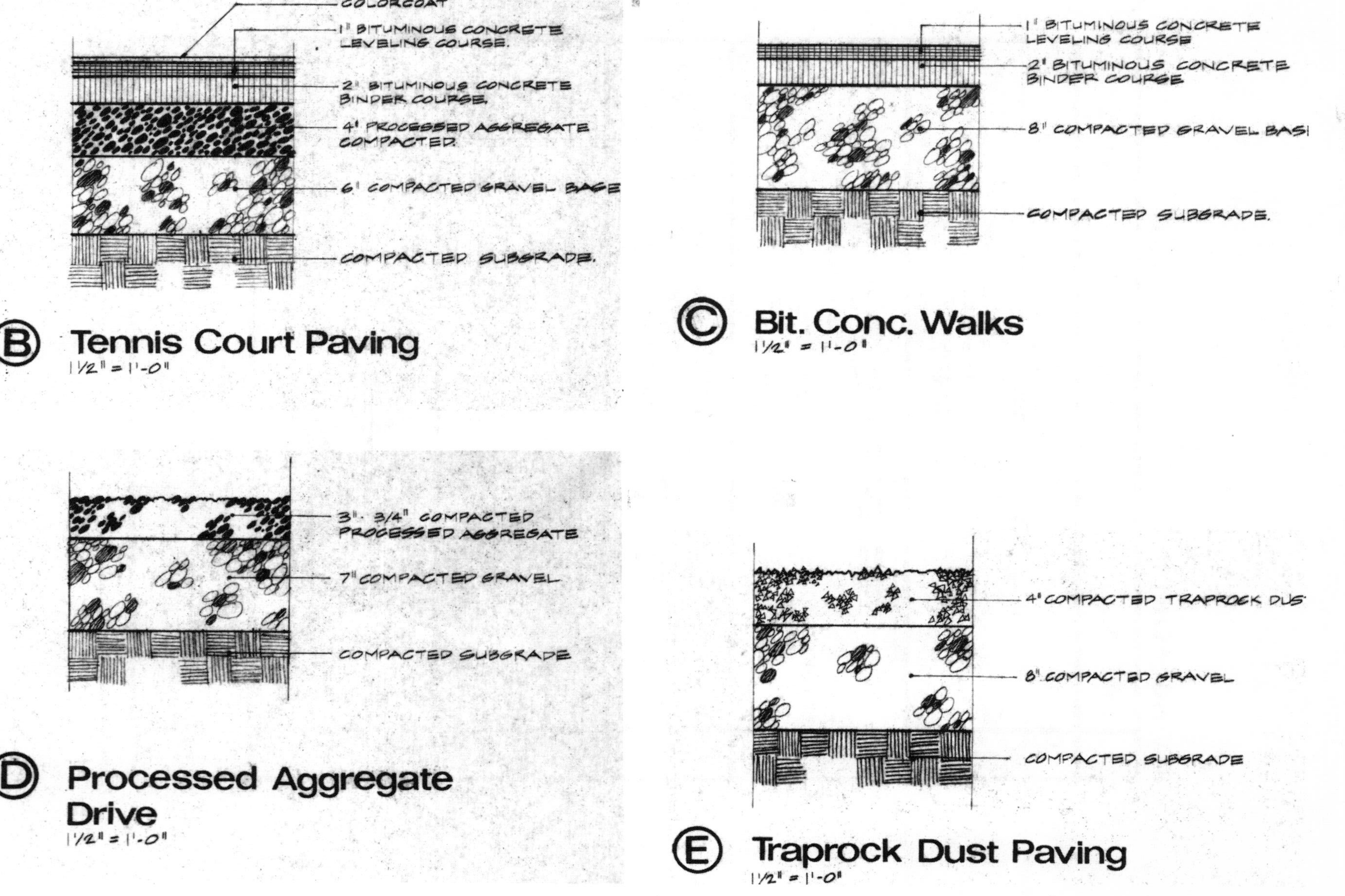

COLORCOAT
1" BITUMINOUS CONCRETE LEVELING COURSE.
2" BITUMINOUS CONCRETE BINDER COURSE.
4" PROCESSED AGGREGATE COMPACTED.
6" COMPACTED GRAVEL BASE
COMPACTED SUBGRADE.
B Tennis Court Paving
1 1/2" = 1'-0"
1" BITUMINOUS CONCRETE LEVELING COURSE
2" BITUMINOUS CONCRETE BINDER COURSE
8" COMPACTED GRAVEL BASI
COMPACTED SUBGRADE.
C Bit. Conc. Walks
1 1/2" = 1'-0"
3"- 3/4" COMPACTED PROCESSED AGGREGATE
7" COMPACTED GRAVEL
COMPACTED SUBGRADE
D Processed Aggregate Drive
1 1/2" = 1'-0"
4" COMPACTED TRAPROCK DUS
8" COMPACTED GRAVEL
COMPACTED SUBGRADE
E Traprock Dust Paving
1 1/2" = 1'-0"

Figure 4.5 *Paving combinations.*

CR3, inc.

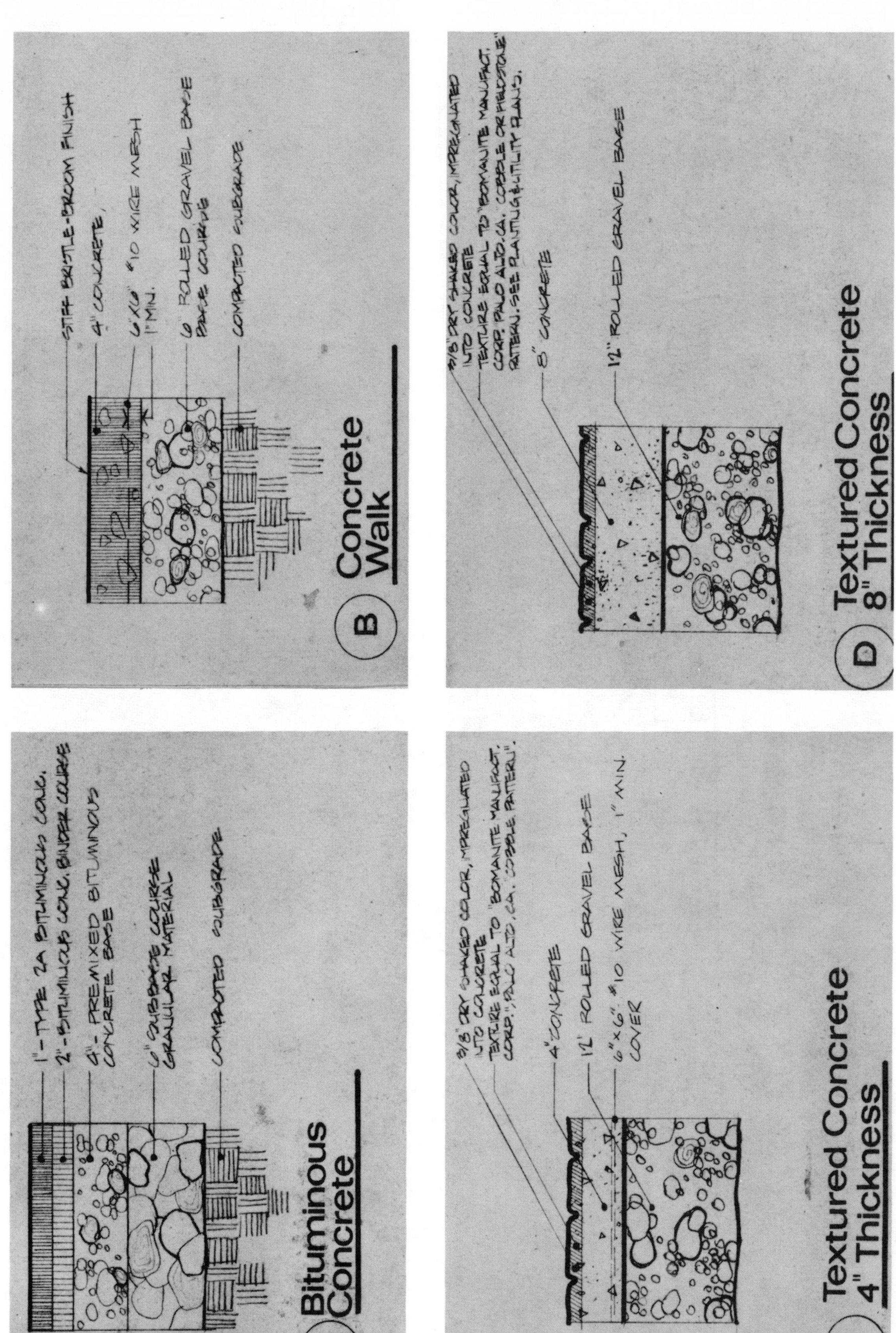
1"–TYPE 2A BITUMINOUS CONC.
2"–BITUMINOUS CONC. BINDER COURSE
4"– PREMIXED BITUMINOUS CONCRETE BASE
6" SUBBASE COURSE GRANULAR MATERIAL
COMPACTED SUBGRADE
A Bituminous Concrete
STIFF BRISTLE-BROOM FINISH
4" CONCRETE,
6"X6" #10 WIRE MESH
1" MIN.
6" ROLLED GRAVEL BASE BASE COURSE
COMPACTED SUBGRADE
B Concrete Walk
3/8" DRY SHAKED COLOR, IMPREGNATED INTO CONCRETE
TEXTURE EQUAL TO "BOMANITE MANUFACT. CORP.", PALO ALTO, CA. "COBBLE PATTERN".
4" CONCRETE
12" ROLLED GRAVEL BASE
6"×6" #10 WIRE MESH, 1" MIN. COVER
C Textured Concrete 4" Thickness
3/8" DRY SHAKED COLOR, IMPREGNATED INTO CONCRETE
TEXTURE EQUAL TO "BOMANITE MANUFACT. CORP. PALO ALTO, CA. "COBBLE OR FIELDSTONE" PATTERN. SEE PLANTING & UTILITY PLANS.
8" CONCRETE
12" ROLLED GRAVEL BASE
D Textured Concrete 8" Thickness

Figure 4.6 *Paving combinations.*

Johnson and Dee

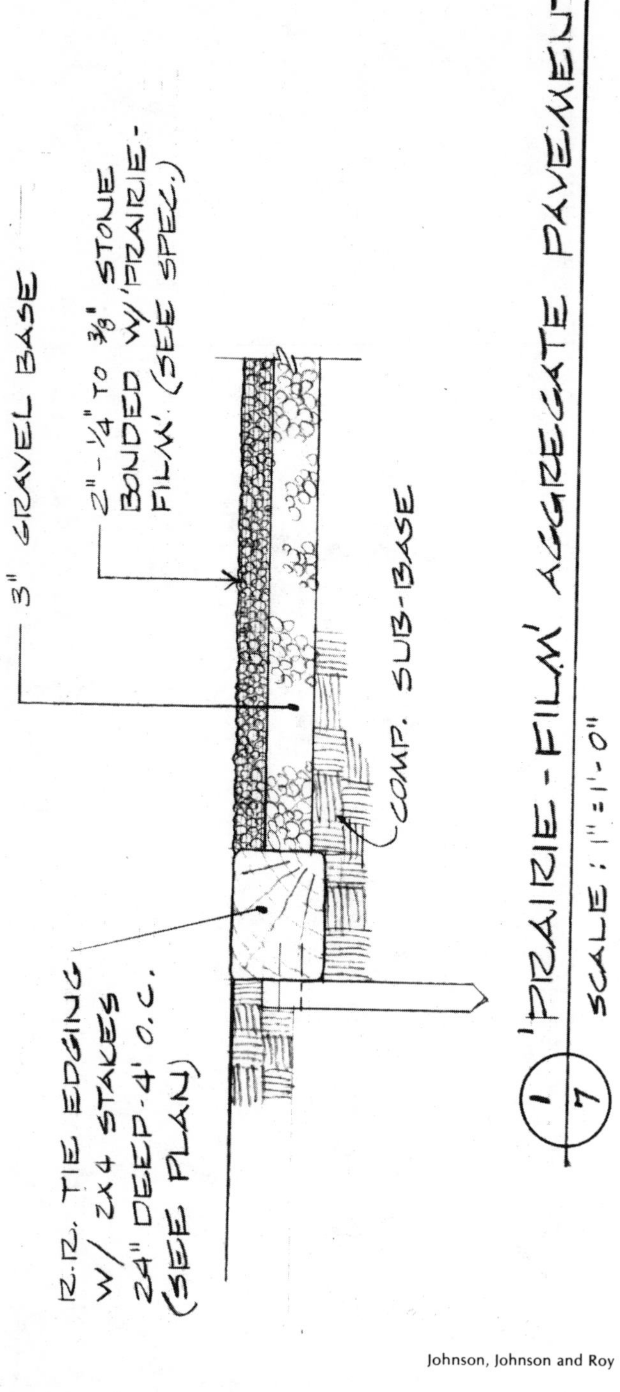
3" GRAVEL BASE
2"-1/4" TO 3/8" STONE BONDED W/'PRAIRIE-FILM.' (SEE SPEC.)
COMP. SUB-BASE
R.R. TIE EDGING W/ 2X4 STAKES 24" DEEP-4' O.C. (SEE PLAN)
1/7
'PRAIRIE-FILM' AGGREGATE PAVEMENT
SCALE: 1" = 1'-0"

Johnson, Johnson and Roy

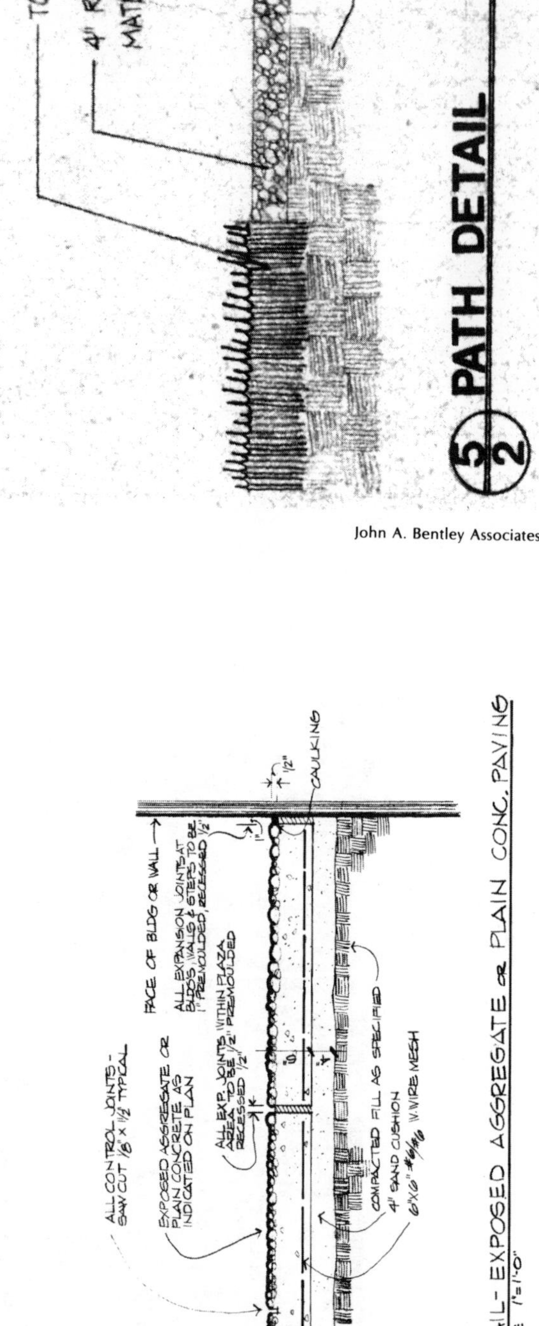
TOPSOIL 4" DEPTH
4" ROLLED GRANULAR MATERIAL. SEE SPEC.
SUBSOIL
5/2
PATH DETAIL
CAULKING
FACE OF BLDG OR WALL
COMPACTED FILL AS SPECIFIED
4" SAND CUSHION
3/SD3
DETAIL-EXPOSED AGGREGATE or PLAIN CONC. PAVING
SCALE 1"=1'-0"

John A. Bentley Associates

Johnson, Johnson and Roy

Figure 4.7 *Paving combinations.*

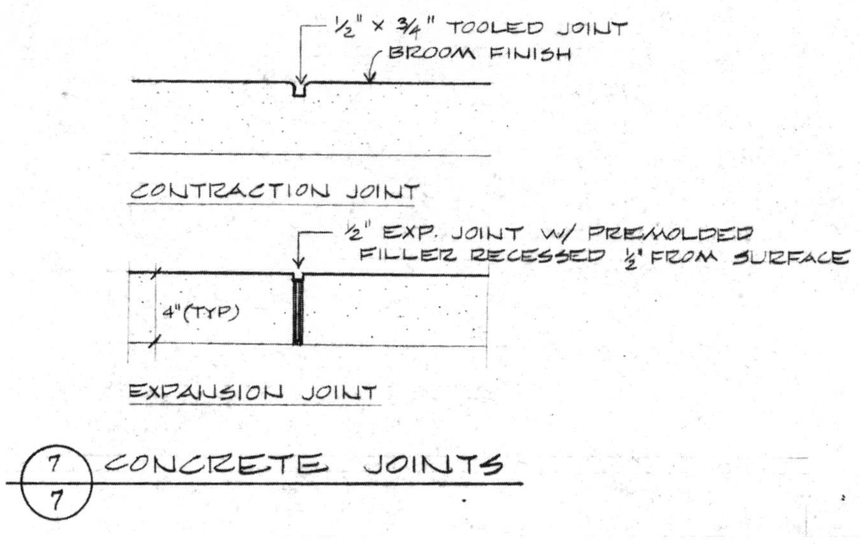

½" x ¾" TOOLED JOINT
BROOM FINISH
CONTRACTION JOINT
½" EXP. JOINT W/ PREMOLDED FILLER RECESSED ½" FROM SURFACE
4"(TYP)
EXPANSION JOINT
7
7
CONCRETE JOINTS

Figure 4.8 *Paving joints.* Johnson, Johnson and Roy

Color coatings can be used on asphalt, such as line striping and sealers, but none of these should be applied earlier than 30 days following paving material placement. Asphaltic concrete gradually turns gray and some users may find it desirable to apply a coat of black asphalt emulsion to restore color. For play areas and tennis courts, acrylic latex paints or emulsions compatible with asphalt can be applied in colors to enhance the playing surface.

The surface treatment for concrete includes several possibilities. One is to expose the aggregate through the use of chemical retardants, by brushing and washing before final set, or by sand blasting after set. The least expensive approach for finishing concrete is to either float finish or use a broom to create a uniform texture. The broom finish provides a texture which increases the safety when the pavement is wet or slick from freezing rain.

Stains and pigments can be added to concrete for color. These in combination with various patterns stamped into the paving surface create imitations of other kinds of paving at less cost.

EXPANSION-CONTRACTION JOINTS

The exact placement of expansion joints will vary across the country depending upon temperature fluctuations in any particular area. In the mid-west, as a general rule of thumb, expansion joints are placed every 30 feet in sidewalks, and larger sections of concrete may be divided up into 15 to 20 foot squares. Contraction joints are generally based upon a module of the width of the material; in other words, a five foot sidewalk may have contraction joints every five feet. To be effective a contraction joint must be one-fourth of the depth of the concrete. These can either be tooled or sawn in place after the concrete is set.

Patterns can be created for aesthetic value, at the same time serving as expansion joints. This can be accomplished with such materials as 2 x 4's of redwood placed in a modular pattern. The redwood allows the concrete to expand and contract at will. These wood dividers will heave and move upward out of the paving during freeze-thaw cycles. In order to prevent this, 16 penny galvanized nails can be driven alternately into each side of the 2 x 4 at 12 inch intervals.

BRICK PAVING

Brick pavers can be placed over 3 to 4 inches of concrete using a ¾-inch mortar setting bed and mortar joints. The joints need to be carefully tooled to seal them against moisture penetration. The use of liquid latex in place of water when preparing mortar will ensure greater durability, strength, and resistance to frost damage.

Brick pavers may also be placed over a 4-inch "full-depth" asphaltic concrete. The base course is placed directly on the soil. On top of the full-depth asphaltic concrete, a bituminous setting bed ¾ inch in depth is added and a precision surface created. A cold neoprene or a hot asphalt cement tack coat is applied just before the pavers are laid in place. In severe

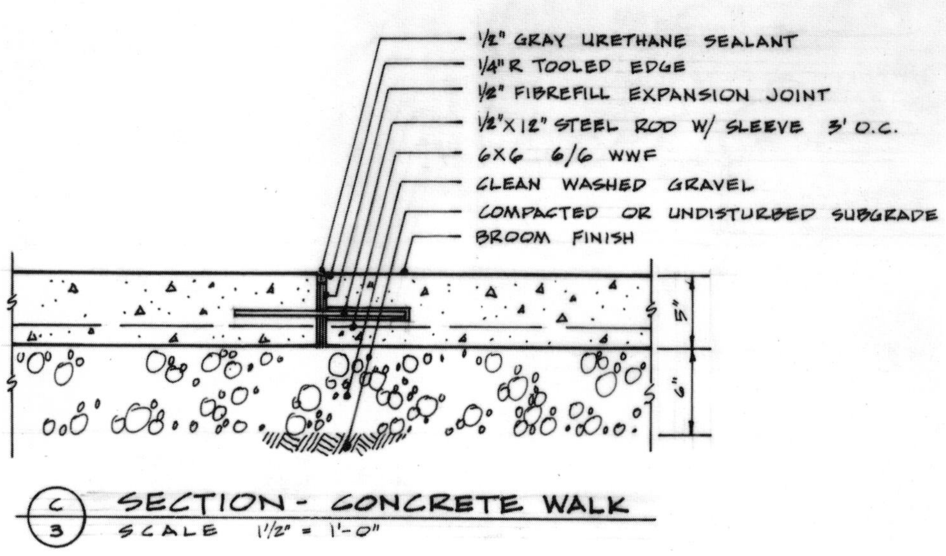
1/2" GRAY URETHANE SEALANT
1/4" R TOOLED EDGE
1/2" FIBREFILL EXPANSION JOINT
1/2"X12" STEEL ROD W/ SLEEVE 3' O.C.
6X6 6/6 WWF
CLEAN WASHED GRAVEL
COMPACTED OR UNDISTURBED SUBGRADE
BROOM FINISH
5"
6"
C
3
SECTION - CONCRETE WALK
SCALE 1 1/2" = 1'-0"

Figure 4.9 *Paving joints.* Walker-Harris-Associates-Inc.

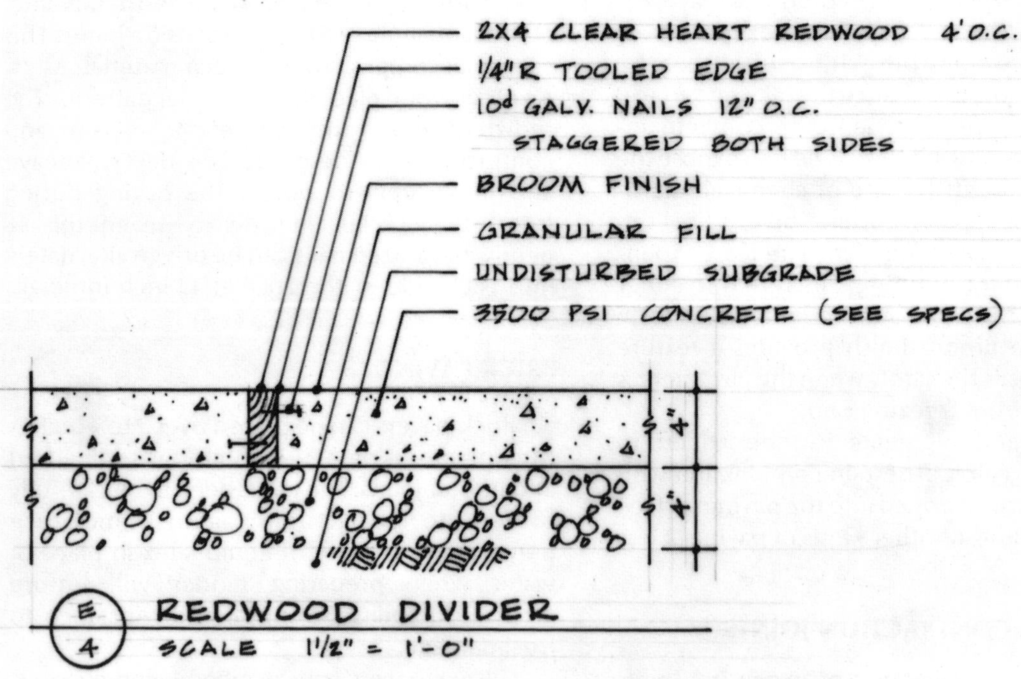
2X4 CLEAR HEART REDWOOD 4' O.C.
1/4" R TOOLED EDGE
10d GALV. NAILS 12" O.C.
STAGGERED BOTH SIDES
BROOM FINISH
GRANULAR FILL
UNDISTURBED SUBGRADE
3500 PSI CONCRETE (SEE SPECS)
4"
4"
E
4
REDWOOD DIVIDER
SCALE 1 1/2" = 1'-0"

Figure 4.10 *Paving joints.* Walker-Harris-Associates-Inc.

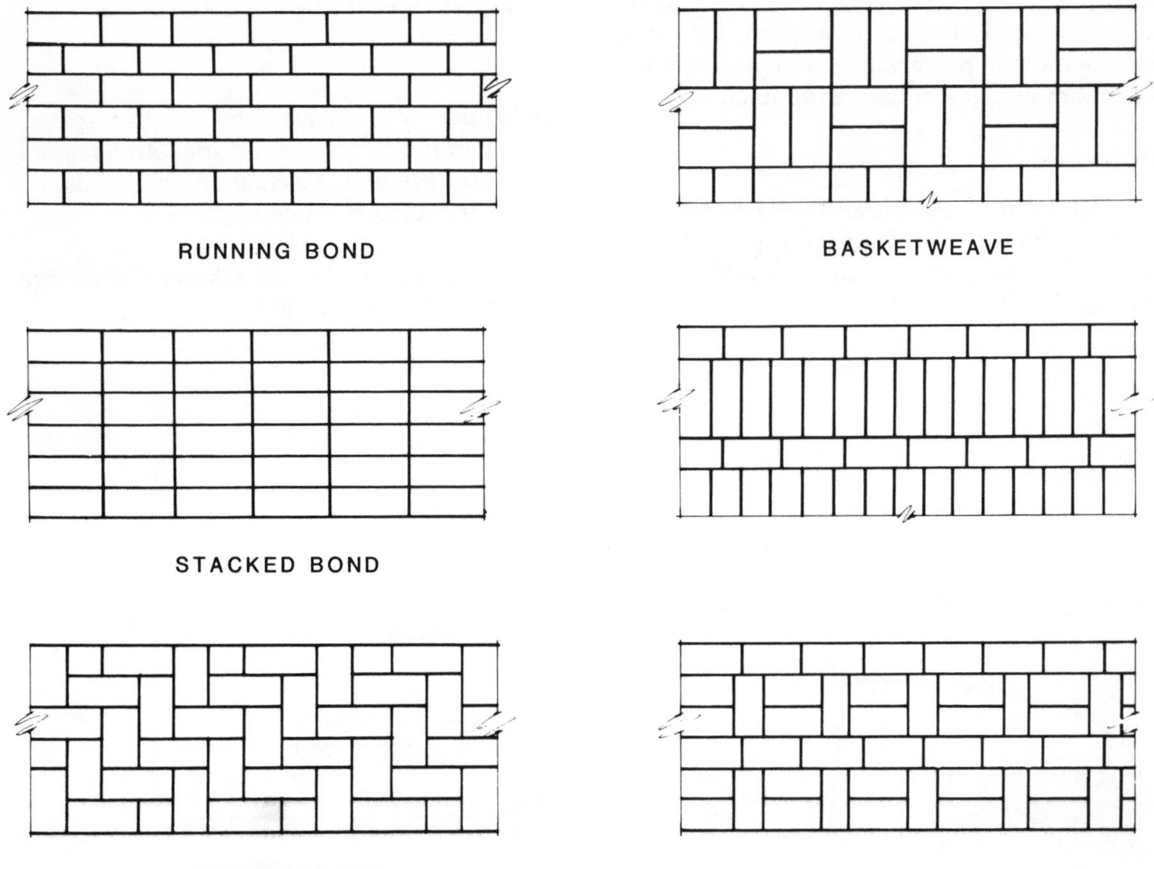
RUNNING BOND
BASKETWEAVE
STACKED BOND
HERRINGBONE

Figure 4.11 *Frequently used brick paving patterns.*

freezing-thawing conditions moisture may get between some of the pavers and cause them to break loose so this technique should be used with caution under such extreme conditions.

Brick may also be laid on a sand base depending upon the soil subbase. The sand may range in depth from 2 to 4 inches. Sand should not be used over loose gravel, as the sand will gradually work down into the gravel and cause settling of the brick. The brick are easier to lay after the sand has been tamped and carefully leveled and a layer of 15-pound asphalt-impregnated felt placed over the sand. The brick are laid directly on the felt and dry sand is brushed into the joints, which will be rather tight if they have been carefully hand set adjacent to each other. If the joints are not uniformly tight, a mixure of sand and cement can be swept into them to improve stability and reduce growth of grass and weeds. Bricks set in this fashion will need some kind of an edging designed to prevent them from shifting and moving. Edgings are described and illustrated in Chapter 5.

STONE

Stone may be utilized in the same manner as brick and in the same kinds of situations, except that stone laid over the asphaltic concrete or concrete base may be much thinner than when it is used over sand. Some stone, like slate, may only be ¾ inch thick when it is laid in a mortar setting bed, whereas if it is laid on sand it will need to be 1½ to 2 inches thick to be stable. The type, quality, thickness and color needs to be precisely identified on the drawings to ensure installation to the designer's expectations.

WOOD

Sections of square, rectangular, or round timbers can be sawn 4 to 6 inches thick and set in a sand or gravel base. The wood will need preservative treatment to increase its resistance to decay. New pressure-treated timber probably will hold up quite well. Sections of new 6 x 6's can be set in 4 inches of sand with tight joints and will have a neat, attractive appearance. A more natural or rustic appearance can be achieved by cutting sections from old trees, soaking them in preservative, and placing them at random in a gravel base and mulch.

DRAINAGE

All paving materials and surfaces must be sloped to drain. A minimum is one percent or 1/8 inch to the foot. Preferably it should be two percent or 1/4 inch to the foot.

REFERENCES FOR FURTHER READING

Bellafiore, V.J. "Pavement in Landscape," *Handbook of Landscape Architectural Construction.* Washington, DC: Landscape Architecture Foundation, 1973.

Halprin, L. *Cities.* Revised Edition. Cambridge, MA: MIT Press, 1973.

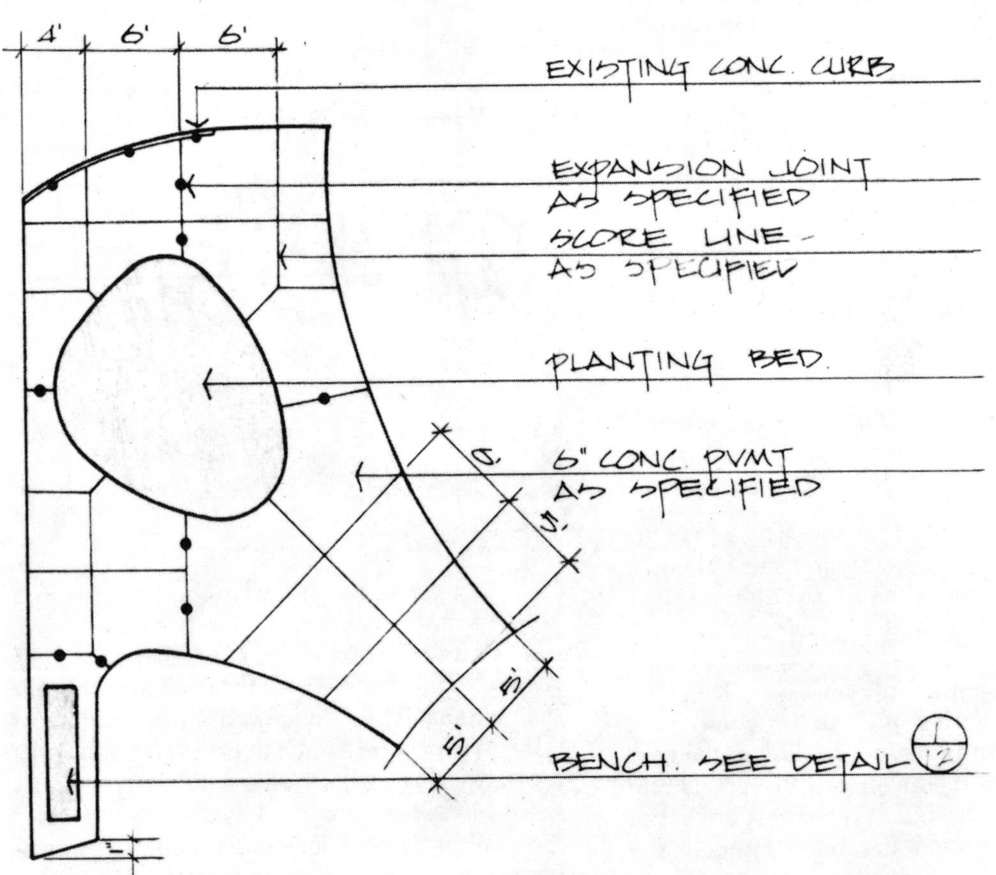

4'
6'
6'
EXISTING CONC. CURB
EXPANSION JOINT AS SPECIFIED
SCORE LINE - AS SPECIFIED
PLANTING BED.
6" CONC. PVMT AS SPECIFIED
6'
5'
5'
5'
BENCH. SEE DETAIL
1/12

6/12
CONC. ENTRANCE/SCORING (ALT. #6)
PLAN
1" = 1'-0"

Figure 4.12 *Paving joints in plan view.*

Bonnell and Associates

BENEFICIAL
LOANS

Figure 4.13 *Paving pattern stamped into concrete.* Johnson and Dee

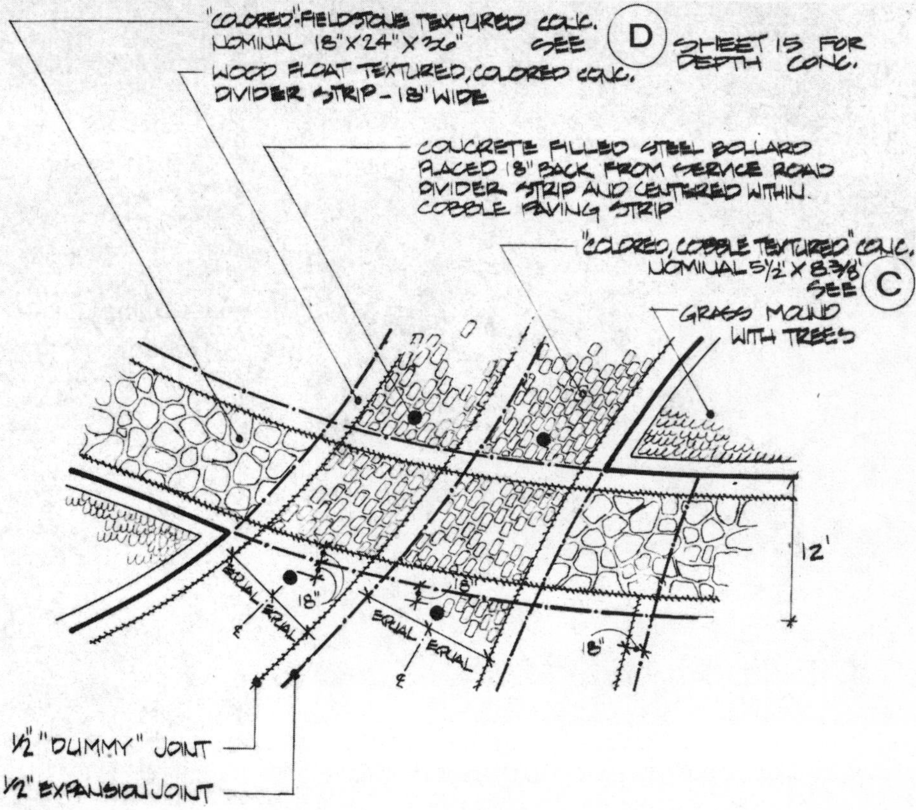
"COLORED"-FIELDSTONE TEXTURED CONC.
NOMINAL 18"X24"X36"
SEE D SHEET 15 FOR DEPTH CONC.
WOOD FLOAT TEXTURED, COLORED CONC.
DIVIDER STRIP - 18" WIDE
CONCRETE FILLED STEEL BOLLARD
PLACED 18" BACK FROM SERVICE ROAD
DIVIDER STRIP AND CENTERED WITHIN.
COBBLE PAVING STRIP
"COLORED, COBBLE TEXTURED" CONC.
NOMINAL 5½" X 8⅜"
SEE C
GRASS MOUND
WITH TREES
12'
18"
EQUAL
EQUAL
18"
EQUAL
EQUAL
18"
½" "DUMMY" JOINT
½" EXPANSION JOINT

Figure 4.14 *Layout for paving in Figure 4.13. See details on page 53.* Johnson and Dee

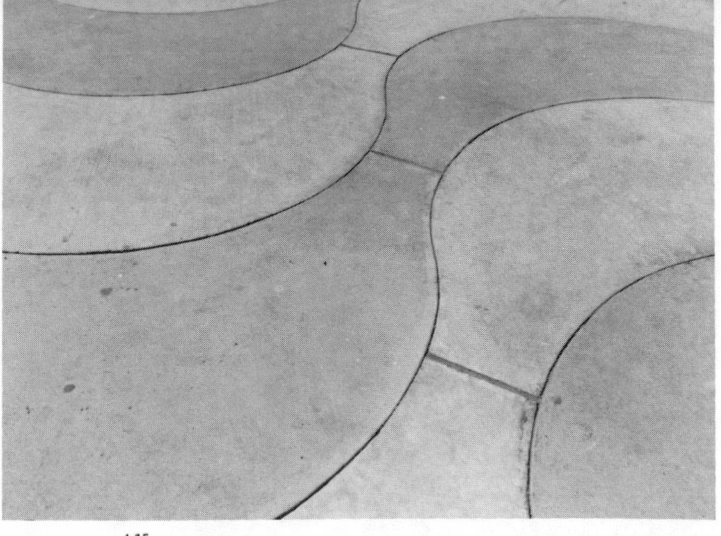

4.15

4.18

4.16

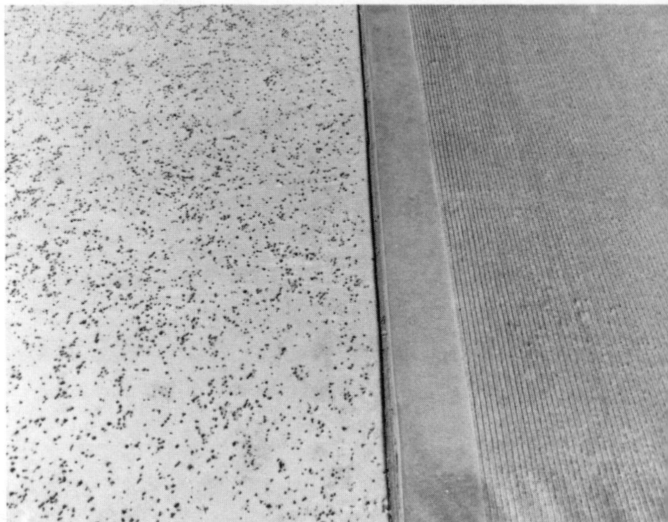

4.19

4.17

Figures 4.15 – 4.16 *A variety of patterns in concrete paving.*

Figure 4.17 *Modular squares made more interesting with an offset.*

Figure 4.18 *Angles repeat lines in the unseen building to the right.*

Figure 4.19 *Precision wire-cut finish on right. Left panel finish created with salt crystals – a technique to be used only in frost-free climates.*

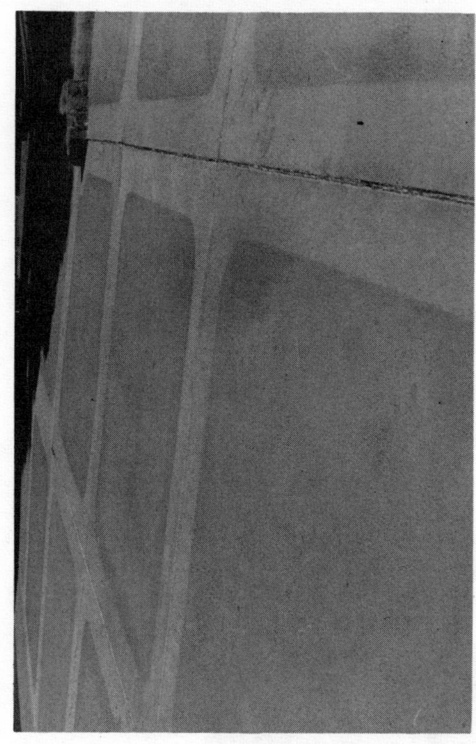

4.20

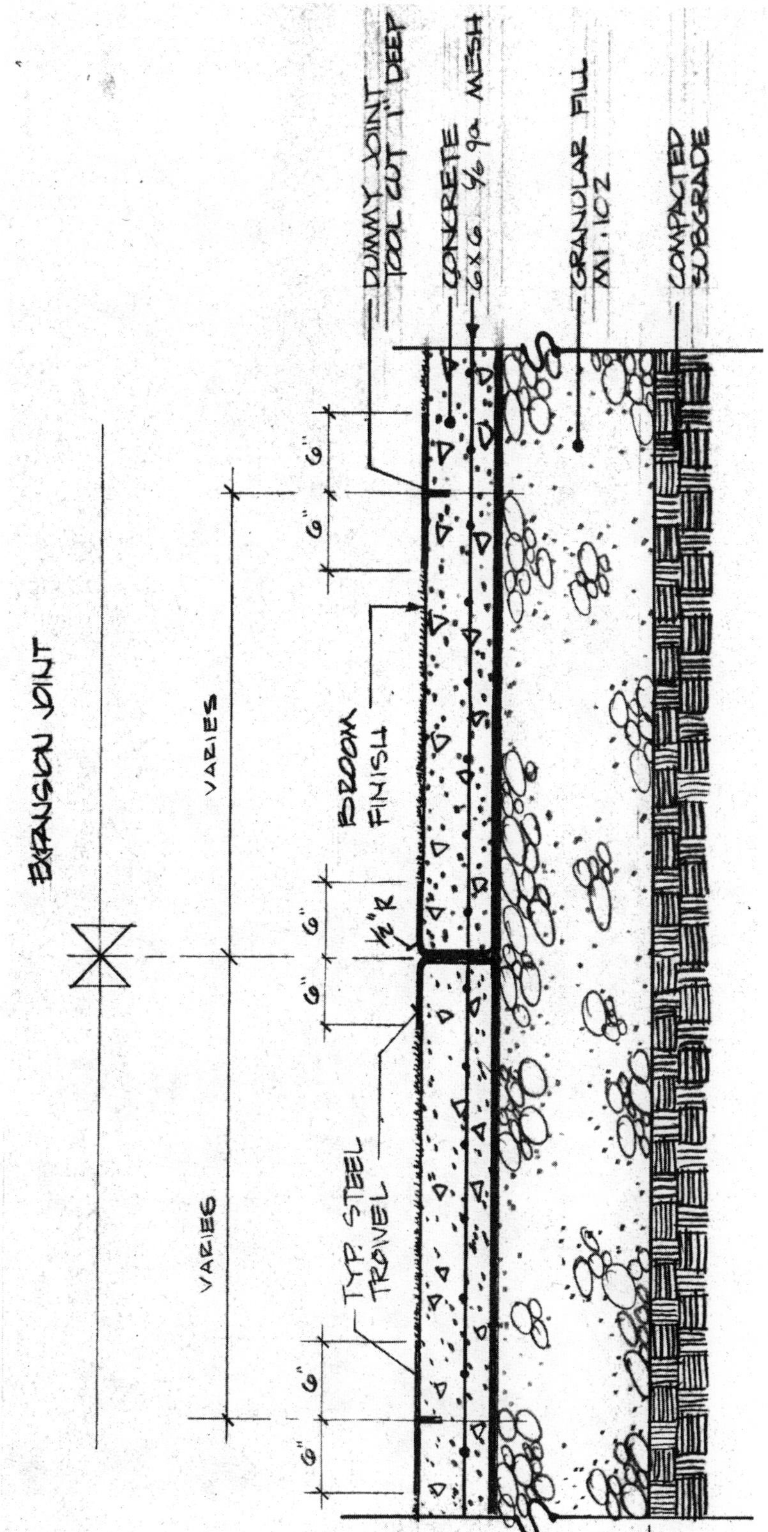

4.21

Saratoga Associates

Figure 4.20 *Contract of broom and smooth finish concrete.*

Figure 4.21 *Concrete paving with broom finish and tooled edges.*

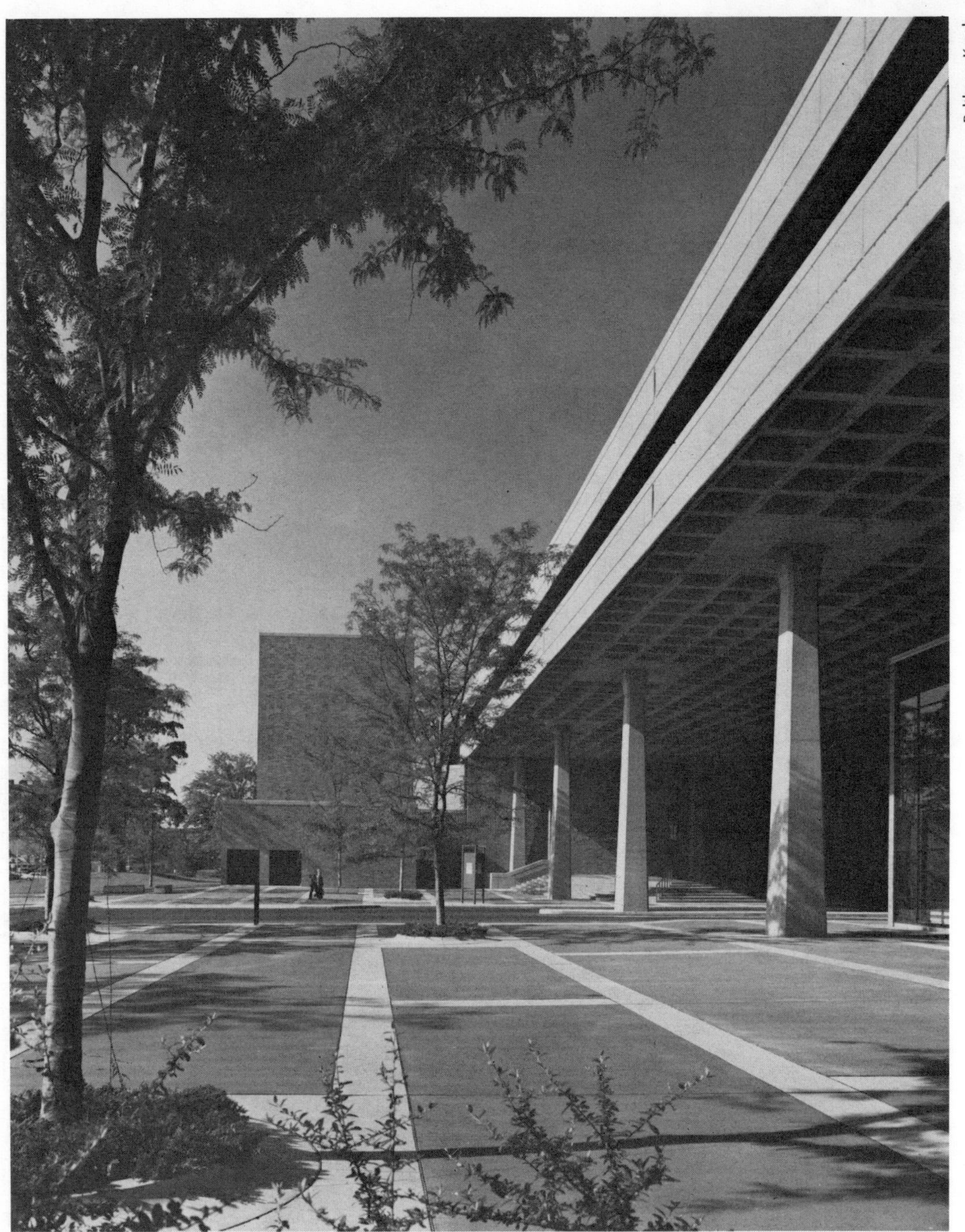

Balthazar Korab

Bonnell and Associates

Figure 4.22 *Black iron oxide mixed with the concrete darkened the large panels of paving and created the contrast shown.*

4.23

4.24

B
A
E
R
BANK

4.25

Figures 4.23 - 4.25 *A variety of patterns using colored concrete.*

4.26

4.27

4.28

Sasaki Associates

Figures 4.26 – 4.28 *Exposed aggregate concrete adds color and texture to paving surfaces.*

4.29

4.30

4.31

Sasaki Associates

Figure 4.29 Change in size and color of aggregate can be used to emphasize design patterns.

Figure 4.30 *A pattern of rectangles.*

Figure 4.31 *Each panel has been pre-cast using brown aggregate and white concrete. Panels are crowned and water drains to and down the gap between them.*

4.32

4.33

Figure 4.32 *Squares of exposed aggregate created with 2x4 redwood dividers.*

Figure 4.33 *Exposed aggregate squares with dividers of smooth concrete. Note placement of expansion joint.*

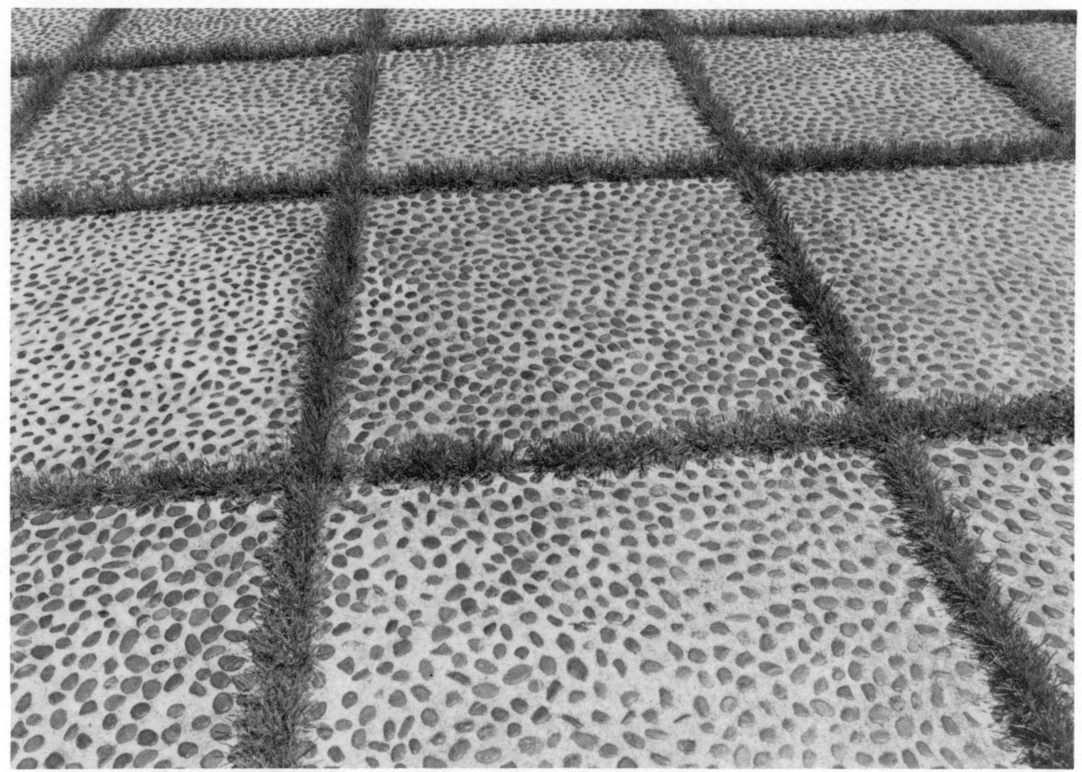

4.34

4.35

Figure 4.34 *Black smooth pebbles contrast against light concrete. Squares with grass dividers in a low traffic area.*

Figure 4.35 *Small squares in grass harmonize, yet contrast with larger squares to the right.*

4.36

4.37

Figures 4.36 – 4.39 *Several pattern combinations using brick and exposed aggregate concrete.*

4.38 M. Paul Friedberg and Partners

4.39 M. Paul Friedberg and Partners

4.40

4.41

Figures 4.40 – 4.41 *Curvilinear and modular patterns defined with the use of brick.*

4.42

4.43

Figure 4.42 *Granite strips with exposed aggregate concrete.*

Figure 4.43 *Hexagonal pavers harmonize with cast iron tree grates.*

4.44

4.45 Nebraska Dept. of Roads

I. Didrichsons, Nebraska Dept. of Roads

4.46

Figures 4.44 – 4.45 *Pre-cast concrete pavers.*

Figures 4.46 – 4.47 *"Turfblock" pre-cast pavers for such areas as overflow parking or other low traffic situations.*

Figure 4.48 *"Checkerblock" paver detail.*

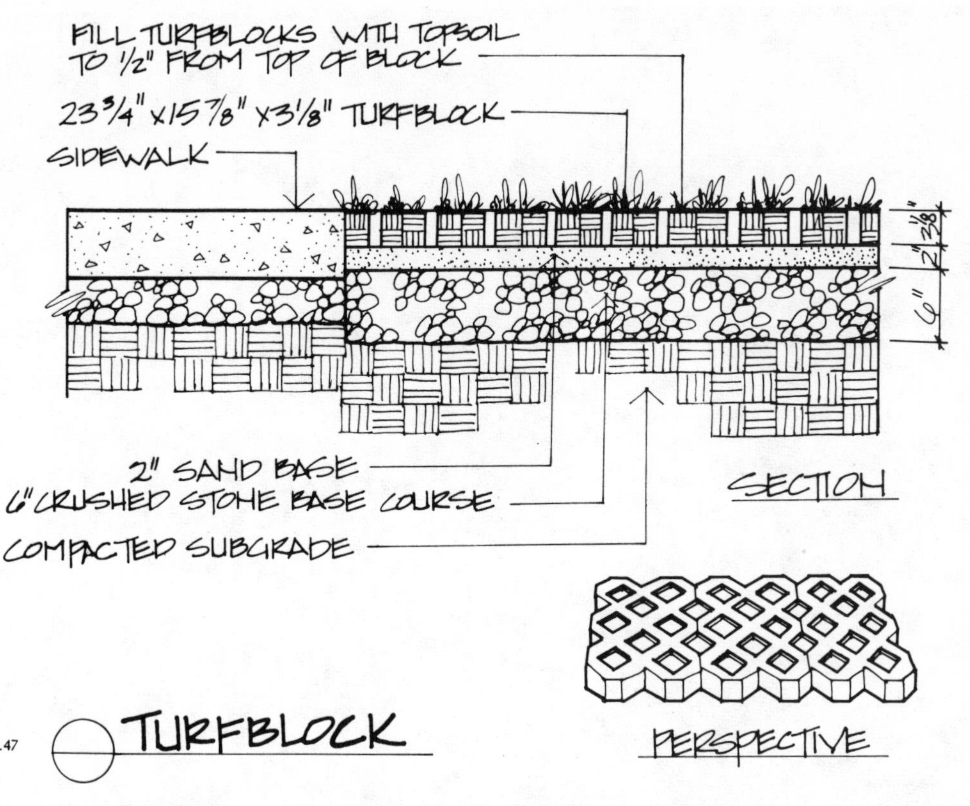
FILL TURFBLOCKS WITH TOPSOIL TO 1/2" FROM TOP OF BLOCK
23 3/4" x 15 7/8" x 3 1/8" TURFBLOCK
SIDEWALK
2" SAND BASE
6" CRUSHED STONE BASE COURSE
COMPACTED SUBGRADE
SECTION
PERSPECTIVE

4.47 TURFBLOCK

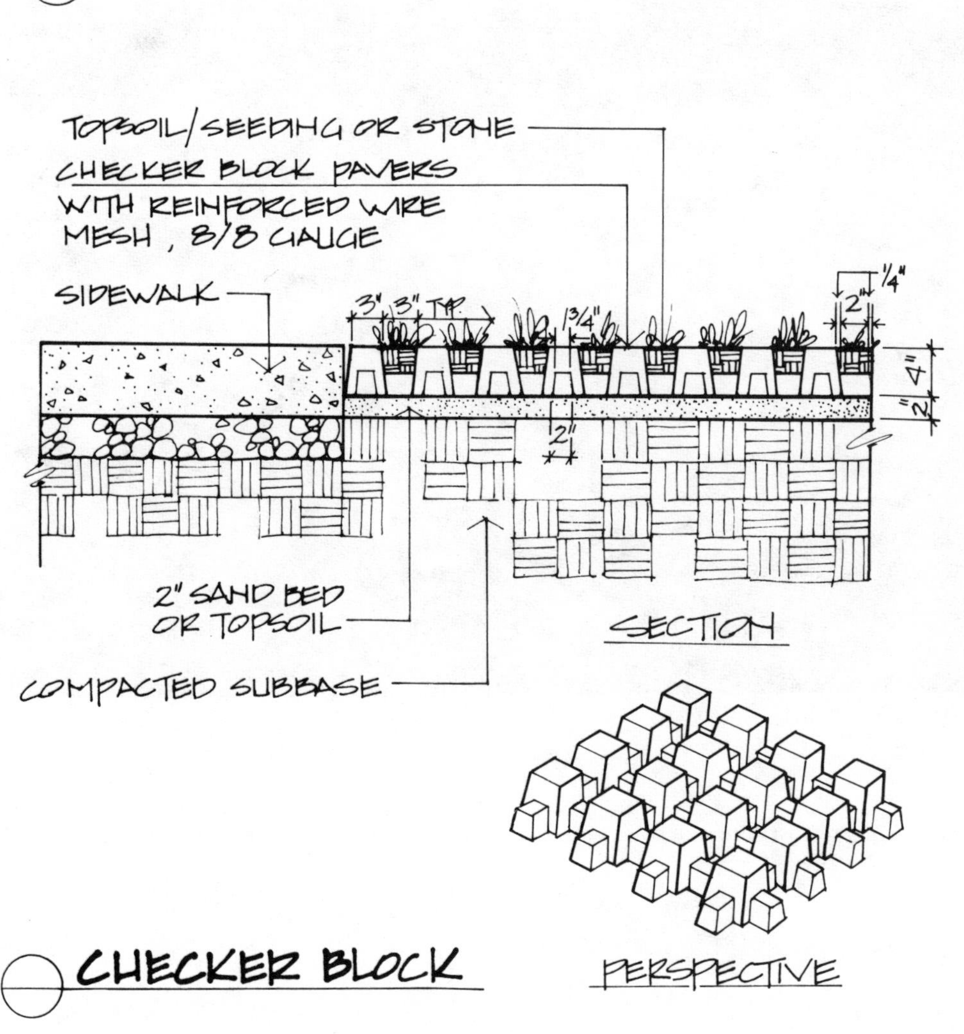
TOPSOIL/SEEDING OR STONE
CHECKER BLOCK PAVERS WITH REINFORCED WIRE MESH, 8/8 GAUGE
SIDEWALK
3" 3" TYP.
1 3/4"
1/4"
2"
4"
2"
2" SAND BED OR TOPSOIL
COMPACTED SUBBASE
SECTION
PERSPECTIVE

4.48 CHECKER BLOCK

Bob Porth, Hedrich-Blessing

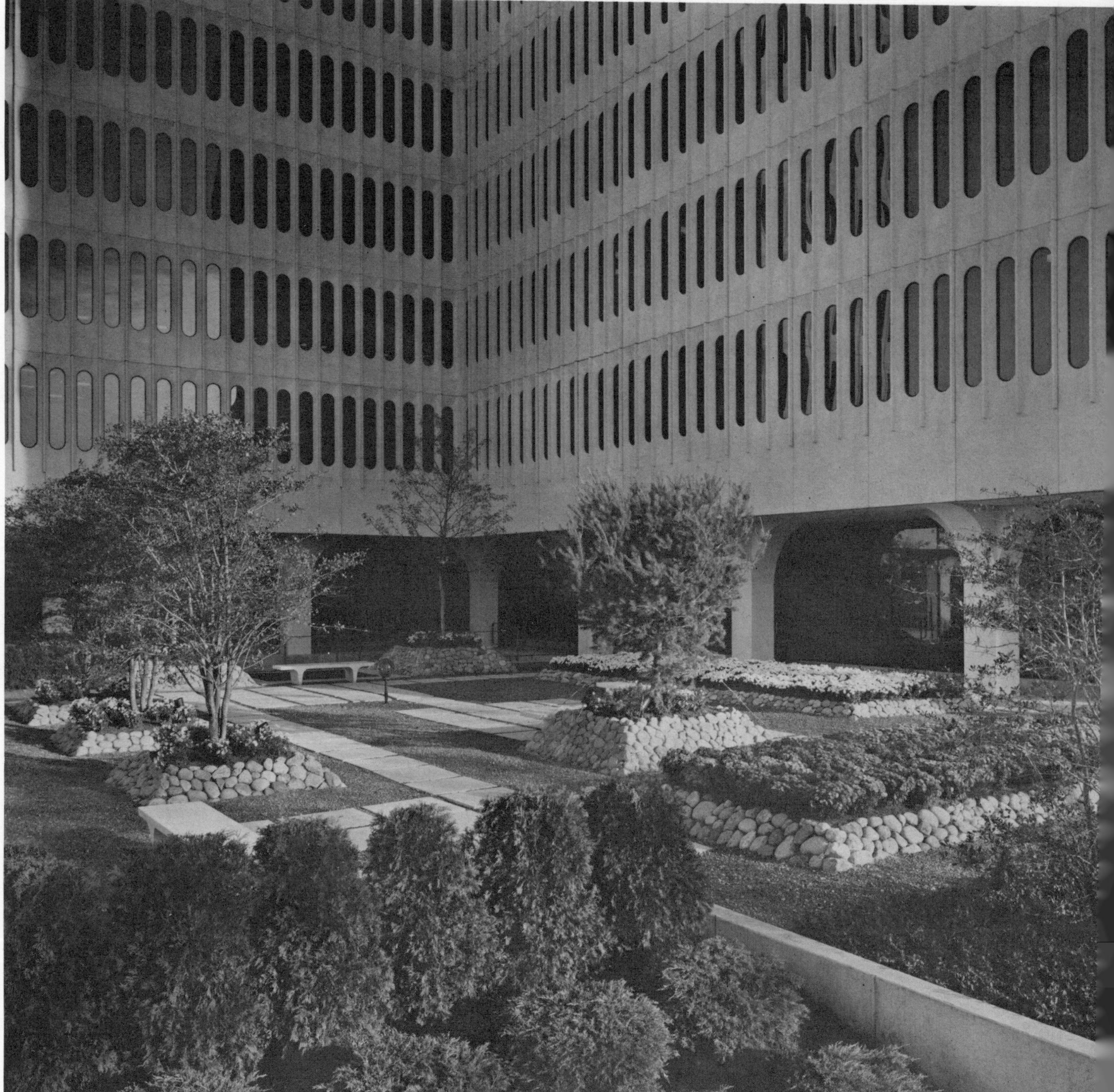

4.49

Theodore Brickman Co.

Figure 4.49 – 4.53 *Pre-cast concrete pavers are available in a variety of shapes and sizes.*

4.50

4.51

4.52

4.53 Betonwerk Munderkingen GmbH

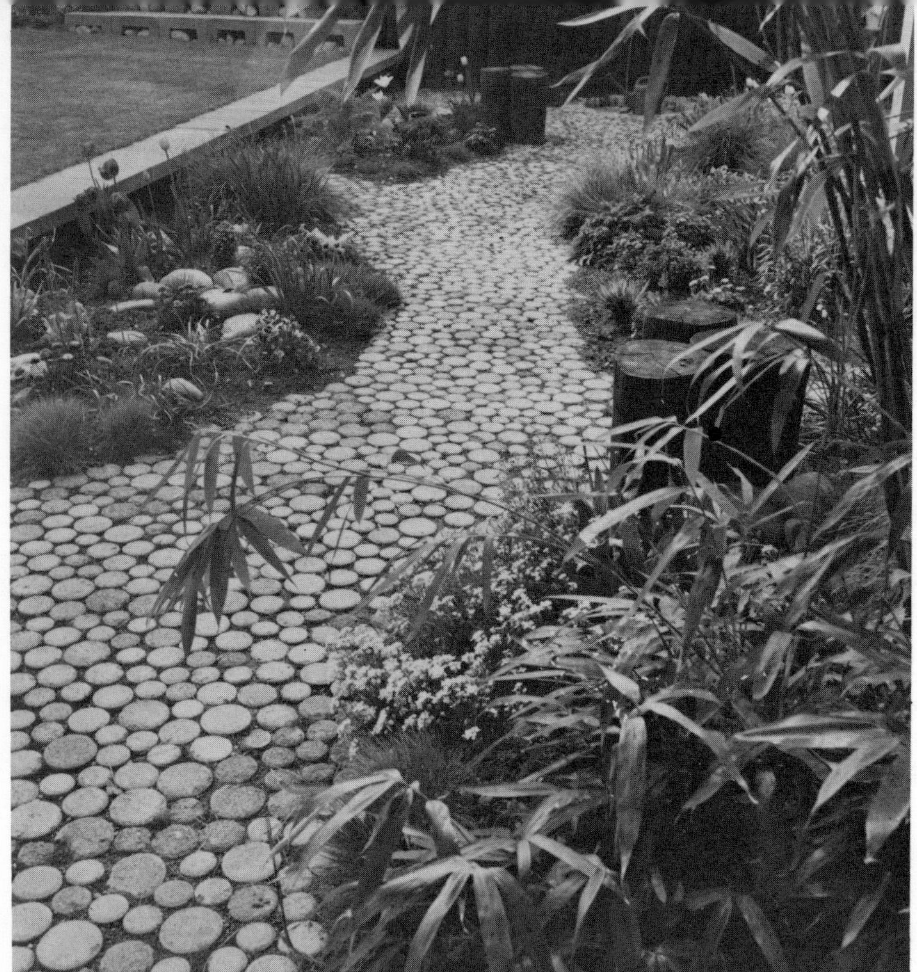

4.54

Betonwerk Munderkingen GmbH

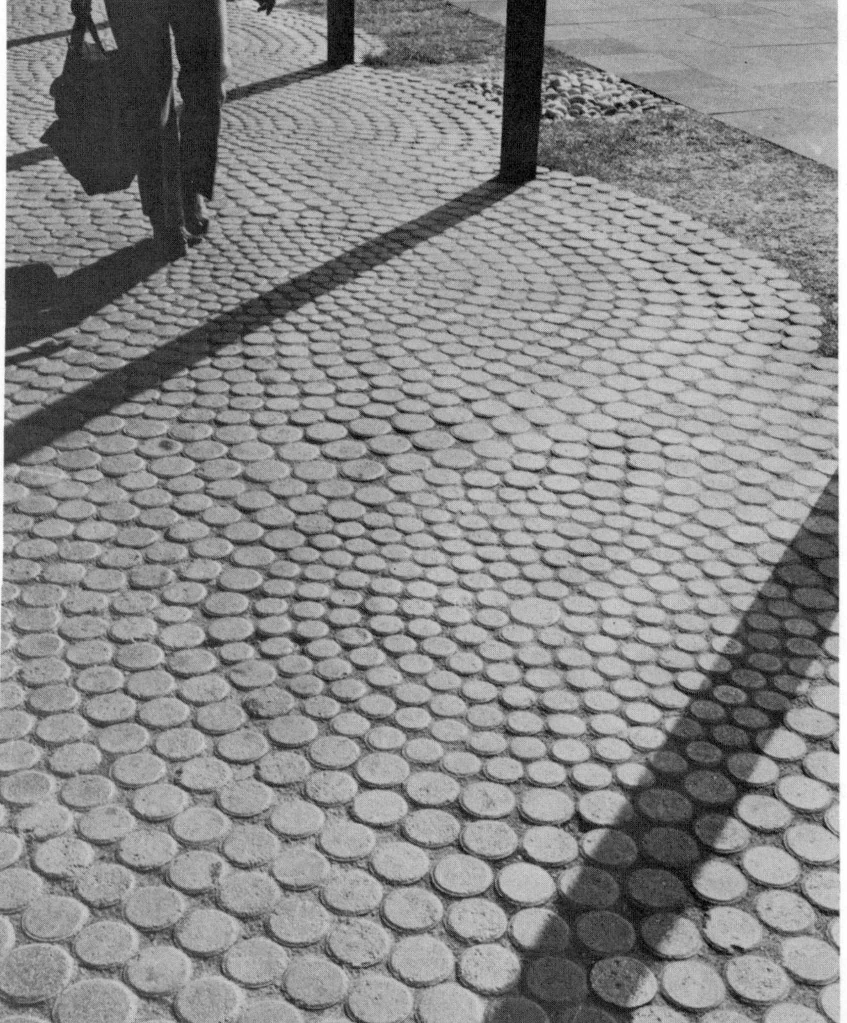

4.55

Figures 4.54 – 4.55 *Round pre-cast pavers.*

4.56

4.57

Bomanite Corporation

Figures 4.56 – 4.57 *Patterns stamped into concrete.*

4.58 Bomanite Corporation

4.59

Figures 4.58 – 4.60 *A few of several patterns available to stamp into the surface of cast-in-place concrete. Color can be added to stimulate the color of brick, stone, etc.*

Figures 4.61 – 4.62 *Brick paving patterns.*

4.60 Bomanite Corporation

4.61 Edward D. Stone, Jr. and Associates

4.62 Edward D. Stone, Jr. and Associates

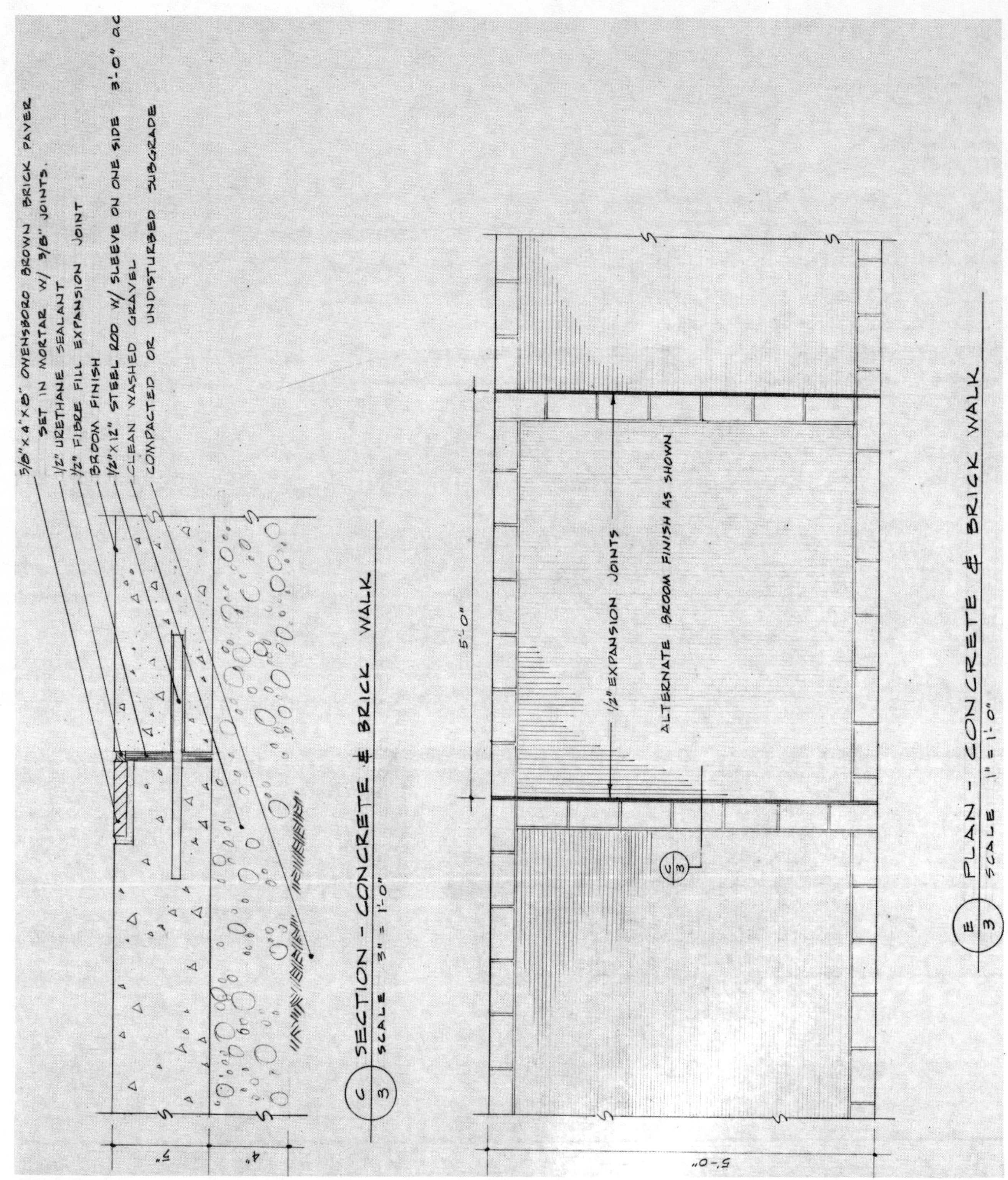

3/8"x4"x8" OWENSBORO BROWN BRICK PAVER
SET IN MORTAR W/ 3/8" JOINTS.
1/2" URETHANE SEALANT
1/2" FIBRE FILL EXPANSION JOINT
BROOM FINISH
1/2"x12" STEEL ROD W/ SLEEVE ON ONE SIDE 3'-0" O.C.
CLEAN WASHED GRAVEL
COMPACTED OR UNDISTURBED SUBGRADE
4"
4"
C 3 SECTION - CONCRETE & BRICK WALK
SCALE 3" = 1'-0"
5'-0"
1/2" EXPANSION JOINTS
ALTERNATE BROOM FINISH AS SHOWN
C 3
5'-0"
E 3 PLAN - CONCRETE & BRICK WALK
SCALE 1" = 1'-0"

Figure 4.63 *Brick and concrete combination.*

Walker-Harris-Associates-Inc.

4.64

4.65

Figures 4.64 – 4.65 *Public spaces and shopping malls paved with brick.*

4.66 Sasaki Associates

4.67

4.68 Browning-Day-Pollak-Associat

Figure 4.66 *Brick in a fishscale pattern interwoven with regular concrete paving.*

Figure 4.67 *Brick in a free-form edged with concrete and enclosed in a circle of pre-cast concrete panels.*

Figure 4.68 *Brick squares with white concrete dividers.*

A. E. Bye and Associates

Figure 4.69 *Hexagonal brick pavers in an urban park.*

4.70 Cole Associates Inc.

4.71

4.72

Figures 4.70 – 4.72 *Brick paving.*

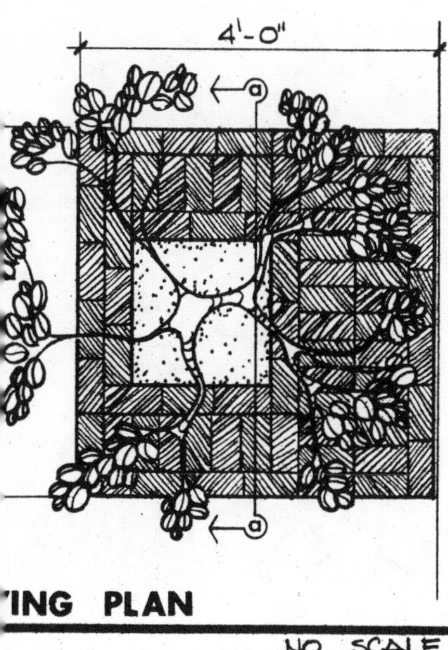
4'-0"
'ING PLAN
NO SCALE

4.73 Saratoga Associates

4.74 Snell Environmental Group

4.75 Environmental Planning and Design

4.76

Figure 4.73 *Paving plan.*
Figure 4.74 *Brick paving and terraces.*
Figure 4.75 *Brick with white concrete strip.*
Figure 4.76 *Brick on edge with marble strip.*

4.77

LaPorte County Landscaping

4.78

4.79

4.80

4.81

4.82

William A. Behnke Associates

4.83

4.84

4.85

Figure 4.77 *Used brick edged with old railroad ties.*

Figure 4.78 *Brick and pre-cast concrete panels.*

Figure 4.79 *Stone squares in a circular pattern.*

Figures 4.80 – 4.81 *Square granite pavers, modular pattern.*

Figure 4.82 *Square granite pavers, fishscale pattern.*

Figure 4.83 *Terrazo pavers.*

Figure 4.84 *Stone pavers.*

Figure 4.85 *Slate squares.*

4.86

4.88

4.87

Figure 4.86 *Granite cobblestone with dark slate for accent.*

Figure 4.87 *Irregular pieces of granite form a path in an oriental style garden.*

Figure 4.88 *Granite stepping stones in a gold fish pond.*

4.89
4.92
4.90
4.93
4.91
4.94

Figures 4.89 – 4.94 *Miscellaneous stone paving patterns.*

4.95

4.97

4.96

4.98

Figures 4.95 – 4.98 *Miscellaneous stone paving patterns.*

4.99

4.101

4.100

4.102

Figures 4.99 – 4.102 *Miscellaneous stone paving patterns.*

4.103

4.104

Figure 4.103 *Six inch slices of old railroad ties placed in a sand bed. Joints and cracks filled with sand.*

Figure 4.104 *Exposed aggregate squares surrounded by asphalt in a sitting area at the entrance of an arboretum.*

Figure 4.105 *Asphalt plaza and curvilinear walks in a city redevelopment area.*

Figures 4.106 – 4.107 *Paving details.*

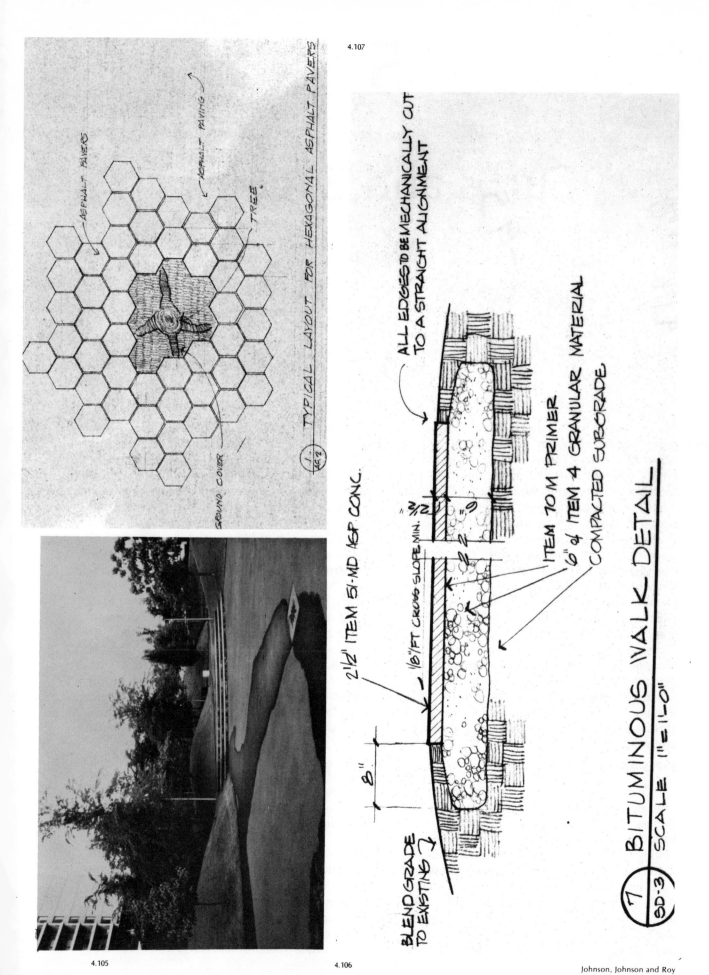

4.107

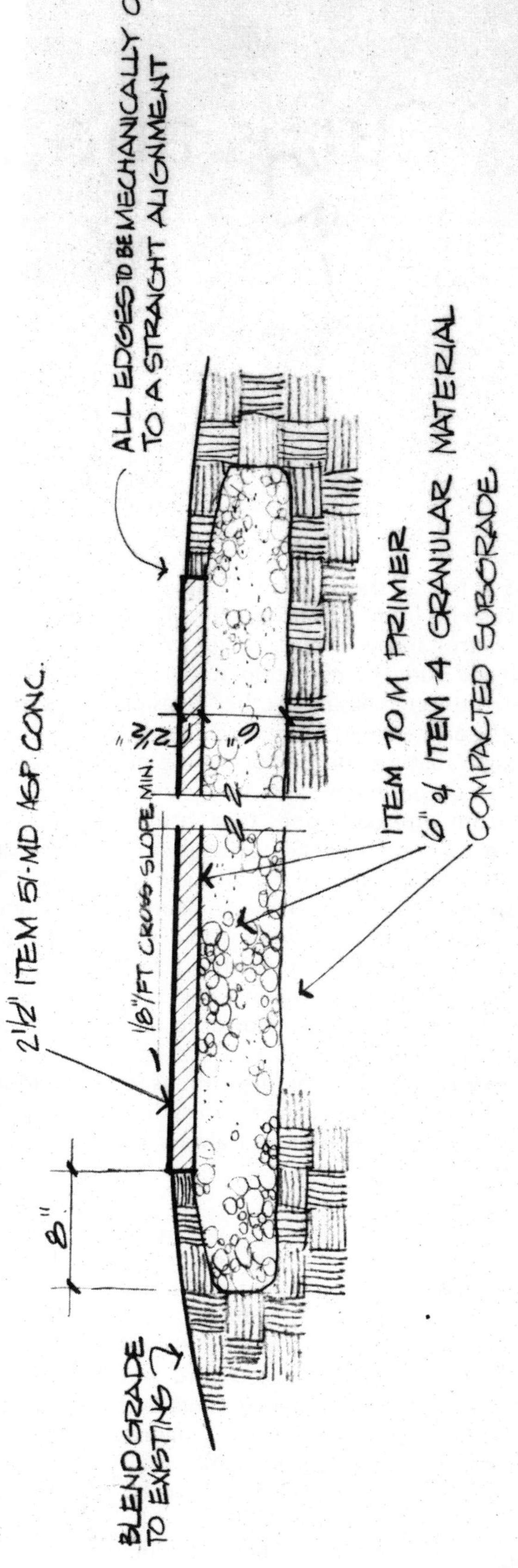
ALL EDGES TO BE MECHANICALLY CUT TO A STRAIGHT ALIGNMENT
2 1/2" ITEM 51-MD ASP CONC.
1/8"/FT CROSS SLOPE MIN.
2 1/2"
6"
8"
BLEND GRADE TO EXISTING
ITEM 70 M PRIMER
6" of ITEM 4 GRANULAR MATERIAL
COMPACTED SUBGRADE
7
SD-3
BITUMINOUS WALK DETAIL
SCALE 1"=1'-0"

4.105

4.106

Johnson, Johnson and Roy

5

Curbs and Edgings

Curbs serve as traffic control devices separating vehicles from pedestrians. They also aid in the control and flow of drainage water. With a curb and gutter combination, water can be channelled to catch basins or other types of inlets. Curbs and edgings help to define the lines and edges that may be part of the design characteristics of pavement and to create a transition from one pavement to another. Edgings, such as a vertical metal or plastic strip between the grass and the mulching of a planting bed, can serve to make maintenance easier. The edging will inhibit the growth of the grass into the bed. An edging which is a few inches wide may also serve as a mowing strip allowing the wheel of the lawn mower to ride along the top of the edging material. Curbs and narrower edgings both provide increased stability to the edge of certain materials like asphalt, ensuring that the edge will always be uniform and neat.

TYPES AND SIZES

Concrete is perhaps the most frequently used edging material, especially for curbs and gutters. There are a number of configurations from straight, vertical curbs to a combination vertical curb and gutter to a rolled curb and gutter. Some state highway departments and local municipalities require certain configurations to be used in the projects within their jurisdiction. Expansion joints and contraction joints are required and in many instances the addition of reinforcing steel will be desirable.

Brick and stone can be used as veneers over concrete to serve as curbs or curb and gutter combinations or as edgings. High quality SW rated pavers and high quality mortar will be required because of the severe exposure, especially in those parts of the country subjected to freezing-thawing conditions.

Granite has been used as the vertical curbing material predominantly in the northeastern part of the United States for many years. It is durable and can be removed and reused when roads are changed. It is available in a number of sizes and also in precut curves to allow a uniform radius around the corner.

Metals can be used for edgings. Steel is the most common and in some parts of the country is available in three different sizes in 16 and 20 foot lengths, ⅛ inch thick by 4 inches high, or 3/16-inch thick by 4 inches high, or ¼ inch thick by 5 inches high. This steel is finished with green or black paint, depending upon the designer's selection and can be bent to fit any kind of curb or can be used in straight pieces and bent to any desired corner such as 90 degrees. The thinnest of the steel units is used for most light duty situations such as lawn edging or tree rings, while the heavier ones are used for driveway edgings, asphalt walks, etc. Stakes are placed at 30-inch intervals along the steel edging but in some freeze-thaw conditions will not be sufficient to hold the edging in place without its heaving. If this is the case, the edging will need to be driven back down to finish grade in the spring time. This problem is also true of some of

5.1

5.2 Sasaki Associates

5.3

the other thin type edgings described hereafter.

Aluminum occasionally is used as an edging material. It is a very light-weight corrugated item which crushes readily and is not recommended for most site work.

There are several edging products utilizing plastics on the market. Some are simple edging similar in thickness and other aspects to the steel edging described earlier. These are held in place by stakes with a loop at the top. They can be bent and formed into a number of design configurations. In severe freeze-thaw situations they are especially subject to heaving. Plastics, however, tend to be less expensive than metal and easier to install.

Wood can be used as an edging material. The most frequent use is made of 2 x 4's laid in straight lines. Because this wood is in contact with the soil, it will need to be one of the woods, such as Redwood, Cedar, or Cypress, with natural characteristics to resist decay or be a pressure-treated wood utilizing pentachlorophenol or chromated copper arsenate. For some gentle curves it is possible to use ½ inch by 4-inch strips of redwood either singly or laminated for increased width. Other than this, wood will generally be confined to straight lines use. Heavier edgings and mowing strips of wood can be old railroad ties or new penta-treated timbers (4x4's or 4x6's) laid in a flush or raised position These items can be held in place by drilling holes in the wood members and driving in pipe or steel reinforcing rods.

REFERENCES FOR FURTHER READING

Ramsey, C.G., and Sleeper, H.R. *Architectural Graphics Standards.* 7th Edition. New York: Wiley, 1981.

Figure 5.1 *Custom designed pre-cast curb and gutter.*

Figure 5.2 *Granite curb.*

Figure 5.3 *Concrete curb and gutter.*

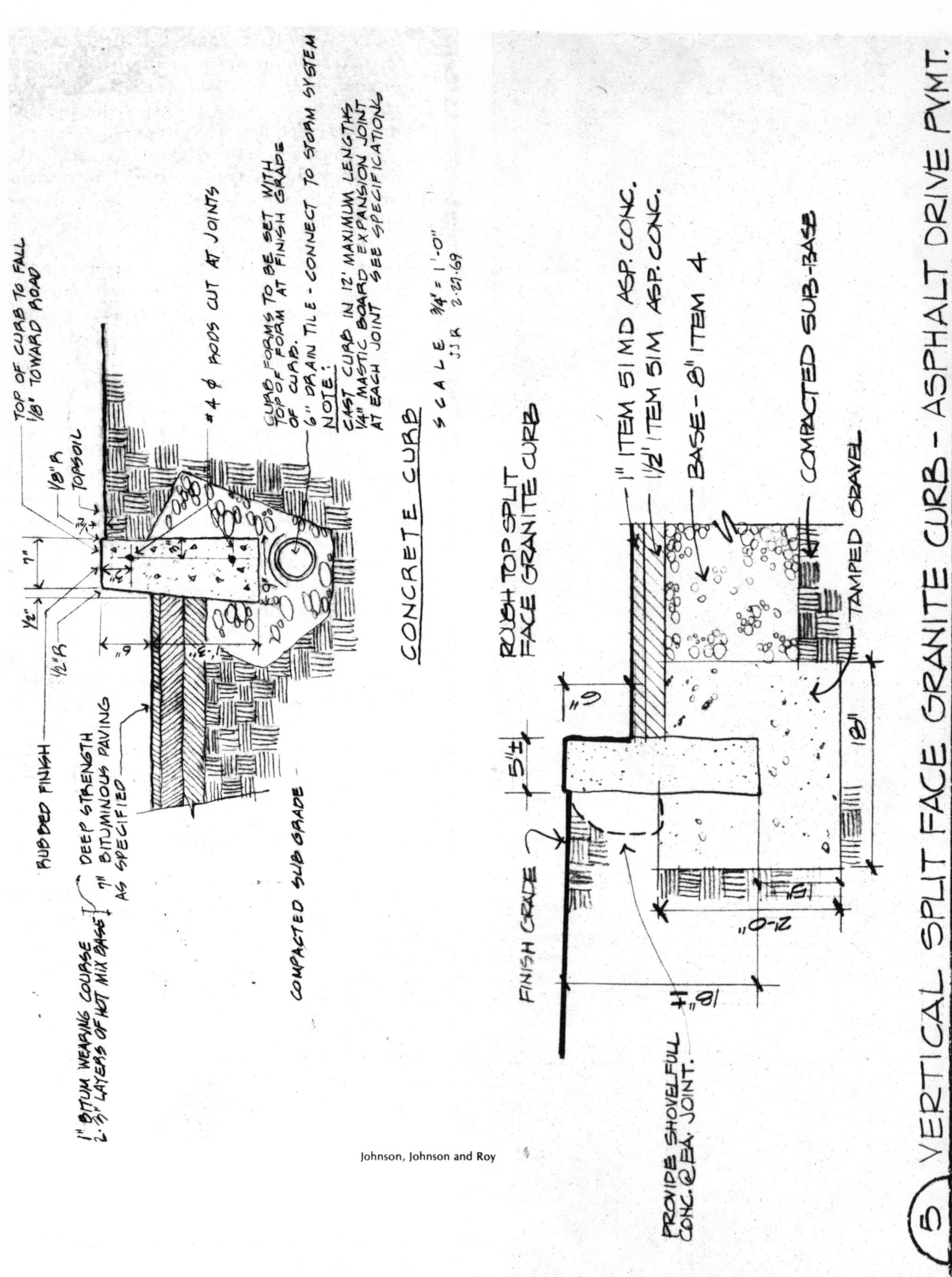

TOP OF CURB TO FALL 1/8" TOWARD ROAD
1/8" R
TOPSOIL
#4 ∅ RODS CUT AT JOINTS
CURB FORMS TO BE SET WITH TOP OF FORM AT FINISH GRADE OF CURB.
6" DRAIN TILE - CONNECT TO STORM SYSTEM
NOTE:
CAST CURB IN 12' MAXIMUM LENGTHS
1/4" MASTIC BOARD EXPANSION JOINT AT EACH JOINT SEE SPECIFICATIONS
CONCRETE CURB
SCALE 3/4" = 1'-0"
RUBBED FINISH
1/2" R
1" BITUM WEARING COURSE
2-3" LAYERS OF HOT MIX BASE
DEEP STRENGTH 7" BITUMINOUS PAVING AS SPECIFIED
COMPACTED SUB GRADE
BUSH TOP SPLIT FACE GRANITE CURB
1" ITEM 51 MD ASP. CONC.
1 1/2" ITEM 51M ASP. CONC.
BASE - 8" ITEM 4
COMPACTED SUB-BASE
TAMPED GRAVEL
FINISH GRADE
PROVIDE SHOVELFULL CONC. @ EA. JOINT.
5 VERTICAL SPLIT FACE GRANITE CURB - ASPHALT DRIVE PVMT.

Johnson, Johnson and Roy

5.5

Johnson, Johnson and Roy

Figures 5.4 – 5.5 *Curb details.*

Bill Hedrich, Hedrich-Blessing

Figure 5.6 *Masonry curb.* Theodore Brickman Co. for Irvin A. Blietz Organization

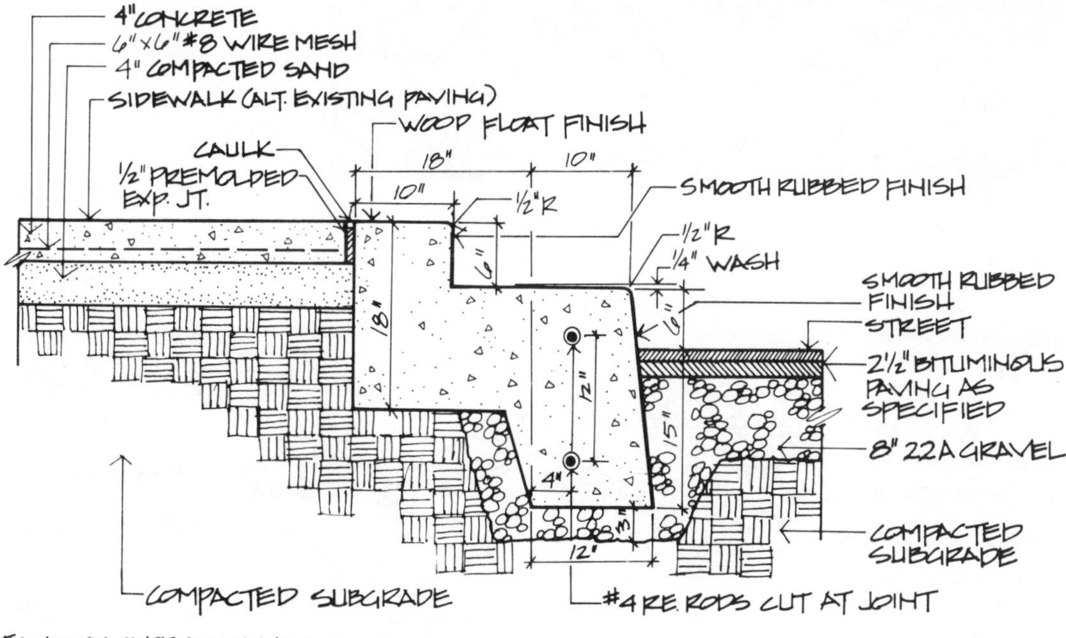
4" CONCRETE
6"x6" #8 WIRE MESH
4" COMPACTED SAND
SIDEWALK (ALT. EXISTING PAVING)
WOOD FLOAT FINISH
CAULK
1/2" PREMOLDED EXP. JT.
18"
10"
10"
1/2"R
SMOOTH RUBBED FINISH
6"
1/2"R
1/4" WASH
6"
SMOOTH RUBBED FINISH
STREET
18"
12"
15"
2 1/2" BITUMINOUS PAVING AS SPECIFIED
8" 22A GRAVEL
4"
3"
12"
COMPACTED SUBGRADE
COMPACTED SUBGRADE
#4 RE. RODS CUT AT JOINT
NOTE: FORM CURB IN 12' MAX. SECTIONS, (4' MIN. FOR CLOSURE)
STEPPED CONCRETE CURB

Figure 5.7 *Curb detail.* Johnson, Johnson and Roy

Figures 5.8 – 5.10 *Three of many different possibilities for brick curbs.*

5.8 Environmental Planning and Design

5.9

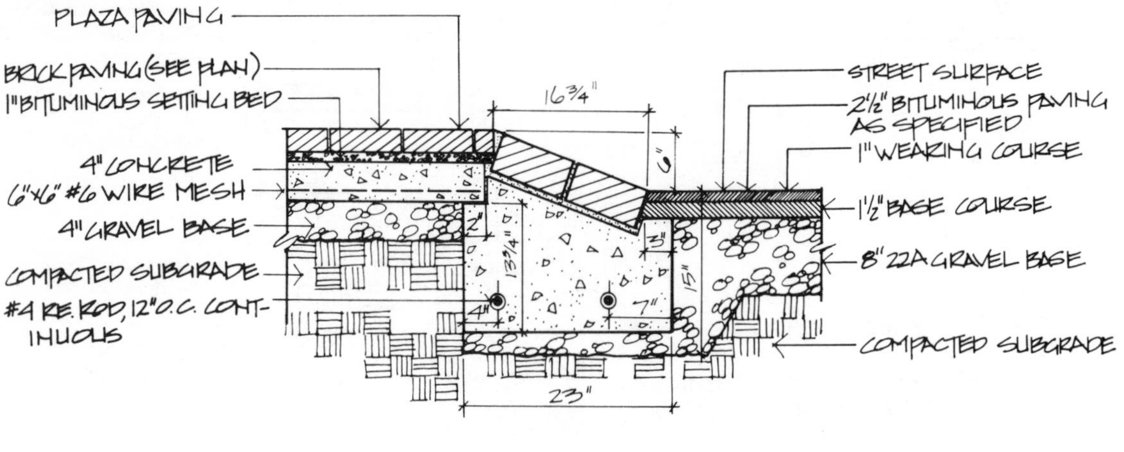
PLAZA PAVING
BRICK PAVING (SEE PLAN)
1" BITUMINOUS SETTING BED
4" CONCRETE
6"x6" #6 WIRE MESH
4" GRAVEL BASE
COMPACTED SUBGRADE
#4 RE. ROD, 12" O.C. CONT-INUOUS
16¾"
6"
13¾"
2"
4"
7"
3"
15"
23"
STREET SURFACE
2½" BITUMINOUS PAVING AS SPECIFIED
1" WEARING COURSE
1½" BASE COURSE
8" 22A GRAVEL BASE
COMPACTED SUBGRADE
DROPPED BRICK CURB

5.10 Johnson, Johnson and Roy

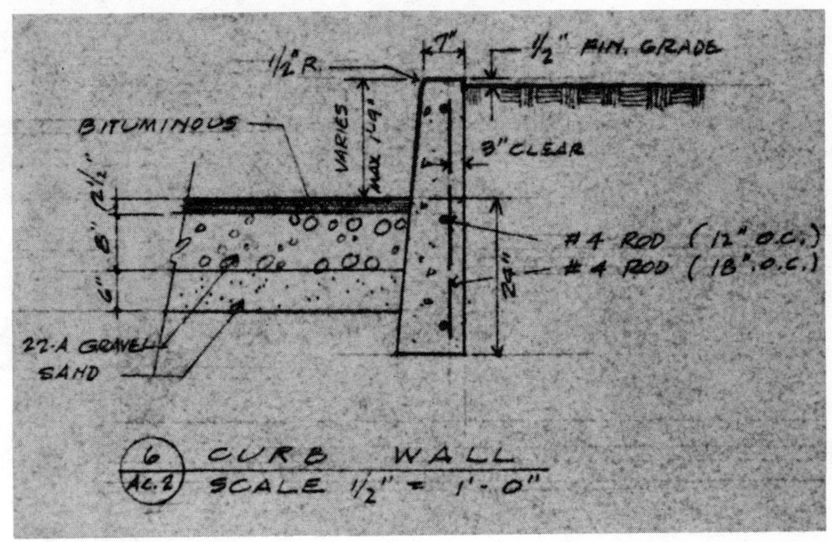
1/2" R.
7"
1/2" FIN. GRADE
BITUMINOUS
VARIES MAX 1'-9"
3" CLEAR
2 1/2"
8"
6"
#4 ROD (12" O.C.)
#4 ROD (18" O.C.)
24"
22-A GRAVEL
SAND
6
AC.2
CURB WALL
SCALE 1/2" = 1'-0"

5.11

Johnson, Johnson and Roy

WHITACRE GREER 4"x8"x2 1/4" ARCH. BRICK PAVERS BY HASTINGS PAVEMENT CO., INC. 3120 COLLEGE PT. CAUSEWAY FLUSHING, N.Y. 11354 COLOR RUSTIC

PLAZA PAVING RUNNING BOND BUTT JOINTS

NORTH

SOUTH

1/4" MORTAR JOINTS ON 2 BRICK HEADER COURSE

RADIUS, INSIDE EDGE OF CURB 28.70'±

SEE SPECS RE EXP. JOINT LOCATIONS

A

A,

PLAN

DROPPED BRICK CURB SEE SECTION DETAIL

BRICK PATTERN

BRICK SIDEWALK PAVING (SEE PLAN)

1" BITUMINOUS SETTING BED

4" CONCRETE

6"x6" #6 WIRE MESH

4" GRAVEL BASE

COMPACTED SUBGRADE

#4 RE ROD, 12" O.C. CONTINUOUS

16 3/4"

1/2"

4" 6"

2 1/4"

8 1/4"

13 3/4"

4"

4"

15"

20"

STREET SURFACE

1" WEARING COURSE

1 1/2" BASE COURSE

8" 22A GRAVEL BASE

COMPACTED SUBBASE

STREET SURFACE

ELEVATION

FACE OF BRICK CURB

SECTION THRU BRICK CURB IN BRICK SIDEWALK AREAS

BRICK CURB & PAVING

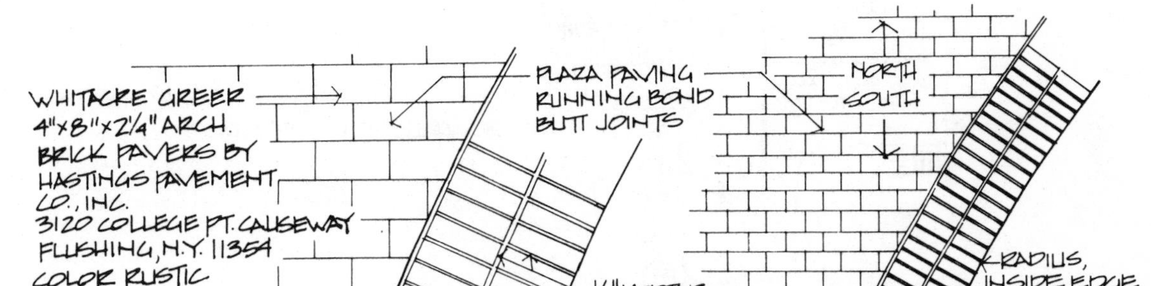

5.12

Johnson, Johnson and Roy

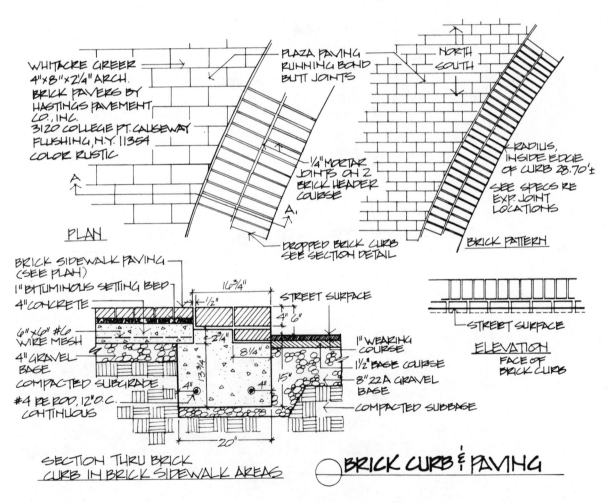

Figures 5.11 – 5.12 *Curb details.*

Figures 5.13 – 5.15 *Vertical concrete curbs.*

5.13

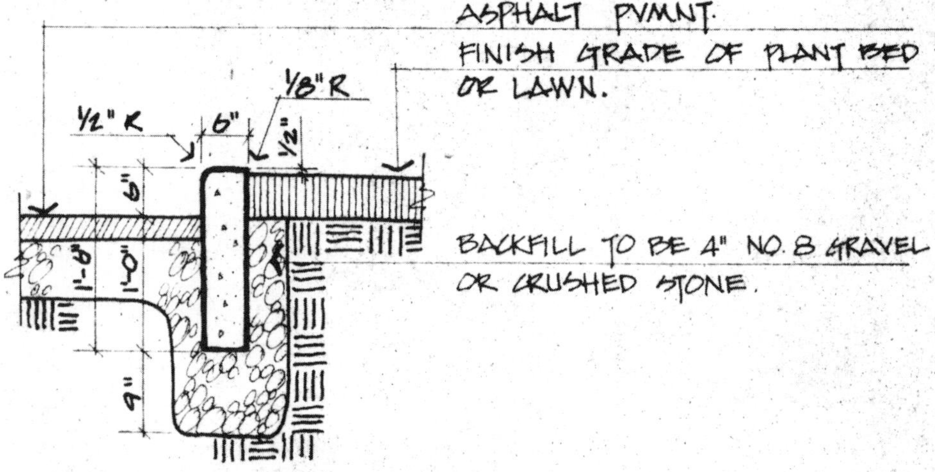
ASPHALT PVMNT.
FINISH GRADE OF PLANT BED OR LAWN.
1/8" R
1/2" R
6"
1/2"
6"
1'-6"
10"
9"
BACKFILL TO BE 4" NO. 8 GRAVEL OR CRUSHED STONE.

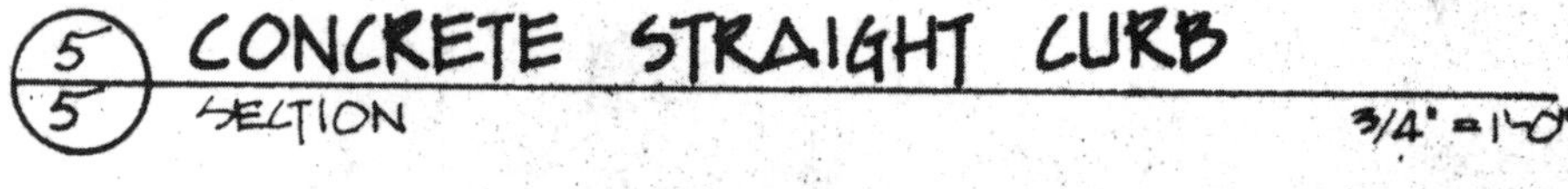
5
5
CONCRETE STRAIGHT CURB
SECTION
3/4" = 1'-0"

5.14

Bonnell and Associates

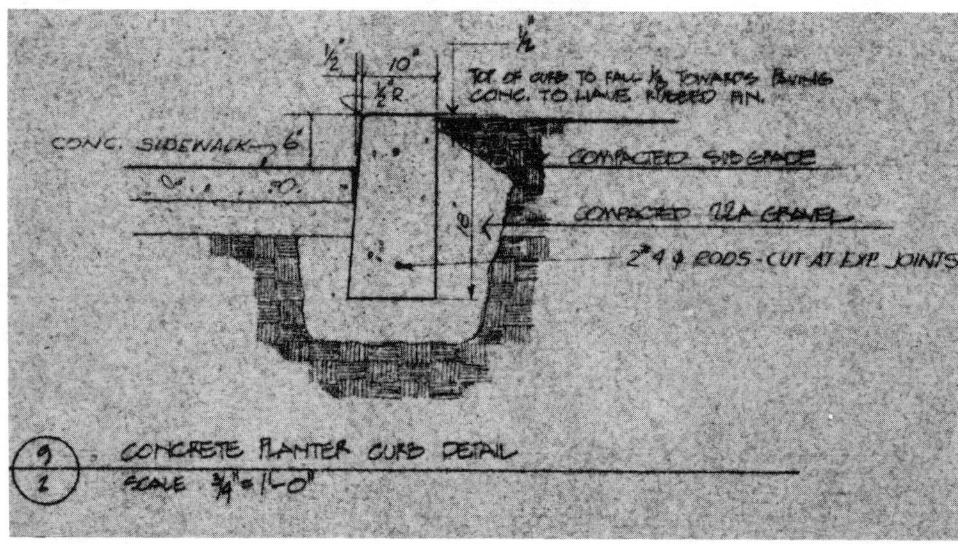
1/2"
10"
1/2" R
1/2"
CONC. SIDEWALK 6"
COMPACTED SUBGRADE
COMPACTED 22A GRAVEL
18"
2 #4 φ RODS - CUT AT EXP. JOINTS
CONCRETE PLANTER CURB DETAIL
SCALE 3/4" = 1'-0"

5.15

Johnson, Johnson and Roy

5.16

Lawrence Halprin and Associates

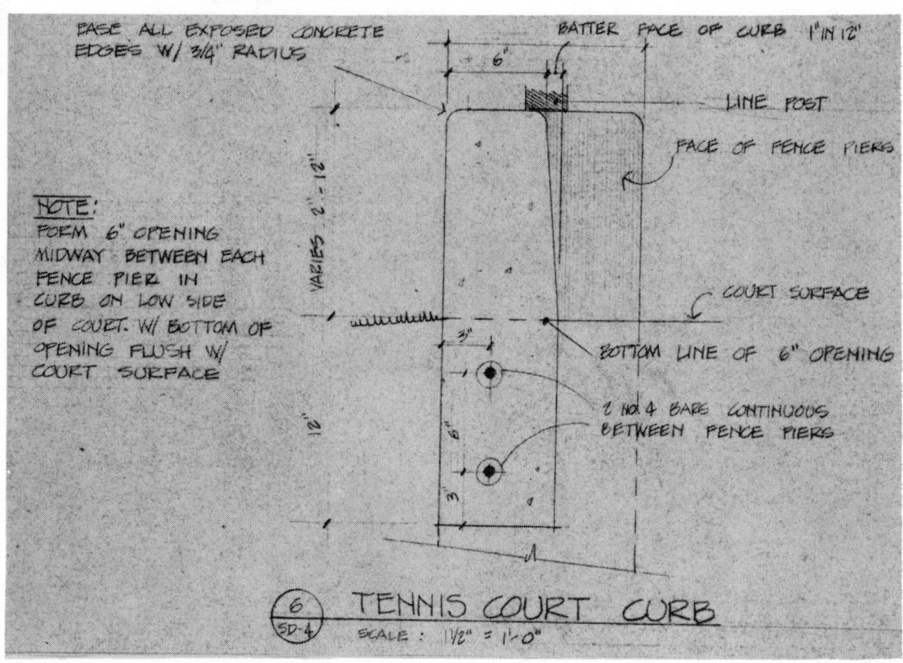

EASE ALL EXPOSED CONCRETE EDGES W/ 3/4" RADIUS
BATTER FACE OF CURB 1" IN 12"
6"
LINE POST
FACE OF FENCE PIERS
NOTE:
FORM 6" OPENING MIDWAY BETWEEN EACH FENCE PIER IN CURB ON LOW SIDE OF COURT. W/ BOTTOM OF OPENING FLUSH W/ COURT SURFACE
VARIES 2" - 12"
COURT SURFACE
BOTTOM LINE OF 6" OPENING
2 NO. 4 BARS CONTINUOUS BETWEEN FENCE PIERS
12"
TENNIS COURT CURB
SCALE : 1½" = 1'-0"

5.17

Johnson, Johnson and Roy

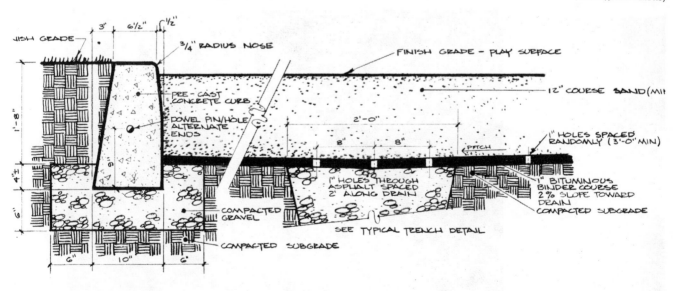

3" 6½" ½"
FINISH GRADE
¾" RADIUS NOSE
FINISH GRADE - PLAY SURFACE
12" COURSE SAND (MI
PRE-CAST CONCRETE CURB
DOWEL PIN/HOLE ALTERNATE ENDS
2'-0"
8" 8"
1" HOLES SPACED RANDOMLY (3'-0" MIN)
PITCH
1'-8"
4"
6"
1" HOLES THROUGH ASPHALT SPACED 2' ALONG DRAIN
1" BITUMINOUS BINDER COURSE 2% SLOPE TOWARD DRAIN
COMPACTED SUBGRADE
COMPACTED GRAVEL
SEE TYPICAL TRENCH DETAIL
COMPACTED SUBGRADE
6" 10" 6"

PLAY SURFACE AND CONCRETE EDGE

5.18

Saratoga Associates

Figures 5.16 – 5.18 *Concrete curbs.*

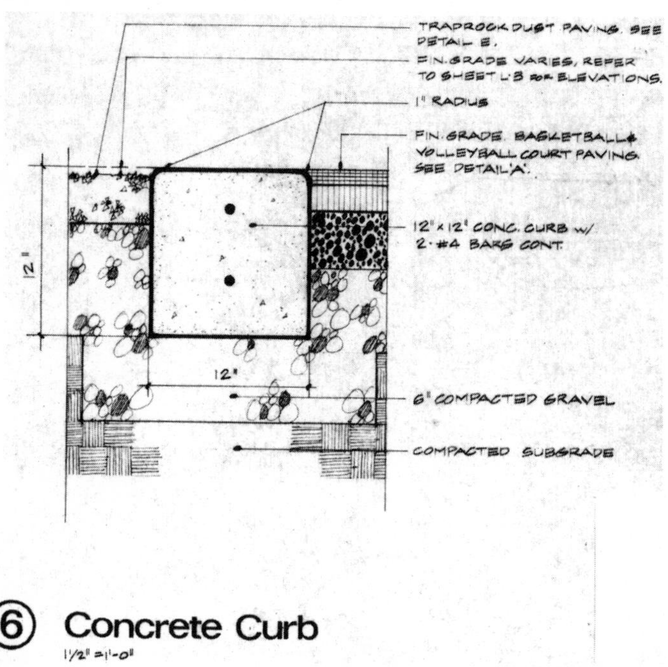
TRAPROCK DUST PAVING. SEE DETAIL E.
FIN. GRADE VARIES, REFER TO SHEET L-3 FOR ELEVATIONS.
1" RADIUS
FIN. GRADE BASKETBALL & VOLLEYBALL COURT PAVING. SEE DETAIL 'A'.
12" x 12" CONC. CURB w/ 2 - #4 BARS CONT.
12"
12"
6" COMPACTED GRAVEL
COMPACTED SUBGRADE
⑥ Concrete Curb
1½" = 1'-0"

5.19 CR3, inc.

5.20

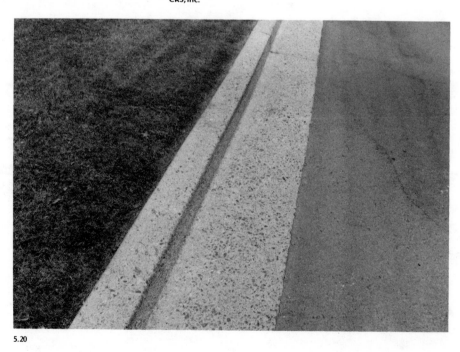

Figures 5.19 – 5.20 *Concrete curbs.*

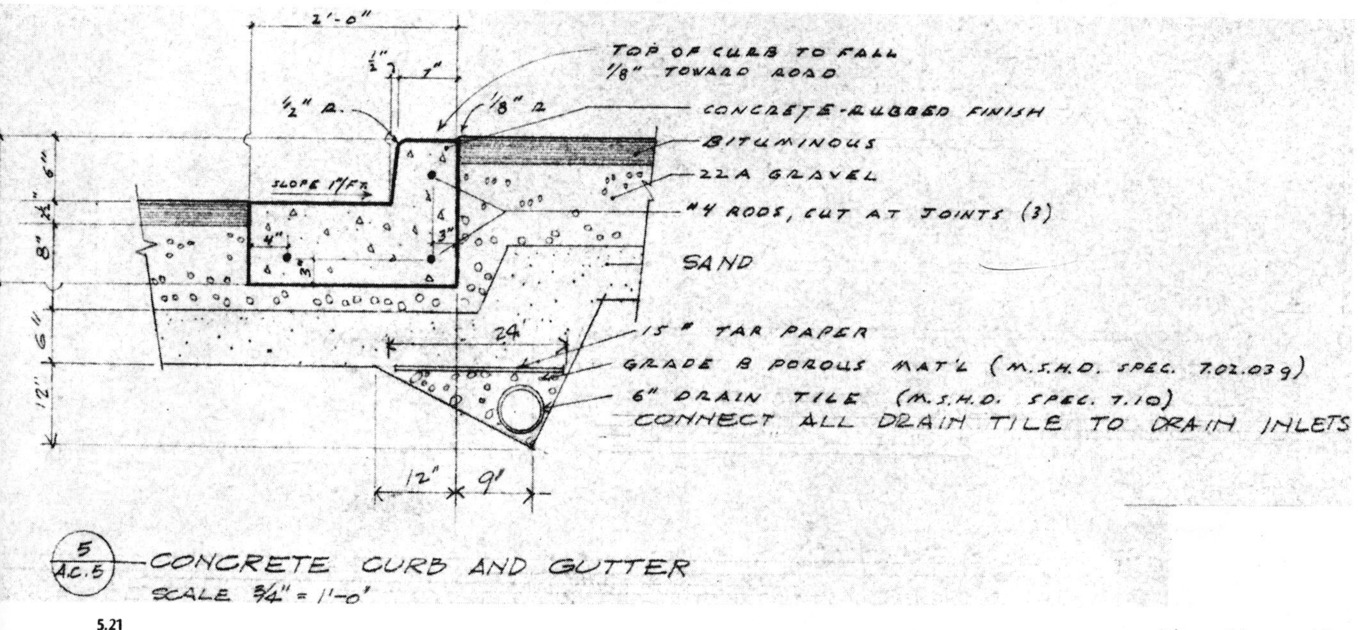

2'-0"
TOP OF CURB TO FALL 1/8" TOWARD ROAD
1/2" R.
1/8" R
CONCRETE-RUBBED FINISH
BITUMINOUS
22A GRAVEL
SLOPE 1"/FT.
#4 RODS, CUT AT JOINTS (3)
SAND
15 # TAR PAPER
GRADE B POROUS MAT'L (M.S.H.D. SPEC. 7.02.039)
6" DRAIN TILE (M.S.H.D. SPEC. 7.10)
CONNECT ALL DRAIN TILE TO DRAIN INLETS
CONCRETE CURB AND GUTTER
SCALE 3/4" = 1'-0"

5.21

Johnson, Johnson and Roy

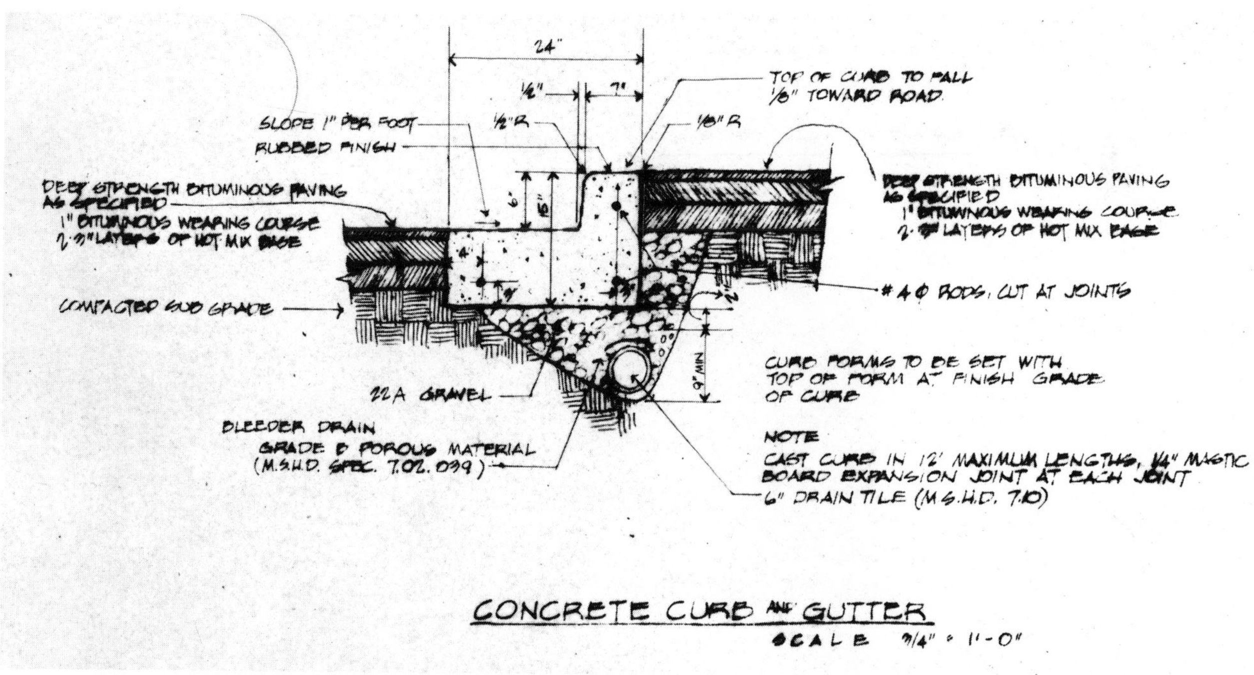

24"
TOP OF CURB TO FALL 1/8" TOWARD ROAD
SLOPE 1" PER FOOT
RUBBED FINISH
1/2"R
1/8"R
DEEP STRENGTH BITUMINOUS PAVING AS SPECIFIED
1" BITUMINOUS WEARING COURSE
2-3" LAYERS OF HOT MIX BASE
COMPACTED SUB GRADE
#4 Φ RODS, CUT AT JOINTS
CURB FORMS TO BE SET WITH TOP OF FORM AT FINISH GRADE OF CURB
22A GRAVEL
BLEEDER DRAIN
GRADE B POROUS MATERIAL (M.S.H.D. SPEC. 7.02.039)
NOTE
CAST CURB IN 12' MAXIMUM LENGTHS, 1/4" MASTIC BOARD EXPANSION JOINT AT EACH JOINT
6" DRAIN TILE (M.S.H.D. 7.10)
CONCRETE CURB AND GUTTER
SCALE 3/4" = 1'-0"

5.22

Johnson, Johnson and Roy

Figures 5.21 – 5.22 *Concrete curbs and gutters.*

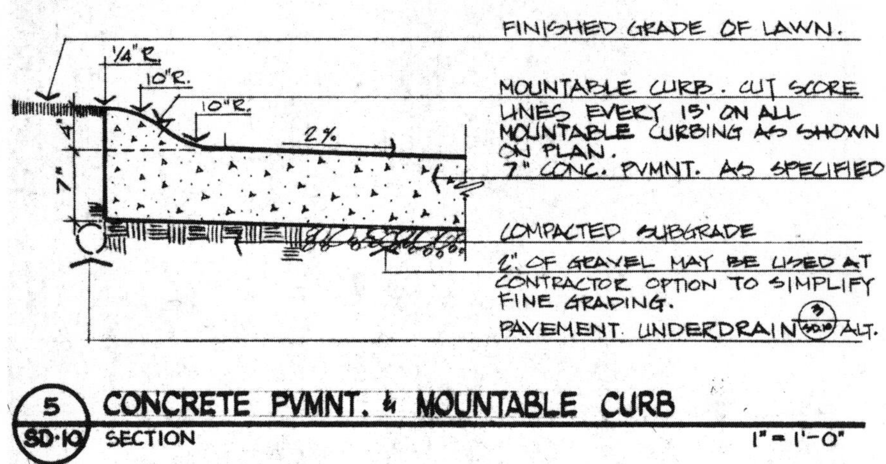

FINISHED GRADE OF LAWN.
1/4" R.
10" R.
10" R.
2%
7"
MOUNTABLE CURB. CUT SCORE LINES EVERY 15' ON ALL MOUNTABLE CURBING AS SHOWN ON PLAN.
7" CONC. PVMNT. AS SPECIFIED
COMPACTED SUBGRADE
2" OF GRAVEL MAY BE USED AT CONTRACTOR OPTION TO SIMPLIFY FINE GRADING.
PAVEMENT UNDERDRAIN 3 SD-10 ALT.
5 SD-10
CONCRETE PVMNT. & MOUNTABLE CURB
SECTION
1" = 1'-0"

5.23 Bonnell and Associates

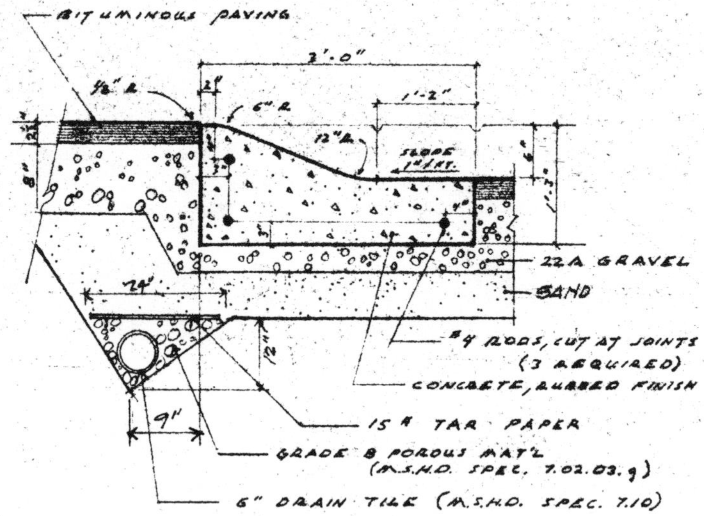

BITUMINOUS PAVING
3'-0"
1'-2"
6" R
12" R
SLOPE 1"/1FT.
22A GRAVEL
SAND
24"
12"
9"
#4 RODS, CUT AT JOINTS (3 REQUIRED)
CONCRETE, RUBBED FINISH
15# TAR PAPER
GRADE B POROUS MAT'L (M.S.H.D. SPEC. 7.02.03.g)
6" DRAIN TILE (M.S.H.D. SPEC. 7.10)

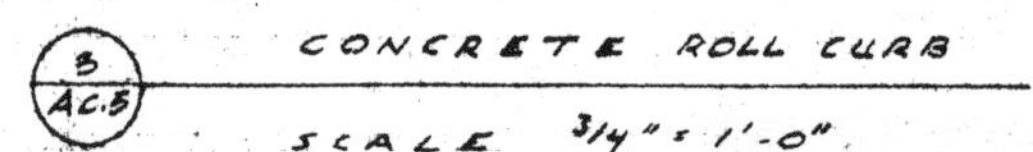

3 AC.5
CONCRETE ROLL CURB
SCALE 3/4" = 1'-0"

5.24 Johnson, Johnson and Roy

Figures 5.23 – 5.25 *Rolled concrete curbs and gutters.*

5.25

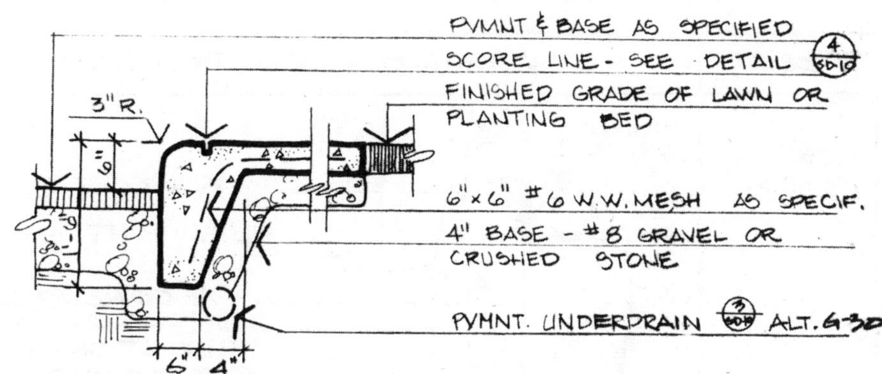
PVMNT & BASE AS SPECIFIED
SCORE LINE - SEE DETAIL 4 SD10
FINISHED GRADE OF LAWN OR PLANTING BED
3" R.
6"x6" #6 W.W. MESH AS SPECIF.
4" BASE - #8 GRAVEL OR CRUSHED STONE
PVMNT. UNDERDRAIN 3 SD19 ALT. G-30
6"
4"

CROSS SLOPE ON WALK TO BE 2% OR AS SHOWN ON GRADING PLAN. LIGHT BROOM FINISH PERPENDICULAR TO CURB. NO EDGING TOOL MARKS PERMITTED.

8
SD·10
INTEGRAL CONCRETE CURB AND WALK
SECTION
1/2" = 1'-0"

5.26 Bonnell and Associates

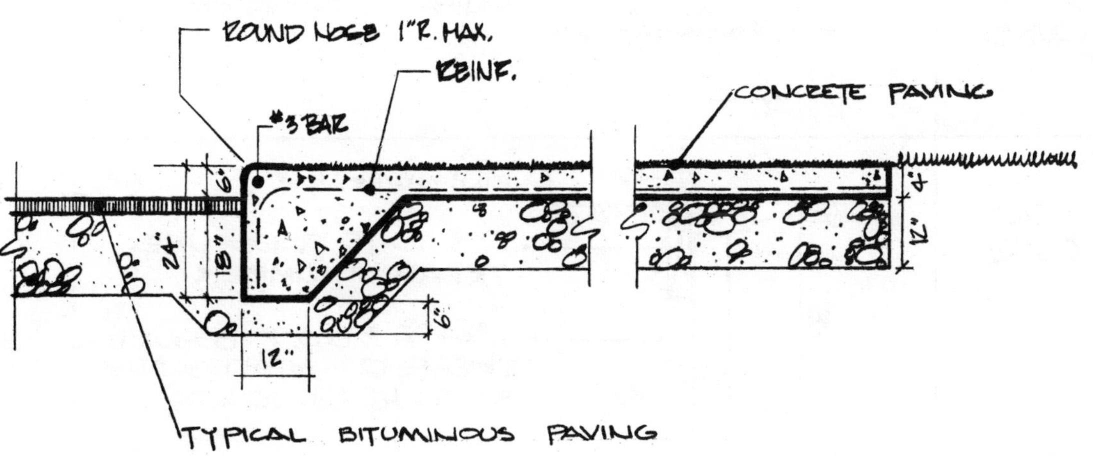
ROUND NOSE 1"R. MAX.
REINF.
#3 BAR
CONCRETE PAVING
6"
24"
18"
4"
12"
6"
12"
TYPICAL BITUMINOUS PAVING

INTEGRAL CONCRETE CURB

NO SCALE

5.27 Saratoga Associates

Figures 5.26 – 5.27 *Integral curb and walk.*

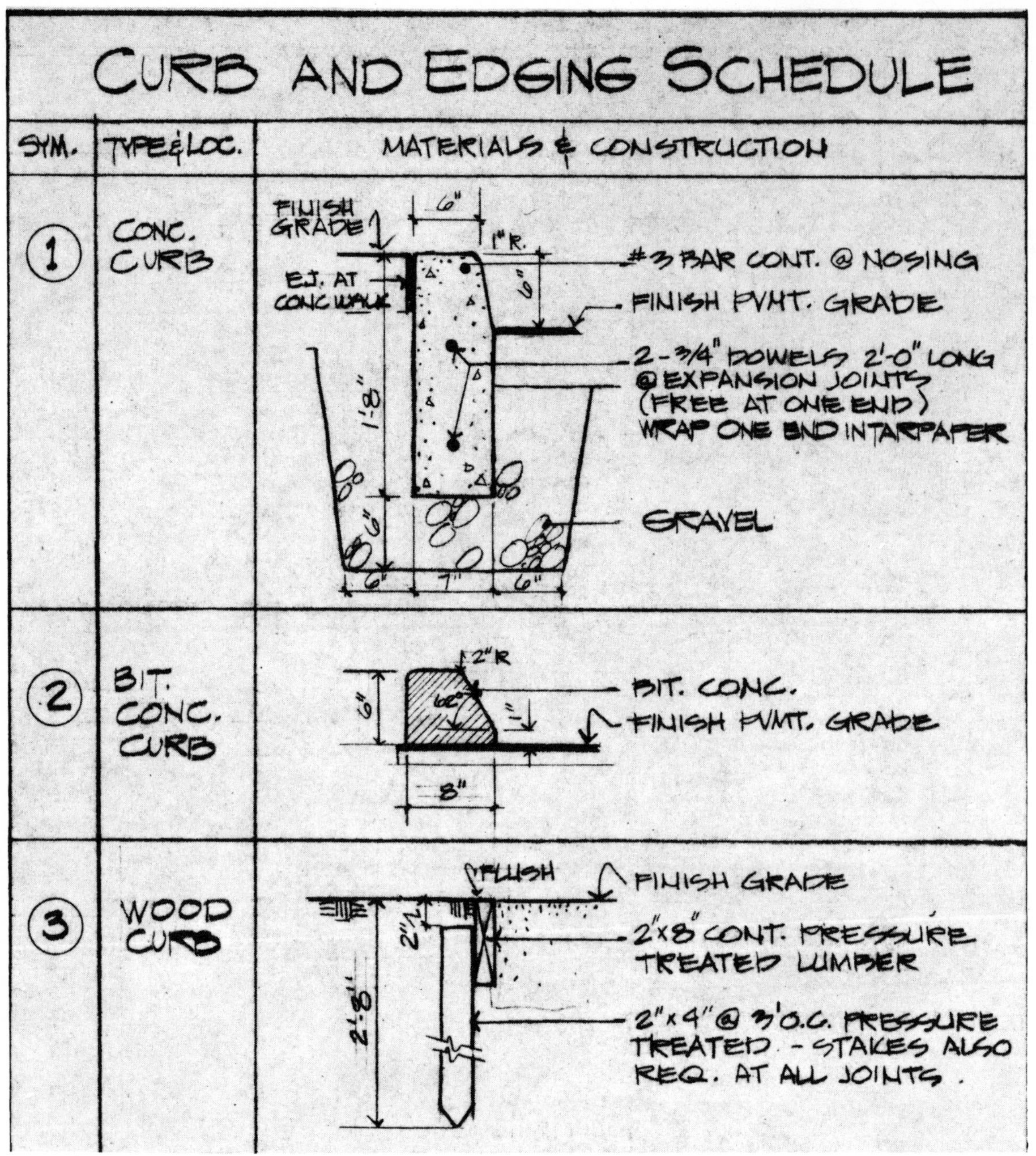
CURB AND EDGING SCHEDULE
SYM.
TYPE & LOC.
MATERIALS & CONSTRUCTION
1
CONC. CURB
FINISH GRADE
6"
1" R.
#3 BAR CONT. @ NOSING
E.J. AT CONC. WALK
6"
FINISH PVMT. GRADE
2-3/4" DOWELS 2'-0" LONG @ EXPANSION JOINTS (FREE AT ONE END) WRAP ONE END IN TARPAPER
1'-8"
GRAVEL
6"
6"
7"
6"
2
BIT. CONC. CURB
2" R
BIT. CONC.
6"
62°
FINISH PVMT. GRADE
8"
3
WOOD CURB
FLUSH
FINISH GRADE
2"x8" CONT. PRESSURE TREATED LUMBER
2 1/2"
2'-8"
2"x4" @ 3'O.C. PRESSURE TREATED - STAKES ALSO REQ. AT ALL JOINTS.

5.28

CR3, inc.

Figures 5.28 –5.29 *A technique for placing several curb and edging details on drawings.*

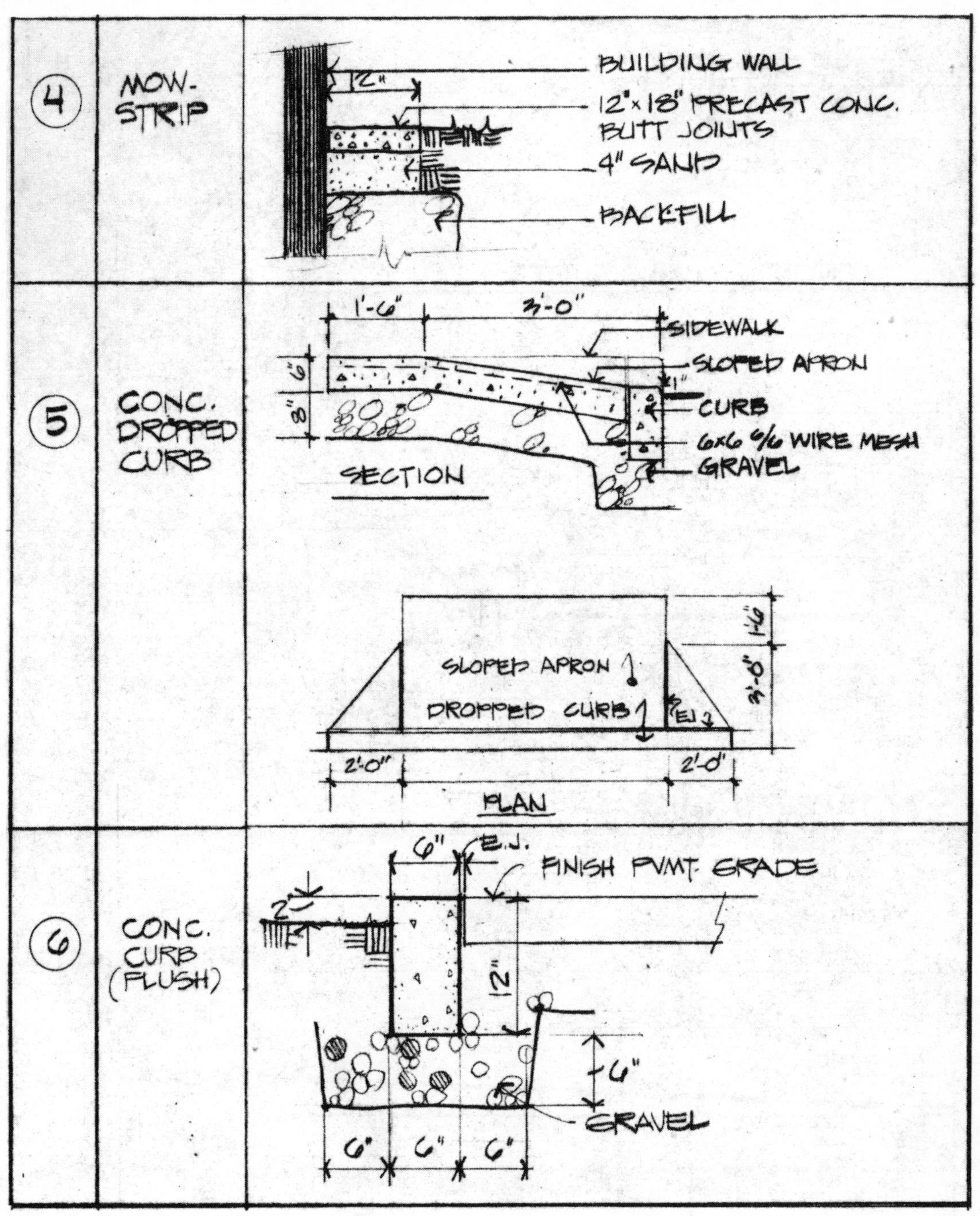
4
MOW-STRIP
BUILDING WALL
2"
12"x18" PRECAST CONC. BUTT JOINTS
4" SAND
BACKFILL
5
CONC. DROPPED CURB
1'-6"
3'-0"
SIDEWALK
SLOPED APRON
6"
8"
1"
CURB
6x6 6/6 WIRE MESH
GRAVEL
SECTION
SLOPED APRON
DROPPED CURB
EJ
1'-6"
3'-0"
2'-0"
2'-0"
PLAN
6
CONC. CURB (FLUSH)
6"
E.J.
FINISH PVMT. GRADE
2"
12"
6"
GRAVEL
6"
6"
6"
5.29

CR3, inc.

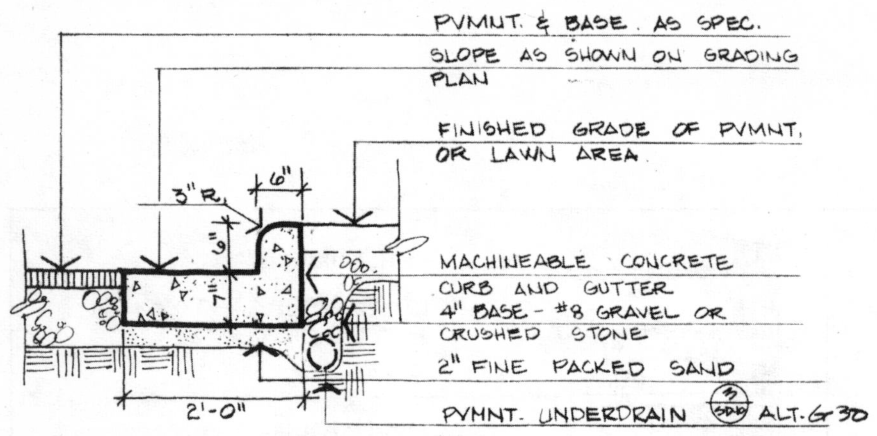
PVMNT. & BASE. AS SPEC.
SLOPE AS SHOWN ON GRADING PLAN
FINISHED GRADE OF PVMNT. OR LAWN AREA.
3" R.
6"
6"
MACHINEABLE CONCRETE CURB AND GUTTER
4" BASE - #8 GRAVEL OR CRUSHED STONE
2" FINE PACKED SAND
2'-0"
PVMNT. UNDERDRAIN 3/SD-10 ALT. G-30

10/SD-10 CONCRETE CURB & GUTTER
SECTION 3/4" = 1'-0"

5.30 Bonnell and Associates

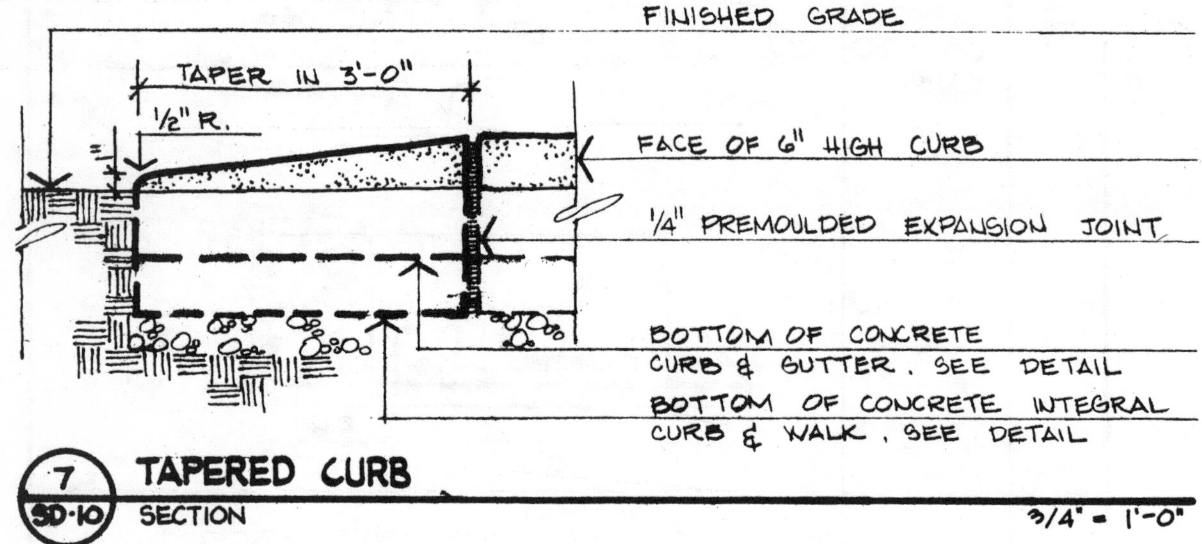
FINISHED GRADE
TAPER IN 3'-0"
1/2" R.
FACE OF 6" HIGH CURB
1/4" PREMOULDED EXPANSION JOINT
BOTTOM OF CONCRETE CURB & GUTTER. SEE DETAIL
BOTTOM OF CONCRETE INTEGRAL CURB & WALK. SEE DETAIL
7/SD-10 TAPERED CURB
SECTION
3/4" = 1'-0"

5.31

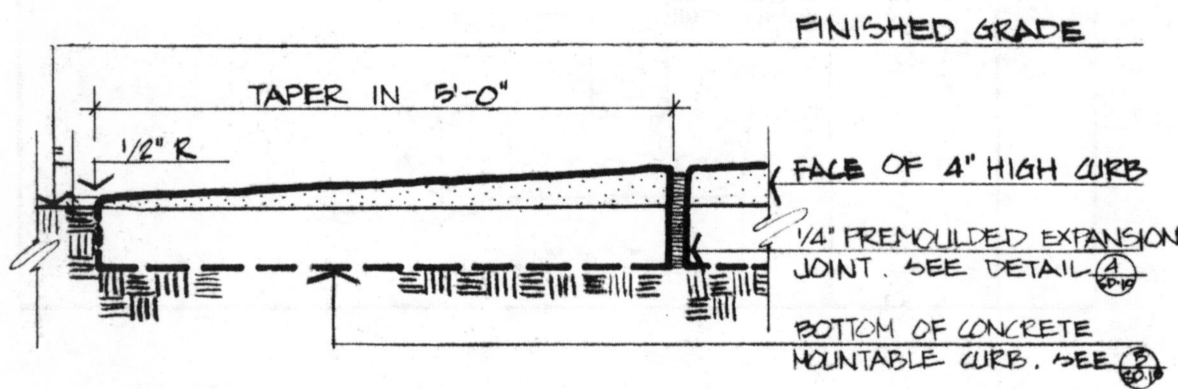
FINISHED GRADE
TAPER IN 5'-0"
1/2" R
FACE OF 4" HIGH CURB
1/4" PREMOULDED EXPANSION JOINT. SEE DETAIL 4/SD-10
BOTTOM OF CONCRETE MOUNTABLE CURB. SEE 5/SD-10

6/SD-10 TAPERED MOUNTABLE CURB
SECTION
3/4" = 1'-0"

Figures 5.30 – 5.32 *Curb details.* Bonnell and Associates

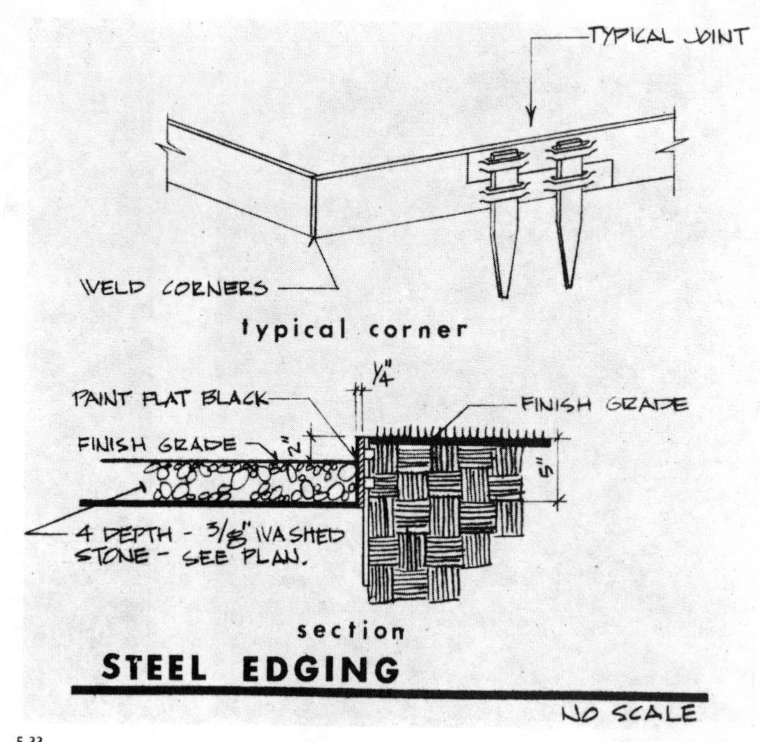
TYPICAL JOINT
WELD CORNERS
typical corner
1/4"
PAINT FLAT BLACK
FINISH GRADE
FINISH GRADE
2"
5"
4 DEPTH - 3/8" WASHED STONE - SEE PLAN.
section
STEEL EDGING
NO SCALE

5.33

Saratoga Associates

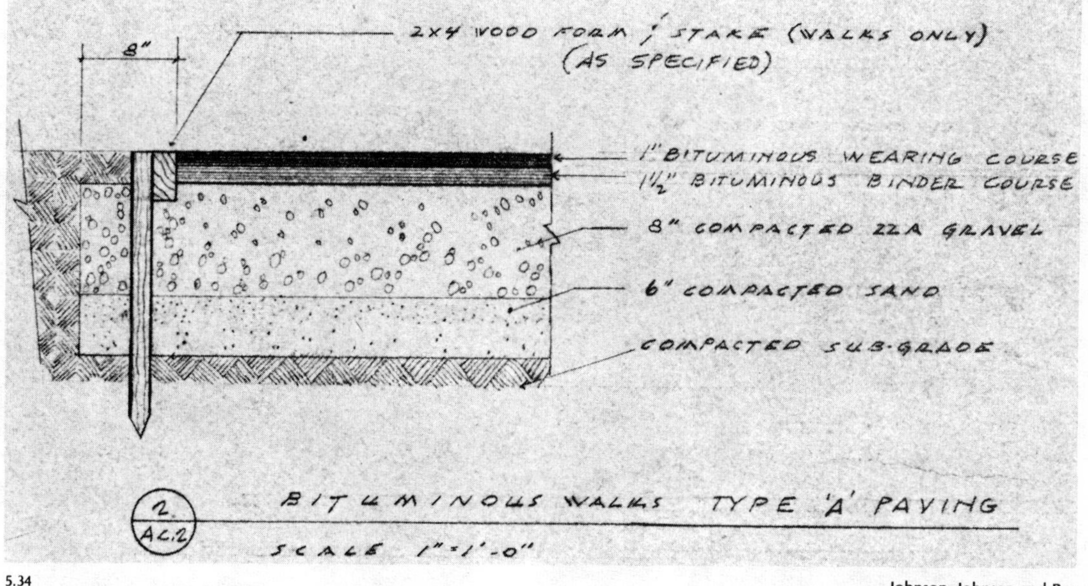
8"
2x4 WOOD FORM & STAKE (WALKS ONLY)
(AS SPECIFIED)
1" BITUMINOUS WEARING COURSE
1½" BITUMINOUS BINDER COURSE
8" COMPACTED 22A GRAVEL
6" COMPACTED SAND
COMPACTED SUB-GRADE
2
AC.2
BITUMINOUS WALKS TYPE 'A' PAVING
SCALE 1"=1'-0"

5.34

Johnson, Johnson and Roy

Figures 5.33 – 5.34 *Edging details.*

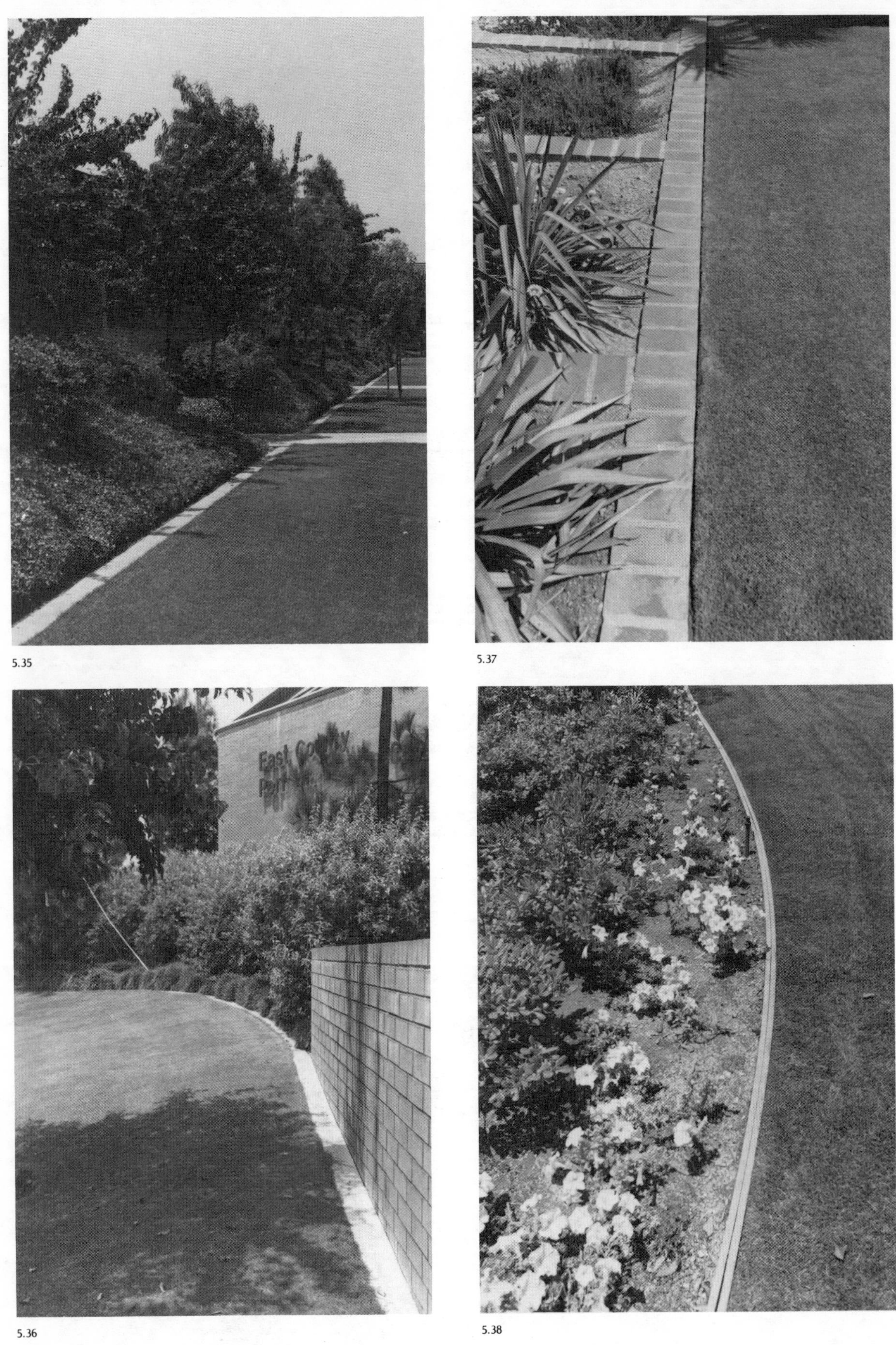

5.35

5.37

5.36

5.38

Figures 5.35 – 5.38 *Concrete, brick and redwood edgings.*

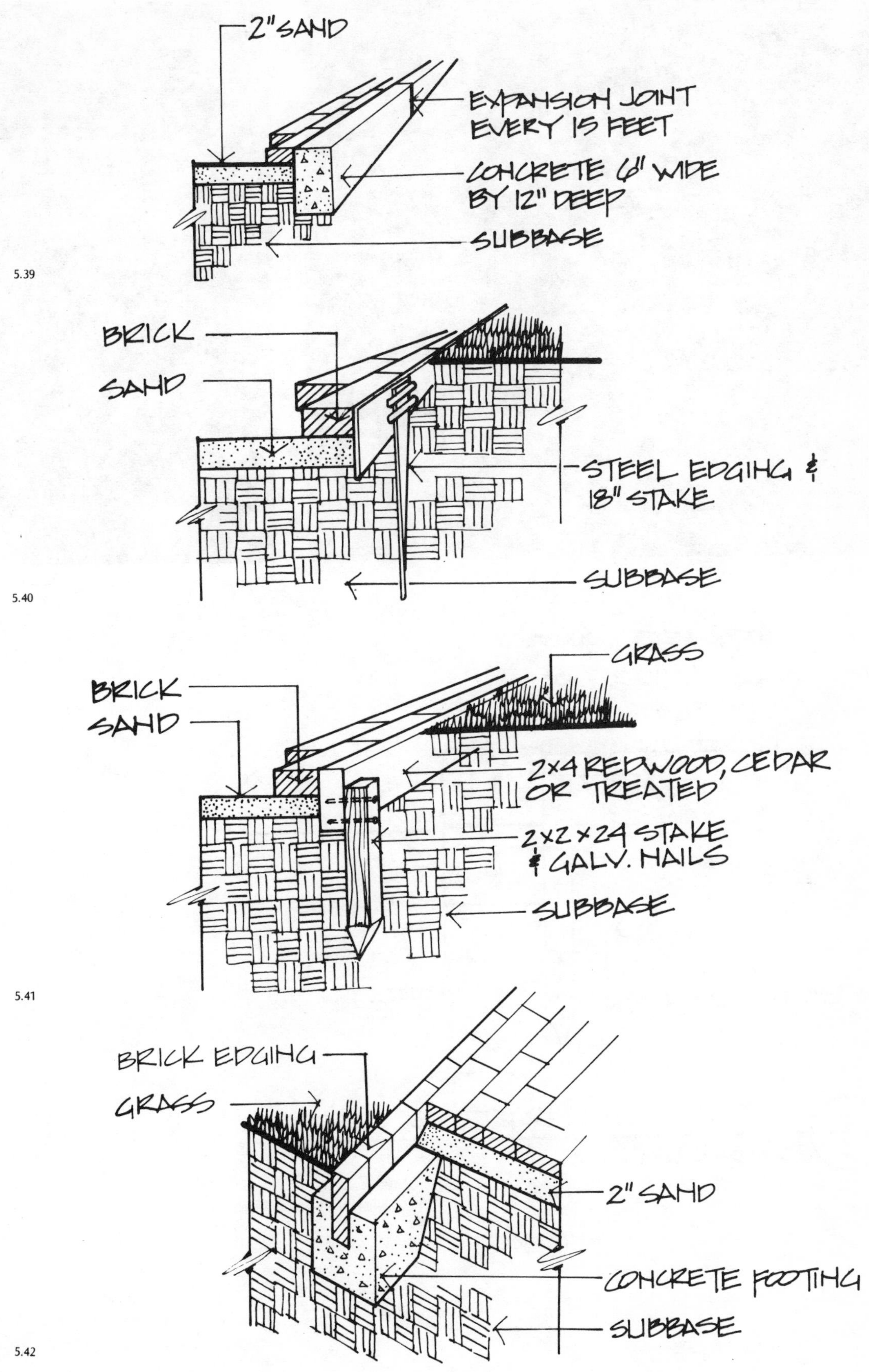
2" SAND
EXPANSION JOINT EVERY 15 FEET
CONCRETE 6" WIDE BY 12" DEEP
SUBBASE
5.39
BRICK
SAND
STEEL EDGING & 18" STAKE
SUBBASE
5.40
GRASS
BRICK
SAND
2×4 REDWOOD, CEDAR OR TREATED
2×2×24 STAKE & GALV. NAILS
SUBBASE
5.41
BRICK EDGING
GRASS
2" SAND
CONCRETE FOOTING
SUBBASE
5.42

Figures 5.39 – 5.42 *Edging details.*

5.43

5.44 LaPorte County Landscaping

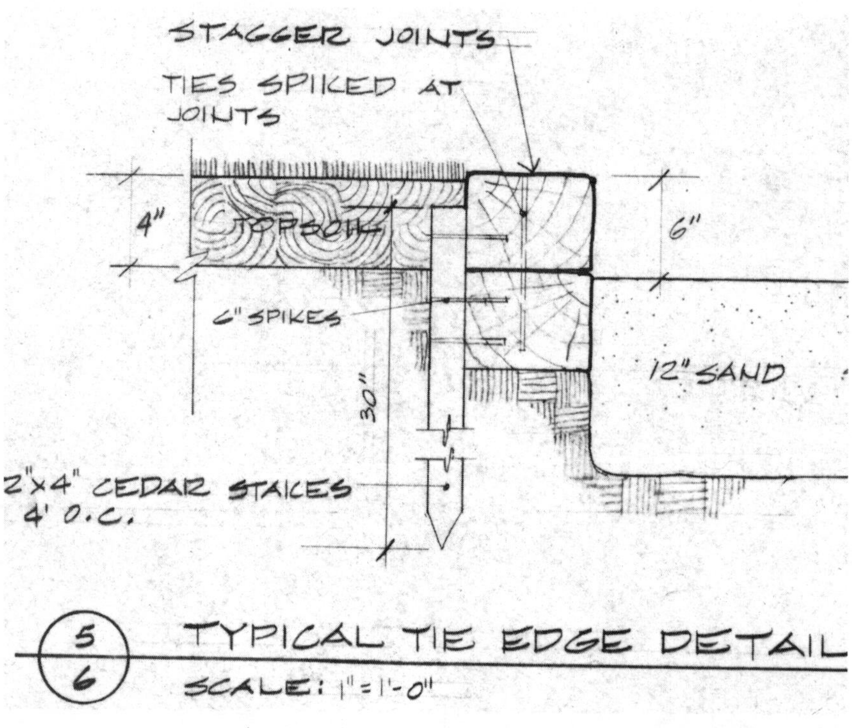

STAGGER JOINTS
TIES SPIKED AT JOINTS
4"
TOPSOIL
6"
6" SPIKES
12" SAND
30"
2"x4" CEDAR STAKES 4' O.C.
5
6
TYPICAL TIE EDGE DETAIL
SCALE: 1" = 1'-0"

5.45 Johnson, Johnson and Roy

Figures 5.43 – 5.48 *Various ways timber can be used as edging.*

5.46 Doede, Inc.

5.47

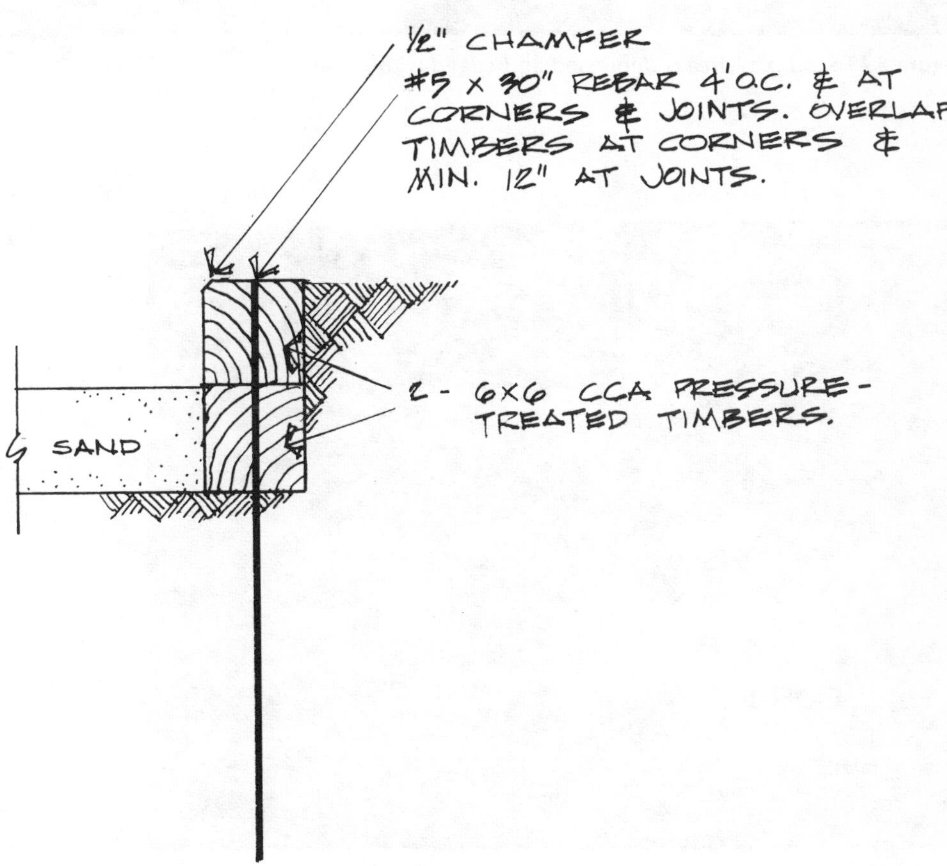

1/2" CHAMFER
#5 x 30" REBAR 4' O.C. & AT CORNERS & JOINTS. OVERLAP TIMBERS AT CORNERS & MIN. 12" AT JOINTS.
2 - 6x6 CCA PRESSURE-TREATED TIMBERS.
SAND
A
5
TIMBER EDGING

5.48 Walker-Harris-Associates-Inc.

Figure 5.49 *Sand play area is depressed and edged with stone.*

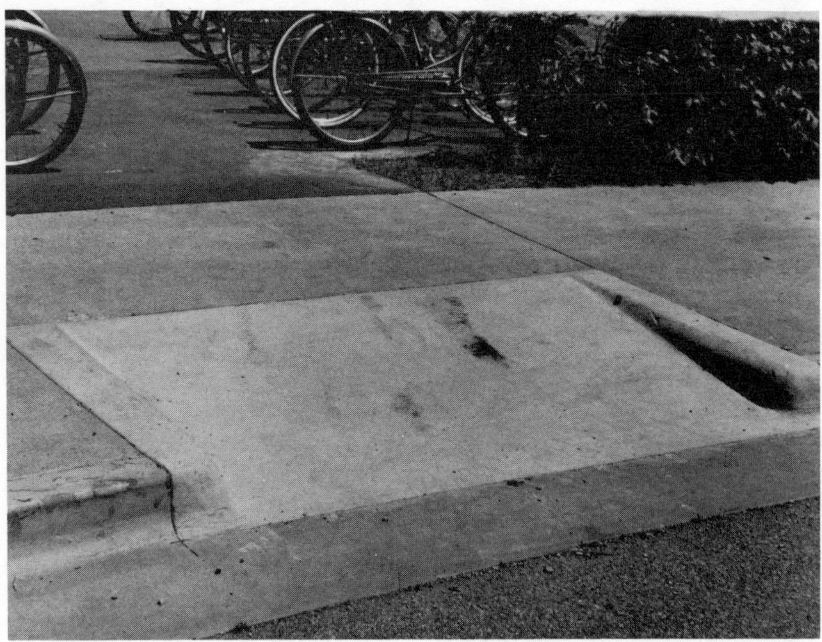

Figure 5.50 *Curb cut which is dangerous, pedestrians can trip and fall over ramp's vertical edges.*

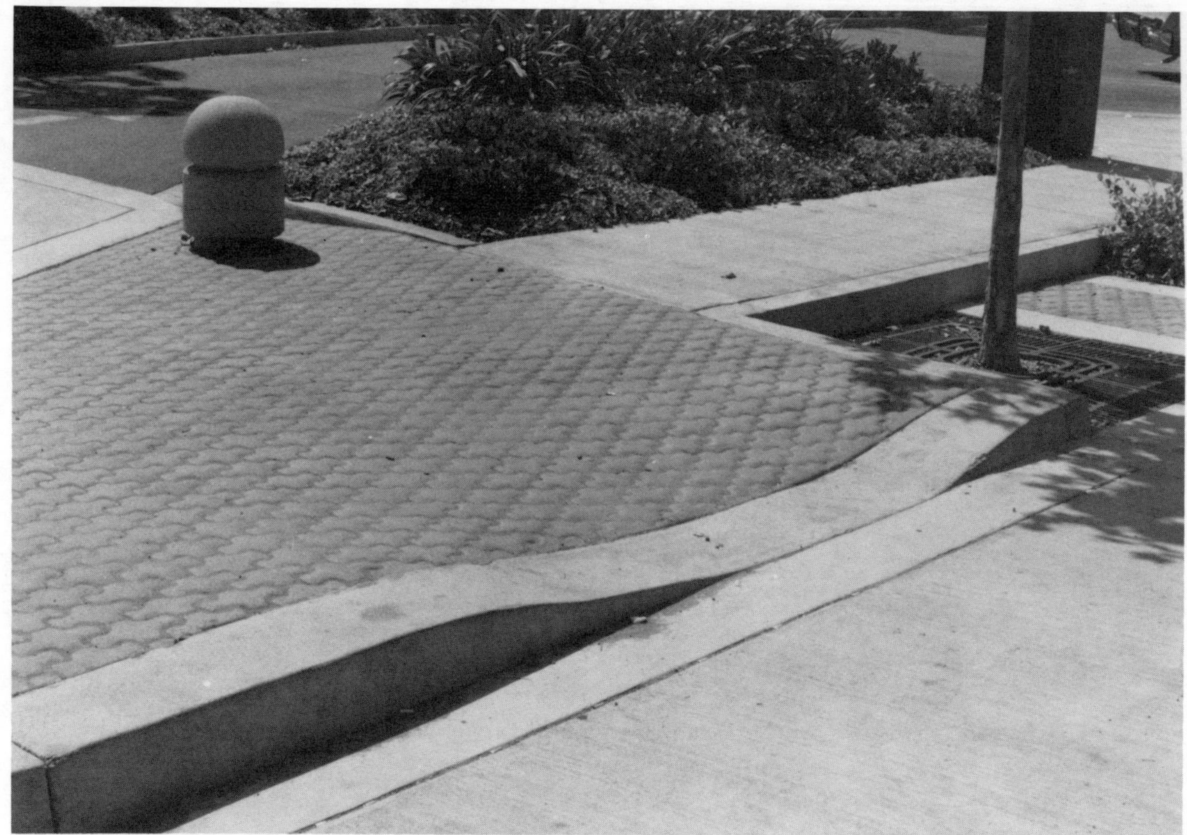

5.51

MAX. RAMP GRADIENT = 17%

3'-0" MIN.

2'-0" MIN.

5.52

Figures 5.51 - 5.52 *Curb cut and detail.*

Figure 5.53 *A gentle and subtle curb cut achieved with brick and granite.*

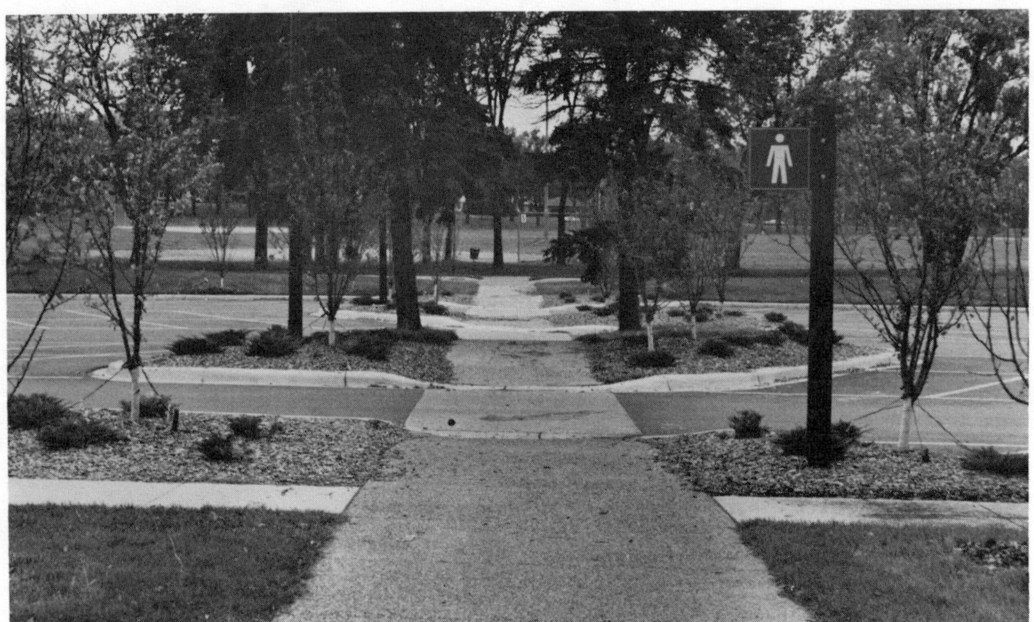

Interdesign, Inc.

Figure 5.54 *Curb cuts through each parking island provide uninterrupted flow of pedestrians and wheelchairs.*

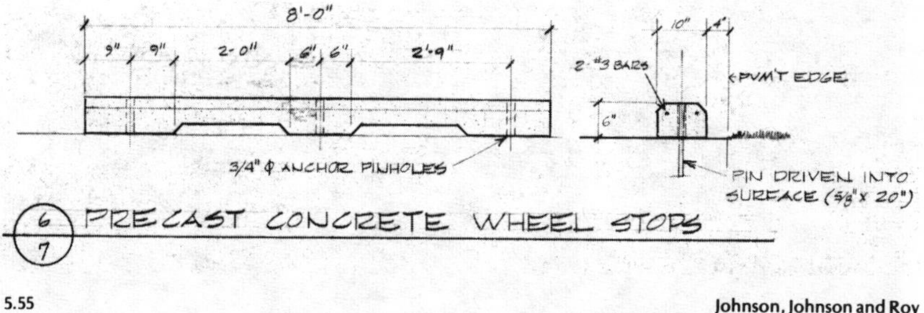
8'-0"
9"
9"
2-0"
6"
6"
2'-9"
3/4" ϕ ANCHOR PINHOLES
10"
4"
2-#3 BARS
PVM'T EDGE
6"
PIN DRIVEN INTO SURFACE (5/8" x 20")
6/7 PRECAST CONCRETE WHEEL STOPS

5.55 Johnson, Johnson and Roy

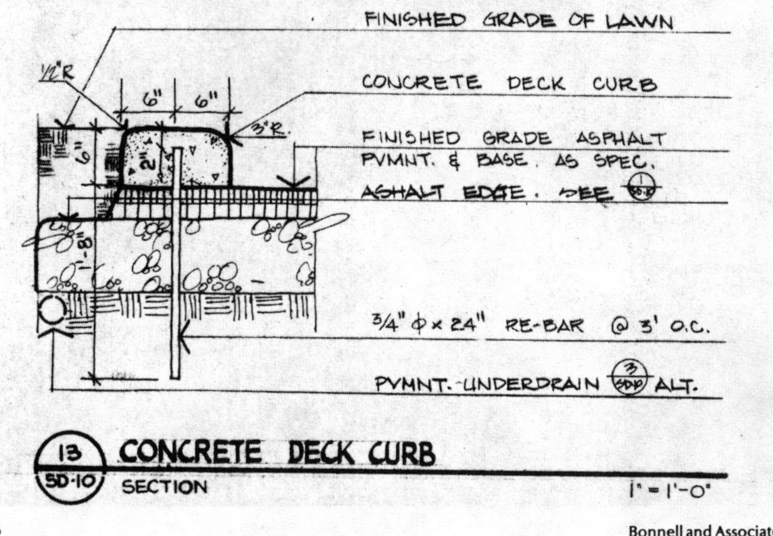
FINISHED GRADE OF LAWN
CONCRETE DECK CURB
1/2"R
6"
6"
3"R.
FINISHED GRADE ASPHALT PVMNT. & BASE. AS SPEC.
ASPHALT EDGE. SEE
3/4" ϕ x 24" RE-BAR @ 3' O.C.
PVMNT.-UNDERDRAIN ALT.
13/SD-10 CONCRETE DECK CURB
SECTION
1" = 1'-0"

5.56 Bonnell and Associates

Figures 5.55 – 5.56 *Wheelstop and deck curb details.*

Figure 6.1 *Steps between multi-level planters.*

6

Steps And Ramps

Pedestrian travel from one horizontal plane to a higher or lower horizontal plane can be accomplished through the use of steps or ramps. Steps consume less horizontal distance in relation to the vertical change while ramps consume greater horizontal distance. For most people ramps are easier to negotiate, while steps cause greater strain and increase the use of physical energy. Of the two, steps are the most expensive to construct because of the additional forming required.

Considerable variety can be created in the design of steps and ramps, particularly steps. The most popular material used in construction is concrete. Exposed aggregate or brick and stone veneers can be used for additional variety at additional cost. Steps can also be constructed from wood timbers.

Ramps can be constructed of concrete or asphaltic concrete. Other materials are possible but may not be practical since most ramps need to be designed for wheel chair use.

PHYSICAL CHARACTERISTICS OF STEPS

As a general rule steps should be a minimum of four feet in width. The number of risers needed to achieve the vertical rise will be determined by the vertical distance between the two horizontal planes. However, as a general rule a minimum of three risers should be used in any one grouping. A single riser generally is quite hazardous because it is very difficult to see, especially for people with limited vision. No more than 19 risers should be used in any single group. Eleven risers would be considered optimum between groups of risers. Landings no less than four feet in length can be used to break up groups of risers. Generally, it is possible to use any odd number group of risers with landings to fit any type of slope.

A number of formulas occur in several references relating to riser-tread relationships. The formulas vary considerably and in some instances result in awkward steps if not used with wisdom. Experience has shown that there are three workable riser-tread relationships that can be used in site design. A 6-inch rise and 12-inch tread will fit a two to one (2:1) slope and should be the steepest for outdoor use. Less steep is a 5½ inch rise with a 14-inch tread. This will be easy to form using 2 x 6 lumber. A 5-inch rise and 15-inch tread will fit a three to one (3:1) slope but is a little more difficult for short-legged individuals to negotiate.

Cheek walls can be added to stairs where they lend to the design and can serve as a base for the installation of handrails and/or recessed lighting fixtures. An 8-inch wide mowing strip sloping with and matching the nose of each tread will provide a more finished appearance to the steps and ease maintenance problems.

Steps which are built as part of retaining wall structures generally are tied to the walls with reinforcing rods that have been left protruding from the retaining wall when it is constructed. Steps which are built or constructed independently of any walls are essentially floating on the soil and may move independently of adjacent paving. To prevent hazards from occurring, the use of rods and sleeves at the top and bottom of the steps to tie the adjacent paving to the steps is recommended, or foundations and footings can be constructed underneath the steps. The thickness of the concrete used varies according to the width of the steps. As a general rule, four inches from the base of the riser to a line perpendicular with the bottom of the slope is sufficient for four-foot width steps, five inches for five to six foot wide steps, and for over six feet, six inches.

Some reinforcing is desirable in all steps. The size and amount vary according to the condition of the soil and may require engineering assistance. As a minimum it is recommended that #3 rebar be used 12 inches on center both ways. Expansion joints are needed at the base of the lowest riser and on the outside of the top tread. Expansion joints are also needed on each side of the steps when these are constructed adjacent to retaining walls or buildings.

The treads of all steps should be finished with a rough texture. This may be accomplished by the use of the float finish. Added roughness can be achieved by adding aluminum oxide grains during final finishing. These treads should be sloped slightly for drainage; ⅛ inch per foot is recommended. Risers can be from finished or stone rubbed to match the float finish of the treads. The face of the riser can be battered one inch to create relief from the vertical or shadow lines at the base of the rise to help individuals with limited vision differentiate the risers from the treads. This latter technique is highly recommended for most public situations. However, the shadow lines cannot be higher than one-third of the height of the riser without creating hazards to those negotiating steps on crutches. If the shadow line is too shallow it will not create a dark enough shadow to be of value. An inch to an inch and a half should be optimum.

At least one handrail is recommended for every set of steps designed for construction in public places. The height of the handrail above the nose of the step can vary vertically from 32 to 33 inches. Steps in public places also need to be lighted at night. This can be accomplished by overhead lighting positioned to light the risers as well as the treads, or recessed lighting within the hand rail is quite effective.

Six-inch timbers can be used for risers as they will have an actual dimension of five and one-half inches which makes an ideal riser height. Timbers can be held in place by drilling vertical holes and driving in 30 to 36 inch #5 rebars, two per riser. For treads, additional timber can be installed, or asphalt concrete can be used, and there are other possibilities. Because smooth wood becomes slick when wet, it should not be used in high pedestrian traffic areas or for the elderly.

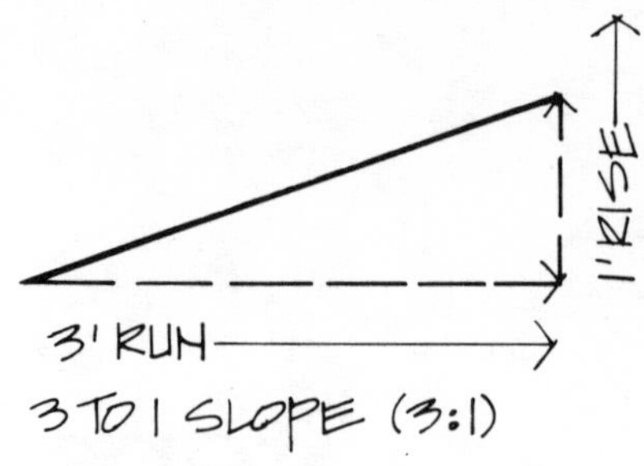
1' RISE
3' RUN
3 TO 1 SLOPE (3:1)

Figure 6.2 *Slope ratio, 1 foot vertical rise in 3 horizontal feet.*

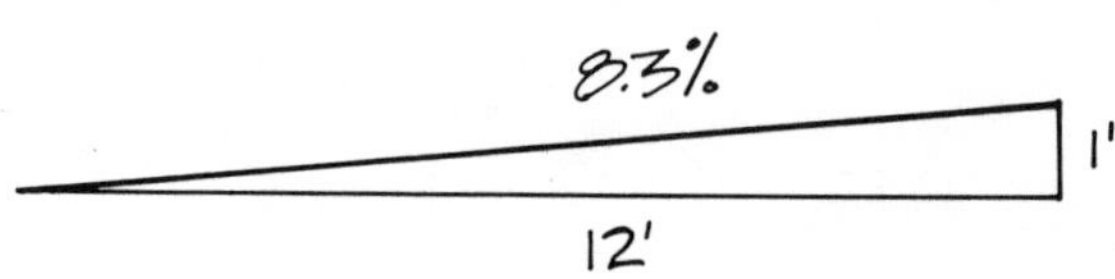
8.3%
1'
12'

Figure 6.3 *Maximum slope for ramps, 1 foot vertical rise in 12 horizontal feet.*

PHYSICAL CHARACTERISTICS OF RAMPS

A ramp slope of 8.3 percent is considered maximum for use by wheelchairs for a distance not exceeding 30 feet. A slope of 14 percent can be used for short distances where two handrails are provided. Longer distances can be broken up intermittently with landings to provide reststops for wheelchair users. For average pedestrian use, a 20 percent slope is considered maximum. Ramps which may be used solely by children or active young adults can tolerate a 30 percent slope for short distances.

Ramps may be constructed of paving material the same thickness and type as adjacent surfaces, though curbs four to six inches above the surface of the paving on each side of the ramp are desirable to keep wheel chairs from rolling off the ramp. Handrails are recommended for wheel chair ramps greater than five percent in slope. A handrail on both sides at 32 inches in height will aid the wheel chair user in maintaining control, and generally the user will use the handrail to move himself forward. For

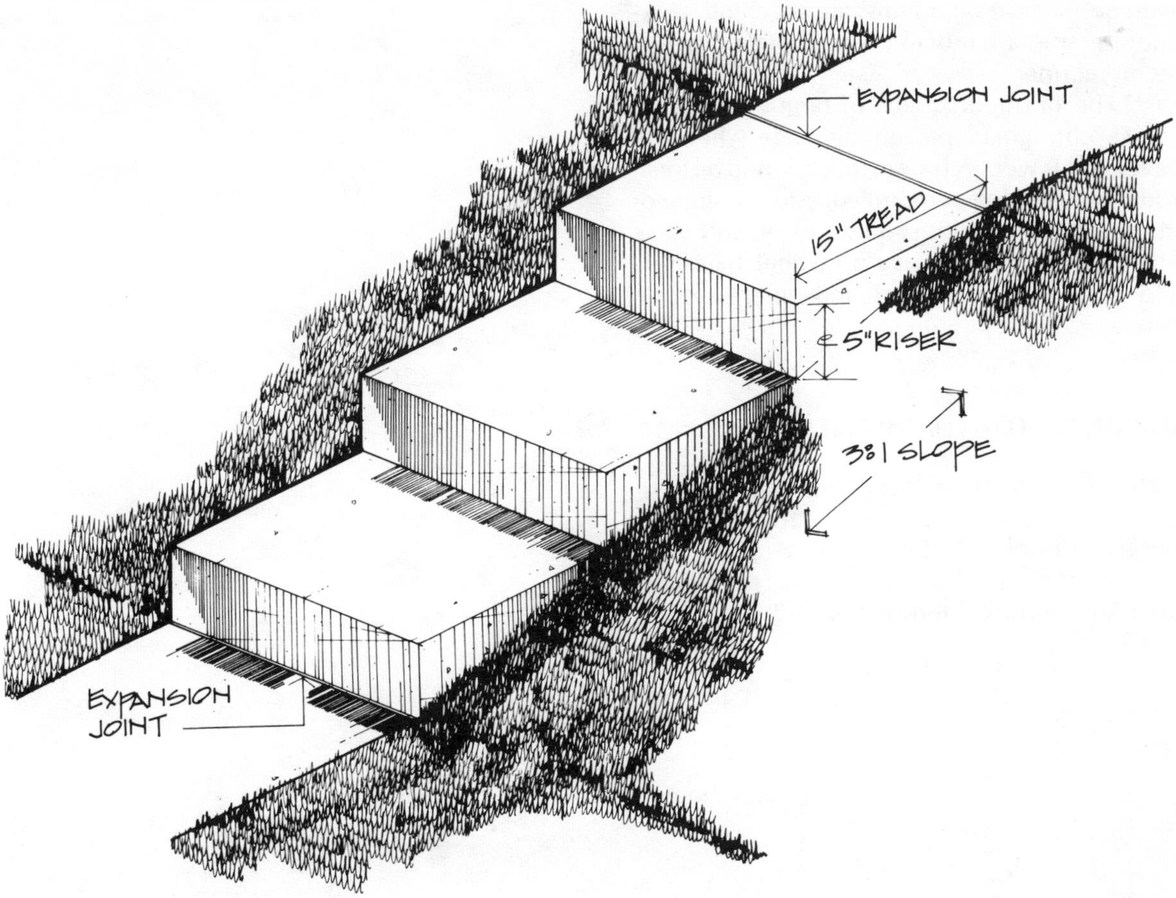

Figure 6.4 *Steps to fit a 3:1 slope.*

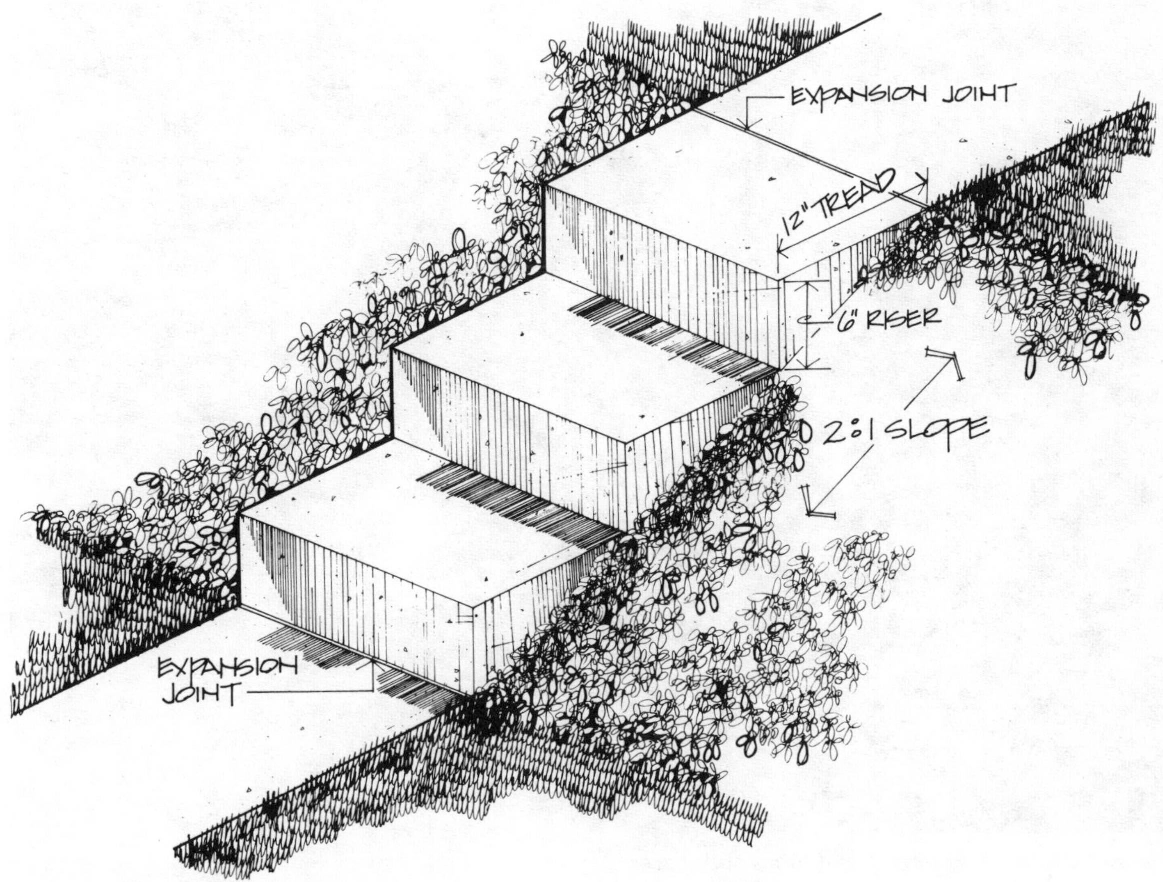
EXPANSION JOINT
12" TREAD
6" RISER
2:1 SLOPE
EXPANSION JOINT

Figure 6.5 *Steps to fit a 2:1 slope.*

average pedestrian ramps approaching maximum grade, a handrail on at least one side is recommended.

The finished surface of ramps should be coarse enough to prevent slippage when the pavement is wet. A broom finish would be ideal with lines running perpendicular to the slope of the ramp. The finish should not be so coarse that it creates a rough ride for wheelchair users and inhibits their upward movement on the ramp.

REFERENCES FOR FURTHER READING

Portland Cement Association. "Concrete – Walks, Drives, Patios and Steps," *Handbook of Landscape Architectural Construction*. Washington, DC: Landscape Architecture Foundation, 1973.

Figure 6.6 *Interesting interplay of forms and spaces.*

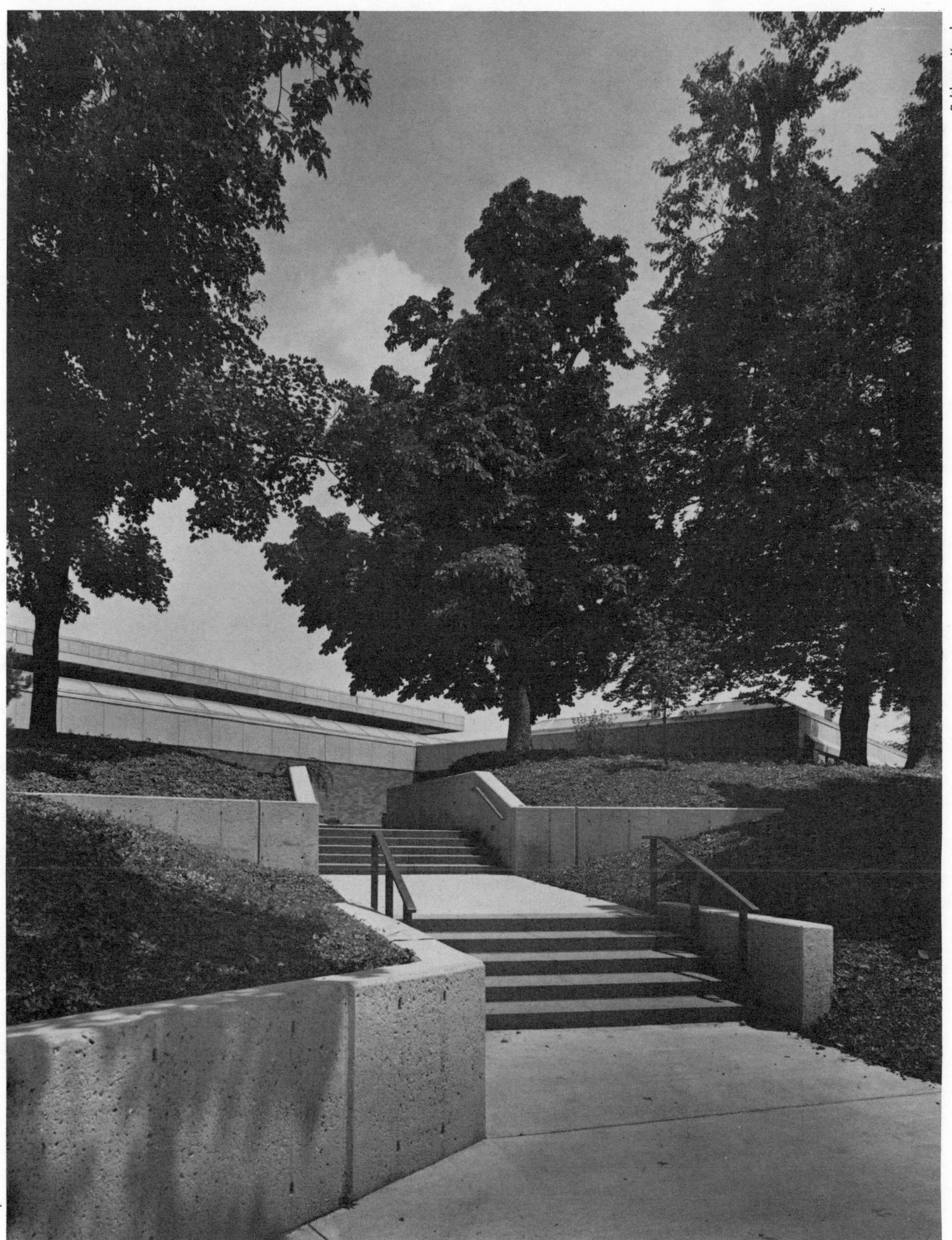
Balthazar Korab

Figure 6.7 *Steps with terraces and landing.*

Bonnell and Associates

6.8 Browning-Day-Pollak-Associates-Inc.

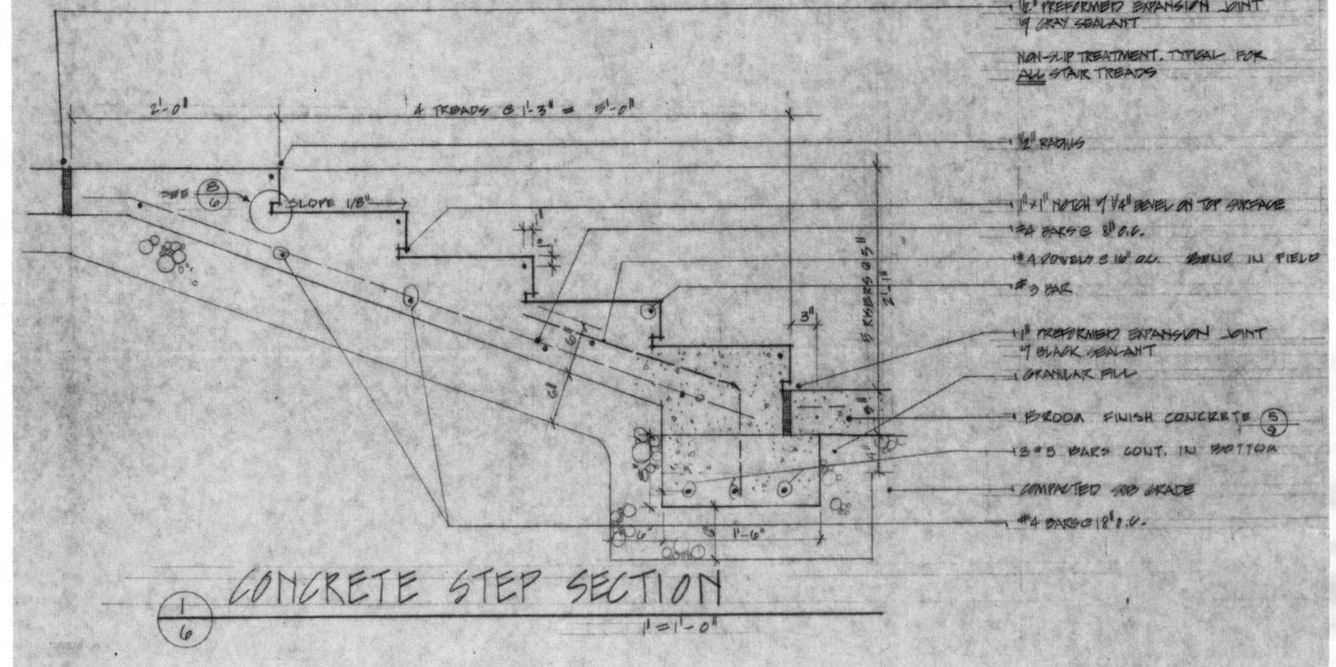

1/2" PREFORMED EXPANSION JOINT
W/ GRAY SEALANT
NON-SLIP TREATMENT, TYPICAL FOR
ALL STAIR TREADS
2'-0"
4 TREADS @ 1'-3" = 5'-0"
1/2" RADIUS
SLOPE 1/8"
1"x1" NOTCH W/ 1/4" BEVEL ON TOP SURFACE
#4 BARS @ 8" O.C.
#4 DOWELS @ 16" O.C. BEND IN FIELD
#3 BAR
3"
1" PREFORMED EXPANSION JOINT
W/ BLACK SEALANT
GRANULAR FILL
BROOM FINISH CONCRETE
3 #5 BARS CONT. IN BOTTOM
COMPACTED SUB GRADE
#4 BARS @ 18" O.C.
1'-6"
CONCRETE STEP SECTION
1" = 1'-0"

6.9 Browning-Day-Pollak-Associates-Inc.

Figures 6.8 – 6.9 *Concrete steps and the detail used for their construction.*

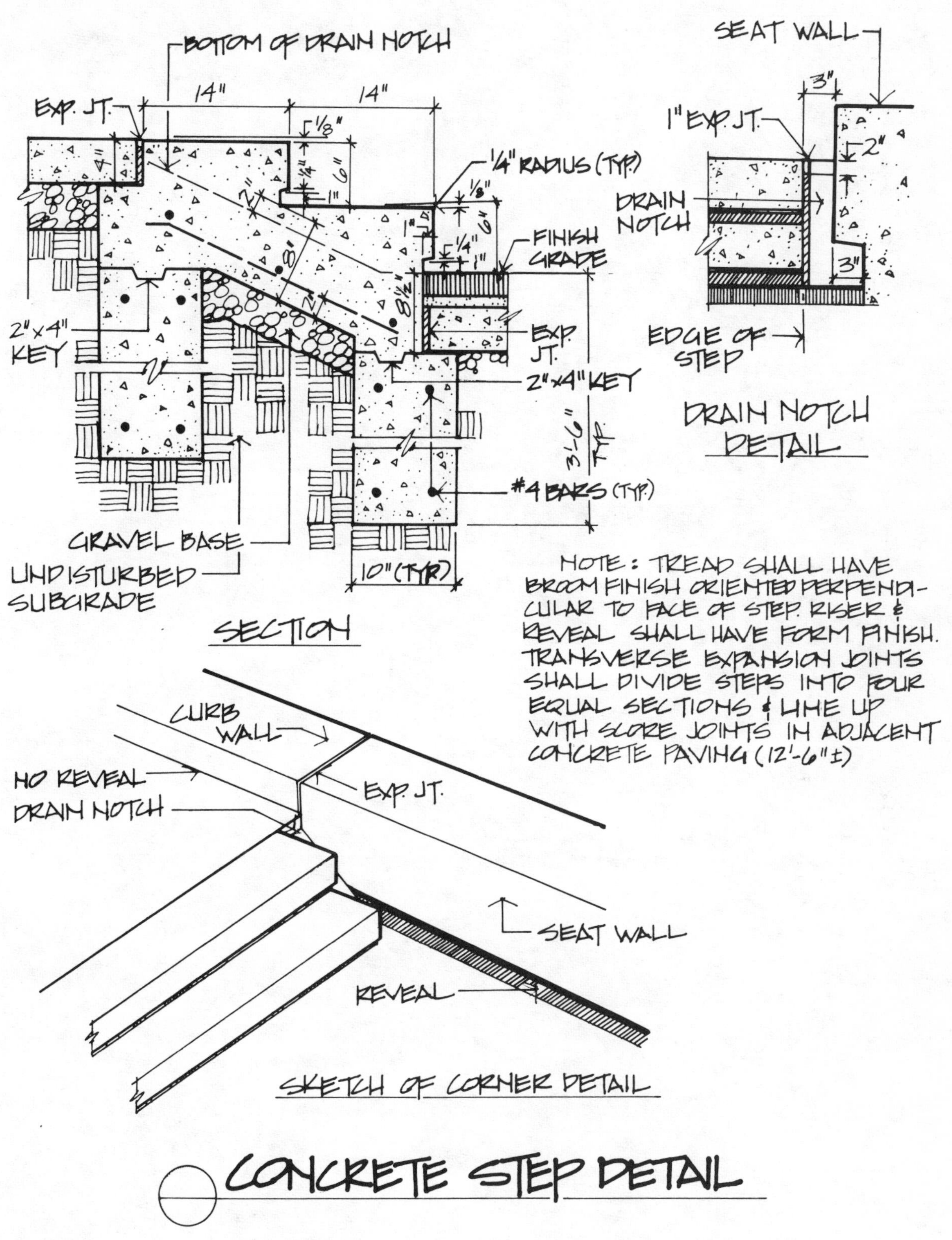
BOTTOM OF DRAIN NOTCH
EXP. JT.
14"
14"
1/8"
1/4"
6"
1"
1/4" RADIUS (TYP.)
1/8"
6"
1"
1/4"
1"
FINISH GRADE
2"x4" KEY
EXP. JT.
2"x4" KEY
3'-6" TYP.
#4 BARS (TYP.)
GRAVEL BASE
UNDISTURBED SUBGRADE
10" (TYP.)
SECTION
SEAT WALL
3"
1" EXP. JT.
2"
DRAIN NOTCH
3"
EDGE OF STEP
DRAIN NOTCH DETAIL
NOTE: TREAD SHALL HAVE BROOM FINISH ORIENTED PERPENDICULAR TO FACE OF STEP. RISER & REVEAL SHALL HAVE FORM FINISH. TRANSVERSE EXPANSION JOINTS SHALL DIVIDE STEPS INTO FOUR EQUAL SECTIONS & LINE UP WITH SCORE JOINTS IN ADJACENT CONCRETE PAVING (12'-6"±)
CURB WALL
NO REVEAL
DRAIN NOTCH
EXP. JT.
SEAT WALL
REVEAL
SKETCH OF CORNER DETAIL
CONCRETE STEP DETAIL

Figure 6.10 *Step detail.*

Johnson, Johnson and Roy

Figure 6.11 *Pre-cast concrete cylinders.*

Photo courtesy of Betonwerk Munderkingen GmbH

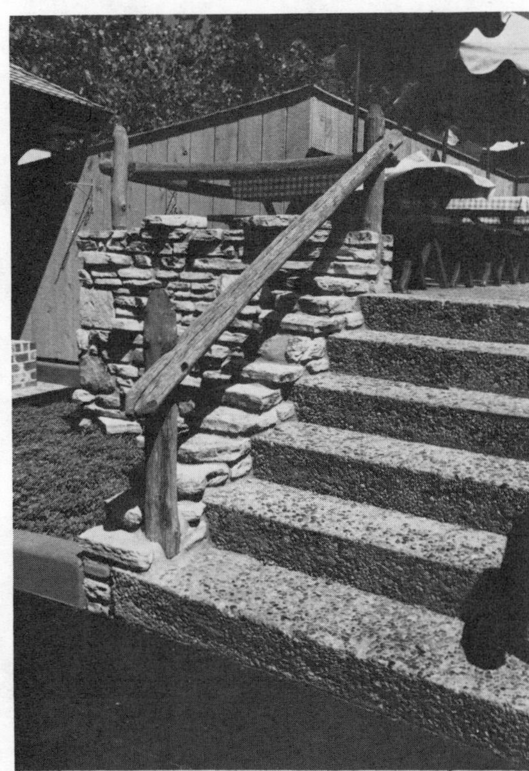

6.12 M. Paul Friedberg and Partners

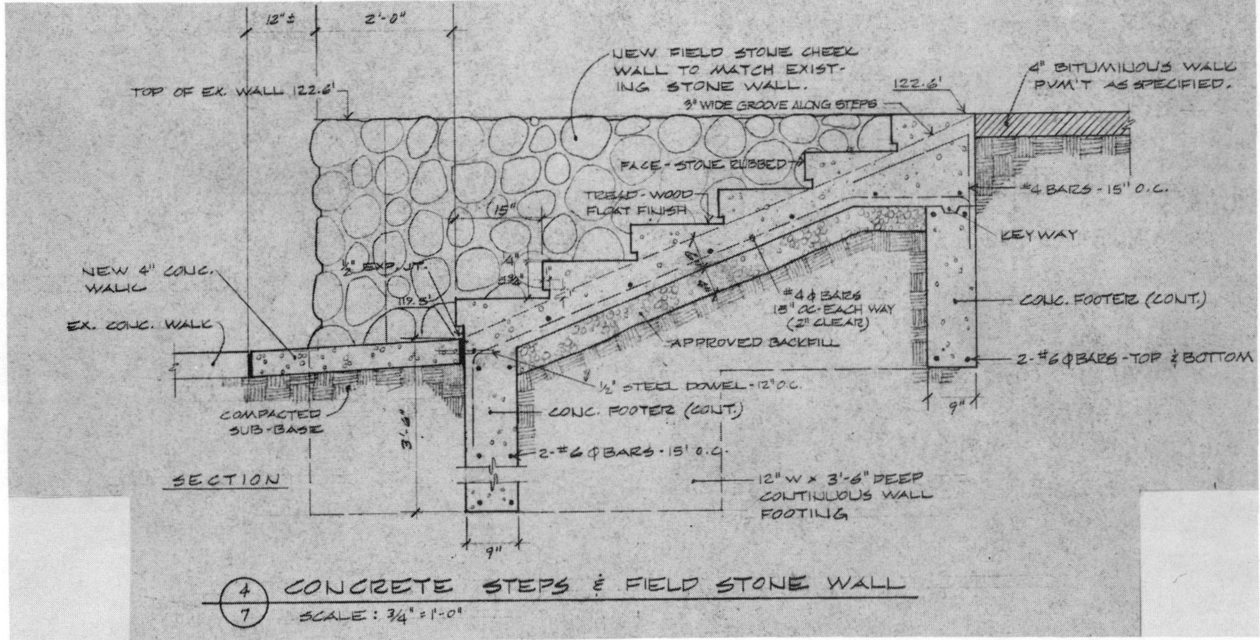

12" ±
2'-0"
TOP OF EX. WALL 122.6'
NEW FIELD STONE CHEEK WALL TO MATCH EXISTING STONE WALL.
122.6'
4" BITUMINOUS WALK PVM'T AS SPECIFIED.
3" WIDE GROOVE ALONG STEPS
FACE-STONE RUBBED
TREAD-WOOD FLOAT FINISH
#4 BARS - 15" O.C.
15"
KEYWAY
NEW 4" CONC. WALK
1/2" EXP. JT.
119.5'
#4 ϕ BARS 15" OC-EACH WAY (2" CLEAR)
CONC. FOOTER (CONT.)
EX. CONC. WALK
APPROVED BACKFILL
2-#6 ϕ BARS - TOP & BOTTOM
1/2" STEEL DOWEL - 12" O.C.
COMPACTED SUB-BASE
CONC. FOOTER (CONT.)
9"
3'-6"
2-#6 ϕ BARS - 15' O.C.
SECTION
12" W x 3'-6" DEEP CONTINUOUS WALL FOOTING
9"
4/7 CONCRETE STEPS & FIELD STONE WALL
SCALE: 3/4" = 1'-0"

6.13 Johnson, Johnson and Roy

Figures 6.12 - 6.13 *Miscellaneous steps and detail.*

6.14

6.15

6.16

6.17

6.18

6.19

Figures 6.14 – 6.19 *Miscellaneous step designs.*

6.20

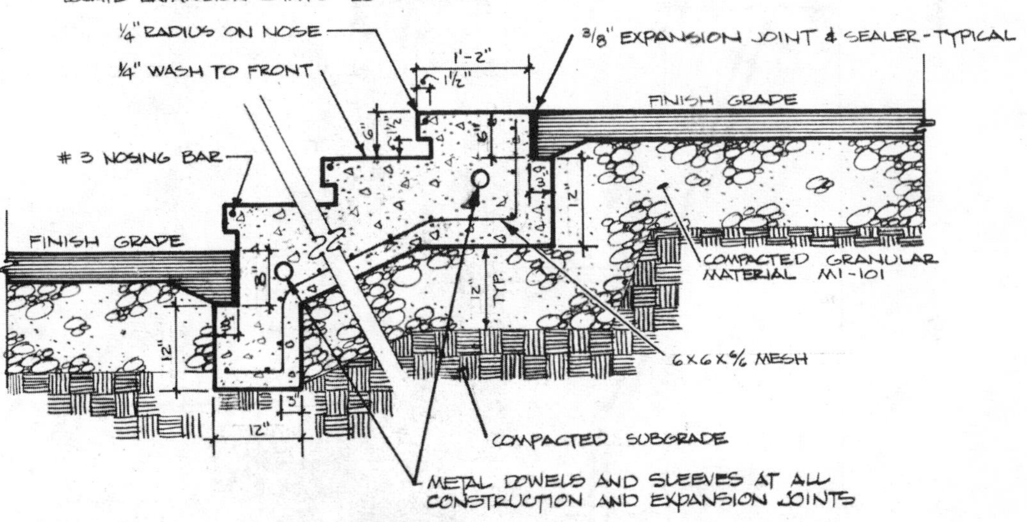
NOTE: NUMBER OF STEPS VARY - SEE PLAN
LOCATE EXPANSION JOINTS - 20' O.C. MAX.
1/4" RADIUS ON NOSE
1/4" WASH TO FRONT
3/8" EXPANSION JOINT & SEALER - TYPICAL
1'-2"
1 1/2"
FINISH GRADE
3 NOSING BAR
FINISH GRADE
COMPACTED GRANULAR MATERIAL M1-101
6x6x6/6 MESH
12"
COMPACTED SUBGRADE
METAL DOWELS AND SLEEVES AT ALL CONSTRUCTION AND EXPANSION JOINTS

f1
CONCRETE STEPS
SCALE 3/4" = 1'-0"

6.21

Saratoga Associates

Figures 6.20 - 6.21 *Steps with shadow in riser.*

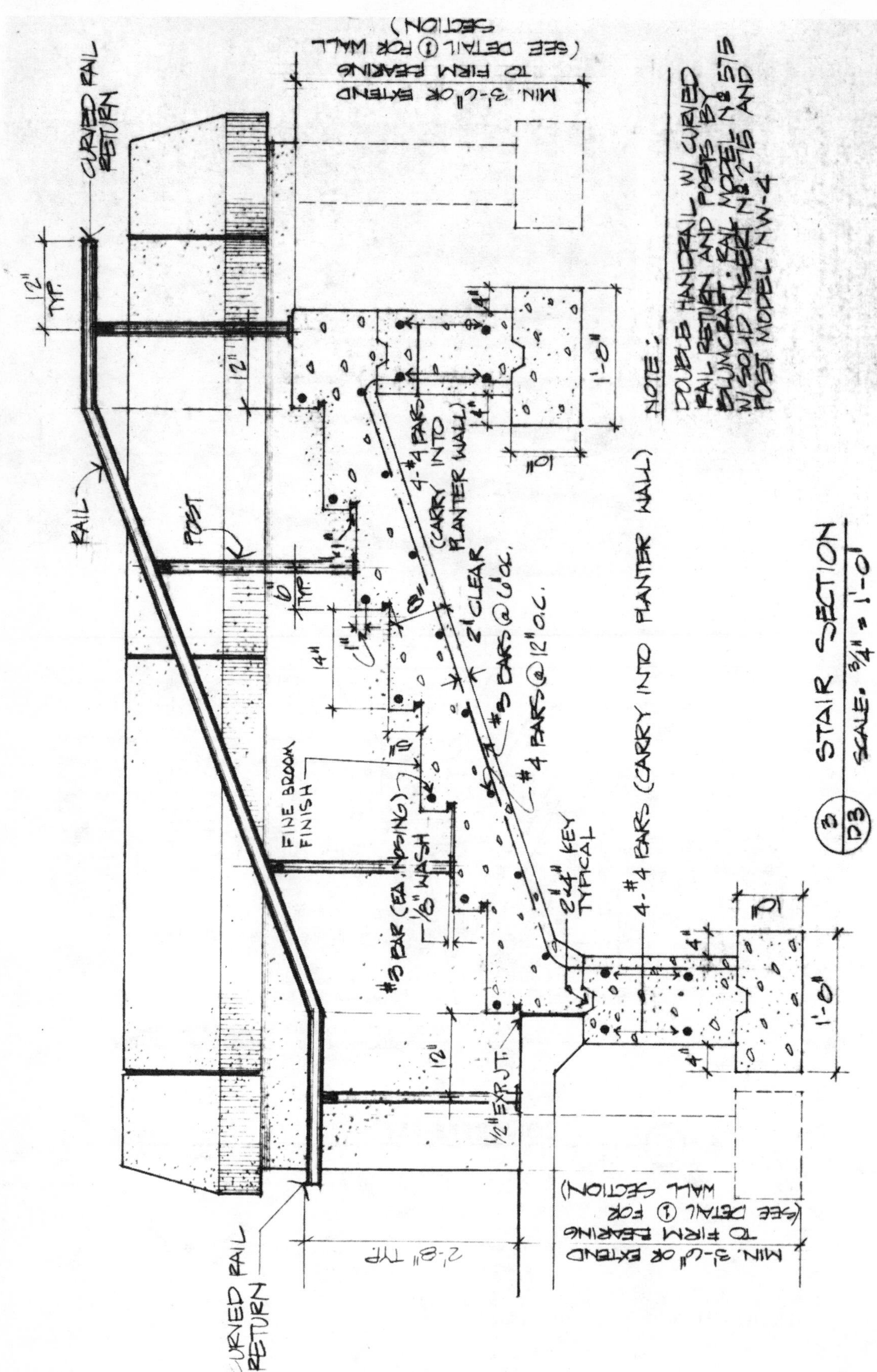

CURVED RAIL RETURN
RAIL
POST
12" TYP.
FINE BROOM FINISH
#3 BAR (EA. NOSING)
1/8" WASH
2 1/4" KEY TYPICAL
4-#4 BARS (CARRY INTO PLANTER WALL)
4-#4 BARS (CARRY INTO PLANTER WALL)
#3 BARS @ 12" O.C.
#3 BARS @ 6" O.C.
2" CLEAR
1/2" EXP. JT.
2'-8" TYP.
MIN. 3'-6" OR EXTEND TO FIRM BEARING (SEE DETAIL ① FOR WALL SECTION)
1'-0"
NOTE:
STAIR SECTION
SCALE: 3/4" = 1'-0"

Figure 6.22 *Concrete step detail.*

CR3, inc.

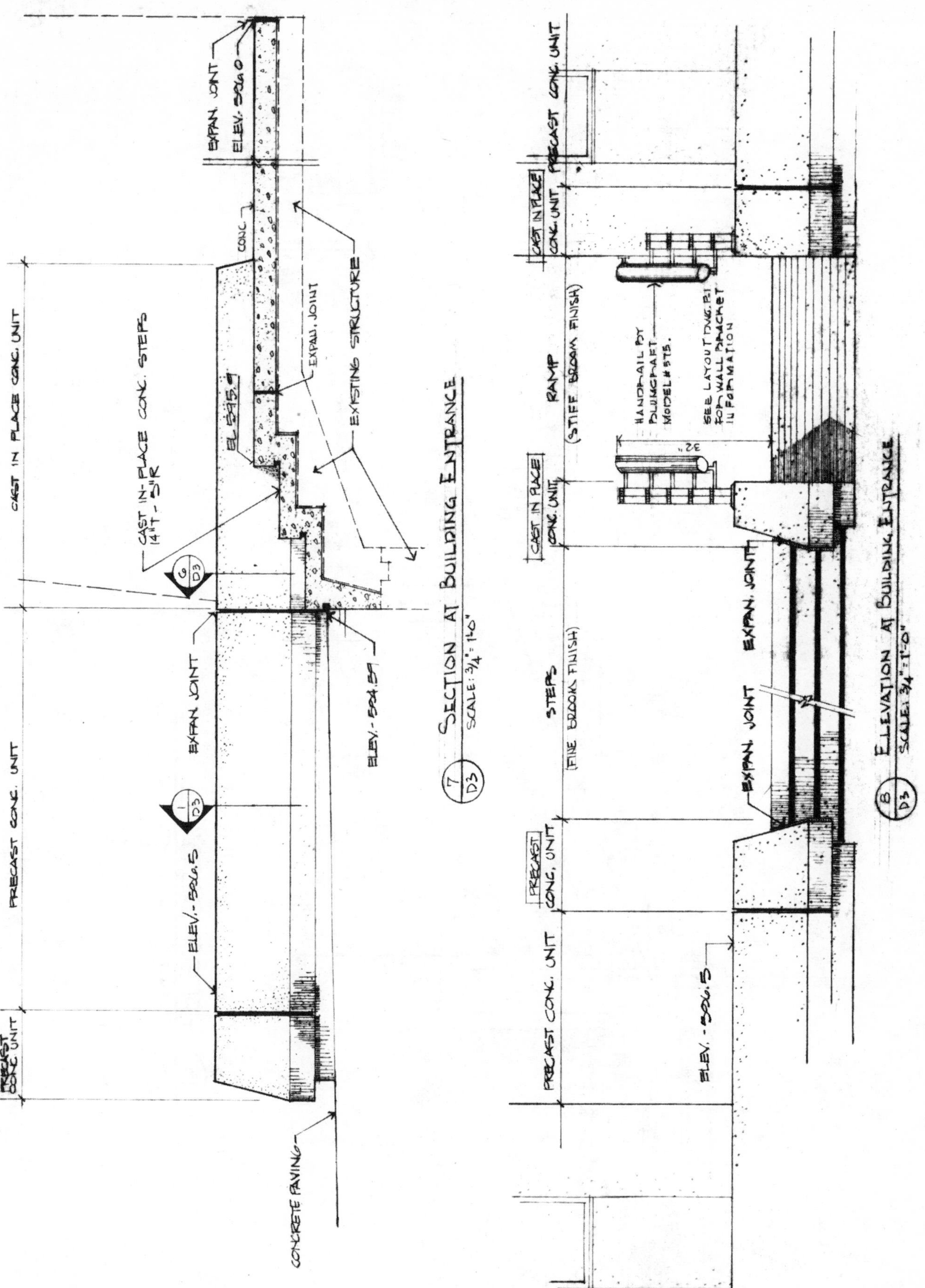
SECTION AT BUILDING ENTRANCE
SCALE: 3/4" = 1'-0"
ELEVATION AT BUILDING ENTRANCE
SCALE: 3/4" = 1'-0"

Figure 6.23 *Concrete step detail.*

CR3, inc.

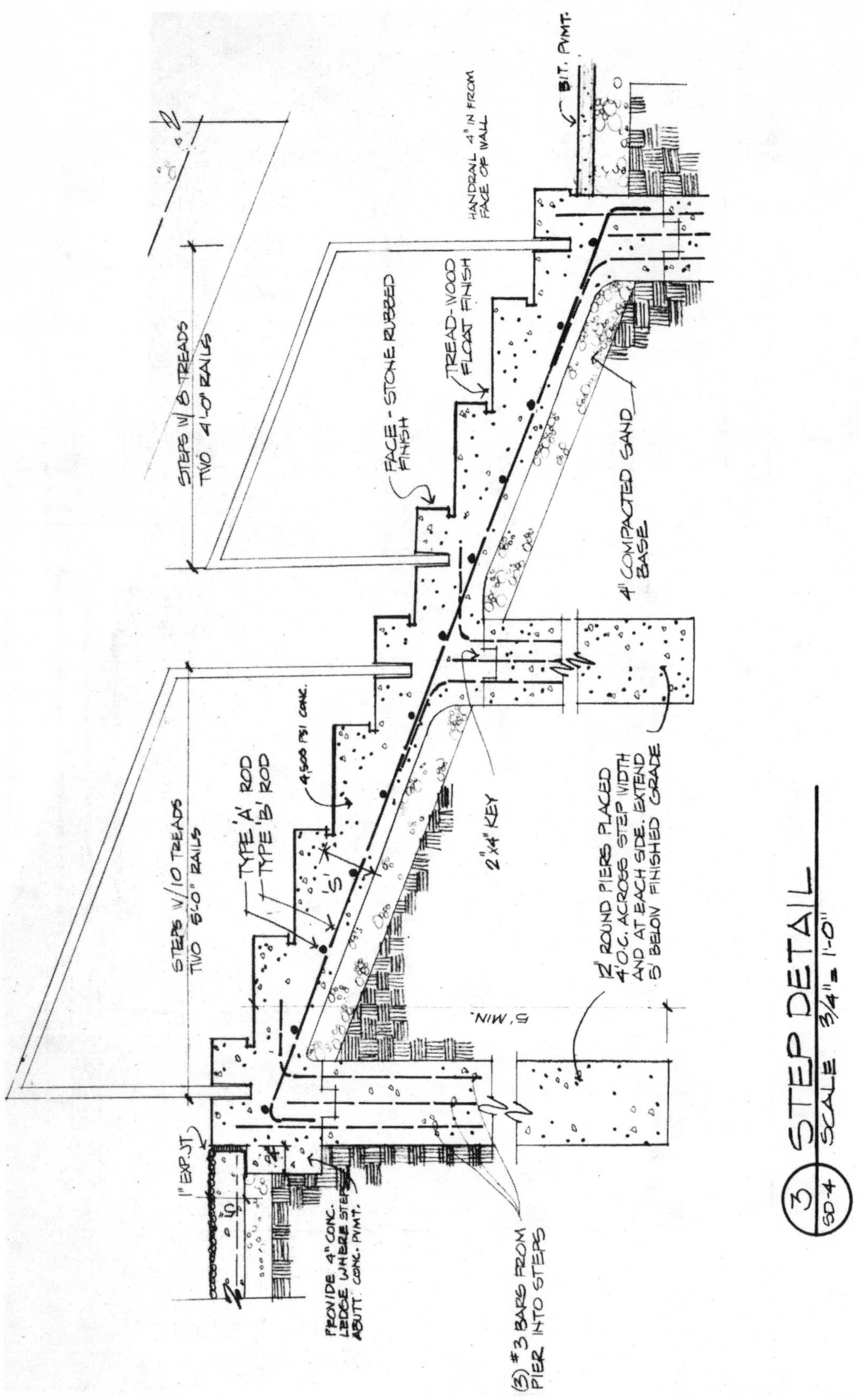

STEPS W/ 8 TREADS
TWO 4'-0" RAILS
HANDRAIL 4" IN FROM FACE OF WALL
BIT. PVMT.
FACE - STONE RUBBED FINISH
TREAD-WOOD FLOAT FINISH
4" COMPACTED SAND BASE
STEPS W/10 TREADS
TWO 5'-0" RAILS
TYPE 'A' ROD
TYPE 'B' ROD
4,500 PSI CONC.
'S'
2"x4" KEY
12" ROUND PIERS PLACED 4' O.C. ACROSS STEP WIDTH AND AT EACH SIDE. EXTEND 5' BELOW FINISHED GRADE
5' MIN.
1" EXP. JT.
PROVIDE 4" CONC. LEDGE WHERE STEPS ABUT. CONC. PVMT.
(3) #3 BARS FROM PIER INTO STEPS
3
SD-4
STEP DETAIL
SCALE 3/4" = 1'-0"

Figure 6.24 *Concrete step detail.*

Johnson, Johnson and Roy

6.25 Sasaki Associates

6.26

6.27

Figures 6.25 – 6.27 *Steps and bicycle ramp.*

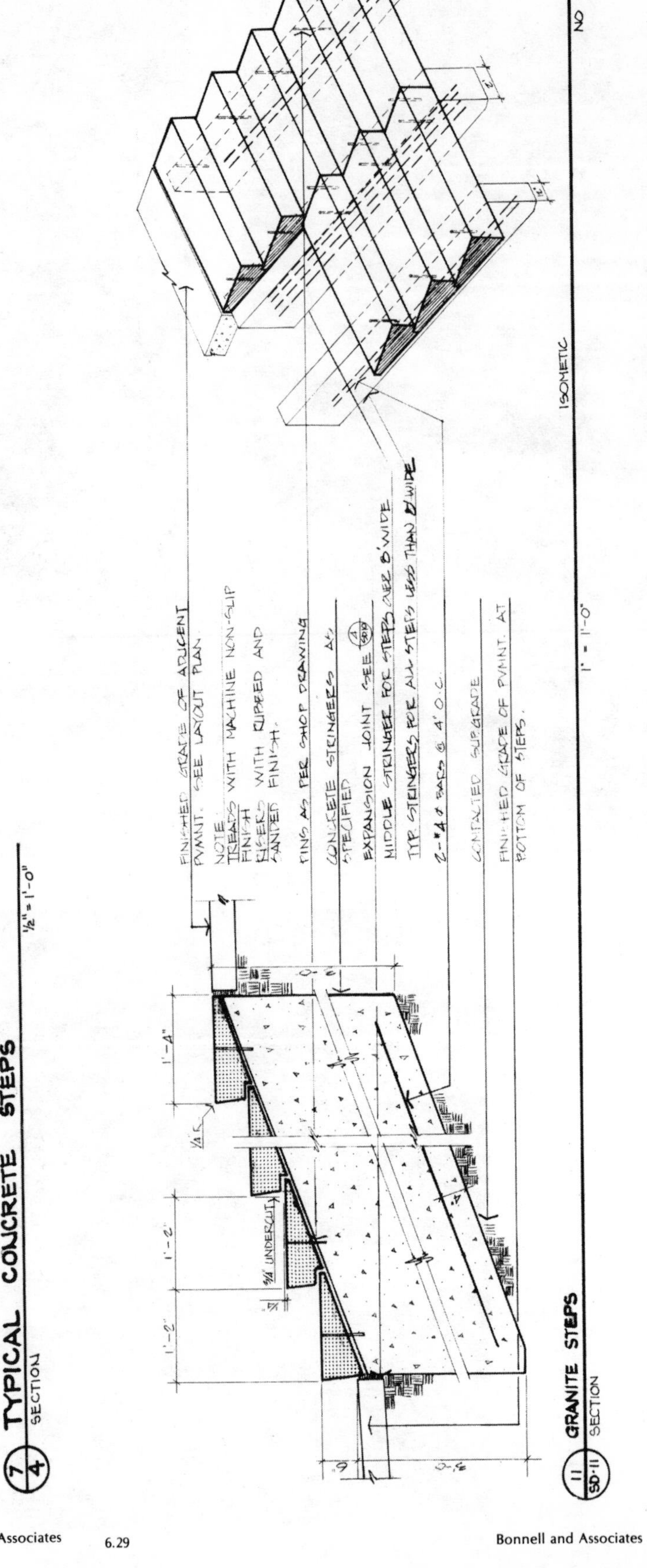

6.28 Bonnell and Associates

6.29 Bonnell and Associates

Figures 6.28 – 6.29 *Step details.*

6.30

6.31

Figures 6.30 – 6.31 *Pre-cast steps.*

6.32 A. E. Bye and Associates

6.34 Browning-Day-Pollak-Associates-Inc.

6.33

6.35 Claire Bennett

Figures 6.32 – 6.35 *Stone and brick steps.*

6.36

6.37

6.38 A. E. Bye

Figures 6.36 – 6.38 *Stone steps.*

6

6.39

6.40

6.41 A. E. Bye and Associates

Figure 6.39 *Pre-cast concrete steps supported on steel brackets and stringers.*

Figure 6.40 *Stone and brick steps.*

Figure 6.41 *Stone steps.*

6.42

6.43

Snell Environmental Group

Figures 6.42 – 6.43 *Wood steps.*

6.44

6.45 Walker-Harris-Associates-Inc.

6.46 Theodore Brickman Co.

Figures 6.44 – 6.46 *Wood steps.*

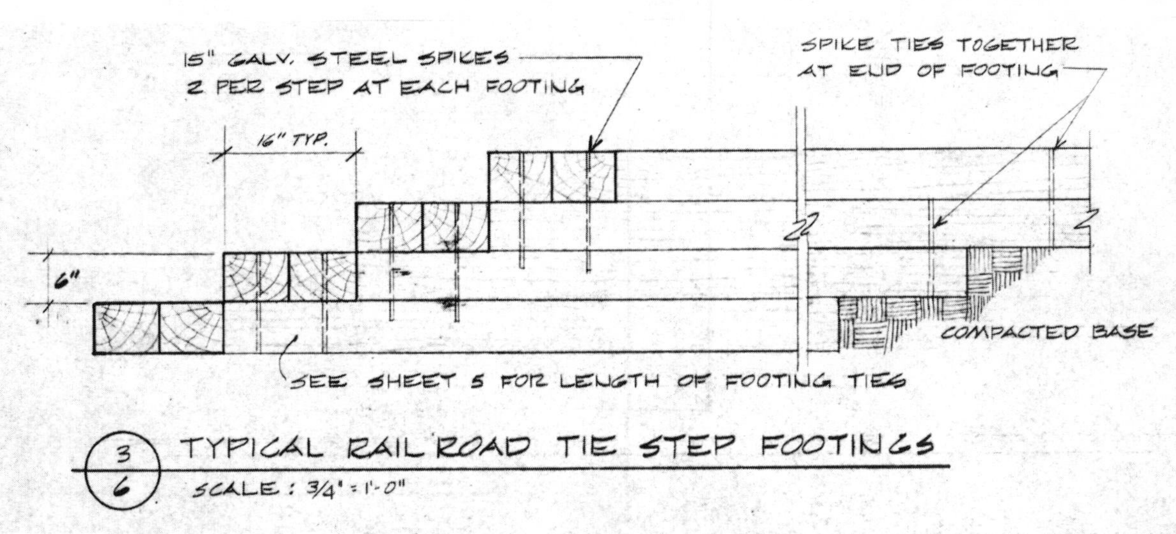
15" GALV. STEEL SPIKES
2 PER STEP AT EACH FOOTING
SPIKE TIES TOGETHER
AT END OF FOOTING
16" TYP.
6"
COMPACTED BASE
SEE SHEET 5 FOR LENGTH OF FOOTING TIES
3
6
TYPICAL RAILROAD TIE STEP FOOTINGS
SCALE: 3/4" = 1'-0"

6.47

Johnson, Johnson and Roy

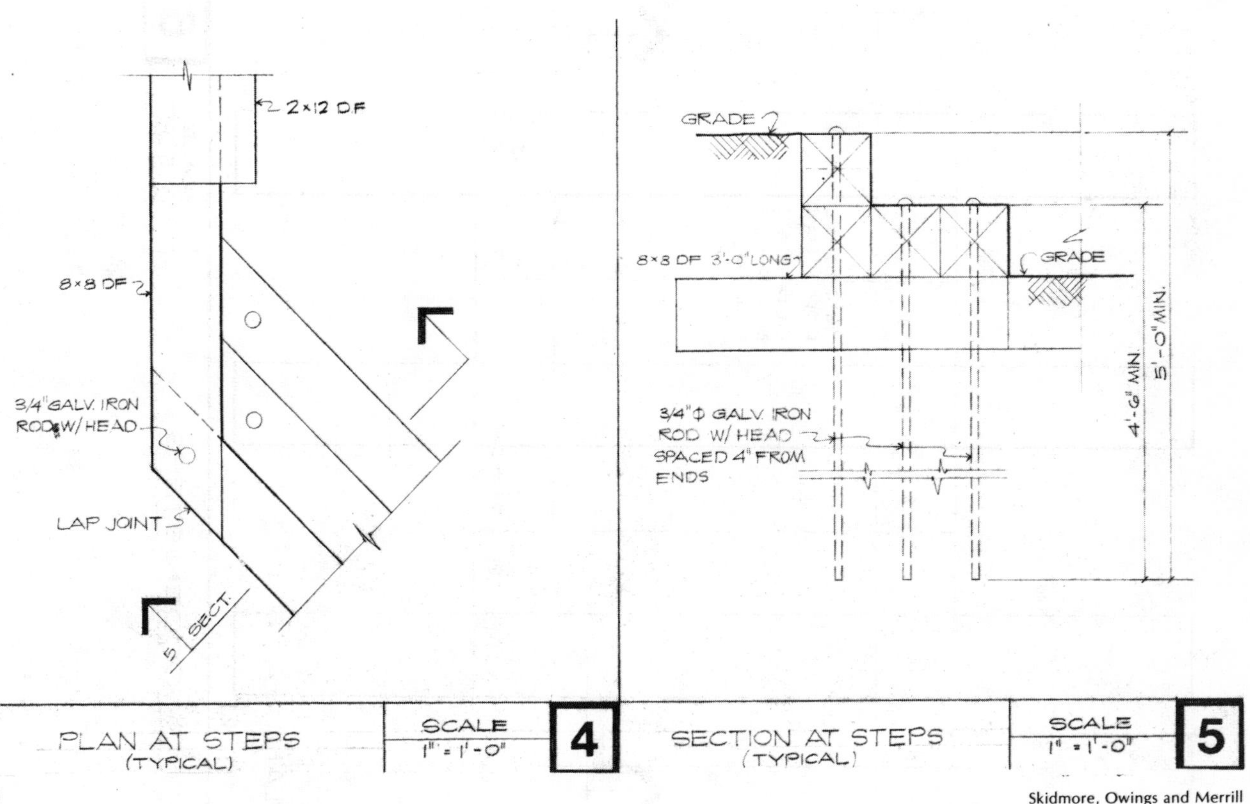
2×12 DF
8×8 DF
3/4" GALV. IRON ROD W/HEAD
LAP JOINT
5 SECT.
PLAN AT STEPS
(TYPICAL)
SCALE
1" = 1'-0"
4
GRADE
8×8 DF 3'-0" LONG
GRADE
3/4" Φ GALV. IRON ROD W/ HEAD SPACED 4" FROM ENDS
4'-6" MIN.
5'-0" MIN.
SECTION AT STEPS
(TYPICAL)
SCALE
1" = 1'-0"
5

6.48

Skidmore, Owings and Merrill

Figures 6.47 – 6.48 *Details for wood steps.*

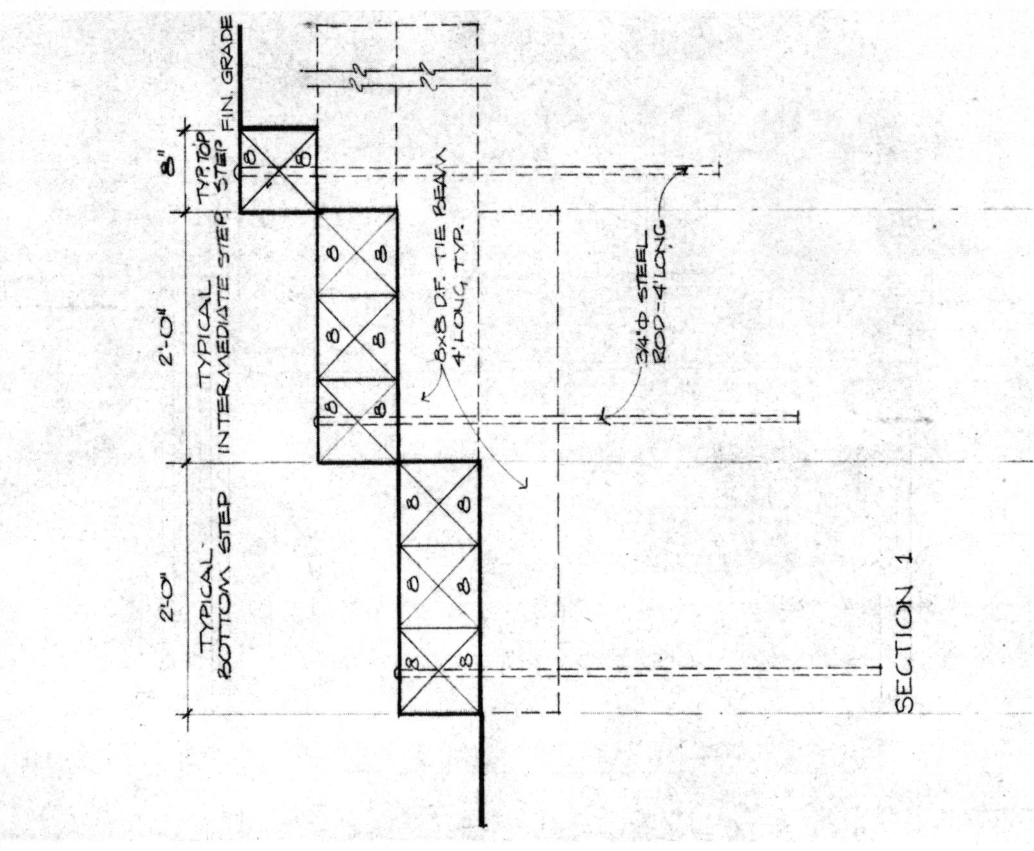
2'-0"
TYPICAL BOTTOM STEP
2'-0"
TYPICAL INTERMEDIATE STEP
8"
TYP. TOP STEP
FIN. GRADE
8x8 D.F. TIE BEAM 4' LONG, TYP.
3/4"Φ STEEL ROD-4' LONG
SECTION 1

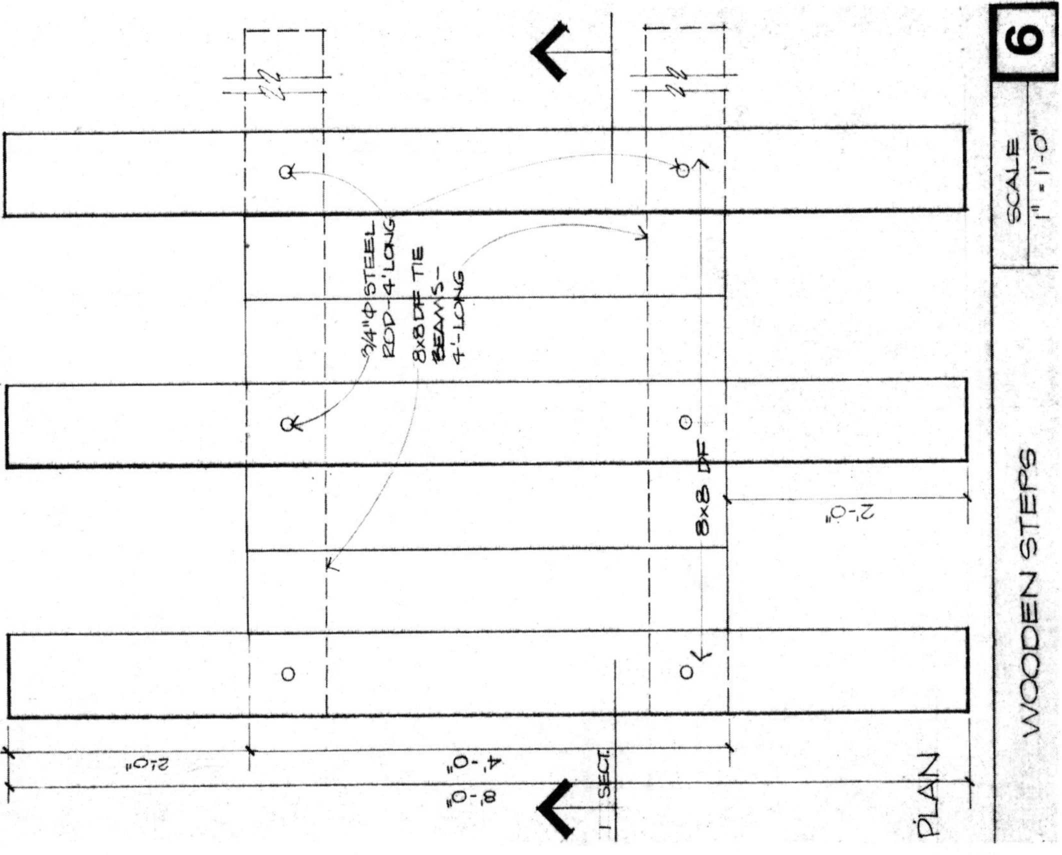
3/4"Φ STEEL ROD-4' LONG
8x8 DF TIE BEAMS-4'-LONG
8x8 DF
2'-0"
2'-0"
4'-0"
8'-0"
1 SECT.
PLAN
WOODEN STEPS
SCALE 1" = 1'-0"
6

Figure 6.49 *Plan and section of wood steps.*

Skidmore, Owings and Merril

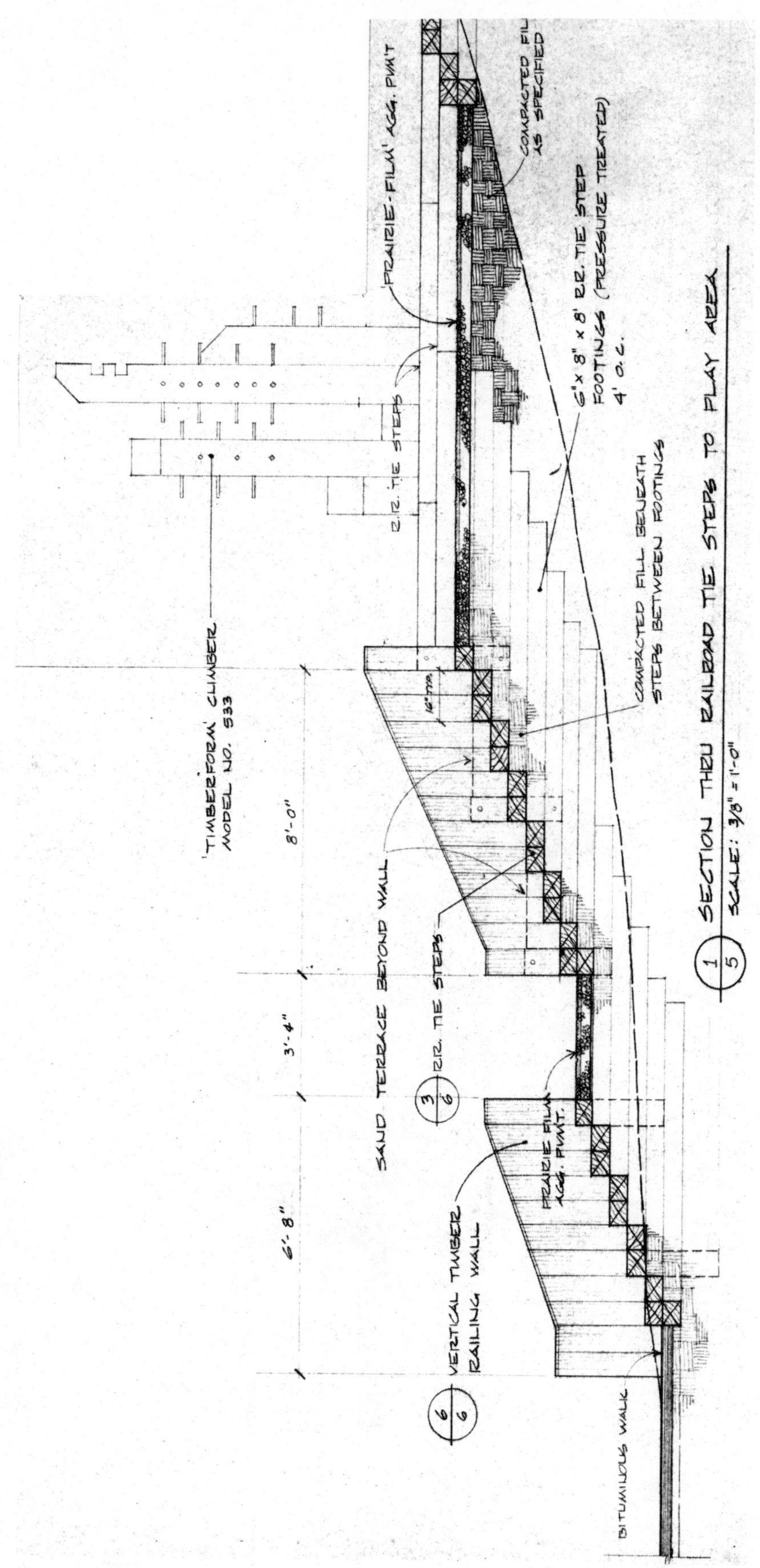
'PRAIRIE-FILM' AGG. PVM'T
AS SPECIFIED
6"x 8" x 8' R.R. TIE STEP FOOTINGS (PRESSURE TREATED) 4' O.C.
R.R. TIE STEPS
'TIMBERFORM' CLIMBER MODEL NO. 533
COMPACTED FILL BENEATH STEPS BETWEEN FOOTINGS
8'-0"
3'-4"
6'-8"
SAND TERRACE BEYOND WALL
3
6
R.R. TIE STEPS
PRAIRIE FILM AGG. PVM'T.
VERTICAL TIMBER RAILING WALL
6
6
BITUMINOUS WALK
1
5
SECTION THRU RAILROAD TIE STEPS TO PLAY AREA
SCALE: 3/8" = 1'-0"

Figure 6.50 *Wood step detail.*

Johnson, Johnson and Roy

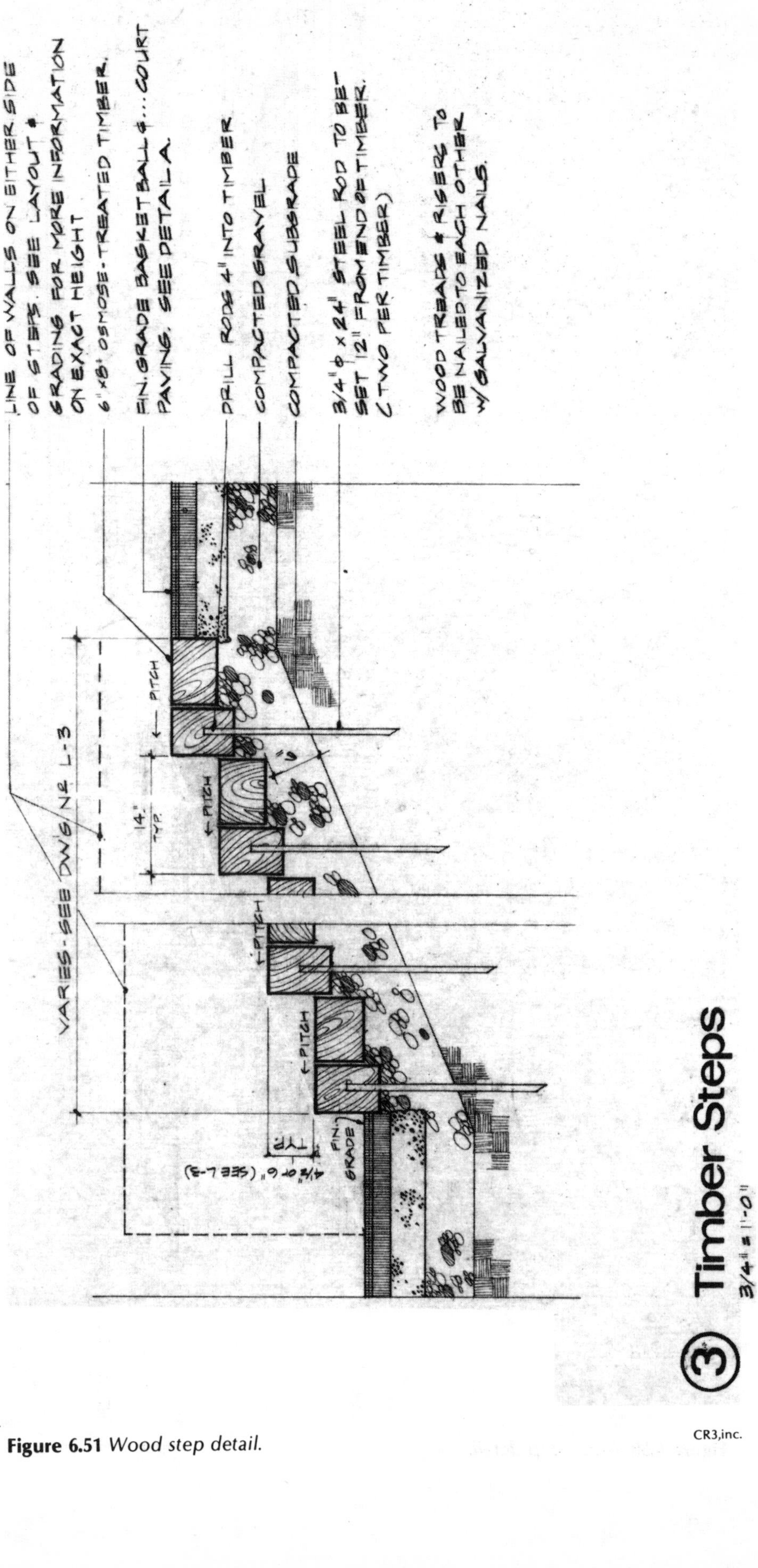

LINE OF WALLS ON EITHER SIDE OF STEPS. SEE LAYOUT & GRADING FOR MORE INFORMATION ON EXACT HEIGHT
6"x8" OSMOSE-TREATED TIMBER.
FIN. GRADE BASKETBALL &... COURT PAVING. SEE DETAIL A.
DRILL RODS 4" INTO TIMBER
COMPACTED GRAVEL
COMPACTED SUBGRADE
3/4" ø x 24" STEEL ROD TO BE SET 12" FROM END OF TIMBER. (TWO PER TIMBER)
WOOD TREADS & RISERS TO BE NAILED TO EACH OTHER W/ GALVANIZED NAILS.
VARIES - SEE DWG NO L-3
14" TYP.
6"
PITCH
4 1/2" or 6" (SEE L-3)
TYP.
FIN. GRADE
3
Timber Steps
3/4" = 1'-0"

Figure 6.51 *Wood step detail.*

CR3,inc.

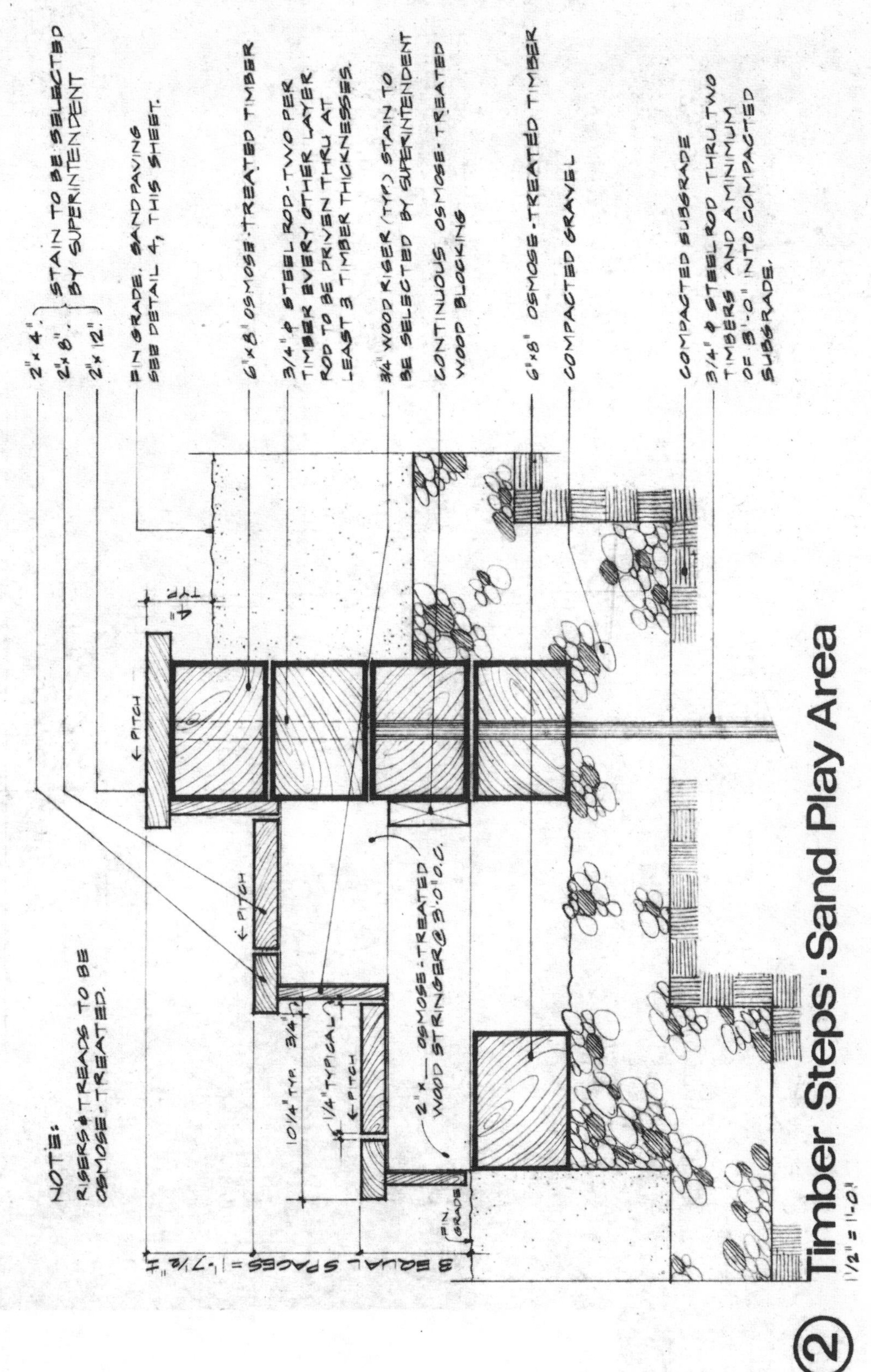
NOTE:
RISERS & TREADS TO BE OSMOSE-TREATED.
2"x 4"
2"x 8"
2"x 12"
STAIN TO BE SELECTED BY SUPERINTENDENT
FIN GRADE. SAND PAVING SEE DETAIL 4, THIS SHEET.
6"x8" OSMOSE-TREATED TIMBER
3/4" ⌀ STEEL ROD - TWO PER TIMBER EVERY OTHER LAYER ROD TO BE DRIVEN THRU AT LEAST 3 TIMBER THICKNESSES.
3/4" WOOD RISER (TYP.) STAIN TO BE SELECTED BY SUPERINTENDENT
CONTINUOUS OSMOSE-TREATED WOOD BLOCKING
6"x8" OSMOSE-TREATED TIMBER
COMPACTED GRAVEL
COMPACTED SUBGRADE
3/4" ⌀ STEEL ROD THRU TWO TIMBERS AND A MINIMUM OF 3'-0" INTO COMPACTED SUBGRADE.
← PITCH
← PITCH
← PITCH
4" TYP.
10 1/4" TYP.
3/4"
1/4" TYPICAL
2"x __ OSMOSE-TREATED WOOD STRINGER @ 3'-0" O.C.
FIN. GRADE
8 EQUAL SPACES = 1'-7 1/2" ±
② Timber Steps · Sand Play Area
1 1/2" = 1'-0"

Figure 6.52 *Wood step detail.*

CR3, inc.

6.53 Howard, Needles, Tammen & Bergendoff

Figures 6.53 – 6.59 *Wood steps, perrons, and details.*

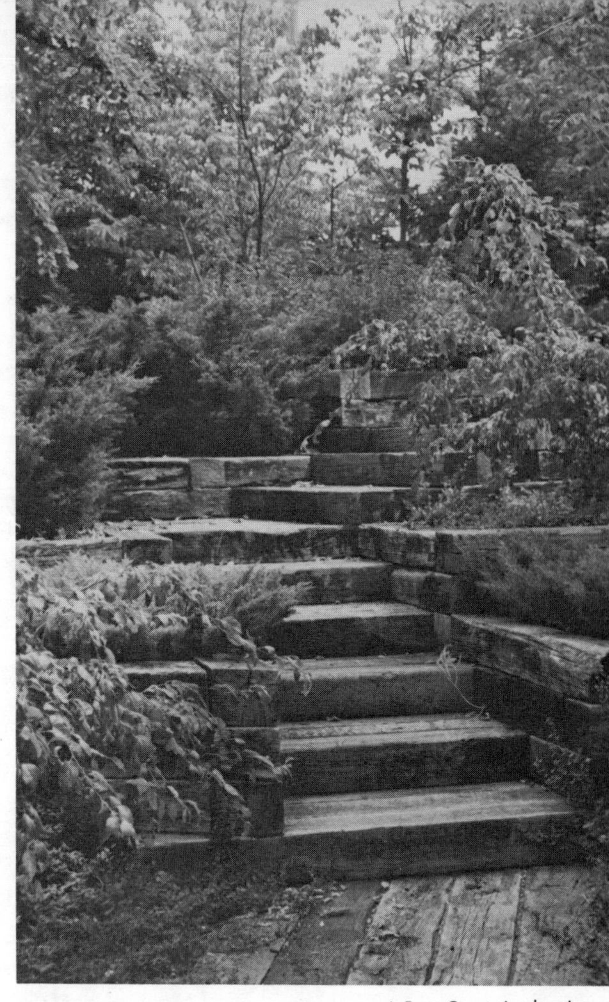

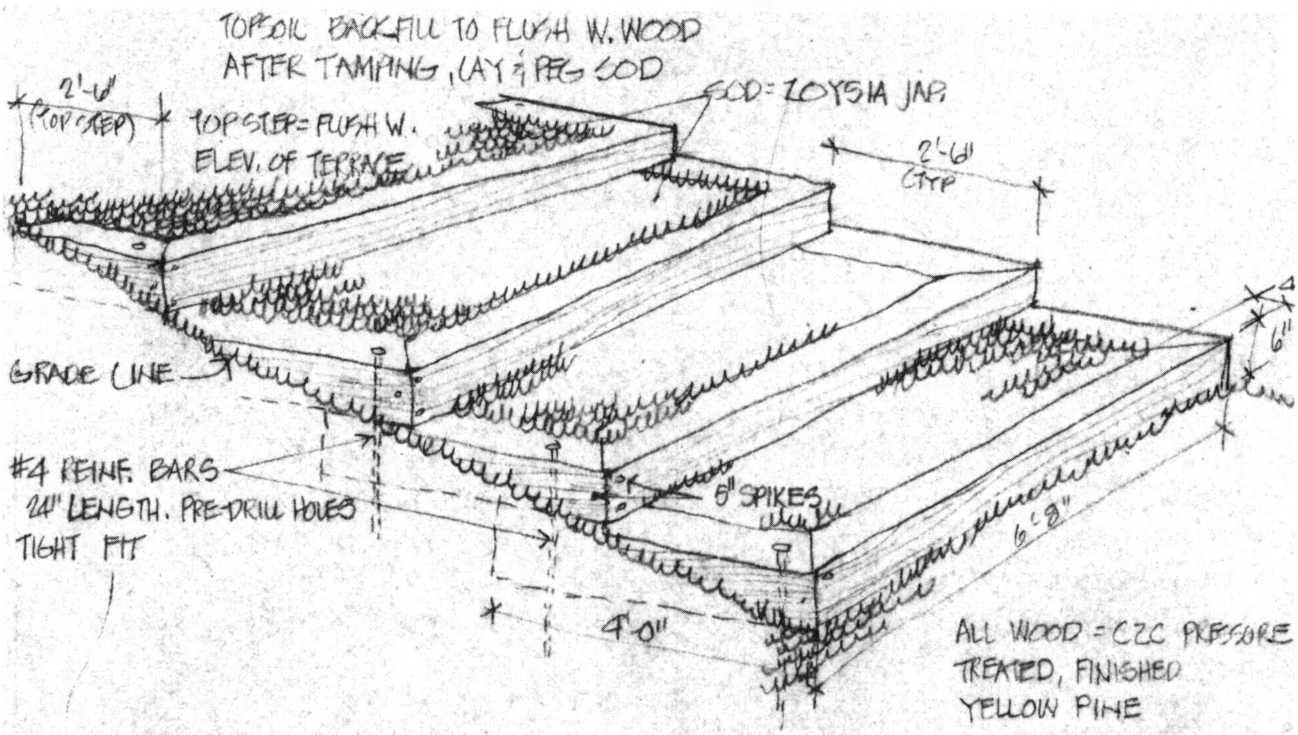

6.54 LaPorte County Landscaping

TOPSOIL BACKFILL TO FLUSH W. WOOD
AFTER TAMPING, LAY & PEG SOD

2'-6" (TOP STEP)

TOP STEP = FLUSH W.
ELEV. OF TERRACE

SOD = ZOYSIA JAP.

2'-6" (TYP)

4

6"

GRADE LINE

#4 REINF. BARS
24" LENGTH. PRE-DRILL HOLES
TIGHT FIT

5" SPIKES

6'-8"

4'-0"

ALL WOOD = CZC PRESSURE
TREATED, FINISHED
YELLOW PINE

DETAIL - STEPS

NOT TO SCALE

WOOD RISERS, GRASS TREADS

6.55 John A. Bentley Associates

6.56 Theodore Brickman Co.

6.57 Browning-Day-Pollak-Associates-Inc.

6.58 Bailey and Associates

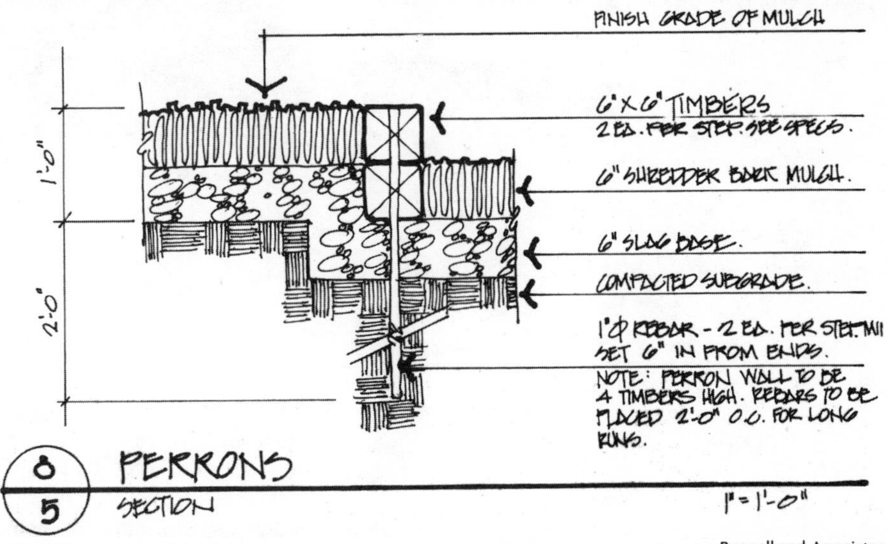
FINISH GRADE OF MULCH
6"X6" TIMBERS
2 EA. PER STEP. SEE SPECS.
6" SHREDDER BARK MULCH.
6" SLAG BASE.
COMPACTED SUBGRADE.
1"Φ REBAR - 2 EA. PER STEP. MI
SET 6" IN FROM ENDS.
NOTE: PERRON WALL TO BE
4 TIMBERS HIGH. REBARS TO BE
PLACED 2'-0" O.C. FOR LONG
RUNS.
1'-0"
2'-0"
8
5
PERRONS
SECTION
1" = 1'-0"

6.59 Bonnell and Associates

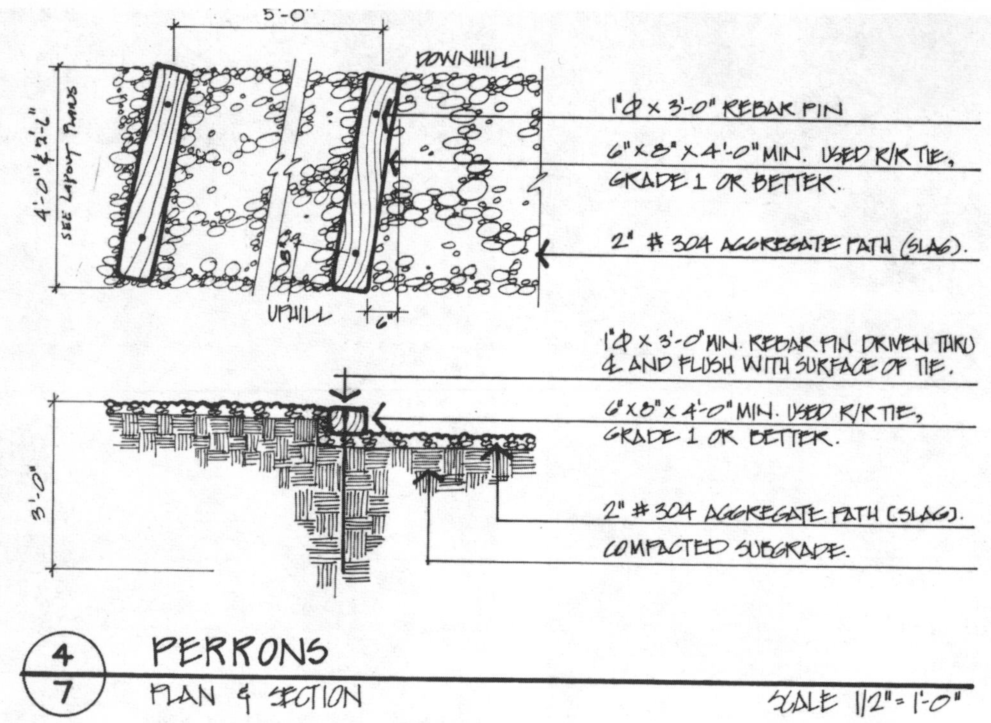

5'-0"
DOWNHILL
UPHILL
6"
4'-0" & 2'-6"
SEE LAYOUT PLANS
1"⌀ x 3'-0" REBAR PIN
6"x8"x4'-0" MIN. USED R/R TIE, GRADE 1 OR BETTER.
2" # 304 AGGREGATE PATH (SLAG).
1"⌀ x 3'-0" MIN. REBAR PIN DRIVEN THRU ℄ AND FLUSH WITH SURFACE OF TIE.
6"x8"x4'-0" MIN. USED R/R TIE, GRADE 1 OR BETTER.
3'-0"
2" # 304 AGGREGATE PATH (SLAG).
COMPACTED SUBGRADE.
4
7
PERRONS
PLAN & SECTION
SCALE 1/2" = 1'-0"

6.60

Bonnell and Associates

6.61

6.62

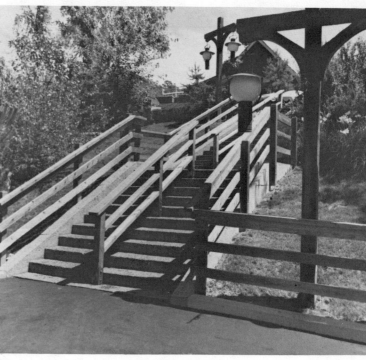

Figure 6.60 *Perron detail.*

Figure 6.61 *Pre-cast concrete units were staggered up the slope in a sweeping S curve. The remainder of the tread is asphalt.*

Figure 6.62 *Steps at a recreation resort.*

6.63

6.65

6.64

6.66

Figures 6.63 – 6.67 *Wheelchair and pedestrian ramps.*

6.67

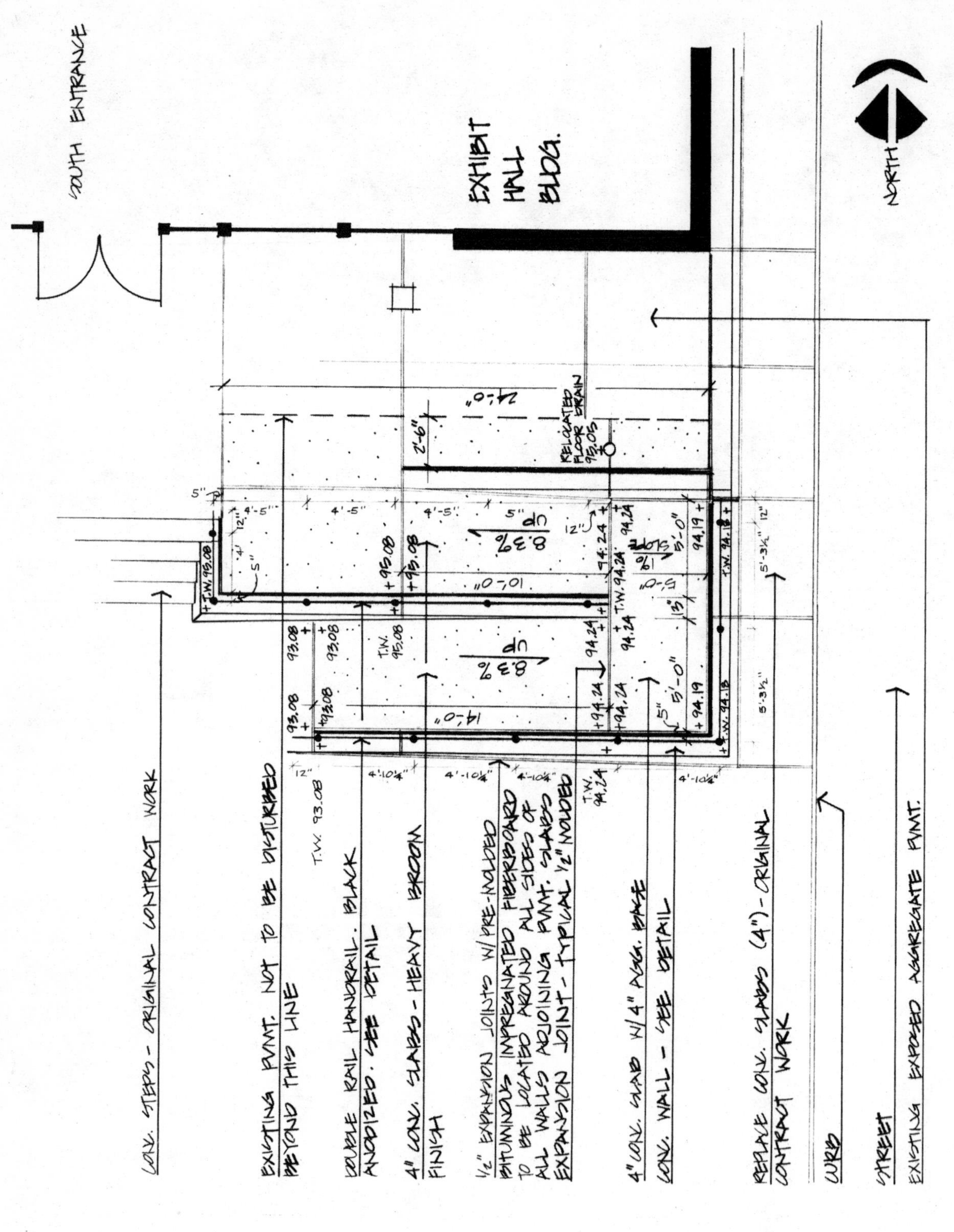
SOUTH ENTRANCE
EXHIBIT HALL BLDG.
NORTH
RELOCATED FLOOR DRAIN
8.37% UP
8.37% UP
CONC. STEPS - ORIGINAL CONTRACT WORK
EXISTING PVMT. NOT TO BE DISTURBED BEYOND THIS LINE
DOUBLE RAIL HANDRAIL. BLACK ANODIZED. SEE DETAIL
4" CONC. SLABS - HEAVY BROOM FINISH
1/2" EXPANSION JOINTS W/ PRE-MOLDED BITUMINOUS IMPREGNATED FIBERBOARD TO BE LOCATED AROUND ALL SIDES OF ALL WALLS ADJOINING PVMT. SLABS EXPANSION JOINT - TYPICAL 1/2" MOLDED
4" CONC. SLAB W/ 4" AGG. BASE
CONC. WALL - SEE DETAIL
REPLACE CONC. SLABS (4") - ORIGINAL CONTRACT WORK
CURB
STREET
EXISTING EXPOSED AGGREGATE PVMT.
LAYOUT PLAN
SCALE: 1/4" = 1'-0"

Figure 6.68 *Wheelchair ramp plan.*

Bonnell and Associates

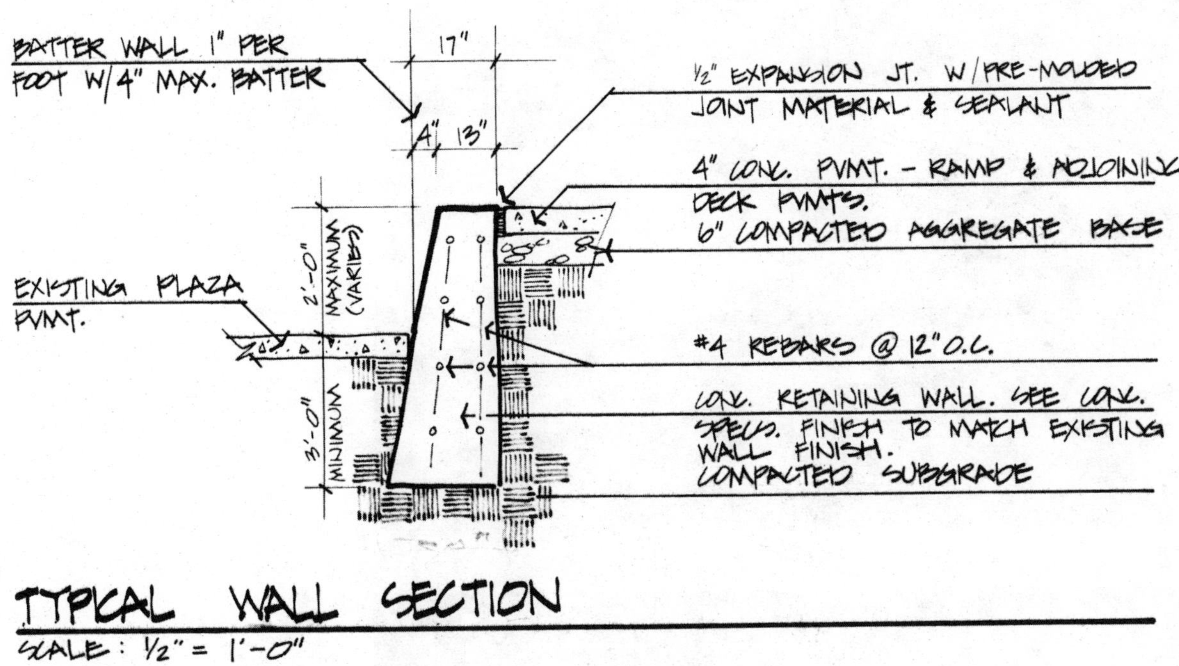
BATTER WALL 1" PER
FOOT W/4" MAX. BATTER
17"
4"
13"
1/2" EXPANSION JT. W/PRE-MOLDED
JOINT MATERIAL & SEALANT
4" CONC. PVMT. - RAMP & ADJOINING
DECK PVMTS.
6" COMPACTED AGGREGATE BASE
EXISTING PLAZA
PVMT.
2'-0" MAXIMUM (VARIES)
#4 REBARS @ 12" O.C.
3'-0" MINIMUM
CONC. RETAINING WALL. SEE CONC.
SPECS. FINISH TO MATCH EXISTING
WALL FINISH.
COMPACTED SUBGRADE
TYPICAL WALL SECTION
SCALE: 1/2" = 1'-0"

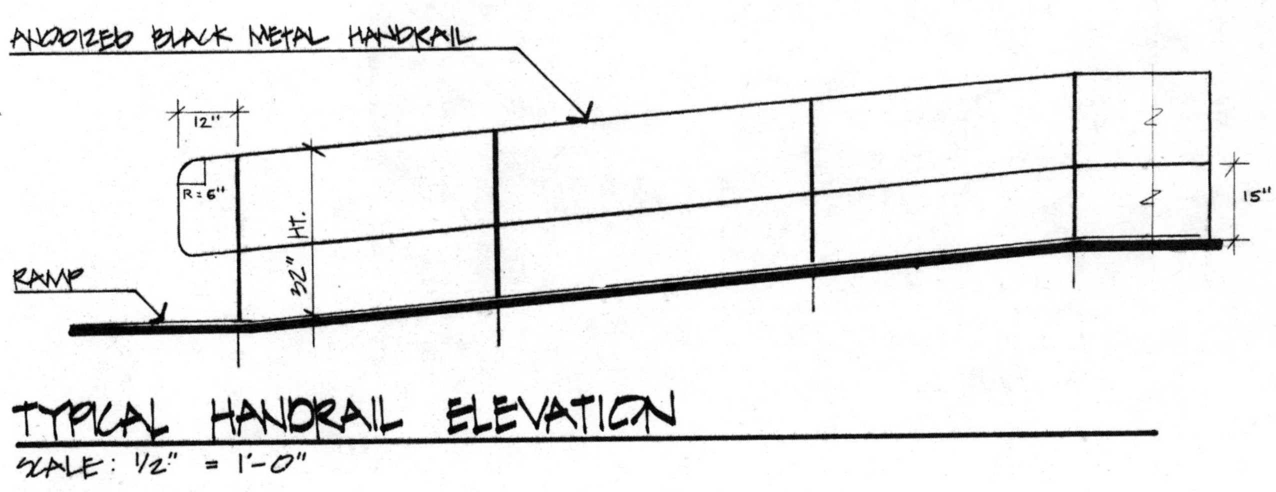
ANODIZED BLACK METAL HANDRAIL
12"
R=6"
32" HT.
15"
RAMP
TYPICAL HANDRAIL ELEVATION
SCALE: 1/2" = 1'-0"

Figure 6.69 *Wheelchair ramp elevation and section.*

Bonnell and Associates

6.70

6.71

Figures 6.70 – 6.73 *Several types of ramps.*

6.72 Browning-Day-Pollak-Associates—Inc.

6.73 Sasaki Associates

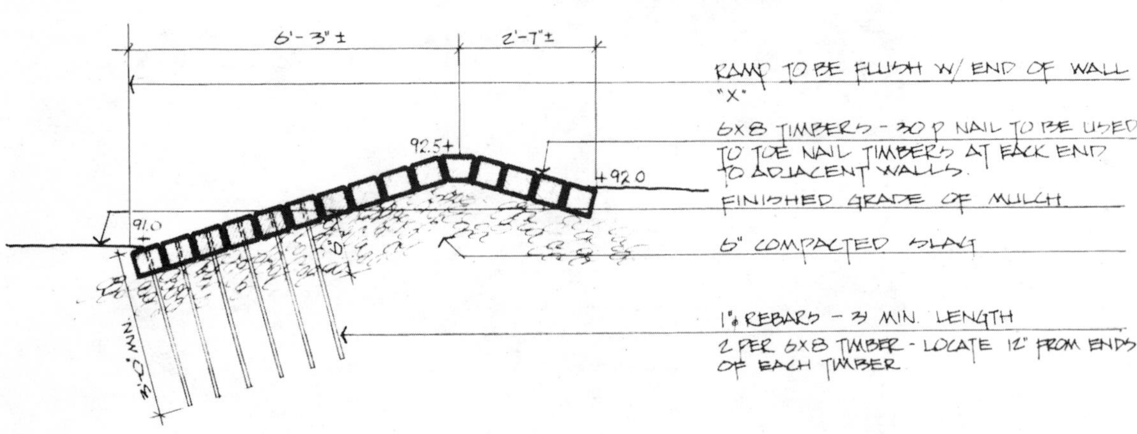

6'-3" ±
2'-7" ±
RAMP TO BE FLUSH W/ END OF WALL "X"
6X8 TIMBERS - 30 P NAIL TO BE USED TO TOE NAIL TIMBERS AT EACH END TO ADJACENT WALLS.
92.5+
+92.0
91.0
FINISHED GRADE OF MULCH
6" COMPACTED SLAG
1"ø REBARS - 3' MIN. LENGTH
2 PER 6X8 TIMBER - LOCATE 12" FROM ENDS OF EACH TIMBER
3'-0" MIN.

5/12
TIMBER RAMP
SECTION
1/2" = 1'-0"

Figure 6.74 *Timber ramp for a play area.*

Bonnell and Associates

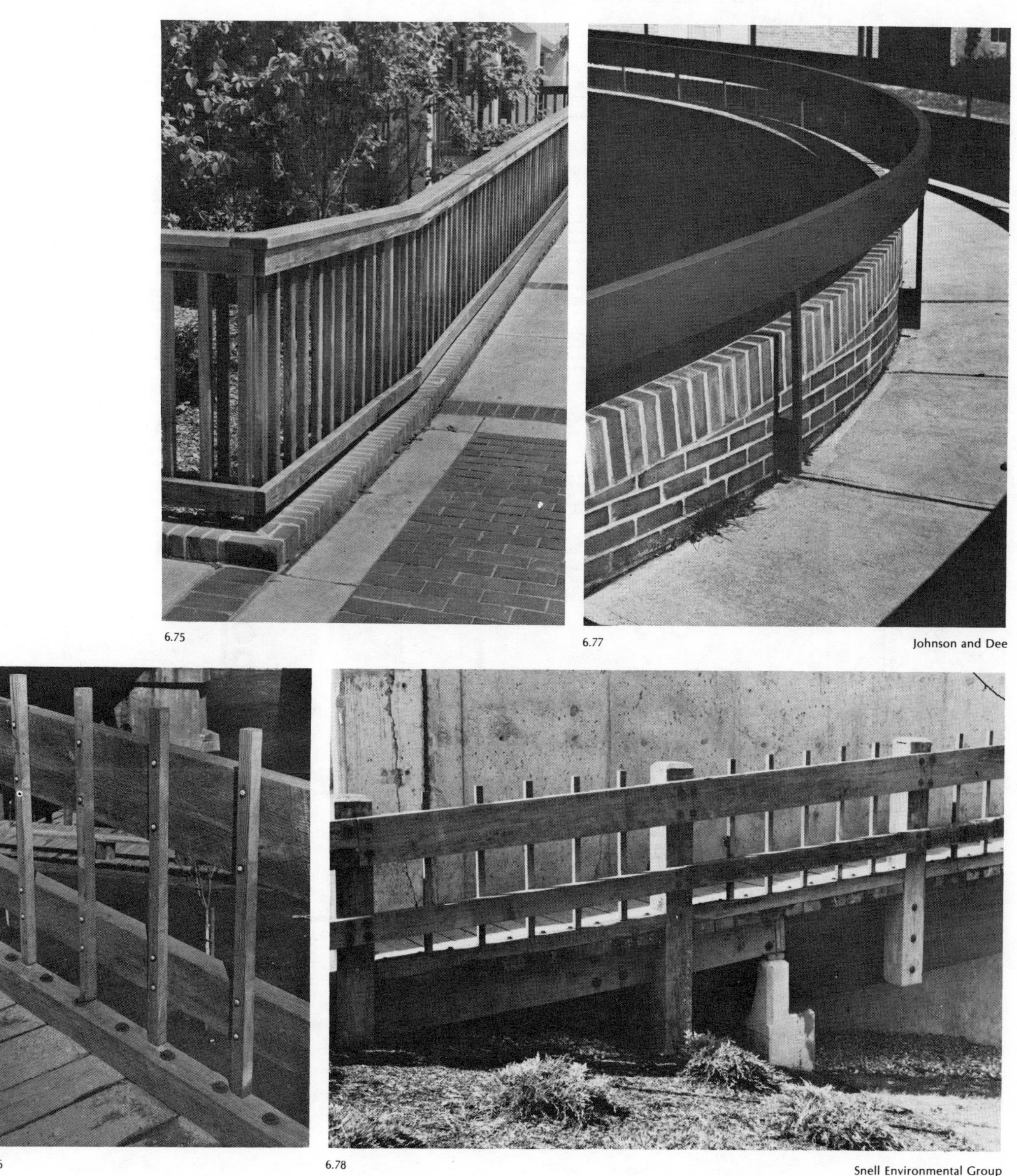

6.75

6.77

Johnson and Dee

76

6.78

Snell Environmental Group

Figures 6.75 – 6.78 *Various railing designs for ramps.*

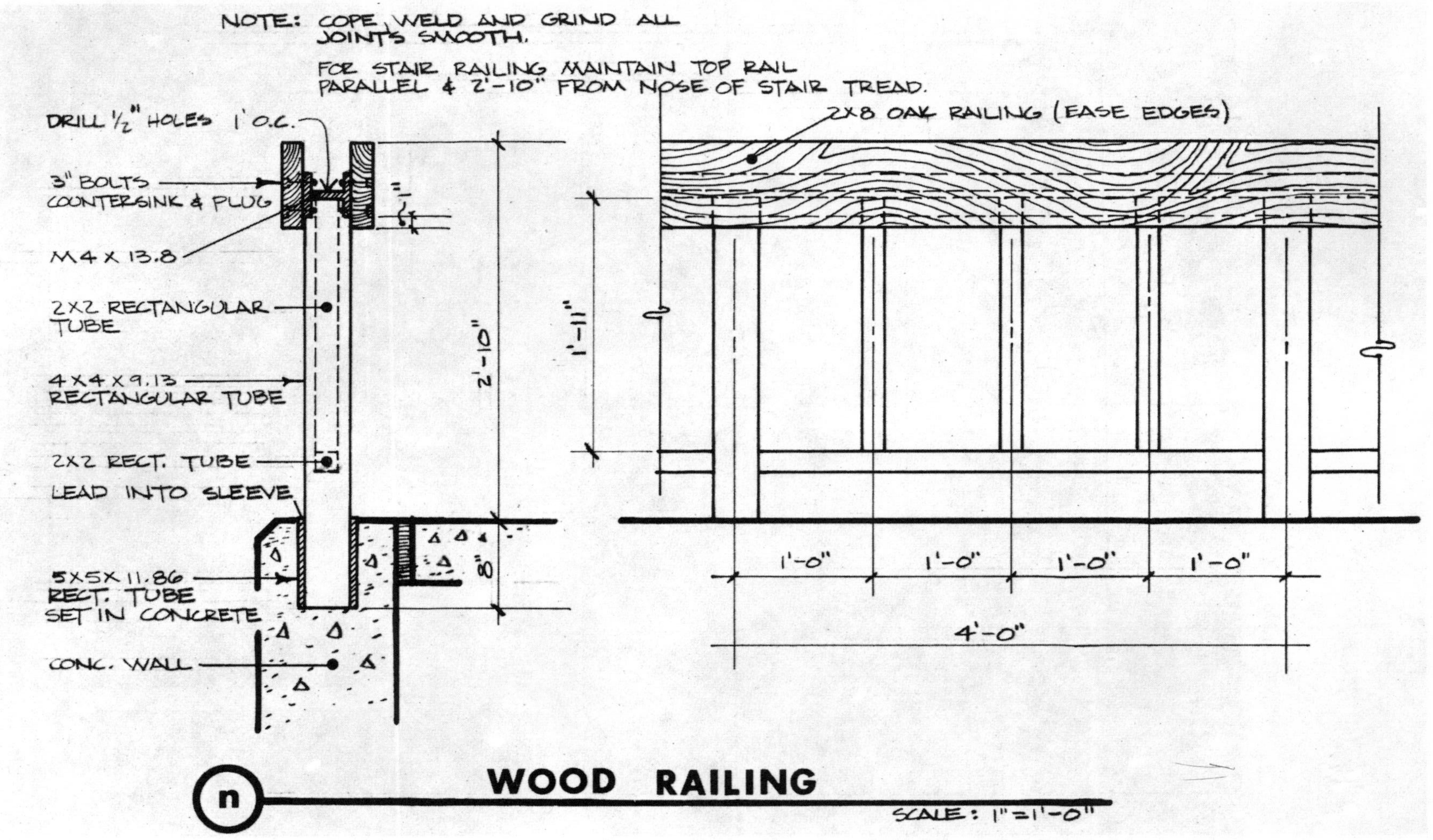
NOTE: COPE WELD AND GRIND ALL JOINTS SMOOTH.
FOR STAIR RAILING MAINTAIN TOP RAIL PARALLEL & 2'-10" FROM NOSE OF STAIR TREAD.
2X8 OAK RAILING (EASE EDGES)
DRILL 1/2" HOLES 1' O.C.
3" BOLTS COUNTERSINK & PLUG
M4 X 13.8
2X2 RECTANGULAR TUBE
4X4X9.13 RECTANGULAR TUBE
2X2 RECT. TUBE
LEAD INTO SLEEVE
5X5X11.86 RECT. TUBE SET IN CONCRETE
CONC. WALL
1"
2'-10"
1'-11"
8"
1'-0"
1'-0"
1'-0"
1'-0"
4'-0"
n
WOOD RAILING
SCALE: 1"=1'-0"

Figure 6.79 *Railing detail.*

Saratoga Associates

The Poppy Shop

6.80

6.82

6.81 William A. Behnke Associates

6.83

Figures 6.80 – 6.83 *Variety of railing designs.*

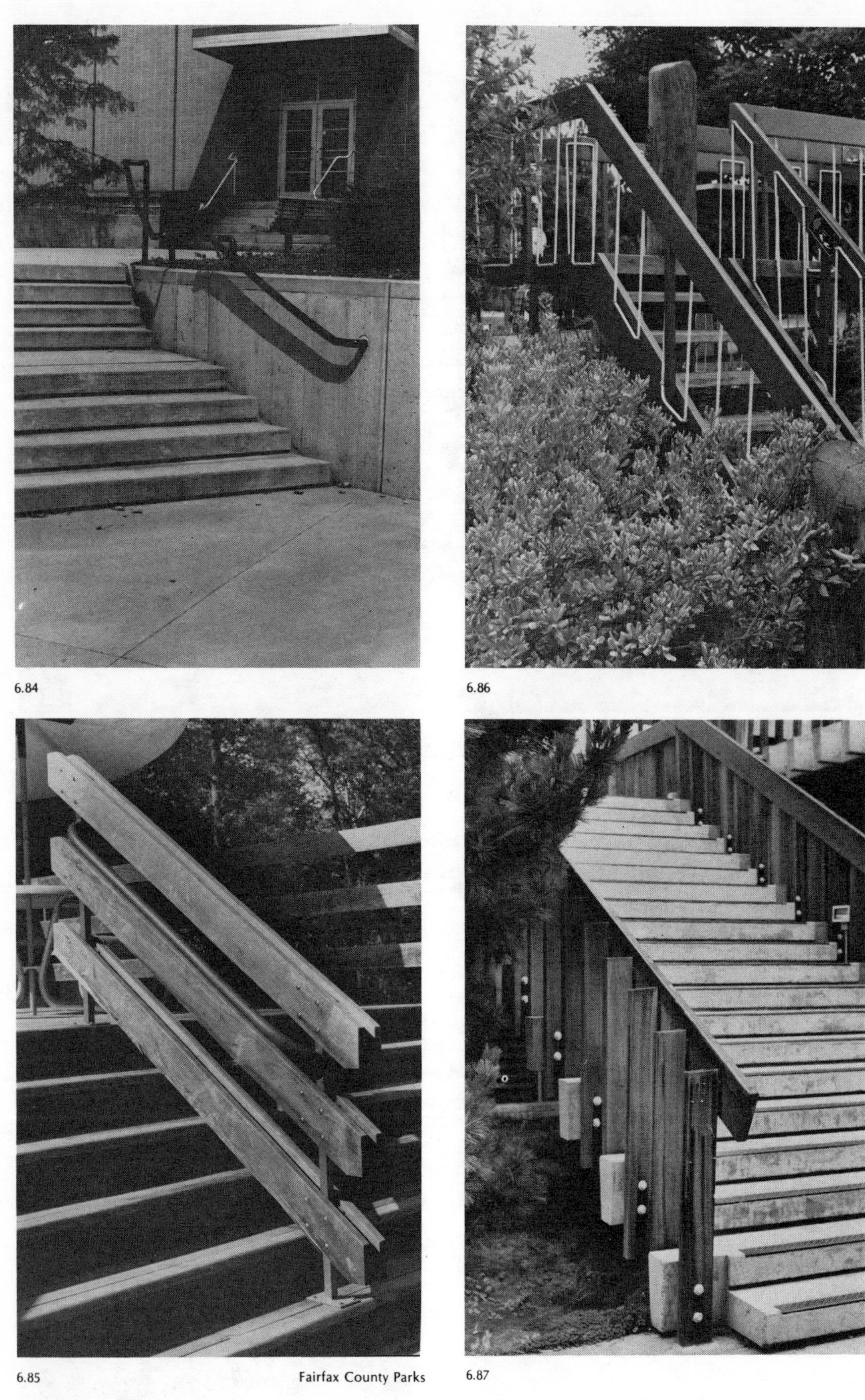

6.84

6.86

6.85 Fairfax County Parks

6.87

Figures 6.84 – 6.87 *Step railings.*

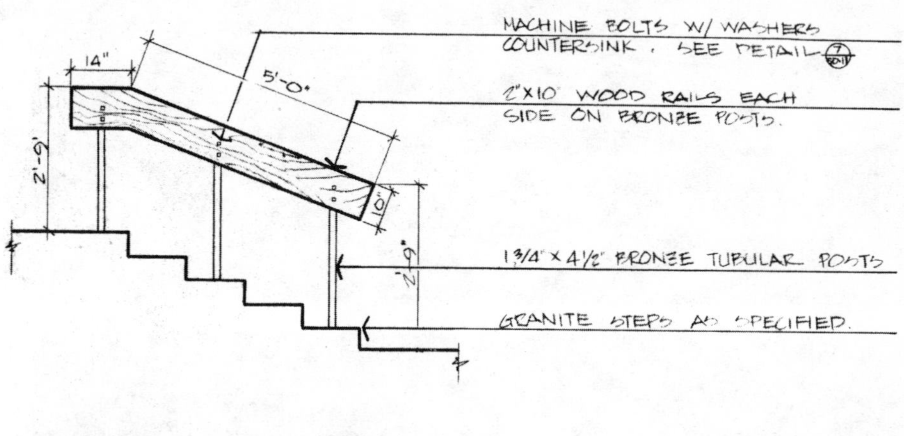

MACHINE BOLTS W/ WASHERS COUNTERSINK. SEE DETAIL 7 SD-11
2"X10" WOOD RAILS EACH SIDE ON BRONZE POSTS.
1 3/4" X 4 1/2" BRONZE TUBULAR POSTS
GRANITE STEPS AS SPECIFIED.
14"
5'-0"
2'-9"
10"
10 SD-11
DOUBLE WOOD HANDRAIL
SECTION
1/2" = 1'-0"

6.88

Bonnell and Associates

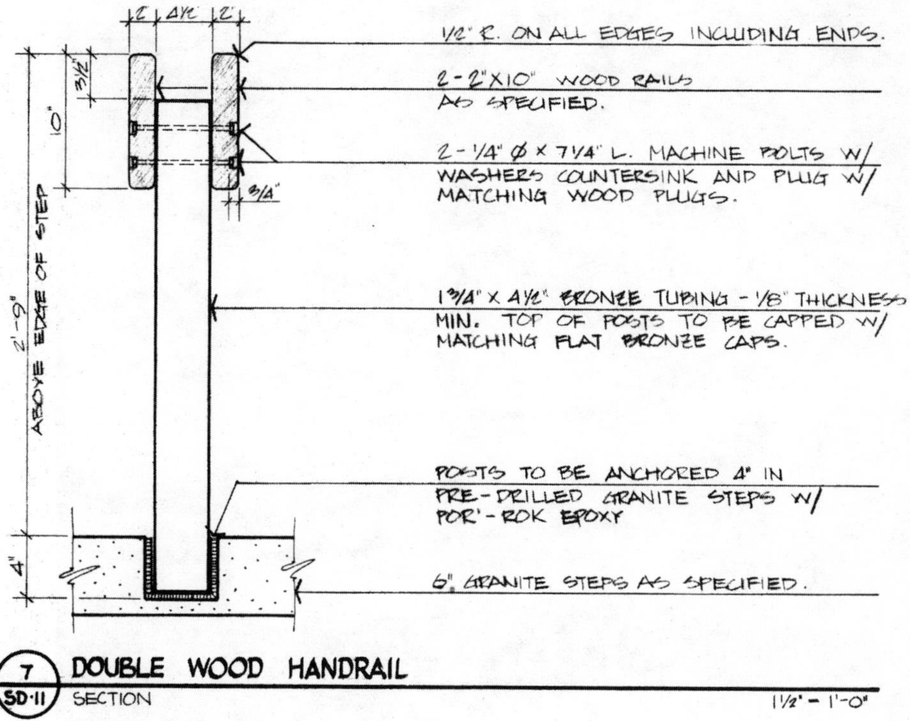

1/2" R. ON ALL EDGES INCLUDING ENDS.
2-2"X10" WOOD RAILS AS SPECIFIED.
2-1/4" Ø X 7 1/4" L. MACHINE BOLTS W/ WASHERS COUNTERSINK AND PLUG W/ MATCHING WOOD PLUGS.
1 3/4" X 4 1/2" BRONZE TUBING - 1/8" THICKNESS MIN. TOP OF POSTS TO BE CAPPED W/ MATCHING FLAT BRONZE CAPS.
POSTS TO BE ANCHORED 4" IN PRE-DRILLED GRANITE STEPS W/ POR'-ROK EPOXY
6" GRANITE STEPS AS SPECIFIED.
2'-9" ABOVE EDGE OF STEP
3/4"
7 SD-11
DOUBLE WOOD HANDRAIL
SECTION
1 1/2" = 1'-0"

6.89

Bonnell and Associates

Figures 6.88 - 6.89 *Railing details.*

Environmental Planning and Design

Photo courtesy of L and J Specialty Corp.

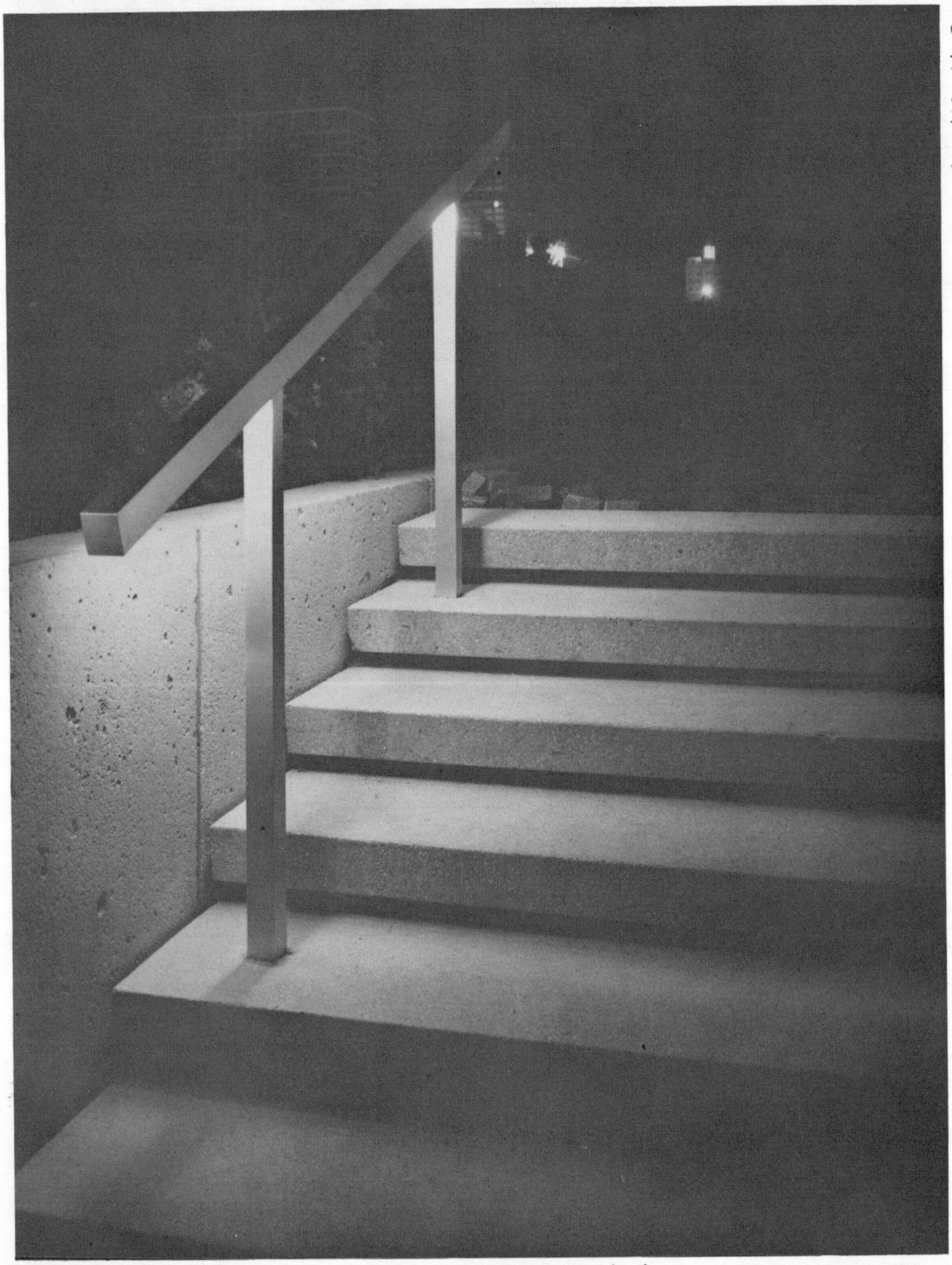

Figure 6.90 *Cheekwall design variations and lighted handrail.*

Edward Durrell Stone

7

Walls

FREE-STANDING WALLS

Brick, stone, clay tile, concrete block, or precast concrete units or a combination of any or all of these materials can be used in the construction of free-standing walls. The principal focus of this section will be upon brick, but much of the discussion will be applicable to the use of the other materials.

Because any material which is used in the construction of a wall is fully exposed to the weather, it should be high quality and resistant to damage by freezing and thawing. Brick must be SW grade, hard fired with low moisture absorbancy. The other materials such as stone, concrete block, precast concrete units, etc., must also be of such a quality to resist moisture absorption.

The footings for walls generally will be concrete with some reinforcing. The exact size of the footing and the amount of reinforcing will be dependent upon soil conditions, but generally the size of the footing will not be less than ten inches deep by sixteen inches wide with two #3 rebars continuous. The footing will be at a depth not less than the frost line in those areas of the country where freezing occurs or as necessary to counteract wind forces. Generally this means three feet or deeper except for low walls in frost-free areas, which can be shallower.

For brick walls, the foundation might be concrete block which will reduce the amount of labor required and represent a cost saving depending upon the availability of materials and the relative cost to each other. Three courses of brick is equal to one course of block, each representing eight inches in height. In some cases it might be more practical to begin laying the brick on top of the footing and go all the way to the top of the wall.

In most walls, horizontal reinforcing will be desirable. A nine gauge truss-type steel reinforcing can be installed each six courses. For eight-inch-thick walls, this will effectively tie the two rows of brick together because the reinforcing lays across both rows.

In areas of potential wind damage additional vertical reinforcement will be needed. The Brick Institute recommends that for ten PSF wind pressure a straight brick wall should not be higher than three-fourths of the wall thickness squared. This would be four feet for an eight-inch wall. Reinforced concrete piers extending from the top of the wall down to three to four feet below grade, with a brick veneer to match the adjoining wall, can be used to compensate for wind pressure. The exact size and spacing will need to be calculated relative to wind pressures typical of the site based upon data available from the Brick Insititute. Buttresses and offsets can also be used to strengthen a wall space where space will allow.

Serpentine walls, while expensive from a labor standpoint, are attractive and self-reinforcing if built according to this formula: for a four-inch-thick wall, the radius of curvature should be no more than twice the height of the wall above ground line and the depth of curvature no less than one-half of the height.

Running bond is the most typical and commonly used pattern for laying bricks in walls. There are a number of other pattens possible including stacked, English, and Flemmish bonds. These can also be varied with brick recessed or projecting outward to create shadows or combined with other material such as title or decorative concrete block.

All walls need some sort of coping or cap. Brick can be laid in a row block pattern on top of natural stone, or precast concrete units can be used. Steel channel can be used but it is disadvantageous because it requires occasional painting in order to prevent corrosion and streaking of rust down the wall.

The quality of mortar is important because it will be the weakest part of the wall. Type "S" is recommended and it consists of one part portland cement, one-half part hydrated lime, and four and one-half parts sand by volume. The use of liquid latex in place of water when preparing the mix will ensure greater durability, strength, and resistance to frost damage.

There are many kinds and styles of mortar joints, but there are two which provide the best seal against moisture intrusion into the joints. These two styles are the concave and V-shaped joints. The tool seals the surface of the mortar and reduces moisture from creeping into the joint, thus inhibiting or minimizing future freeze-thaw damage.

For long walls, expansion joints are needed in order to relieve the stress and minimize the possibility of cracking. These are vertical joints in the walls which, according to the National Concrete Masonary Association, should be placed every 50 feet.

Many masonry walls are affected by the deposit of water-soluble salts on the outside surface of the wall, which is called efflorescence. It is usually rather white in color and unsightly. High quality brick and mortar generally will minimize the occurrence of efflorescence, but should it occur it can be cleaned with a mild solution of muriatic acid.

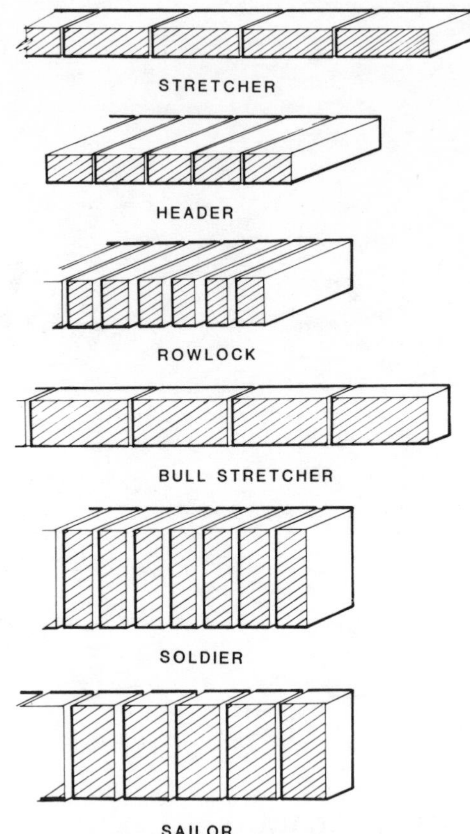
STRETCHER
HEADER
ROWLOCK
BULL STRETCHER
SOLDIER
SAILOR

Figure 7.1 *Commonly used terms for various positions of brick.*

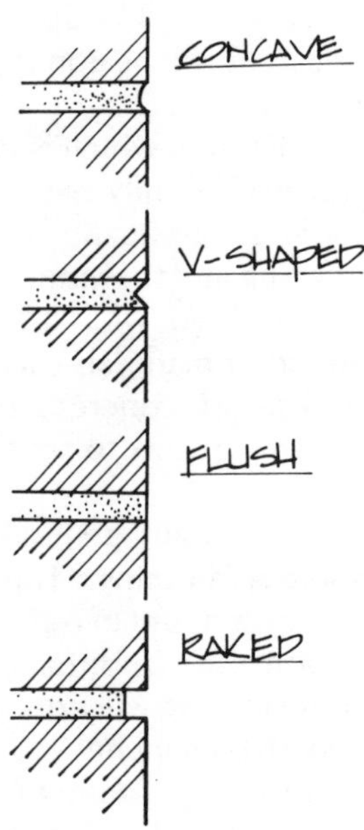
CONCAVE
V-SHAPED
FLUSH
RAKED

Figure 7.2 *Four common finishes for mortar joints.*

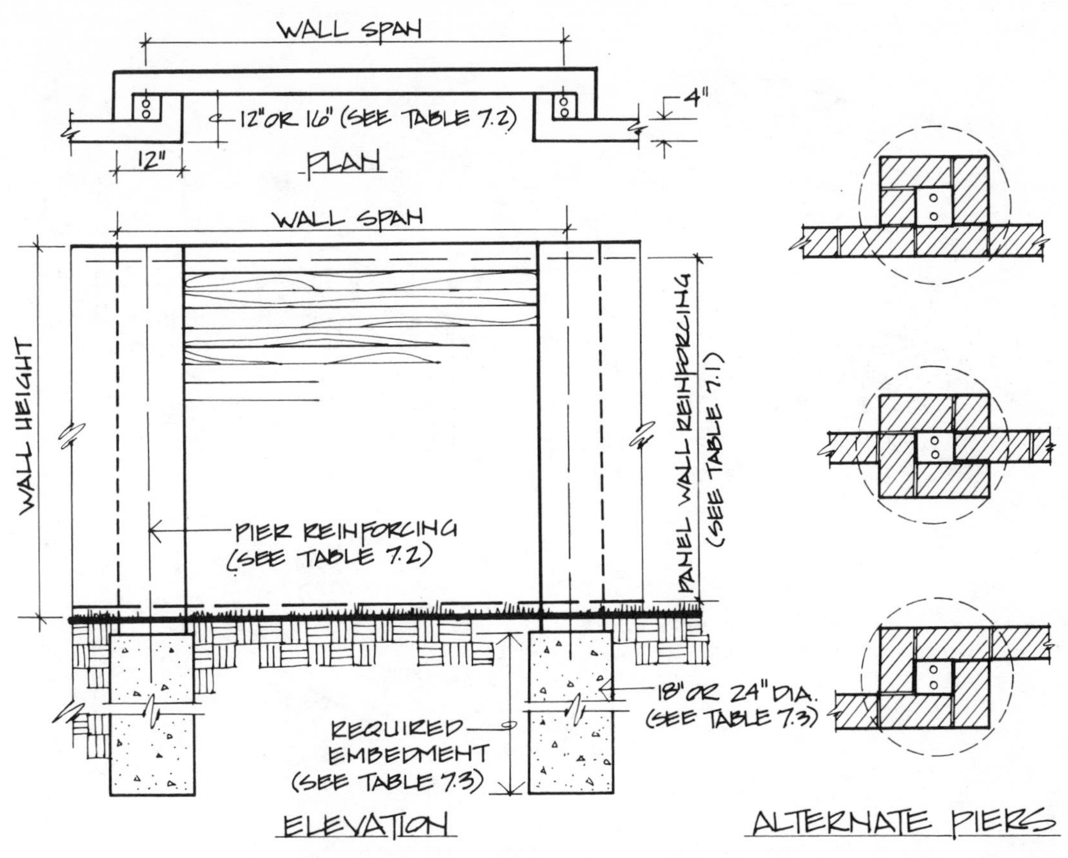
WALL SPAN
4"
12"OR 16" (SEE TABLE 7.2)
12"
PLAN
WALL SPAN
WALL HEIGHT
PANEL WALL REINFORCING (SEE TABLE 7.1)
PIER REINFORCING (SEE TABLE 7.2)
18"OR 24" DIA. (SEE TABLE 7.3)
REQUIRED EMBEDMENT (SEE TABLE 7.3)
ELEVATION
ALTERNATE PIERS
PIER AND PANEL GARDEN WALL

TABLE 7.1 Panel Wall Reinforcing Steel

Wall Span, ft	Vertical Spacing, in.								
	Wind Load, 10 psf			Wind Load, 15 psf			Wind Load, 20 psf		
	A	B	C	A	B	C	A	B	C
8	45	30	19	30	20	12	23	15	9.5
10	29	19	12	19	13	8.0	14	10	6.0
12	20	13	8.5	13	9.0	5.5	10	7.0	4.0
14	15	10	6.5	10	6.5	4.0	7.5	5.0	3.0
16	11	7.5	5.0	7.5	5.0	3.0	6.0	4.0	2.5

Note: A = 2 - no. 2 bars
B = 2 - 3/16-in. diam wires
C = 2 - 9-gage wires

TABLE 7.2 Pier Reinforcing Steel

Wall Span, ft	Wind Load, 10 psf			Wind Load, 15 psf			Wind Load, 20 psf		
	Wall Height, ft			Wall Height, ft			Wall Height, ft		
	4	6	8	4	6	8	4	6	8
8	2#3	2#4	2#5	2#3	2#5	2#6	2#4	2#5	2#5
10	2#3	2#4	2#5	2#4	2#5	2#7	2#4	2#6	2#6
12	2#3	2#5	2#6	2#4	2#6	2#6	2#4	2#6	2#7
14	2#3	2#5	2#6	2#4	2#6	2#6	2#5	2#5	2#7
16	2#4	2#5	2#7	2#4	2#6	2#7	2#5	2#6	2#7

[a] Within heavy lines 12 × 16-in. pier required. All other values obtained with 12 × 12-in. pier.

TABLE 7.3 Required Embedment for Pier Foundation

Wall Span, ft	Wind Load, 10 psf			Wind Load, 15 psf			Wind Load, 20 psf		
	Wall Height, ft			Wall Height, ft			Wall Height, ft		
	4	6	8	4	6	8	4	6	8
8	2′-0″	2′-3″	2′-9″	2′-3″	2′-6″	3′-0″	2′-3″	2′-9″	3′-0″
10	2′-0″	2′-6″	2′-9″	2′-3″	2′-9″	3′-3″	2′-6″	3′-0″	3′-3″
12	2′-3″	2′-6″	3′-0″	2′-3″	3′-0″	3′-3″	2′-6″	3′-3″	3′-6″
14	2′-3″	2′-9″	3′-0″	2′-6″	3′-0″	3′-3″	2′-9″	3′-3″	3′-9″
16	2′-3″	2′-9″	3′-0″	2′-6″	3′-3″	3′-6″	2′-9″	3′-3″	4′-0″

[a] Within heavy lines 24-in. diam. foundation required. All other values obtained with 18-in. diam. foundation.

Courtesy of the Brick Institute

Figure 7.3 *Brick wall detail.*

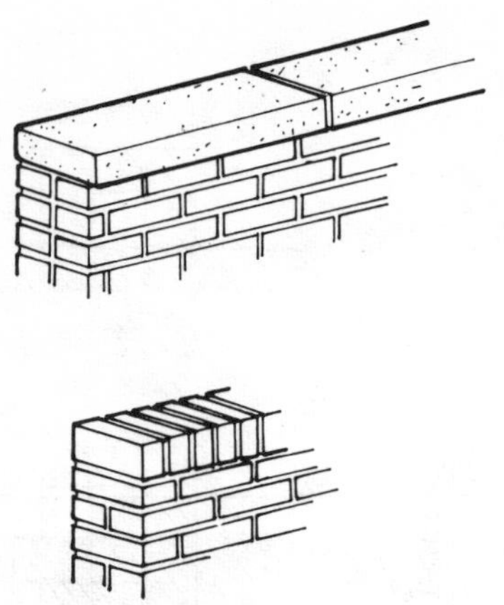

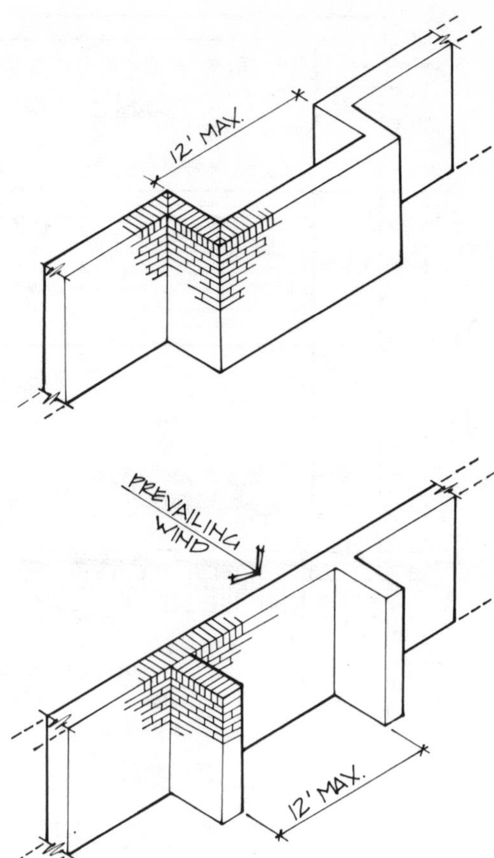
12' MAX.
PREVAILING WIND
12' MAX.

Figure 7.4 *Stone or pre-cast concrete and rowlock brick are just two of several possible caps for a wall.*

Figure 7.5 *Walls may be reinforced against strong winds with offsets or buttresses.*

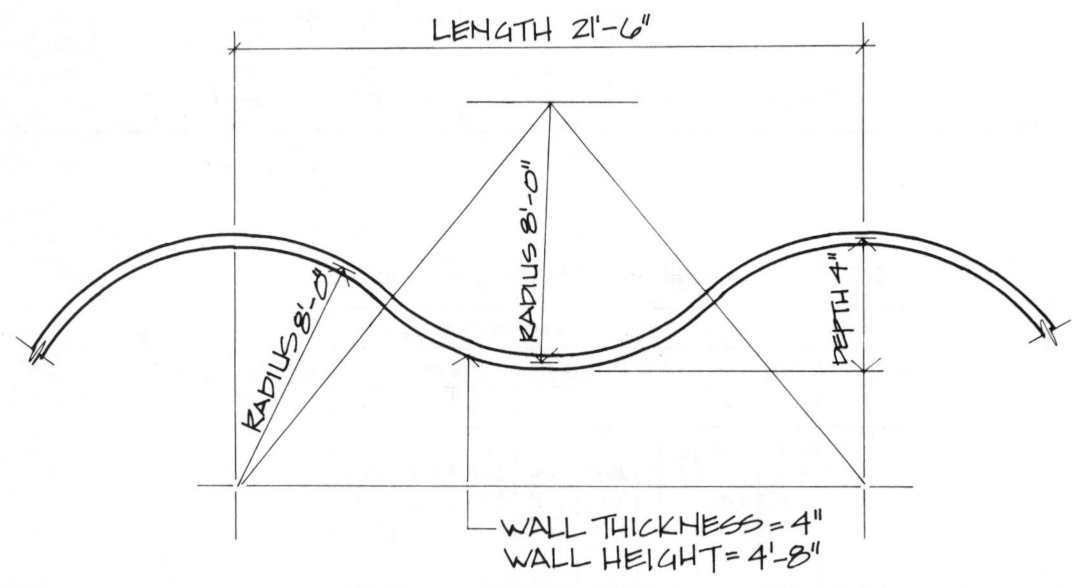
LENGTH 21'-6"
RADIUS 8'-0"
RADIUS 8'-0"
DEPTH 4"
WALL THICKNESS = 4"
WALL HEIGHT = 4'-8"

Figure 7.6 *Typical layout of a serpentine wall.*

RETAINING WALLS AND SLOPE RETENTION SYSTEMS

Whenever, in the development of the land, changes of grade create unstable soil conditions some type of retaining or slope retention system may be needed. For slopes that are 45 degrees or less, some type of riprap either stone or broken concrete or logs, might be used. When slopes become steeper than 45 degrees and begin approaching vertical, cribbing or dry-stone gravity-type retaining walls can be considered. Cribbing can either be timbers, precast reinforced concrete, or metal panels.

Vertical changes of grade can be in several forms. The lowest might be simply a raised planter where a simple concrete or masonry wall by its own mass can retain the adjacent soil without difficulty. For vertical changes up to three feet and when the soil on the high side is level, simple reinforced concrete walls will perform well without difficult designing. For higher vertical changes or where the soil slopes upward (surcharge), careful designing of the retaining wall must be accomplished in order to ensure that the wall will not overturn or slide forward and thus fail to retain the soil. Retaining walls may be one of two different types: reinforced concrete cantilever walls which may be either L-shaped or inverted T-shape or gravity walls which depend upon their own mass to achieve stability. Gravity walls may be either monolithic concrete or stone.

A computer can be used to accurately calculate the forces affecting the design of a retaining wall and will allow the designer to use a structural design that meets the needs of the site with least cost to the Owner. This is especially recommended for those walls where "H" exceeds 6 feet as shown in the tables which are provided in this section, or where unusual soil or surcharge conditions occur on the site involved.

Walls may be form finished with a wide variety of textures using commercially available polystyrene or elastomeric form liners. Many of the textures illustrated in this book can be recreated with form liners. Other techniques involve using an air hammer with a bush fitting to roughen the surface of the concrete after it has cured. On some retaining walls a 1-inch chamfered edge may add to its attractiveness.

Illustrated in this chapter are a number of approaches to the design of retaining walls which can improve their aesthetic appearance. Also illustrated are various techniques for other types of slope retention systems. Where reinforced concrete is used for vertical retaining walls, the face of the concrete which is exposed can be covered with veneers of other materials which will improve their appearance. These might be brick, stone, or precast concrete panels.

Walls may be form finished with texture added by the use of rough wood which has been sand blasted to expose the grain. The wood may be of varying thickness to create vertical or horizontal shadow patterns across the face of the retaining wall. Another technique for improving the raw appearance of concrete is the use of bush hammering, where, after the concrete is fully cured, an air hammer can be used with a bush fitting to roughen the surface of the concrete. Chemical retardants can be used on the forms which will allow the aggregate to be exposed after the forms have been removed by brushing and washing of the surface with water. Uniform tapered wood strips can be used vertically in the forms to create a uniform textural pattern. Also rubber mats can be inserted on the inside of the form to provide certain types of patterns and textures. On some retaining walls a one-inch chamfered edge may add to its attractiveness.

In most cases, retaining walls will accumulate hydraulic pressure or water behind them, except for dry stone walls where the water can seep through. For soils where water accumulation behind a wall is a possibility, two techniques for relieving the hydraulic pressure are possible. One is the use of weep holes in the front base of the wall, or drainage tile can be installed behind the wall and directed toward a storm sewage system. Weep holes may be simply small holes drilled through the wall after it is set, or two inch PVC pipe can be used with a screen to cover the pipe behind the wall with six inches of gravel. Very large retaining walls may use four-inch clay tile for weep holes. The holes from clay tile, however, are too large for many design situations and are less desirable. The four-inch tile behind the wall which is drained into a sewage storm system can be either clay tile in a gravel bed with the top half of the joints covered with 15-pound asphalt impregnated felt or corrugated polyethylene pipe with small slits to allow the water to percolate from the gravel bed into the tile or pipe. The spacing of weep holes should generally be no more than ten feet apart in order to insure that the hydraulic pressure is adequately relieved.

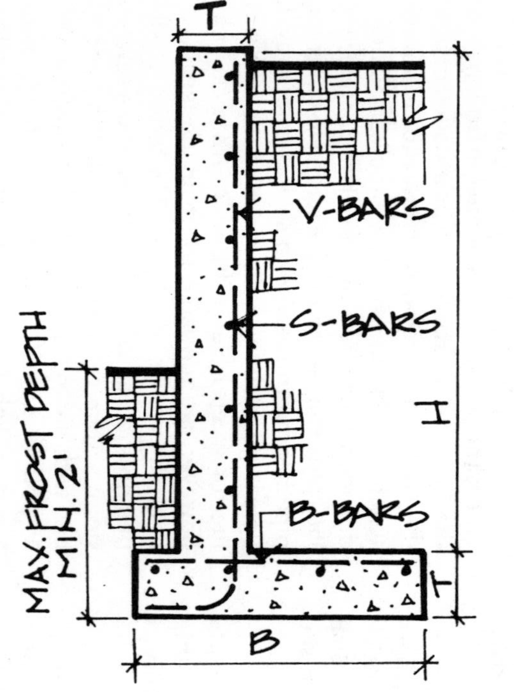

T
V-BARS
S-BARS
H
B-BARS
MAX. FROST DEPTH
MIN. 2'
T
B

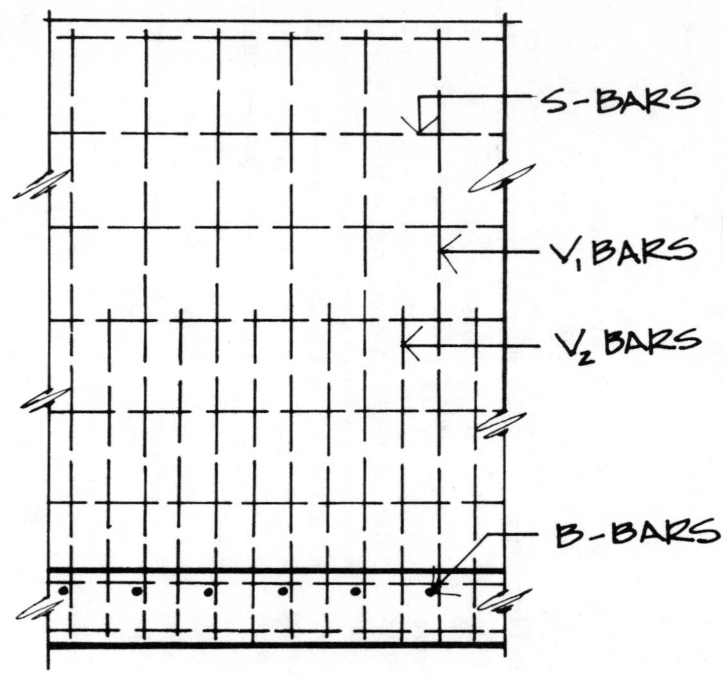

S-BARS
V_1 BARS
V_2 BARS
B-BARS

H	B	T	Vol. Conc.	V-Bars		Lengths		B-Bars			S-Bars			Reinforcement
ft.	ft.-in.	in.	Cu. yd. per lin. ft.	Size (dia.)	Spacing	V^1-Bars	V^2-Bars	Size (dia.)	Spacing	Length	Number	Size (dia.)	Spacing	Lb. per lin. ft.
5	2-9	10	.24	¼″	12″	6′-6″	—	¼″	12″	2′-4″	8	⅜″	12″	4.5
6	3-4	10	.29	¼″	7″	7′-6″	—	¼″	7″	3′-0″	10	⅜″	12″	6.8
7	3-10	10	.33	⅜″	9″	8′-4″	—	⅜″	9″	3′-6″	12	⅜″	12″	10.4
8	4-6	12	.46	½″	12″	9′-8″	5′-0″	½″	12″	4′-2″	13	⅜″	12″	12.6
9	5-0	12	.52	½″	9″	10′-8″	5′-4″	½″	9″	4′-8″	15	⅜″	12″	16.9
10	5-6	12	.57	⅝″	11″	11′-8″	6′-2″	⅝″	11″	5′-2″	16	⅜″	12″	22.1

Courtesy of Portland Cement Association

Figure 7.7 *Cantilever retaining walls without surcharge.*

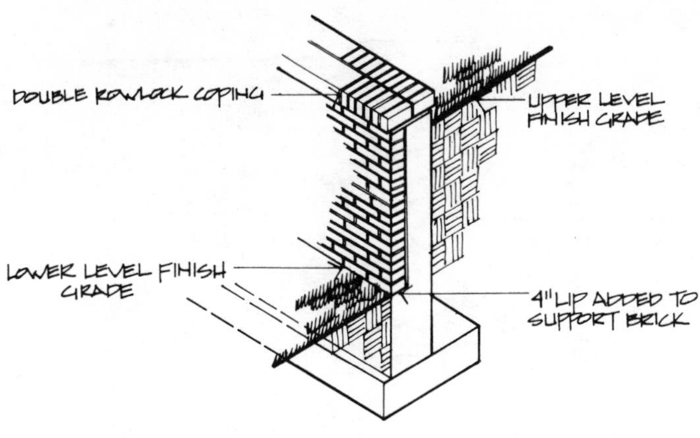
DOUBLE ROWLOCK COPING
UPPER LEVEL FINISH GRADE
LOWER LEVEL FINISH GRADE
4" LIP ADDED TO SUPPORT BRICK

Figure 7.8 *Brick veneer on a retaining wall.*

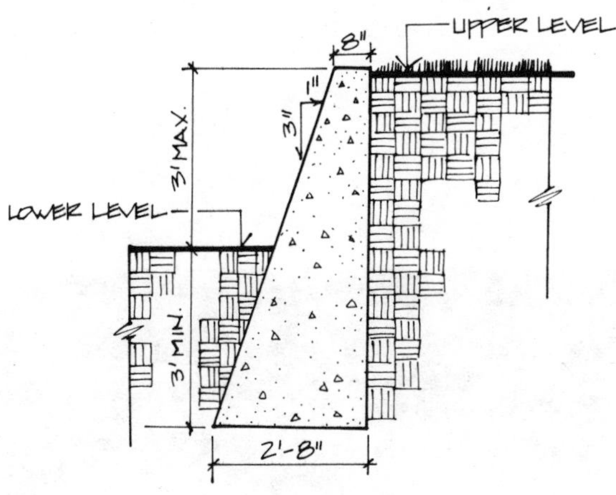
UPPER LEVEL
8"
1"
3"
3' MAX.
LOWER LEVEL
3' MIN.
2'-8"

Figure 7.9 *Gravity type retaining wall.*

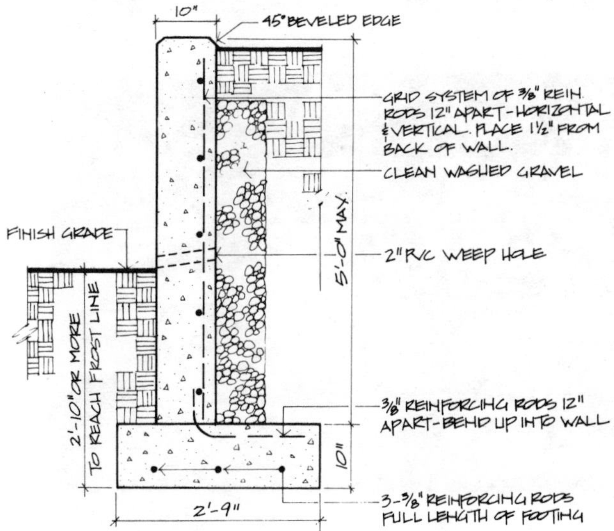
10"
45° BEVELED EDGE
GRID SYSTEM OF 3/8" REIN. RODS 12" APART - HORIZONTAL & VERTICAL. PLACE 1½" FROM BACK OF WALL.
CLEAN WASHED GRAVEL
FINISH GRADE
5'-0" MAX.
2" PVC WEEP HOLE
2'-10" OR MORE TO REACH FROST LINE
3/8" REINFORCING RODS 12" APART - BEND UP INTO WALL
10"
2'-9"
3-3/8" REINFORCING RODS FULL LENGTH OF FOOTING

Figure 7.10 *One solution using Figure 7.7.*

Weep holes may be disadvantageous in some situations because the water seeping from behind the wall carries minerals and sediments which stand and discolor the paving at the base of the wall.

Because concrete is not completely waterproof and to eliminate the possibility of surface staining, streaking, and efflorescence, it is desirable to waterproof the back side of the wall. This can be accomplished by applying a coat of asphalt emulsion, a layer of six-mil polyethylene, and an additional layer of asphalt emulsion. In planters where some protection against freezing of the soil in a sideways direction is desirable, or to provide expansion of the soil in the planter without damage to the walls, one-to two-inch-thick polystyrene foam can be placed along the sides of the planter after the last coat of asphalt emulsion has been applied.

Long retaining walls will require some provision for expansion and contraction of the concrete. These vertical joints, however, can separate horizontally in a perpendicular direction to the wall unless some technique is provided to prevent it. There are two possibilities: one is to provide a key using a tapered 2 x 4 vertically in the first pour, and the second is to install steel rods, 12 inches in length and a minimum of one-half inch in diameter, horizontally in the vertical joint at 12-inch intervals with a sleeve on one end of the rod. The sleeve allows the rod to move in one side of the wall during expansion and contraction but prevents the wall from separating horizontally, perpendicular to the wall. The thickness of the joints should be about a half an inch with a water resistant fiber fill provided. In order to prevent water seepage through the joint vinyl waterstops will need to be used. The type which is most adaptable is one with a double flange on one side to allow it to be nailed to the forms. The joint, in order to reduce unsightliness, can be covered with a gray urethane sealant.

Install expansion joints every 100 feet and contraction joints (1 inch wide tapered to ½ inch depth) every 25 feet.

Timber Walls

Logs, railroad ties and timbers can be used to retain soil. Several different techniques can be used in designing retaining walls to ensure their stability. Horizontally placed timbers can be held in place by (1) vertical steel I beams anchored below grade, (2) closely spaced vertical timbers, posts, or pre-cast concrete units also anchored below grade, or (3) deadmen, anchored back into the slope. A deadman might be a timber attached to the wall or a steel cable bolted to the wall and to a concrete anchor several feet behind the wall.

Vertical timbers can also be used. For low walls without surcharge they may be installed below grade to a depth equal to the height above grade. Some technique for keeping the timbers in alignment may be required.

REFERENCES FOR FURTHER READING

Munson, A.E. *Construction Design for Landscape Architects.* New York: McGraw-Hill, 1974.

Ramsey, C.G., and Sleeper, H.R. *Architectural Graphics Standards.* 7th Edition. New York: Wiley, 1981.

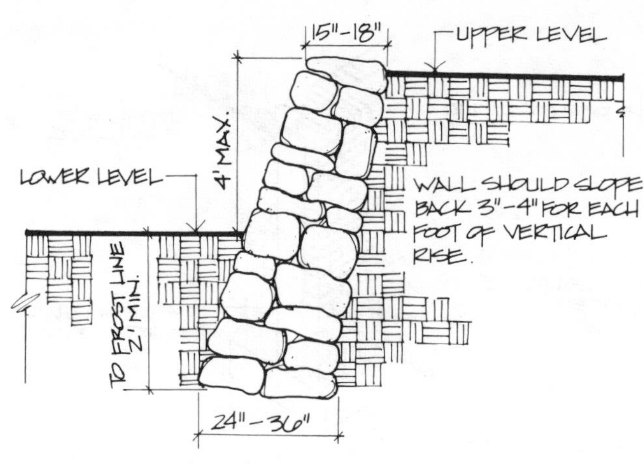

15"–18"
UPPER LEVEL
4' MAX.
LOWER LEVEL
WALL SHOULD SLOPE BACK 3"–4" FOR EACH FOOT OF VERTICAL RISE.
TO FROST LINE 2' MIN.
24"–36"

Figure 7.11 *Detail for a dry stone wall.*

7.12
7.14
7.13
7.15

Figures 7.12 – 7.21 *Wall patterns and textures.*

7.16

7.19

7.17

7.20

7.18

7.21

7.22

7.24

7.23

7.25

Figures 7.22 – 7.29 *Wall patterns and textures.*

7.26

7.28

7.27

7.29

7.30

Michael Painter

7.31

7.32

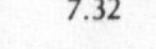

7.33

7.34

Figures 7.30 – 7.33 *Various patterns in brick walls.*

Figure 7.34 *Clay tile (4") forms the center of this wall.*

7.35 Environmental Planning and Design

7.38

7.36

7.39

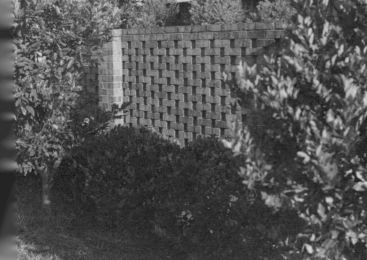

7.37

Figures 7.35 – 7.38 *Brick wall variations.*
Figure 7.39 *Brick wall with offsets.*

7.40

7.42

7.41

7.43 Doede, Inc.

7.44

Figures 7.40 – 7.47 *Additional design variations in brick walls.*

Figure 7.41 *Pre-cast concrete cap. Note underside grove for drip and serrated metal top to discourage trespassers.*

Figure 7.45 *Serpentine wall at a zoo.*

7.45

7.46

7.47

7.48

7.49

7.50

7.51

7.52

7.53

7.54

7.56

7.55

7.57

Figure 7.48 *Four inch thick brick wall held in place with steel channel.*

Figures 7.49 – 7.57 *Design variations in concrete block.*

Figure 7.53 *Stacked bond pattern.*

Figure 7.58 *Pre-cast concrete panels serve as a railing for the patio beyond and as a retaining wall (lower half).*

7.58

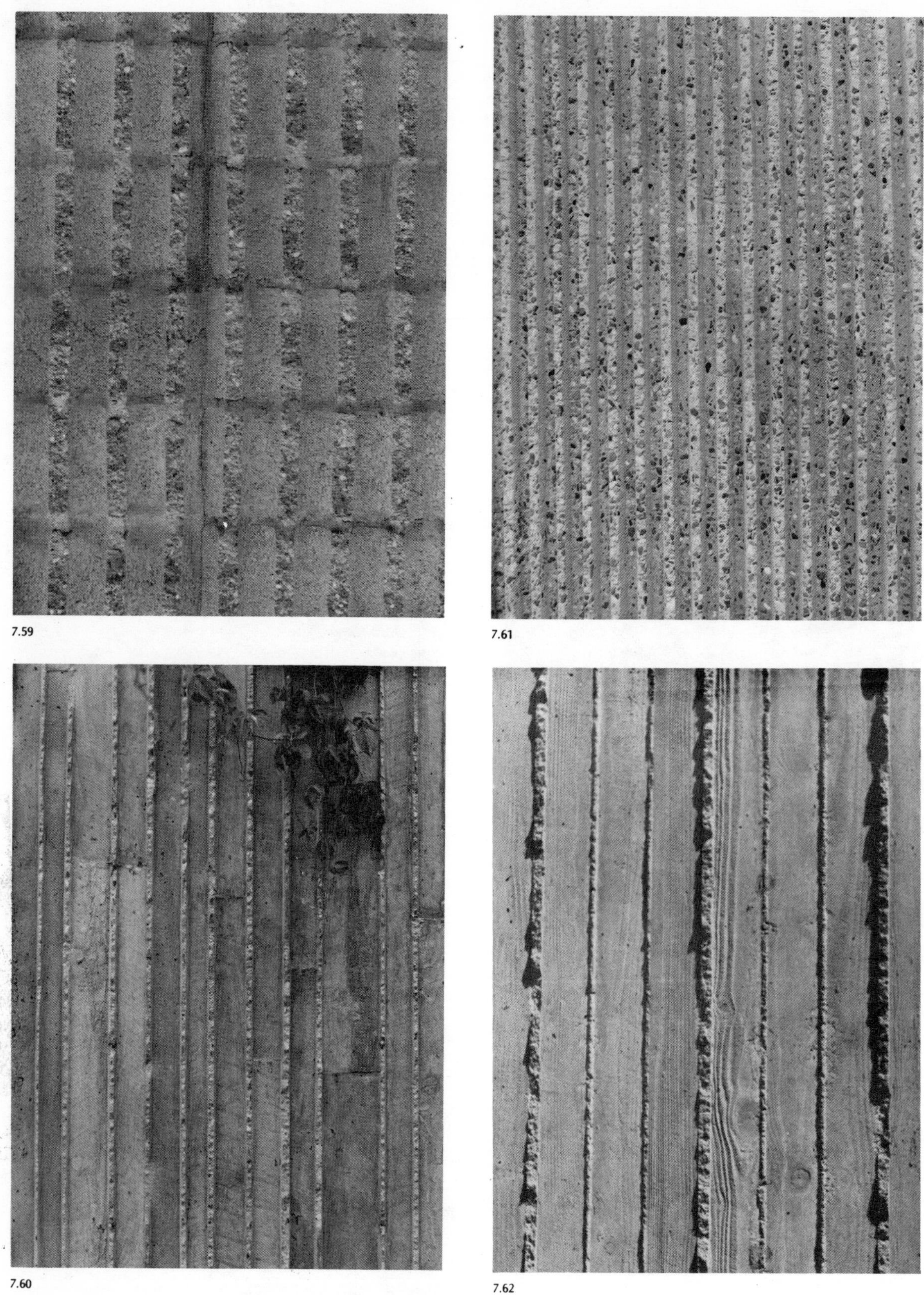
7.59
7.61
7.60
7.62

Figure 7.59 *Concrete block with textured face.*
Figures 7.60 – 7.65 *Surface textures on concrete walls.*
Figure 7.66 *Granite rectangles.*

7.63

7.64

7.65

7.66

7.67

7.68

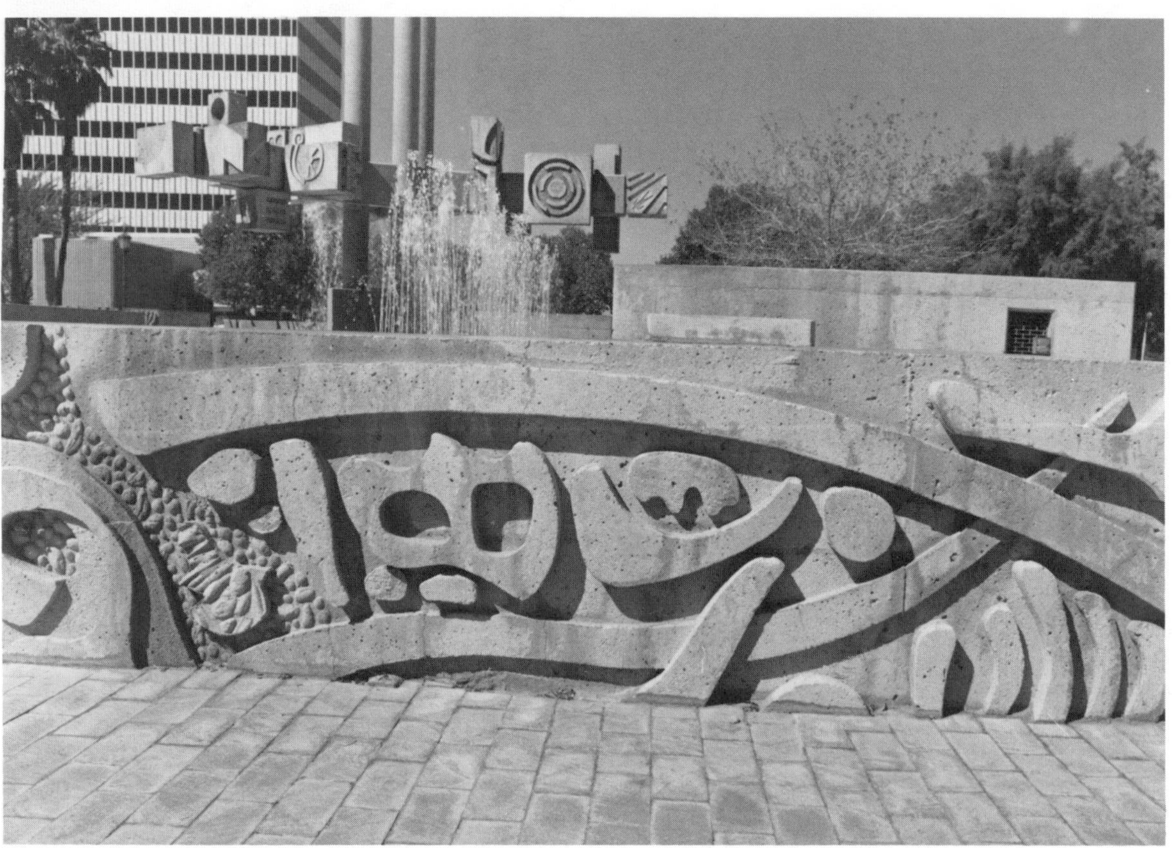
7.69

Figures 7.67 – 7.70 *Wall variations which express movement.*

7.70

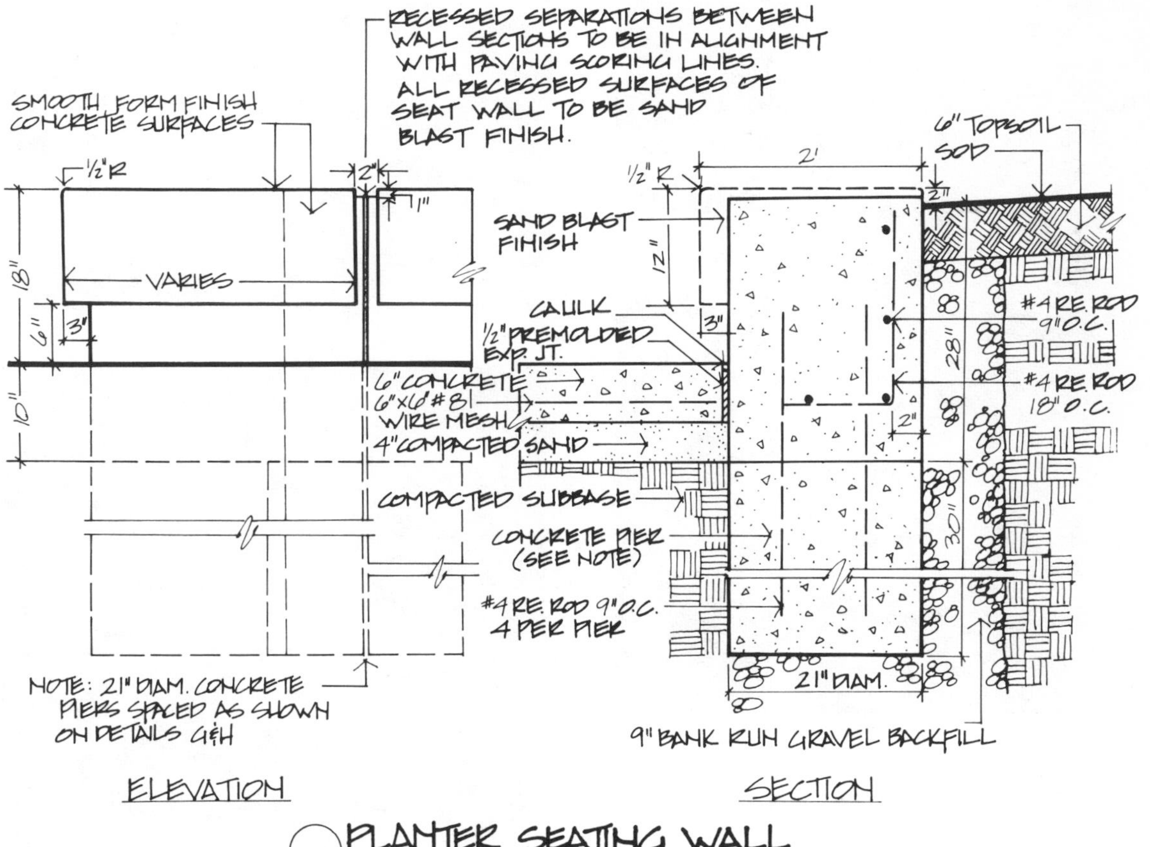

RECESSED SEPARATIONS BETWEEN WALL SECTIONS TO BE IN ALIGNMENT WITH PAVING SCORING LINES. ALL RECESSED SURFACES OF SEAT WALL TO BE SAND BLAST FINISH.
SMOOTH FORM FINISH CONCRETE SURFACES
1/2" R
2"
1"
18"
VARIES
6"
3"
10"
NOTE: 21" DIAM. CONCRETE PIERS SPACED AS SHOWN ON DETAILS G&H
ELEVATION
6" TOPSOIL
SOD
2'
1/2" R
2"
SAND BLAST FINISH
12"
CAULK
3"
1/2" PREMOLDED EXP. JT.
6" CONCRETE
6"x6" #81 WIRE MESH
4" COMPACTED SAND
#4 RE. ROD 9" O.C.
28"
#4 RE. ROD 18" O.C.
2"
COMPACTED SUBBASE
CONCRETE PIER (SEE NOTE)
30"
#4 RE. ROD 9" O.C. 4 PER PIER
21" DIAM.
9" BANK RUN GRAVEL BACKFILL
SECTION
PLANTER SEATING WALL

7.71

Johnson, Johnson and Roy

7.72

7.73

7.74

7.75

7.76

Figure 7.72 *Course textured wall designed by Frank Lloyd Wright.*

Figure 7.73 *Square granite blocks.*

Figure 7.74 *Pre-cast tilt up panels.*

Figures 7.75 – 7.76 *Field and native stone.*

7.77

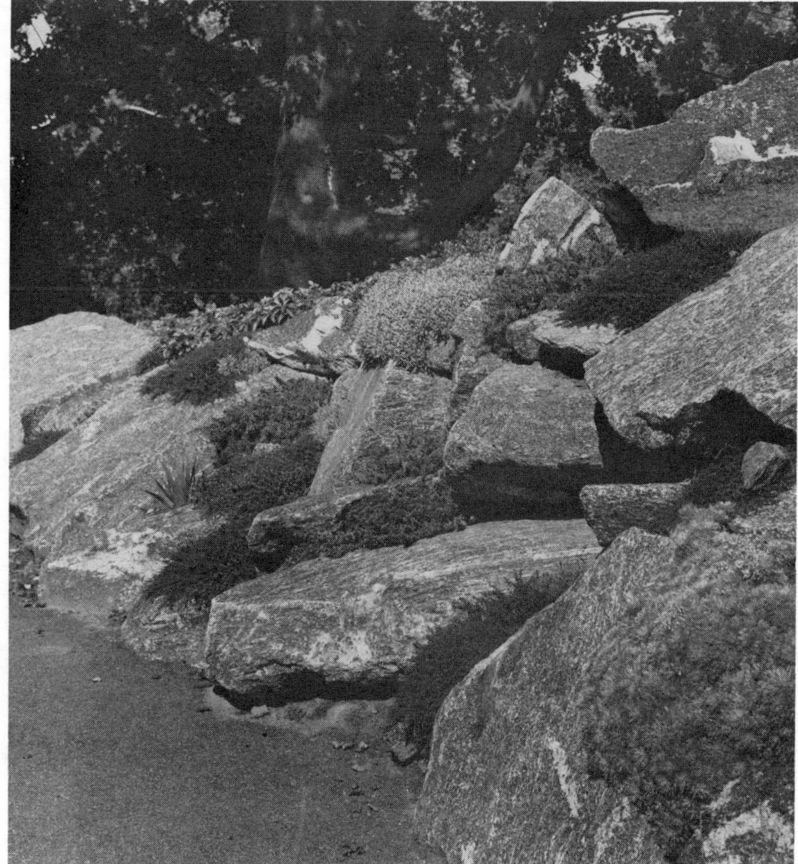

7.78

A. E. Bye and Associates

Figures 7.77 – 7.78 *Stone used to retain slopes.*

7.79

7.81 William A. Behnke Associates

7.80

7.82 U.S. Forest Service, Ozark N.F.

7.83 U.S. Forest Service, George Washington N.F.

Figures 7.79 – 7.83 *Different ways stone can be used to retain slopes.*

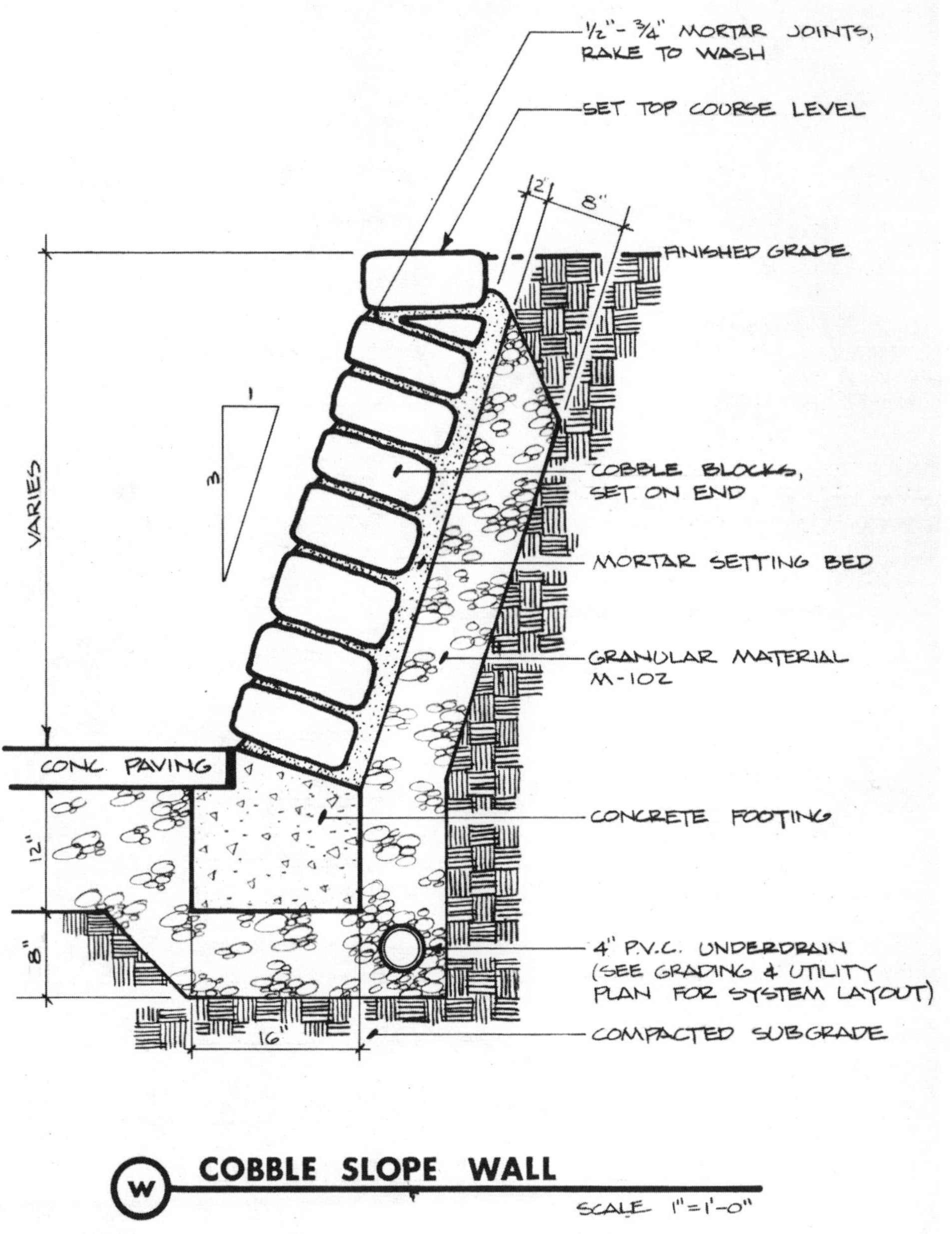
½"- ¾" MORTAR JOINTS, RAKE TO WASH
SET TOP COURSE LEVEL
2"
8"
FINISHED GRADE
1
3
VARIES
COBBLE BLOCKS, SET ON END
MORTAR SETTING BED
GRANULAR MATERIAL M-102
CONC. PAVING
CONCRETE FOOTING
12"
8"
4" P.V.C. UNDERDRAIN (SEE GRADING & UTILITY PLAN FOR SYSTEM LAYOUT)
16"
COMPACTED SUBGRADE
W
COBBLE SLOPE WALL
SCALE 1"=1'-0"

Figure 7.84 *Stone wall.*

Saratoga Associates

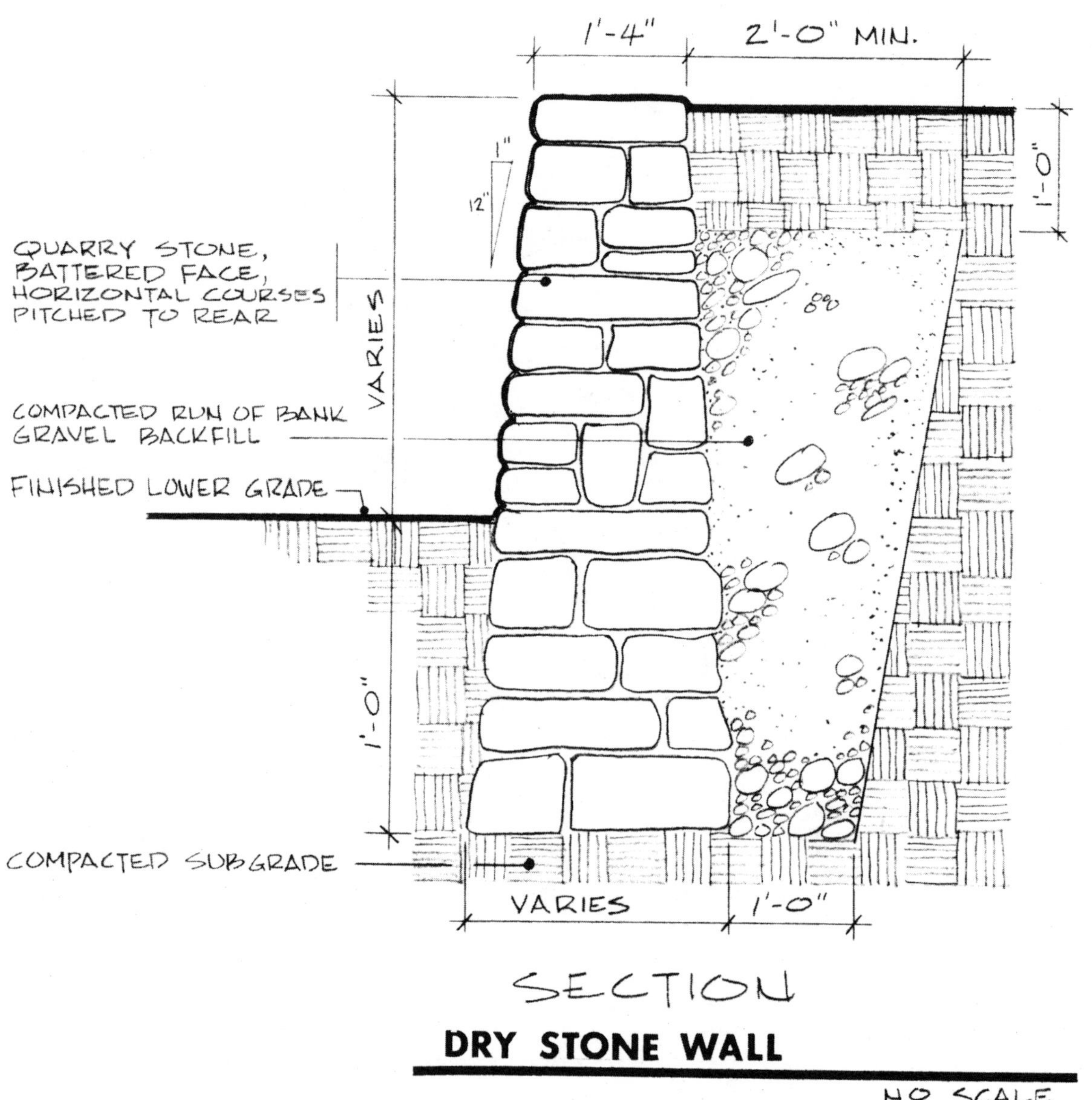
1'-4"
2'-0" MIN.
1"
12"
1'-0"
QUARRY STONE,
BATTERED FACE,
HORIZONTAL COURSES
PITCHED TO REAR
VARIES
COMPACTED RUN OF BANK
GRAVEL BACKFILL
FINISHED LOWER GRADE
1'-0"
COMPACTED SUBGRADE
VARIES
1'-0"
SECTION
DRY STONE WALL
NO SCALE

Figure 7.85 *Dry stone wall.*

Saratoga Associates

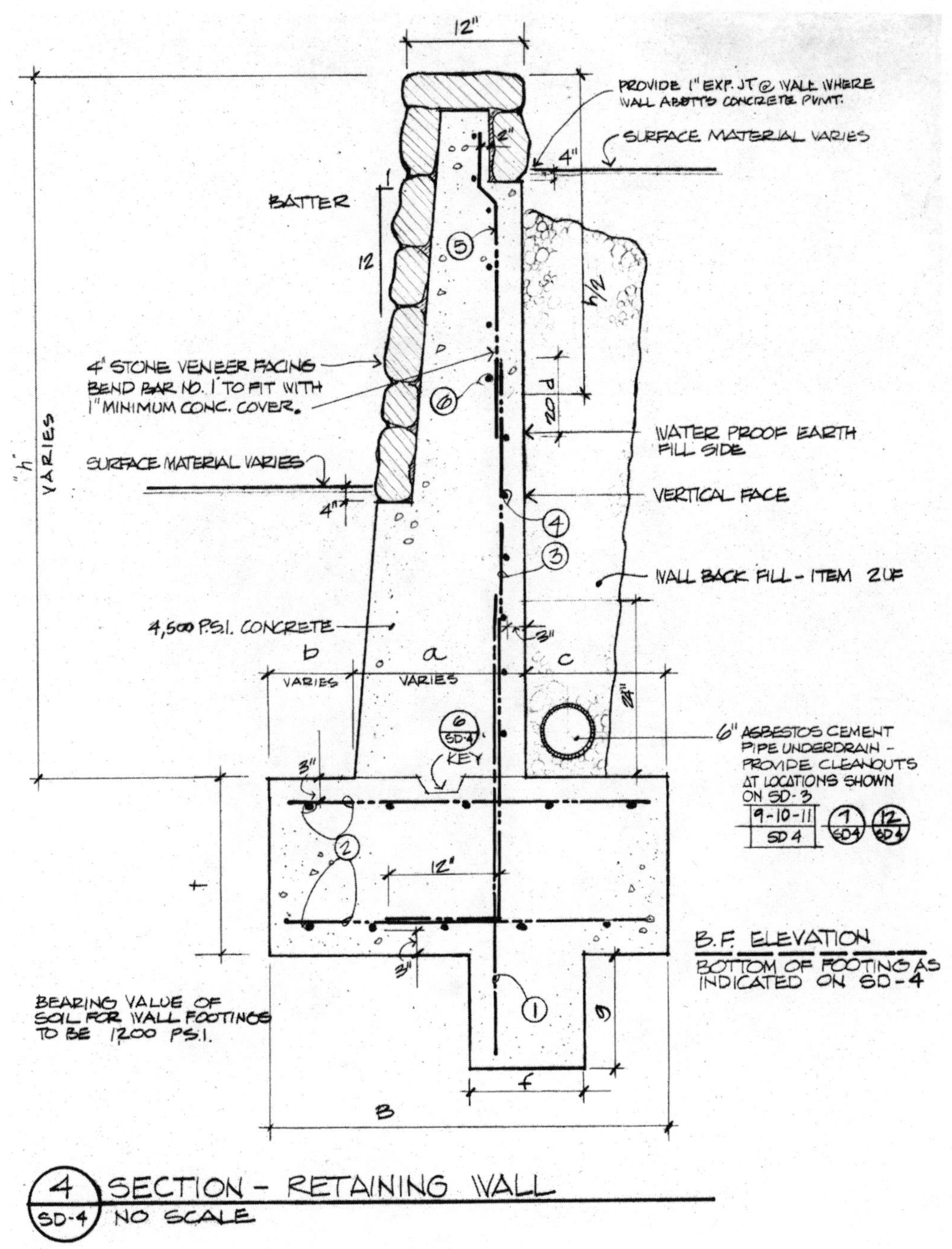
12"
PROVIDE 1" EXP. JT @ WALL WHERE WALL ABUTTS CONCRETE PVMT.
SURFACE MATERIAL VARIES
2"
4"
BATTER
1
12
5
h/2
4" STONE VENEER FACING
BEND BAR NO. 1 TO FIT WITH 1" MINIMUM CONC. COVER.
6
d
20d
WATER PROOF EARTH FILL SIDE
"h" VARIES
SURFACE MATERIAL VARIES
4"
VERTICAL FACE
4
3
WALL BACK FILL - ITEM 2UF
4,500 P.S.I. CONCRETE
3"
b
a
c
VARIES
VARIES
24"
6" ASBESTOS CEMENT PIPE UNDERDRAIN - PROVIDE CLEANOUTS AT LOCATIONS SHOWN ON SD-3
6 SD-4
KEY
3"
9-10-11 SD 4
7 SD4
12 SD4
2
t
12"
B.F. ELEVATION
BOTTOM OF FOOTING AS INDICATED ON SD-4
3"
1
g
BEARING VALUE OF SOIL FOR WALL FOOTINGS TO BE 1200 PS.I.
f
B
4 SD-4
SECTION - RETAINING WALL
NO SCALE

Figure 7.86 *Stone veneer retaining wall.*

Johnson, Johnson and Roy

7.87

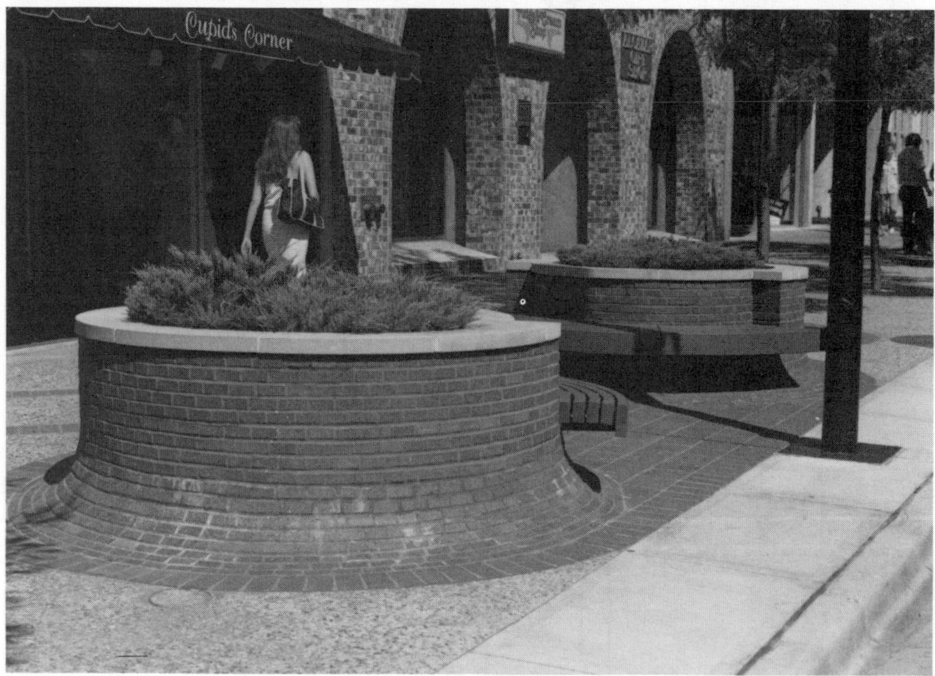
Cupid's Corner

7.88

Figures 7.87 - 7.88 *Brick veneer retaining walls.*

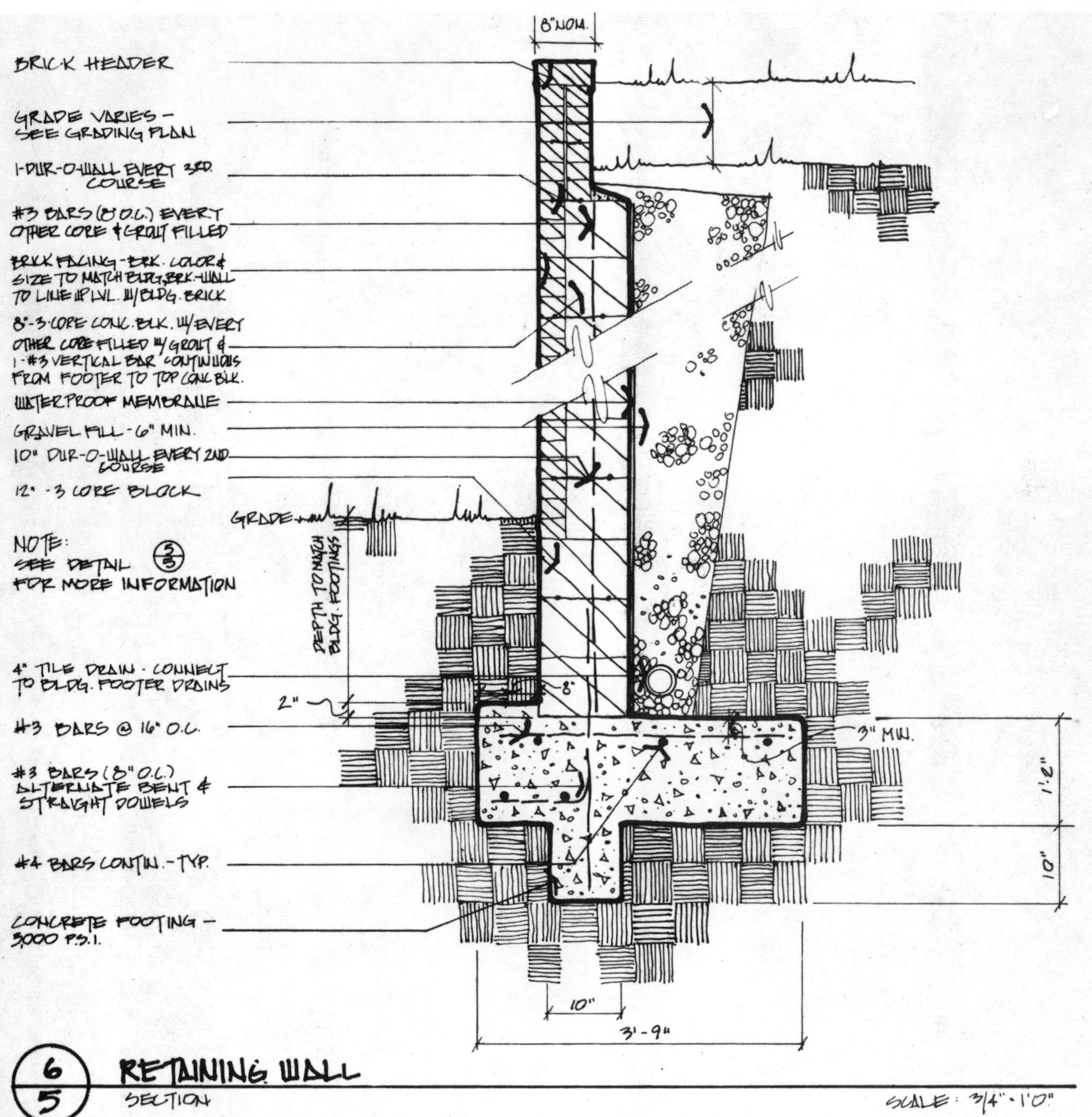
8" NOM.
BRICK HEADER
GRADE VARIES – SEE GRADING PLAN
1-DUR-O-WALL EVERY 3RD. COURSE
#3 BARS (8" O.C.) EVERY OTHER CORE & GROUT FILLED
BRICK FACING - BRK. COLOR & SIZE TO MATCH BLDG. BRK. - WALL TO LINE UP LVL. W/BLDG. BRICK
8"-3-CORE CONC. BLK. W/EVERY OTHER CORE FILLED W/GROUT & 1-#3 VERTICAL BAR CONTINUOUS FROM FOOTER TO TOP CONC. BLK.
WATERPROOF MEMBRANE
GRAVEL FILL - 6" MIN.
10" DUR-O-WALL EVERY 2ND COURSE
12" - 3 CORE BLOCK
GRADE
NOTE: SEE DETAIL 5/5 FOR MORE INFORMATION
DEPTH TO MATCH BLDG. FOOTINGS
4" TILE DRAIN - CONNECT TO BLDG. FOOTER DRAINS
8"
2"
#3 BARS @ 16" O.C.
3" MIN.
#3 BARS (8" O.C.) ALTERNATE BENT & STRAIGHT DOWELS
1'-2"
#4 BARS CONTIN. - TYP.
10"
CONCRETE FOOTING – 3000 P.S.I.
10"
3'-9"
6/5
RETAINING WALL
SECTION
SCALE: 3/4" = 1'-0"

Figure 7.89 *Brick and block retaining wall.*

Bonnell and Associates

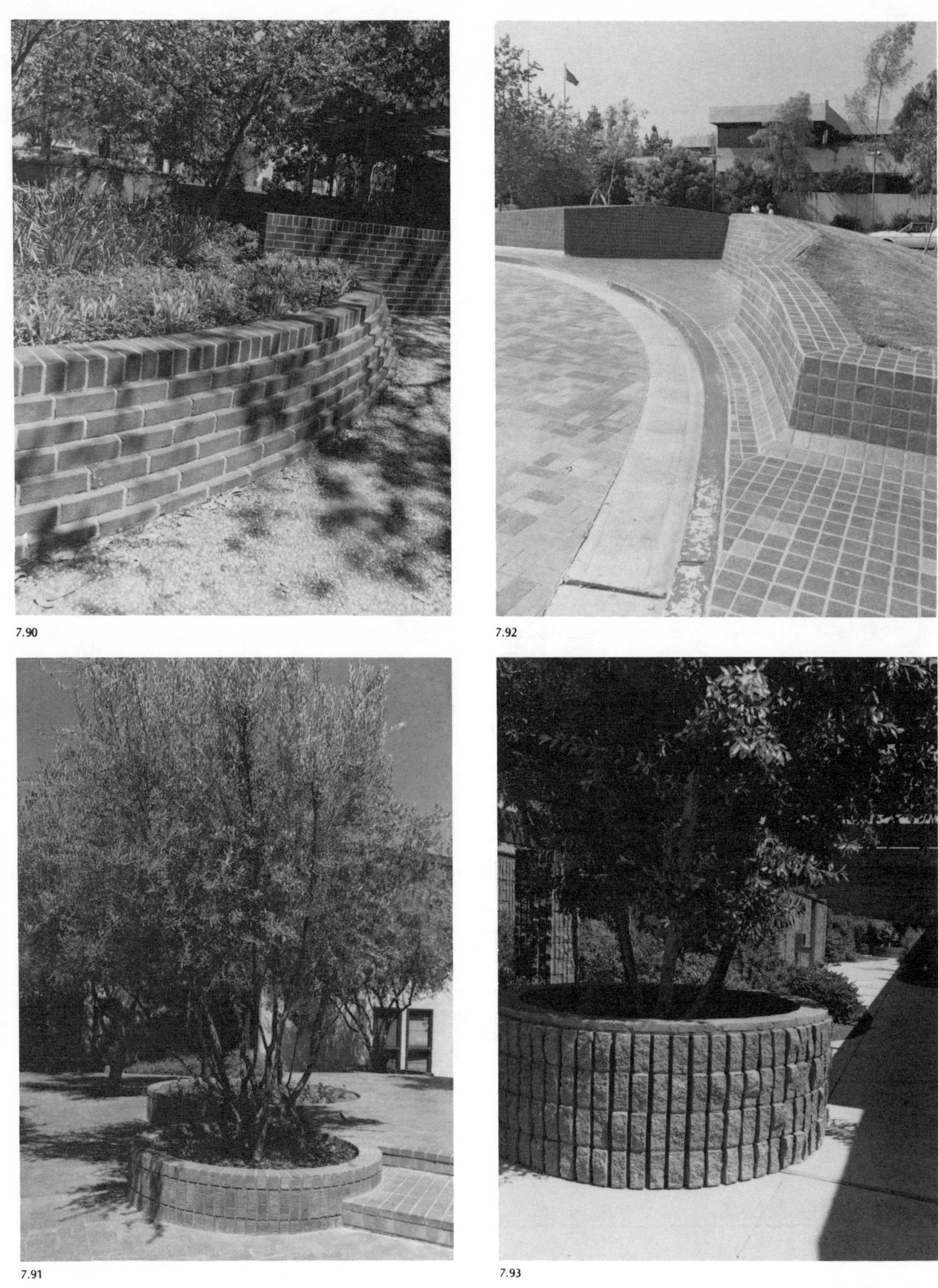

7.90

7.92

7.91

7.93

Figures 7.90 – 7.93 *Brick retaining walls.*

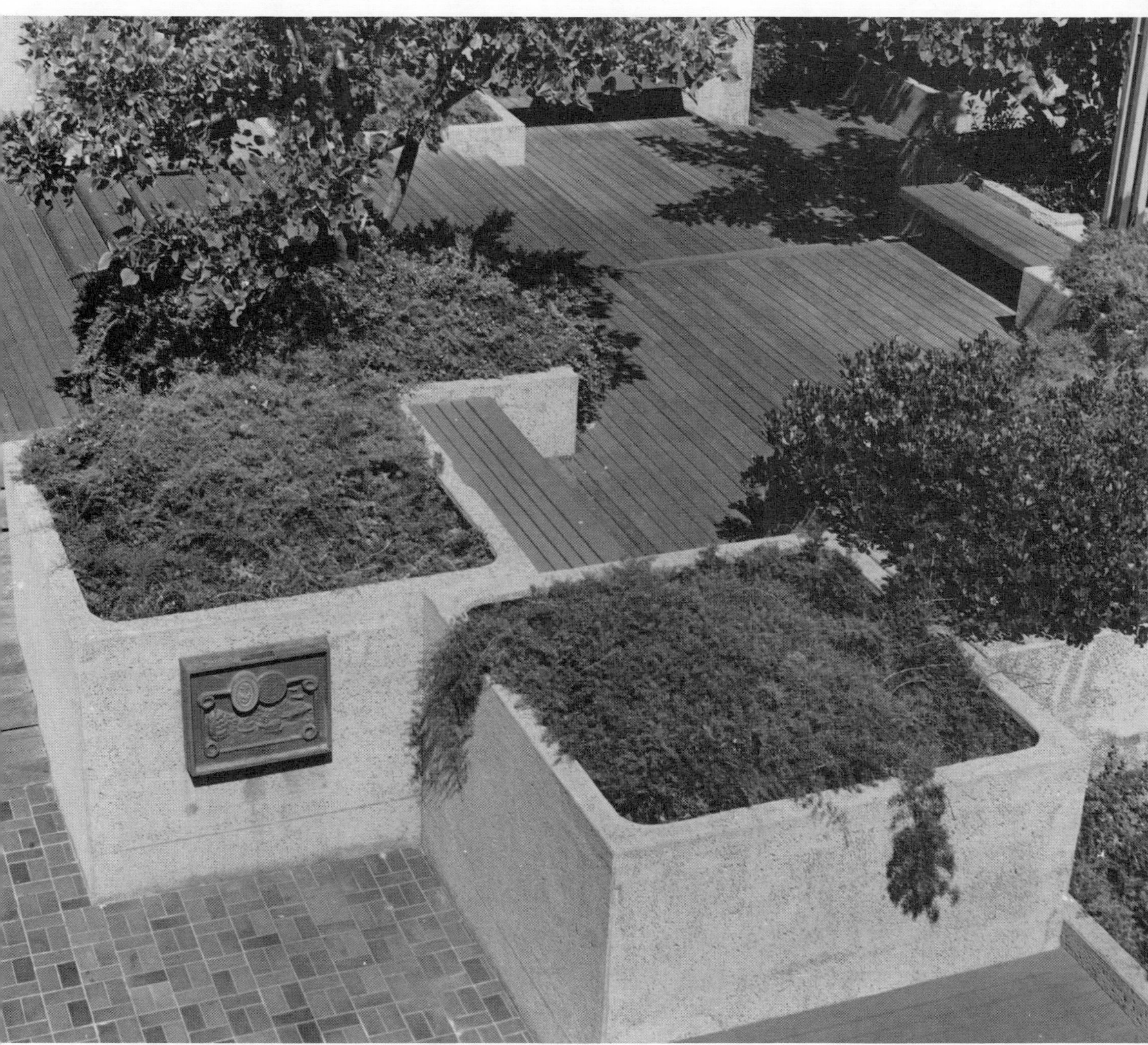

Figure 7.94 *Series of raised planters on a west coast waterfront.*

7.95

7.96

7.97

Figures 7.95 – 7.97 *Various design patterns for raised planters – retaining walls.*

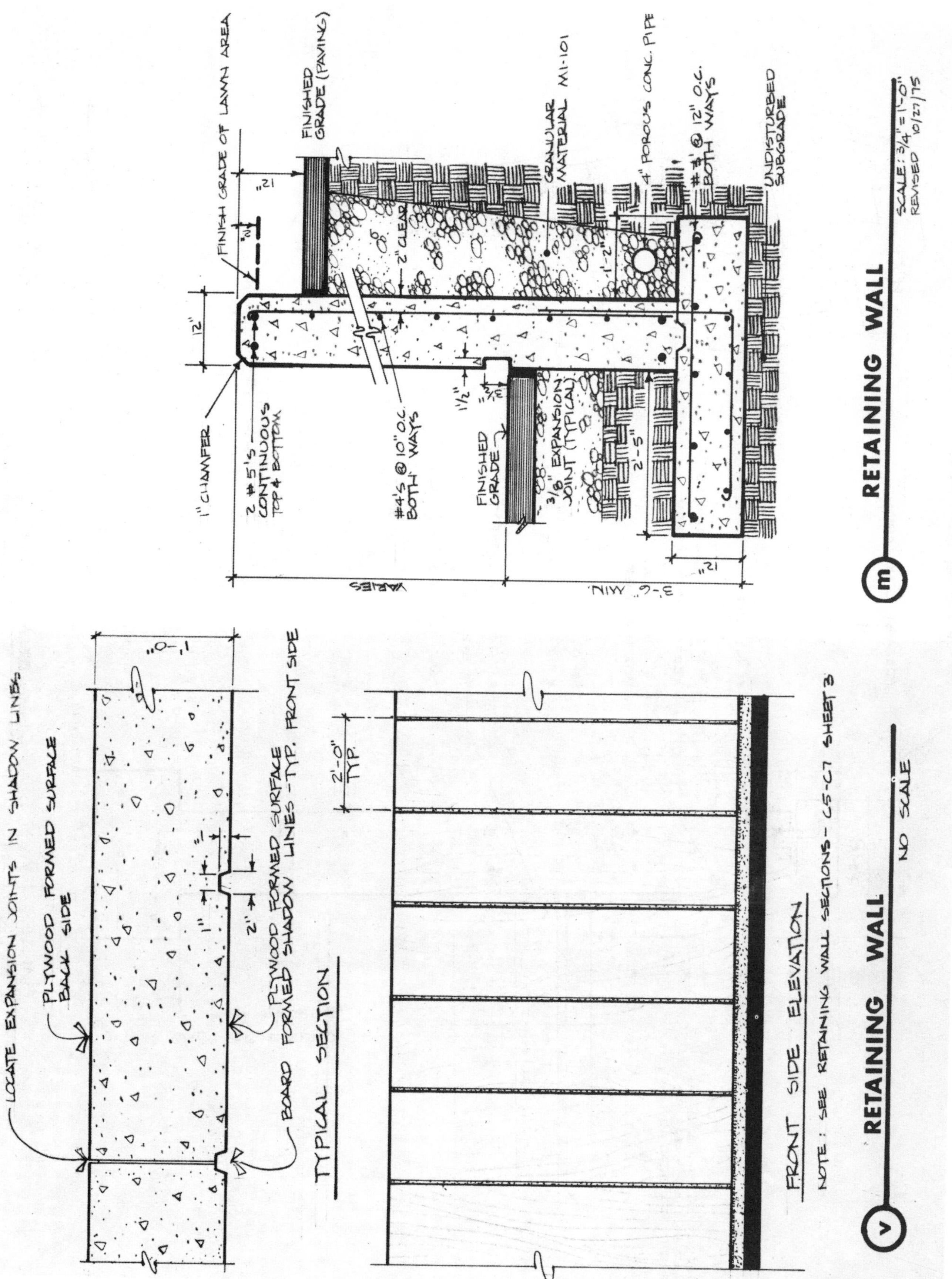

1" CHAMFER
2 #5'S CONTINUOUS TOP & BOTTOM
12"
FINISH GRADE OF LAWN AREA
12"
FINISHED GRADE (PAVING)
2" CLEAR
#4'S @ 10" O.C. BOTH WAYS
1 1/2"
FINISHED GRADE
3/8" EXPANSION JOINT (TYPICAL)
GRANULAR MATERIAL MI-101
4" POROUS CONC. PIPE
1'-2"
2'-5"
#3'S @ 12" O.C. BOTH WAYS
UNDISTURBED SUBGRADE
12"
VARIES
3'-6" MIN.
m
RETAINING WALL
SCALE: 3/4"=1'-0"
REVISED 10/27/75
LOCATE EXPANSION JOINTS IN SHADOW LINES
PLYWOOD FORMED SURFACE BACK SIDE
1'-0"
1"
1"
2"
PLYWOOD FORMED SURFACE BOARD FORMED SHADOW LINES - TYP. FRONT SIDE
TYPICAL SECTION
2'-0" TYP.
FRONT SIDE ELEVATION
NOTE: SEE RETAINING WALL SECTIONS - C5-C7 SHEET 3
v
RETAINING WALL
NO SCALE

Figure 7.98 *Retaining wall sections and elevation.*

Saratoga Associates

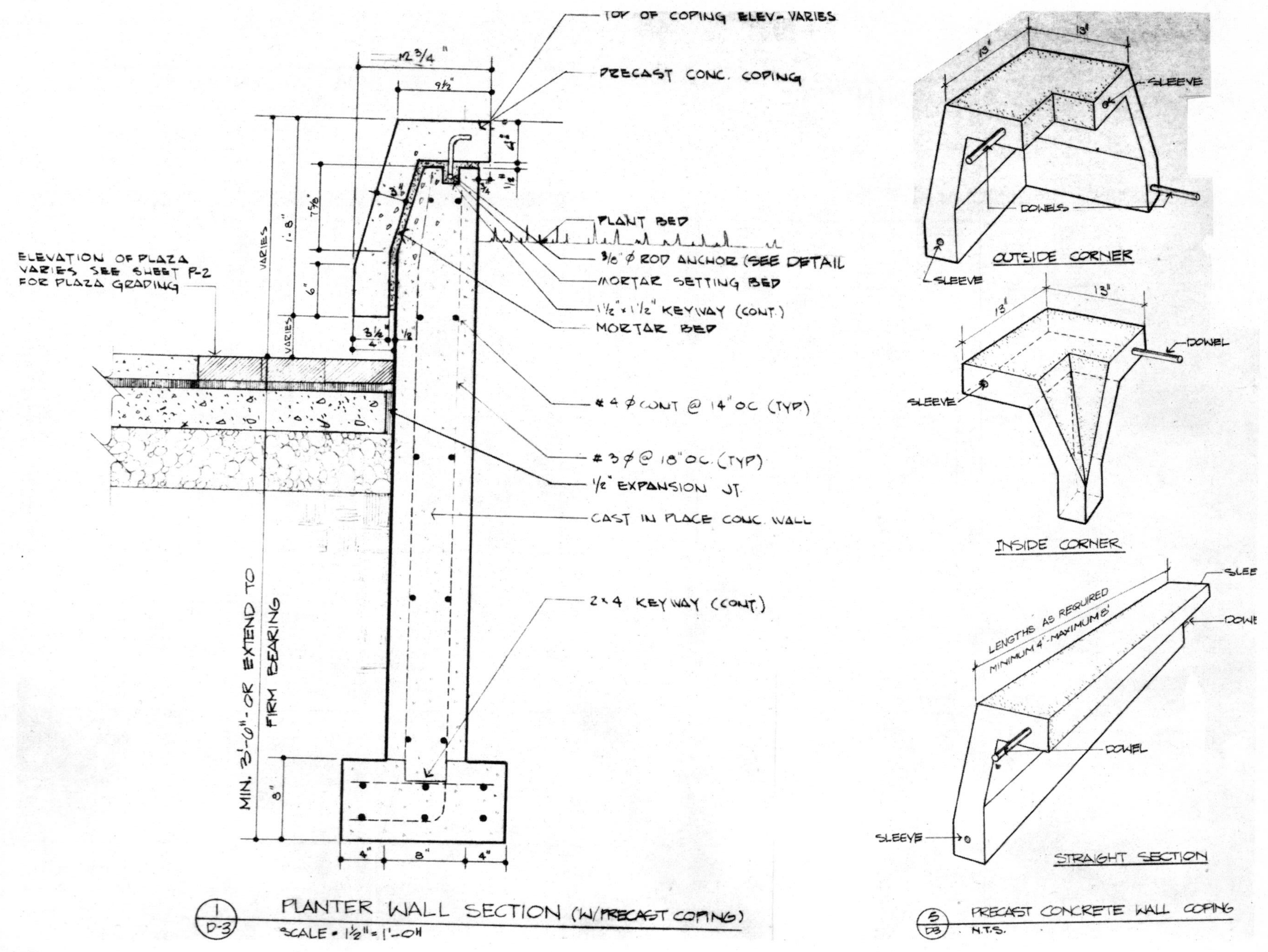
TOP OF COPING ELEV.- VARIES
PRECAST CONC. COPING
12 3/4"
9 1/2"
PLANT BED
3/8" ø ROD ANCHOR (SEE DETAIL
MORTAR SETTING BED
1 1/2" x 1 1/2" KEYWAY (CONT.)
MORTAR BED
ELEVATION OF PLAZA VARIES SEE SHEET P-2 FOR PLAZA GRADING
VARIES
1'-8"
7 5/8"
6"
3 1/8"
4"
1/8"
4 ø CONT @ 14" OC (TYP)
3 ø @ 18" OC. (TYP)
1/2" EXPANSION JT.
CAST IN PLACE CONC. WALL
2 x 4 KEYWAY (CONT.)
MIN. 3'-6" OR EXTEND TO FIRM BEARING
8"
4"
8"
4"
PLANTER WALL SECTION (W/PRECAST COPING)
SCALE • 1 1/2" = 1'-0"
1 D-3
13"
13"
SLEEVE
DOWELS
SLEEVE
OUTSIDE CORNER
13"
13"
DOWEL
SLEEVE
INSIDE CORNER
LENGTHS AS REQUIRED
MINIMUM 4' - MAXIMUM 8'
SLEE
DOWE
DOWEL
SLEEVE
STRAIGHT SECTION
PRECAST CONCRETE WALL COPING
N.T.S.
5 D3

7.100

7.101

7.102

Figure 7.100 *Pre-cast veneer retaining wall.*

Figure 7.101 *Stone planters.*

Figure 7.102 *Exposed aggregate concrete wall with shadow recess.*

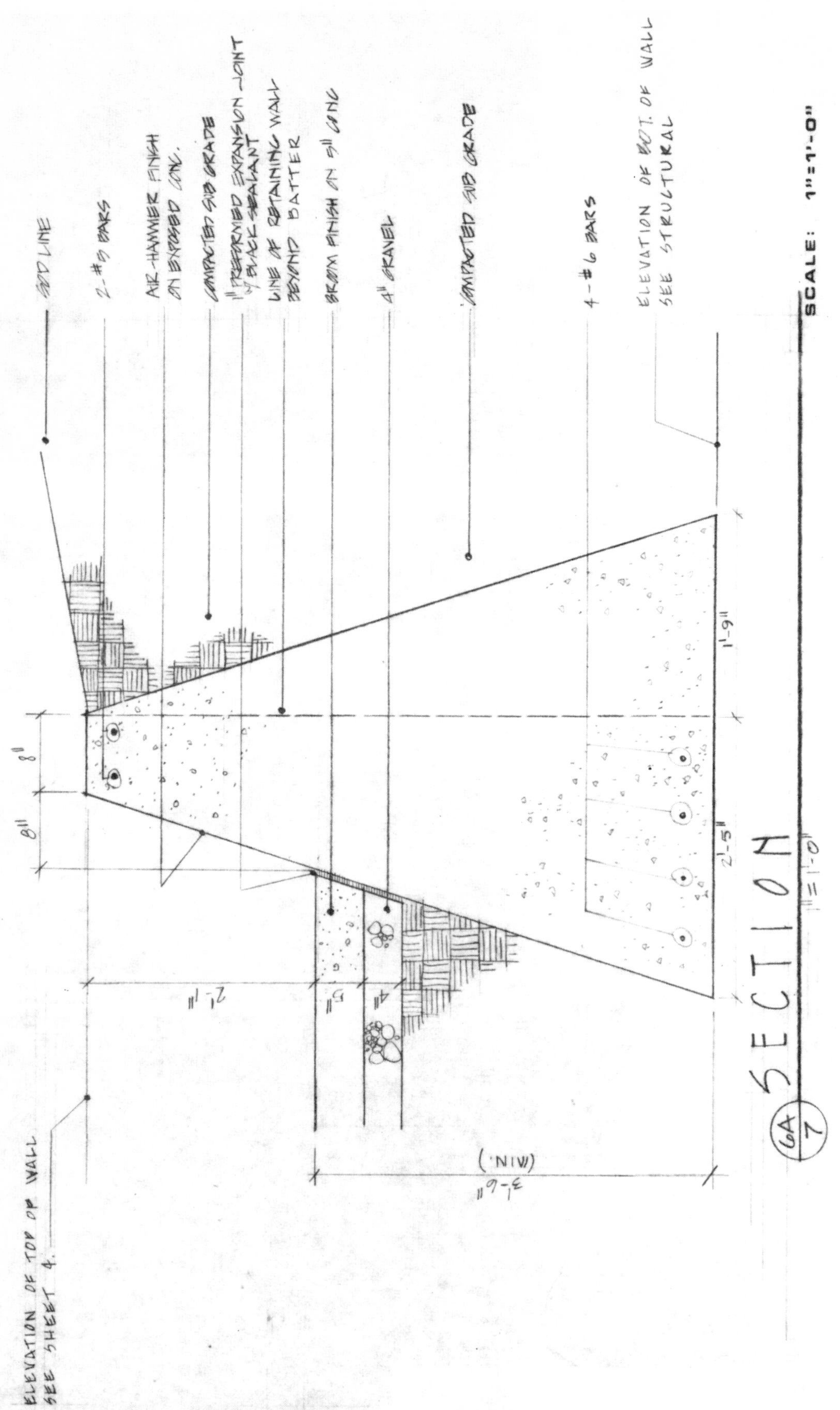

SOD LINE
2-#5 BARS
AIR-HAMMER FINISH ON EXPOSED CONC.
COMPACTED SUB GRADE
1" PREFORMED EXPANSION JOINT W/ BLACK SEALANT
LINE OF RETAINING WALL BEYOND BATTER
BROOM FINISH ON 5" CONC
4" GRAVEL
COMPACTED SUB GRADE
4-#6 BARS
ELEVATION OF BOT. OF WALL SEE STRUCTURAL
ELEVATION OF TOP OF WALL SEE SHEET 4.
8"
8"
2'-1"
5"
4"
3'-6" (MIN.)
1'-9"
2'-5"
SECTION 1"=1'-0"
6A 7
SCALE: 1"=1'-0"

Browning-Day-Pollak-Associates-Inc.

Figure 7.103 *Concrete retaining wall (gravity type). Reinforcing steel was used because of possible settling of subgrade. See Figure 7.104.*

7.104

Browning-Day-Pollak-Associates-Inc.

7.105

Figure 7.104 *See Figure 7.103.*

Figure 7.105 *Textured retaining wall with cantilevered planters.*

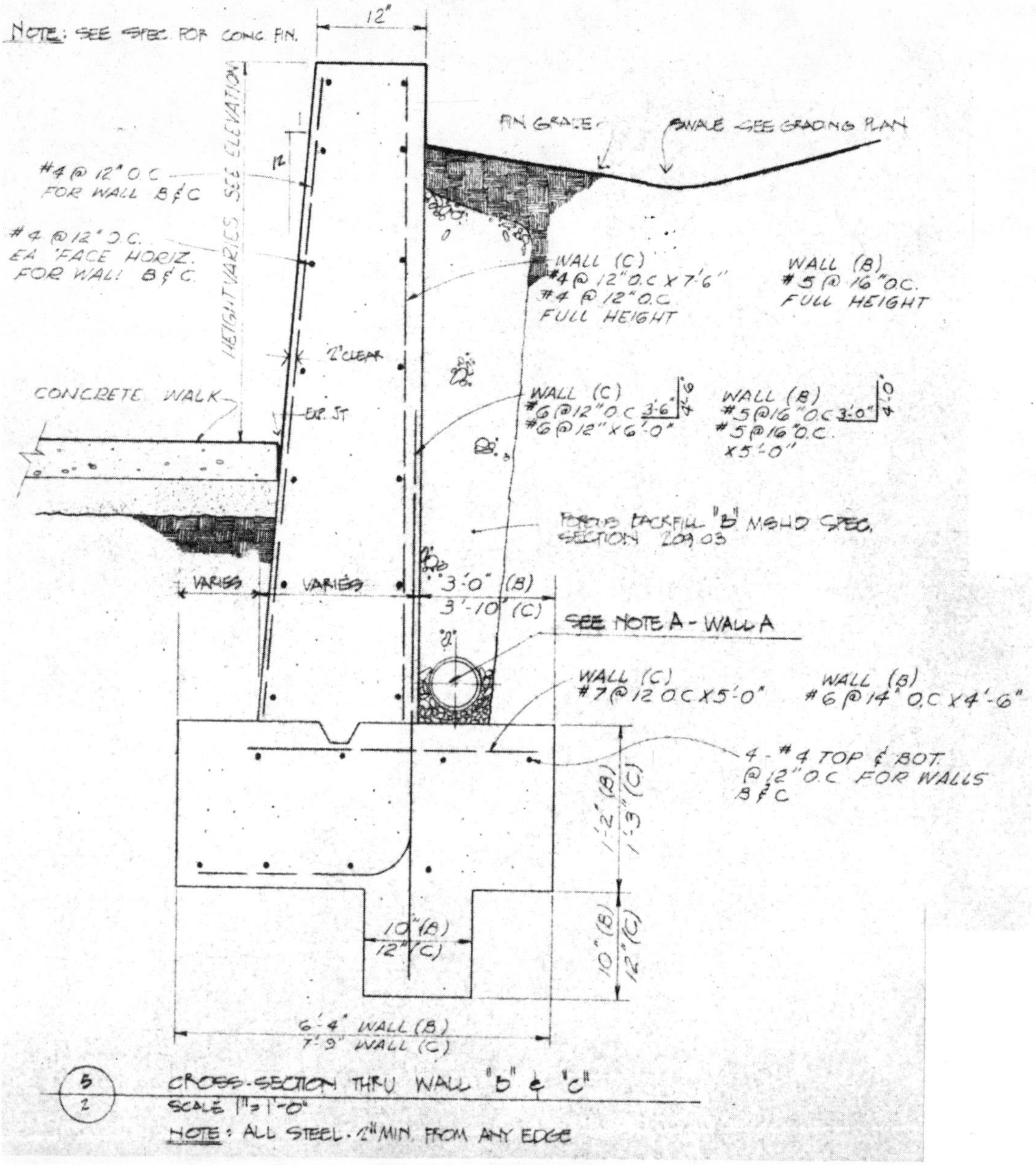

NOTE: SEE SPEC. FOR CONC. FIN.

12"

FIN GRADE

SWALE - SEE GRADING PLAN

#4 @ 12" O.C. FOR WALL B & C

#4 @ 12" O.C. EA. FACE HORIZ. FOR WALL B & C

HEIGHT VARIES SEE ELEVATION

WALL (C) #4 @ 12" O.C. X 7'-6" #4 @ 12" O.C. FULL HEIGHT

WALL (B) #5 @ 16" O.C. FULL HEIGHT

2" CLEAR

CONCRETE WALK

EXP. JT.

WALL (C) #6 @ 12" O.C. 3'-6" 4'-6" #6 @ 12" x 6'-0"

WALL (B) #5 @ 16" O.C. 3'-0" 4'-0" #5 @ 16" O.C. x 5'-0"

POROUS BACKFILL "B" MSHD SPEC. SECTION 209.03

VARIES VARIES 3'-0" (B) 3'-10" (C)

SEE NOTE A - WALL A

WALL (C) #7 @ 12 O.C. X 5'-0"

WALL (B) #6 @ 14" O.C. X 4'-6"

4 - #4 TOP & BOT. @ 12" O.C. FOR WALLS B & C

1'-2" (B) 1'-3" (C)

10" (B) 12" (C)

10" (B) 12" (C)

6'-4" WALL (B) 7'-9" WALL (C)

CROSS-SECTION THRU WALL "B" & "C"
SCALE 1" = 1'-0"
NOTE: ALL STEEL 2" MIN. FROM ANY EDGE

7.106

Johnson, Johnson and Roy

Figures 7.106 – 7.107 *Concrete retaining walls.*

7.107

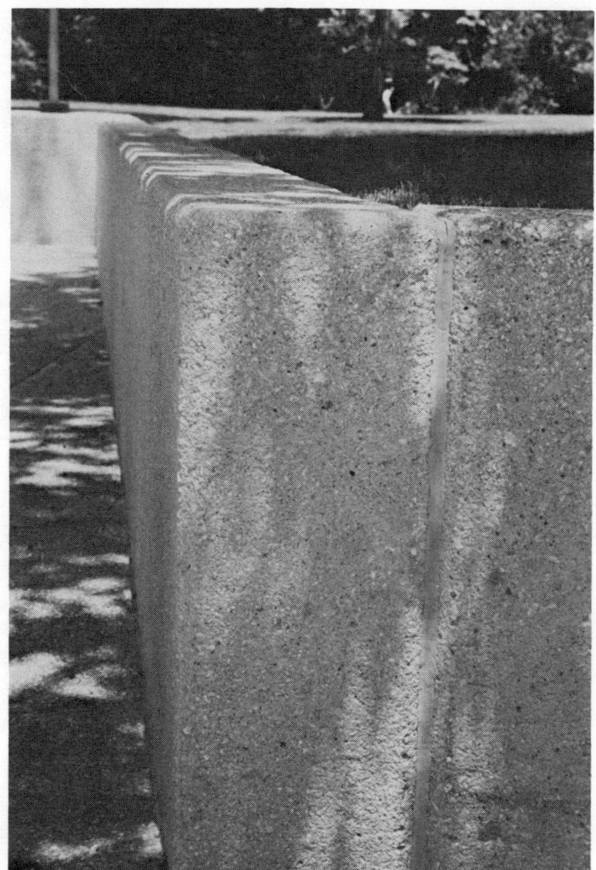

Figure 7.109 *Expansion joint with vinyl waterstop in center and gray urethane sealant. Sides of joint are beveled and corners are chamfered. Surface was textured with a bush-hammer.*

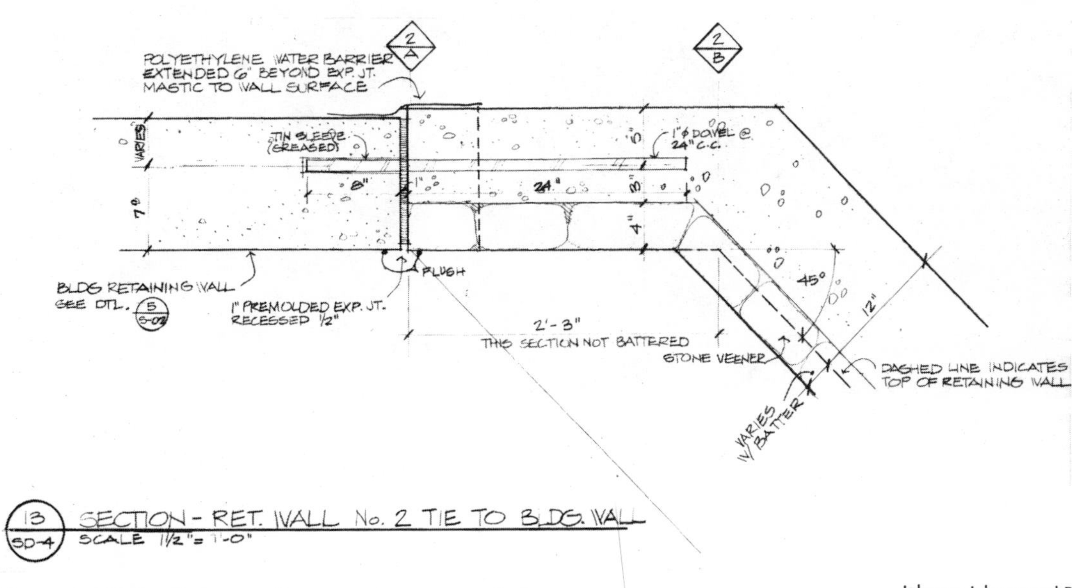

2
A
2
B
POLYETHYLENE WATER BARRIER
EXTENDED 6" BEYOND EXP. JT.
MASTIC TO WALL SURFACE
VARIES
TIN SLEEVE
(GREASED)
1"ϕ DOWEL @
24" C.C.
8"
1"
24"
3"
4"
7'
FLUSH
BLDG RETAINING WALL
SEE DTL. 5 S-02
1" PREMOLDED EXP. JT.
RECESSED ½"
2'-3"
THIS SECTION NOT BATTERED
STONE VEENER
45°
12"
DASHED LINE INDICATES
TOP OF RETAINING WALL
VARIES
W/ BATTER
13
SD-4
SECTION - RET. WALL No. 2 TIE TO BLDG. WALL
SCALE 1½" = 1'-0"

Johnson, Johnson and Roy

Figure 7.108 *Retaining wall joint utilzing steel dowel to control horizontal movement. Polyethylene water barrier is used in place of a waterstop which may be less effective, but the only choice possible when joining an existing wall.*

7.110

7.111

Figures 7.110 – 7.117 *Design variations in retaining walls.*

Figure 7.112 *Illustrates the aesthetic qualities of a terraced arrangement when space allows.*

7.112

7.115

7.113 Sasaki Associates

7.116 Environmental Planning and Design

7.114

7.117

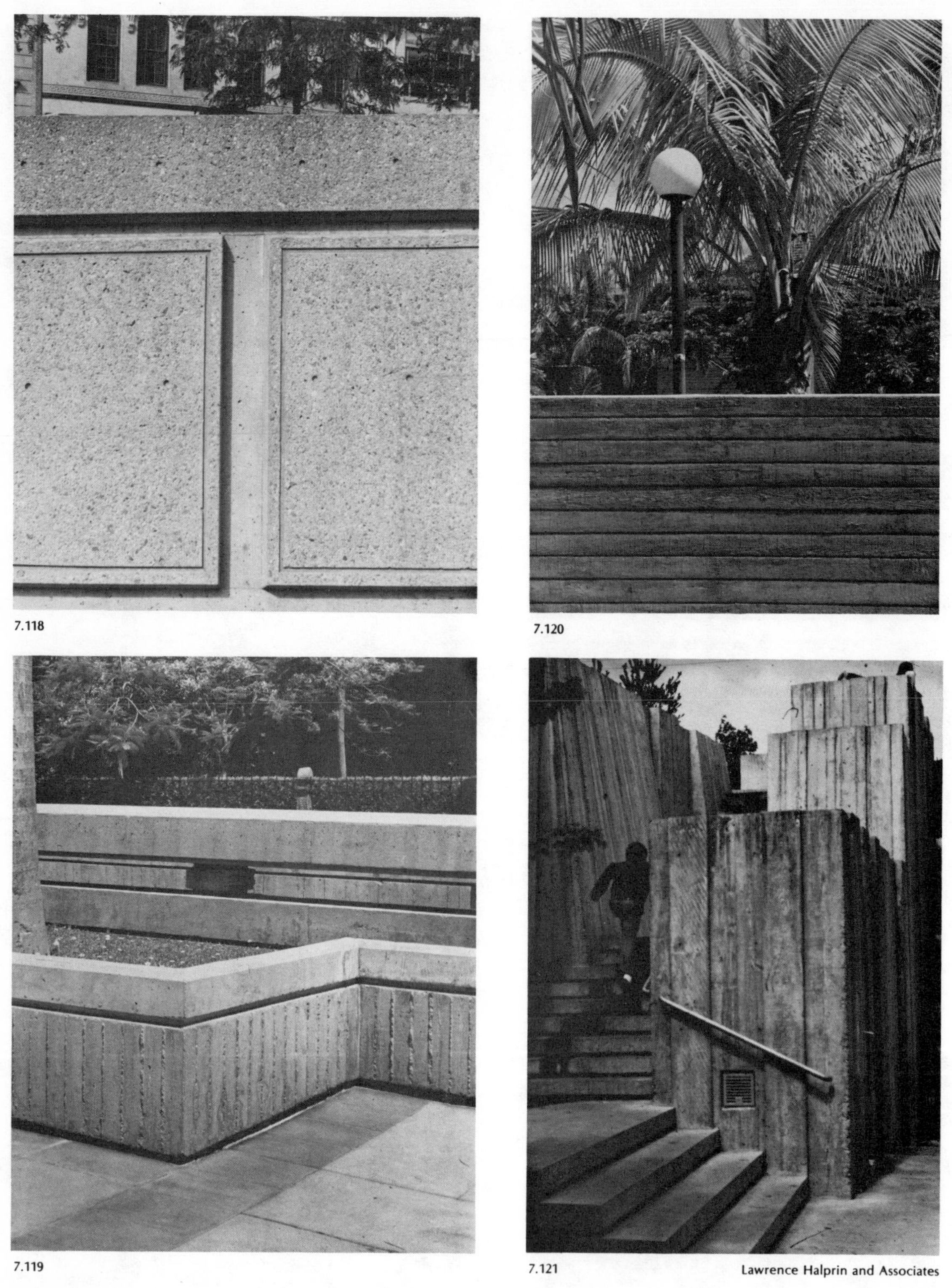

7.118

7.120

7.119

7.121 Lawrence Halprin and Associates

Figures 7.118 – 7.123 *Surface textures and shadow lines in concrete retaining walls.*

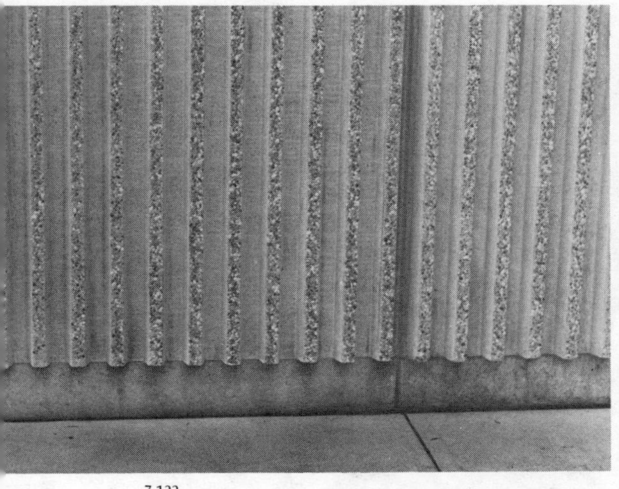
7.122

7.123

Figure 7.124 *Pre-cast concrete cylinders.* Betonwerk Munderkingen GmbH

7.125

7.127 Fairfax County Parks

7.126

7.128 Sverdrup and Parcel

Figure 7.125 *Stepped wall serves as seating for the adjacent plaza.*

Figure 7.126 *Terraced wood retaining walls.*

Figure 7.127 *Pre-cast concrete cribbing.*

Figure 7.128 *Play structure – retaining wall combination.*

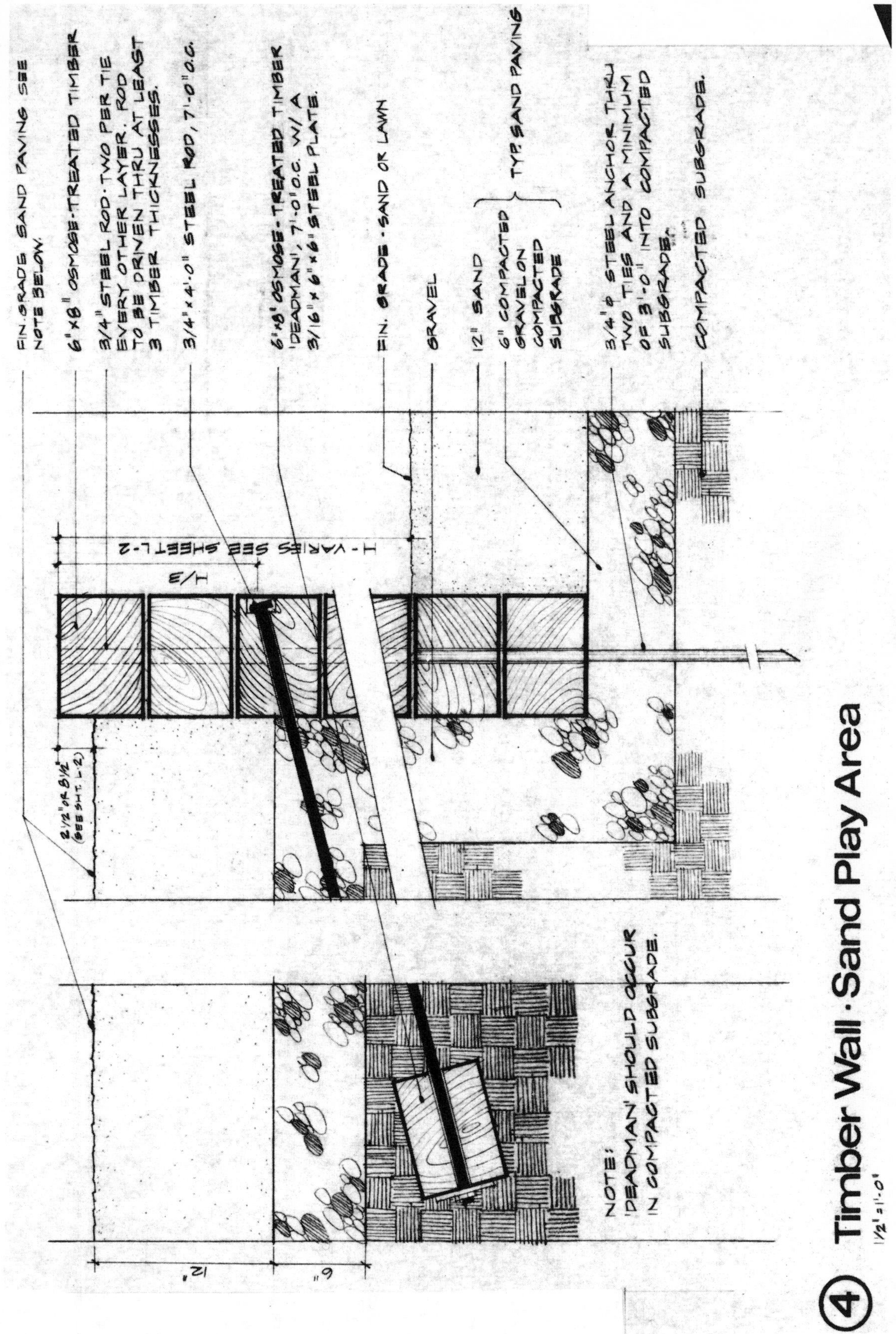
FIN. GRADE SAND PAVING SEE NOTE BELOW.
6"x8" OSMOSE-TREATED TIMBER
3/4" STEEL ROD: TWO PER TIE EVERY OTHER LAYER. ROD TO BE DRIVEN THRU AT LEAST 3 TIMBER THICKNESSES.
3/4"x4'-0" STEEL ROD, 7'-0" O.C.
6"x8' OSMOSE-TREATED TIMBER 'DEADMAN', 7'-0" O.C. W/ A 3/16"x6"x6" STEEL PLATE.
FIN. GRADE - SAND OR LAWN
GRAVEL
12" SAND
6" COMPACTED GRAVEL ON COMPACTED SUBGRADE
TYP. SAND PAVING
3/4"Ø STEEL ANCHOR THRU TWO TIES AND A MINIMUM OF 3'-0" INTO COMPACTED SUBGRADE.
COMPACTED SUBGRADE.
H-VARIES SEE SHEET L-2
H/3
2 1/2" OR 3 1/2" (SEE SHT. L-2)
12"
6"
NOTE: 'DEADMAN' SHOULD OCCUR IN COMPACTED SUBGRADE.
4 Timber Wall · Sand Play Area
1/2" = 1'-0"

Figure 7.129 *Wood retaining wall with deadman detail.*

CR3, inc.

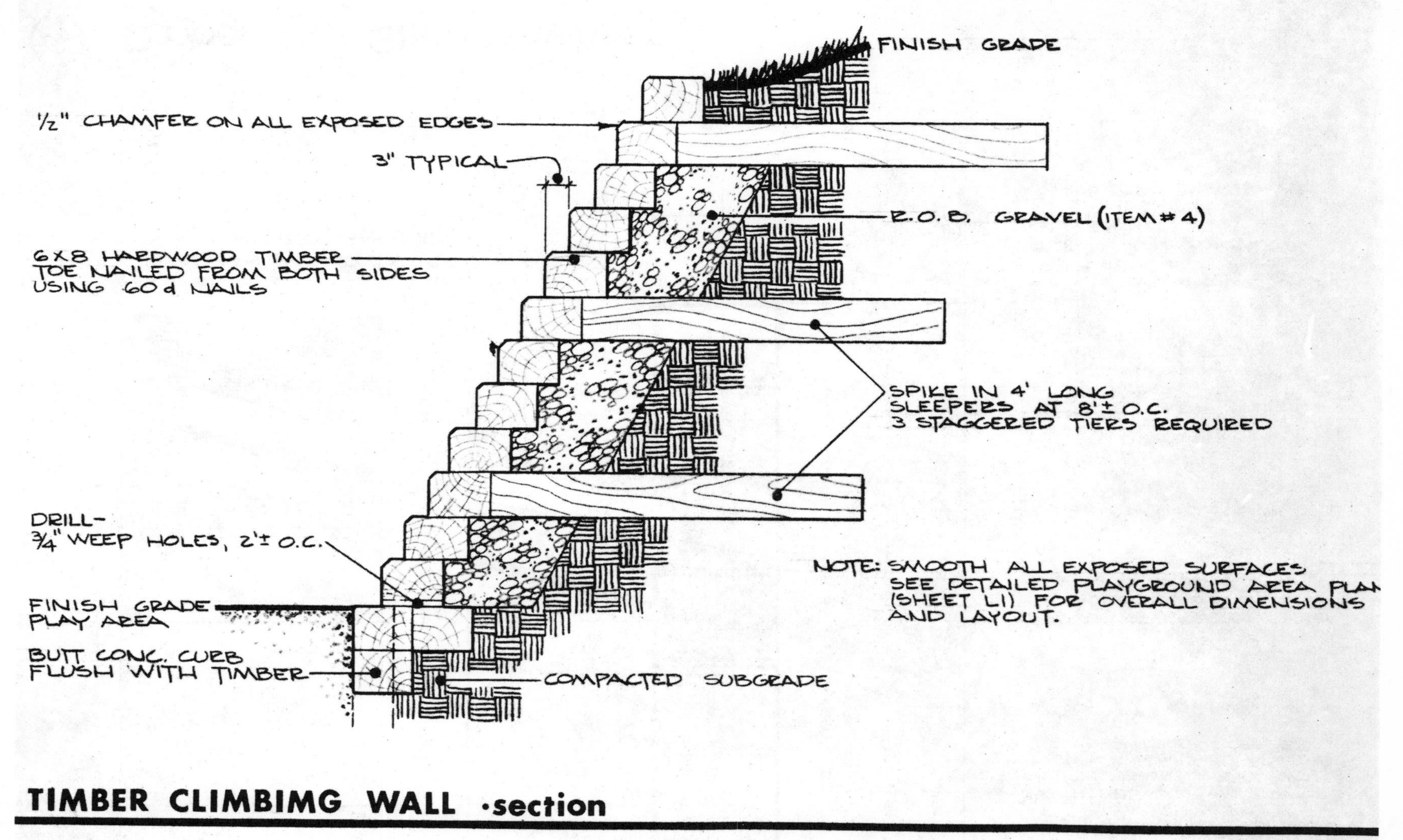

FINISH GRADE
1/2" CHAMFER ON ALL EXPOSED EDGES
3" TYPICAL
R.O.B. GRAVEL (ITEM # 4)
6X8 HARDWOOD TIMBER
TOE NAILED FROM BOTH SIDES
USING 60d NAILS
SPIKE IN 4' LONG
SLEEPERS AT 8'± O.C.
3 STAGGERED TIERS REQUIRED
DRILL-
3/4" WEEP HOLES, 2'± O.C.
NOTE: SMOOTH ALL EXPOSED SURFACES
SEE DETAILED PLAYGROUND AREA PLAN
(SHEET L1) FOR OVERALL DIMENSIONS
AND LAYOUT.
FINISH GRADE
PLAY AREA
BUTT CONC. CURB
FLUSH WITH TIMBER
COMPACTED SUBGRADE
TIMBER CLIMBIMG WALL ·section

Figure 7.130 *Wood retaining wall.*

Saratoga Associates

7.131

7.132 Browning-Day-Pollak-Associates—Inc.

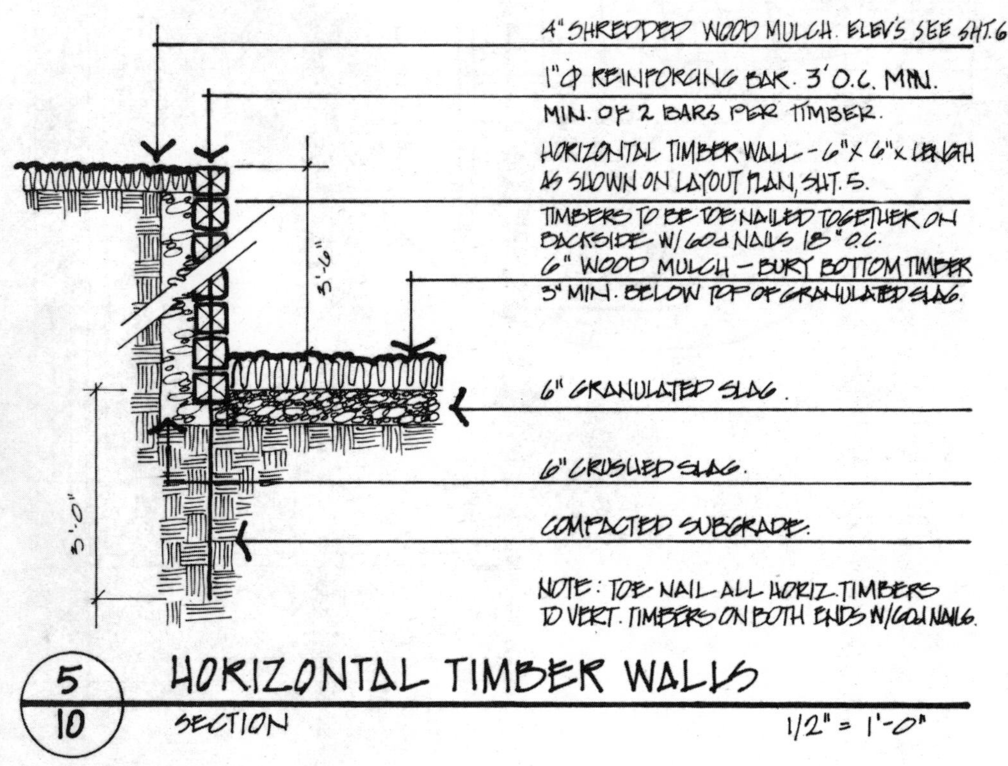
4" SHREDDED WOOD MULCH. ELEV'S SEE SHT. 6
1" ⌀ REINFORCING BAR. 3' O.C. MIN.
MIN. OF 2 BARS PER TIMBER.
HORIZONTAL TIMBER WALL - 6" x 6" x LENGTH
AS SHOWN ON LAYOUT PLAN, SHT. 5.
TIMBERS TO BE TOE NAILED TOGETHER ON
BACKSIDE W/ 60d NAILS 18" O.C.
6" WOOD MULCH - BURY BOTTOM TIMBER
3" MIN. BELOW TOP OF GRANULATED SLAG.
3'-6"
6" GRANULATED SLAG.
6" CRUSHED SLAG.
COMPACTED SUBGRADE.
3'-0"
NOTE: TOE NAIL ALL HORIZ. TIMBERS
TO VERT. TIMBERS ON BOTH ENDS W/ 60d NAILS.
5
10
HORIZONTAL TIMBER WALLS
SECTION
1/2" = 1'-0"

7.133

Figures 7.131 – 7.133 *Timber retaining walls.*

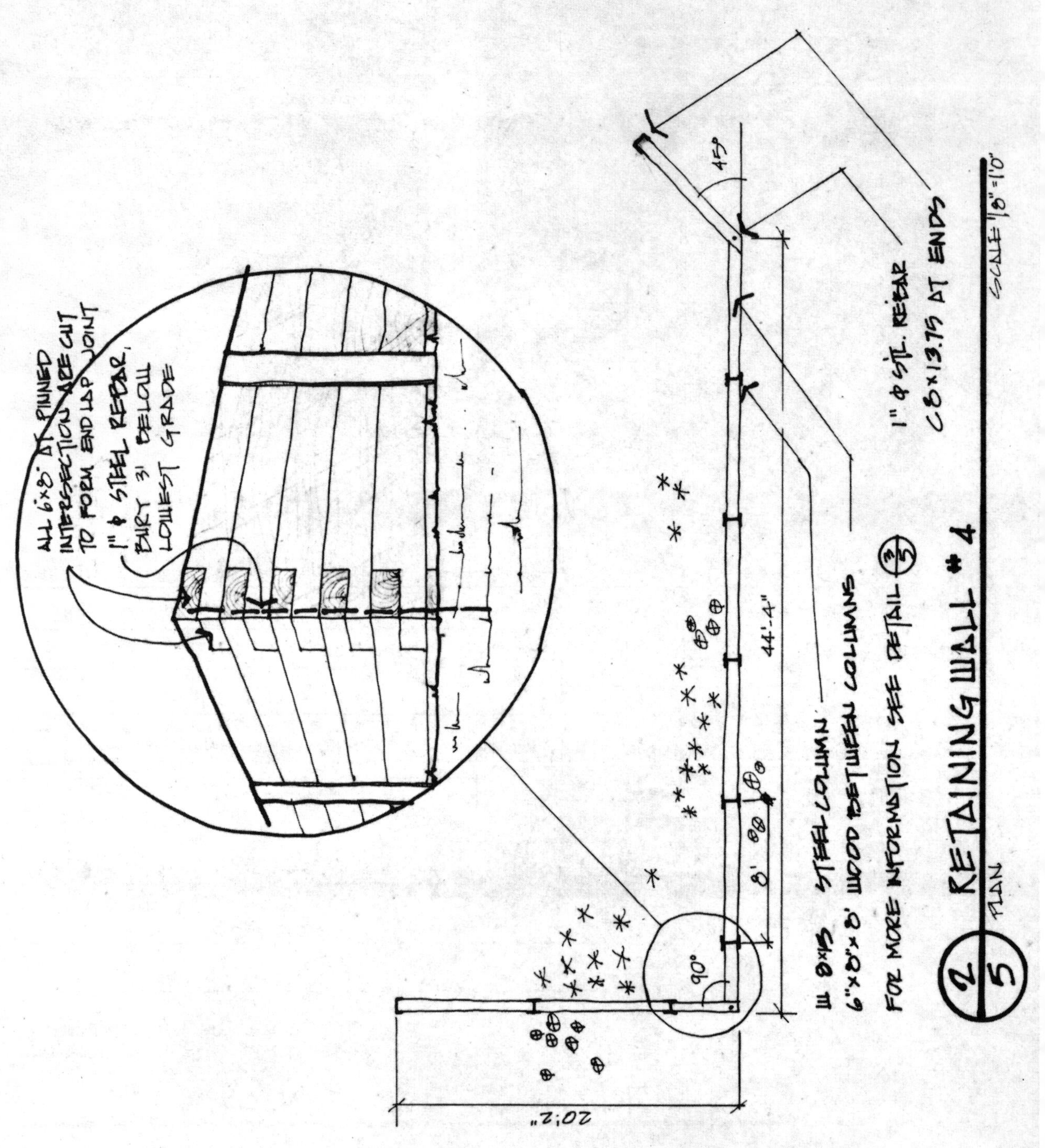

ALL 6x8' AT PINNED INTERSECTION ARE CUT TO FORM END LAP JOINT
1" φ STEEL REBAR, BURY 3' BELOW LOWEST GRADE
20'2"
90°
8'
44'-4"
45°
W 8x15 STEEL COLUMN
6"x8"x8' WOOD BETWEEN COLUMNS
1" φ STL. REBAR
C8x13.75 AT ENDS
FOR MORE INFORMATION SEE DETAIL 3/5
2/5
RETAINING WALL # 4
PLAN
SCALE 1/8"=1'0"

7.134

Bonnell and Associates

Figures 7.134 – 7.135 *Wood and steel retaining wall.*

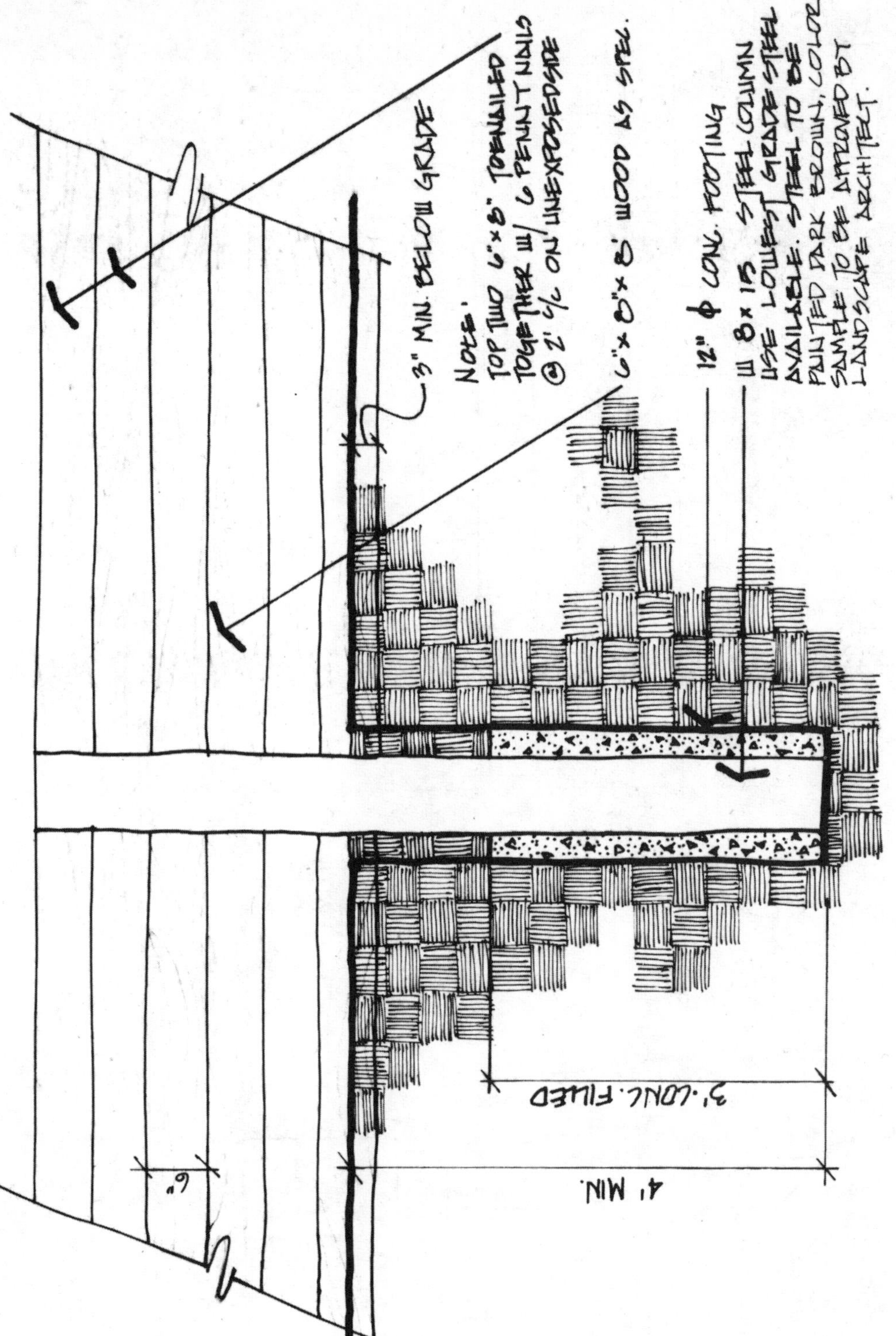
3" MIN. BELOW GRADE
NOTE:
TOP TWO 6"x8" TOENAILED TOGETHER W/ 6 PENNY NAILS @ 2' O/C ON UNEXPOSED SIDE
6"x8"x8' WOOD AS SPEC.
12" ϕ CONC. FOOTING
W 8x15 STEEL COLUMN USE LOWEST GRADE STEEL AVAILABLE. STEEL TO BE PAINTED DARK BROWN, COLOR SAMPLE TO BE APPROVED BY LANDSCAPE ARCHITECT.
NO SCALE
3' CONC. FILLED
4' MIN.
6"
3
5
RETAINING WALL
SECTION/ELEVATION

7.135

Bonnell and Associates

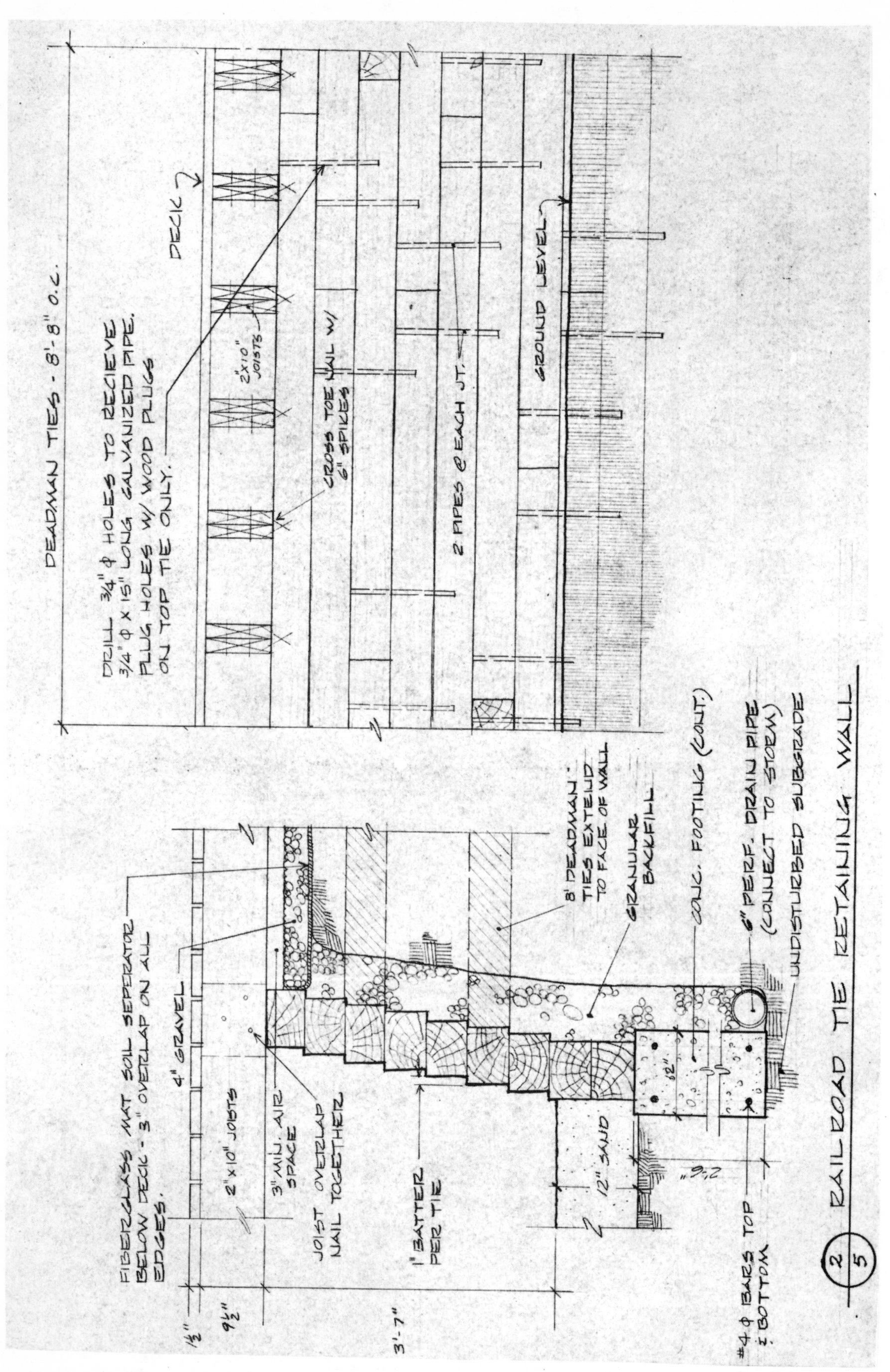
DEADMAN TIES - 8'-8" O.C.
DRILL 3/4" φ HOLES TO RECIEVE 3/4" φ X 15" LONG GALVANIZED PIPE. PLUG HOLES W/ WOOD PLUGS ON TOP TIE ONLY.
DECK
2"X10" JOISTS
CROSS TOE NAIL W/ 6" SPIKES
2 PIPES @ EACH JT.
GROUND LEVEL
FIBERGLASS MAT SOIL SEPERATOR BELOW DECK - 3" OVERLAP ON ALL EDGES.
4" GRAVEL
2"X10" JOISTS
3" MIN. AIR SPACE
JOIST OVERLAP NAIL TOGETHER
1" BATTER PER TIE
12" SAND
8' DEADMAN TIES EXTEND TO FACE OF WALL
GRANULAR BACKFILL
CONC. FOOTING (CONT.)
6" PERF. DRAIN PIPE (CONNECT TO STORM)
UNDISTURBED SUBGRADE
#4 φ BARS TOP & BOTTOM
1½"
9½"
3'-7"
2/5
RAILROAD TIE RETAINING WALL

Figures 7.136 – 7.137 *Retaining wall details.*

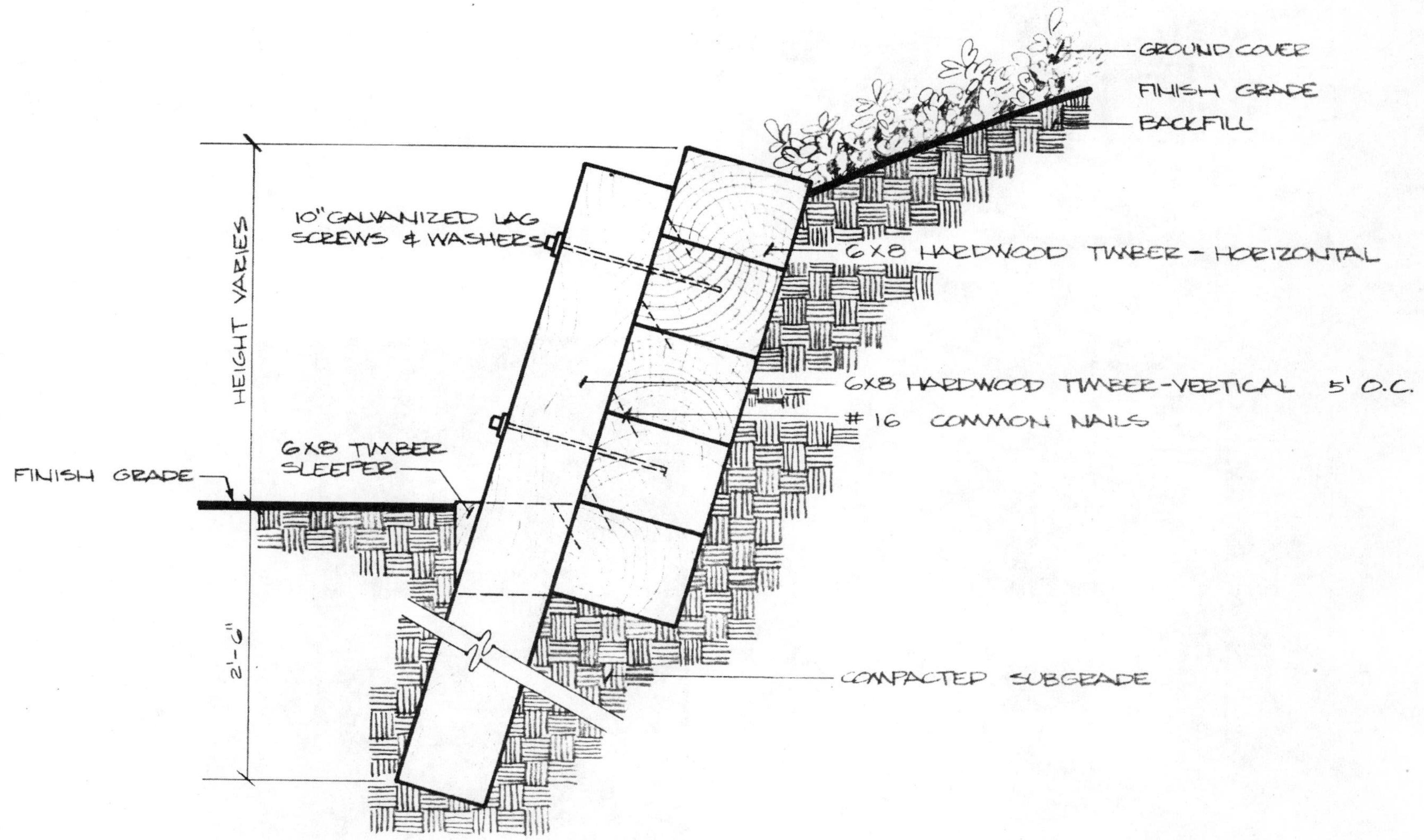

GROUND COVER
FINISH GRADE
BACKFILL
HEIGHT VARIES
10" GALVANIZED LAG SCREWS & WASHERS
6X8 HARDWOOD TIMBER - HORIZONTAL
6X8 HARDWOOD TIMBER-VERTICAL 5' O.C.
#16 COMMON NAILS
6X8 TIMBER SLEEPER
FINISH GRADE
2'-6"
COMPACTED SUBGRADE

TIMBER RETAINING WALL

SCALE: 1½" = 1'-0"

7.138

Sverdrup and Parcel

7.139

Bailey and Associates

Figure 7.138 *Timber retaining wall with buttresses.*
Figure 7.139 *Timber retaining wall with deadmen.*

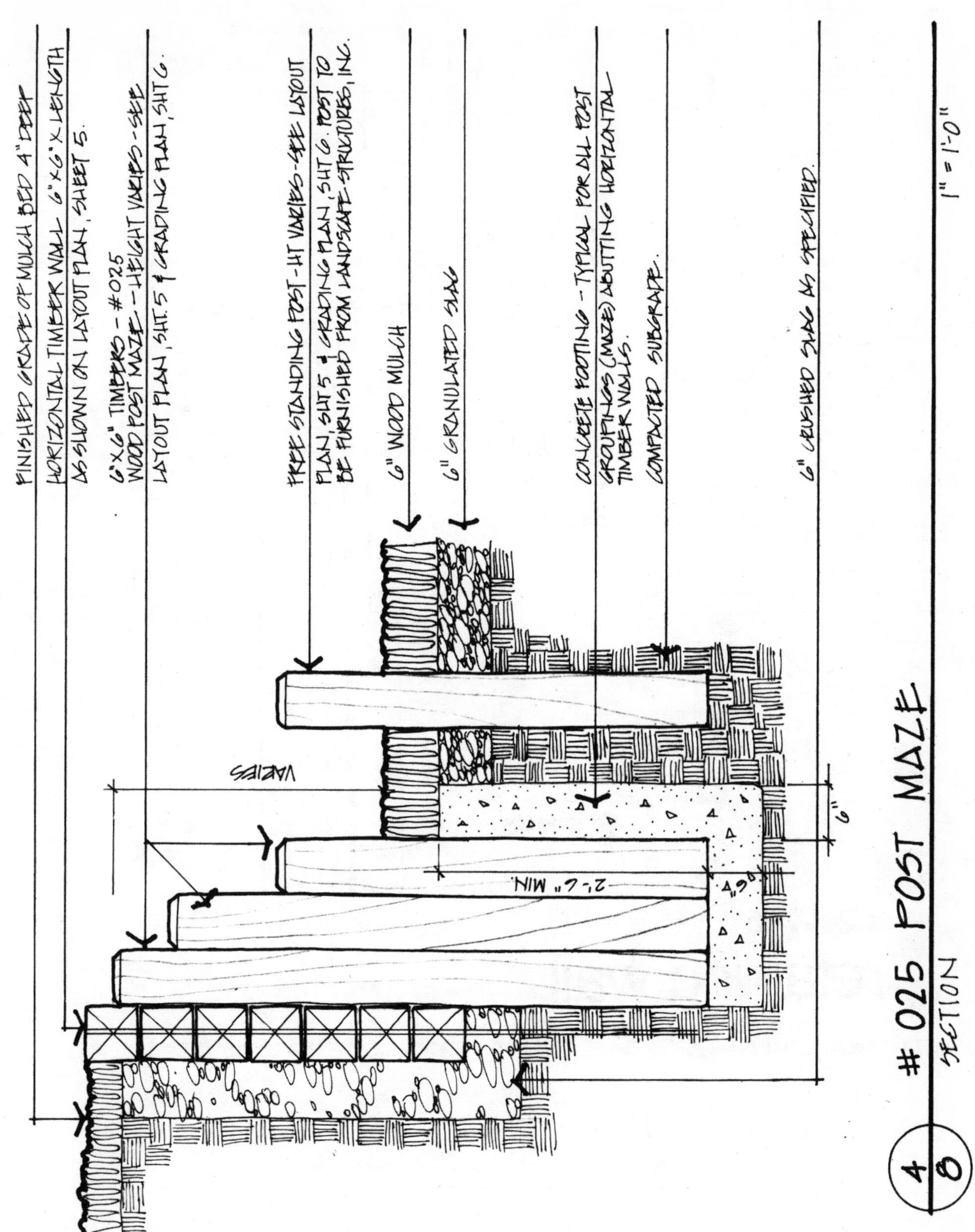
FINISHED GRADE OF MULCH BED 4" DEEP
HORIZONTAL TIMBER WALL 6"x6" x LENGTH AS SHOWN ON LAYOUT PLAN, SHEET 5.
6"x6" TIMBERS - #025 WOOD POST MAZE - HEIGHT VARIES - SEE LAYOUT PLAN, SHT. 5 & GRADING PLAN, SHT 6.
FREE STANDING POST - HT VARIES - SEE LAYOUT PLAN, SHT 5 & GRADING PLAN, SHT 6. POST TO BE FURNISHED FROM LANDSCAPE STRUCTURES, INC.
6" WOOD MULCH
6" GRANULATED SLAG
CONCRETE FOOTING - TYPICAL FOR ALL POST GROUPINGS (MAZE) ABUTTING HORIZONTAL TIMBER WALLS.
COMPACTED SUBGRADE.
6" CRUSHED SLAG AS SPECIFIED.
VARIES
2'-6" MIN.
6"
4
8
#025 POST MAZE
SECTION
1" = 1'-0"

Figure 7.140 *Retaining wall detail.*

Bonnell and Associates

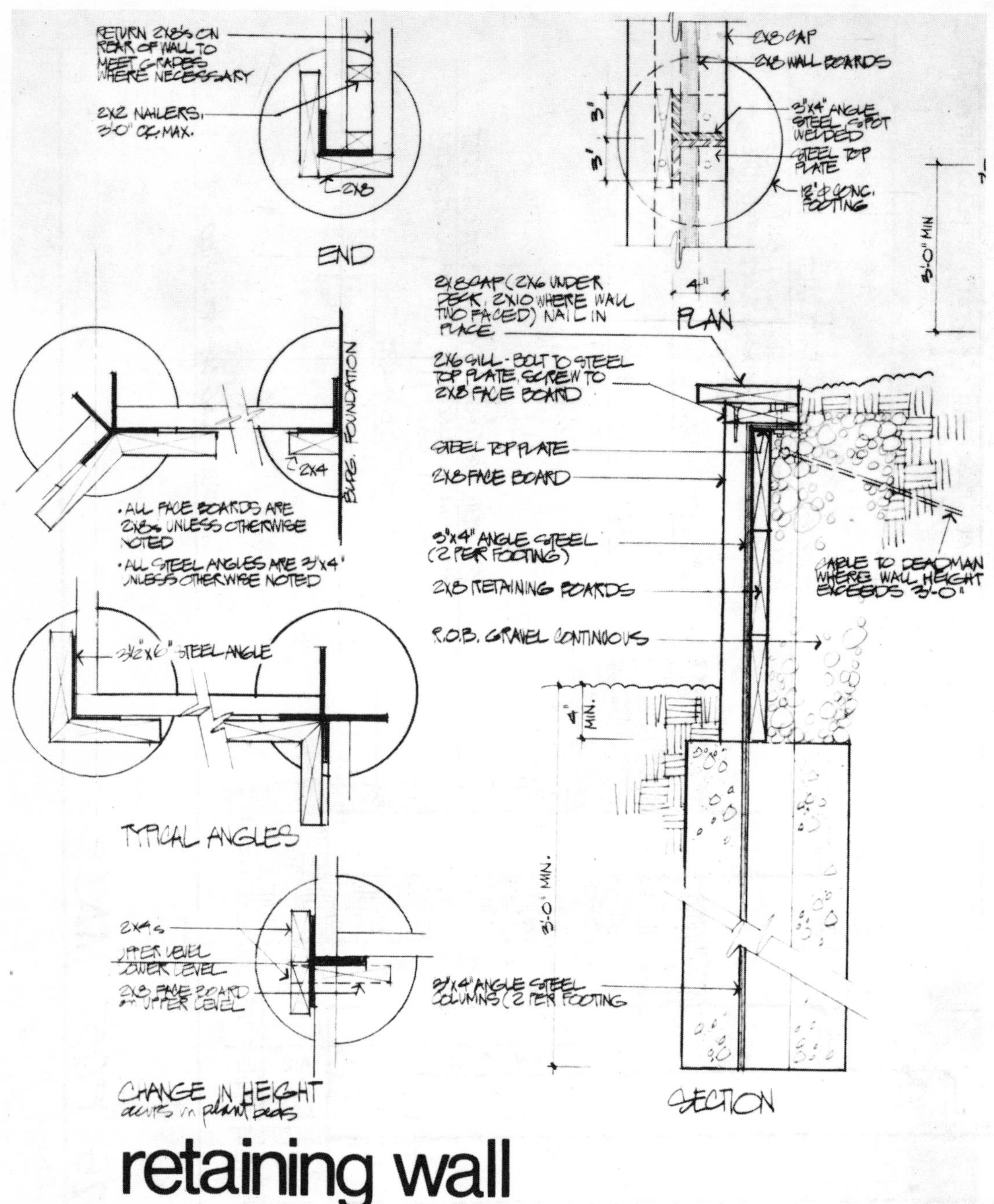
RETURN 2X8'S ON REAR OF WALL TO MEET GRADES WHERE NECESSARY
2X2 NAILERS, 3'-0" O.C. MAX.
2X8
END
2X8 CAP
2X8 WALL BOARDS
3"x4" ANGLE STEEL SPOT WELDED
STEEL TOP PLATE
12" ⌀ CONC. FOOTING
3'
3'
4"
PLAN
3'-0" MIN
2X8 CAP (2X6 UNDER DECK, 2X10 WHERE WALL TWO FACED) NAIL IN PLACE
2X6 SILL - BOLT TO STEEL TOP PLATE, SCREW TO 2X8 FACE BOARD
STEEL TOP PLATE
2X8 FACE BOARD
3"x4" ANGLE STEEL (2 PER FOOTING)
2X8 RETAINING BOARDS
R.O.B. GRAVEL CONTINUOUS
CABLE TO DEADMAN WHERE WALL HEIGHT EXCEEDS 3'-0"
4" MIN.
3'-0" MIN.
3"x4" ANGLE STEEL COLUMNS (2 PER FOOTING)
SECTION
BLDG. FOUNDATION
2X4
• ALL FACE BOARDS ARE 2X8's UNLESS OTHERWISE NOTED
• ALL STEEL ANGLES ARE 3"x4" UNLESS OTHERWISE NOTED
3½"x6" STEEL ANGLE
TYPICAL ANGLES
2X4's
UPPER LEVEL
LOWER LEVEL
2X8 FACE BOARD AT UPPER LEVEL
CHANGE IN HEIGHT
occurs in plant beds
retaining wall

Figure 7.141 *Retaining wall details.*

Reimann/Buechner Partnership

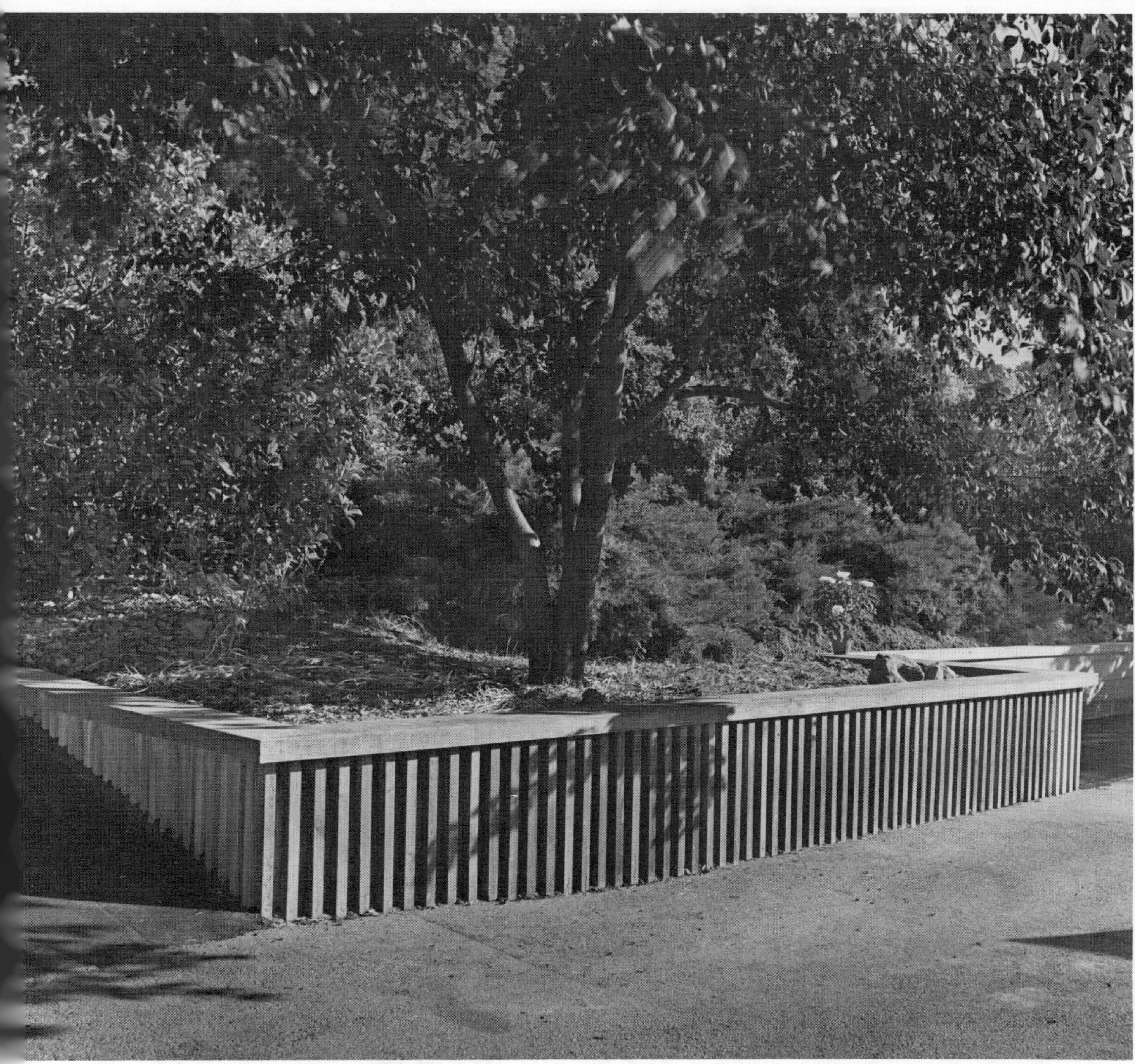

Figure 7.142 *Wood retaining wall.*

Barbeau Engh, Courtesy of California Redwood Association

7.143

7.144

Figure 7.143 – 7.147 *Retaining walls and details.*

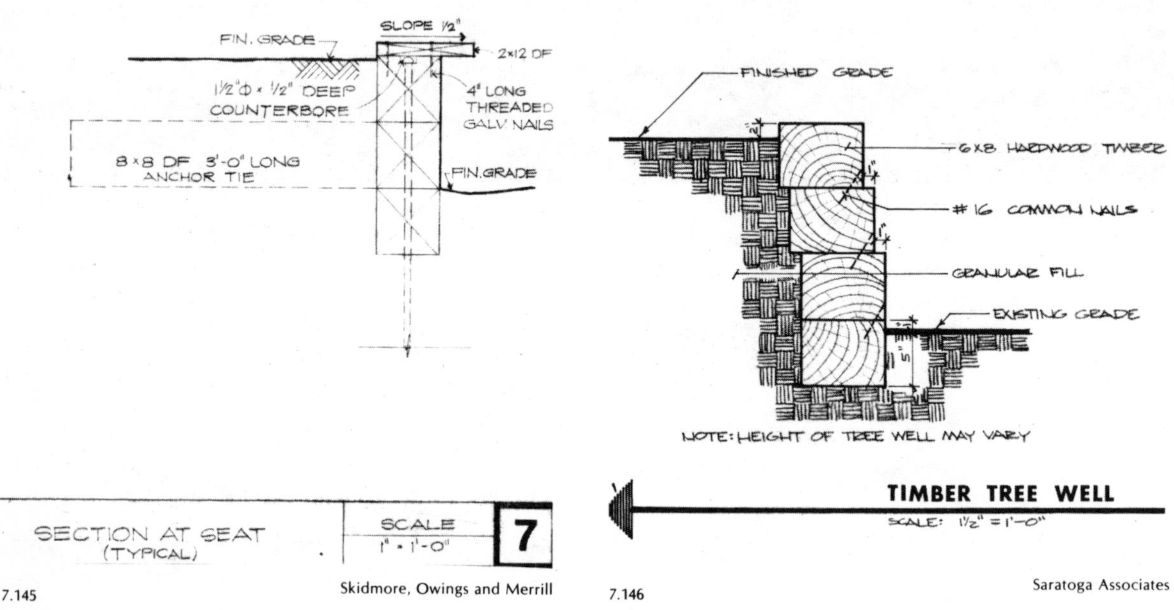
SLOPE ½"
FIN. GRADE
2×12 DF
1½"Φ × ½" DEEP COUNTERBORE
4" LONG THREADED GALV. NAILS
8×8 DF 3'-0" LONG ANCHOR TIE
FIN. GRADE
SECTION AT SEAT (TYPICAL)
SCALE 1" = 1'-0"
7
FINISHED GRADE
6×8 HARDWOOD TIMBER
#16 COMMON NAILS
GRANULAR FILL
EXISTING GRADE
NOTE: HEIGHT OF TREE WELL MAY VARY
TIMBER TREE WELL
SCALE: 1½" = 1'-0"

7.145 Skidmore, Owings and Merrill

7.146 Saratoga Associates

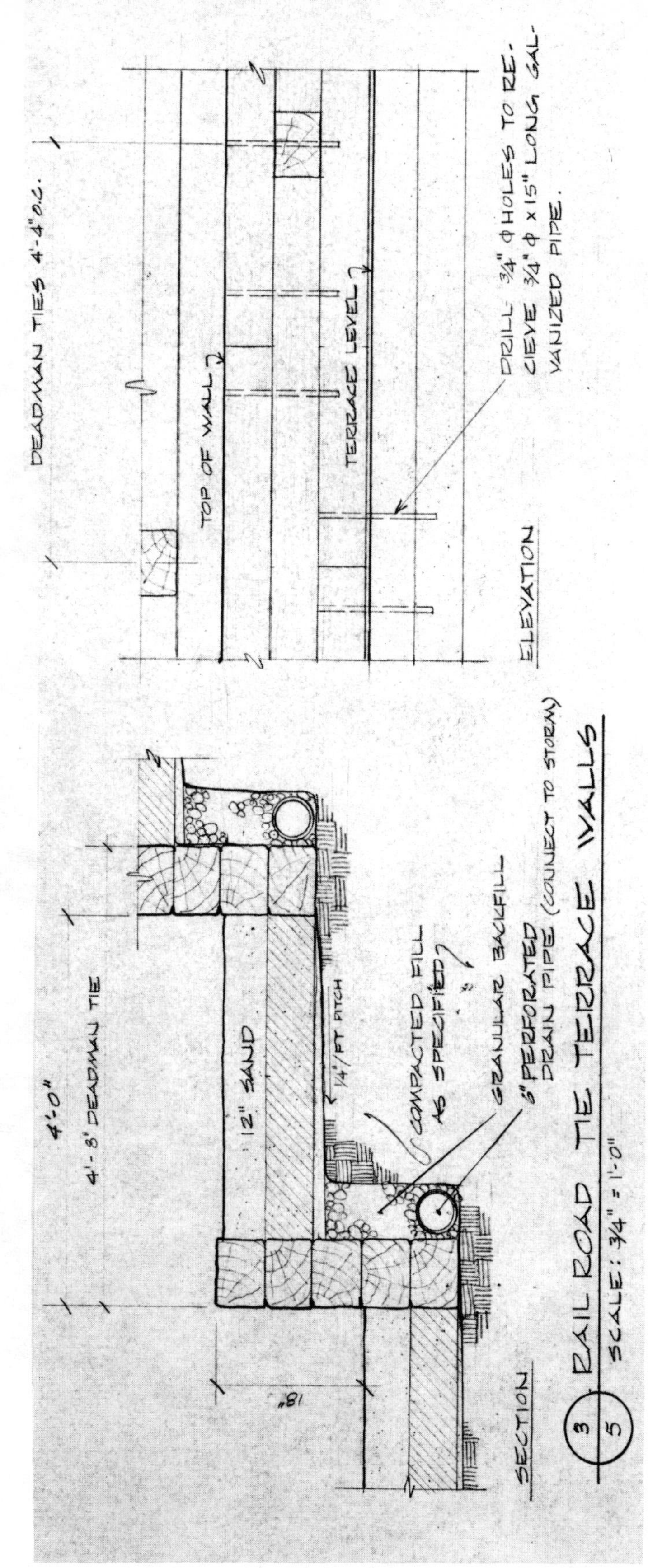
DEADMAN TIES 4'-4" O.C.
TOP OF WALL
TERRACE LEVEL
DRILL 3/4" ϕ HOLES TO RE-
CIEVE 3/4" ϕ x 15" LONG GAL-
VANIZED PIPE.
ELEVATION
4'-0"
4'-8" DEADMAN TIE
12" SAND
1/4"/FT PITCH
COMPACTED FILL
AS SPECIFIED
GRANULAR BACKFILL
6" PERFORATED
DRAIN PIPE (CONNECT TO STORM)
18"
SECTION
3
5
RAIL ROAD TIE TERRACE WALLS
SCALE: 3/4" = 1'-0"

7.147

Johnson, Johnson and Roy

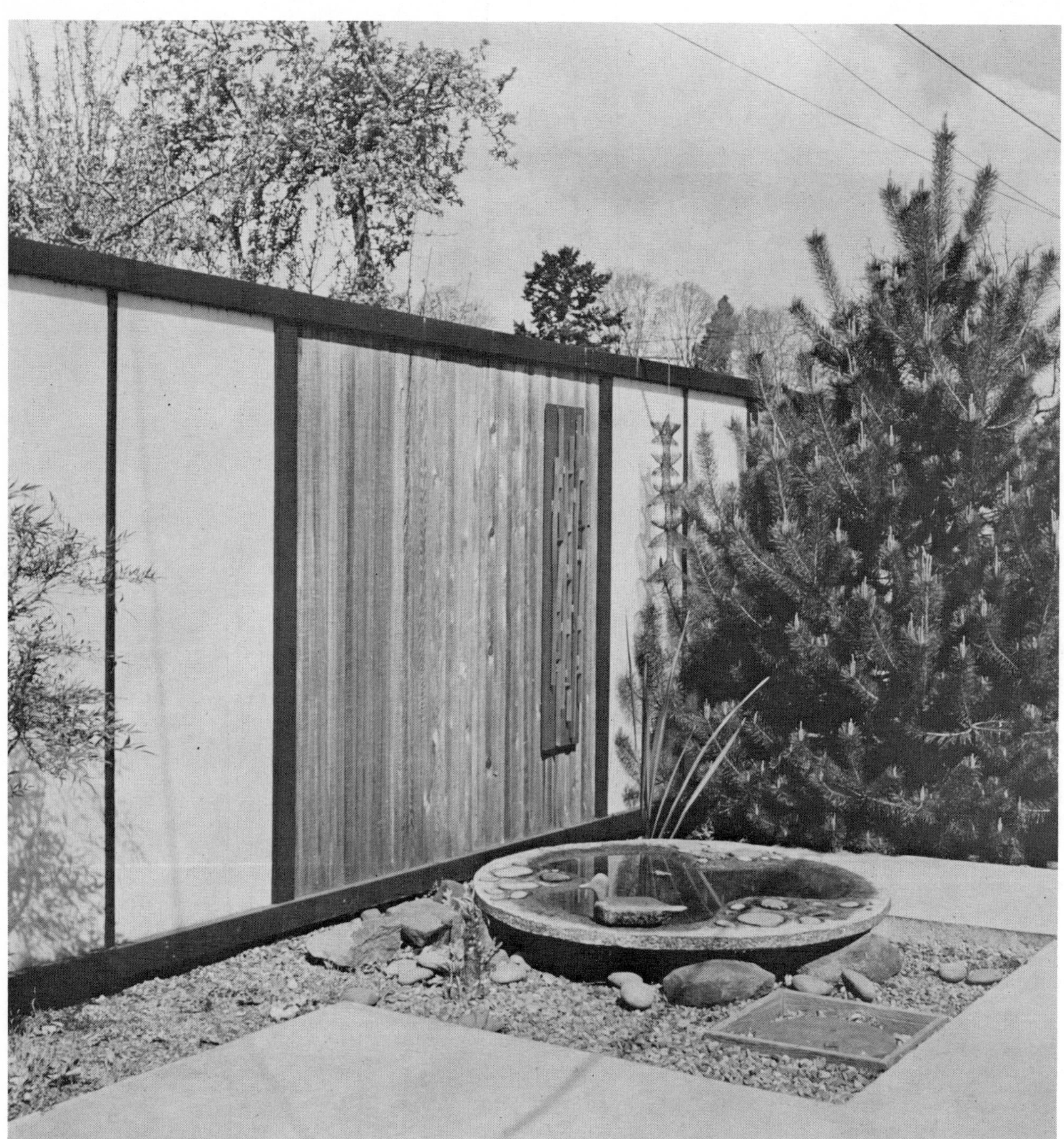

Tom Burns, courtesy of Western Wood Products Association

Figure 8.1 *Custom designed wood fence.*

James and Bonnie Bartell

8

Fences

Fences serve to provide privacy (when solid), discourage trespassing, reduce wind and modify climate, control human and animal traffic, define property lines, identify and emphasize entrances, and create and define outdoor space.

Many styles and designs can be created from both wood and metal, which are the most commonly used materials in fencing. Metal fences include chainlink, wrought iron, and pipe. Wrought iron is highly ornamental and used in classic design situations, though it has some comtemporary applications as well. Chainlink is quite common and in many situations can be classified as incompatible and unsightly. It consists of woven fabric made of heavy gauge (9 or 11) galvanized steel wire and galvanized steel pipes for posts and rails. Some manufactures offer vinyl coatings for color, and slats which can be inserted in the fabric to provide privacy. Chainlink fences are common where security is needed and at industrial sites.

Wood is a natural material which harmonizes with most sites, and there are many creative ways it can be used in fence design. The design should conform to local regulations, if there are any.

A design will be influenced by whether a fence is to be merely a physical barrier or a visual barrier. Four feet of height may be enough for a physical barrier, while six feet on level ground will provide visual privacy. Whether the fence will need to pass air or be air tight is a question the designer will need to answer.

The fence may be highly decorative and a work of art in and of itself or a simple structure acting as a backdrop for planting or a unifying force for other portions of the design.

The materials which make up a wood fence include posts, rails, boards, and fasteners. There is economy in using standard lumber dimensions.

Posts may be typically four by four's in an eight-foot length (a common size), though for short fences 12 foot lengths cut in half might be used. For short fences which pass air to a 2 to 2½ foot depth of bury for the post below finished grade may be adequate, wherease 3 feet are needed for 6-foot fences, and more should be used for fences which are higher. Merely tamping the soil around the post in its hole is not adequate where soil is soft, or is made soft by springthaws, or where high winds occur. In the case of solid fences 6 feet in height, a 12-inch-diameter hole with the posts completely surrounded with concrete for the full depth is recommended in order to provide sufficient resistance to wind. Adding some gravel to the bottom of the post hole will aid in leveling and provide a pocket for excess moisture away from the wood.

Besides being set into holes, posts may also be set on top of concrete walls or 12-inch-diameter concrete columns by using steel angles or double straps, which are set into the concrete and bolted to the post.

If the design of the fence calls for the rails to be laid flat rather than on edge, spacing for the posts at 6 feet or closer is recommended in order to prevent sagging of the rail. When spacing posts 8 feet apart, 2 x 4 rails on edge generally will not sag. Rather than butting the rail to the post and toenailing, it is better to either dado the post and insert the railing into the dado or cross lap the rail on the side of the post and nail directly into the post. Butting and toenailing do not provide sufficient strength and structural integrity for the fence.

All nails and fastenings should be galvanized or otherwise corrosion resistant.

The boards which are attached to the rails may be of any number of sizes and character; flat boards 4 inches in width and up to 12 inches in width may be used, though 6 and 8 inches are the most common. There are also a wide variety of pickets, grape stakes, and other narrow materials which also can be nailed to the rails. For short fences, two rails are usually adequate, whereas three rails should be used for fences 6 feet or more in height to prevent warping and movement of the boards.

If a gate is needed it can be designed to harmonize with the design of the fence. Structurally it will be a square or retangular frame with a diagonal brace running from the top of the frame on the latch side down to the opposite corner near the hinges. Such hardware as hinges, and latches should be of sturdy quality and resistant to weathering and corrosion. The post to which the gate is attached may need to be larger and/or deeper in order to make it sturdy enough to handle the extra strain.

Fences constructed of redwood or cedar may be allowed to weather to their natural gray color, or they can be stained or painted. Other types of woods will need to be stained or painted on a regular basis unless they have been pressure treated with a preservative such as pentachlorophenol or chromated copper arsenate. Painting and staining will, in most instances, increase long term maintenance costs and if not properly maintained can become rather unsightly as it begins to wear off.

When space allows, there are other techniques which can be utilized for reinforcing fences against wind damage. This involves the use of offsets spaced periodically in the fence or buttresses. In either case, a two-foot width seems to be the most effective as a minimum.

REFERENCES FOR FURTHER READING

Rouse Co. "Fences," *Handbook of Landscape Architectural Construction*. Washington, DC: Landscape Architecture Foundation, 1973.

Ramsey, C.G., and Sleeper, H.R. *Architectural Graphics Standards*. 7th Edition. New York: Wiley, 1981.

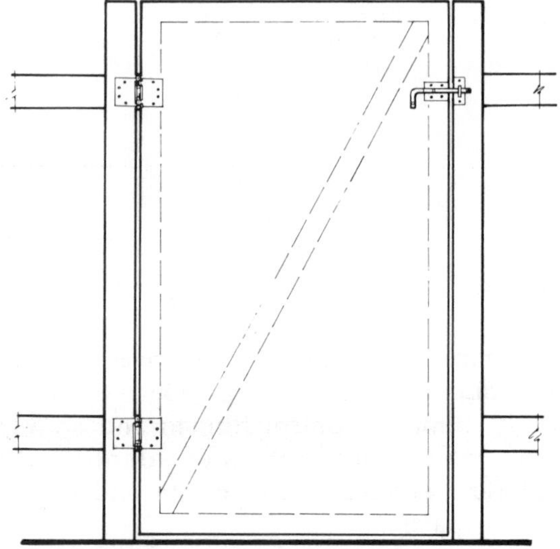

Figure 8.2 *Correct position for a diagonal brace in a gate.*

Figure 8.3 *Steel frame for a wood gate. Note position of bracing.*

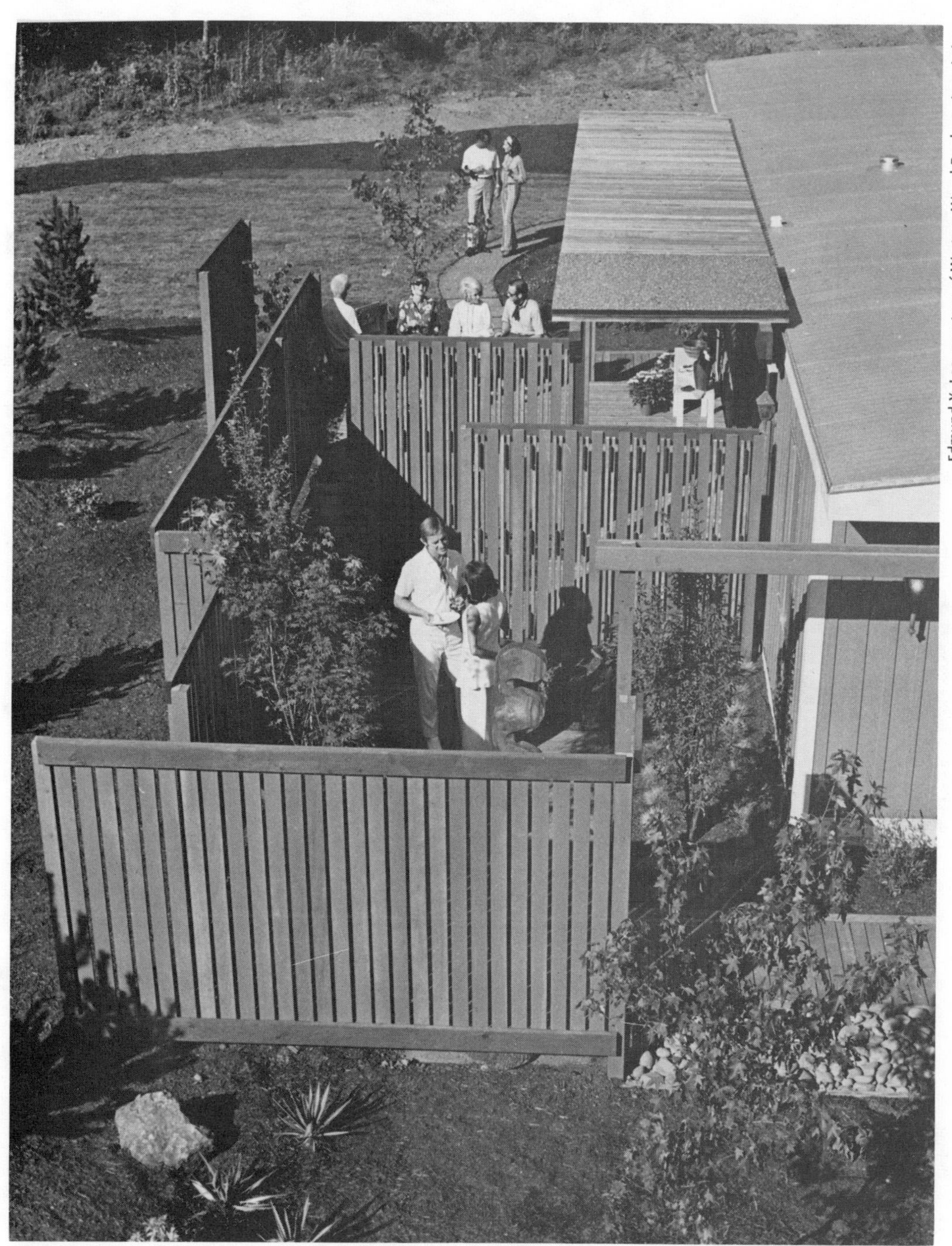

Edmund Y. Lee, courtesy of Western Wood Products Association

Alex Pierce, Environment 21/E. A. Maddox

Figure 8.4 *Fences add interest to otherwise drab mobile home developments as they create varying spaces and provide privacy.*

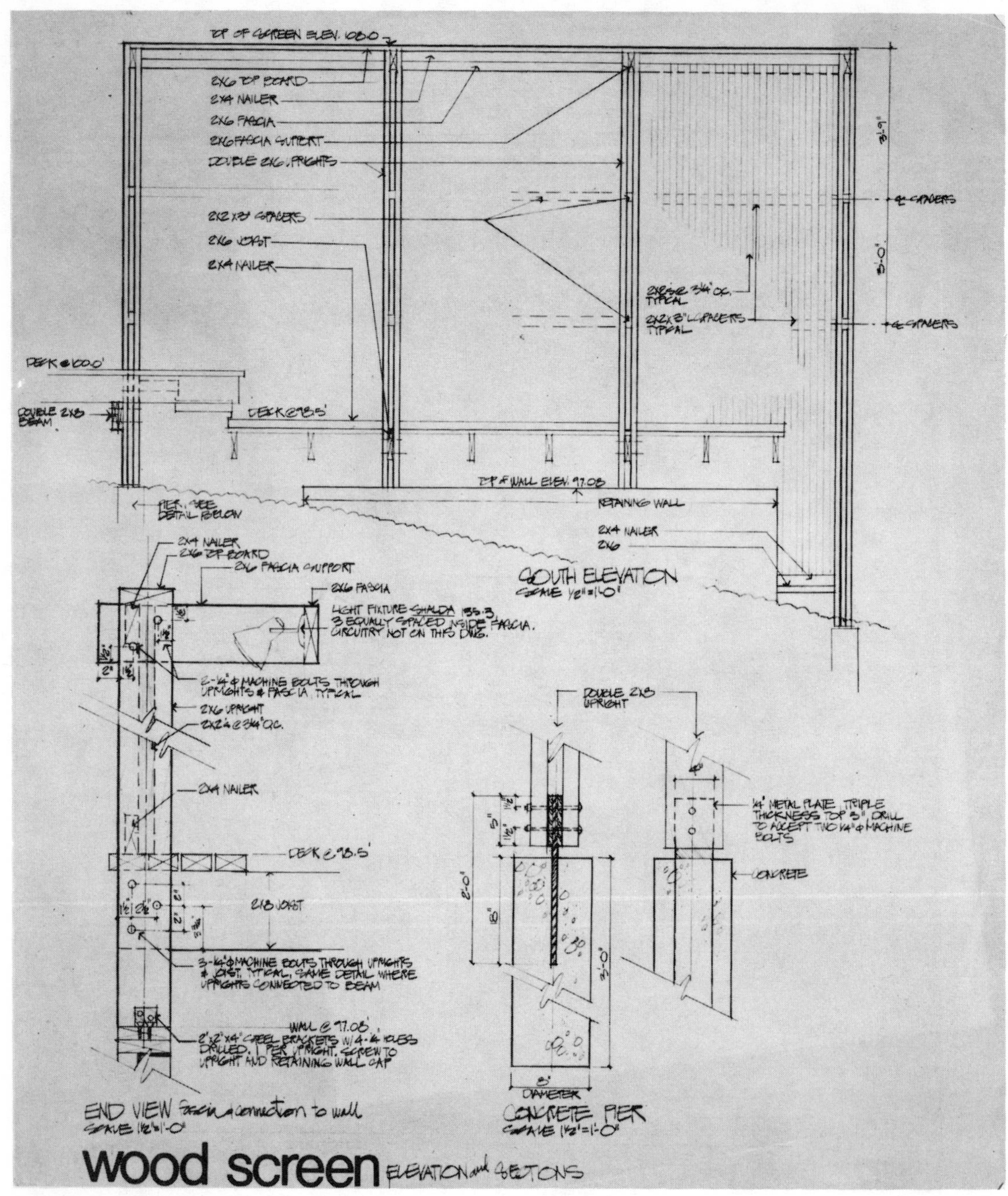
SOUTH ELEVATION
END VIEW
CONCRETE PIER
wood screen

Figure 8.5 *Fence details.*

Reimann/Buechner Partnership

8.6

8.7

8.8

Figures 8.6 – 8.8 *Wood fences in a variety of designs.*

8.9

8.12

2875

8.10

8.13

8.11

8.14

Figures 8.9 – 8.18 *Variety of designs for wood fences.*

8.15

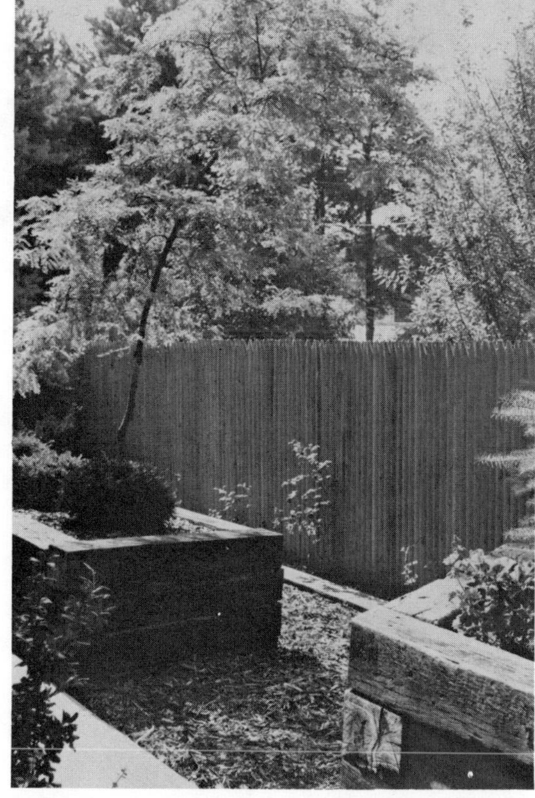

8.16 LaPorte County Landscaping

8.17 LaPorte County Landscaping

8.18 LaPorte County Landscaping

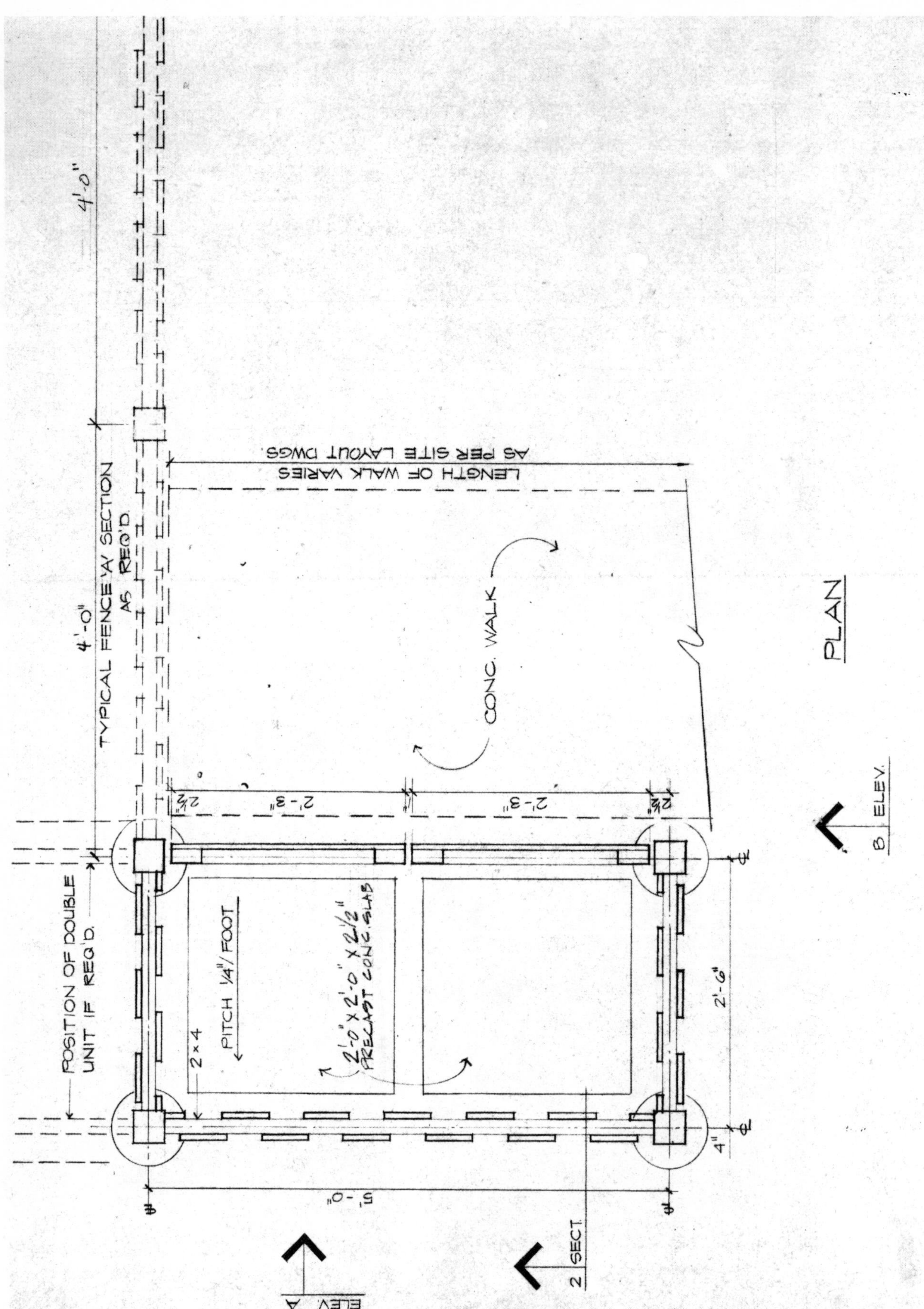
POSITION OF DOUBLE UNIT IF REQ'D.
TYPICAL FENCE 'A' SECTION AS REQ'D.
4'-0"
4'-0"
LENGTH OF WALK VARIES AS PER SITE LAYOUT DWGS.
CONC. WALK
PLAN
2'-3"
2'-3"
2x4
PITCH 1/4"/FOOT
2'-0" x 2'-0" x 2 1/2" PRECAST CONC. SLAB
2'-6"
4"
5'-0"
2 SECT.
B ELEV.
ELEV. A

Figure 8.19 *Plan for a wood fence.*

Skidmore, Owings and Merrill

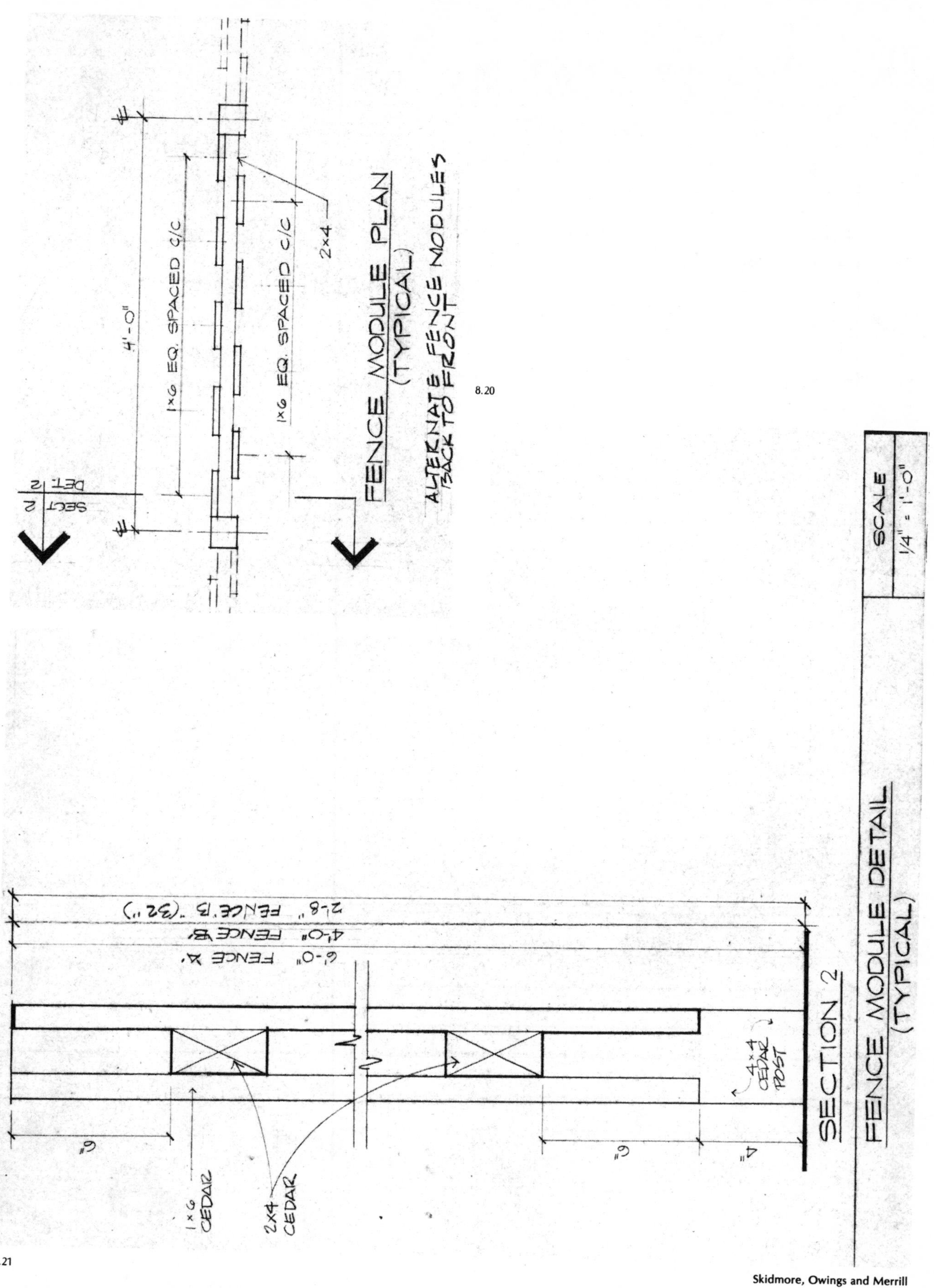
FENCE MODULE PLAN
(TYPICAL)
ALTERNATE FENCE MODULES BACK TO FRONT
4'-0"
1×6 EQ. SPACED C/C
1×6 EQ. SPACED C/C
2×4
SECT 2
DET. 2
SECTION 2
FENCE MODULE DETAIL
(TYPICAL)
SCALE
1/4" = 1'-0"
1×6 CEDAR
2×4 CEDAR
4×4 CEDAR POST
6"
6"
4"

8.20

8.21

Skidmore, Owings and Merrill

Figures 8.20 – 8.21 *Fence details.*

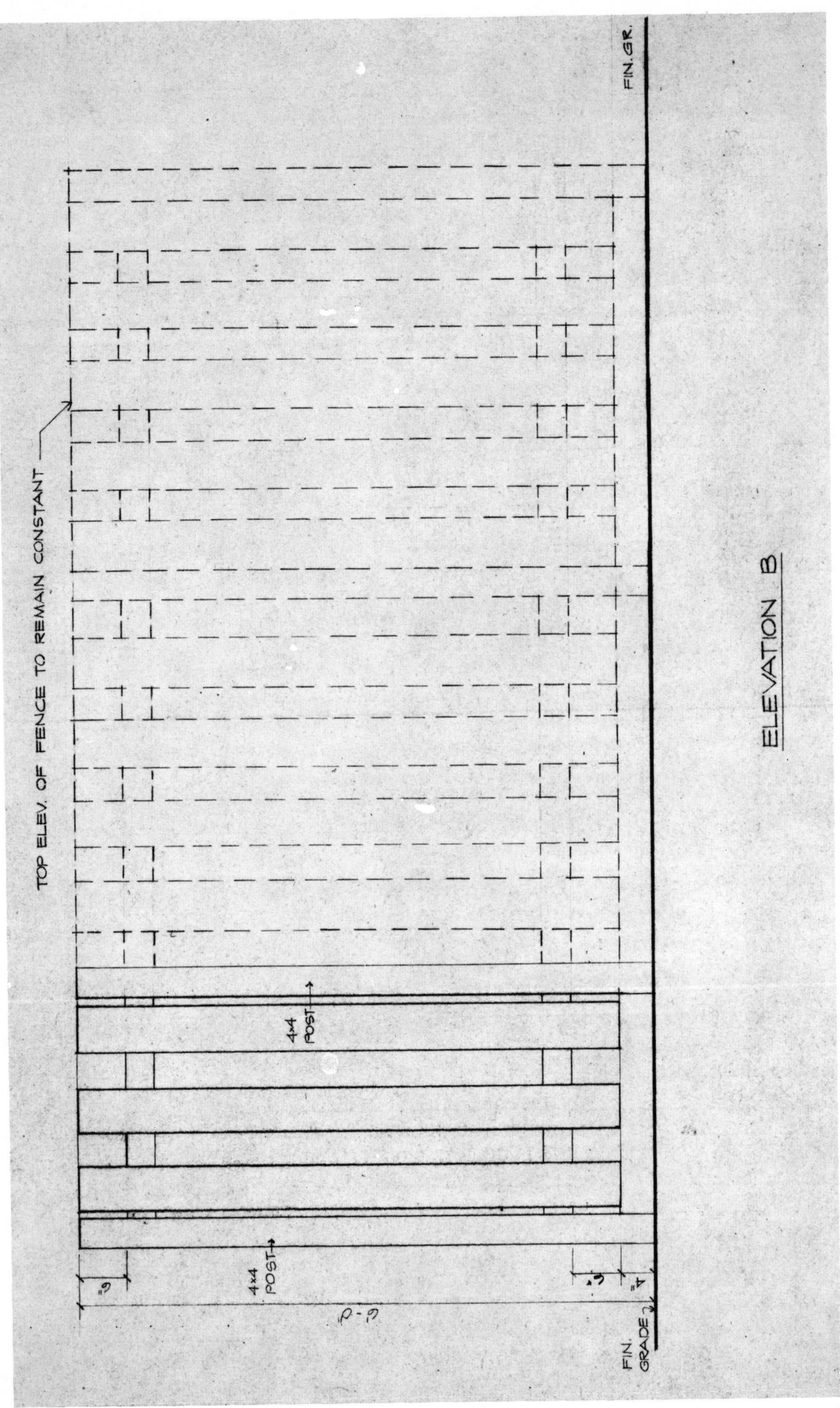
TOP ELEV. OF FENCE TO REMAIN CONSTANT
FIN. GR.
4x4 POST
4x4 POST
FIN. GRADE
ELEVATION B

Figure 8.22 *Elevation view of a wood fence.*

Skidmore, Owings and Merrill

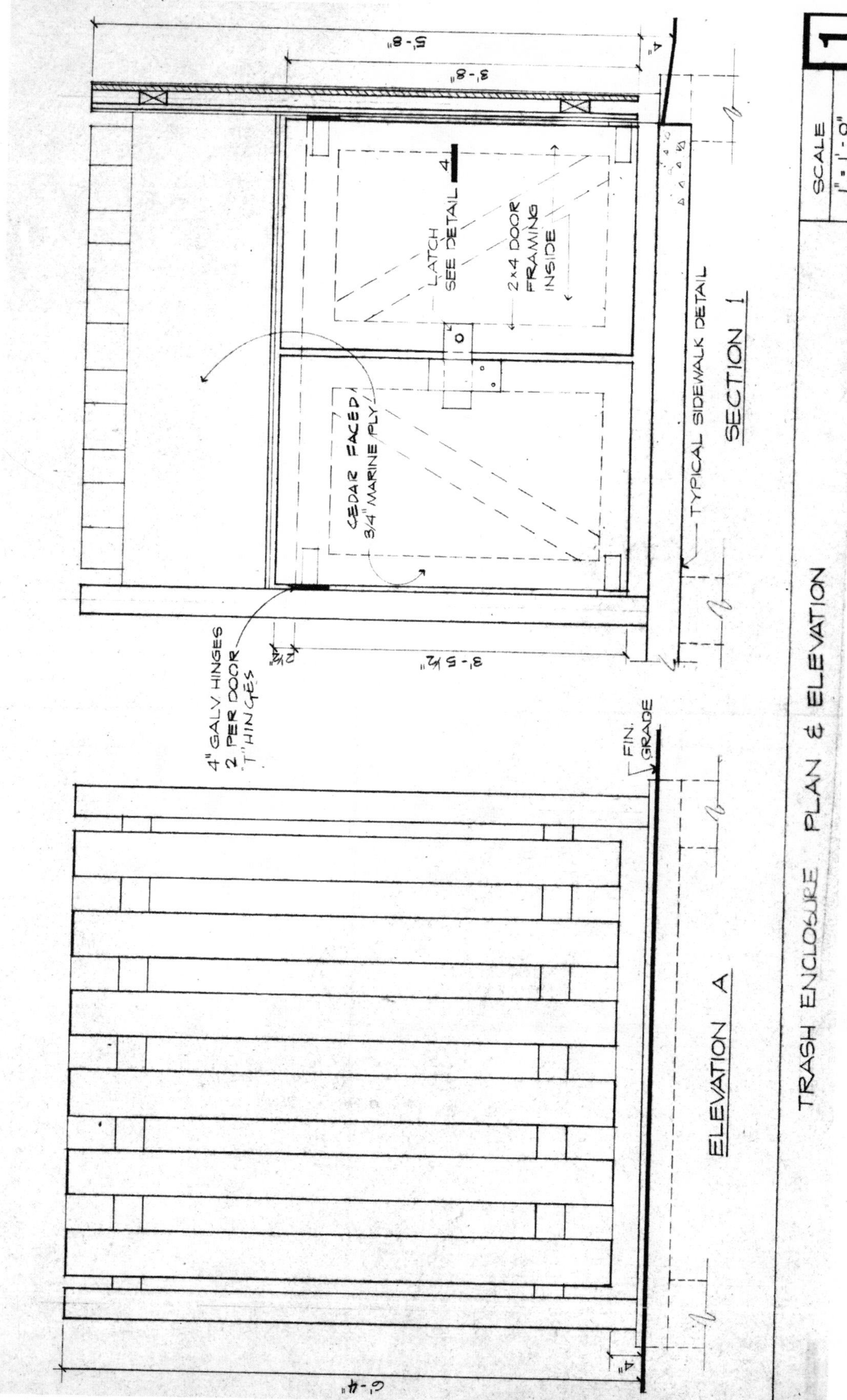
TRASH ENCLOSURE PLAN & ELEVATION
SCALE 1" = 1'-0"
1
ELEVATION A
SECTION 1
TYPICAL SIDEWALK DETAIL
FIN. GRADE
4" GALV HINGES
2 PER DOOR
"T" HINGES
CEDAR FACED
3/4" MARINE PLY
LATCH
SEE DETAIL 4
2x4 DOOR
FRAMING
INSIDE
5'-8"
3'-8"
3'-5 1/2"
6'-4"
4"

Figure 8.23 *Wood fence elevation and gate details.*

Skidmore, Owings and Merrill

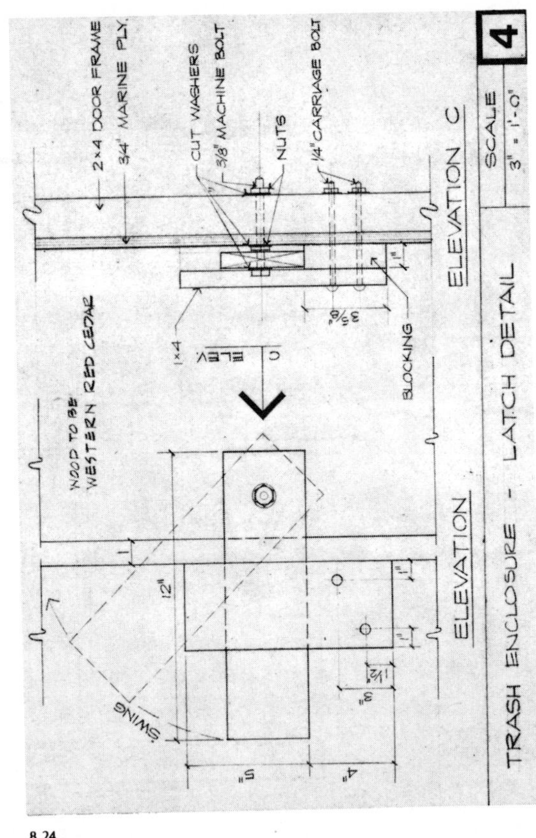

WOOD TO BE WESTERN RED CEDAR
2×4 DOOR FRAME
3/4" MARINE PLY.
CUT WASHERS
3/8" MACHINE BOLT
NUTS
1/4" CARRIAGE BOLT
1×4
ELEV C
BLOCKING
SWING
ELEVATION
ELEVATION C
TRASH ENCLOSURE - LATCH DETAIL
SCALE 3" = 1'-0"
4

8.24

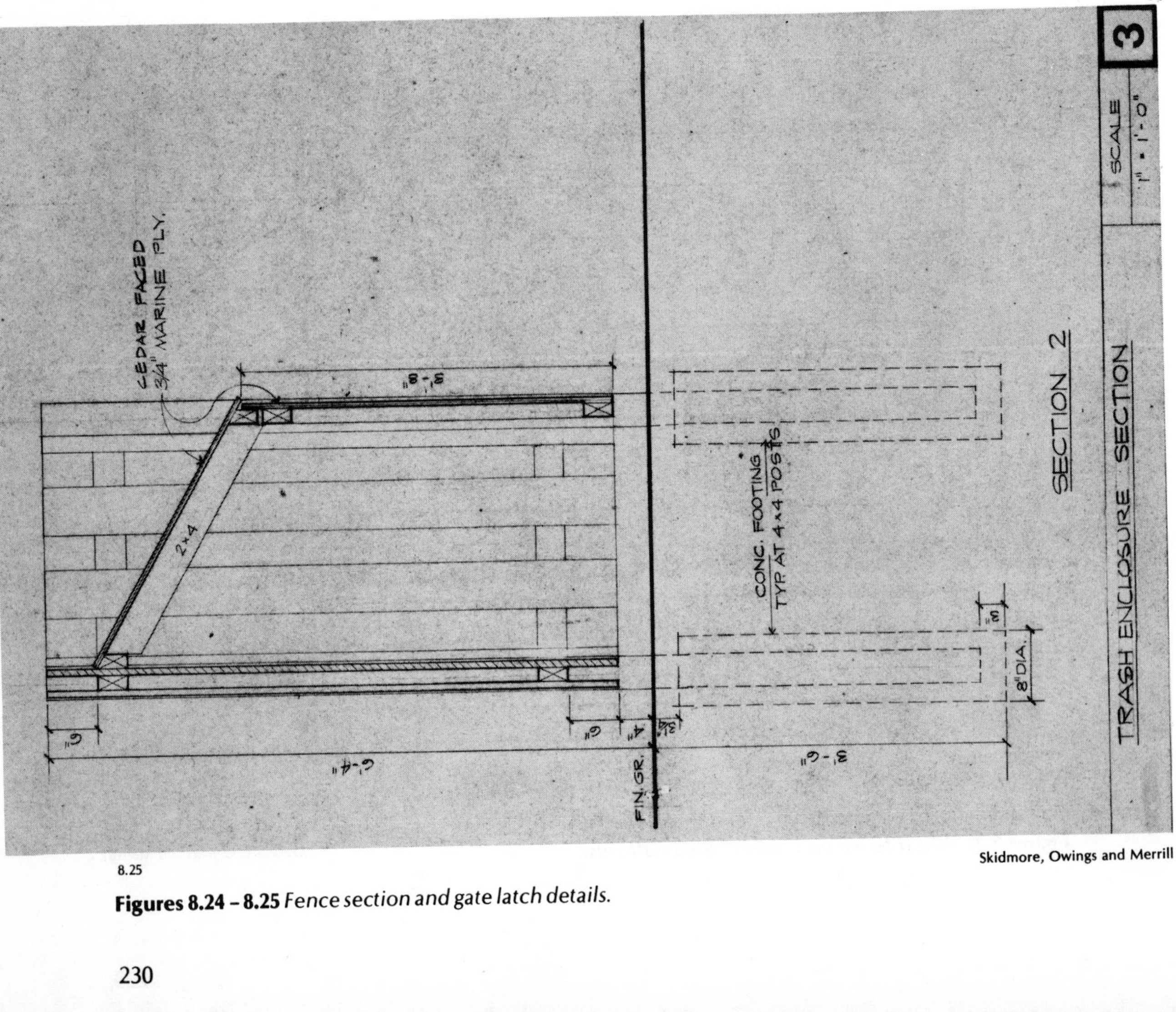

8.25

Skidmore, Owings and Merrill

Figures 8.24 – 8.25 *Fence section and gate latch details.*

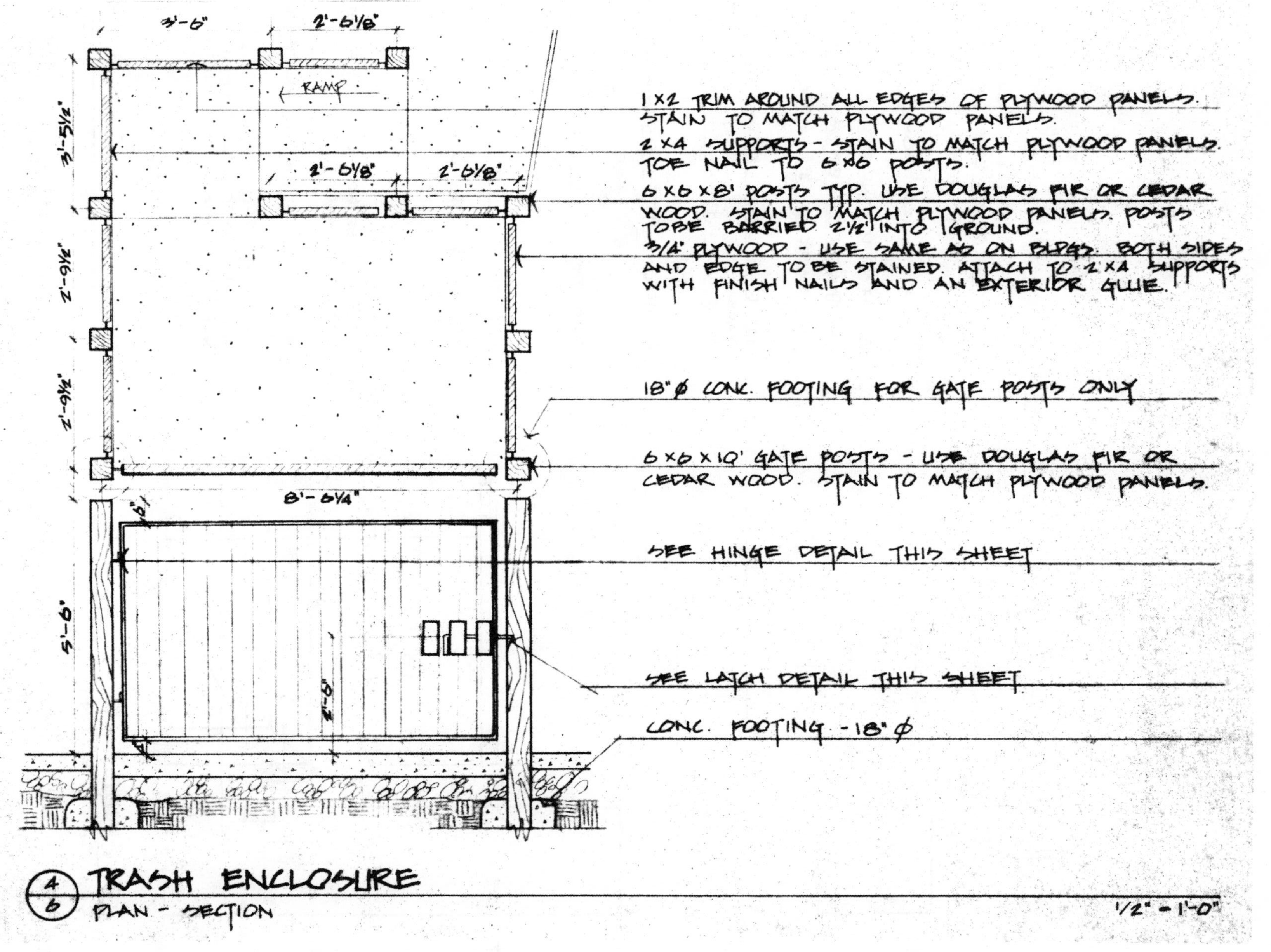
3'-6"
2'-6 1/8"
RAMP
3'-5 1/2"
2'-6 1/8"
2'-6 1/8"
2'-9 1/2"
2'-9 1/2"
8'-6 1/4"
5'-6"
1 X 2 TRIM AROUND ALL EDGES OF PLYWOOD PANELS. STAIN TO MATCH PLYWOOD PANELS.
2 X 4 SUPPORTS - STAIN TO MATCH PLYWOOD PANELS. TOE NAIL TO 6 X 6 POSTS.
6 X 6 X 8' POSTS TYP. USE DOUGLAS FIR OR CEDAR WOOD. STAIN TO MATCH PLYWOOD PANELS. POSTS TO BE BARRIED 2 1/2' INTO GROUND.
3/4" PLYWOOD - USE SAME AS ON BLDGS. BOTH SIDES AND EDGE TO BE STAINED. ATTACH TO 2 X 4 SUPPORTS WITH FINISH NAILS AND AN EXTERIOR GLUE.
18" ∅ CONC. FOOTING FOR GATE POSTS ONLY
6 X 6 X 10' GATE POSTS - USE DOUGLAS FIR OR CEDAR WOOD. STAIN TO MATCH PLYWOOD PANELS.
SEE HINGE DETAIL THIS SHEET
SEE LATCH DETAIL THIS SHEET
CONC. FOOTING - 18" ∅
4/6
TRASH ENCLOSURE
PLAN - SECTION
1/2" = 1'-0"

Figure 8.26 *Fence plan and section.*

Bonnell and Associates

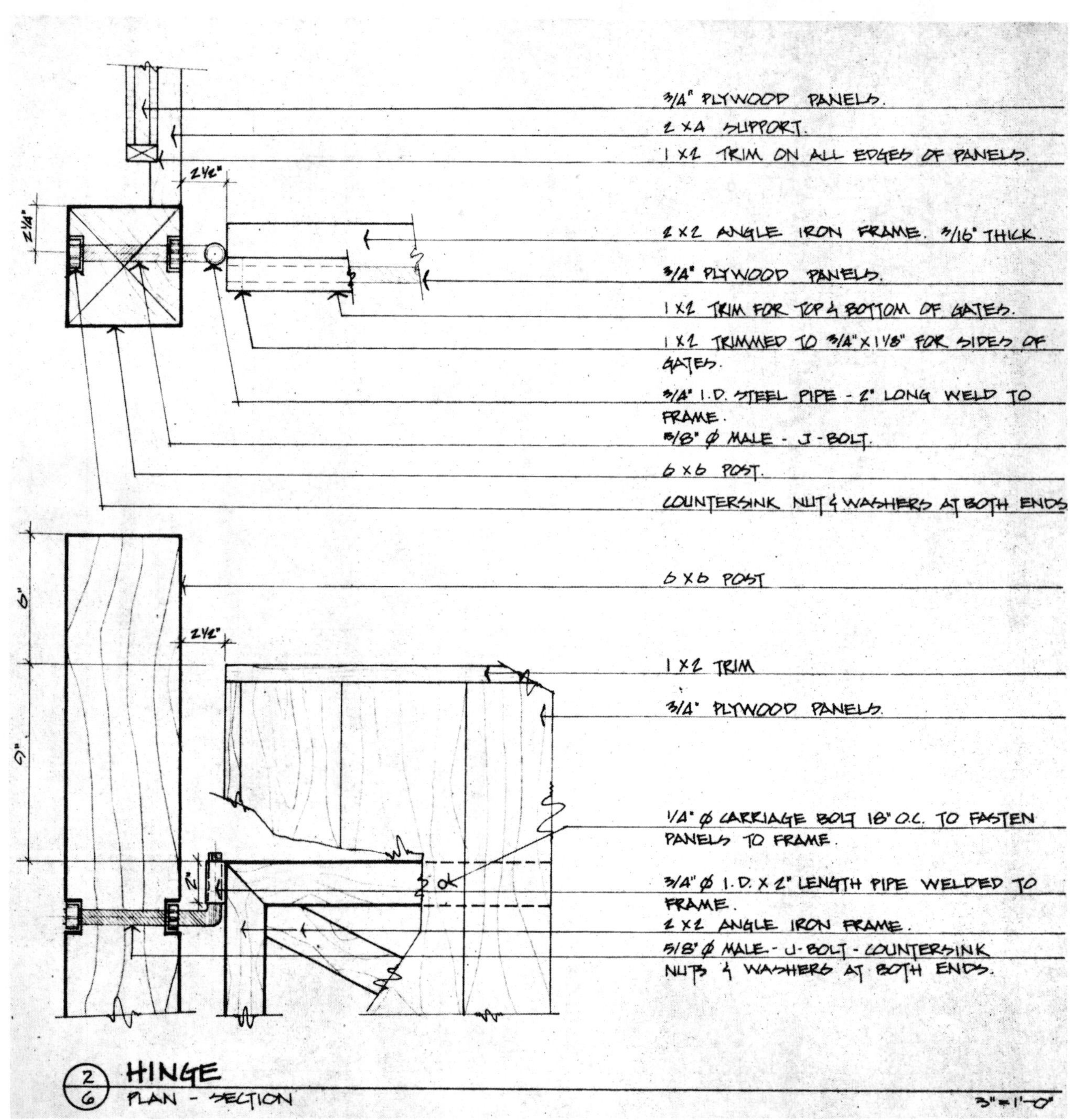

3/4" PLYWOOD PANELS.
2 X 4 SUPPORT.
1 X 2 TRIM ON ALL EDGES OF PANELS.
2 1/2"
2 1/4"
2 X 2 ANGLE IRON FRAME. 3/16" THICK.
3/4" PLYWOOD PANELS.
1 X 2 TRIM FOR TOP & BOTTOM OF GATES.
1 X 2 TRIMMED TO 3/4" X 1 1/8" FOR SIDES OF GATES.
3/4" I.D. STEEL PIPE - 2" LONG WELD TO FRAME.
5/8" ϕ MALE - J - BOLT.
6 X 6 POST.
COUNTERSINK NUT & WASHERS AT BOTH ENDS
6"
6 X 6 POST
2 1/2"
1 X 2 TRIM
3/4" PLYWOOD PANELS.
6"
1/4" ϕ CARRIAGE BOLT 18" O.C. TO FASTEN PANELS TO FRAME.
3/4" ϕ I.D. X 2" LENGTH PIPE WELDED TO FRAME.
2 X 2 ANGLE IRON FRAME.
5/8" ϕ MALE - J - BOLT - COUNTERSINK NUTS & WASHERS AT BOTH ENDS.
2/6 HINGE
PLAN - SECTION
3" = 1'-0"

Figure 8.27 *Gate details.*

Bonnell and Associates

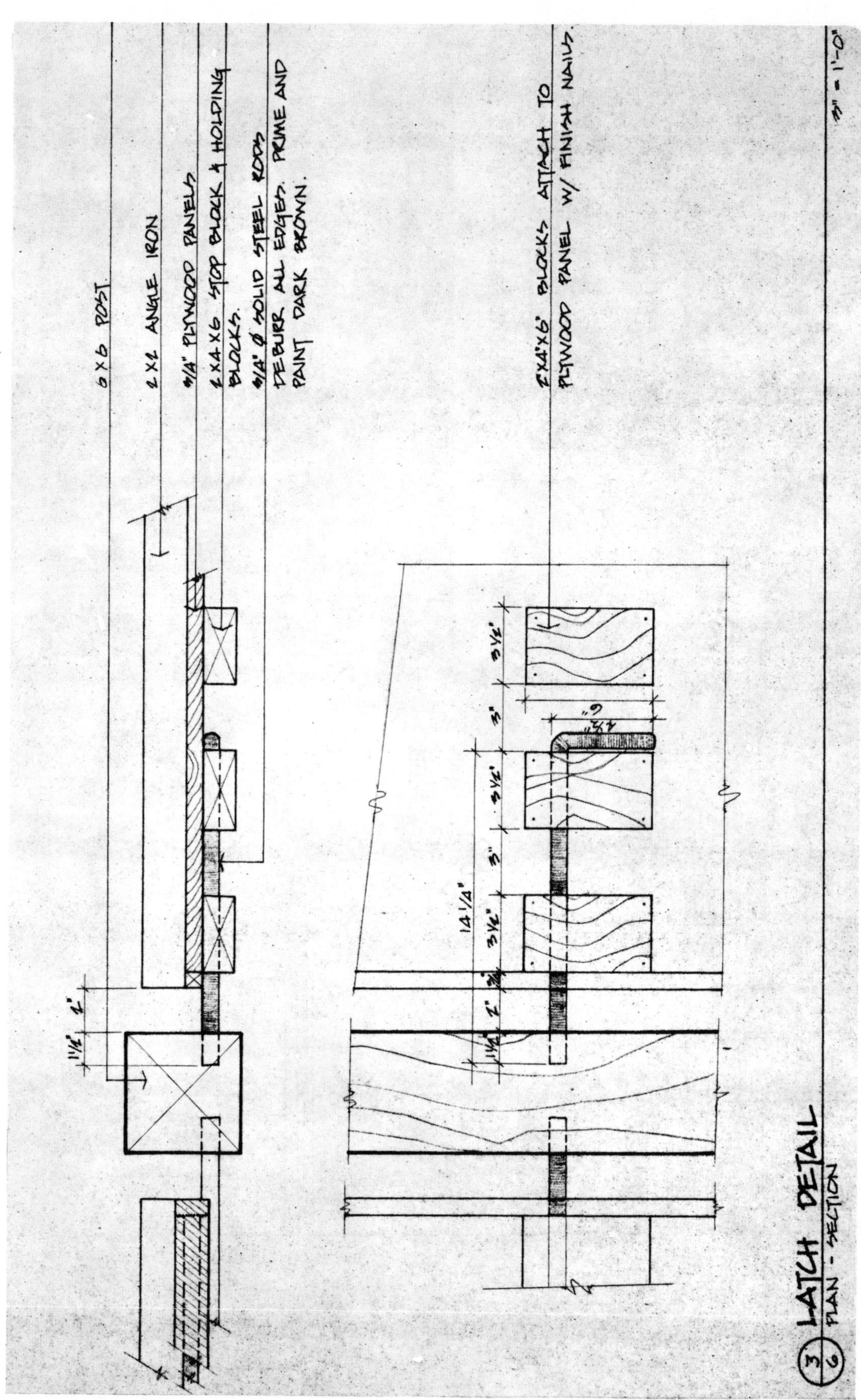
6 X 6 POST
2 X 2 ANGLE IRON
3/4" PLYWOOD PANELS
2 X 4 X 6 STOP BLOCK & HOLDING BLOCKS.
3/4" ∅ SOLID STEEL RODS
DEBURR ALL EDGES. PRIME AND PAINT DARK BROWN.
2"X4"X6" BLOCKS ATTACH TO PLYWOOD PANEL W/ FINISH NAILS.
14 1/4"
LATCH DETAIL
PLAN - SECTION
3" = 1'-0"

Figure 8.28 *Gate details.*

Bonnell and Associates

8.29

8.30

4"x4" POST
2"x6" RAIL
1"x6" BOARD
5/4"x3" BATTEN

PLAN

LUMBER FOR 8' LONG FENCE
2 - 2x6's ; 8'-0" LONG
1 - 4x4 ; 10'-0" LONG
15 - 1x6's ; 6'-0" LONG
15 - 5/4x3 ; 6'-0" LONG

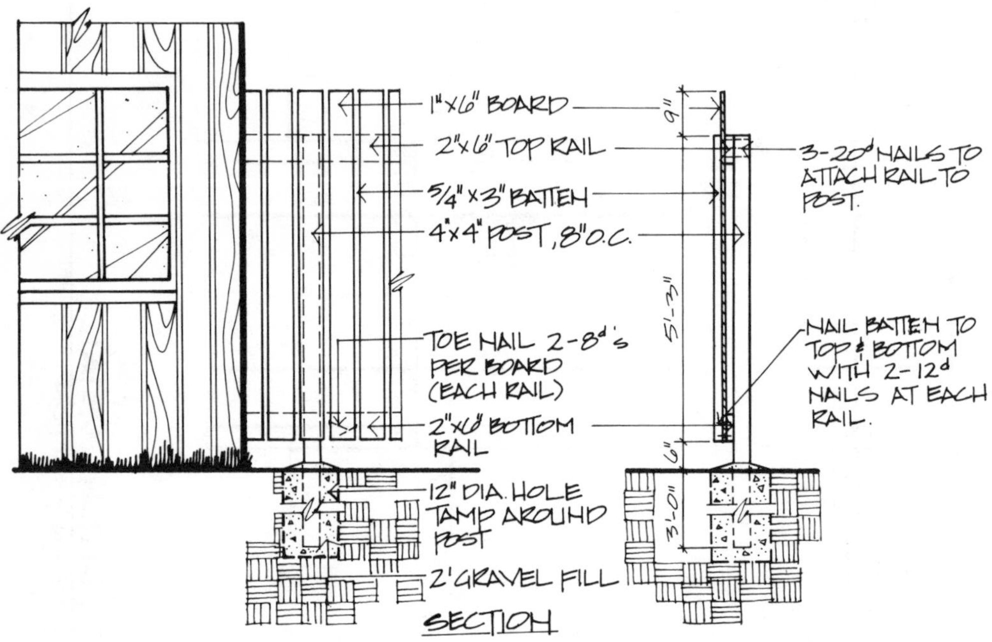
1"x6" BOARD
2"x6" TOP RAIL
5/4"x3" BATTEN
4"x4" POST, 8" O.C.
TOE NAIL 2-8d's PER BOARD (EACH RAIL)
2"x6" BOTTOM RAIL
12" DIA. HOLE TAMP AROUND POST
2' GRAVEL FILL
SECTION
9"
5'-3"
6"
3'-0"
3-20d NAILS TO ATTACH RAIL TO POST.
NAIL BATTEN TO TOP & BOTTOM WITH 2-12d NAILS AT EACH RAIL.

FENCE DETAIL

Western Wood Products Association

8.31 Kirk, Wallace and McKinley — Charles R. Pearson, courtesy of Western Wood Products Association

8.33 Lloyd Bond — Tom Burns, courtesy of Western Wood Products Association

8.32 Lloyd Bond — Tom Burns, courtesy of Western Wood Products Association

8.34 Paul Hayden Kirk — Charles R. Pearson, courtesy of Western Wood Products Association

Figures 8.29 – 8.34 *Design variations in wood fences.*

Phil Palmer, courtesy of California Redwood Association

8.35

John Vogley

Morley Baer, courtesy of California Redwood Association

8.36

Robert Cornwall

Figures 8.35 – 8.36 *Fence design variations.*

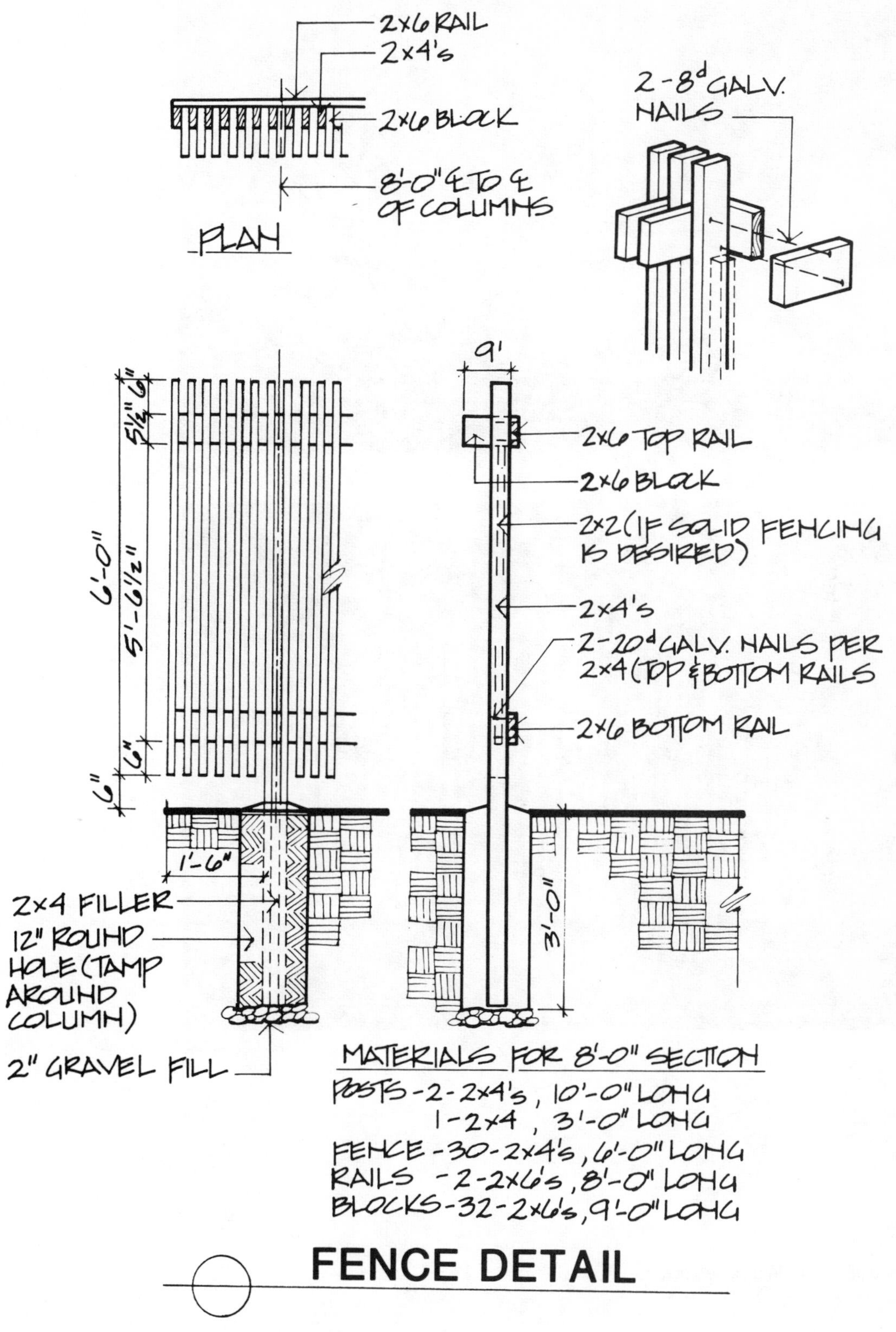
2×6 RAIL
2×4'S
2×6 BLOCK
8'-0" ℄ TO ℄ OF COLUMNS
PLAN
2-8d GALV. NAILS
9'
2×6 TOP RAIL
2×6 BLOCK
2×2 (IF SOLID FENCING IS DESIRED)
2×4'S
2-20d GALV. NAILS PER 2×4 (TOP & BOTTOM RAILS
2×6 BOTTOM RAIL
5½"
6"
6'-0"
5'-6½"
6"
6"
1'-6"
3'-0"
2×4 FILLER
12" ROUND HOLE (TAMP AROUND COLUMN)
2" GRAVEL FILL
MATERIALS FOR 8'-0" SECTION
POSTS - 2 - 2×4'S, 10'-0" LONG
1 - 2×4, 3'-0" LONG
FENCE - 30 - 2×4'S, 6'-0" LONG
RAILS - 2 - 2×6'S, 8'-0" LONG
BLOCKS - 32 - 2×6'S, 9'-0" LONG
FENCE DETAIL

Figure 8.37 *Fence details.*

Western Wood Products Association

Tom Burns, courtesy of Western Wood Products Association

8.38 Lloyd Bond

8.39 Doede, Inc.

Figures 8.38 - 8.42 *Wood fences.*

8.40 Alan Seder

Tom Burns, courtesy of Western Wood Products Association

8.41 A. O. Bumgardner

Charles R. Pearson, courtesy of Western Wood Products Association

8.42 Frits Loonsten

8.43

8.44

8.45

8.46

Figures 8.43 – 8.49 *Wood fences.*

8.47

8.48 Bailey and Associates

8.49

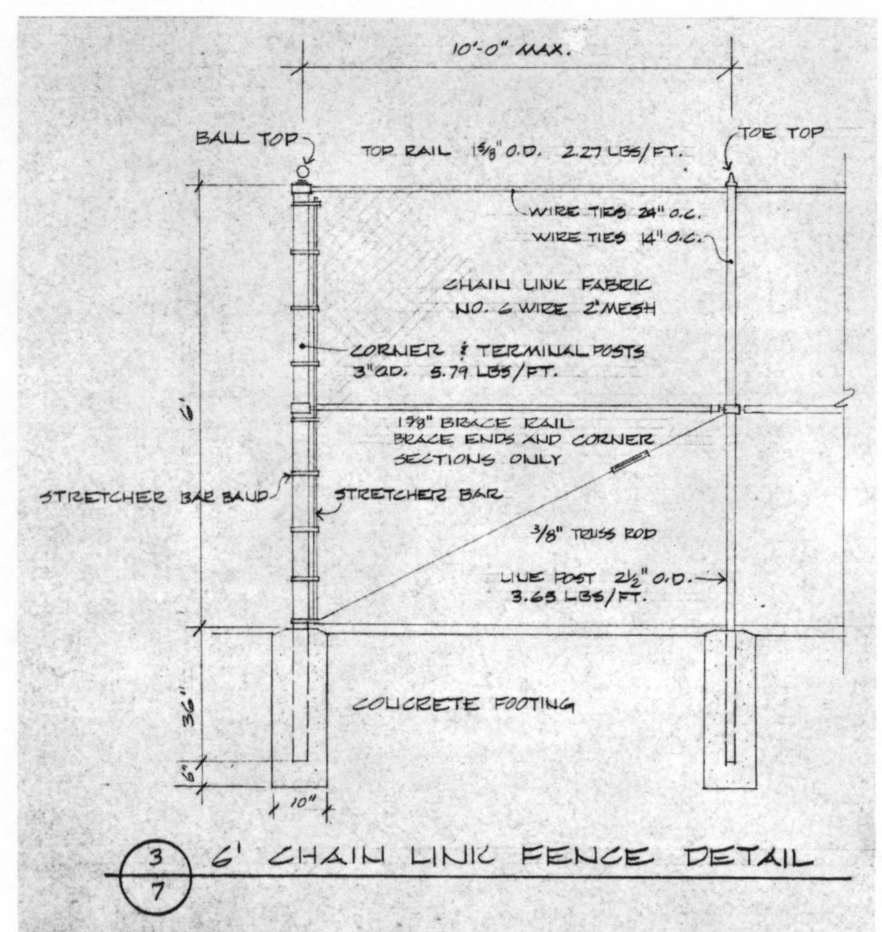

10'-0" MAX.
BALL TOP
TOP RAIL 1 5/8" O.D. 2.27 LBS/FT.
TOE TOP
WIRE TIES 24" O.C.
WIRE TIES 14" O.C.
CHAIN LINK FABRIC
NO. 6 WIRE 2" MESH
CORNER & TERMINAL POSTS
3" O.D. 5.79 LBS/FT.
6'
1 5/8" BRACE RAIL
BRACE ENDS AND CORNER
SECTIONS ONLY
STRETCHER BAR BAND
STRETCHER BAR
3/8" TRUSS ROD
LINE POST 2 1/2" O.D.
3.65 LBS/FT.
CONCRETE FOOTING
36"
6"
10"
3
7
6' CHAIN LINK FENCE DETAIL

8.50 Johnson, Johnson and Roy

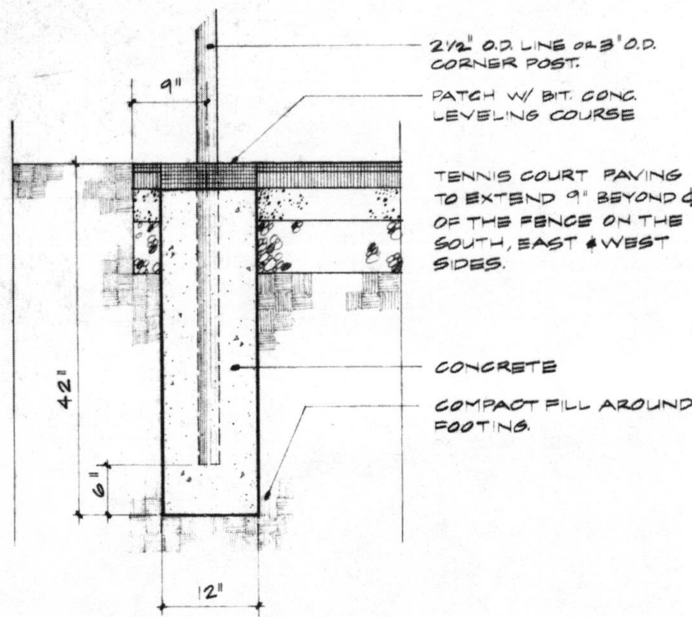

2 1/2" O.D. LINE OR 3" O.D.
CORNER POST.
9"
PATCH W/ BIT. CONC.
LEVELING COURSE
TENNIS COURT PAVING
TO EXTEND 9" BEYOND ¢
OF THE FENCE ON THE
SOUTH, EAST & WEST
SIDES.
CONCRETE
COMPACT FILL AROUND
FOOTING.
42"
6"
12"

5 Fence Post Footing
3/4" = 1'-0" TENNIS COURT SITUATION

CR3, inc.

Figures 8.50 – 8.51 *Details for a chain link fence.*

Figures 8.52 – 8.57 *Variety of designs for metal fences.*

8.52

8.55

8.53

8.56

8.54

8.57

8.58

8.59

8.60

8.61

Figures 8.58 – 8.61 *Metal fences.*

9

Structures: Decks, Shelters and Bridges

DECKS

Decks extend space in a horizontal plane at floor level or at edges of hillsides. The extension of living space in a home or a similar extension of usable space for commercial, recreational or other kinds of facilities makes the design of a deck a worthwhile consideration. They are popular for children because the space dries quickly after a storm and children can play on them long before other spaces such as lawn areas have dried sufficiently for play activity. Overhead structures may be open in character providing partial shade or temporary shade or permanent protection from sun and rain.

The design construction of structures must conform to local building codes and any local regulations such as restrictive covenants. The shape and size of any structure will be influenced by Owner's needs, views, prevailing winds, orientation to the sun, topography of site, etc.

The principal material used in structures as described and illustrated herein is wood, though metals, especially in fasteners, are important, as well as paints and plastics for various finishes. The designer should be familiar with these materials, their techniques of use, and construction methods, before commencing design, in order to achieve the greatest efficiency, performance, aesthetics and safety.

Wood used as structures will need to be naturally resistant to decay or pressure treated with preservatives conforming to the standards of the American Wood Preservers Association or Federal Specifications TT-W-57i. Wood (other than those with an inherent decay resistance) in contact with soil should be penta-treated. Other wood above the ground can be preserved with water-borne preservatives such as chromated copper arsenate, which will accept paints and stains where colors are desired for design harmony. Otherwise the wood can weather to a natural gray which varies in tone from species to species.

Metals will need to be hot dipped galvanized, cadmium plated, or primed and painted to minimize corrosion. Rusting nails and metal parts will stain the wood and eventually lose their strength and holding power.

The various components of structures include posts, beams, joists, planking, railings, steps, roofing, etc. Not all, such as steps and roofing, would be used in any one design project; however, the way these components relate to each other is illustrated in this chapter. There are several methods of determining the size and spacing of the components to be used. One is through complex mathematical formulas for determining reflection, bending moments, horizontal shear, allowable stresses, etc. Those who wish to pursue this approach may consult the references listed at the end of this chapter.

Structural Design

The following is a description of some of the common structural design terms in a deflection formula with an example calculation:

1. Load: There are two kinds, dead load and live load. Dead load is the weight of the materials in the structure, including permanently attached fixtures and equipment. Live load is the people who may use the structure, moveable furniture and equipment, and snow.
2. Span: If a beam is supported at each end, the length of the beam and the span are equal. Otherwise, the span is measured from the center of one support to the center of the next support.
3. Allowable Stresses: These have been established for the various woods and can be referred to in the publications of the National Forest Products Association as listed in the references. They are subject to adjustment for duration of the load such as a heavy snow remaining in place for several days.
4. Modulus of Elasticity: A measure of the stiffness of lumber. It varies according to the variety of species of wood. The figure is larger for Douglas Fir than for Redwood.
5. Moment of Inertia: This is computed from a cross-section of a beam $\frac{bh^3}{12}$ with "b" as the horizontal dimension and "h" as the vertical dimension. For a 2 x 4 laid flat, "b" would be 3½ inches and "h" would be 1½ inches, whereas if the 2 x 4 is on edge, "b" would be 1½ inches and "h" would be 3½ inches. After computation, the moment of inertia for the flat 2 x 4 is .984 and the 2 x 4 on edge is 5.359.
6. Deflection: One of the methods for selection of a beam is to determine its deflection or sag between supports. The maximum deflection will occur at the center of the span. To prevent excessive movement of a beam in service, the deflection should be limited to $\frac{L}{360}$ of the span expressed in inches. The formula for computing deflection is $D = \frac{5}{384} \times \frac{WL^3}{EI}$. D = deflection in inches, L = length of span in inches, E = modulus of elasticity, I = moment of inertia, and W = uniformly distributed load in pounds.

The load guidelines are generally 40 pounds per square foot (p.s.f.) of live load for most situations on decks plus an allowance of an additional ten pounds p.s.f. for dead load. This can be used also for footbridges built strictly for pedestrians. If small bridges will handle motorcycles, carts, small tractors, etc., the load calculations should be raised to 100 p.s.f. Adding a large planter with soil to the surface of the deck does not constitute a uniform load and the weight of that particular point may well exceed the 40 p.s.f. live load.

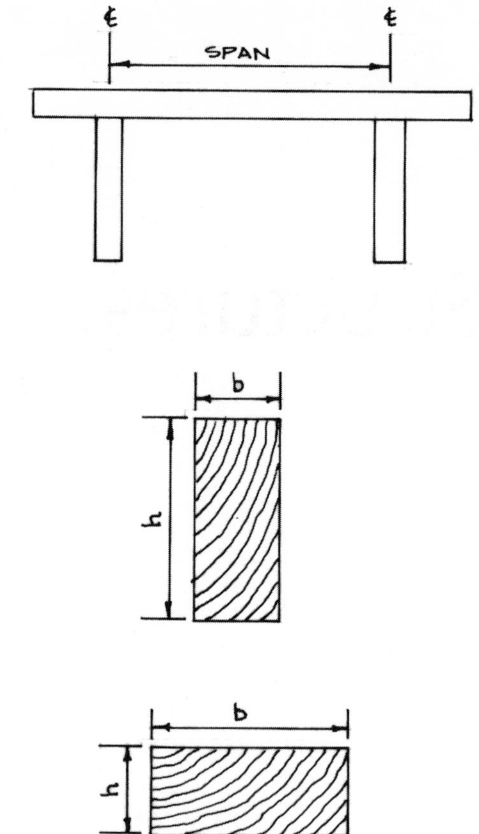

SPAN
b
h
b
h

Figure 9.1 *Structural design factors.*

An example of the deflection formula in use is as follows: In a preliminary design, a 4 x 8 was tentatively selected for a beam for the deck with beams spaced 4 feet apart and supports 10 feet apart. L = 120 inches. Maximum deflection based upon $\frac{L}{360}$ = .33 inches, and E = 1,500,000, which is the modulus elasticity for Southern Yellow Pine. I = 111.148 for a 4 x 8 beam. With a combined live and dead load of 50 p.s.f. and a load area of 40 square feet (4 x 10) or beam spacing x span), the load is computed to be 2,000 pounds. On the basis of the formula the deflection is calculated to be .27 inches, slightly less than the .33 inches permitted. Thus the beam is large enough to use and is safe.

Tables have been developed as a general guide for component selection in most situations, and they can be used to save time in calculations. The tables are divided into three groups with the wood species for each identified at the bottom of the table.

Rather than using the tables, greater accuracy at less cost can be achieved in beam design and size selection by using a computer. A designer can arrive at a technical structural design solution faster with less frustration with calculations and the Owner will save money with less materials being used, or a structure that is safer.

Most structures will begin with footings (down to the frost line or no less than two-foot depth for stability), to which the posts are attached. The posts in turn support the beam. Whether or not joists are used depends upon the design. A low deck close to the ground may not have sufficient room available to use joists. More beams closer together will solve the problem. Based on the chart for "allowable spans of deck boards or planking," a five foot spacing of the beams is possible for Group 1 wood species.

In situations involving upper level decks where use will be made of the space below, a minimum number of supporting beams and posts will probably be desirable. This will require larger beams and posts and the use of joists to distribute the load to the fewer number of beams.

When ¼ or ⅛ inch space is provided between the deck boards, drainage can readily occur and the deck can be flat. If tongue and groove planking, deck boards, or plywood is used, the deck will need to be sloped in order to provide drainage.

Footings will generally be concrete and sized to handle the load in relation to the bearing capabilities of the soil. Consult local sources for soil information. At a minimum, a 16-inch by 16-inch square 10 inches deep is recommended for footings.

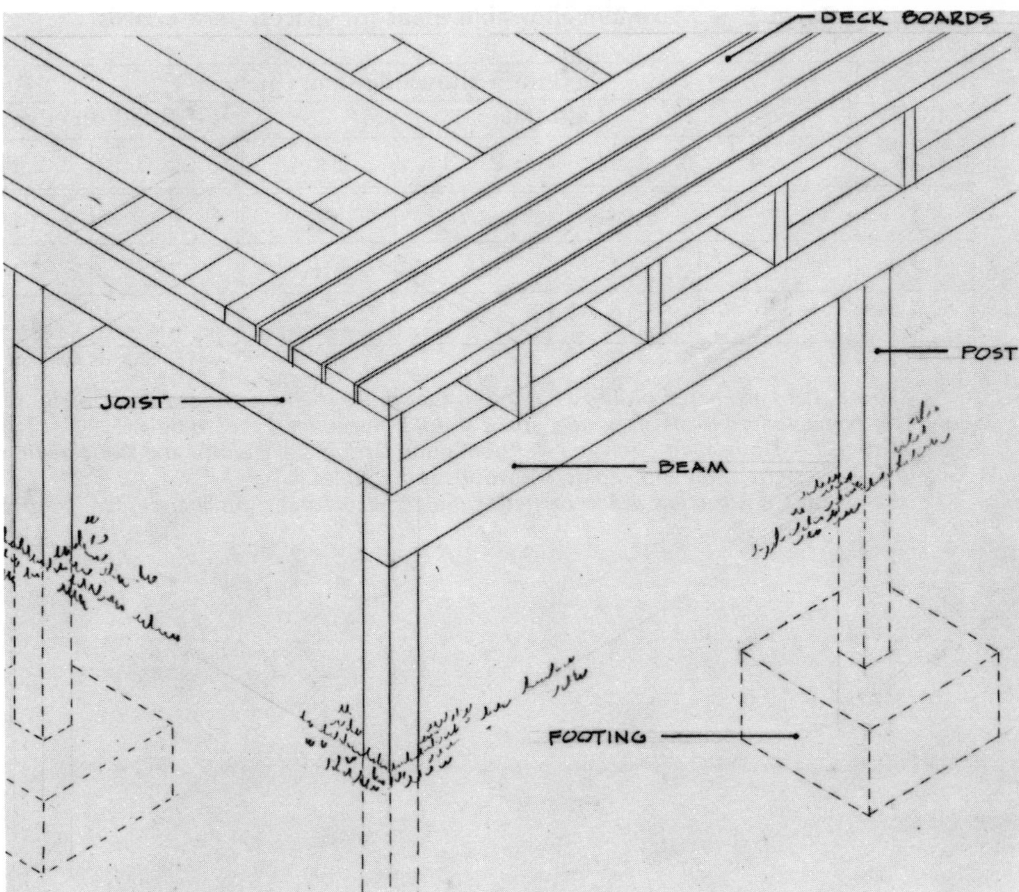
DECK BOARDS
POST
JOIST
BEAM
FOOTING

Figure 9.2 *Identification and relationship of deck components.*

Table 1. — Minimum post sizes (wood beam supports)[1]

Species group[2]	Post size (in.)	Load area[3] beam spacing x post spacing (sq. ft.)									
		36	48	60	72	84	96	108	120	132	144
1	4x4	Up to 12-ft. heights →				Up to 10-ft. heights →			Up to 8-ft. heights →		
	4x6					Up to 12-ft. heights →				Up to 10-ft →	
	6x6									Up to 12-ft →	
2	4x4	Up to 12-ft. →		Up to 10-ft. hts. →			Up to 8-ft. heights →				
	4x6			Up to 12-ft. hts. →			Up to 10-ft. heights →				
	6x6						Up to 12-ft. heights →				
3	4x4	Up to 12′	Up to 10′ →		Up to 8-ft. hts. →			Up to 6-ft. heights →			
	4x6		Up to 12′ →		Up to 10-ft. hts. →			Up to 8-ft. heights →			
	6x6				Up to 12-ft. heights →						

U.S.D.A. Handbook No. 432

[1]*Based on 40 p.s.f. deck live load plus 10 p.s.f. dead load. Grade is Standard and Better for 4- × 4-inch posts and No. 1 and Better for larger sizes.*

[2]*Group 1 — Douglas-fir-larch and southern pine; Group 2 — Hem-fir and Douglas-fir south; Group 3 — Western pines and cedars, redwood, and spruces.*

[3]*Example: If the beam supports are spaced 8 feet, 6 inches, on center and the posts are 11 feet, 6 inches, on center, then the load area is 98. Use next larger area 108.*

Table 2. — Maximum allowable spans for spaced deck boards[1]

Species group[2]	Maximum allowable span (inches)[3]					
	Laid flat				Laid on edge	
	1 x 4	2 x 2	2 x 3	2 x 4	2 x 3	2 x 4
1	16	60	60	60	90	144
2	14	48	48	48	78	120
3	12	42	42	42	66	108

U.S.D.A. Handbook No. 432

[1]*These spans are based on the assumption that more than one floor board carries normal loads. If concentrated loads are a rule, spans should be reduced accordingly.*

[2]*Group 1 — Douglas-fir-larch and southern pine; Group 2 — Hem-fir and Douglas-fir south; Group 3 — Western pines and cedars, redwood, and spruces.*

[3]*Based on Construction grade or Better (Select Structural, Appearance, No. 1 or No. 2).*

Table 3. — Minimum beam sizes and spans[1]

Species group[2]	Beam size (in.)	Spacing between beams[3] (ft.) 4	5	6	7	8	9	10	11	12
1	4x6	Up to 6-ft. spans	→	→						
	3x8	Up to 8-ft.	→	Up to 7′ →	Up to 6-ft. spans	→	→			
	4x8	Up to 10′	Up to 9′ →	Up to 8′ →	Up to 7-ft.	→	Up to 6-ft. spans	→	→	
	3x10	Up to 11′	Up to 10′ →	Up to 9′ →	Up to 8-ft.	→	Up to 7-ft.	→	Up to 6-ft.	→
	4x10	Up to 12′	Up to 11′ →	Up to 10′ →	Up to 9-ft.	→	Up to 8-ft.	→	Up to 7-ft.	→
	3x12		Up to 12′ →	Up to 11′ →	Up to 10′ →	Up to 9-ft.	→	Up to 8-ft. spans	→	→
	4x12			Up to 12-ft.	→	Up to 11′ →	Up to 10-ft.	→	Up to 9-ft.	→
	6x10					Up to 12′ →	Up to 11′ →	Up to 10-ft. spans	→	→
	6x12						Up to 12-ft. spans	→	→	→
2	4x6	Up to 6-ft.	→							
	3x8	Up to 7-ft.	→	Up to 6-ft.	→					
	4x8	Up to 9′	Up to 8′ →	Up to 7-ft.	→	Up to 6-ft.	→			
	3x10	Up to 10′	Up to 9′ →	Up to 8′ →	Up to 7-ft.	→	Up to 6-ft. spans	→	→	
	4x10	Up to 11′	Up to 10′ →	Up to 9′ →	Up to 8-ft.	→	Up to 7-ft. spans	→	→	Up to 6′
	3x12	Up to 12′	Up to 11′ →	Up to 10′ →	Up to 9′ →	Up to 8-ft.	→	Up to 7-ft. spans	→	→
	4x12		Up to 12′ →	Up to 11′ →	Up to 10-ft.	→	Up to 9-ft.	→	Up to 8-ft.	→
	6x10			Up to 12′ →	Up to 11′ →	Up to 10-ft.	→	Up to 9-ft. spans	→	→
	6x12				Up to 12-ft. spans	→	→	Up to 11-ft.	→	Up to 10′
3	4x6	Up to 6′								
	3x8	Up to 7′	Up to 6′ →							
	4x8	Up to 8′	Up to 7′ →	Up to 6-ft.	→					
	3x10	Up to 9′	Up to 8′ →	Up to 7′ →	Up to 6-ft. spans	→	→			
	4x10	Up to 10′	Up to 9′ →	Up to 8-ft.	→	Up to 7-ft.	→	Up to 6-ft. spans	→	→
	3x12	Up to 11′	Up to 10′ →	Up to 9′ →	Up to 8′ →	Up to 7-ft. spans	→	→	Up to 6-ft.	→
	4x12	Up to 12′	Up to 11′ →	Up to 10′ →	Up to 9-ft.	→	Up to 8-ft.	→	Up to 7-ft.	→
	6x10		Up to 12′ →	Up to 11′ →	Up to 10′ →	Up to 9-ft.	→	Up to 8-ft. spans	→	→
	6x12			Up to 12-ft.	→	Up to 11-ft.	→	Up to 10-ft.	→	Up to 8′

[1]*Beams are on edge. Spans are center to center distances between posts or supports. (Based on 40 p.s.f. deck live load plus 10 p.s.f. dead load. Grade is No. 2 or Better; No. 2, medium grain southern pine.)*

[2]*Group 1 — Douglas fir-larch and southern pine; Group 2 — Hem-fir and Douglas-fir south; Group 3 — Western pines and cedars, redwood, and spruces.*

[3]*Example: If the beams are 9 feet, 8 inches apart and the species is Group 2, use the 10-ft column; 3×10 up to 6-ft. spans, 4×10 or 3×12 up to 7-ft. spans, 4×12 or 6×10 up to 9-ft spans, 6×12 up to 11-ft. spans.*

U.S.D.A. Handbook No. 432

Table 4. — Maximum allowable spans for deck joists[1]

Species group[2]	Joist size (inches)	Joist spacing (inches)		
		16	24	32
1	2x6	9′-9″	7′-11″	6′-2″
	2x8	12′-10″	10′-6″	8′-1″
	2x10	16′-5″	13′-4″	10′-4″
2	2x6	8′-7″	7′-0″	5′-8″
	2x8	11′-4″	9′-3″	7′-6″
	2x10	14′-6″	11′-10″	9′-6″
3	2x6	7′-9″	6′-2″	5′-0″
	2x8	10′-2″	8′-1″	6′-8″
	2x10	13′-0″	10′-4″	8′-6″

[1]Joists are on edge. Spans are center distances between beams or supports. Based on 40 p.s.f. deck live loads plus 10 p.s.f. dead load. Grade is No. 2 or Better; No. 2 medium grain southern pine.
[2]Group 1 — Douglas-fir-larch and southern pine; Group 2 — Hem-fir and Douglas-fir south; Group 3 — Western pines and cedars, redwood, and spruces. *U.S.D.A. Handbook No. 432*

Fasteners

Nails are the most commonly used fasteners. They are the least expensive and easiest to use. However, they have the poorest holding power and will fail or pull out in most stress situations. Nails which are spirally grooved or have deformed shanks hold the best, but may not always be available in rust resistant form. Nails should be long enough to penetrate the receiving member by a minimum of one and one-half inches unless that member is thinner. A ten penny (10^d) nail would be maximum for nailing two 2 x 4's together. When nailing a 2 x 4 deckboard flat to a 4 x 8, a 16^d nail would provide good holding power. In a situation where splitting may occur, especially for larger nails or spikes, predrilling three-fourths of the diameter of the nail is desirable. For two-inch-thick boards four and six inches wide laid flat, two nails per joint are recommended. For wider boards, three nails per joint would be needed. For some woods, such as yellow pine, predrill within 6 inches of the end before nailing to avoid immediate or delayed splitting.

Screws, lag screws and bolts are recommended for railings, steps, benches, etc., where impact and movement stresses are involved. Screws come in three types. These types are flat head, oval head, and round head. Screws should be long enough to penetrate the receiving member by a minimum of one inch. Pre-drilling three-fourths of the diameter to the screw will be necessary. Flat and oval head screws are best for most exposed situations as they protrude the least and are less likely to catch clothing or become uncomfortable to sit on or touch.

Lag screws are used to fasten large members where bolts cannot be used. Holes will need to be pre-drilled three-quarters of the diameter of the screw and a washer used under head. If used for seats or railings they can be counter sunk so that the head is flush with the surface, but only on members thicker than two inches.

Bolts are the best fasteners as they provide the best rigidity. There are two types: carriage (with a rounded head) and machine. Carriage bolts are best for situations exposed to skin contact, though after weathering they will be difficult to remove as the head will turn in the wood. Holes are drilled to the exact diameter of the bolts, and washers are used under the nuts of carriage bolts and both ends of machine bolts. As a rough guide, one-fourth-inch diameter bolts can be used for two- to three-inch-thick members; three-eighths-inch bolts for three- to six-inch members, and one-half-inch diameter bolts for four-inch and larger wood members. A minimum of two bolts staggered per joint is recommended, increasing to three or more for members six inches or larger.

Other metal items that may be used in structures include steel pipe flanges, post flanges, T-cleats, straps, angles, beam hangers and any members of custom design and fabricated products. Ways in which any or all of these can be used are illustrated in this chapter.

Bracing

Decks or other structures which stand free or independent of other major structures will need to be braced to prevent unwanted movement. Two by fours can be used for braces less than 8 feet in length and 2 x 6's for those more than 8 feet. Fasten braces with bolts or lag screws.

Railings

A railing is generally not needed for decks or structures which are low. Check local building codes for exact requirements. Some codes require a minimum railing height of 36 inches when any deck is 48 inches or higher above grade.

There is a wide variety of design possibilities for railings, but only a few are illustrated in this chapter. In general, some minimums need to be observed. The railing should be rigid and capable of supporting at least 20 p.s.f. of lateral load. Posts should not be more than 6 feet apart to support a 2 x 4 rail. Posts may be a part of the structure and extend through the deck boards or be attached to beams. Fasteners other than nails, except in small intermediate rails, are recommended.

Benches can be combined with railings for additional utility and function and can be integrally designed and constructed. Support members can be wood bolted to joists extending up through the decking or fabricated metal straps attached to the surface of the deck.

Stairs

A railing is not required when one or two steps are used for low decks but may be desirable for elderly and handicapped persons. Principles governing the heights of railings and other step characteristics are the same as discussed earlier in Chapter 6.

Wood stairs generally utilize stringers and treads. Stringers can be 2 x 10's or 2 x 12's attached to the deck and to a firm base, probably concrete. Two stringers can support treads up to 48 inches in width except for Group 3 wood species which are limited to 42 inches.

Stringers can be notched to hold treads, or cleats can be attached. The latter are stronger. Nails, by themselves, are not recommended as fasteners on stairs.

The riser-tread relationship may be a little steeper than for other outdoor steps according to prevailing practice. Risers over seven inches are not recommended. The product of a riser-tread relationship may be between 72 and 75; a 7-inch riser would mean a 10½-inch tread. If two 2 x 6's were used for a tread with the members spaced ¼ inch apart, the resulting 11¼ inch tread would relate to a 6½ inch rise, and most people would find that combination comfortable.

SHELTERS

Shelters and overhead structures may be open in character, providing partial or temporary shade, or roofed over for permanent protection from sun and rain.

The components, joining techniques, bracing, etc., are similar to decks. Because of wind and/or snow loads the loading for most areas of the country are the same as for decks; thus, the tables can be used for selecting component sizes. Consult local sources for loading recommendations in areas of no snow and light wind.

Many different design possibilities are available for roof design. The roof may be an open structure providing little shade but interesting shadow patterns, or it may support vines or temporary canvas panels. It can be flat or sloped; it may be partially open with closely spaced wood strips or completely solid. For solid roofing, truss design, built up roofs, etc., consult the references at the end of the chapter.

Illustrated in this chapter are several designs for open or partial open overhead structures and shelters.

BRIDGES

There are five different types of fixed bridges: simple beam, arch, truss, cantilever and suspension. For most site design situations, the simple beam type is commonly used. Suspension types are sometimes used in recreation areas over deep ravines, etc.

Components for simple beam type bridges will consist generally of beams, planking, and railings, with the beams supported by concrete buttresses (or abutments) at each end or posts or combination of both. The tables can be used for selecting beams for bridges limited to pedestrians. For other bridges the structures must be designed for heavy loads (100 p.s.f. or more) using the formulas found in the references. In most cases, stronger railings than those for decks are also needed. Laminated beams are becoming popular for use in wood bridge design and construction.

The comments made earlier in the section on decks about using a computer to select beam sizes also applies here. In addition a designer may want to check into several different brands of commercially available pre-designed bridges.

DESIGN PROCESS

The best designs are not created by simply sketching the shape and size of the structure and then sizing the components to fit. Such a technique may result in components out of scale to each other and/or inefficient use of materials. The design concept will need to be altered and modified as the size of the components selected are evaluated, reselected, etc.

Site conditions may dictate which direction the beams will run but otherwise there is a choice. The direction of the beam will dictate the direction of the joist (if used) and deck boards. Deck boards running parallel to the direction of view may tend to elongate the distance, which may or may not be desirable depending upon the decision of the designer. Two or three different design possibilities may be sketched out and cost estimates prepared according to the materials and labor required for erection to determine the comparative costs between one design and another.

REFERENCES FOR FURTHER READING

Anderson, L.O., Heebrink, T.B., and Oviatt, A.E. *Construction Guides for Exposed Wood Decks.* Agriculture Handbook #432, U.S. Forest Service. Washington, DC: USGPO, 1972.

Breeden, J.B. "Decks and Overhead Structures," *Handbook of Landscape Architectural Construction.* Washington, DC: Landscape Architecture Foundation, 1973.

National Design Specifications for Stress-Grade Lumber and its Fastenings (revised supplement). Washington, DC: National Forest Products Association, 1974.

Ramsey, C.G., and Sleeper, H.R. *Architectural Graphics Standards.* 7th Edition. New York: Wiley, 1981.

Sunset Editors. *Decks: How to Plan and Build.* Menlo Park, CA: Lane Publishing Co., 1980.

Wood Structural Design Data. Washington, DC: National Forest Products Association, 1970.

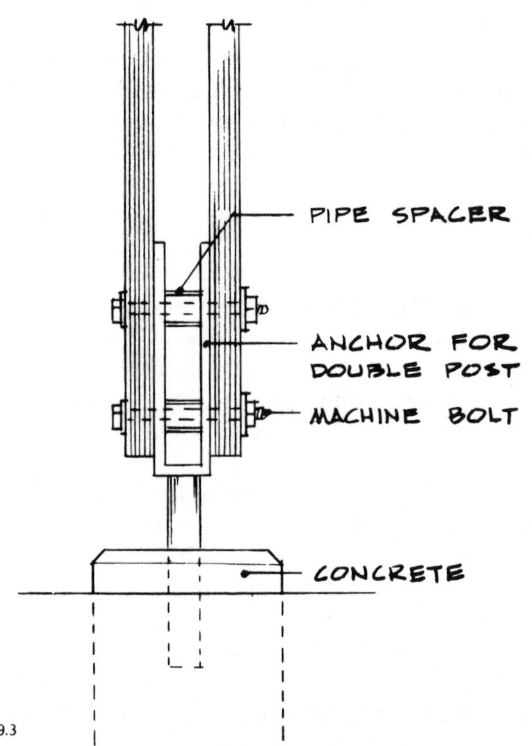
PIPE SPACER
ANCHOR FOR DOUBLE POST
MACHINE BOLT
CONCRETE
9.3

Figures 9.3 - 9.5 *Post to footing connections.*

Figure 9.6 - 9.7 *Joist to beam, joist and beam to building connections.*

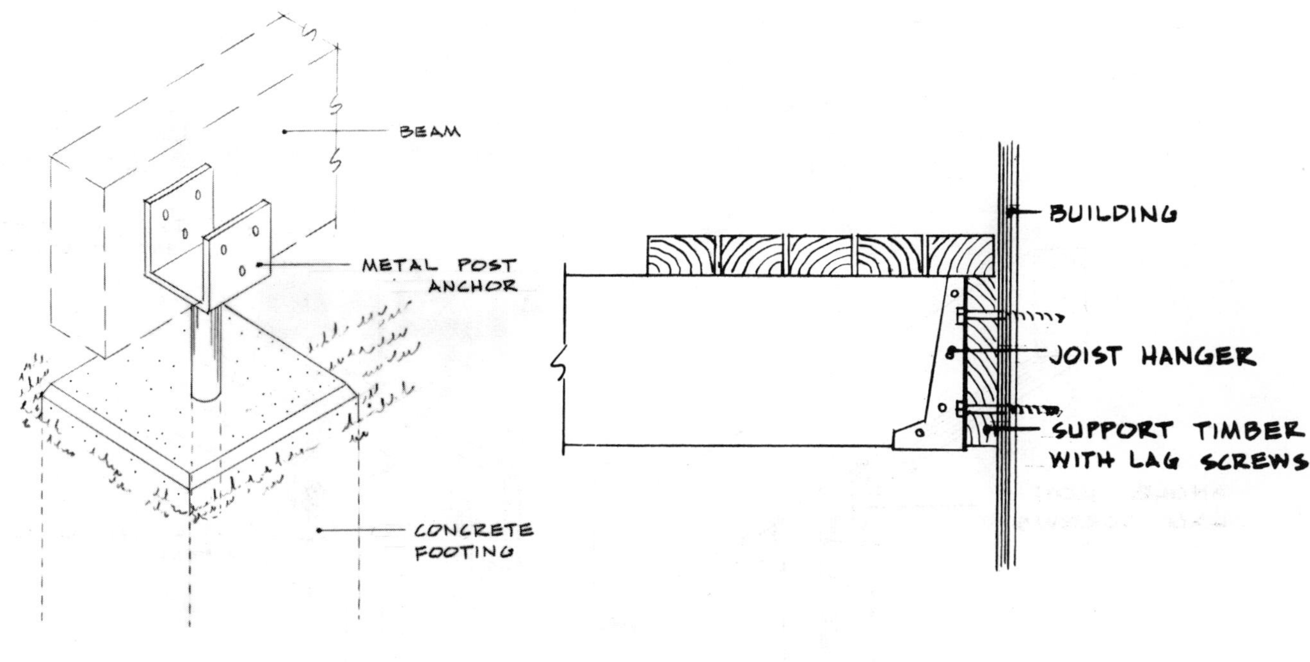
BEAM
METAL POST ANCHOR
CONCRETE FOOTING
BUILDING
JOIST HANGER
SUPPORT TIMBER WITH LAG SCREWS

9.6

9.4

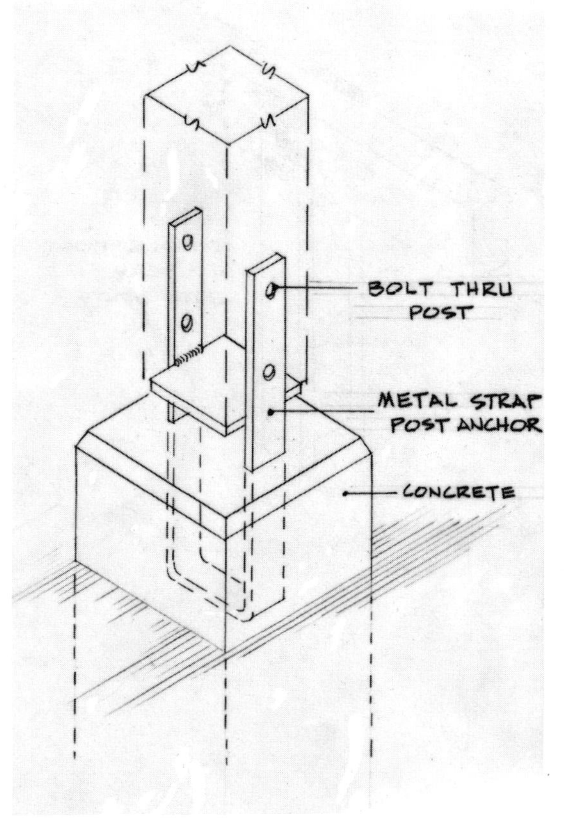
BOLT THRU POST
METAL STRAP POST ANCHOR
CONCRETE

9.5

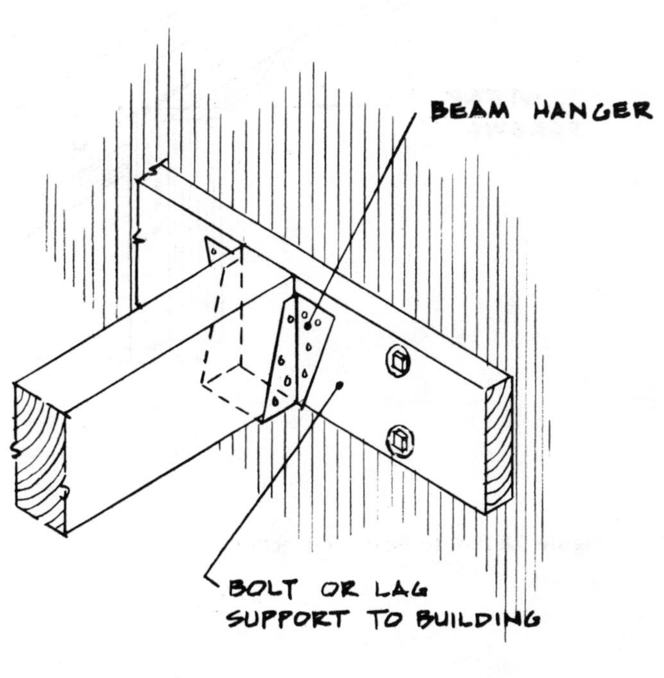
BEAM HANGER
BOLT OR LAG SUPPORT TO BUILDING

9.7

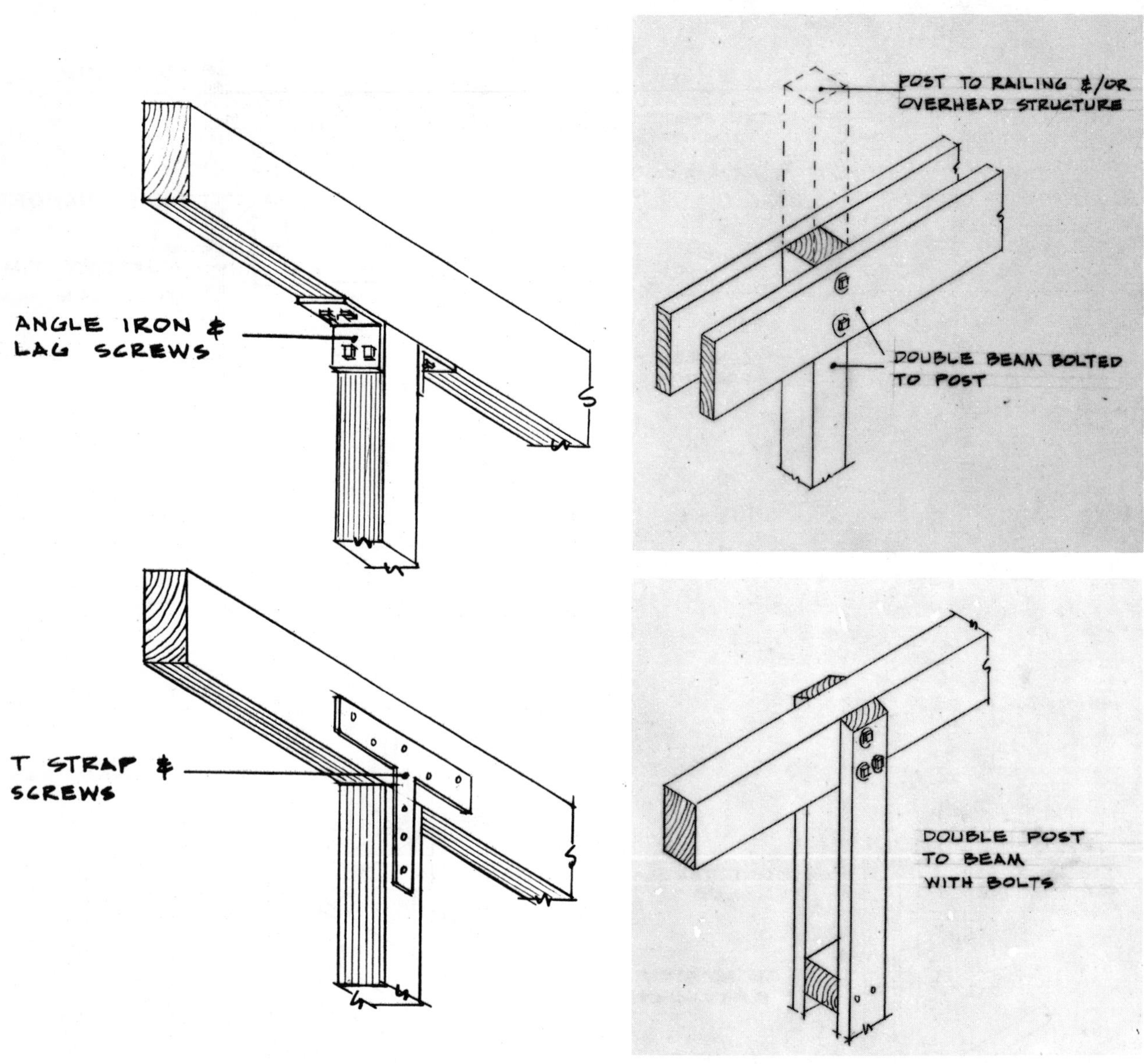
ANGLE IRON &
LAG SCREWS
T STRAP &
SCREWS
POST TO RAILING &/OR
OVERHEAD STRUCTURE
DOUBLE BEAM BOLTED
TO POST
DOUBLE POST
TO BEAM
WITH BOLTS

Figure 9.8 *Post to beam connections.*

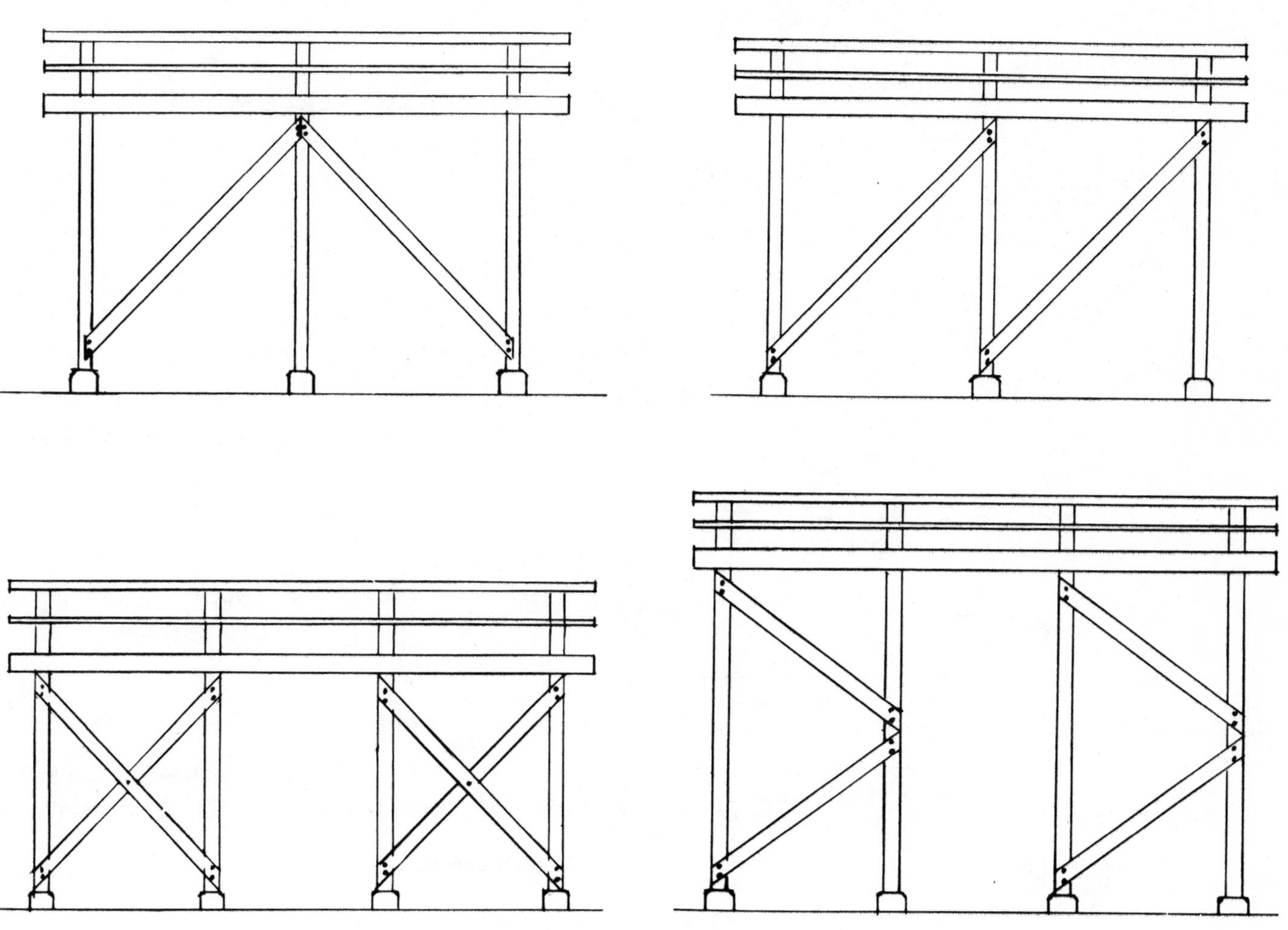

Figure 9.9 *Post bracing patterns for hillside decks.*

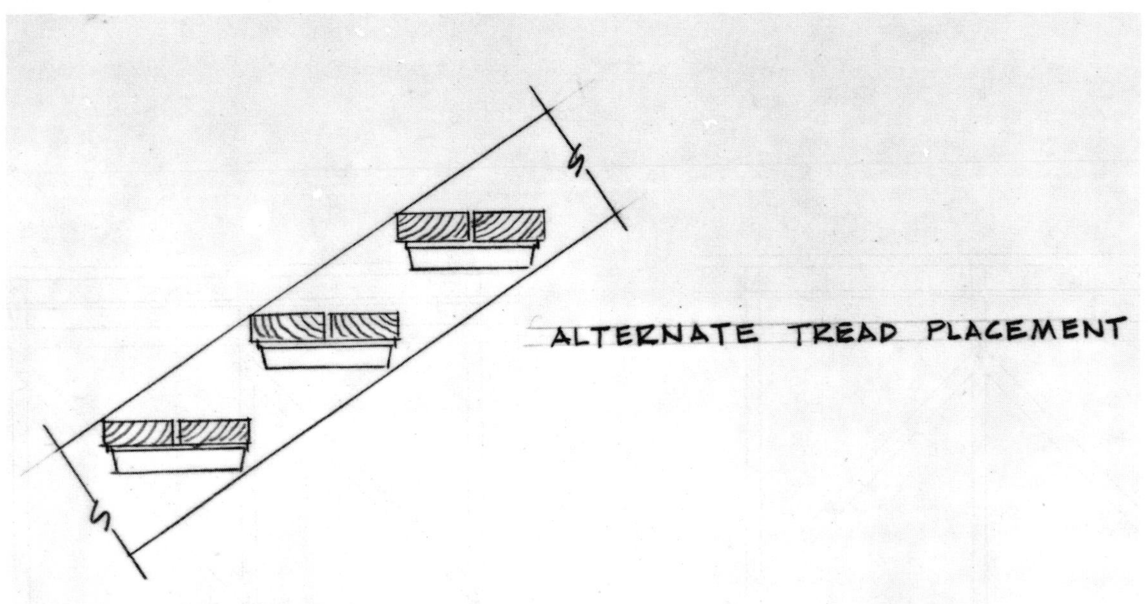
ALTERNATE TREAD PLACEMENT

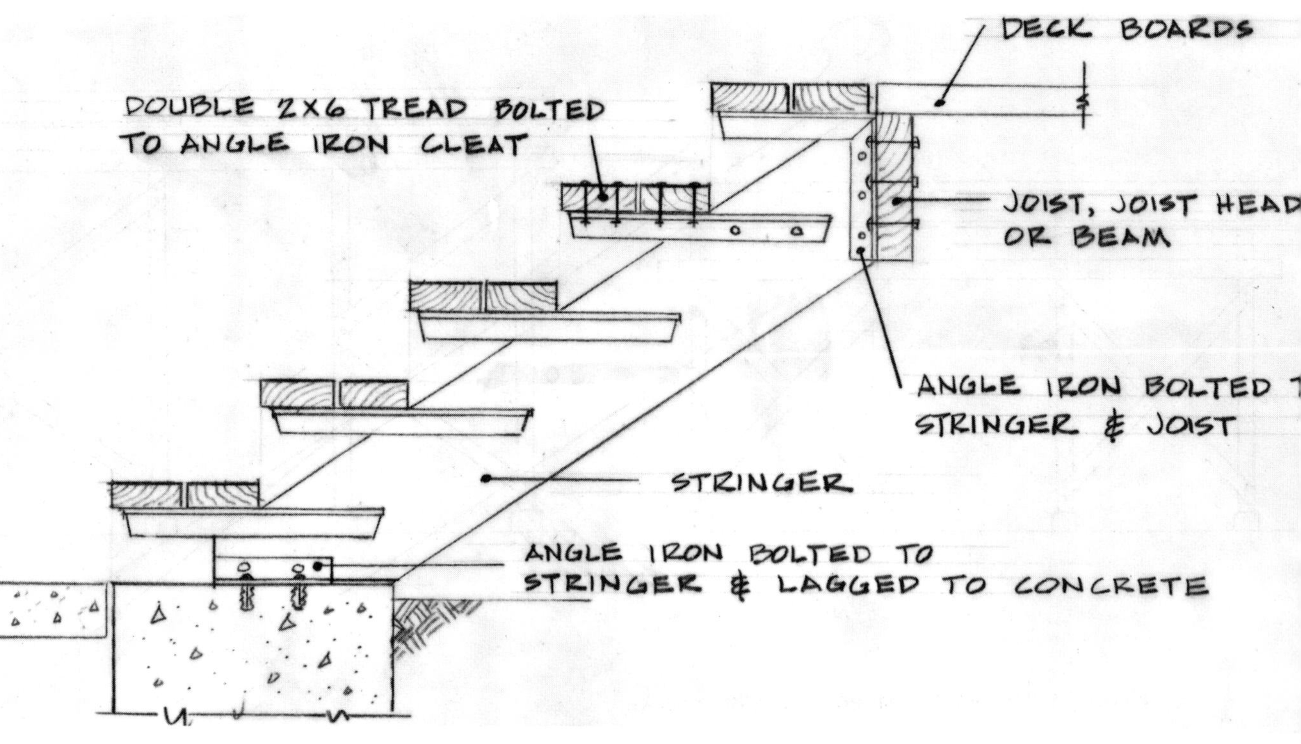
DECK BOARDS
DOUBLE 2X6 TREAD BOLTED
TO ANGLE IRON CLEAT
JOIST, JOIST HEAD
OR BEAM
ANGLE IRON BOLTED T
STRINGER & JOIST
STRINGER
ANGLE IRON BOLTED TO
STRINGER & LAGGED TO CONCRETE

Figure 9.10 *Stair connections.*

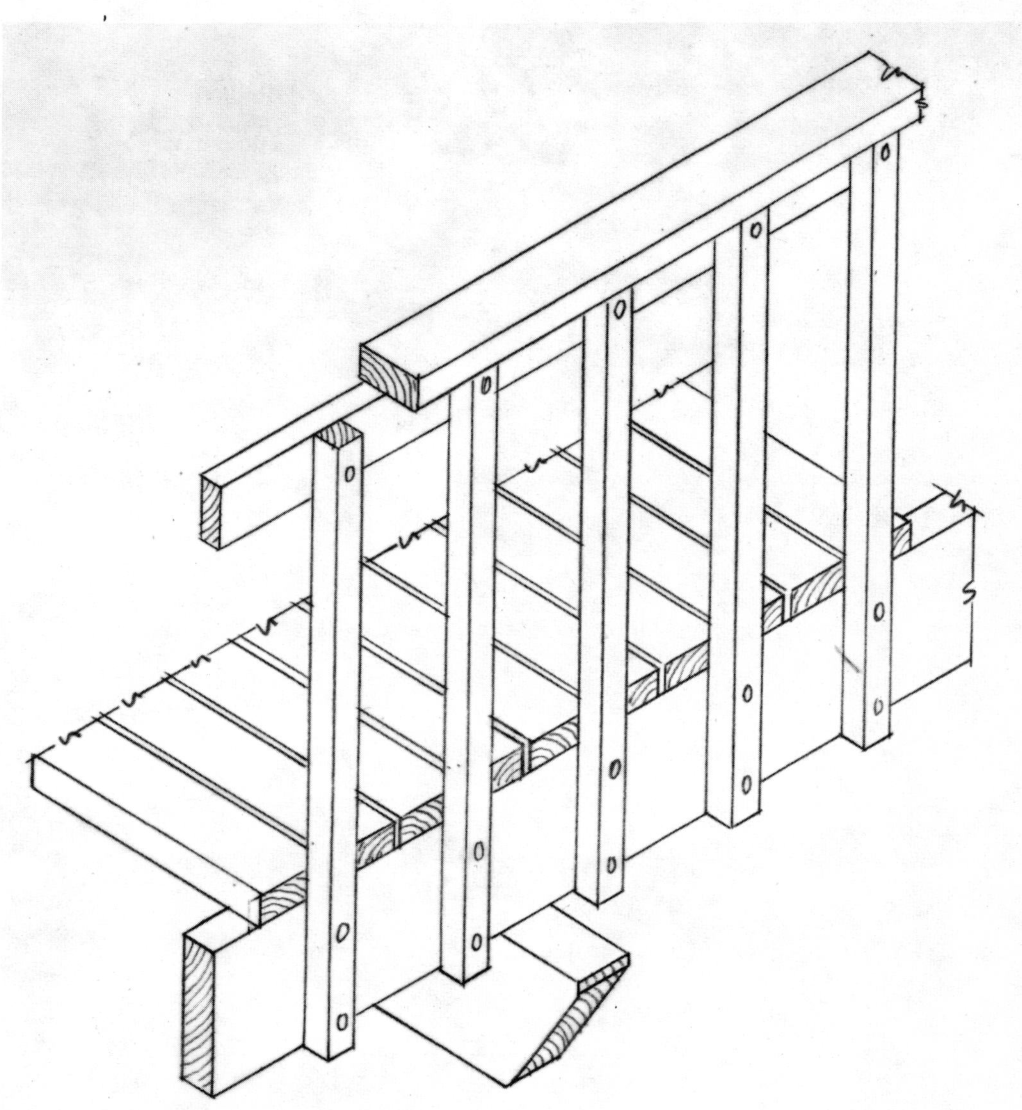

Figure 9.11 *One of many design possibilities tor a railing.*

Ed Dull, courtesy of Western Wood Products Association

9.12

Alex Pierce

Figures 9.12 - 9.13 *Deck and fire pit with details.*

LUMBER REQUIRED:

1-4×12 : 8'-0" LONG
18-5/4×4 : 10-0"
20-5/4×4 : 8'-0"
9-4×4(TREAT): 8'-0"
2-2×6 : 8'-0"
28-2×4 : 10'-0"
40-2×4 : 6'-0"
32-2×4 : 8'-0"
4-4×4(TREAT): 10'-0" LONG

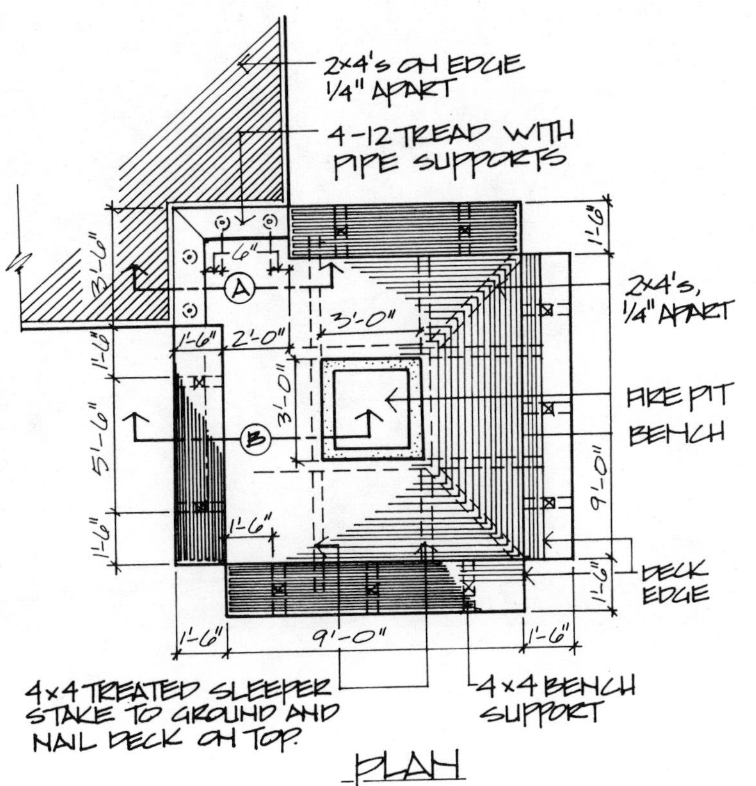
2×4's ON EDGE
1/4" APART
4-12 TREAD WITH
PIPE SUPPORTS
3'-6"
6"
A
3'-0"
1'-6"
2'-0"
1'-6"
3'-0"
B
5'-6"
1'-6"
1'-6"
2×4's,
1/4" APART
FIRE PIT
BENCH
9'-0"
1'-6"
DECK
EDGE
1'-6"
9'-0"
1'-6"
4×4 TREATED SLEEPER
STAKE TO GROUND AND
NAIL DECK ON TOP.
4×4 BENCH
SUPPORT
PLAN

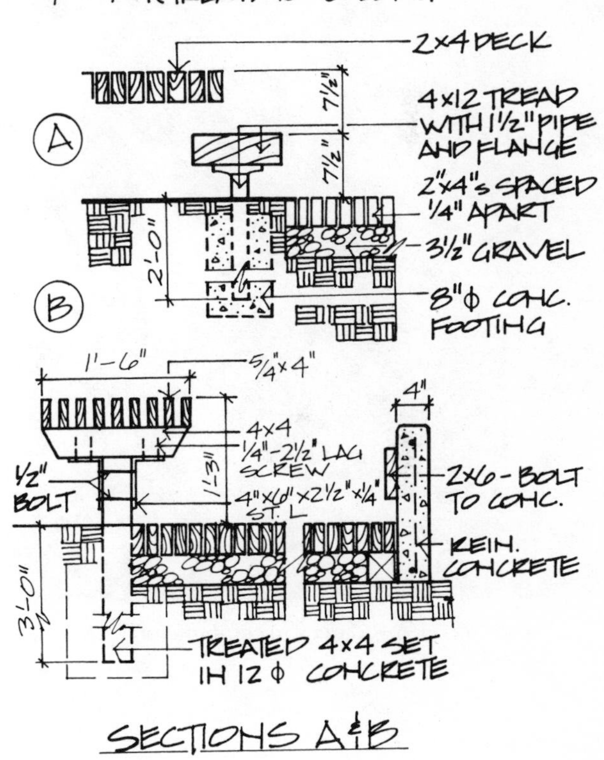
2×4 DECK
7 1/2"
A
7 1/2"
4×12 TREAD
WITH 1 1/2" PIPE
AND FLANGE
2"×4"s SPACED
1/4" APART
2'-0"
3 1/2" GRAVEL
B
8" φ CONC.
FOOTING
1'-6"
5/4"×4"
4"
4×4
1/4"-2 1/2" LAG
SCREW
1'3"
1/2"
BOLT
4"×6"×2 1/2"×1/4"
ST. L
2×6-BOLT
TO CONC.
REIN.
CONCRETE
3'-0"
TREATED 4×4 SET
IN 12 φ CONCRETE
SECTIONS A&B

STEP-DOWN FIREPIT

9.13

Western Wood Products Association

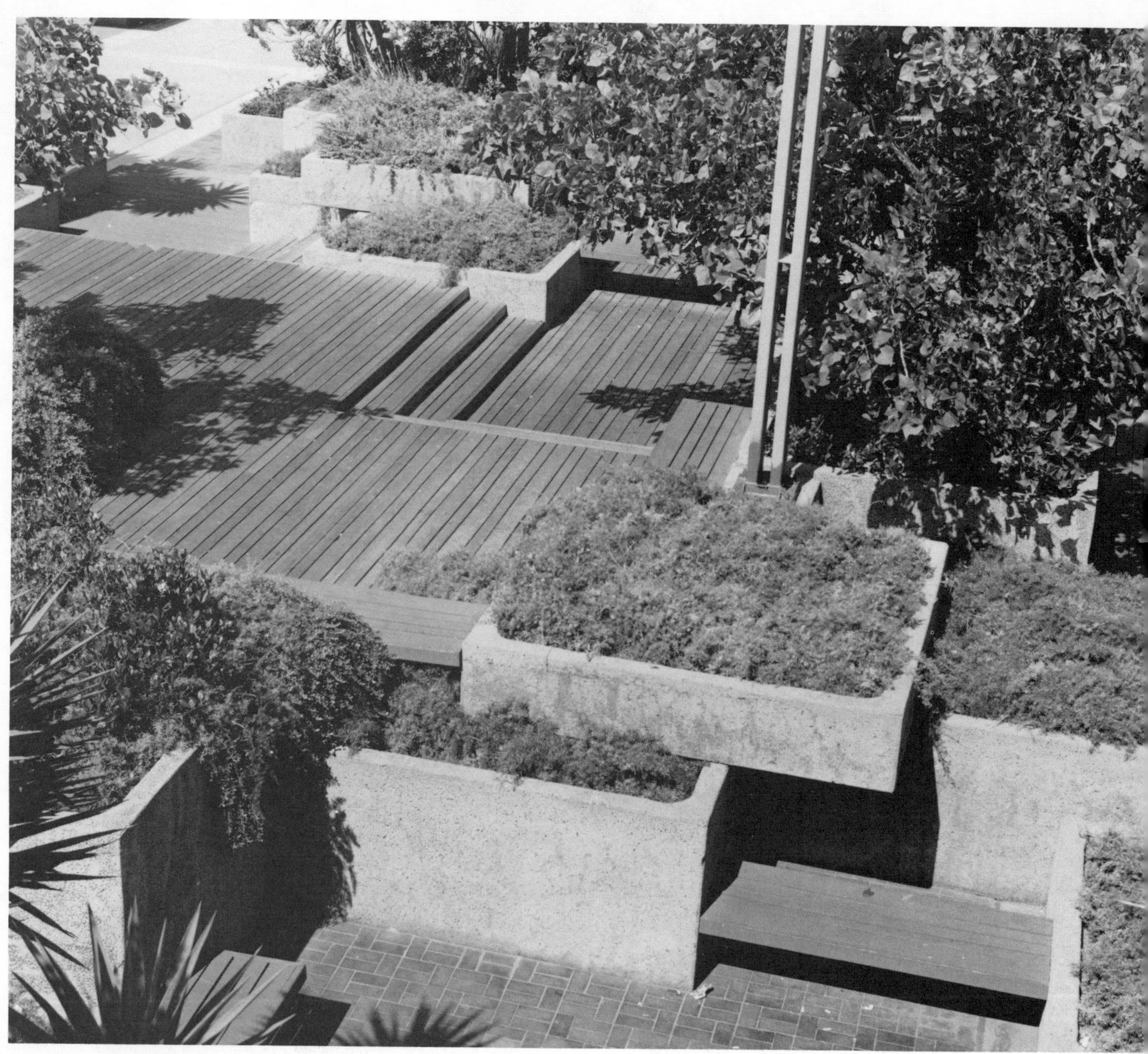

Figure 9.14 *Wood deck in combination with concrete planters.*

9.15

Theodore Brickman Co.

9.16

LaPorte County Landscaping

Figure 9.15 *Deck and shelter combination.*

Figure 9.16 *Wood bridge crosses a dry gravel moat to a wood deck in another portion of the meandering moat. Two poles from the deck center hold up "snow fence" type shelter.*

Charles R. Pearson, Western Wood Products Association

9.17 Blair and Zaik

Charles R. Pearson, Western Wood Products Association

9.18 Blair and Zaik

Figures 9.17 – 9.20 *Wood decks.*

California Redwood Association

9.19

Western Wood Products Association

9.20

Arthur W. Erfeldt

Charles R. Pearson, courtesy of Western Wood Products Association

9.21

Lawrence Halprin

9.22

Doede, Inc.

9.23

9.24

Figures 9.21 – 9.24 *Wood decks.*

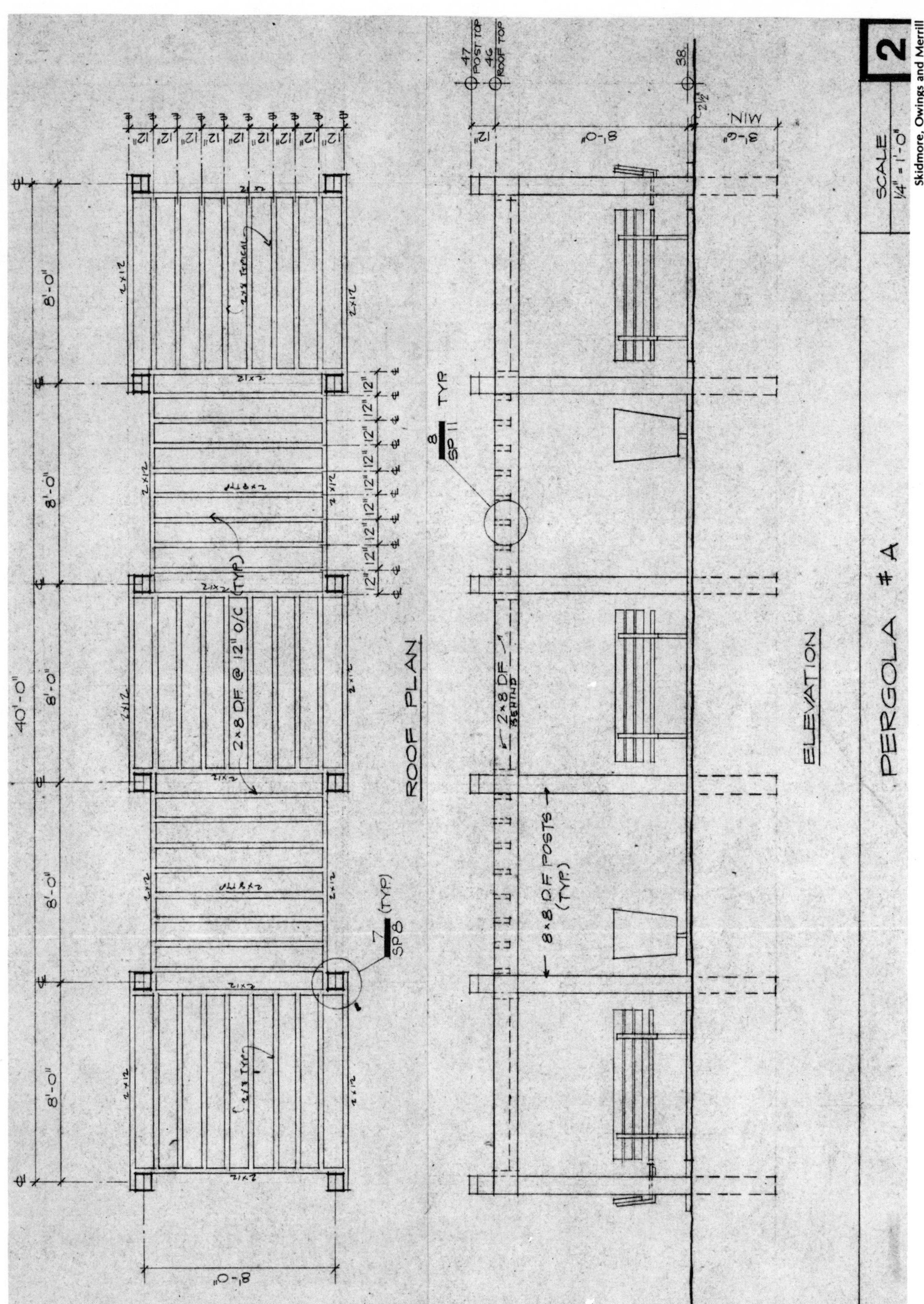
ROOF PLAN
2×8 DF @ 12" O/C (TYP)
40'-0"
8'-0"
ELEVATION
8×8 DF POSTS (TYP)
2×8 DF BEHIND
POST TOP
ROOF TOP
PERGOLA # A
SCALE
1/4" = 1'-0"
2
Skidmore, Owings and Merrill

Figure 9.25 *Pergola details.*

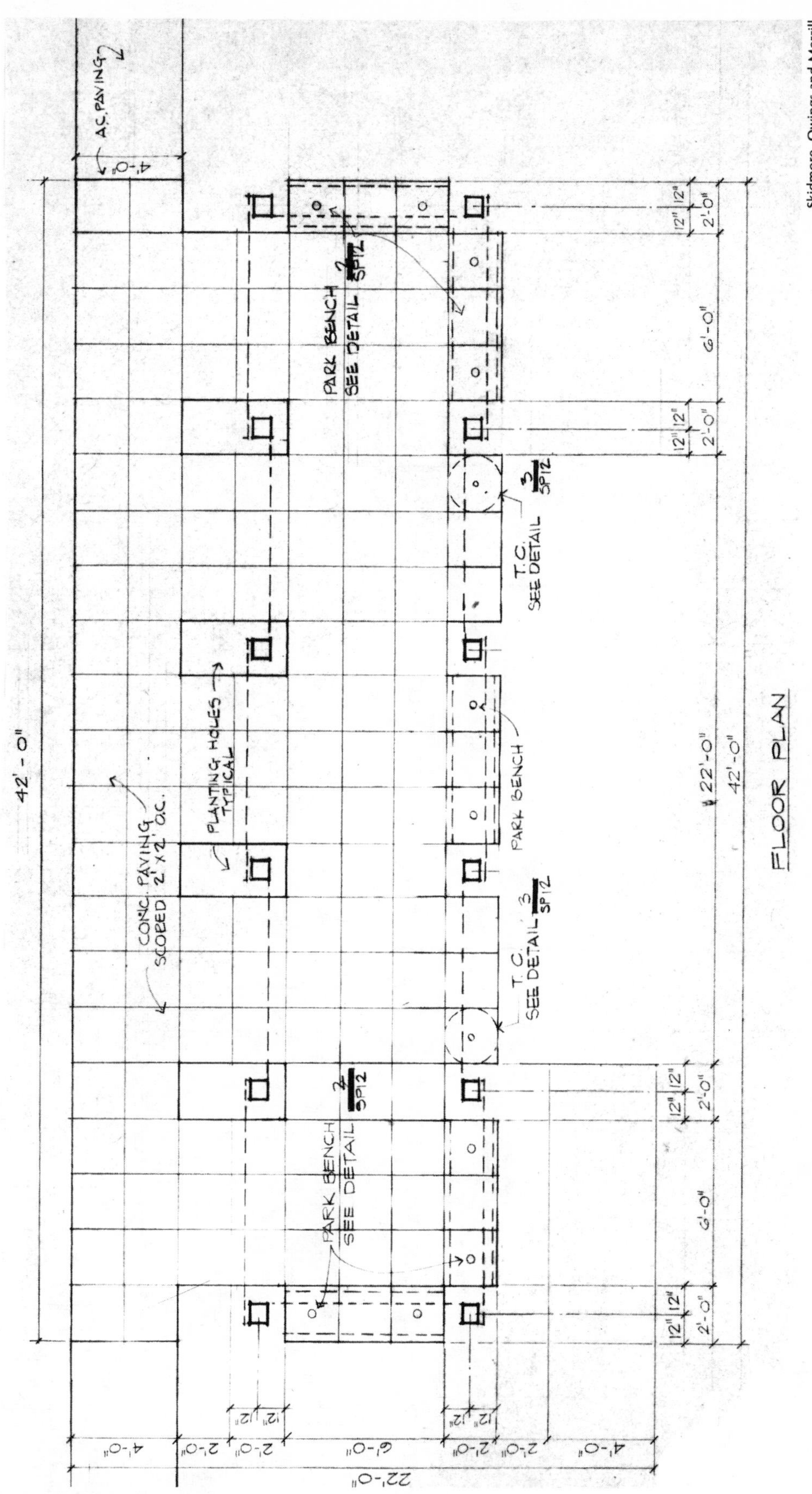
FLOOR PLAN
42' - 0"
AC PAVING
CONC. PAVING SCORED 2' X 2' O.C.
PLANTING HOLES TYPICAL
PARK BENCH SEE DETAIL
PARK BENCH
T.C. SEE DETAIL
22'-0"
6'-0"
2'-0"
4'-0"
12"

Skidmore, Owings and Merrill

Figure 9.26 *Pergola details.*

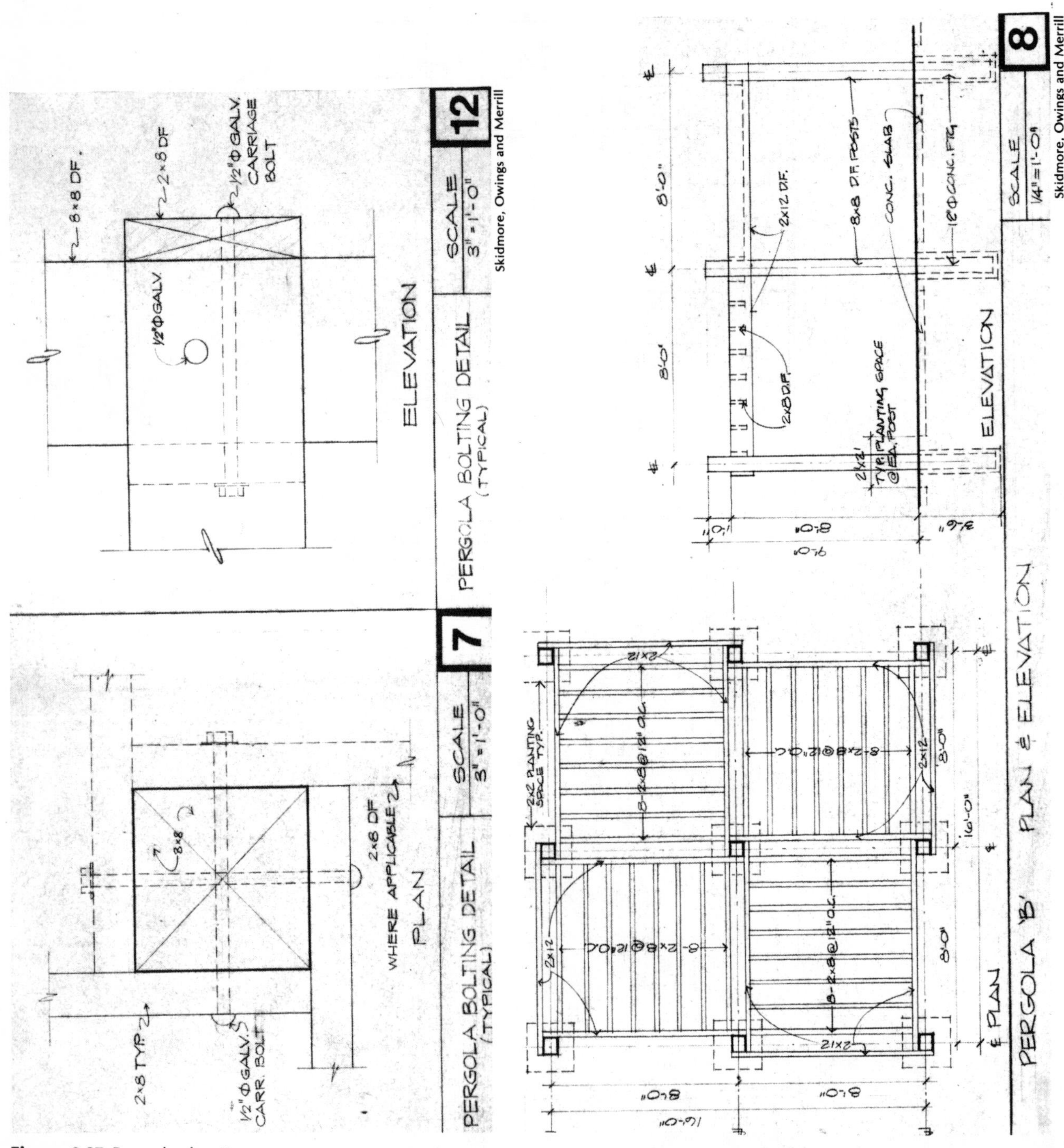
PERGOLA BOLTING DETAIL
(TYPICAL)
SCALE
3" = 1'-0"
7
PLAN
2×8 TYP.
1/2" Φ GALV. CARR. BOLT
2×8 DF WHERE APPLICABLE
8×8
PERGOLA BOLTING DETAIL
(TYPICAL)
SCALE
3" = 1'-0"
12
ELEVATION
8×8 DF.
2×8 DF
1/2" Φ GALV. CARRIAGE BOLT
1/2" Φ GALV.
Skidmore, Owings and Merrill
PERGOLA 'B' PLAN & ELEVATION
SCALE
1/4" = 1'-0"
8
ELEVATION
8×8 D.F. POSTS
CONC. SLAB
18" Φ CONC. FTG.
2x12 D.F.
2x8 D.F.
TYP. PLANTING SPACE @ EA. POST
℄ PLAN
8-2×8 @ 12" O.C.
2x12
2x2 PLANTING SPACE TYP.
16'-0"
8'-0"
Skidmore, Owings and Merrill

Figure 9.27 *Pergola details.*

9.28

9.29

9.30

Maurice Wrangell

Figures 9.28 – 9.30 *Pergola.*

9.31 Sasaki Associates

9.32 Sasaki Associates

Figures 9.31 – 9.32 *Shelter at an east coast waterfront park.*

9.33 William A. Behnke Associates

9.34 William A. Behnke Associates

Figures 9.33 – 9.34 *Shelter and pergola.*

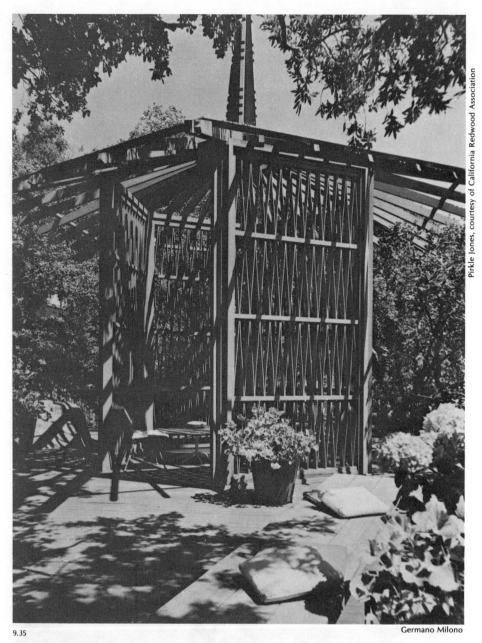

Pirkle Jones, courtesy of California Redwood Association

9.35

Germano Milono

9.36

Figures 9.35 – 9.38 *Gazebo and shelters.*

9.37

9.38

9.39 California Redwood Association

9.40 Ned Rucker

Phil Palmer, courtesy of California Redwood Association

9.41 California Redwood Association

9.42

Figures 9.39 – 9.41 *Shelter and deck combinations.*

Figures 9.42 – 9.47 *Miscellaneous shelters, many of which are in parks.*

Figure 9.48 *Amphitheater. The lawn on the left serves as seating.*

9.43

9.46

9.44

9.47

9.45

9.48

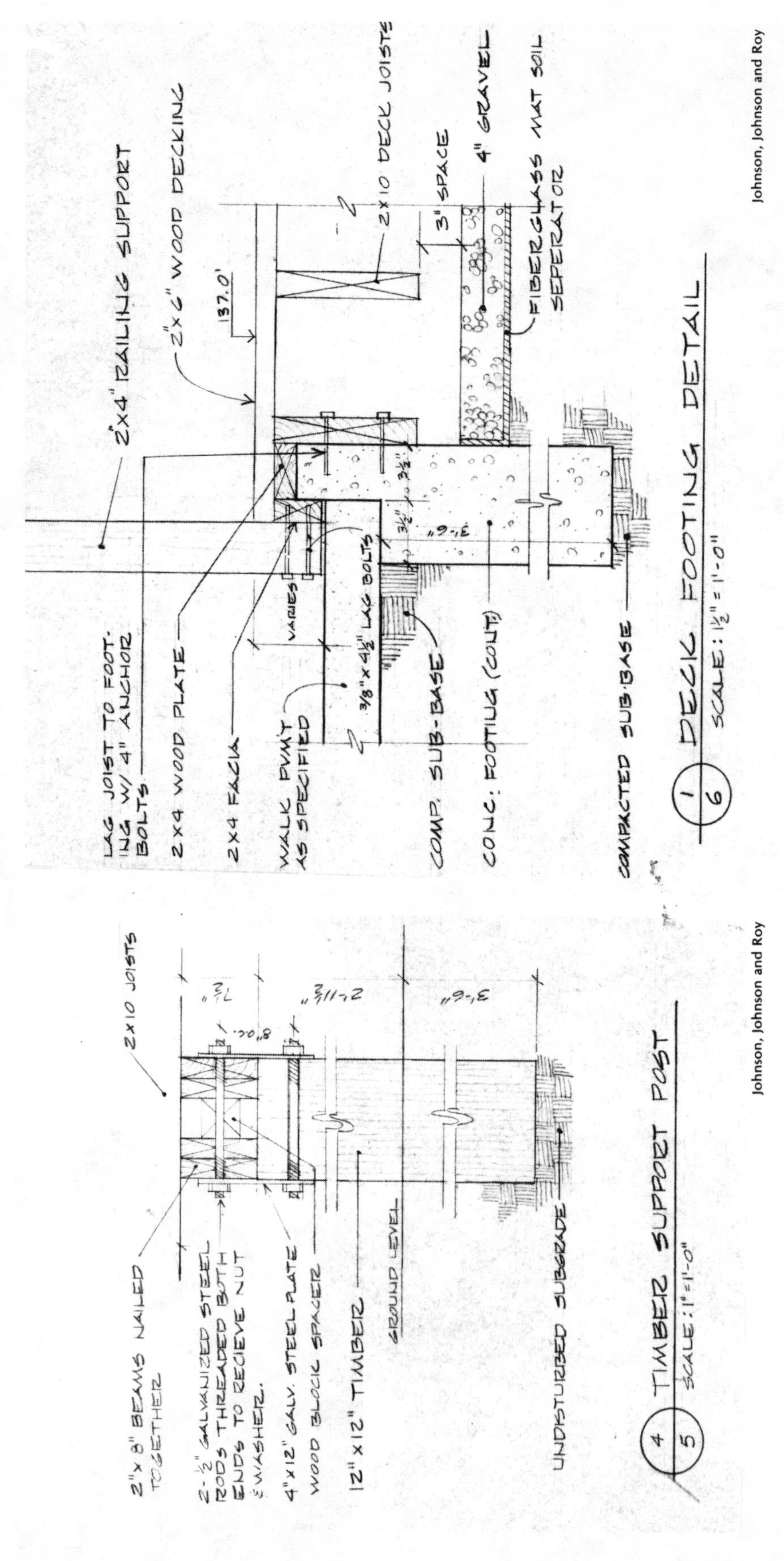
2"x 8" BEAMS NAILED TOGETHER
2 - ½" GALVANIZED STEEL RODS THREADED BOTH ENDS TO RECIEVE NUT & WASHER.
4"x 12" GALV. STEEL PLATE
WOOD BLOCK SPACER
12" x 12" TIMBER
GROUND LEVEL
UNDISTURBED SUBGRADE
2x10 JOISTS
TIMBER SUPPORT POST
SCALE: 1" = 1'-0"
Johnson, Johnson and Roy
LAG JOIST TO FOOTING W/ 4" ANCHOR BOLTS
2x4 WOOD PLATE
2x4 FACIA
WALK PVMT AS SPECIFIED
COMP. SUB-BASE
CONC. FOOTING (CONT.)
COMPACTED SUB-BASE
2x4" RAILING SUPPORT
2"x 6" WOOD DECKING
2x10 DECK JOISTS
3" SPACE
4" GRAVEL
FIBERGLASS MAT SOIL SEPERATOR
3/8" x 4½" LAG BOLTS
VARIES
DECK FOOTING DETAIL
SCALE: 1½" = 1'-0"
Johnson, Johnson and Roy

Figure 9.49 *Deck details.*

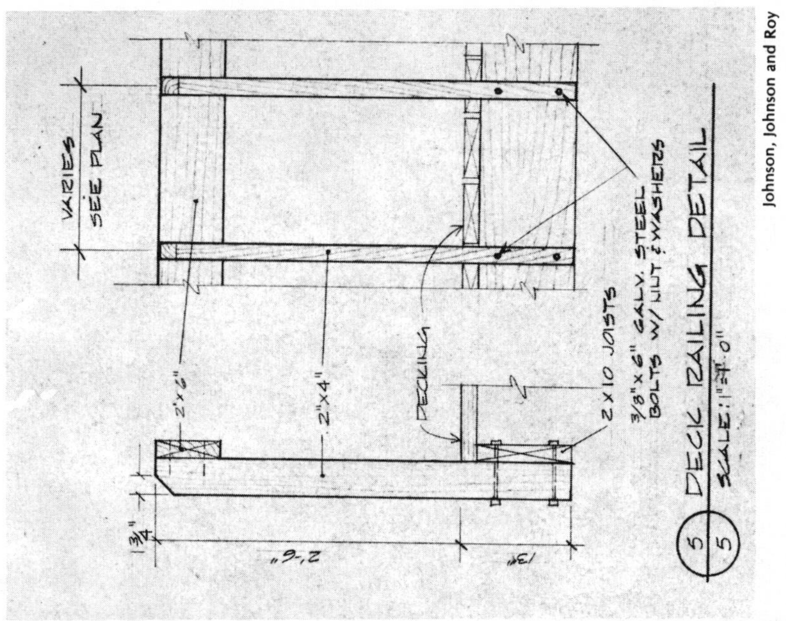
VARIES
SEE PLAN
2"x6"
2"x4"
DECKING
2X10 JOISTS
3/8" x 6" GALV. STEEL BOLTS W/ NUT & WASHERS
1 3/4"
2'-6"
13"
5
5
DECK RAILING DETAIL
SCALE: 1"=1'-0"

Johnson, Johnson and Roy

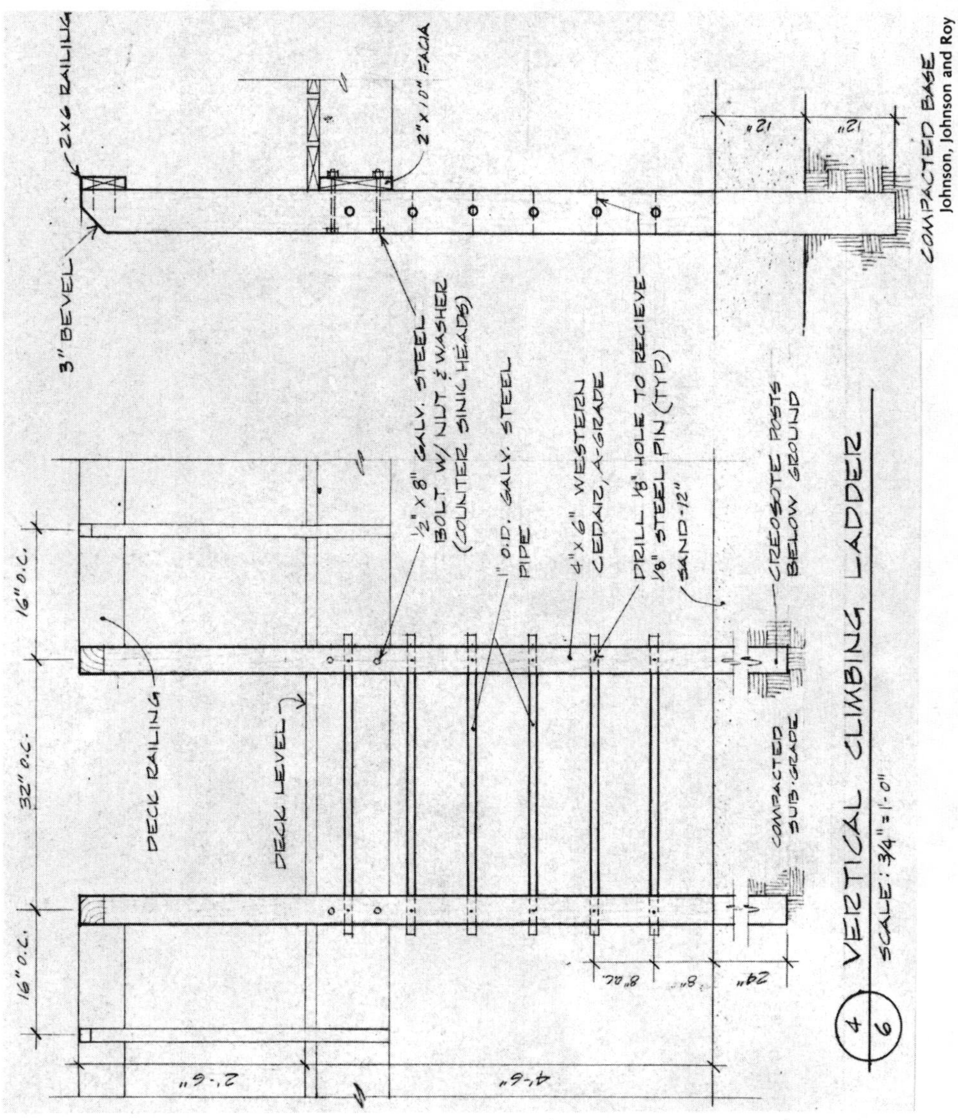
16" O.C.
32" O.C.
16" O.C.
DECK RAILING
DECK LEVEL
3" BEVEL
2X6 RAILING
2"X10" FACIA
1/2" X 8" GALV. STEEL BOLT W/ NUT & WASHER (COUNTER SINK HEADS)
1" O.D. GALV. STEEL PIPE
4"X6" WESTERN CEDAR, A-GRADE
DRILL 1/8" HOLE TO RECIEVE 1/8" STEEL PIN (TYP)
SAND-12"
CREOSOTE POSTS BELOW GROUND
COMPACTED SUB-GRADE
COMPACTED BASE
2'-6"
4'-6"
8" O.C.
8"
24"
12"
12"
4
6
VERTICAL CLIMBING LADDER
SCALE: 3/4"=1'-0"

Johnson, Johnson and Roy

Figure 9.50 *Deck details.*

9.51 Bailey and Associates

9.52

Figures 9.51 – 9.52 *Shelters and decks over water.*

9.53 California Dept. of Transportation

9.54

Figure 9.53 *Shelter at a roadside reststop.*
Figure 9.54 *Shelter in an arboretum.*

9.55

9.57

9.56

9.58

Figures 9.55 – 9.58 *Various designs of landscape structures.*

9.59

9.60

9.61

9.62

9.63

Figures 9.59 – 9.63 *Variety of designs for bridges.*

9.64

9.65

9.66

9.67

9.68

9.69

9.70 Interdesign, Inc.

9.72 Interdesign, Inc.

9.71 Environmental Planning and Design

9.73

9.74 U.S. Forest Service

Figure 9.64 *Pedestrian bridge at a shopping center.*
Figure 9.65 *Vehicular and pedestrian bridge in a park.*
Figure 9.66 *Bridge over a stream in a park.*
Figure 9.67 *Golf course bridge.*
Figure 9.68 *Vehicular bridge on a college campus.*
Figure 9.69 *Office courtyard.*
Figures 9.70 – 9.74 *Bridges in parks.*

9.75

9.77

9.76

9.78

Figures 9.75 – 9.78 *Bridges with a close-up of related handrails.*
Figures 9.79 – 9.80, 9.82 – 9.83 *Bridges in parks.*
Figure 9.81 *Water garden in a botanical park.*

9.79

9.80

9.81

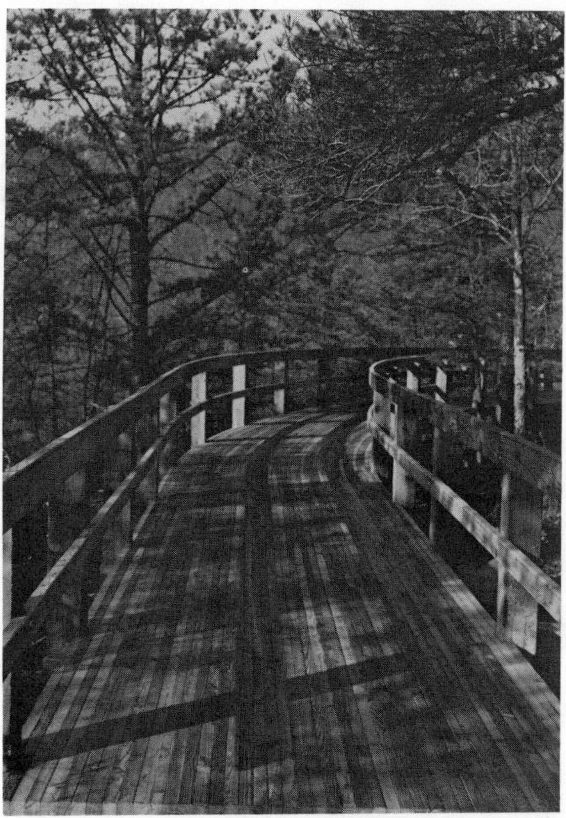

9.82 U.S. Forest Service, George Washington N.F.

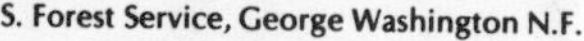

9.83

9.84

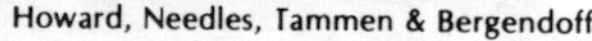

Howard, Needles, Tammen & Bergendoff

9.85 Walker-Harris-Associates-Inc.

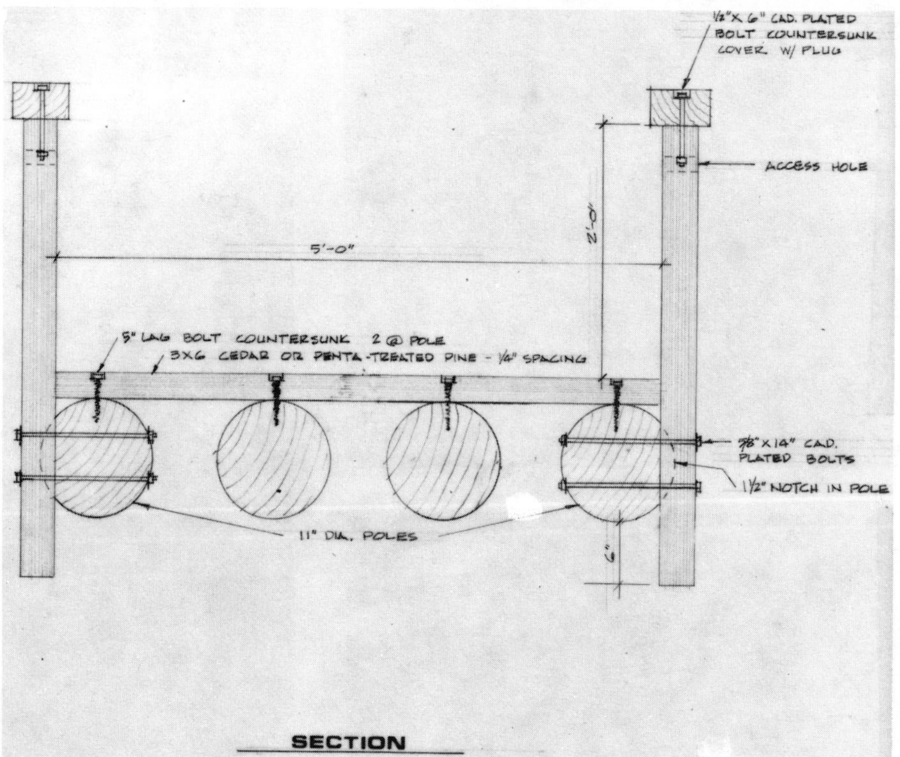
1/2"X 6" CAD. PLATED
BOLT COUNTERSUNK
COVER W/ PLUG
ACCESS HOLE
2'-0"
5'-0"
5" LAG BOLT COUNTERSUNK 2 @ POLE
3X6 CEDAR OR PENTA-TREATED PINE - 1/4" SPACING
5/8" X 14" CAD.
PLATED BOLTS
1 1/2" NOTCH IN POLE
11" DIA. POLES
6"
SECTION

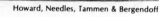

9.86 Walker-Harris-Associates-Inc.

Figure 9.84 *Bridge between the beach and bathhouse at a national park.*

Figures 9.85 – 9.86 *Bridge and detail for a nature trail in the Midwest.*

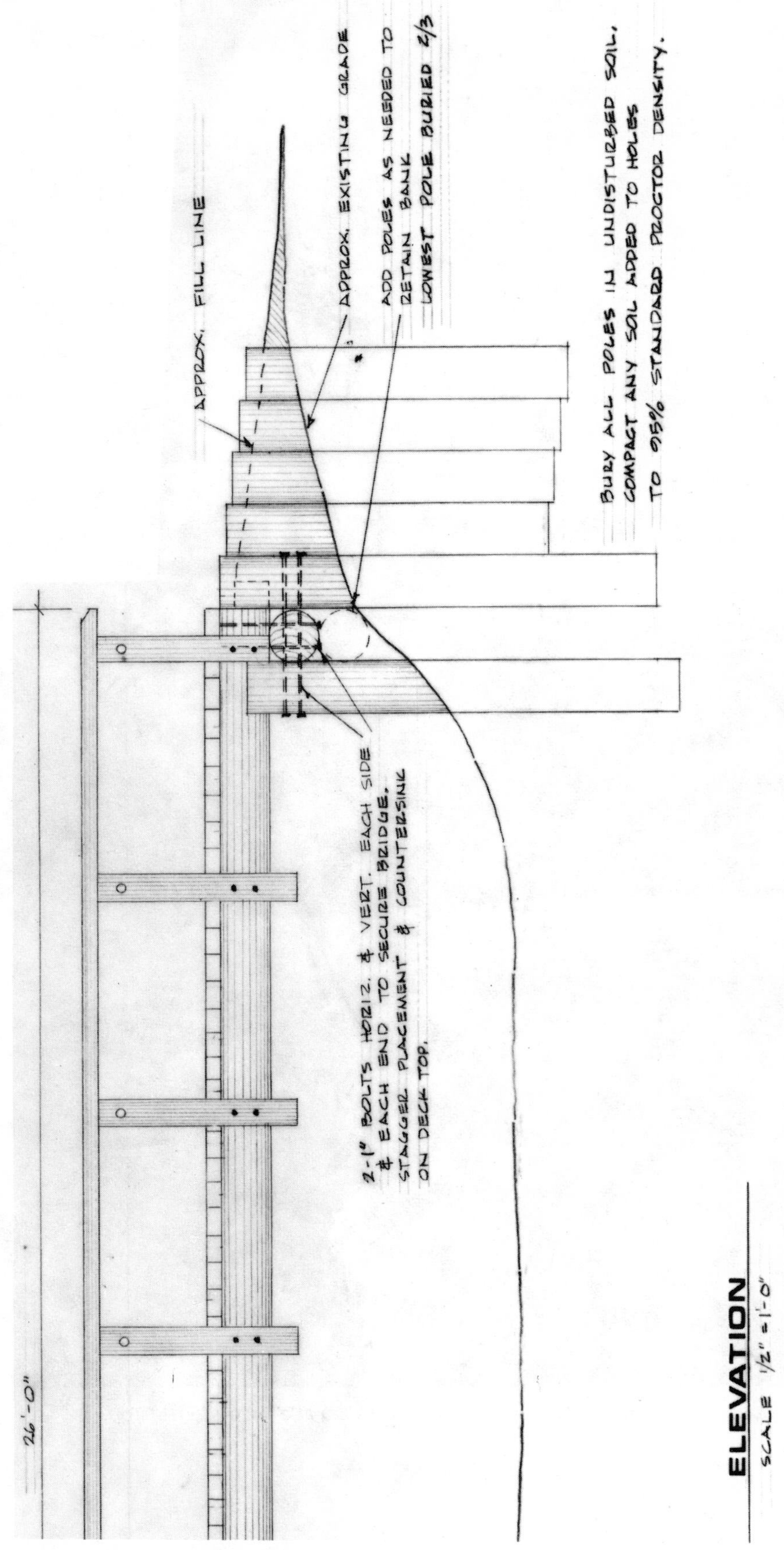

APPROX. FILL LINE
APPROX. EXISTING GRADE
ADD POLES AS NEEDED TO RETAIN BANK
LOWEST POLE BURIED 2/3
BURY ALL POLES IN UNDISTURBED SOIL, COMPACT ANY SOIL ADDED TO HOLES TO 95% STANDARD PROCTOR DENSITY.
2-1" BOLTS HORIZ. & VERT. EACH SIDE & EACH END TO SECURE BRIDGE. STAGGER PLACEMENT & COUNTERSINK ON DECK TOP.
26'-0"
ELEVATION
SCALE 1/2" = 1'-0"

Figure 9.87 *Bridge detail. See Figures 9.85 and 9.86.*

Nebraska Department of Roads

Figure 9.88 *Rough form-finish concrete bridge over a stream at a roadside reststop.*

10

Play and Recreation Equipment

There is an infinite variety of playground equipment currently on the market. The variety of styles, design, and use of materials represent wide-ranging thought and philosophy regarding children's play activities. There are many playgrounds containing equipment which has been custom designed. In some cases the custom designed playground equipment of today becomes a mass produced catalog item tomorrow.

The site designer is faced with a decision in designing playgrounds, whether to select catalog items or custom design. When selecting catalog items it is fairly simple to select those particular products which satisfy the clients' needs and have the contractor follow the manufacturer's instructions for installation. It is necessary during custom designing to research materials and carefully design the equipment to fit human (childrens') dimensions. Safety must be considered in the design phase. Metals that are used need to be corrosion resistant. Wood needs to be either redwood or pressure treated timbers utilizing non-toxic preservatives.

Playground owners are faced with a number of maintenance problems of which the designer should be aware. Metals which are not galvanized and require painting are subject to wear and constant corrosion. Frequent repainting and touch up are required. Quite frequently fasteners work loose and must be tightened. Cables loosen and require tightening with a turnbuckle.

Loose materials such as sand or fine gravel get into the shoes and cuffs of children and are carried away. Even though they must be replaced periodically, they are, along with wood chips, much softer cushioning materials for play areas than asphalt which is sometimes used. Sand can also become a play activity in and of itself with children using it to build sand castles, etc. Timbers and other materials need to have rounded or chamfered edges in order to reduce the harshness and any danger that might come from children striking sharp edges when they fall on or run into them.

Most play areas will need to be drained in order to prevent or minimize water accumulation and maximize the time use availability of the play area.

REFERENCES FOR FURTHER READING

Ramsey, C.G., and Sleeper, H.R. *Architectural Graphics Standards.* 7th Edition. New York: Wiley, 1981.

Jack Sterling

Figure 10.1 Sculptural playground.

Bonnell and Associates

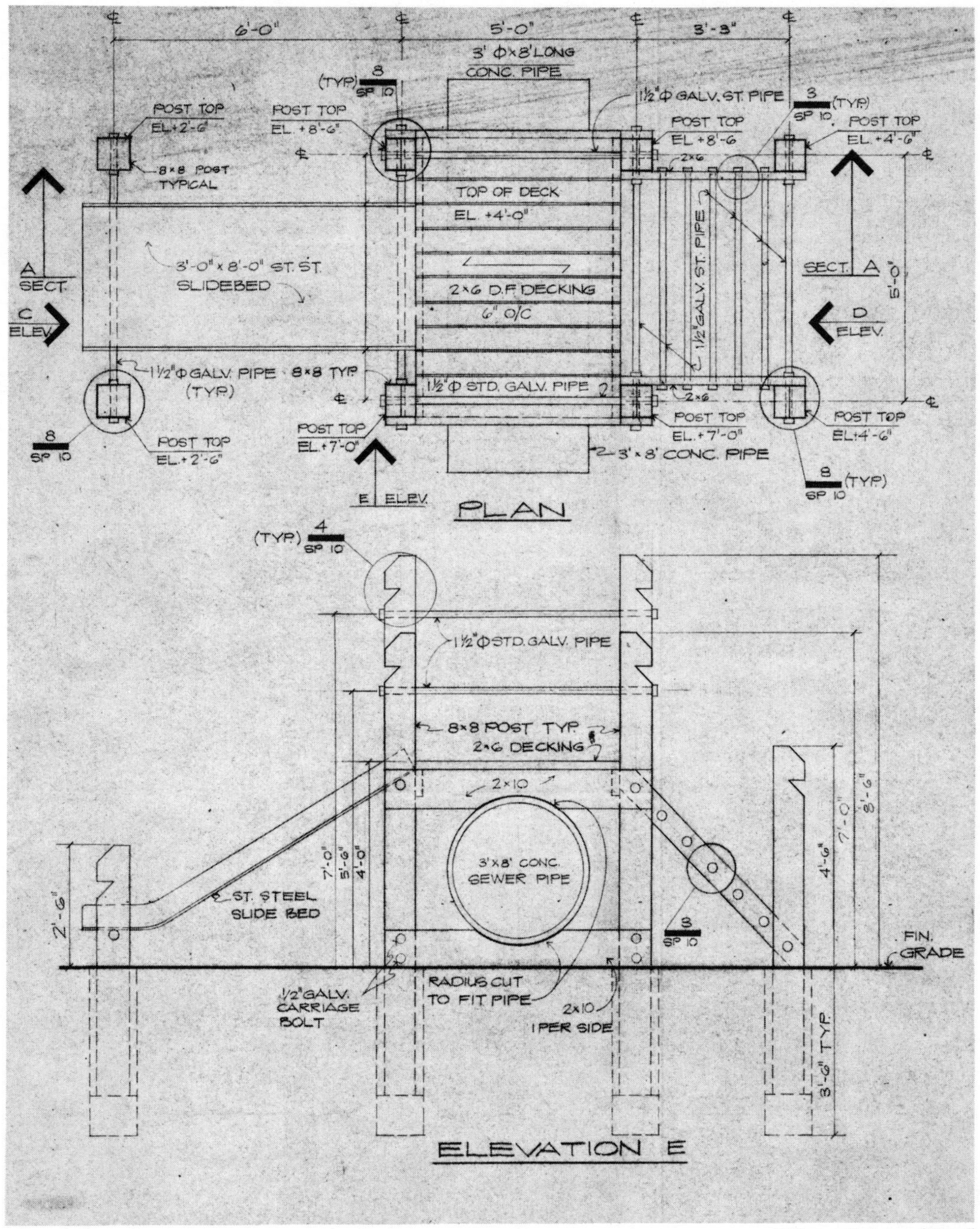
PLAN
ELEVATION E
3' Φ x 8' LONG CONC. PIPE
TOP OF DECK EL. +4'-0"
2x6 D.F. DECKING 6" O/C
3'-0" x 8'-0" ST. ST. SLIDEBED
8x8 POST TYPICAL
3'x8' CONC. SEWER PIPE
ST. STEEL SLIDE BED
1/2" GALV. CARRIAGE BOLT
RADIUS CUT TO FIT PIPE
2x10 1 PER SIDE
FIN. GRADE

Figure 10.2 *Timber play equipment details.*

Skidmore, Owings and Merrill

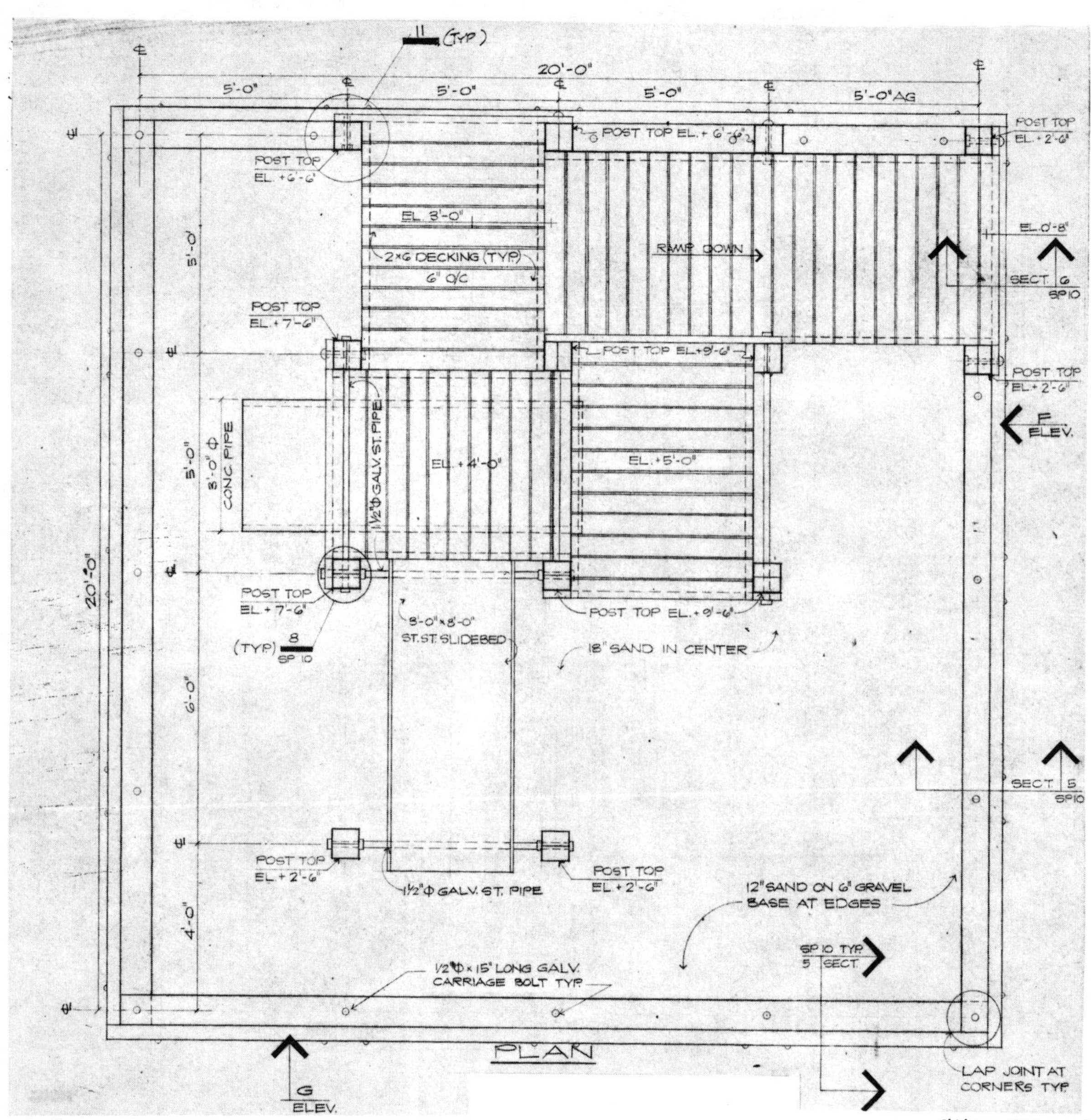

PLAN
20'-0"
5'-0"
5'-0"
5'-0"
5'-0" AG
POST TOP EL. +6'-6"
POST TOP EL. +7'-6"
POST TOP EL. +9'-6"
POST TOP EL. +2'-6"
EL. 3'-0"
2×6 DECKING (TYP.) 6" O/C
RAMP DOWN
EL. 0'-8"
SECT. 6 SP10
EL. +4'-0"
EL. +5'-0"
8'-0" Φ CONC PIPE
1½"Φ GALV. ST. PIPE
8'-0"×8'-0" ST. ST. SLIDEBED
18" SAND IN CENTER
F ELEV.
SECT. 5 SP10
12" SAND ON 6" GRAVEL BASE AT EDGES
½"Φ×15" LONG GALV. CARRIAGE BOLT TYP.
LAP JOINT AT CORNERS TYP.
G ELEV.

Skidmore, Owings and Merrill

Figure 10.3 *Timber play equipment details.*

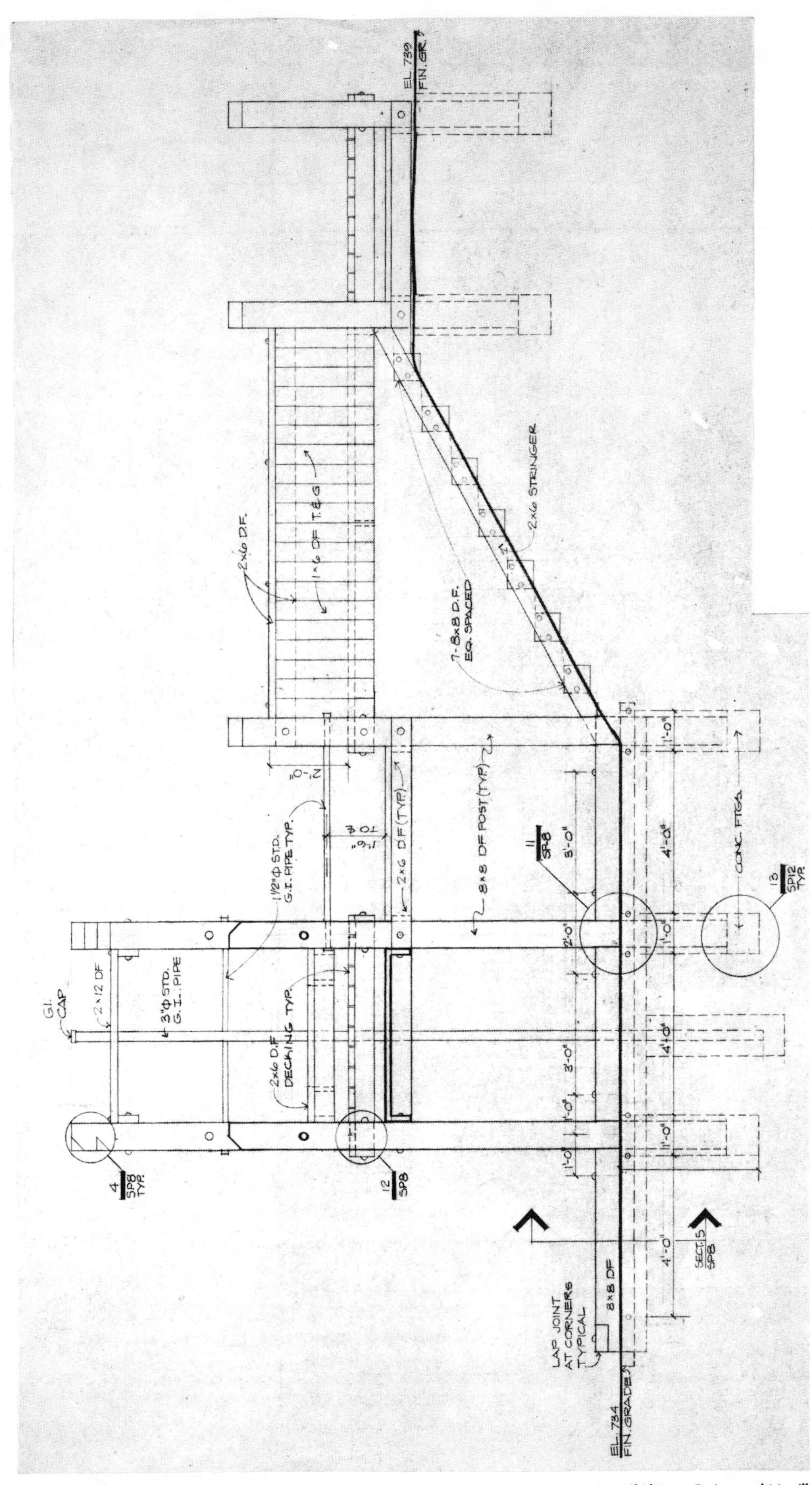
EL. 739
FIN. GR.
2x6 D.F.
1x6 DF T&G
2x6 STRINGER
7-8x8 D.F.
EQ. SPACED
8x8 DF POST (TYP)
2x6 DF (TYP)
1 1/2"Φ STD.
G.I. PIPE TYP.
G.I.
CAP
2x12 DF
3"Φ STD.
G.I. PIPE
2x6 D.F
DECKING TYP.
CONC. FTGS.
LAP JOINT
AT CORNERS
TYPICAL
8x8 DF
EL. 734
FIN. GRADE

Skidmore, Owings and Merrill

Figure 10.4 *Timber play equipment details.*

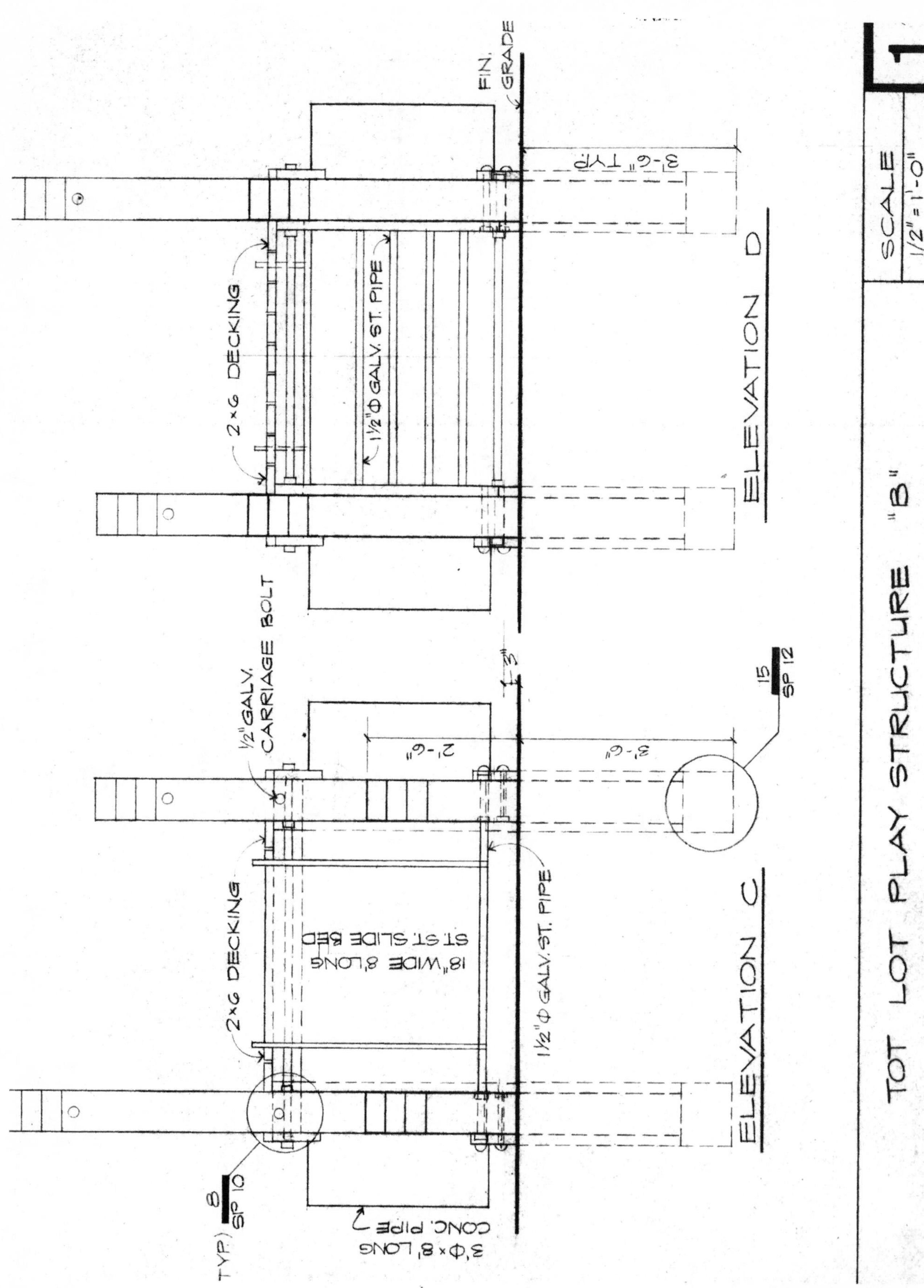
TOT LOT PLAY STRUCTURE "B"
SCALE
1/2" = 1'-0"
1
ELEVATION C
ELEVATION D
2×6 DECKING
1½"Φ GALV. ST. PIPE
18" WIDE 8' LONG
ST. ST. SLIDE BED
1/2" GALV. CARRIAGE BOLT
3'Φ × 8' LONG
CONC. PIPE
FIN. GRADE
3'-6" TYP.
2'-6"
3'-6"
3"
(TYP.)
8
SP 10
15
SP 12

Figure 10.5 *Play structure details.*

Skidmore, Owings and Merrill

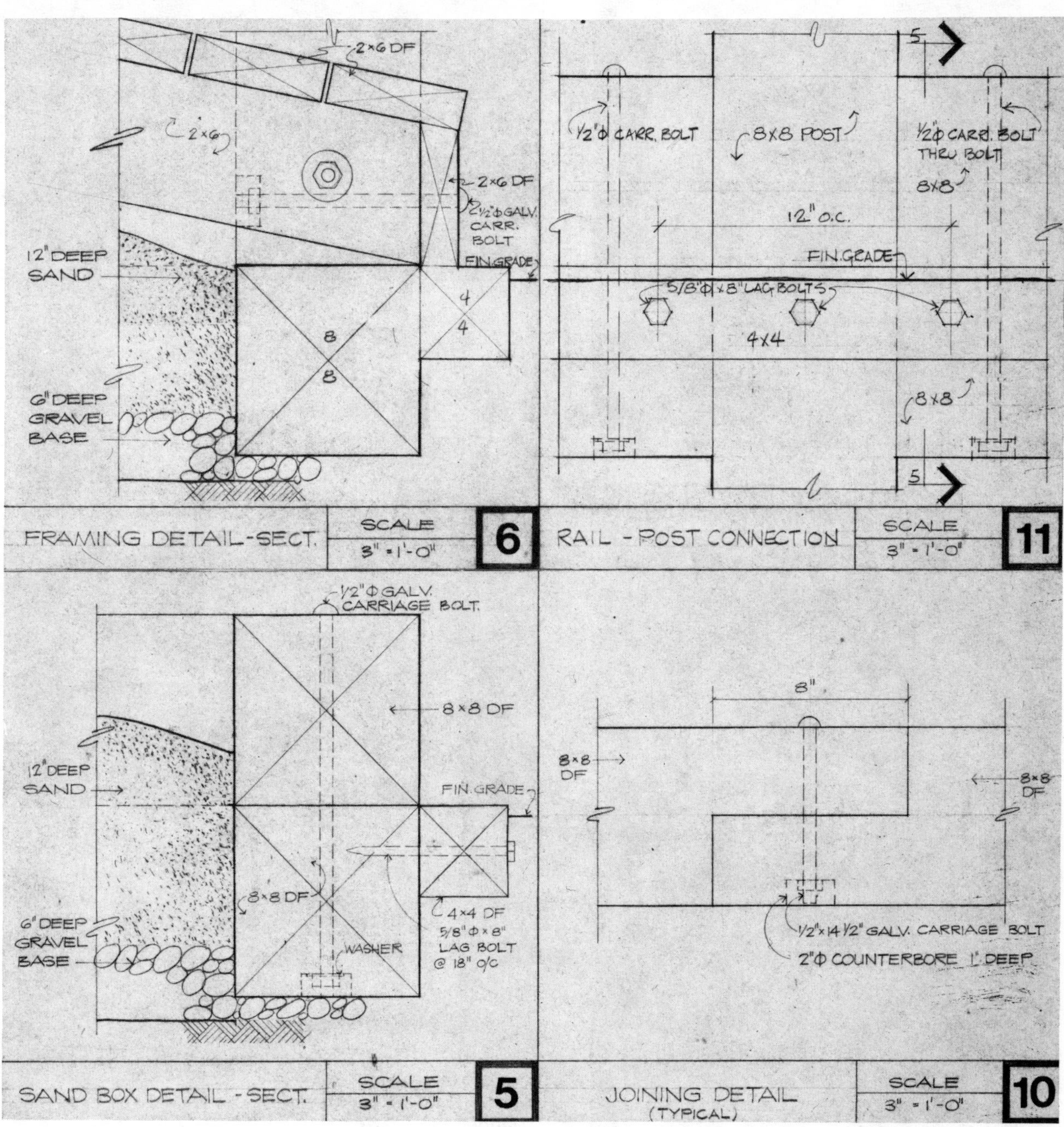
2×6 DF
2×6
2×6 DF
1/2"Φ GALV. CARR. BOLT
12" DEEP SAND
FIN.GRADE
8
8
4
4
6" DEEP GRAVEL BASE
FRAMING DETAIL-SECT.
SCALE
3" = 1'-0"
6
1/2"Φ CARR. BOLT
8X8 POST
1/2"Φ CARR. BOLT THRU BOLT
8X8
12" O.C.
FIN.GRADE
5/8"Φ x 8" LAG BOLTS
4X4
8X8
5
5
RAIL - POST CONNECTION
SCALE
3" = 1'-0"
11
1/2"Φ GALV. CARRIAGE BOLT
8×8 DF
12" DEEP SAND
FIN.GRADE
8×8 DF
4×4 DF
5/8"Φ × 8" LAG BOLT @ 18" o/c
WASHER
6" DEEP GRAVEL BASE
SAND BOX DETAIL - SECT.
SCALE
3" = 1'-0"
5
8"
8×8 DF
8×8 DF
1/2"×14 1/2" GALV. CARRIAGE BOLT
2"Φ COUNTERBORE 1" DEEP
JOINING DETAIL
(TYPICAL)
SCALE
3" = 1'-0"
10

Figure 10.6 *Play structure details.*

Skidmore, Owings and Merrill

10.7

10.9

10.10

10.8

Figures 10.7 – 10.12 *Playground designed by M. Paul Friedberg and Partners.*

Figures 10.13 – 10.16 *Playground designed by Myrick, Newman and Dahlberg.*

10.11

10.12

10.13

10.14

10.15

10.16

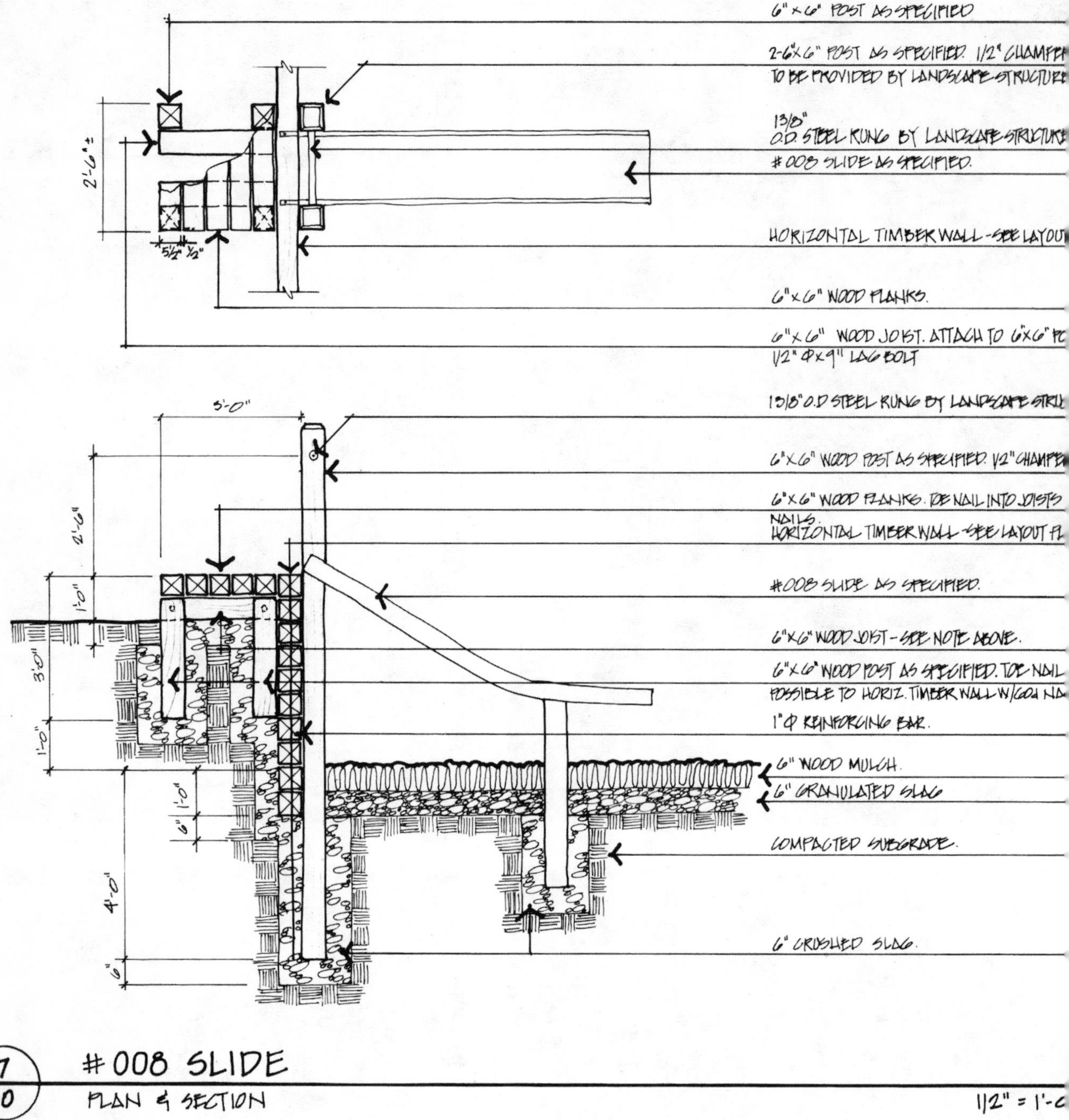
6" × 6" POST AS SPECIFIED
2-6"×6" POST AS SPECIFIED. 1/2" CHAMFER
TO BE PROVIDED BY LANDSCAPE STRUCTURE
13/8" O.D. STEEL RUNG BY LANDSCAPE STRUCTURE
#008 SLIDE AS SPECIFIED.
HORIZONTAL TIMBER WALL - SEE LAYOUT
6"×6" WOOD PLANKS.
6"×6" WOOD JOIST. ATTACH TO 6"×6" PO
1/2" Φ×9" LAG BOLT
13/8" O.D STEEL RUNG BY LANDSCAPE STRU
6"×6" WOOD POST AS SPECIFIED. 1/2" CHAMFER
6"×6" WOOD PLANKS. TOE NAIL INTO JOISTS
NAILS.
HORIZONTAL TIMBER WALL - SEE LAYOUT PL
#008 SLIDE AS SPECIFIED.
6"×6" WOOD JOIST - SEE NOTE ABOVE.
6"×6" WOOD POST AS SPECIFIED. TOE NAIL
POSSIBLE TO HORIZ. TIMBER WALL W/60d NA
1" Φ REINFORCING BAR.
6" WOOD MULCH.
6" GRANULATED SLAG
COMPACTED SUBGRADE.
6" CRUSHED SLAG.
2'-6"±
5½" ½"
5'-0"
2'-6"
1'-0"
3'-0"
1'-0"
1'-0"
6"
4'-0"
6"
7
10
#008 SLIDE
PLAN & SECTION
1/2" = 1'-0

Bonnell and Associates

Figure 10.17 *Play structure details.*

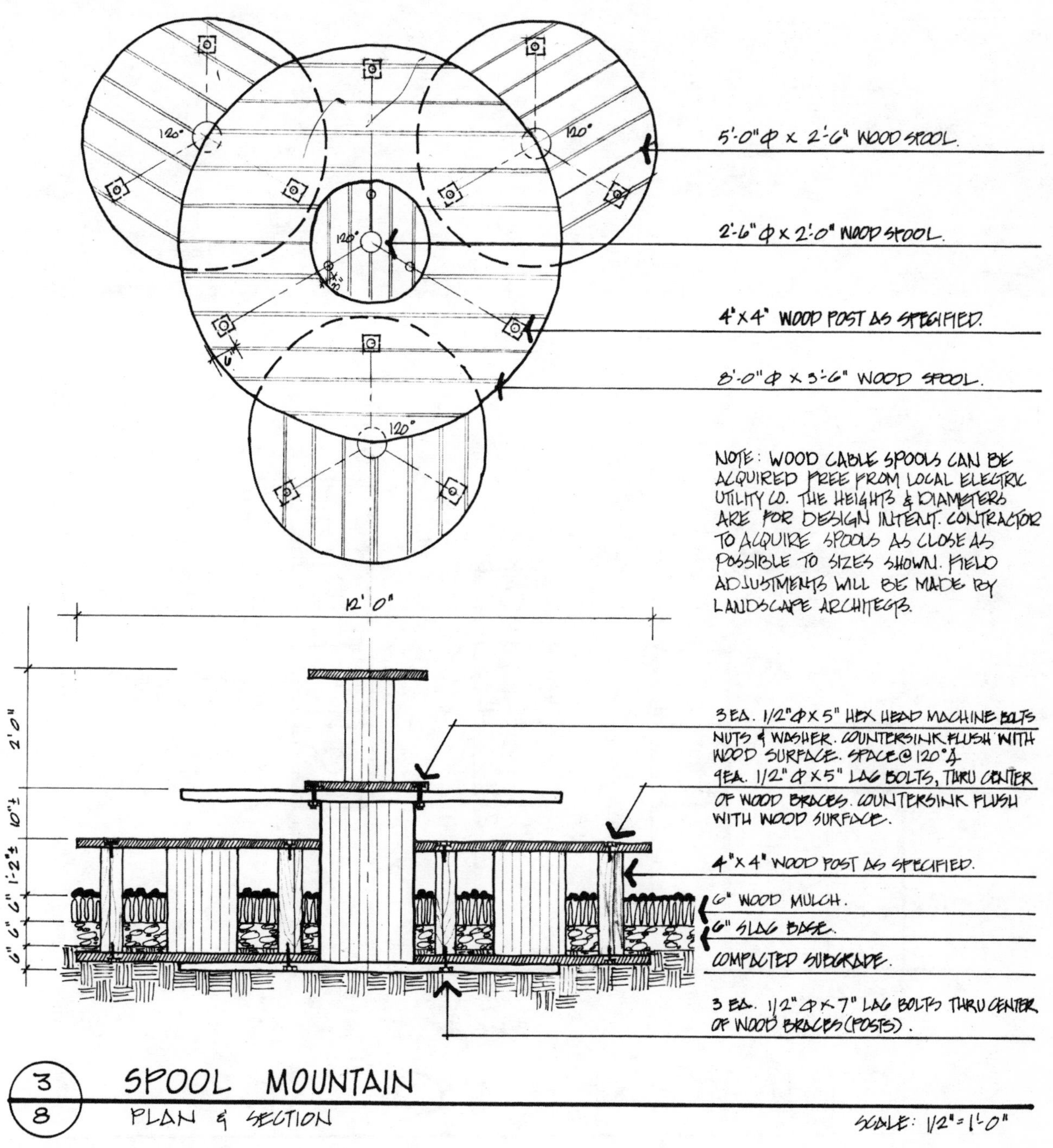
5'-0"Φ x 2'-6" WOOD SPOOL.
2'-6"Φ x 2'-0" WOOD SPOOL.
4"x4" WOOD POST AS SPECIFIED.
8'-0"Φ x 3'-6" WOOD SPOOL.
NOTE: WOOD CABLE SPOOLS CAN BE ACQUIRED FREE FROM LOCAL ELECTRIC UTILITY CO. THE HEIGHTS & DIAMETERS ARE FOR DESIGN INTENT. CONTRACTOR TO ACQUIRE SPOOLS AS CLOSE AS POSSIBLE TO SIZES SHOWN. FIELD ADJUSTMENTS WILL BE MADE BY LANDSCAPE ARCHITECTS.
12' 0"
3 EA. 1/2"Φ X 5" HEX HEAD MACHINE BOLTS NUTS & WASHER. COUNTERSINK FLUSH WITH WOOD SURFACE. SPACE @ 120° Δ
4 EA. 1/2" Φ X 5" LAG BOLTS, THRU CENTER OF WOOD BRACES. COUNTERSINK FLUSH WITH WOOD SURFACE.
4"X4" WOOD POST AS SPECIFIED.
6" WOOD MULCH.
6" SLAG BASE.
COMPACTED SUBGRADE.
3 EA. 1/2" Φ X 7" LAG BOLTS THRU CENTER OF WOOD BRACES (POSTS).
2'0"
10"±
1'-2"±
6"
6"
6"
3
8
SPOOL MOUNTAIN
PLAN & SECTION
SCALE: 1/2"=1'-0"

Figure 10.18 *Play equipment details.*

Bonnell and Associates

10.19

10.20

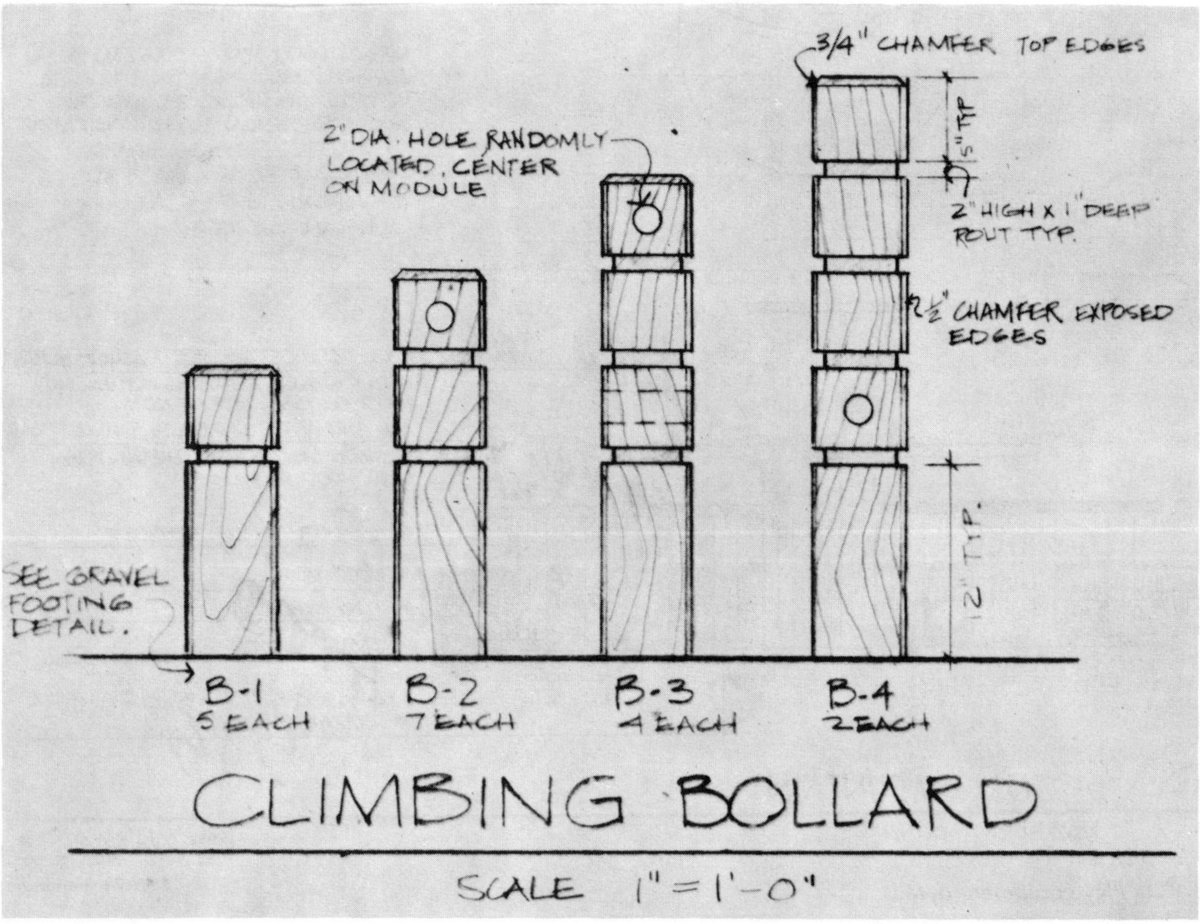

3/4" CHAMFER TOP EDGES
2" DIA. HOLE RANDOMLY LOCATED, CENTER ON MODULE
5" TYP.
2" HIGH x 1" DEEP ROUT TYP.
1/2" CHAMFER EXPOSED EDGES
12" TYP.
SEE GRAVEL FOOTING DETAIL.
B-1
5 EACH
B-2
7 EACH
B-3
4 EACH
B-4
2 EACH
CLIMBING BOLLARD
SCALE 1" = 1'-0"

10.21

Robin Salsbury, Reimann/Buechner Partnership

Figures 10.19 – 10.22 *Play equipment and details.*

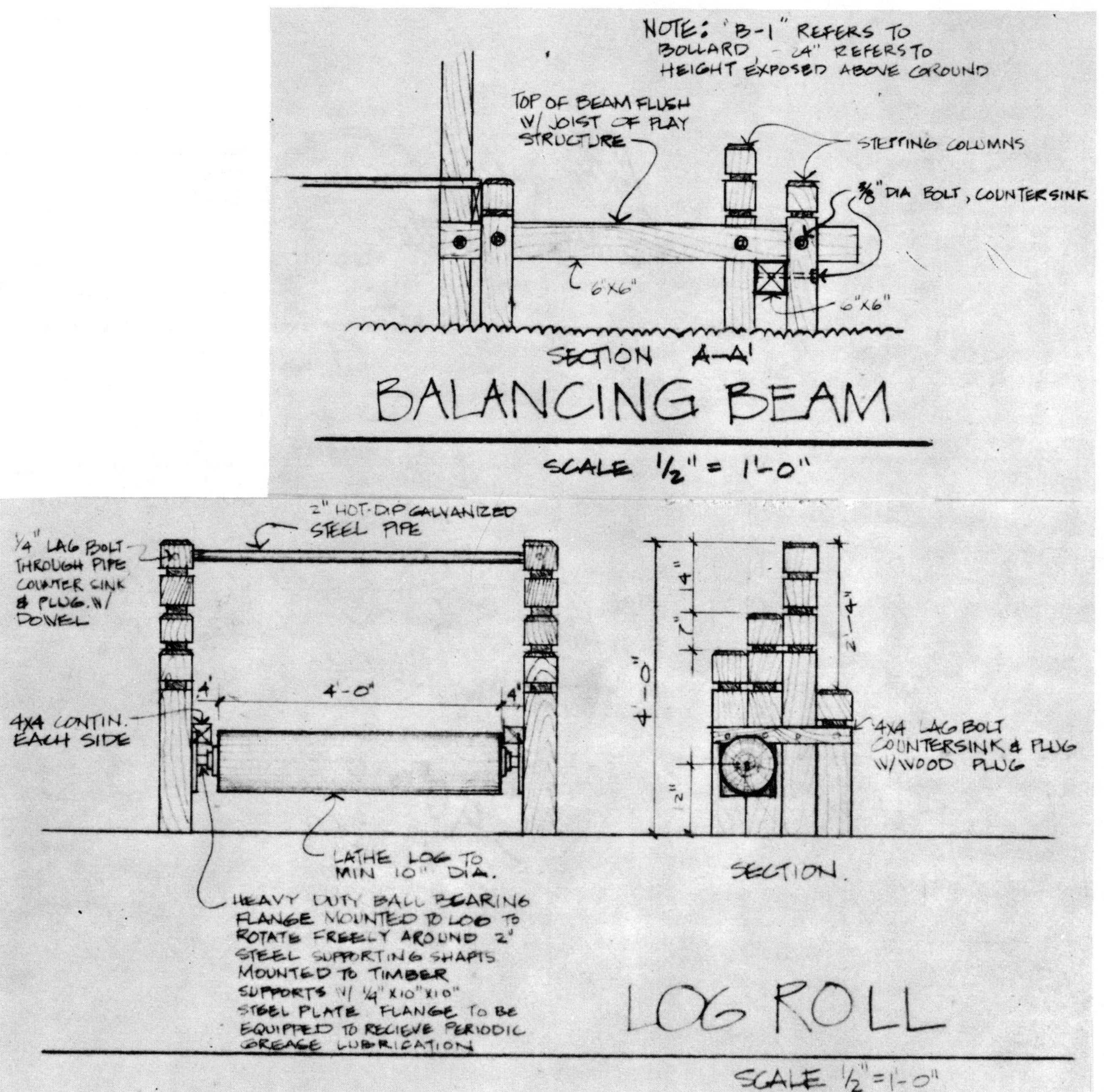
NOTE: "B-1" REFERS TO BOLLARD - 24" REFERS TO HEIGHT EXPOSED ABOVE GROUND
TOP OF BEAM FLUSH W/ JOIST OF PLAY STRUCTURE
STEPPING COLUMNS
3/8" DIA BOLT, COUNTERSINK
6"X6"
6"X6"
SECTION A-A'
BALANCING BEAM
SCALE 1/2" = 1'-0"
2" HOT-DIP GALVANIZED STEEL PIPE
1/4" LAG BOLT THROUGH PIPE COUNTER SINK & PLUG W/ DOWEL
4'
4'-0"
4"
4X4 CONTIN. EACH SIDE
LATHE LOG TO MIN 10" DIA.
HEAVY DUTY BALL BEARING FLANGE MOUNTED TO LOG TO ROTATE FREELY AROUND 2" STEEL SUPPORTING SHAFTS MOUNTED TO TIMBER SUPPORTS W/ 1/4" X10" X10" STEEL PLATE FLANGE TO BE EQUIPPED TO RECIEVE PERIODIC GREASE LUBRICATION
4'-0"
4"
2"
2'-4"
12"
4X4 LAG BOLT COUNTERSINK & PLUG W/WOOD PLUG
SECTION.
LOG ROLL
SCALE 1/2" = 1'-0"

10.22

Robin Salsbury, Reimann/Buechner Partnership

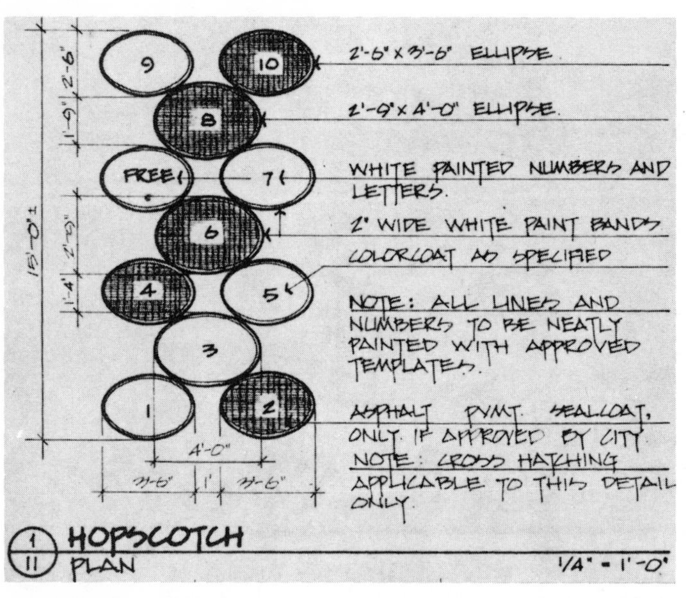
2'-6" x 3'-6" ELLIPSE
2'-9" x 4'-0" ELLIPSE
WHITE PAINTED NUMBERS AND LETTERS.
2" WIDE WHITE PAINT BANDS
COLORCOAT AS SPECIFIED
NOTE: ALL LINES AND NUMBERS TO BE NEATLY PAINTED WITH APPROVED TEMPLATES.
ASPHALT PVMT. SEALCOAT, ONLY IF APPROVED BY CITY
NOTE: CROSS HATCHING APPLICABLE TO THIS DETAIL ONLY.
FREE
1 HOPSCOTCH
11 PLAN
1/4" = 1'-0"

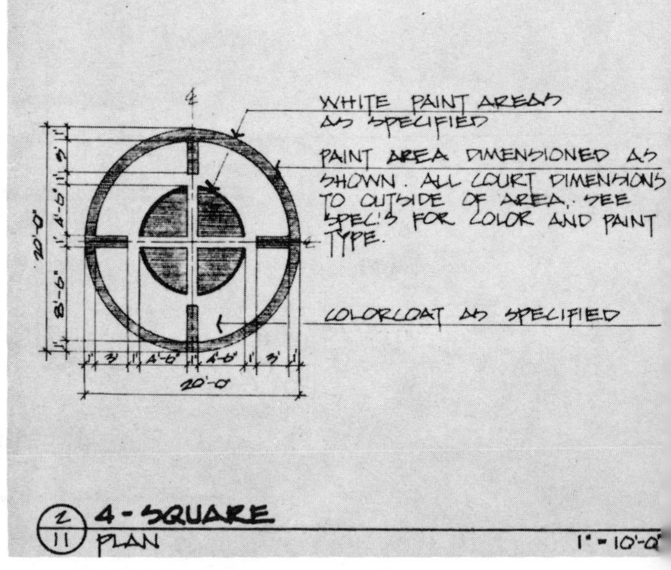
WHITE PAINT AREAS AS SPECIFIED
PAINT AREA DIMENSIONED AS SHOWN. ALL COURT DIMENSIONS TO OUTSIDE OF AREA. SEE SPEC'S FOR COLOR AND PAINT TYPE.
COLORCOAT AS SPECIFIED
20'-0"
2 4-SQUARE
11 PLAN
1" = 10'-0"

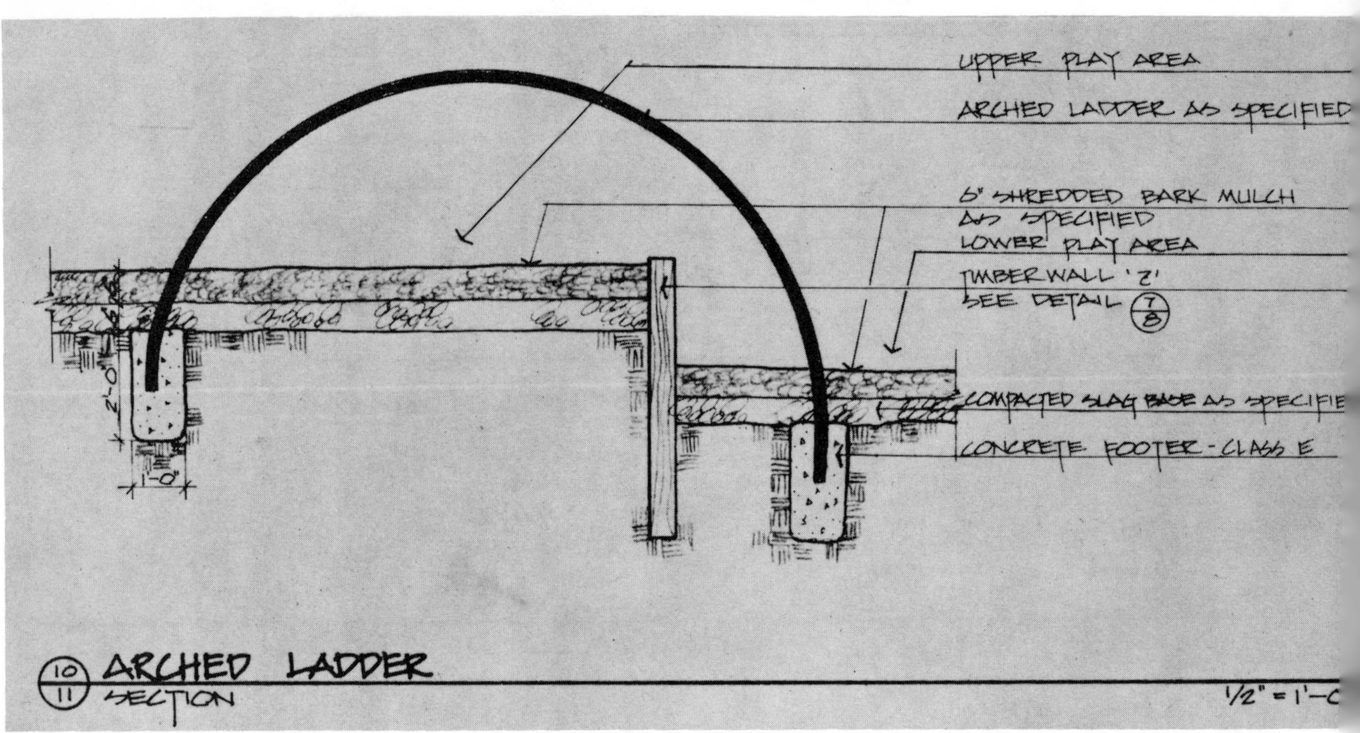
UPPER PLAY AREA
ARCHED LADDER AS SPECIFIED
6" SHREDDED BARK MULCH AS SPECIFIED
LOWER PLAY AREA
TIMBER WALL 'Z' SEE DETAIL 7/8
COMPACTED SLAG BASE AS SPECIFIE
CONCRETE FOOTER - CLASS E
2'-0"
1'-0"
10 ARCHED LADDER
11 SECTION
1/2" = 1'-0

Bonnell and Associ

Figure 10.23 *Play area details.*

10.24 Environmental Planning and Design

10.25 Sverdrup and Parcel

Figures 10.24 – 10.25 *Play areas.*

Jack Sterling

10.26 Bonnell and Associates

10.27 Sverdrup and Parcel

Figures 10.26 – 10.29 *Play areas.*

10.28 Sverdrup and Parcel

10.29 Sverdrup and Parcel

10.30 Sverdrup and Parcel

10.31 Sverdrup and Parcel

Figure 10.30 *Climbing mound with three different slope materials for visual and kinetic variation.*

Figure 10.31 *Play area retaining wall with cantilevered steps.*

10.32 Bailey and Associates

10.34 Sverdrup and Parcel

10.33 Bailey and Associates

10.35

Figures 10.32 – 10.35 *Play areas, equipment and structures.*

10.36

10.38 Bonnell and Associates

10.39 Bonnell and Associates

10.37 Browning-Day-Pollak-Associates-Inc.

Figures 10.36 – 10.41 *Wide variety of design ideas in play areas.*

10.40 Sasaki Associates

10.41 Bonnell and Associates

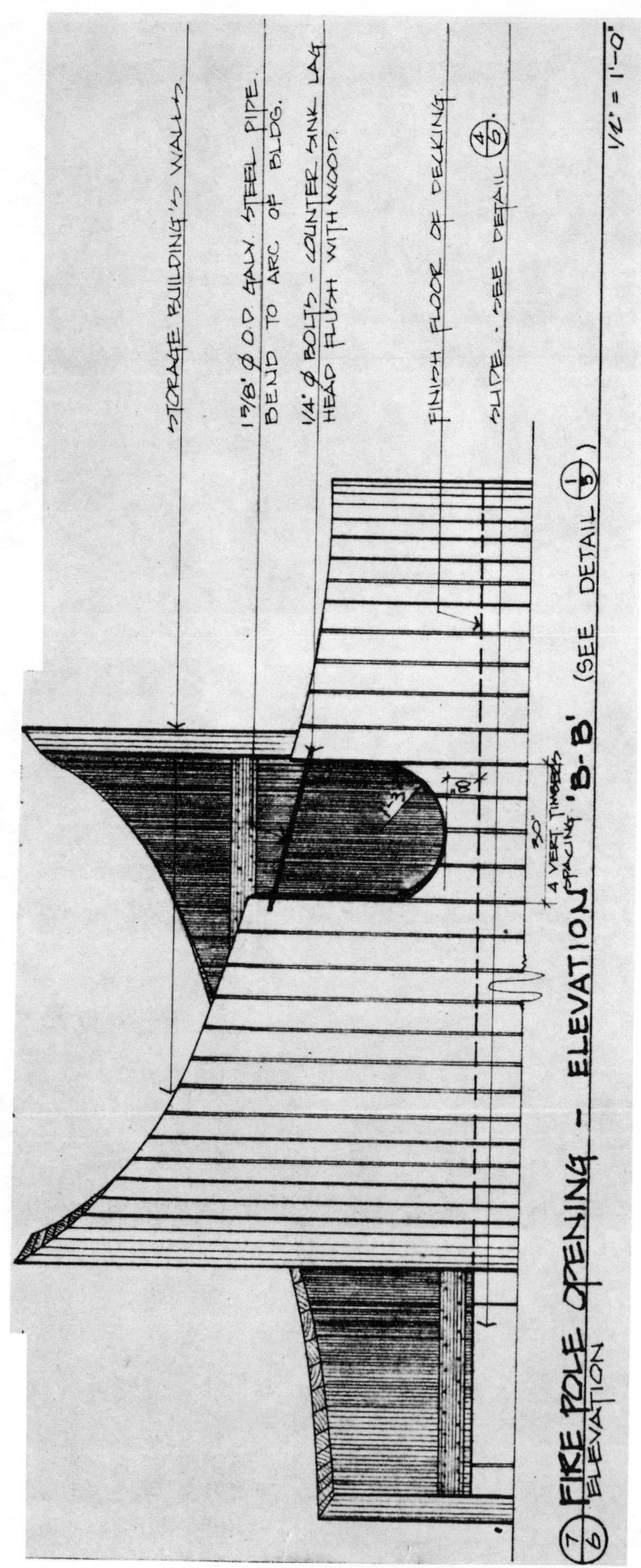
STORAGE BUILDING'S WALLS.
1 5/8" Ø O.D. GALV. STEEL PIPE. BEND TO ARC OF BLDG.
1/4" Ø BOLTS - COUNTER SINK LAG HEAD FLUSH WITH WOOD.
FINISH FLOOR OF DECKING.
SLIDE - SEE DETAIL 4/6
1/2" = 1'-0"
30"
4 VERT. TIMBERS SPACING
7/6 FIRE POLE OPENING - ELEVATION 'B-B' (SEE DETAIL 1/5)
ELEVATION

Figure 10.42 *Play structure detail. See Figure 10.41.*

Bonnell and Associates

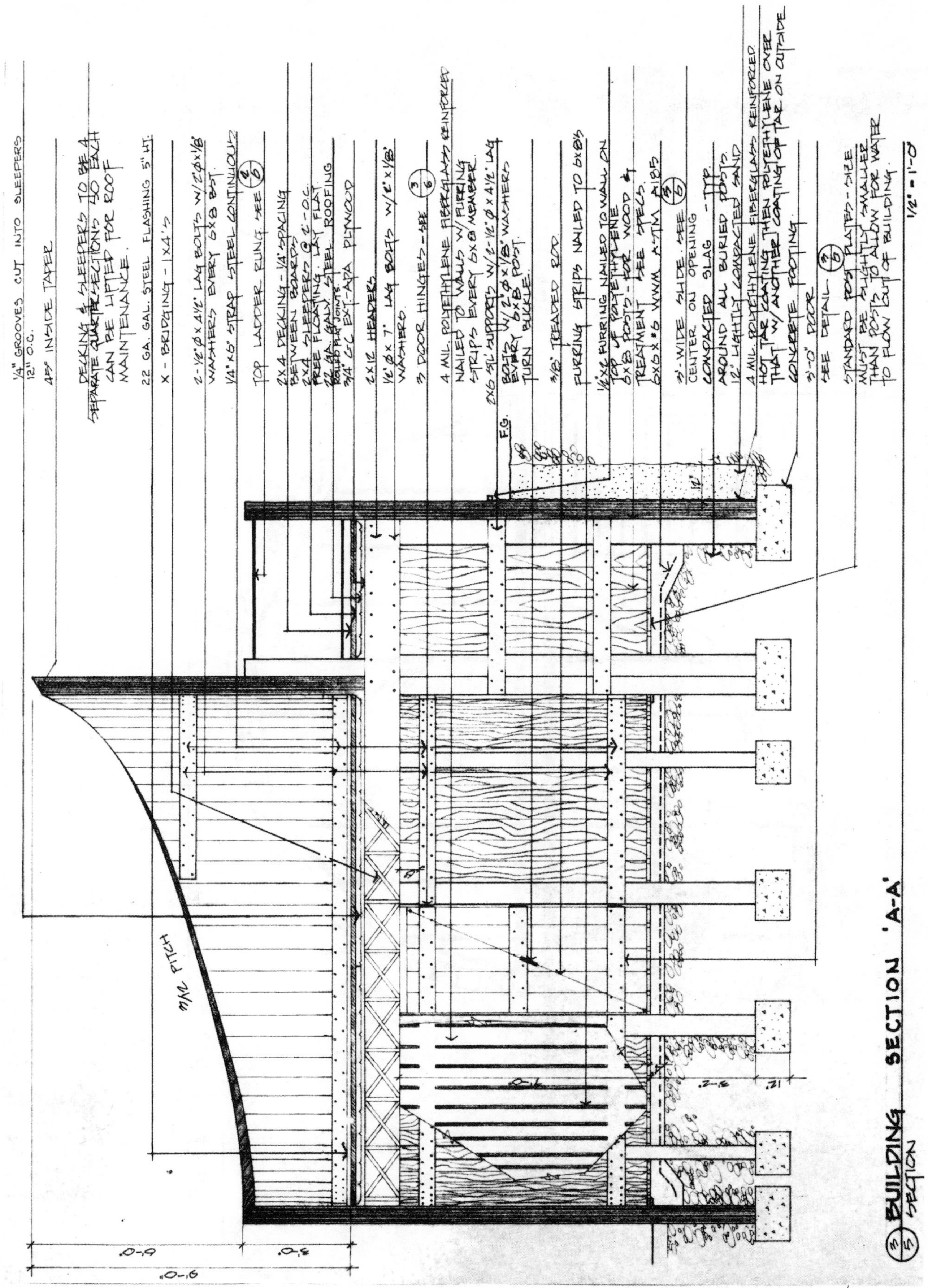
1/4" GROOVES CUT INTO SLEEPERS 12" O.C.
45° INSIDE TAPER
DECKING & SLEEPERS TO BE 4 SEPARATE QUARTER SECTIONS SO EACH CAN BE LIFTED FOR ROOF MAINTENANCE.
22 GA. GAL. STEEL FLASHING 5" HT.
X - BRIDGING - 1X4'S
1/4"X6" STRAP STEEL CONTINUOUS
TOP LADDER RUNG SEE
2X4 DECKING - 1/4" SPACING BETWEEN BOARDS
3/4 C-C EXT-APA PLYWOOD
2X12 HEADERS
3" DOOR HINGES - SEE
TURN BUCKLE
3/8" THREADED ROD
FURRING STRIPS NAILED TO 6X8'S
3' WIDE SLIDE - SEE
CENTER ON OPENING
COMPACTED SLAG
AROUND ALL BURIED POSTS - TYP.
12" LIGHTLY COMPACTED SAND
4 MIL. POLYETHYLENE FIBERGLASS REINFORCED
HOT TAR COATING THEN POLYETHYLENE OVER THAT W/ ANOTHER COATING OF TAR ON OUTSIDE
CONCRETE FOOTING
3'-0" DOOR
SEE DETAIL
STANDARD POST PLATES - SIZE MUST BE SLIGHTLY SMALLER THAN POSTS TO ALLOW FOR WATER TO FLOW OUT OF BUILDING.
1/2" = 1'-0"
7/12 PITCH
F.G.
6'-0"
3'-0"
9'-0"
BUILDING SECTION 'A-A'
SECTION

Figure 10.43 *Play structure detail. See Figures 10.41 and 10.42.*

Bonnell and Associates

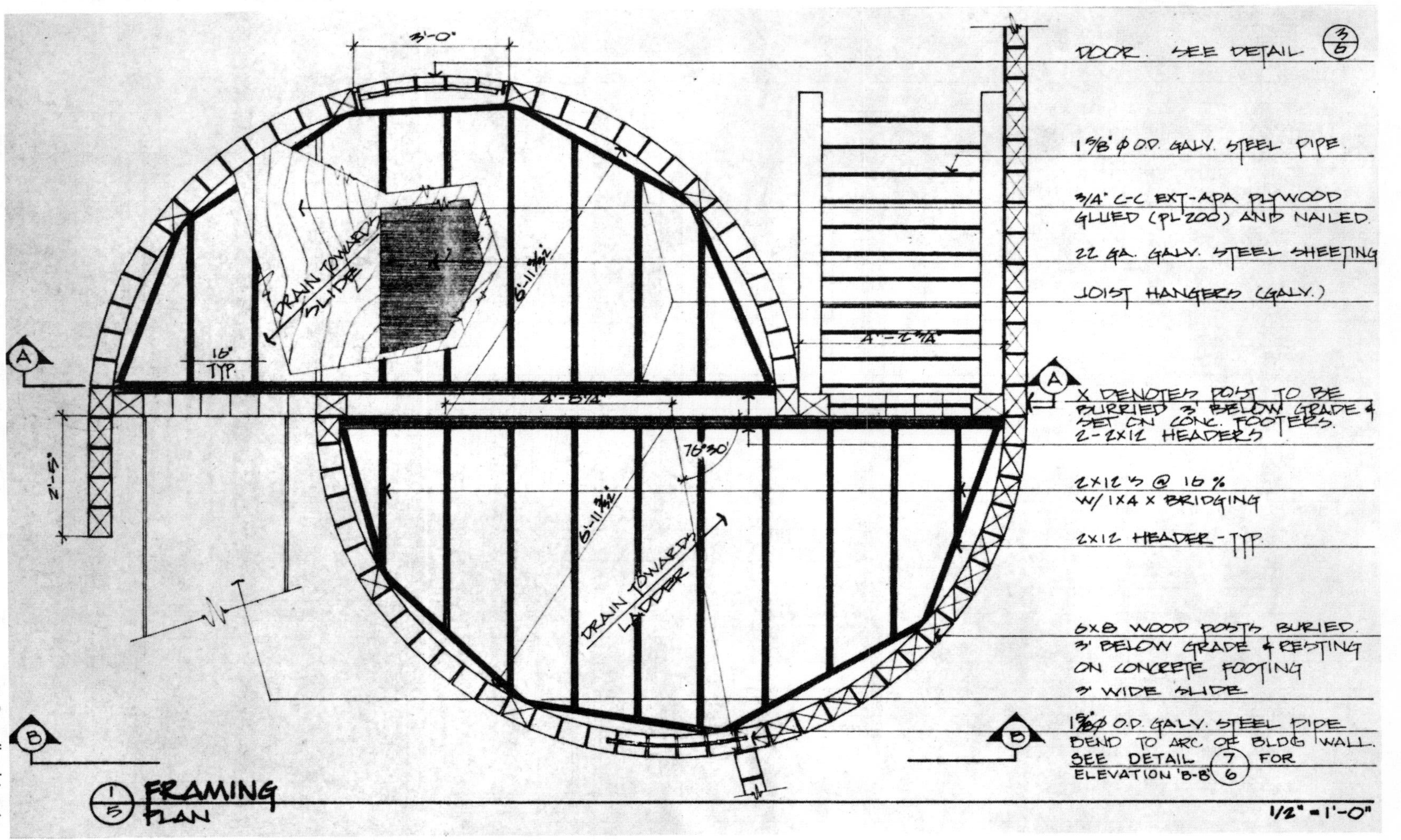
3'-0"
DOOR. SEE DETAIL 3/6
1 5/8" ϕ O.D. GALV. STEEL PIPE
3/4" C-C EXT-APA PLYWOOD
GLUED (PL200) AND NAILED.
22 GA. GALV. STEEL SHEETING
JOIST HANGERS (GALV.)
DRAIN TOWARDS SLIDE
10" TYP.
X DENOTES POST TO BE BURRIED 3' BELOW GRADE & SET ON CONC. FOOTERS.
2-2X12 HEADERS
76°30'
2'-5"
2X12'S @ 16"
W/ 1X4 X BRIDGING
2X12 HEADER - TYP.
DRAIN TOWARDS LADDER
6X8 WOOD POSTS BURIED
3' BELOW GRADE & RESTING
ON CONCRETE FOOTING
3' WIDE SLIDE
1 5/8" ϕ O.D. GALV. STEEL PIPE
BEND TO ARC OF BLDG WALL.
SEE DETAIL 7/6 FOR
ELEVATION 'B-B'
FRAMING PLAN
1/2" = 1'-0"

Figure 10.44 *Play structure details. See Figures 10.41 – 10.43.*

Bonnell and Associates

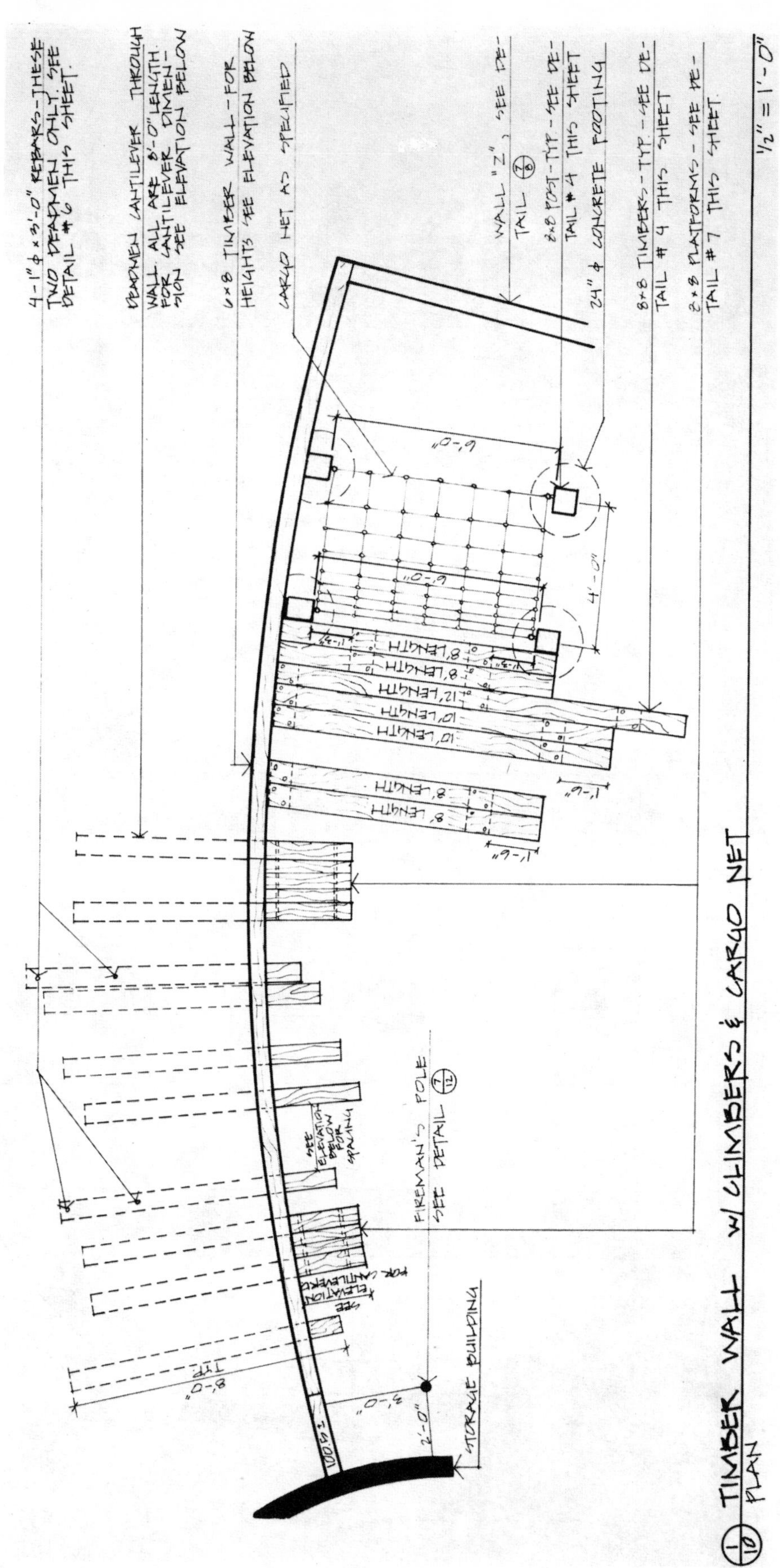

4-1" ⌀ × 3'-0" REBARS - THESE TWO DEADMEN ONLY. SEE DETAIL #6 THIS SHEET
DEADMEN CANTILEVER THROUGH WALL. ALL ARE 8'-0" LENGTH. FOR CANTILEVER DIMENSION SEE ELEVATION BELOW
6×8 TIMBER WALL - FOR HEIGHTS SEE ELEVATION BELOW
CARGO NET AS SPECIFIED
WALL "Z", SEE DETAIL
8×8 POST - TYP - SEE DETAIL #4 THIS SHEET
24" ⌀ CONCRETE FOOTING
8×8 TIMBERS - TYP - SEE DETAIL #4 THIS SHEET
2×8 PLATFORMS - SEE DETAIL #7 THIS SHEET
FIREMAN'S POLE SEE DETAIL
STORAGE BUILDING
8'-0" TYP
TIMBER WALL w/ CLIMBERS & CARGO NET PLAN
1/2" = 1'-0"

Figure 10.45 *Play structure detail. See Figure 10.38.*

Bonnell and Associates

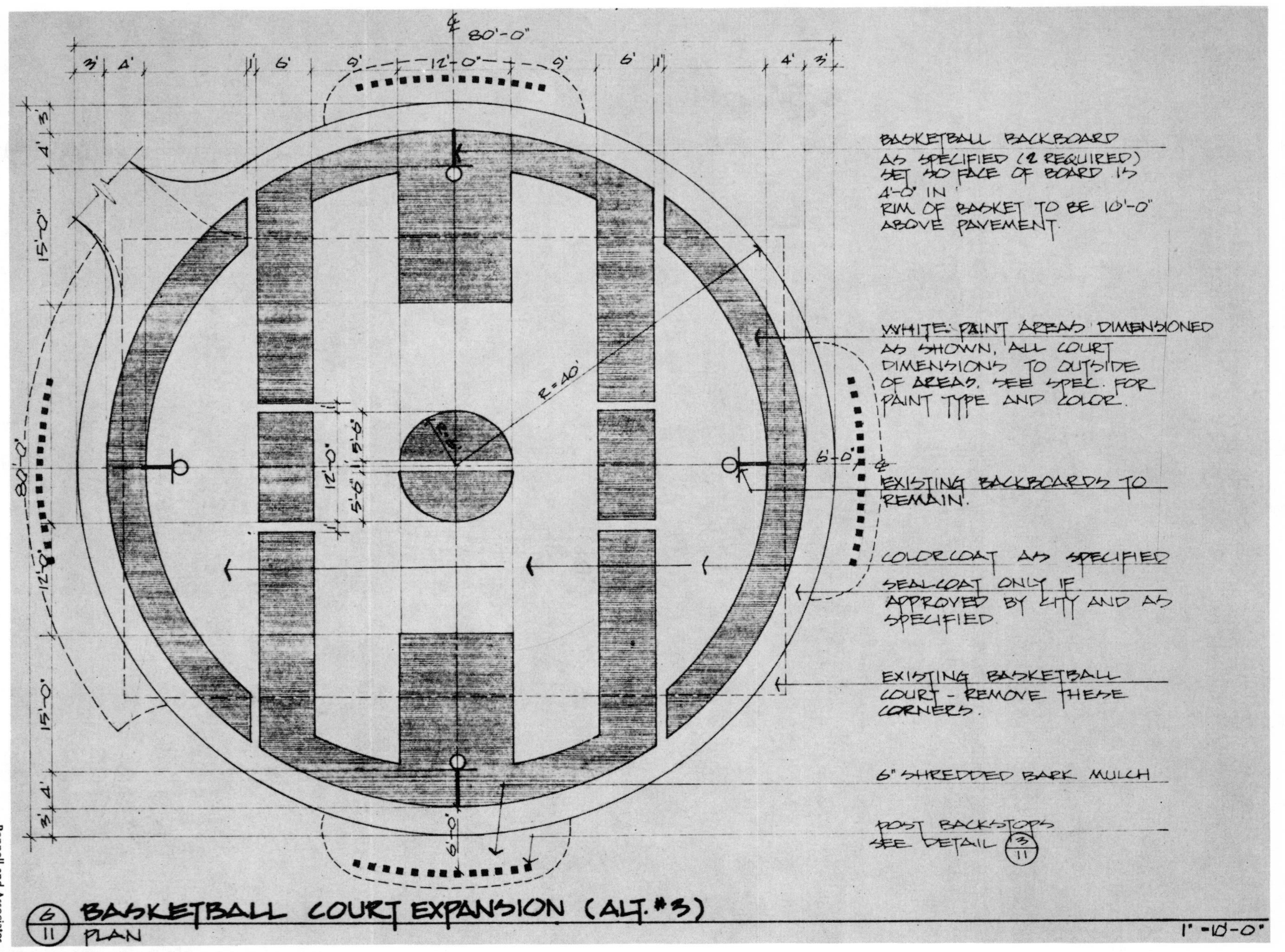

80'-0"
12'-0"
BASKETBALL BACKBOARD AS SPECIFIED (2 REQUIRED) SET SO FACE OF BOARD IS 4'-0" IN RIM OF BASKET TO BE 10'-0" ABOVE PAVEMENT.
WHITE: PAINT AREAS DIMENSIONED AS SHOWN, ALL COURT DIMENSIONS TO OUTSIDE OF AREAS. SEE SPEC. FOR PAINT TYPE AND COLOR.
R=40'
EXISTING BACKBOARDS TO REMAIN.
COLORCOAT AS SPECIFIED
SEAL-COAT ONLY IF APPROVED BY CITY AND AS SPECIFIED
EXISTING BASKETBALL COURT - REMOVE THESE CORNERS.
6" SHREDDED BARK MULCH
POST BACKSTOPS SEE DETAIL 3/11
BASKETBALL COURT EXPANSION (ALT. #3)
PLAN

Bonnell and Associates

Figure 10.46 *Basketball court detail.*

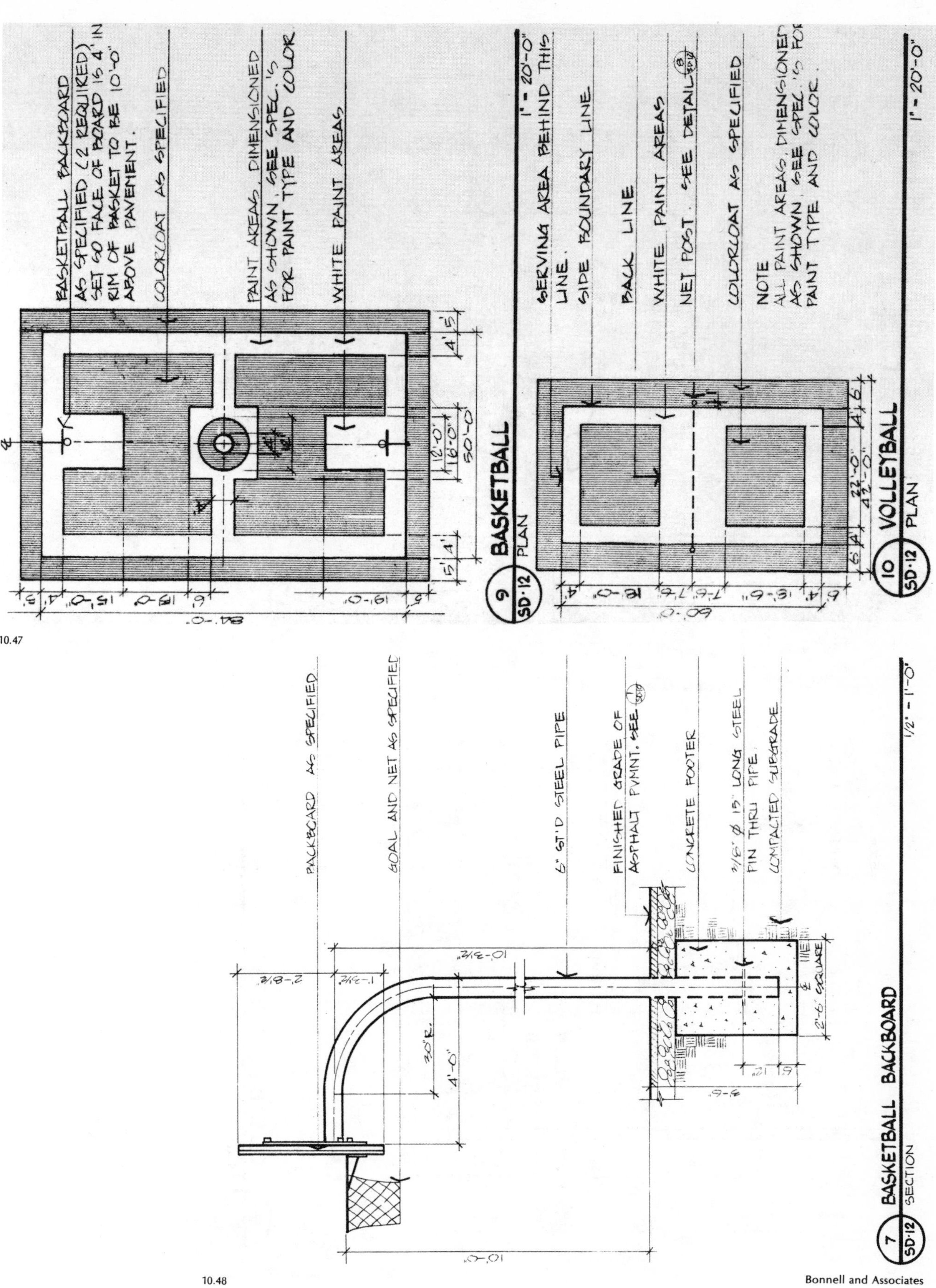
BASKETBALL BACKBOARD AS SPECIFIED (2 REQUIRED) SET 60 FACE OF BOARD IS 4' IN RIM OF BASKET TO BE 10'-0" ABOVE PAVEMENT.
COLORCOAT AS SPECIFIED
PAINT AREAS, DIMENSIONED AS SHOWN, SEE SPEC.'S FOR PAINT TYPE AND COLOR
WHITE PAINT AREAS
12'-0"
16'-0"
50'-0"
84'-0"
9 SD·12 BASKETBALL PLAN
1" = 20'-0"
SERVING AREA BEHIND THIS LINE.
SIDE BOUNDARY LINE
BACK LINE
WHITE PAINT AREAS
NET POST. SEE DETAIL
COLORCOAT AS SPECIFIED
NOTE
ALL PAINT AREAS, DIMENSIONED AS SHOWN, SEE SPEC.'S FOR PAINT TYPE AND COLOR.
22'-0"
42'-0"
60'-0"
10 SD·12 VOLLEYBALL PLAN
1" = 20'-0"
BACKBOARD AS SPECIFIED
GOAL AND NET AS SPECIFIED
6" ST'D STEEL PIPE
FINISHED GRADE OF ASPHALT PVMNT. SEE
CONCRETE FOOTER
3/8" ø 15" LONG STEEL PIN THRU PIPE
COMPACTED SUBGRADE
10'-3/4"
3'0" R.
4'-0"
2'-6" SQUARE
10'-0"
7 SD·12 BASKETBALL BACKBOARD SECTION
1/2" - 1'-0"

10.47

10.48

Bonnell and Associates

Figures 10.47 – 10.48 *Basketball and volleyball details.*

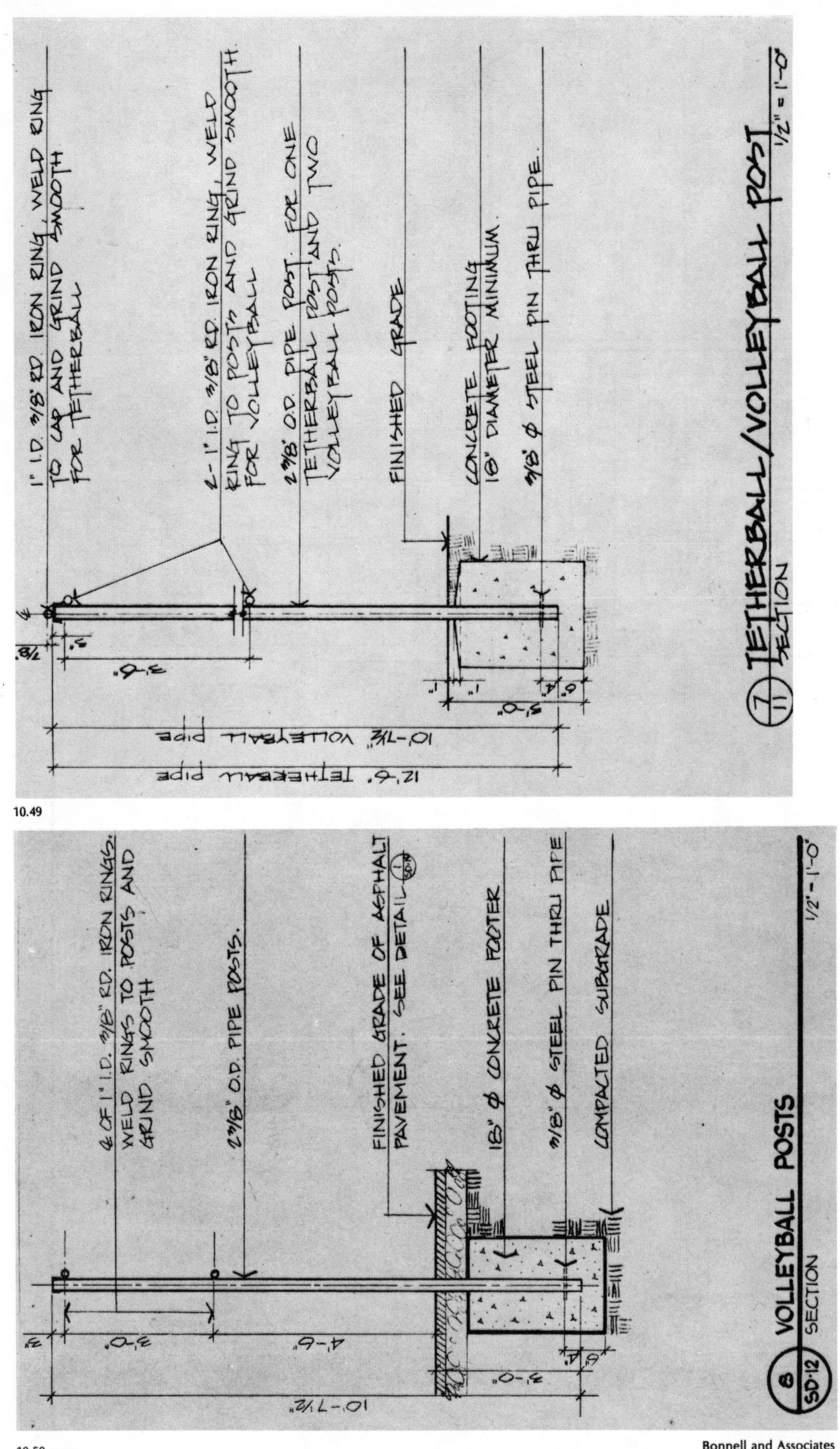
1" I.D. 3/8" RD. IRON RING, WELD RING TO CAP AND GRIND SMOOTH FOR TETHERBALL
2-1" I.D. 3/8" RD. IRON RING, WELD RING TO POSTS AND GRIND SMOOTH FOR VOLLEYBALL
2 7/8" O.D. PIPE POST. FOR ONE TETHERBALL POST AND TWO VOLLEYBALL POSTS.
FINISHED GRADE
CONCRETE FOOTING 18" DIAMETER MINIMUM.
3/8" ϕ STEEL PIN THRU PIPE.
12'-6" TETHERBALL PIPE
10'-7 1/2" VOLLEYBALL PIPE
3'-0"
3'-0"
7
11
TETHERBALL/VOLLEYBALL POST
SECTION
1/2" = 1'-0"

10.49

2 OF 1" I.D. 3/8" RD. IRON RINGS. WELD RINGS TO POSTS AND GRIND SMOOTH
2 7/8" O.D. PIPE POSTS.
FINISHED GRADE OF ASPHALT PAVEMENT. SEE DETAIL
18" ϕ CONCRETE FOOTER
3/8" ϕ STEEL PIN THRU PIPE
COMPACTED SUBGRADE
10'-7 1/2"
3'-0"
4'-6"
3'-0"
8
SD-12
VOLLEYBALL POSTS
SECTION
1/2" = 1'-0"

10.50

Bonnell and Associates

Figures 10.49 – 10.50 *Volleyball and tetherball details.*

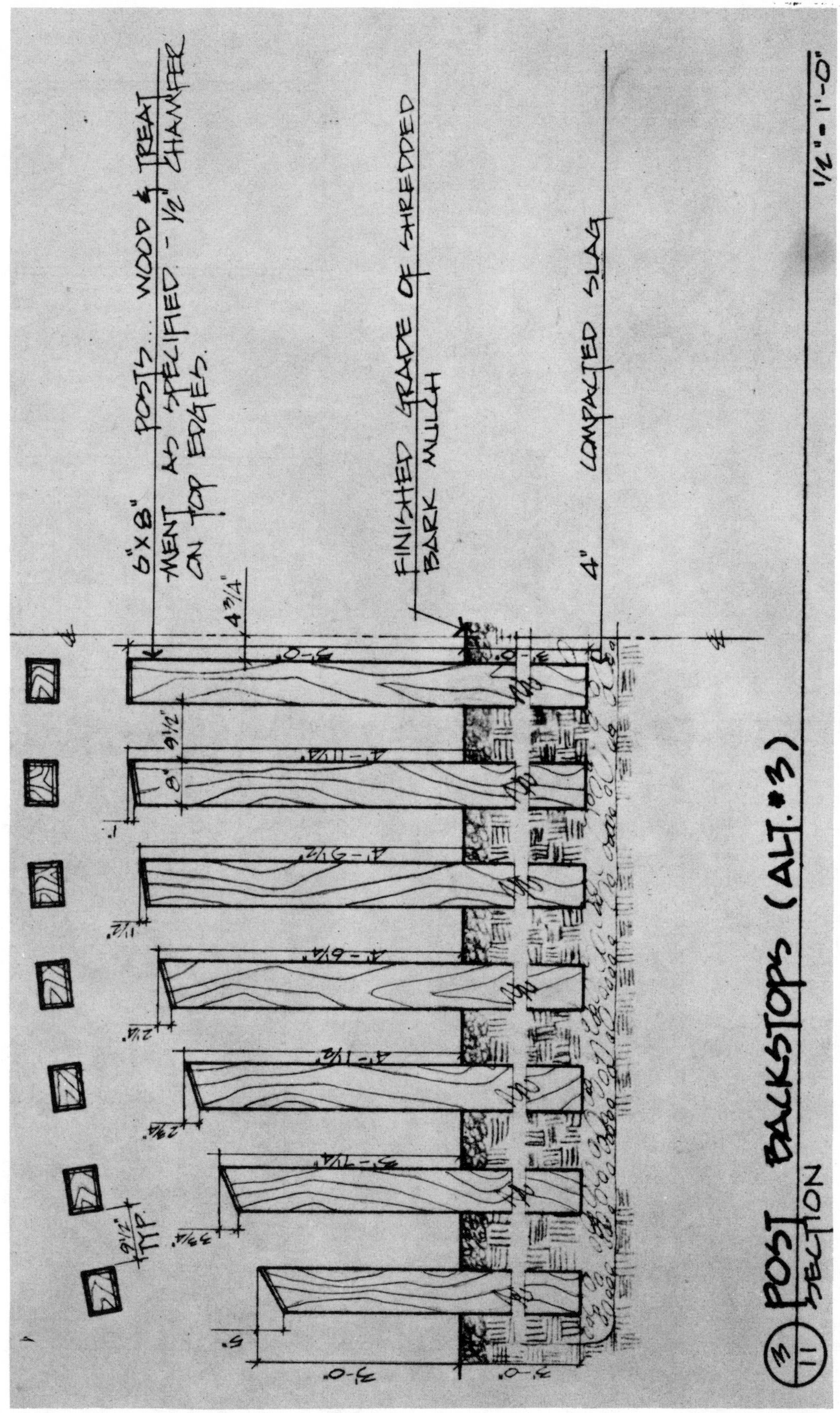

6"X8" POSTS... WOOD & TREATMENT AS SPECIFIED - 1/2" CHAMFER ON TOP EDGES.
FINISHED GRADE OF SHREDDED BARK MULCH
4" COMPACTED SLAG
POST BACKSTOPS (ALT. #3)
SECTION
1/2" = 1'-0"

Bonnell and Associates

Figure 10.51 *Backstop detail.*

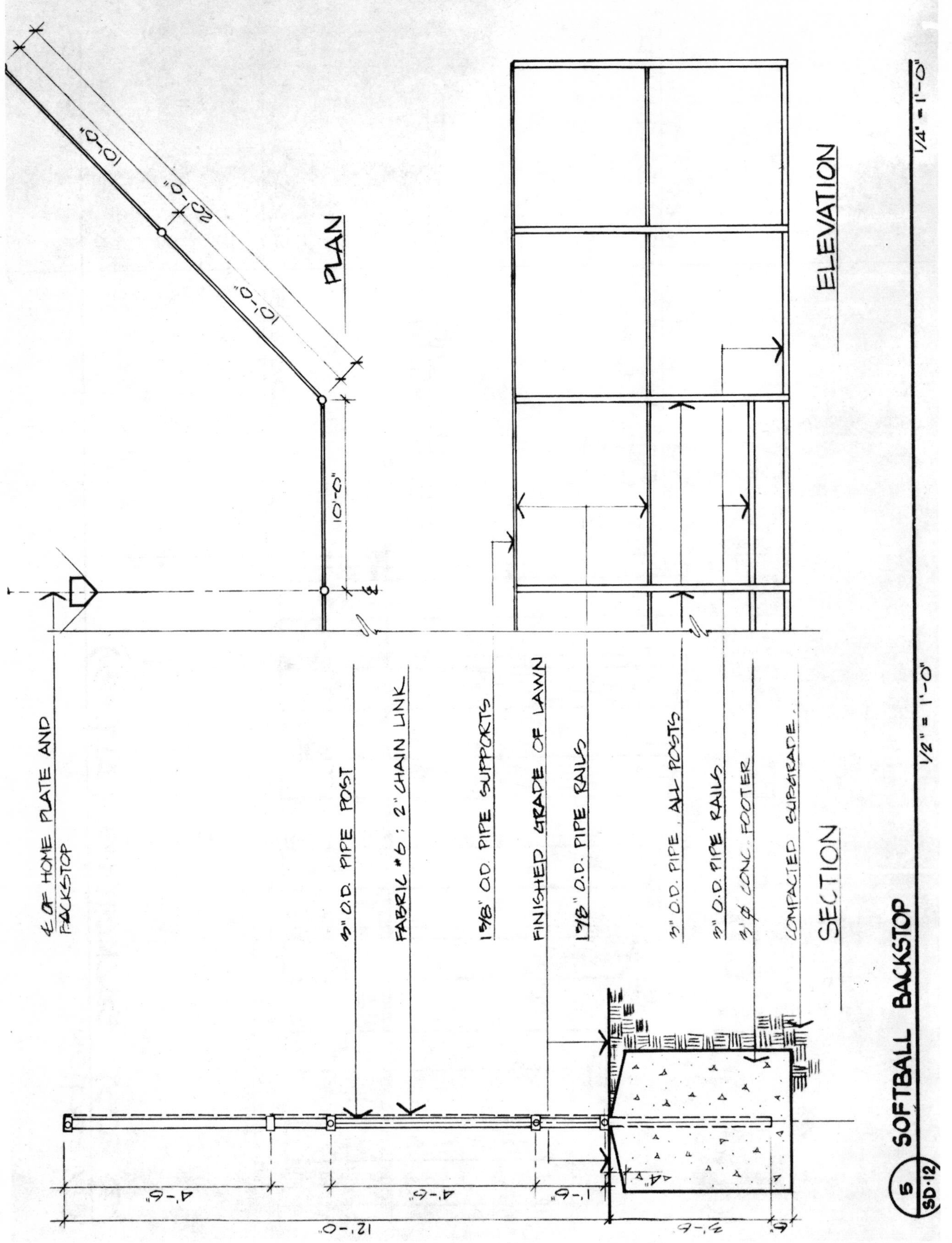
PLAN
10'-0"
20'-0"
10'-0"
10'-0"
ELEVATION
℄ OF HOME PLATE AND BACKSTOP
3" O.D. PIPE POST
FABRIC #6 : 2" CHAIN LINK
1 3/8" O.D. PIPE SUPPORTS
FINISHED GRADE OF LAWN
1 3/8" O.D. PIPE RAILS
3" O.D. PIPE, ALL POSTS
3" O.D. PIPE RAILS
3' Ø CONC. FOOTER
COMPACTED SUBGRADE
SECTION
4'-6"
4'-6"
1'-6"
12'-0"
4'-6"
6"
5
SD-12
SOFTBALL BACKSTOP
1/2" = 1'-0"
1/4" = 1'-0"

Bonnell and Associates

Figure 10.52 *Softball backstop detail.*

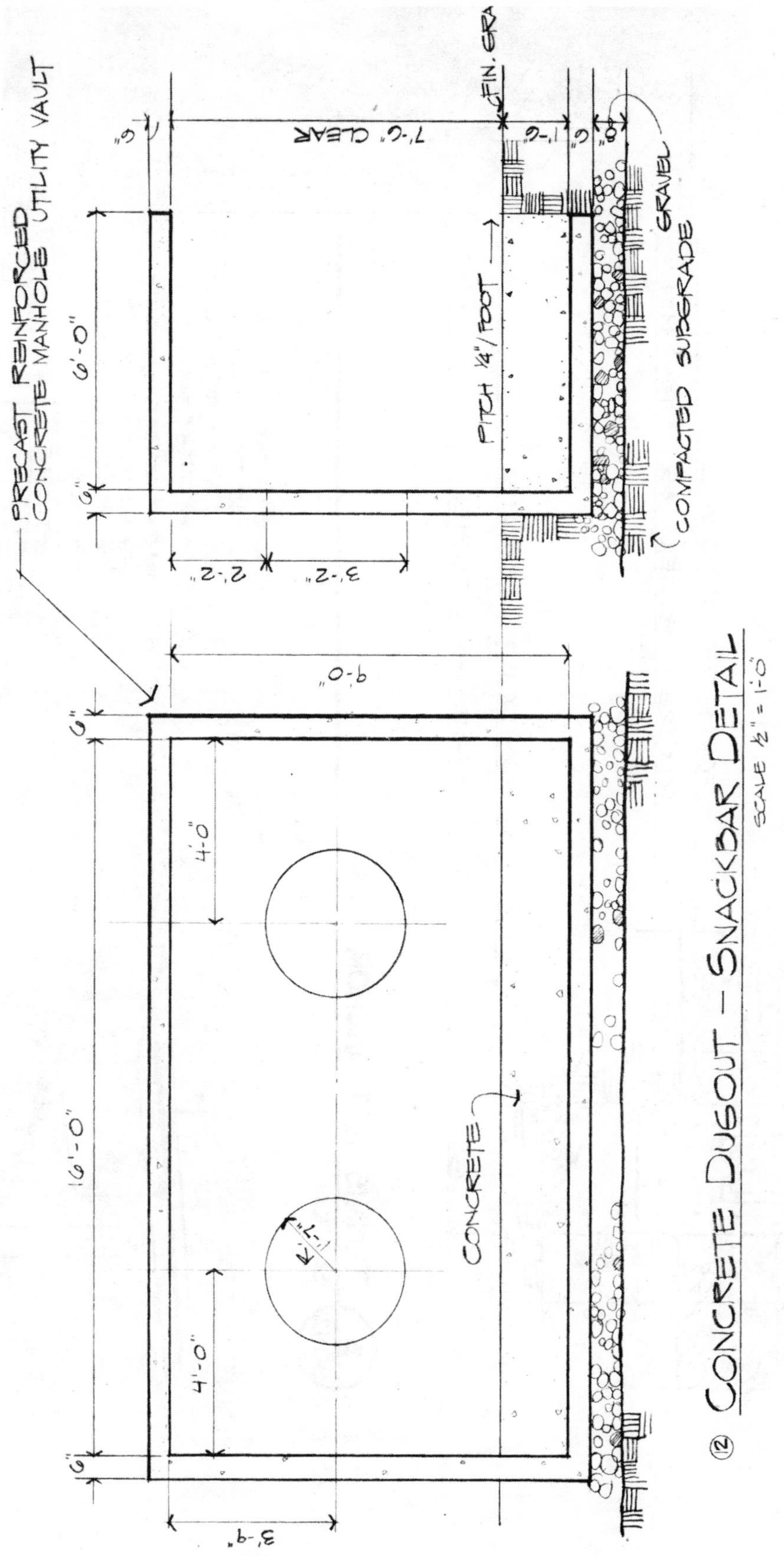
PRECAST REINFORCED CONCRETE MANHOLE UTILITY VAULT
FIN. GRA
7'-0" CLEAR
PITCH 1/4"/FOOT
CONCRETE
GRAVEL
COMPACTED SUBGRADE
⑫ CONCRETE DUGOUT – SNACKBAR DETAIL
SCALE 1/2" = 1'-0"

Figure 10.53 *Dugout detail.*

CR3, inc.

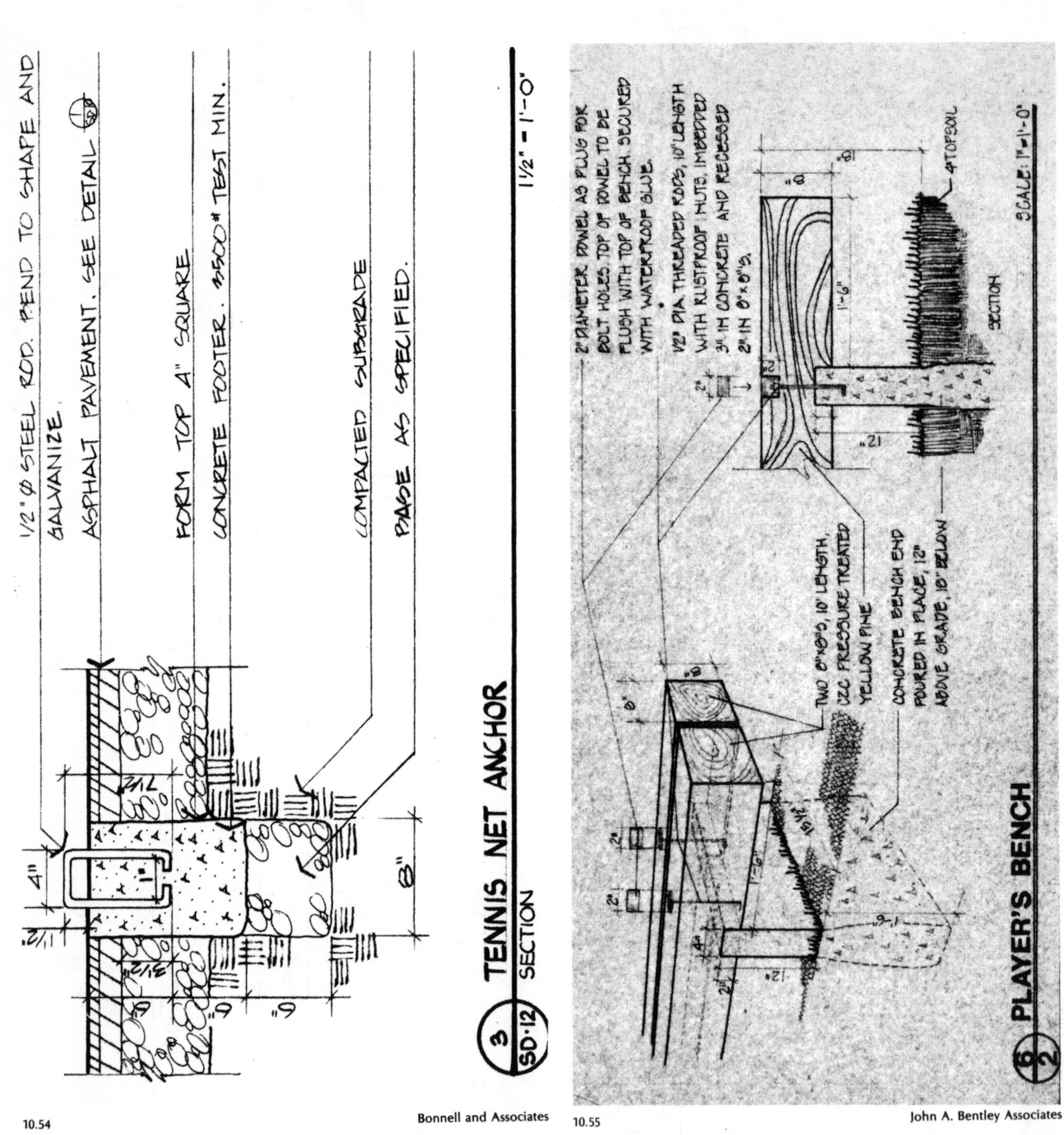

1/2" ∅ STEEL ROD. BEND TO SHAPE AND GALVANIZE.
ASPHALT PAVEMENT. SEE DETAIL
FORM TOP 4" SQUARE
CONCRETE FOOTER. 3500# TEST MIN.
COMPACTED SUBGRADE
BASE AS SPECIFIED.
TENNIS NET ANCHOR
SECTION
1 1/2" = 1'-0"
2" DIAMETER DOWEL AS PLUG FOR BOLT HOLES. TOP OF DOWEL TO BE FLUSH WITH TOP OF BENCH. SECURED WITH WATERPROOF GLUE.
1/2" DIA. THREADED RODS, 10" LENGTH WITH RUSTPROOF NUTS, IMBEDDED 3" IN CONCRETE AND RECESSED 2" IN 8"x8"'S.
TWO 8"x8"'S, 10' LENGTH, CZC PRESSURE TREATED YELLOW PINE
CONCRETE BENCH END POURED IN PLACE, 12" ABOVE GRADE, 10" BELOW
4" TOPSOIL
SECTION
PLAYER'S BENCH
SCALE: 1"=1'-0"

10.54 Bonnell and Associates

10.55 John A. Bentley Associates

Figures 10.54 – 10.55 *Recreation area details.*

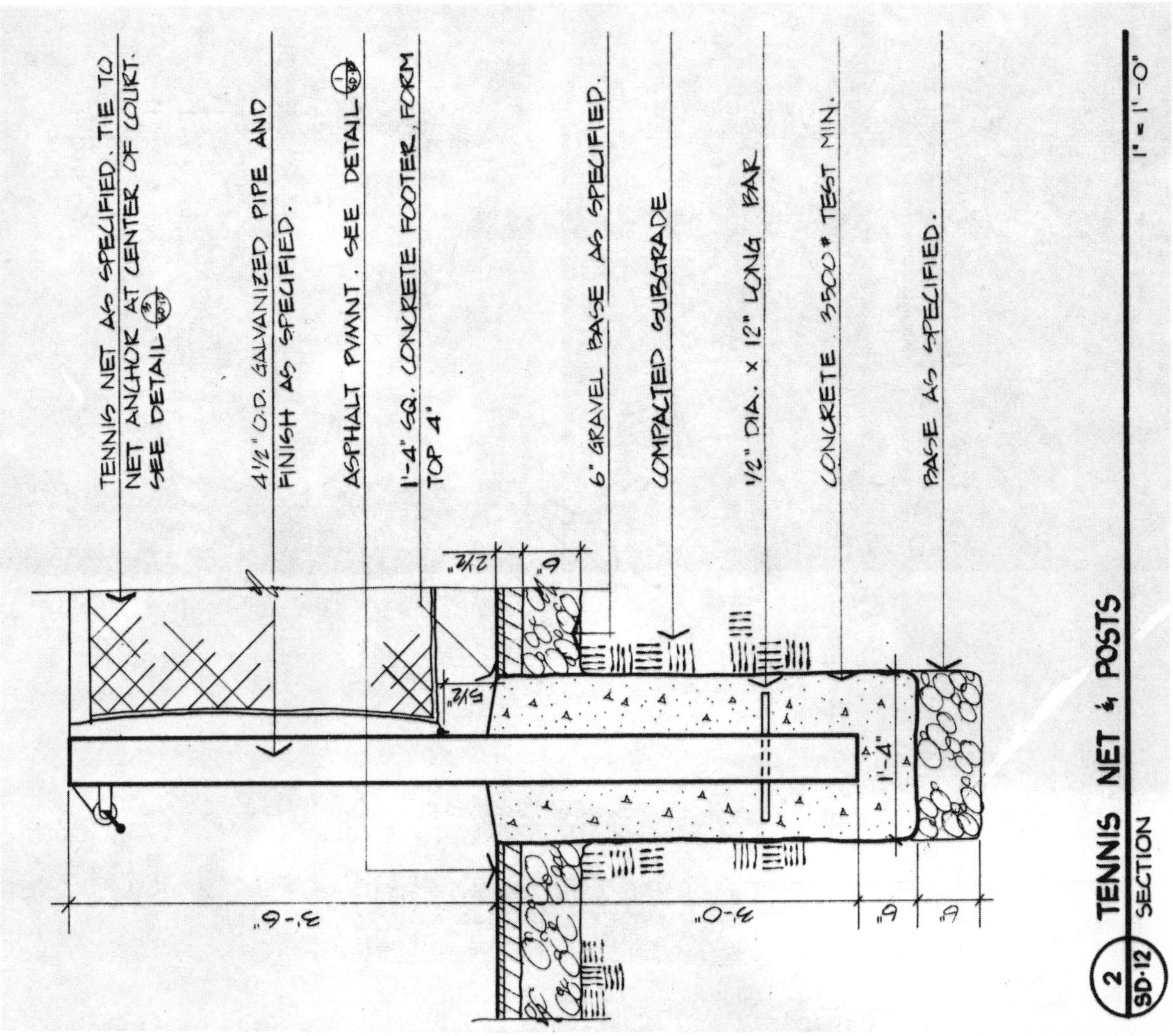

TENNIS NET AS SPECIFIED. TIE TO NET ANCHOR AT CENTER OF COURT. SEE DETAIL

4 1/2" O.D. GALVANIZED PIPE AND FINISH AS SPECIFIED.

ASPHALT PVMNT. SEE DETAIL

1'-4" SQ. CONCRETE FOOTER, FORM TOP 4"

6" GRAVEL BASE AS SPECIFIED.

COMPACTED SUBGRADE

1/2" DIA. x 12" LONG BAR

CONCRETE 3500# TEST MIN.

BASE AS SPECIFIED.

3'-6"

3'-0"

6"

6"

2 1/2"

6"

5 1/2"

1'-4"

2 SD-12 TENNIS NET & POSTS

SECTION

1" = 1'-0"

10.56

Bonnell and Associates

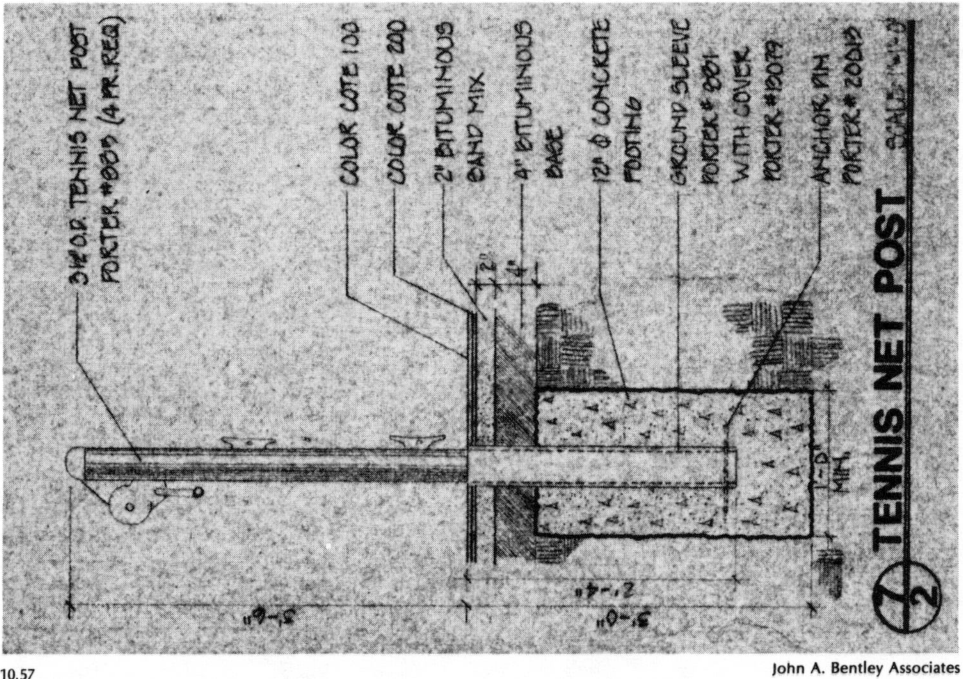

COLOR COTE 100
COLOR COTE 200
2" BITUMINOUS SAND MIX
4" BITUMINOUS BASE
12" Ø CONCRETE FOOTING
GROUND SLEEVE
WITH COVER
ANCHOR PIN
TENNIS NET POST
1'-0" MIN.
3'-6"
3'-0"
2'-4"

10.57

John A. Bentley Associates

Figures 10.56 – 10.57 *Tennis court details.*

10.58 Bailey and Associates 10.59

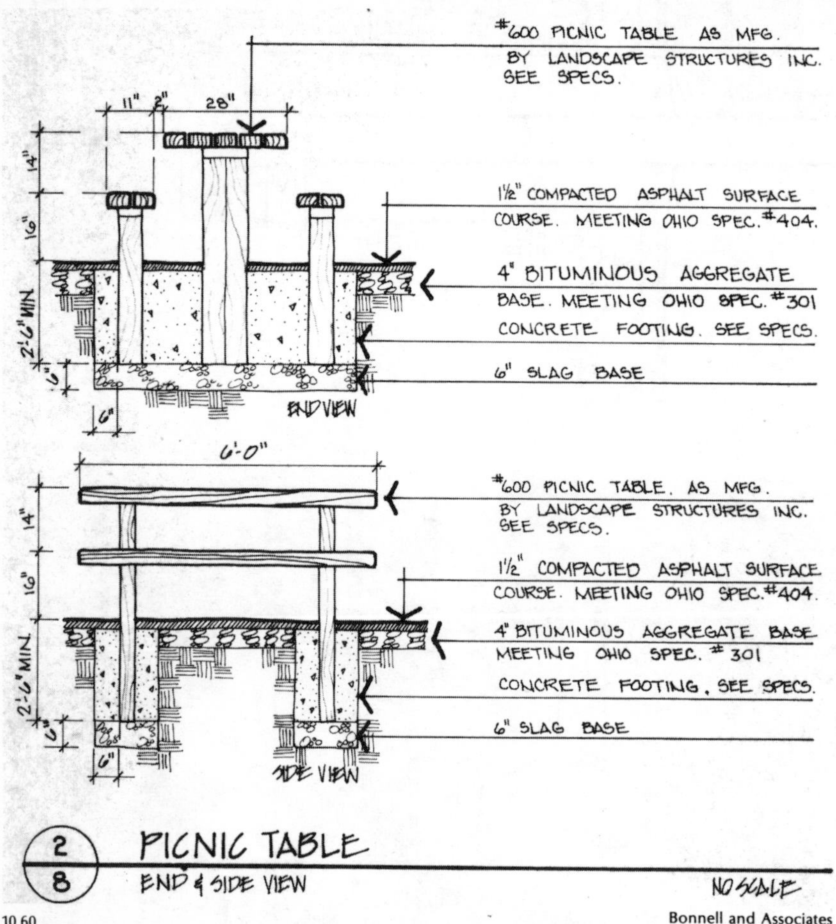
#600 PICNIC TABLE AS MFG.
BY LANDSCAPE STRUCTURES INC.
SEE SPECS.
11" 2" 28"
14"
16"
2'-6" MIN.
6"
6"
1½" COMPACTED ASPHALT SURFACE
COURSE. MEETING OHIO SPEC. #404.
4" BITUMINOUS AGGREGATE
BASE. MEETING OHIO SPEC. #301
CONCRETE FOOTING. SEE SPECS.
6" SLAG BASE
END VIEW
6'-0"
#600 PICNIC TABLE. AS MFG.
BY LANDSCAPE STRUCTURES INC.
SEE SPECS.
1½" COMPACTED ASPHALT SURFACE
COURSE. MEETING OHIO SPEC. #404.
4" BITUMINOUS AGGREGATE BASE
MEETING OHIO SPEC. # 301
CONCRETE FOOTING. SEE SPECS.
6" SLAG BASE
SIDE VIEW
2
8
PICNIC TABLE
END & SIDE VIEW
NO SCALE

10.60 Bonnell and Associates

Figures 10.58 – 10.66 *Picnic tables and details.*

10.61

10.64

10.62

10.65

10.63

10.66

10.67 Snell Environmental Group

10.69

10.68

10.70

10.71 Bailey and Associates

Figures 10.67 – 10.71 *Water related recreation areas.*

11

Site Furniture and Fixtures

Included in this chapter are such items as benches, bollards, flag poles, signs, kiosks, bicycle racks, planters, trash containers, tree grates and guards, and wheel stops. Advertisements in professional journals and magazines, as well as catalogs from suppliers and manufacturers, reveal that many different designs are available and can be ordered and installed without custom designing. Custom design may be desirable, however, to ensure a certain continuity of style or character and uniformity of materials within a particular project. As is true with many other areas of design, some custom designed furniture and fixtures are soon picked up by manufacturers and become mass produced as catalog items.

When custom manufacturing, it is wise to carefully research materials, their durability, and maintenance problems that might incur through their use and to be aware of human dimensions and design for maximum human usage and comfort. The designs and details illustrated in this chapter and the references for further reading will provide some guidelines for sizes, methods, and installation requirements.

LIGHTING

When selecting light fixtures a designer needs to be aware of lighting efficiency. The old standard incandescent light requires the greatest amount of electrical energy and while the initial cost of the fixture might be less than other types such as high pressure sodium, the ultimate cost is something else. The exact cost difference depends upon the current cost of electricity in the area where the site is located. Constantly rising costs suggest that efficient lighting is always the best investment. The National Lighting Bureau has issued figures which offer a comparison between different types of lighting. These comparisons are made on the basis of lumens (a unit or quantity of light output) per watt (a unit of electricity). An incandescent light on average yields from 15 to 24 lumens per watt whereas fluorescent yields 63 to 100 lumens per watt. At the high end is high pressure sodium which yields 79-130 lumens per watt. The life of an incandescent lamp ranges from 750-2500 hours while fluorescent is 12,000-20,000 hours. Thus, the more efficient fixtures require less maintenance.

From the fifth edition of the Illuminating Engineering Society Lighting Handbook, the following are recommended illumination levels. These levels are stated as footcandles (fc) which is the measure of the amount of light falling on a surface.

Indoor recreational sports: 20 fc
Indoor professional sports: 50 fc
Indoor exhibits, drafting rooms: 100 fc
Outdoor recreational sports: 10 fc
Outdoor tournament sports: 30 fc
Parking areas, entry roads: 1-3 fc
General parks and gardens: 0.5 fc
Paths, and steps: 1 fc
Backgrounds, fences, walls, plants: 2 fc
Flower beds, rocks: 5 fc
Lighting plants for emphasis: 5 fc
Garden focal points, large: 10 fc
Garden focal points, small: 20 fc
Malls: 5-10 fc
Building exteriors, light colored - 5-15 fc
Building exteriors, medium colored - 10-30 fc
Building exteriors, dark colored - 20-50 fc

11.1

REFERENCES FOR FURTHER READING

Ewald, W.R. *Street Graphics.* Washington, DC: Landscape Architecture Foundation, 1971.

Ramsey, C.G., and Sleeper, H.R. *Architectural Graphics Standards.* 7th Edition. New York: Wiley, 1981.

11.2

Figures 11.1 - 11.8 *A variety of bench designs.*

11.3

11.4

11.5

11.6

11.7

11.8

11.9

11.12

11.10

11.13

11.11

Figures 11.9 – 11.18 *Several different materials can be used to create benches in a variety of forms and shapes.*

11.14

11.16

11.15

11.17

11.18

11.19

Johnson, Johnson and Roy

Figure 11.19 *Urban Mall.*

Figure 11.20 *College campus sitting area adjacent to a lake.*

Figure 11.21 *Garden area over an underground parking garage for a corporate headquarters.*

11.20

11.21

David Racker and Associates

11.23

Figures 11.22 - 11.23 *Pre-cast concrete and metal benches.*

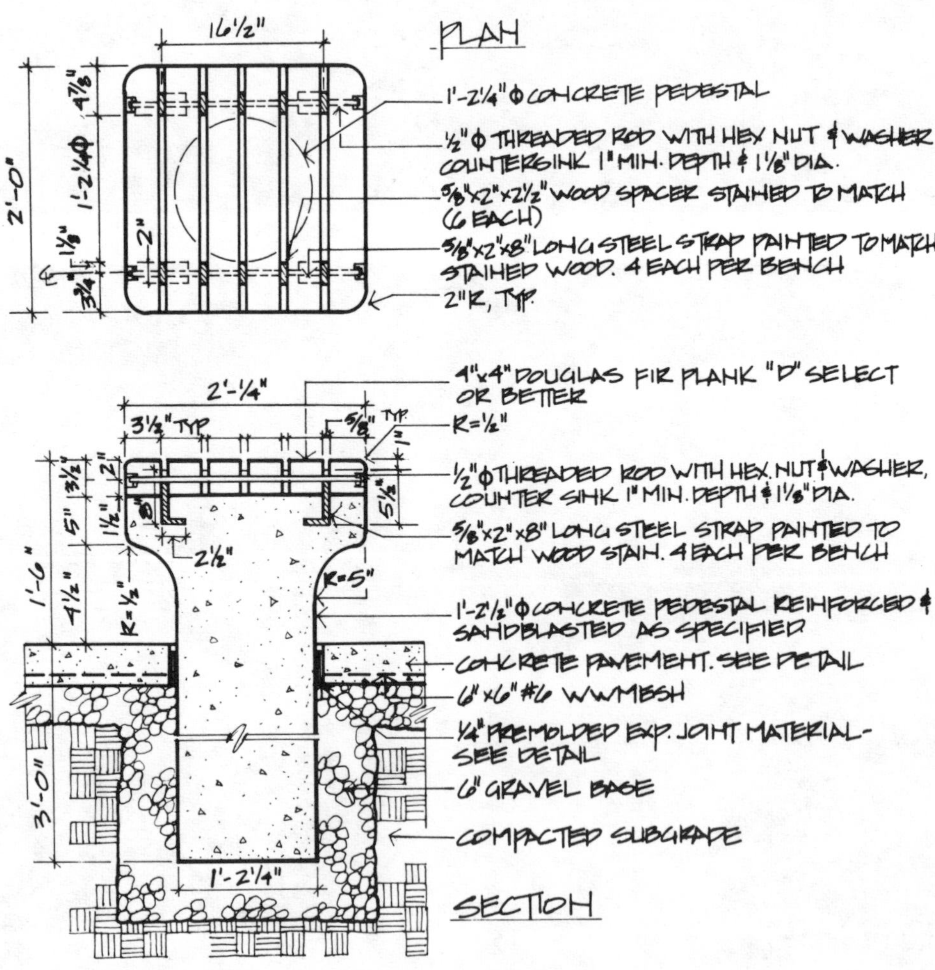

PLAN
16½"
2'-0"
1'-2¼"Φ
4⅞"
1⅛"
2"
¾"
1'-2¼"Φ CONCRETE PEDESTAL
½"Φ THREADED ROD WITH HEX NUT & WASHER. COUNTERSINK 1" MIN. DEPTH & 1⅛" DIA.
⅝"x2"x2½" WOOD SPACER STAINED TO MATCH (6 EACH)
⅝"x2"x8" LONG STEEL STRAP PAINTED TO MATCH STAINED WOOD. 4 EACH PER BENCH
2"R, TYP.
2'-¼"
3½" TYP
⅝" TYP
1"
R=½"
4"x4" DOUGLAS FIR PLANK "D" SELECT OR BETTER
½"Φ THREADED ROD WITH HEX. NUT & WASHER, COUNTER SINK 1" MIN. DEPTH & 1⅛" DIA.
⅝"x2"x8" LONG STEEL STRAP PAINTED TO MATCH WOOD STAIN. 4 EACH PER BENCH
1'-2½"Φ CONCRETE PEDESTAL REINFORCED & SANDBLASTED AS SPECIFIED
CONCRETE PAVEMENT. SEE DETAIL
6"x6" #6 WWMESH
¼" PREMOLDED EXP. JOINT MATERIAL - SEE DETAIL
6" GRAVEL BASE
COMPACTED SUBGRADE
1'-6"
3½"
5"
4½"
1¼"
2½"
R=½"
R=5"
5½"
3'-0"
1'-2¼"
SECTION

PEDESTAL BENCH DETAIL

Figure 11.24 *Bench detail.*

Bonnell and Associates

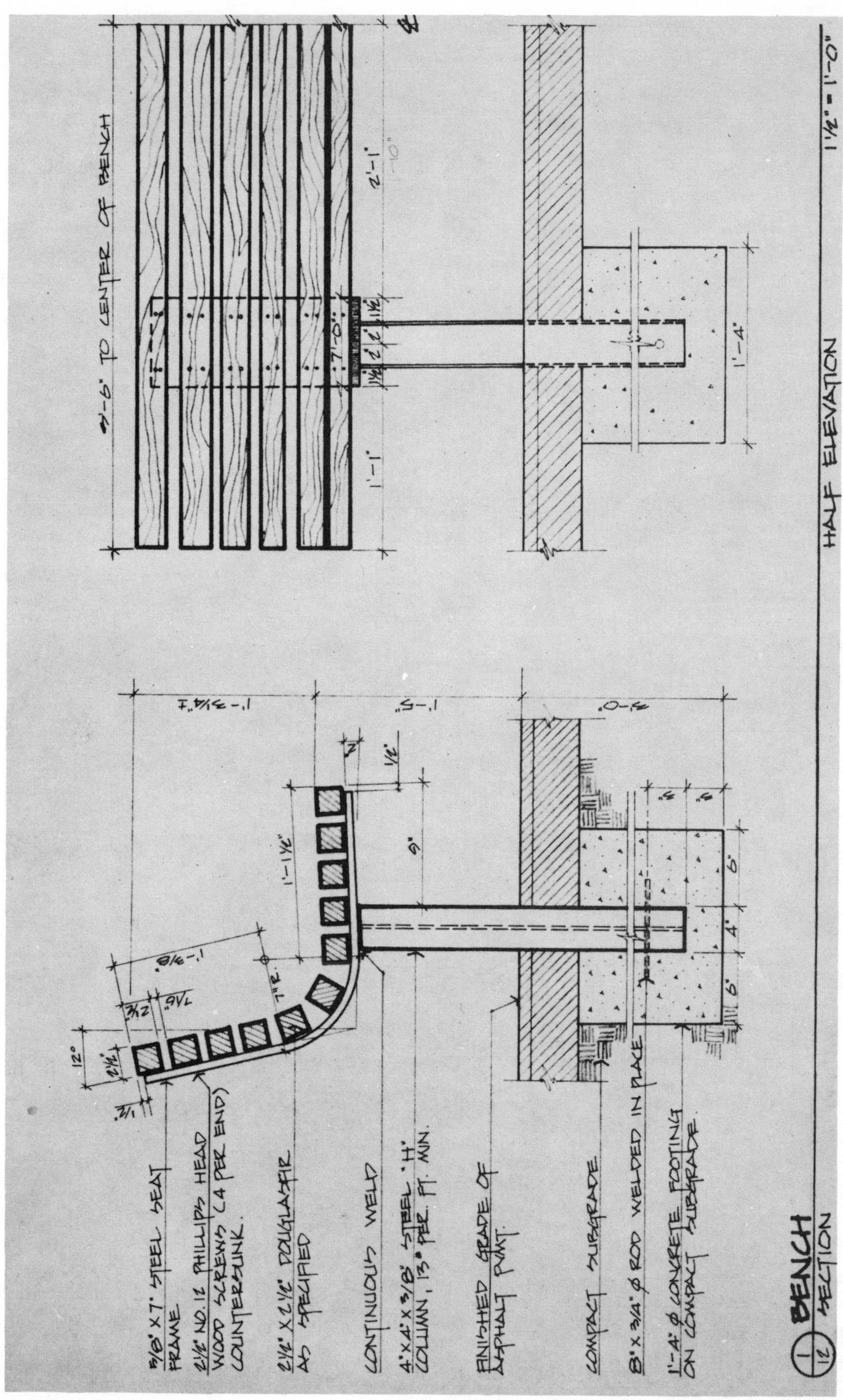
5/8" X 7" STEEL SEAT FRAME
2 1/2" NO. 12 PHILLIPS HEAD WOOD SCREWS (4 PER END) COUNTERSUNK.
2 1/2" X 2 1/2" DOUGLAS FIR AS SPECIFIED
CONTINUOUS WELD
4"X4"X3/8" STEEL 'H' COLUMN, 13# PER. FT. MIN.
FINISHED GRADE OF ASPHALT PVMT.
COMPACT SUBGRADE
8" X 3/4" ø ROD WELDED IN PLACE
1'-4" ø CONCRETE FOOTING ON COMPACT SUBGRADE
BENCH
SECTION
3'-6" TO CENTER OF BENCH
HALF ELEVATION
1 1/2" = 1'-0"

Figure 11.25 *Bench detail.*

Bonnell and Associates

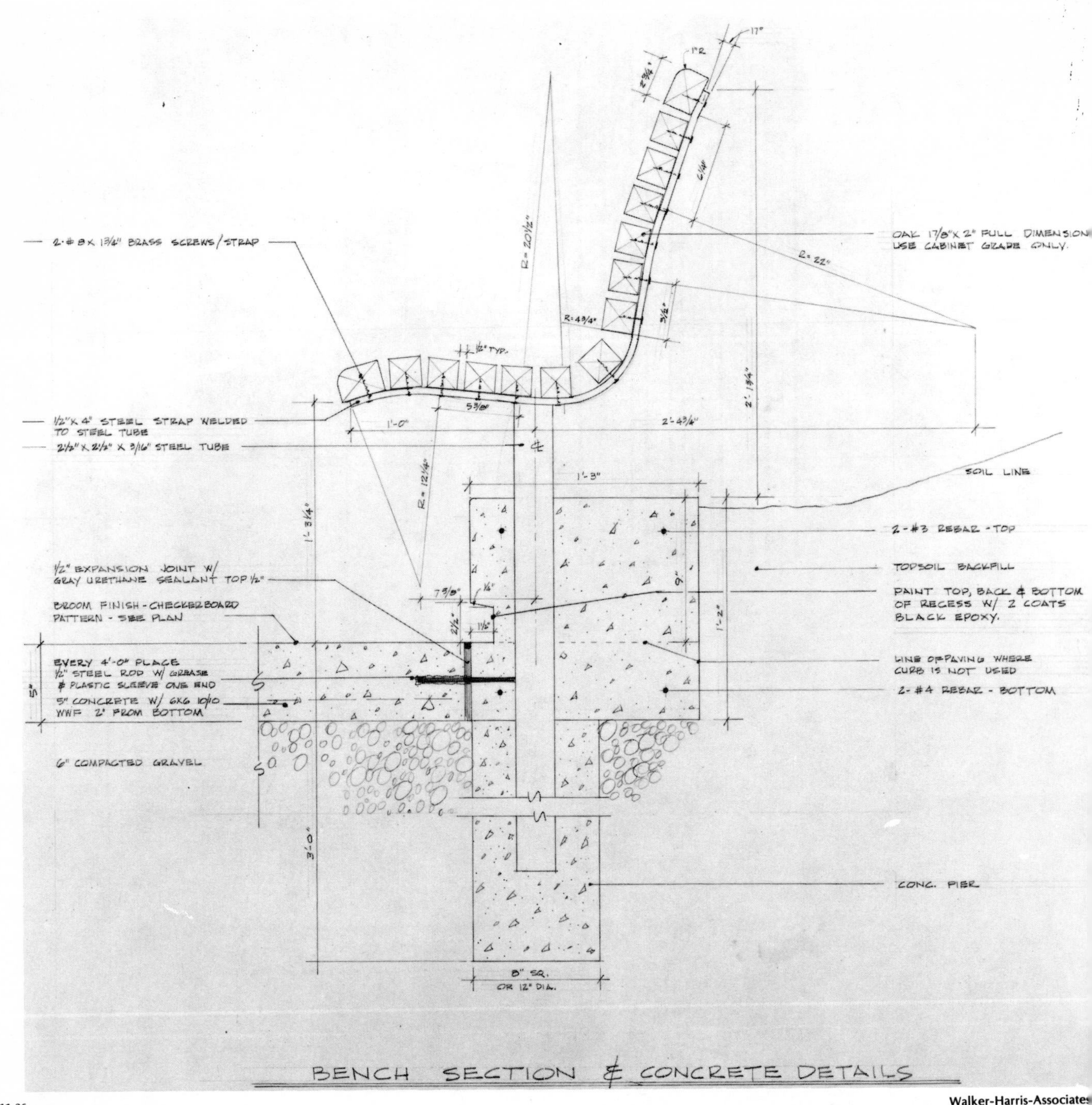
2-#8 x 1 3/4" BRASS SCREWS/STRAP
1/2" x 4" STEEL STRAP WELDED TO STEEL TUBE
2 1/2" x 2 1/2" x 3/16" STEEL TUBE
OAK 1 7/8" x 2" FULL DIMENSION USE CABINET GRADE ONLY.
SOIL LINE
2-#3 REBAR - TOP
TOPSOIL BACKFILL
PAINT TOP, BACK & BOTTOM OF RECESS W/ 2 COATS BLACK EPOXY.
LINE OF PAVING WHERE CURB IS NOT USED
2-#4 REBAR - BOTTOM
1/2" EXPANSION JOINT W/ GRAY URETHANE SEALANT TOP 1/2"
BROOM FINISH - CHECKERBOARD PATTERN - SEE PLAN
EVERY 4'-0" PLACE 1/2" STEEL ROD W/ GREASE & PLASTIC SLEEVE ONE END
5" CONCRETE W/ 6X6 10/10 WWF 2" FROM BOTTOM
6" COMPACTED GRAVEL
CONC. PIER
8" SQ. OR 12" DIA.
BENCH SECTION & CONCRETE DETAILS

11.26

Walker-Harris-Associates

Figures 11.26 - 11.32 *Wood benches, some with similar shapes.*

11.27 Sasaki Associates

11.28

11.29 Lawrence Halprin and Associates

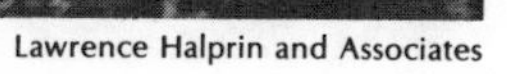

11.30 Sasaki Associates

11.31 Walker-Harris-Associates-Inc.

11.32 Environmental Planning and Design

11.33

LORDS
11.34

11.35

11.36

ROADWAY
11.37

11.38

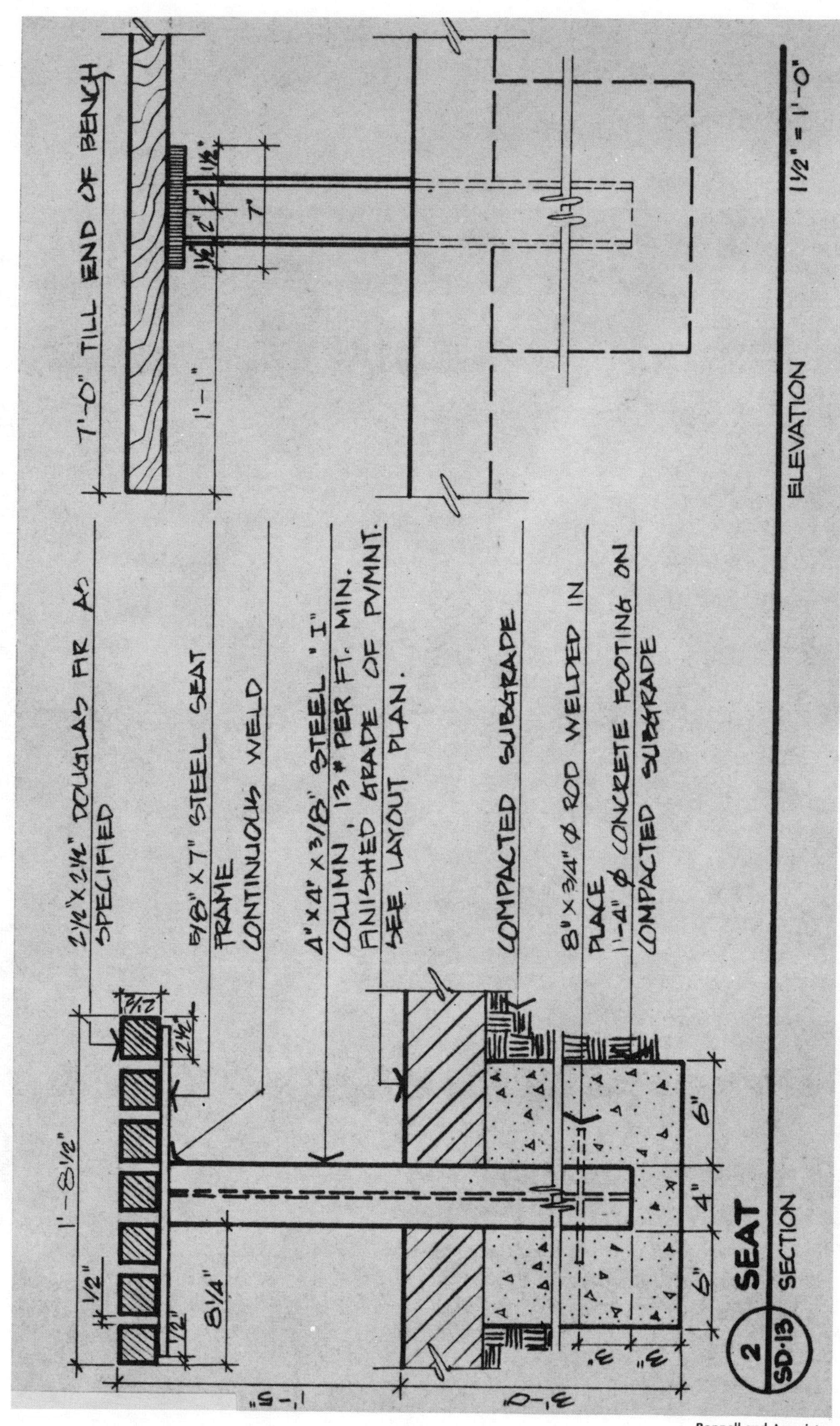

2½"X2½" DOUGLAS FIR AS SPECIFIED
5/8" X 7" STEEL SEAT FRAME
CONTINUOUS WELD
4" X 4" X 3/8" STEEL "I" COLUMN, 13# PER FT. MIN.
FINISHED GRADE OF PVMNT. SEE LAYOUT PLAN.
COMPACTED SUBGRADE
8" X 3/4" Ø ROD WELDED IN PLACE
1'-4" Ø CONCRETE FOOTING ON COMPACTED SUBGRADE
7'-0" TILL END OF BENCH
1'-1"
1'-8½"
8¼"
1'-5"
3'-0"
ELEVATION
1½" = 1'-0"
2
SD-13
SEAT
SECTION

11.39

Bonnell and Associates

Figures 11.33 – 11.38 *Design variations for benches.*

Figure 11.39 *Bench detail.*

Johnson, Johnson and Roy

Figure 11.40 *Construction details for the benches above can be found on the next page.*

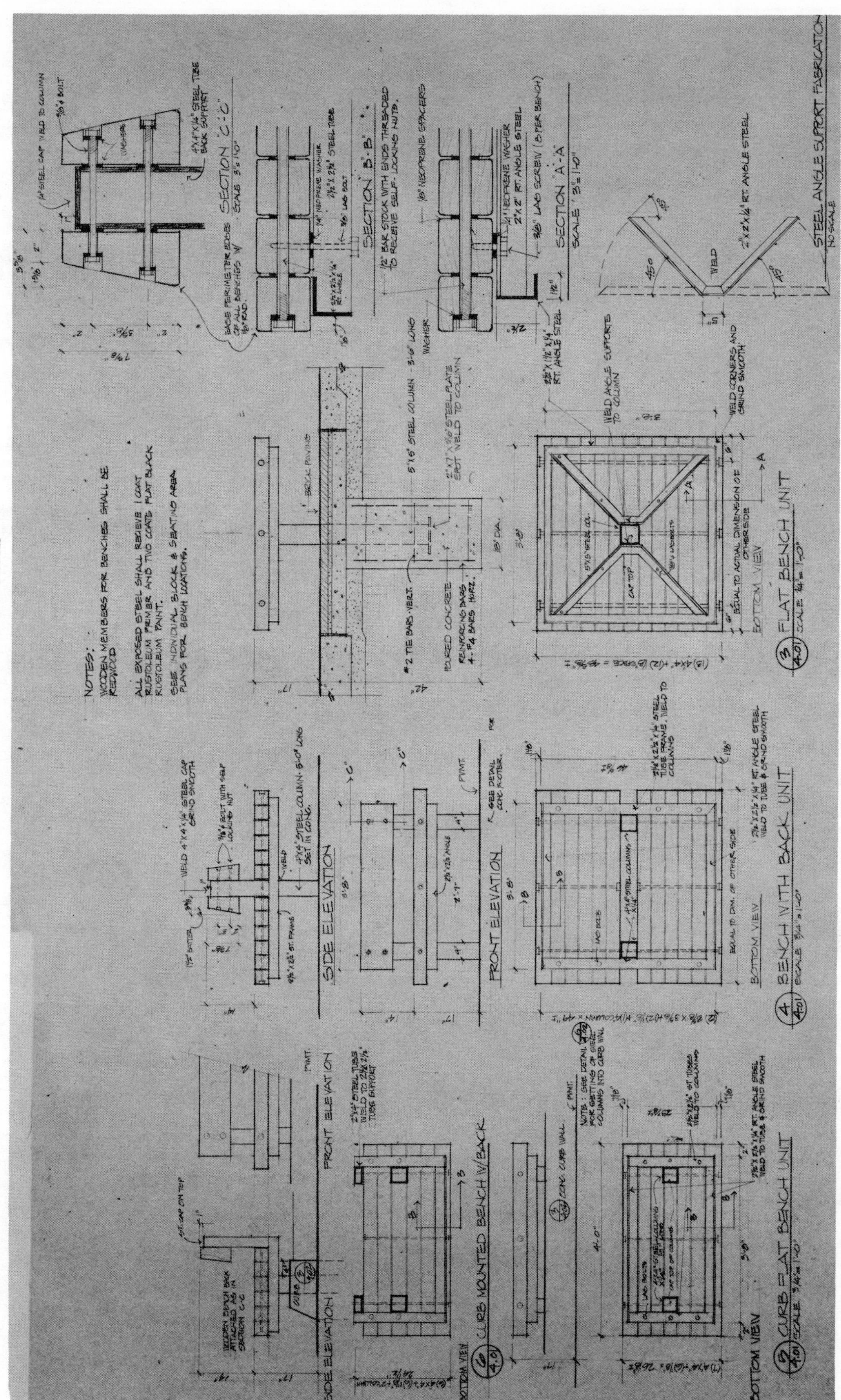
NOTES:
WOODEN MEMBERS FOR BENCHES SHALL BE REDWOOD
SECTION 'C-C'
SECTION 'B-B'
SECTION 'A-A'
STEEL ANGLE SUPPORT FABRICATION
SIDE ELEVATION
FRONT ELEVATION
BOTTOM VIEW
FLAT BENCH UNIT
BENCH WITH BACK UNIT
CURB MOUNTED BENCH W/BACK
CURB FLAT BENCH UNIT

Figure 11.41 *Details for benches in Figure 11.40.*

Johnson, Johnson and Roy

11.42

11.43

11.44

Environmental Planning and Design

11.45

Snell Environmental Group

11.46

11.47

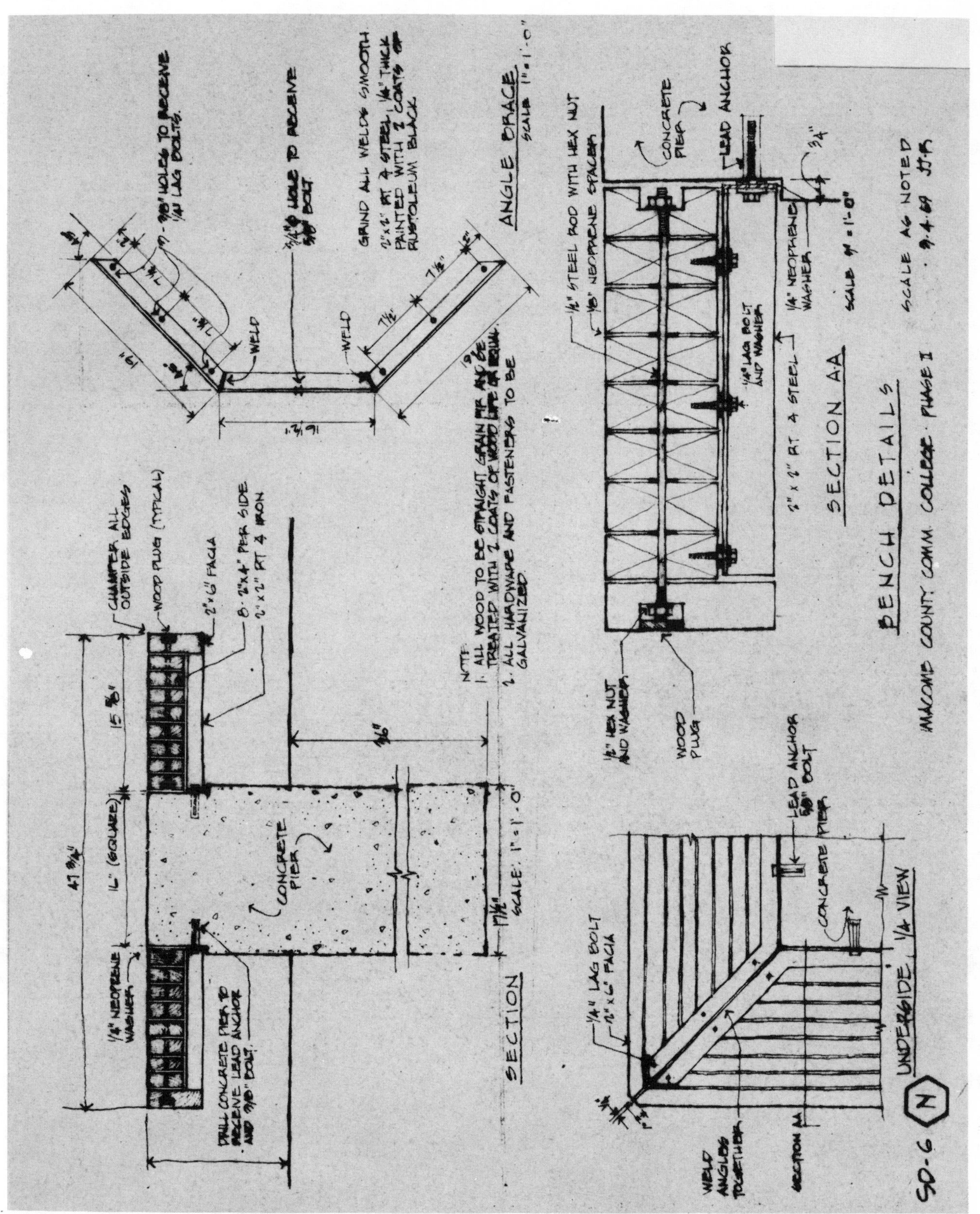
SECTION
SCALE: 1" = 1'-0"
ANGLE BRACE
SECTION A-A
BENCH DETAILS
MACOMB COUNTY COMM. COLLEGE · PHASE I
UNDERSIDE 1/4 VIEW
SO-6

11.48 **Figures 11.42 – 11.47** *Several wood bench designs.*

Figure 11.48 *Bench details.*

Johnson, Johnson and Roy

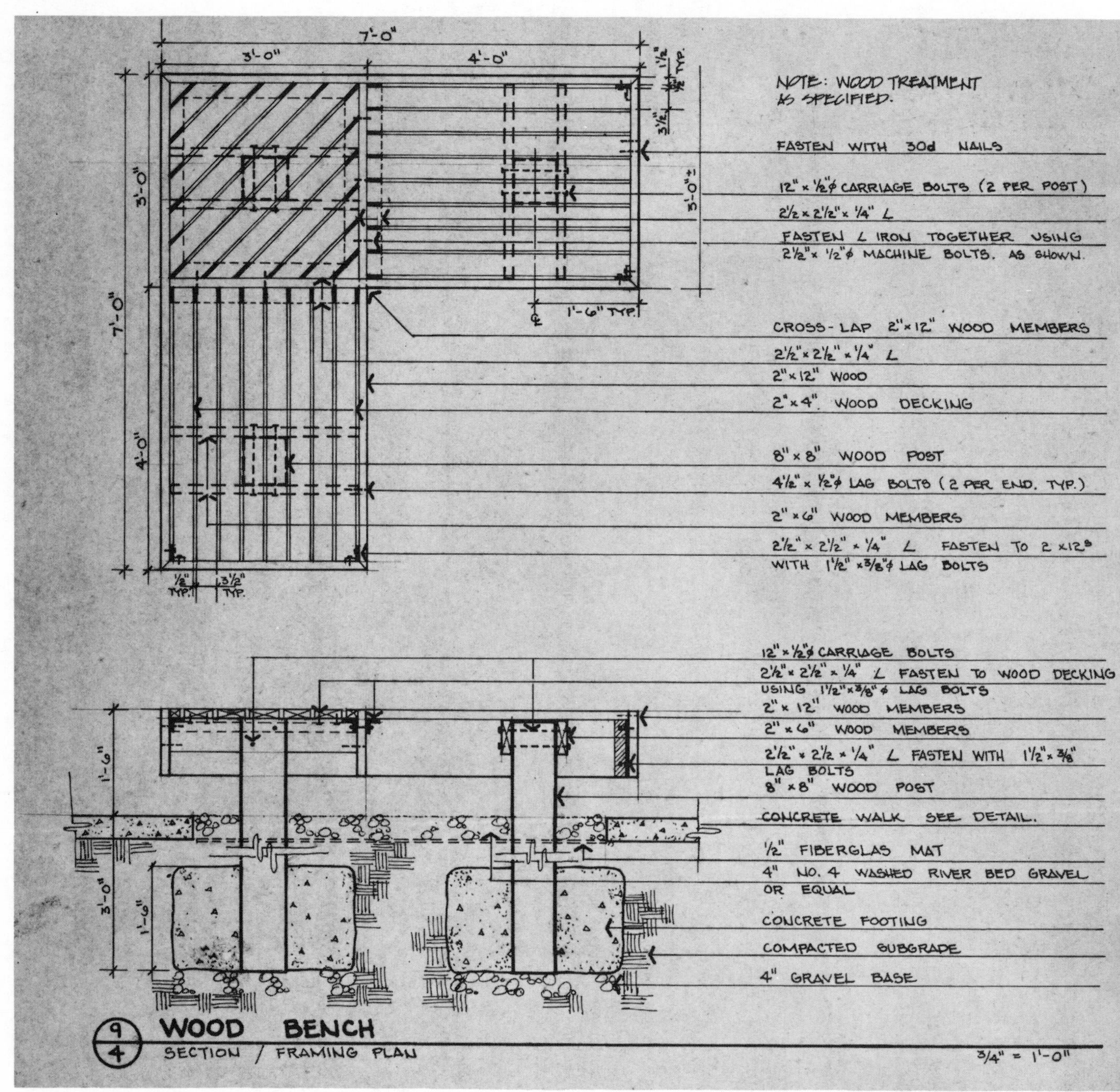
7'-0"
3'-0"
4'-0"
NOTE: WOOD TREATMENT AS SPECIFIED.
FASTEN WITH 30d NAILS
12" x ½"ϕ CARRIAGE BOLTS (2 PER POST)
2½ x 2½" x ¼" L
FASTEN L IRON TOGETHER USING 2½" x ½"ϕ MACHINE BOLTS. AS SHOWN.
1'-6" TYP.
CROSS-LAP 2" x 12" WOOD MEMBERS
2½" x 2½" x ¼" L
2" x 12" WOOD
2" x 4" WOOD DECKING
8" x 8" WOOD POST
4½" x ½"ϕ LAG BOLTS (2 PER END. TYP.)
2" x 6" WOOD MEMBERS
2½" x 2½" x ¼" L FASTEN TO 2 x 12'S WITH 1½" x ⅜"ϕ LAG BOLTS
½" TYP.
3½" TYP.
12" x ½"ϕ CARRIAGE BOLTS
2½" x 2½" x ¼" L FASTEN TO WOOD DECKING USING 1½" x ⅜"ϕ LAG BOLTS
2" x 12" WOOD MEMBERS
2" x 6" WOOD MEMBERS
2½" x 2½ x ¼" L FASTEN WITH 1½" x ⅜" LAG BOLTS
8" x 8" WOOD POST
CONCRETE WALK SEE DETAIL.
½" FIBERGLAS MAT
4" NO. 4 WASHED RIVER BED GRAVEL OR EQUAL
CONCRETE FOOTING
COMPACTED SUBGRADE
4" GRAVEL BASE
1'-6"
3'-0"
9
4
WOOD BENCH
SECTION / FRAMING PLAN
¾" = 1'-0"

Figure 11.49 *Bench details.*

Bonnell and Associates

Figures 11.50 – 11.55 *Benches of varying shapes, sizes and materials.*

11.50 Environmental Planning and Design

11.51

11.52

11.53 Sasaki Associates

11.54

11.55

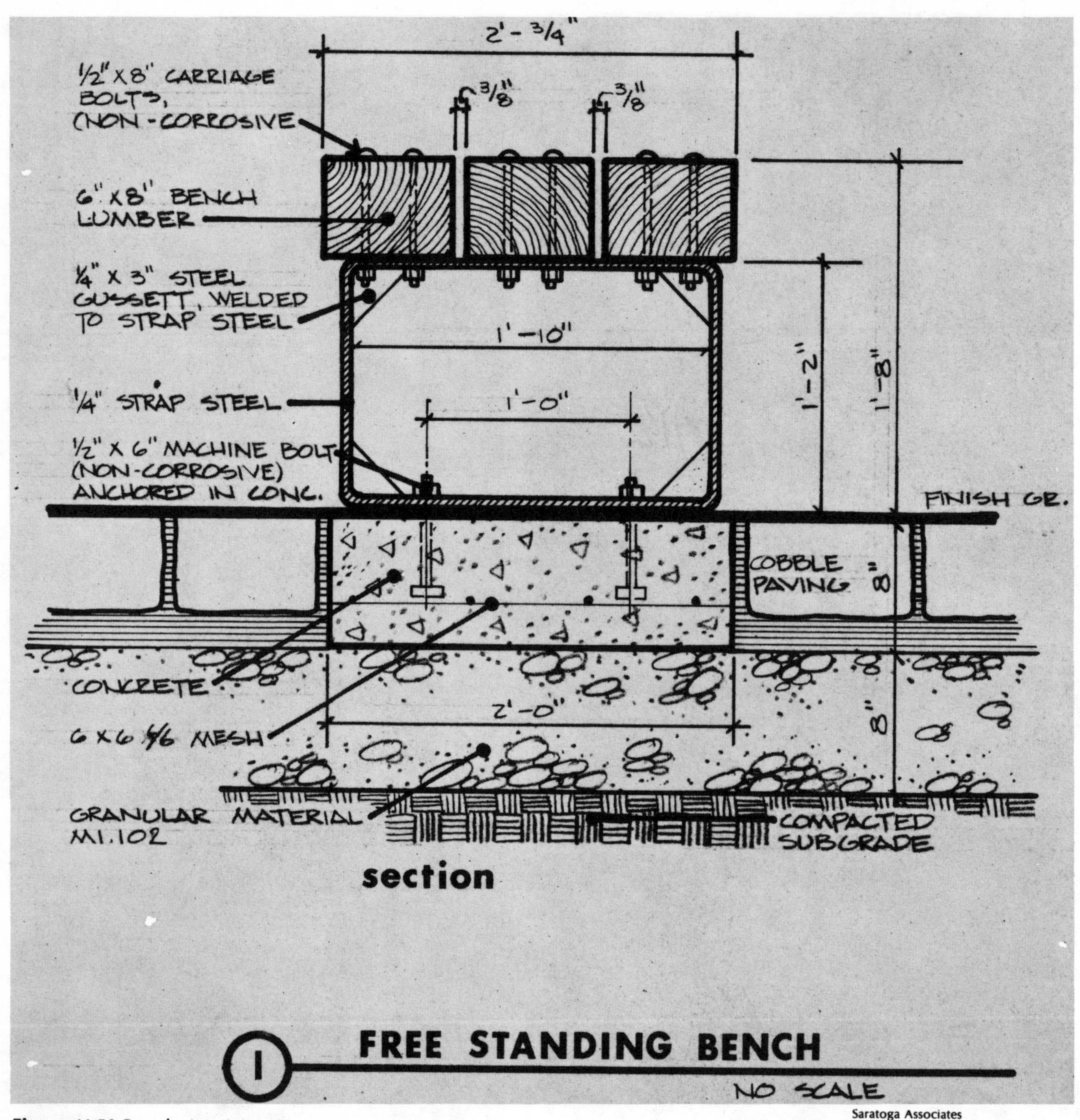

2'-3/4"
1/2" X 8" CARRIAGE BOLTS, (NON-CORROSIVE
3/8"
3/8"
6" X 8" BENCH LUMBER
1/4" X 3" STEEL GUSSETT, WELDED TO STRAP STEEL
1'-10"
1'-2"
1'-8"
1/4" STRAP STEEL
1'-0"
1/2" X 6" MACHINE BOLT (NON-CORROSIVE) ANCHORED IN CONC.
FINISH GR.
COBBLE PAVING
8"
CONCRETE
2'-0"
8"
6 X 6 6/6 MESH
GRANULAR MATERIAL M1.102
COMPACTED SUBGRADE
section
1
FREE STANDING BENCH
NO SCALE

Saratoga Associates

Figure 11.56 *Bench detail.*

11.57

Edward D. Stone Jr. and Associates

11.58

11.59

Environmental Planning and Design

Figures 11.57 – 11.59 *Benches with various base supports.*

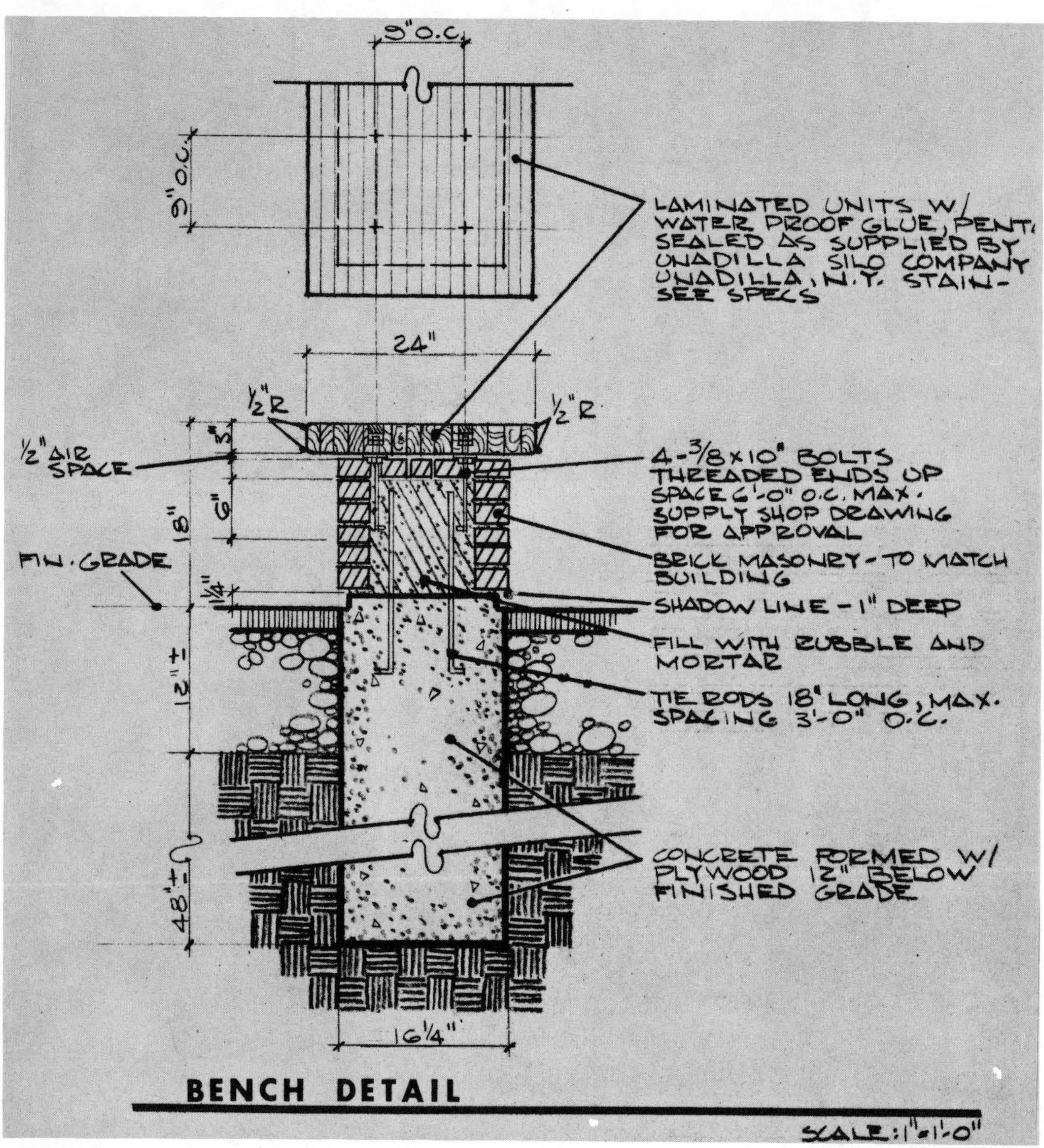
9" O.C.
9" O.C.
LAMINATED UNITS W/ WATER PROOF GLUE, PENTA SEALED AS SUPPLIED BY UNADILLA SILO COMPANY UNADILLA, N.Y. STAIN-SEE SPECS
24"
1/2" R
1/2" R
1/2" AIR SPACE
4-3/8 x 10" BOLTS THREADED ENDS UP SPACE 6'-0" O.C. MAX. SUPPLY SHOP DRAWING FOR APPROVAL
6"
18"
BRICK MASONRY - TO MATCH BUILDING
FIN. GRADE
SHADOW LINE - 1" DEEP
FILL WITH RUBBLE AND MORTAR
12"±
TIE RODS 18" LONG, MAX. SPACING 3'-0" O.C.
CONCRETE FORMED W/ PLYWOOD 12" BELOW FINISHED GRADE
48"±
16 1/4"
BENCH DETAIL
SCALE: 1"=1'-0"

Figure 11.60 *Bench detail.*

Saratoga Associates

Figures 11.61 – 11.66 *Wood benches in a variety of shapes.*

11.61 Sasaki Associates

11.62

11.63 William A. Behnke Associates

11.64 M. Paul Friedberg and Partners

11.65 M. Paul Friedberg and Partners

11.66 Bailey and Associates

Ed Dull, courtesy of Western Wood Products Association

11.67 Alex Pierce

11.68

11.69 Bailey and Associates

Figure 11.67 *Construction details for this bench can be found on page 259.*

Figures 11.68 – 11.69 *Additional benches.*

11.70
11.71
11.72
11.73

Figures 11.70 – 11.73 *Stone and pre-cast concrete benches.*

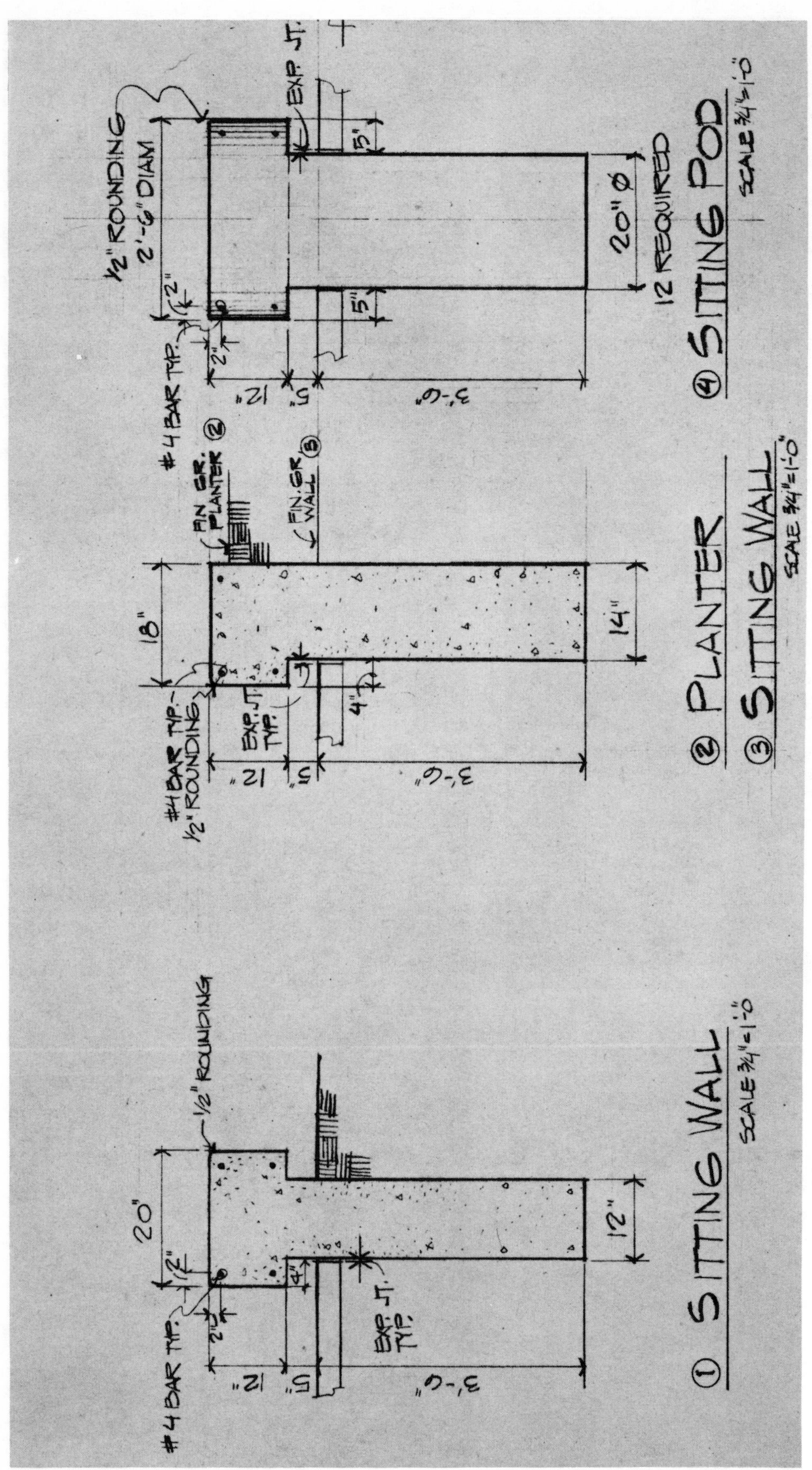
① SITTING WALL
SCALE 3/4"=1'-0"
#4 BAR TYP.
1/2" ROUNDING
EXP. JT. TYP.
20"
12"
3'-6"
② PLANTER
③ SITTING WALL
SCALE 3/4"=1'-0"
#4 BAR TYP.-
1/2" ROUNDING
18"
14"
FIN. GR. PLANTER ②
FIN. GR. WALL ③
④ SITTING POD
SCALE 3/4"=1'-0"
12 REQUIRED
20" Ø
1/2" ROUNDING
2'-6" DIAM
EXP. JT.

Figure 11.74 *Concrete bench details.*

CR3, inc.

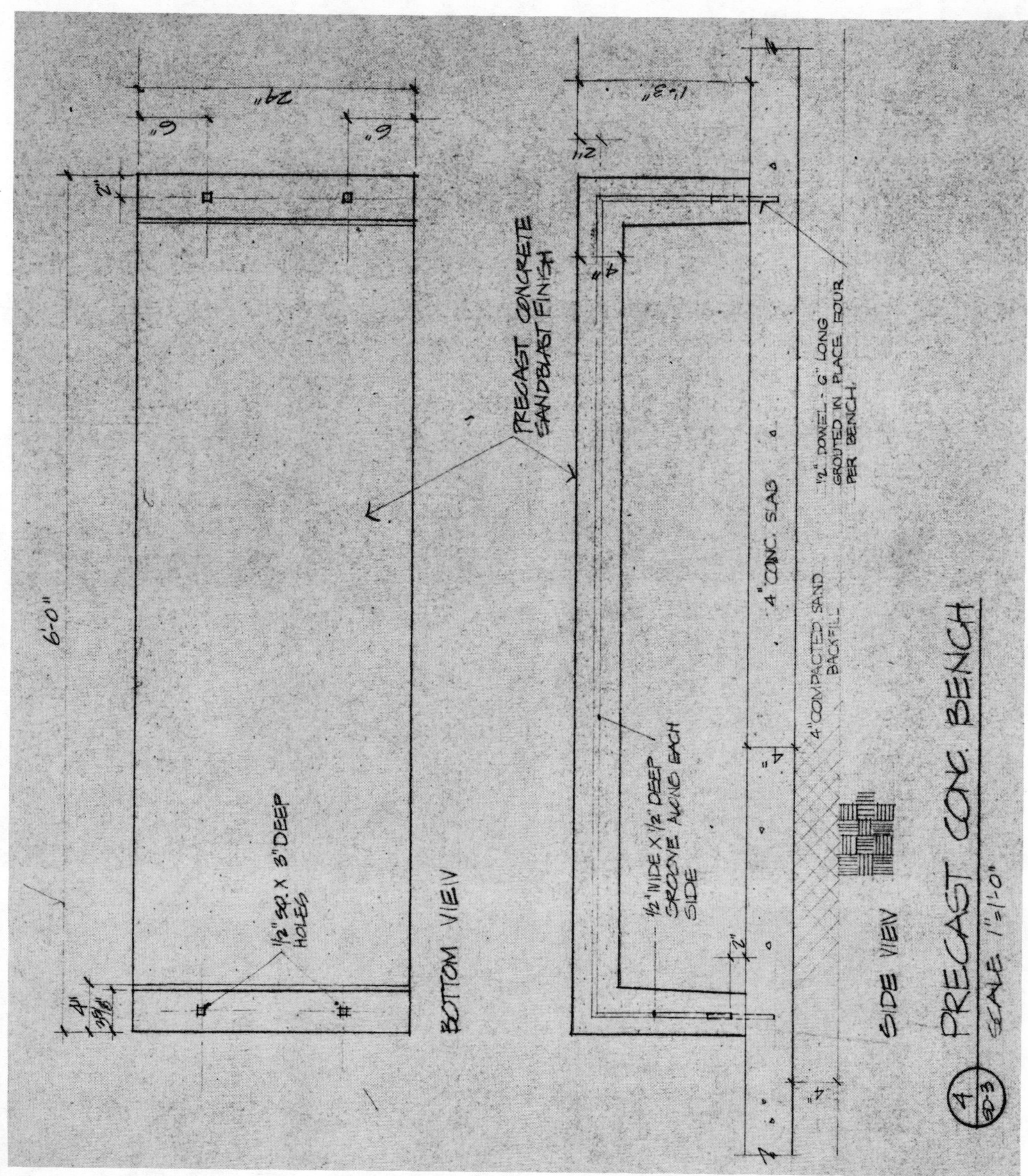
6'-0"
24"
6"
6"
2"
4"
1/2" SQ. X 3" DEEP HOLES
BOTTOM VIEW
PRECAST CONCRETE SANDBLAST FINISH
1'-3"
2"
4"
1/2" WIDE X 1/2" DEEP GROOVE ALONG EACH SIDE
4" CONC. SLAB
4" COMPACTED SAND BACKFILL
1/2" DOWEL - 6" LONG GROUTED IN PLACE FOUR PER BENCH.
SIDE VIEW
PRECAST CONC. BENCH
SCALE 1"=1'-0"
4
SD-3

Figure 11.75 *Concrete bench detail.*

Johnson, Johnson and Roy

11.76 Cole Associates Inc.

11.79 James H. Bassett

11.77

11.80

11.78

11.81

11.82

11.83

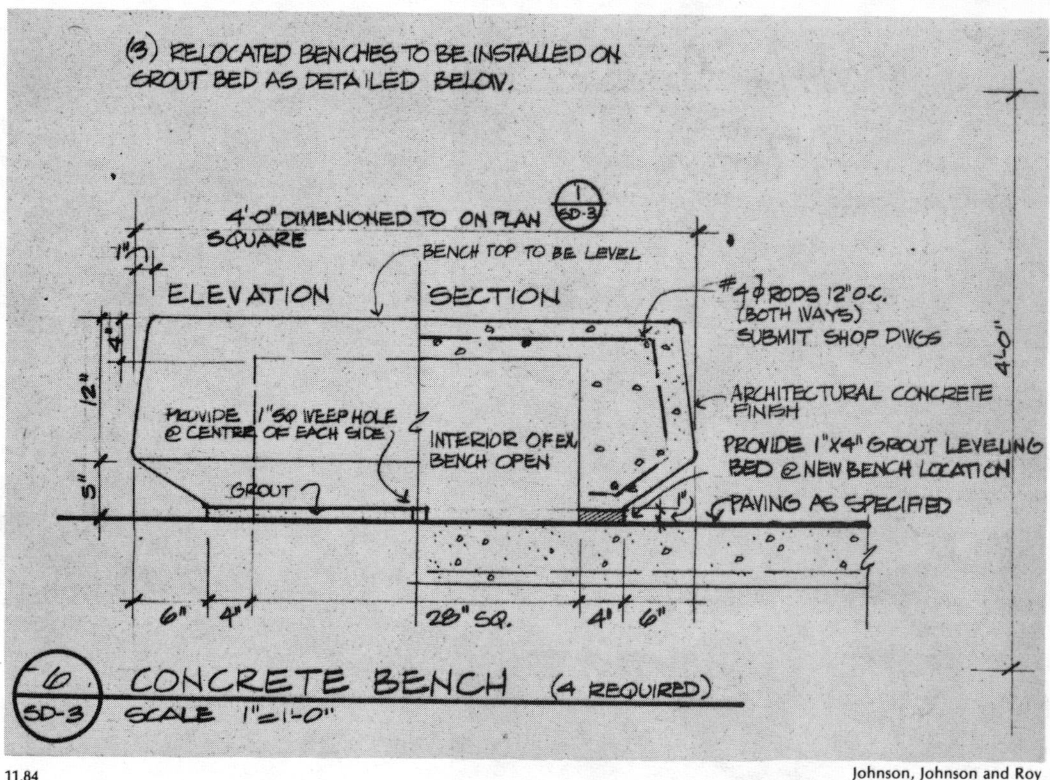

(3) RELOCATED BENCHES TO BE INSTALLED ON GROUT BED AS DETAILED BELOW.
4'-0" DIMENIONED TO ON PLAN SQUARE
1 SD-3
BENCH TOP TO BE LEVEL
1"
ELEVATION
SECTION
#4 ϕ RODS 12" O.C. (BOTH WAYS) SUBMIT SHOP DWGS
4"
12"
5"
ARCHITECTURAL CONCRETE FINISH
PROVIDE 1" SQ WEEP HOLE @ CENTRE OF EACH SIDE
INTERIOR OF BENCH OPEN
PROVIDE 1"X4" GROUT LEVELING BED @ NEW BENCH LOCATION
GROUT
1"
PAVING AS SPECIFIED
6"
4"
28" SQ.
4"
6"
4'-0"
6 SD-3
CONCRETE BENCH (4 REQUIRED)
SCALE 1"=1'-0"

11.84

Johnson, Johnson and Roy

Figures 11.76 – 11.83 *Concrete benches.*

Figure 11.84 *Construction detail for a concrete bench.*

11.85

11.88 Charles Wood

11.86

11.89 Bailey and Associates

11.87 Johnson and Dee

Figures 11.85 – 11.89 *Miscellaneous style and types of benches.*

Figures 11.90 – 11.95 *Bollards of many styles.*

11.90

11.93

11.91

11.94

11.92

11.95

11.96

11.97

11.98

11.99

11.100

11.101

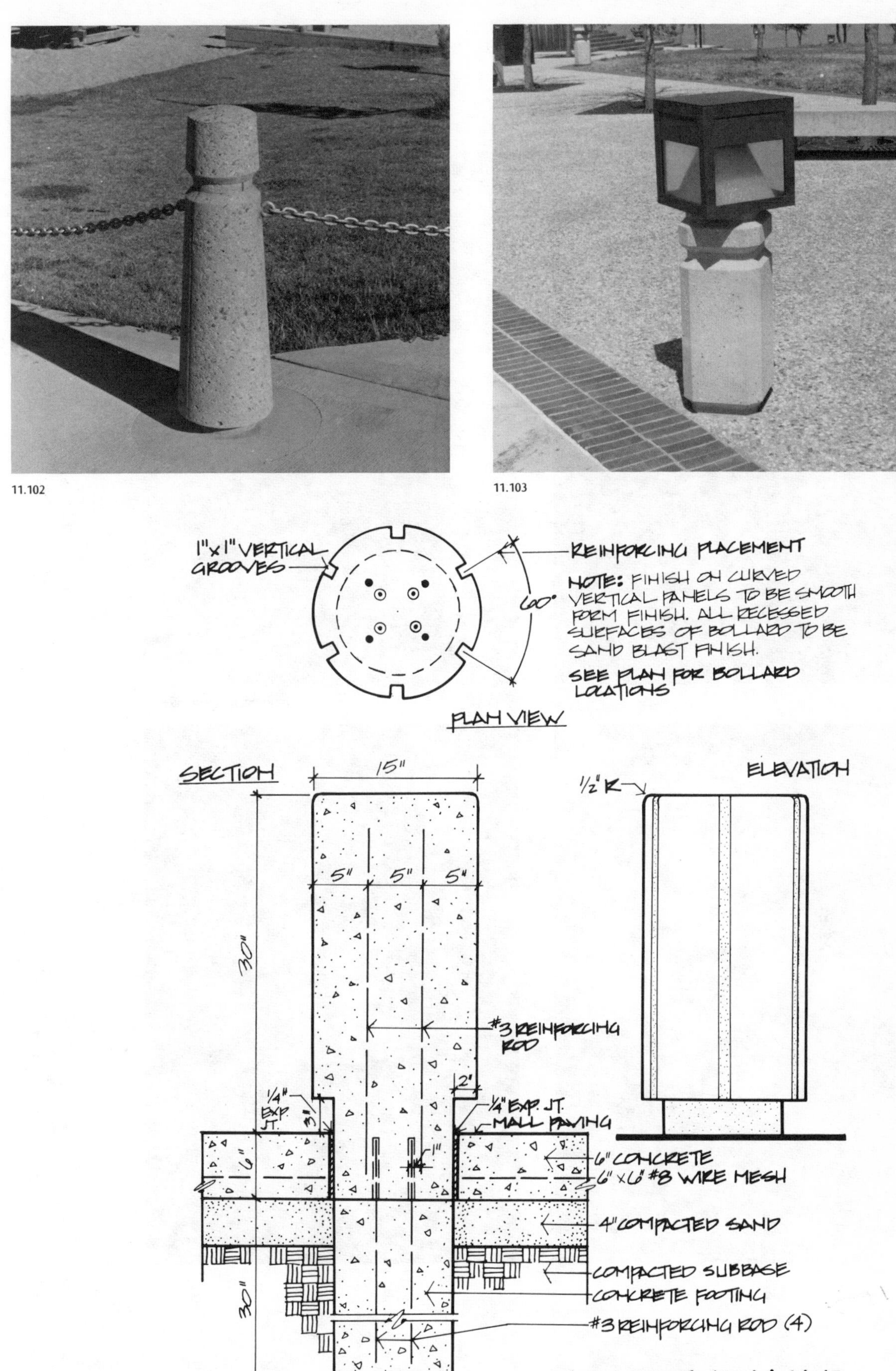
11.102
11.103
1"x1" VERTICAL GROOVES
REINFORCING PLACEMENT
60°
NOTE: FINISH ON CURVED VERTICAL PANELS TO BE SMOOTH FORM FINISH. ALL RECESSED SURFACES OF BOLLARD TO BE SAND BLAST FINISH.
SEE PLAN FOR BOLLARD LOCATIONS
PLAN VIEW
SECTION
15"
5" 5" 5"
30"
#3 REINFORCING ROD
2"
1/4" EXP. JT.
3"
1/4" EXP. JT.
MALL PAVING
1"
6"
6" CONCRETE
6"x6" #8 WIRE MESH
4" COMPACTED SAND
COMPACTED SUBBASE
CONCRETE FOOTING
30"
#3 REINFORCING ROD (4)
11"
ELEVATION
1/2" R
CONCRETE BOLLARD
11.104

Figures 11.96 – 11.104 *Bollards and a detail.*

11.105

11.107 Johnson, Johnson and Roy

11.106

11.108

Figures 11.105 - 11.112 *Concrete bollards, some with recessed lights.*

11.109

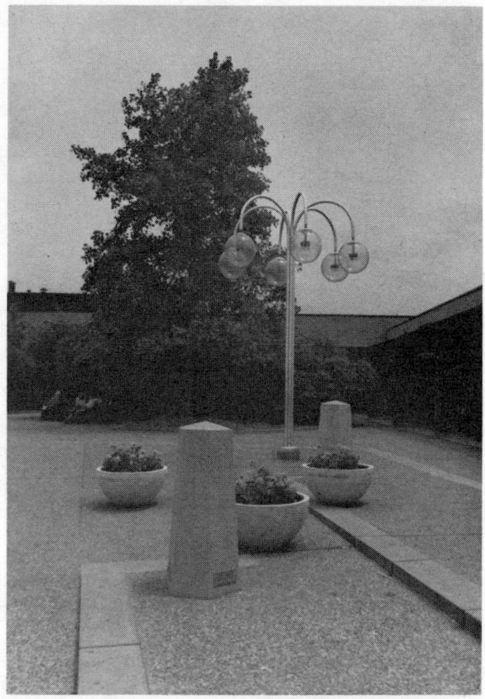

11.111 Lawrence Halprin and Associates

11.110 Sasaki Associates

11.112 James H. Bassett

11.113

11.115

11.114

11.116

YMCA
YMCA
YMCA
YMCA

11.117

M. Paul Friedberg and

Figures 11.113 – 11.117 *Wood and concrete bollards.*

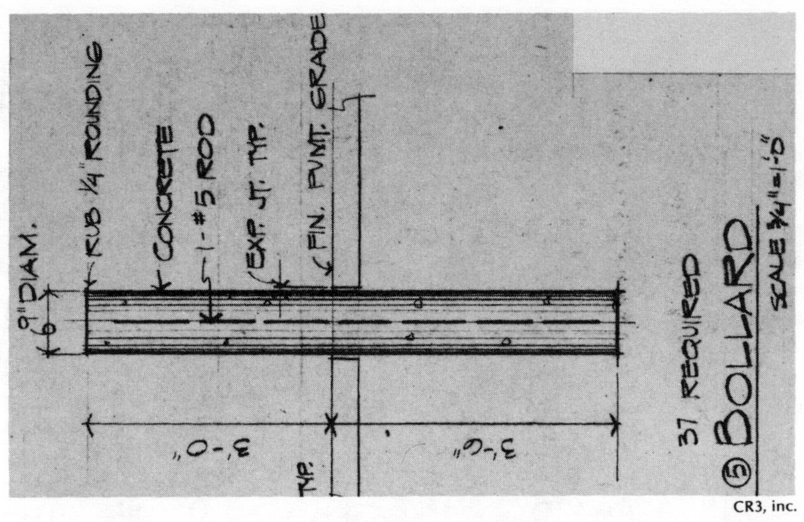
9" DIAM.
6"
RUB 1/4" ROUNDING
CONCRETE
1-#5 ROD
EXP. JT. TYP.
FIN. PVMT. GRADE
3'-0"
3'-6"
TYP.
37 REQUIRED
5 BOLLARD
SCALE 3/4"=1'-0"

CR3, inc.

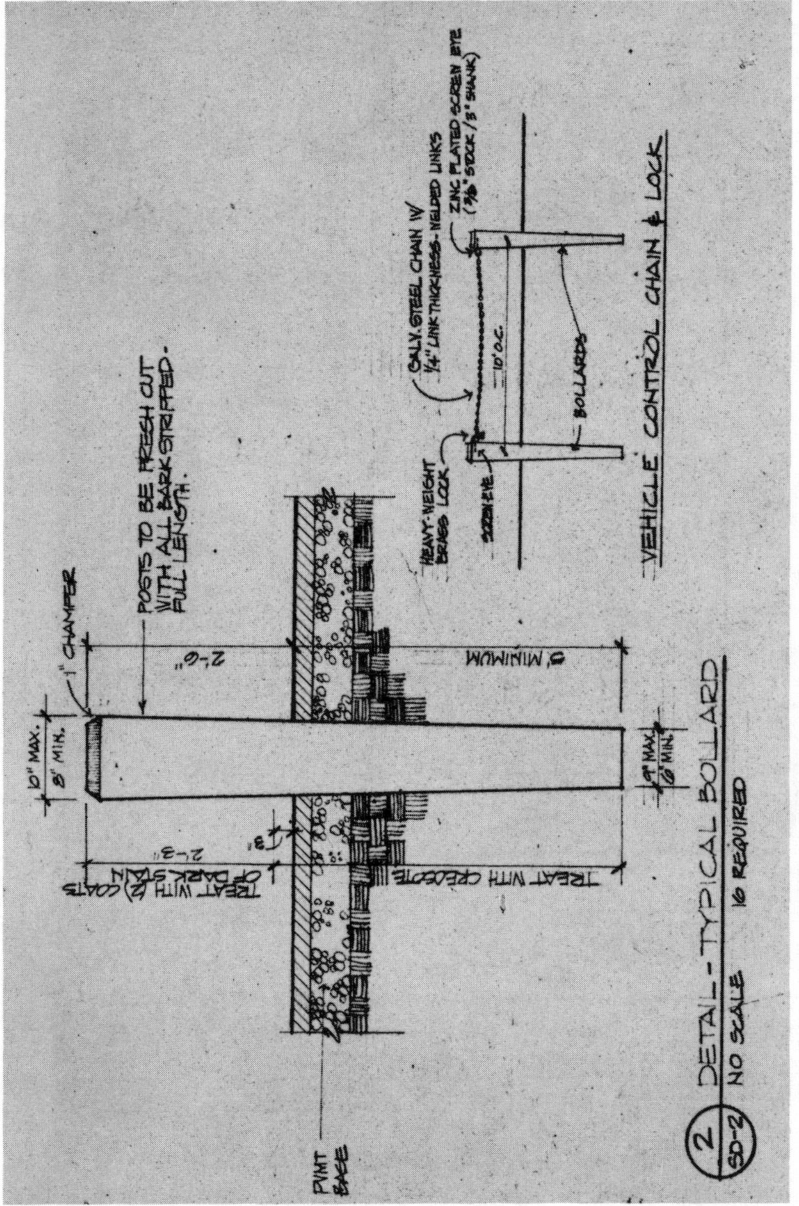
10" MAX.
8" MIN.
1" CHAMFER
POSTS TO BE FRESH CUT WITH ALL BARK STRIPPED-FULL LENGTH.
2'-6"
6' MINIMUM
2'-3"
3"
TREAT WITH (2) COATS OF DARK STAIN
TREAT WITH CREOSOTE
9" MAX.
6" MIN.
PVMT BASE
2 SD-2
DETAIL - TYPICAL BOLLARD
NO SCALE 16 REQUIRED
HEAVY-WEIGHT BRASS LOCK
SCREW EYE
GALV. STEEL CHAIN W/ 1/4" LINK THICKNESS - WELDED LINKS
ZINC PLATED SCREW EYE (3/8" STOCK / 3" SHANK)
10' O.C.
BOLLARDS
VEHICLE CONTROL CHAIN & LOCK

Johnson, Johnson and Roy

Figure 11.118 *Bollard details.*

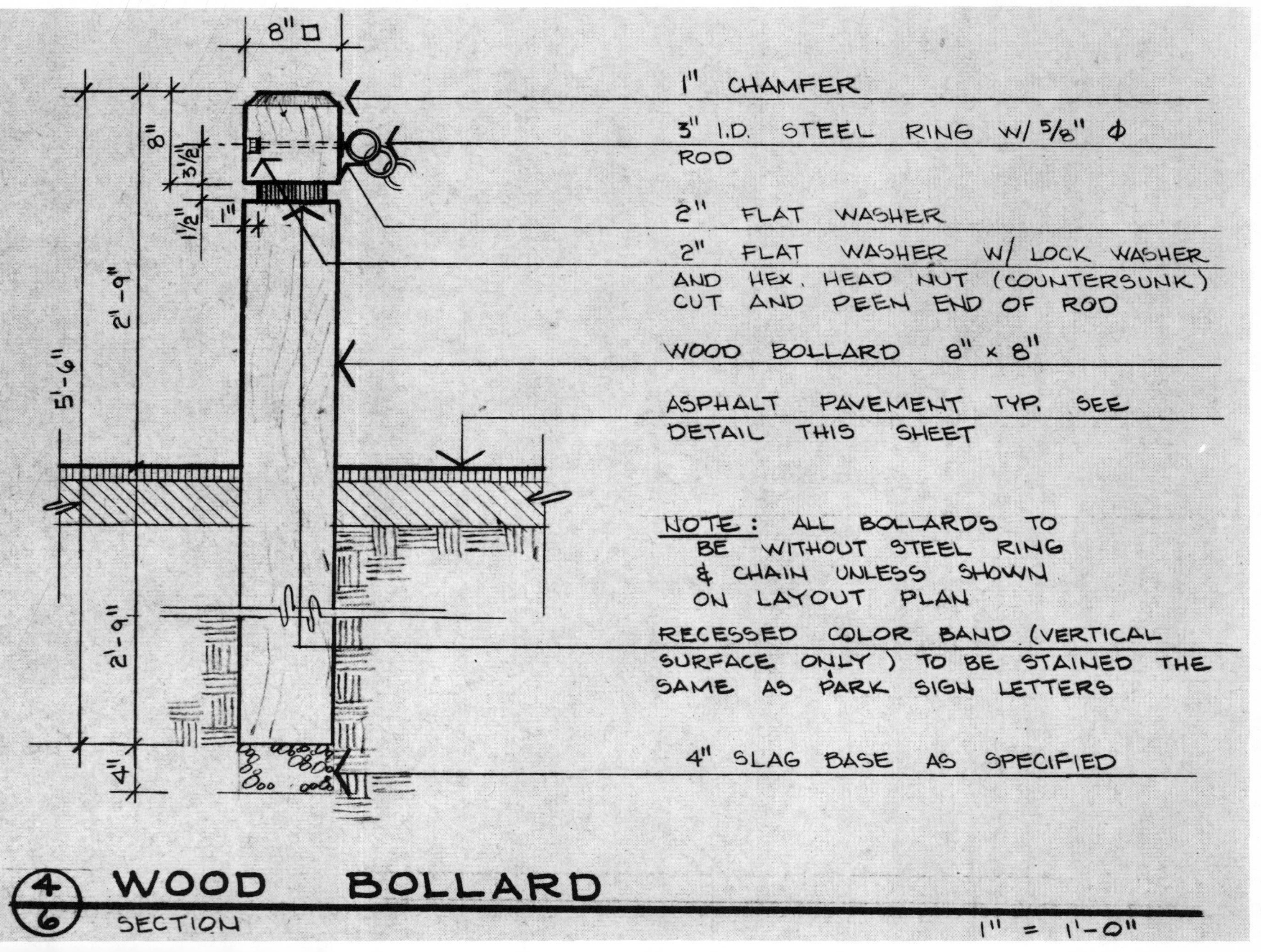
8" □
1" CHAMFER
3" I.D. STEEL RING W/ 5/8" ϕ ROD
2" FLAT WASHER
2" FLAT WASHER W/ LOCK WASHER AND HEX. HEAD NUT (COUNTERSUNK) CUT AND PEEN END OF ROD
WOOD BOLLARD 8" x 8"
ASPHALT PAVEMENT TYP. SEE DETAIL THIS SHEET
NOTE: ALL BOLLARDS TO BE WITHOUT STEEL RING & CHAIN UNLESS SHOWN ON LAYOUT PLAN
RECESSED COLOR BAND (VERTICAL SURFACE ONLY) TO BE STAINED THE SAME AS PARK SIGN LETTERS
4" SLAG BASE AS SPECIFIED
8"
3 1/2"
1 1/2"
1"
2'-9"
2'-9"
4"
5'-6"
4
6
WOOD BOLLARD
SECTION
1" = 1'-0"

Bonnell and Associates

Figure 11.119 *Bollard detail.*

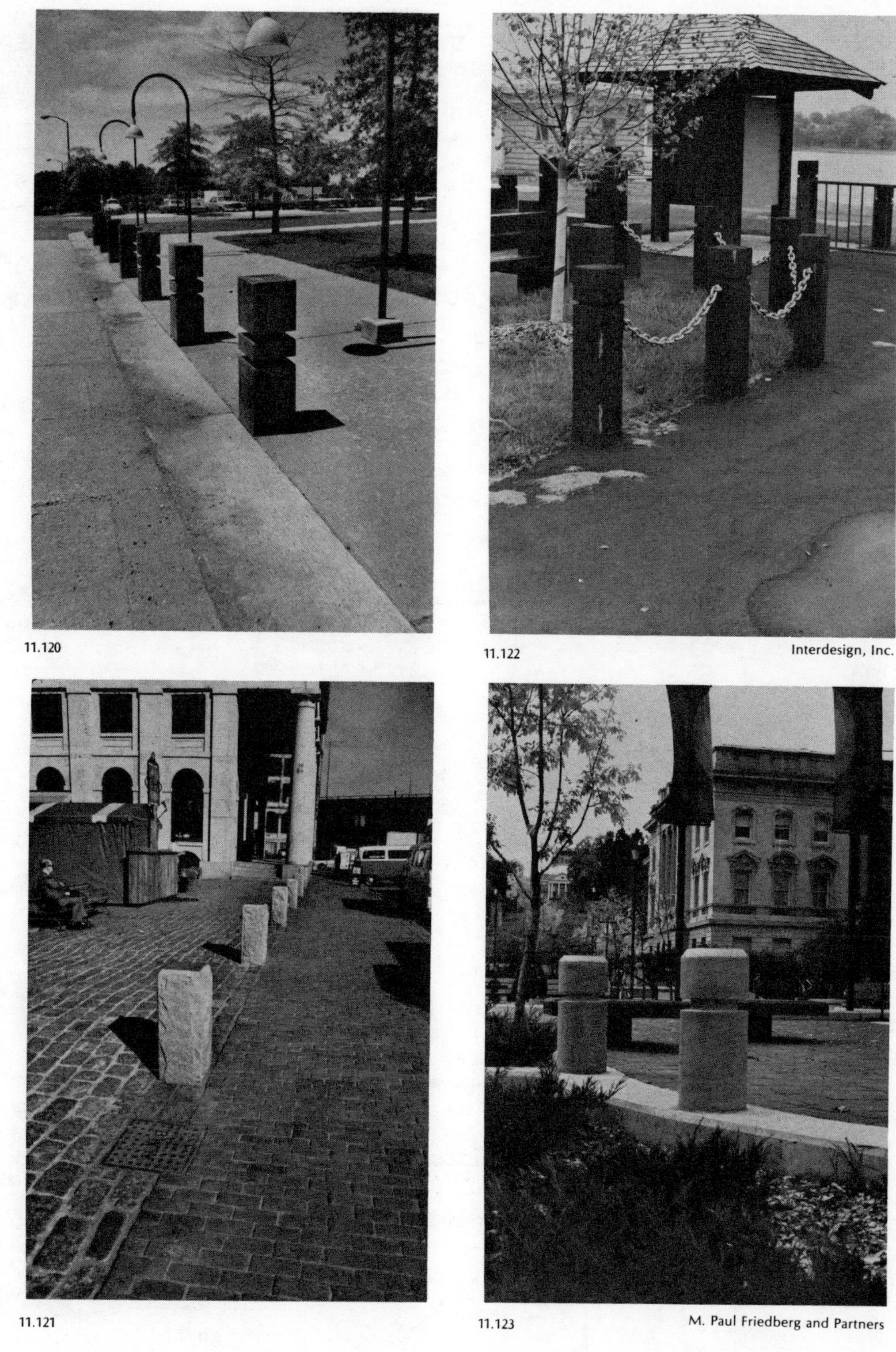

11.120

11.122 Interdesign, Inc.

11.121

11.123 M. Paul Friedberg and Partners

Figures 11.120 - 11.123 *Wood, granite and pre-cast bollards.*

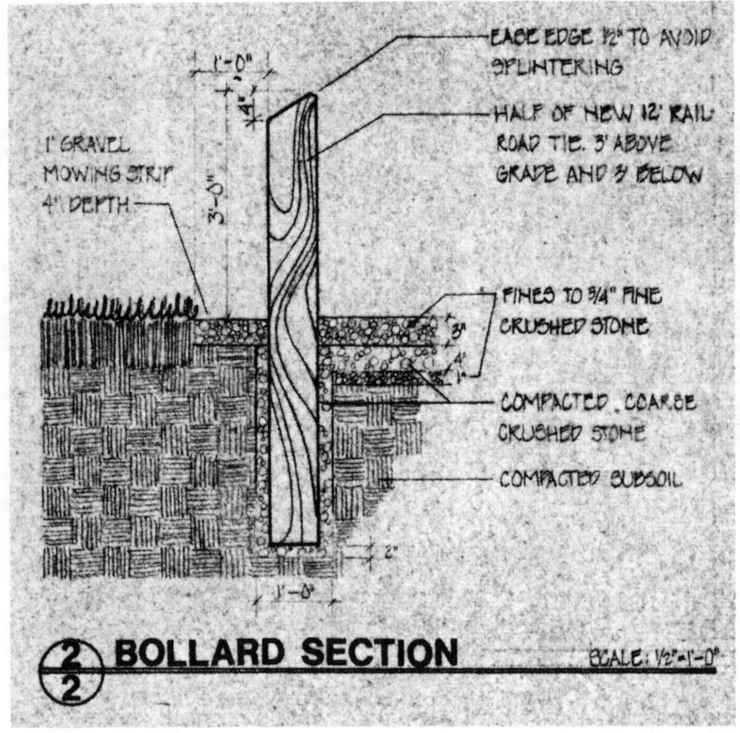
EASE EDGE ½" TO AVOID SPLINTERING
HALF OF NEW 12' RAIL ROAD TIE. 3' ABOVE GRADE AND 3' BELOW
1' GRAVEL MOWING STRIP 4" DEPTH
FINES TO 3/4" FINE CRUSHED STONE
COMPACTED COARSE CRUSHED STONE
COMPACTED SUBSOIL
BOLLARD SECTION
SCALE: ½"=1'-0"

11.124 John A. Bentley Associates

11.126 Lawrence Halprin and Associates

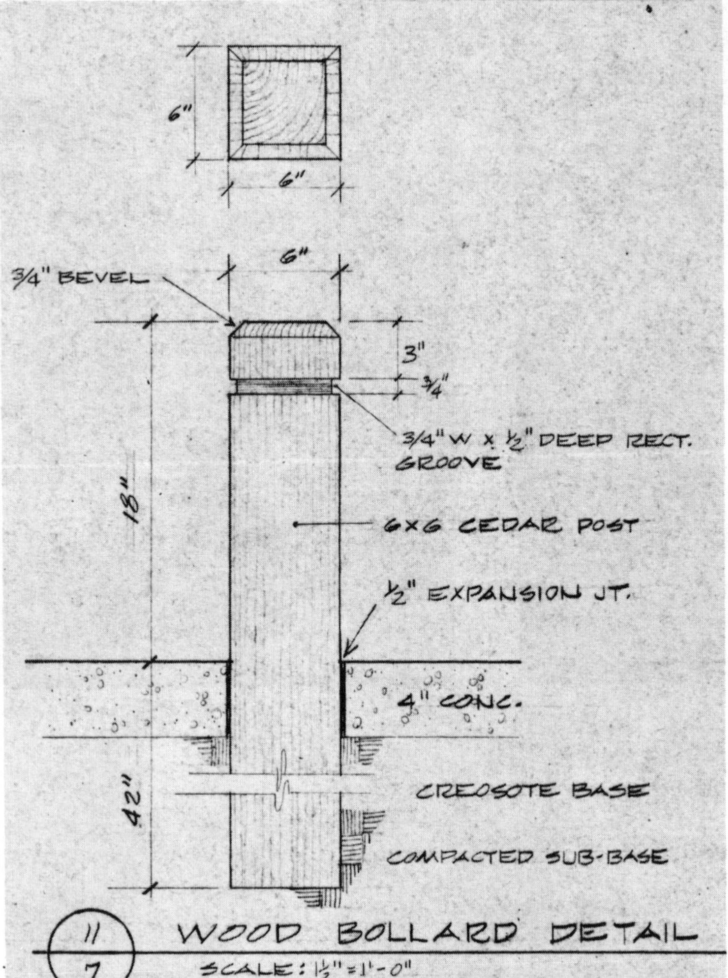
3/4" BEVEL
3/4" W x ½" DEEP RECT. GROOVE
6x6 CEDAR POST
½" EXPANSION JT.
4" CONC.
CREOSOTE BASE
COMPACTED SUB-BASE
WOOD BOLLARD DETAIL
SCALE: 1½"=1'-0"

11.125 Johnson, Johnson and Roy

11.127 James H. Bassett

Figures 11.124 – 11.127 *Bollards and details.*

11.128

11.130

11.129

11.131

Figures 11.128 – 11.131 *Varying design styles in kiosks.*

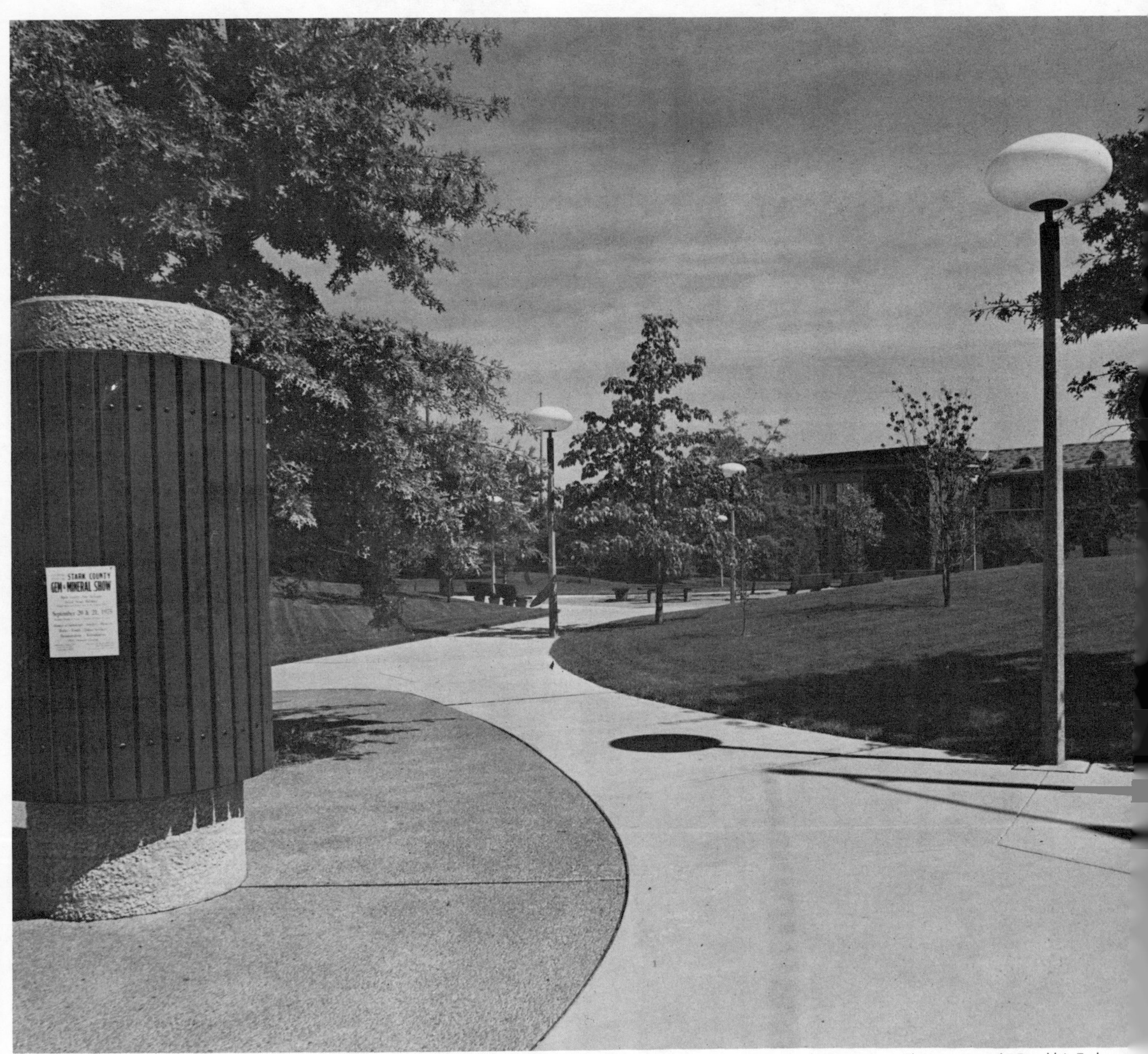
STARK COUNTY
GEM & MINERAL SHOW

Bonnell and Associates   Photo courtesy of: Donald A. Teal

Figure 11.132 *Kiosk in an urban park.*

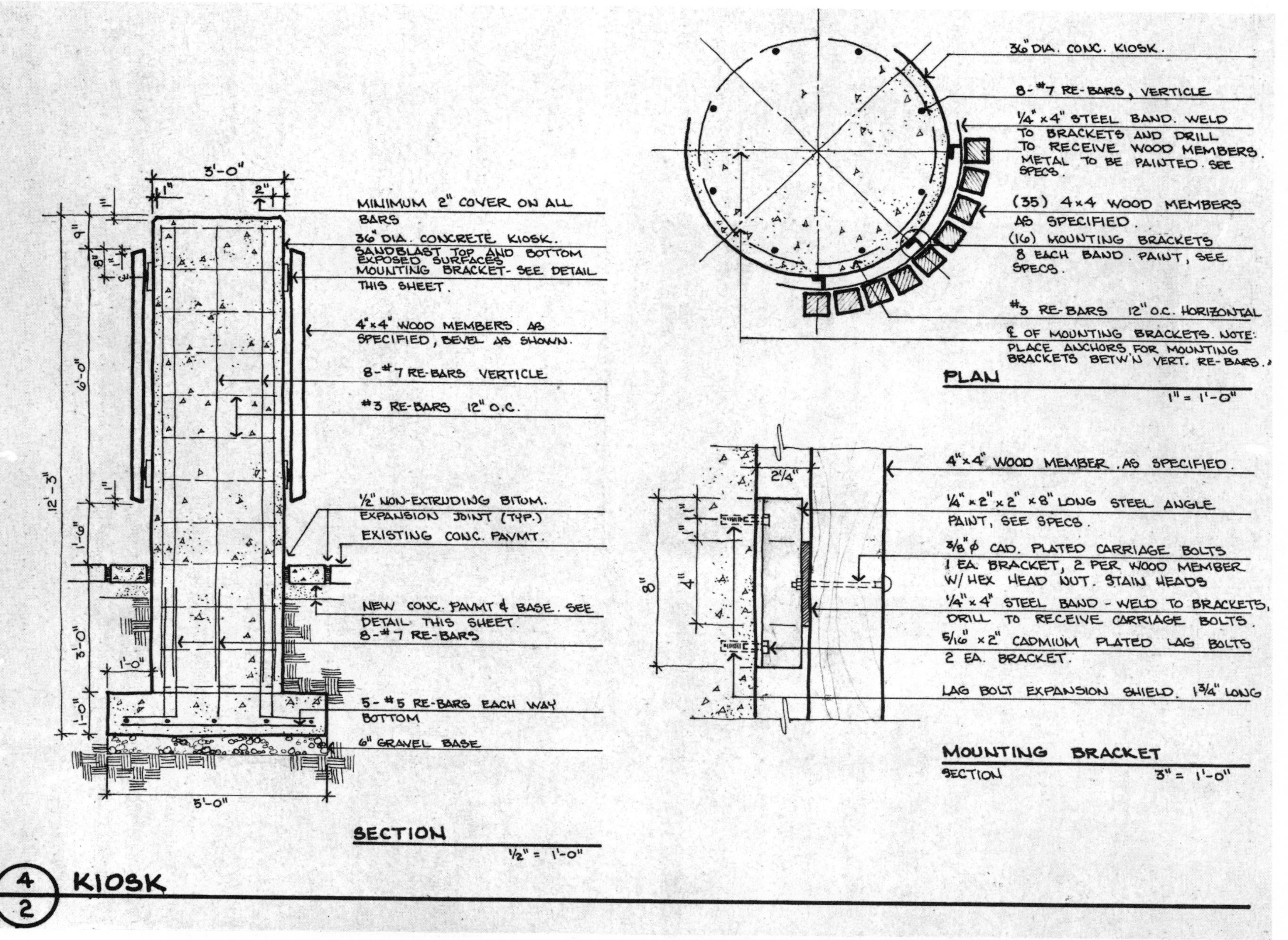

MINIMUM 2" COVER ON ALL BARS
36" DIA. CONCRETE KIOSK.
SANDBLAST TOP AND BOTTOM EXPOSED SURFACES
MOUNTING BRACKET- SEE DETAIL THIS SHEET.
4"x4" WOOD MEMBERS. AS SPECIFIED, BEVEL AS SHOWN.
8-#7 RE-BARS VERTICLE
#3 RE-BARS 12" O.C.
1/2" NON-EXTRUDING BITUM. EXPANSION JOINT (TYP.)
EXISTING CONC. PAVMT.
NEW CONC. PAVMT & BASE. SEE DETAIL THIS SHEET.
8-#7 RE-BARS
5-#5 RE-BARS EACH WAY BOTTOM
6" GRAVEL BASE
3'-0"
5'-0"
12'-3"
SECTION
1/2" = 1'-0"
KIOSK
36" DIA. CONC. KIOSK.
8-#7 RE-BARS, VERTICLE
1/4"x4" STEEL BAND. WELD TO BRACKETS AND DRILL TO RECEIVE WOOD MEMBERS. METAL TO BE PAINTED. SEE SPECS.
(35) 4x4 WOOD MEMBERS AS SPECIFIED.
(16) MOUNTING BRACKETS 8 EACH BAND. PAINT, SEE SPECS.
#3 RE-BARS 12" O.C. HORIZONTAL
℄ OF MOUNTING BRACKETS. NOTE: PLACE ANCHORS FOR MOUNTING BRACKETS BETW'N VERT. RE-BARS.
PLAN
1" = 1'-0"
4"x4" WOOD MEMBER. AS SPECIFIED.
1/4"x2"x2"x8" LONG STEEL ANGLE PAINT, SEE SPECS.
3/8"ϕ CAD. PLATED CARRIAGE BOLTS 1 EA. BRACKET, 2 PER WOOD MEMBER W/ HEX HEAD NUT. STAIN HEADS
1/4"x4" STEEL BAND - WELD TO BRACKETS, DRILL TO RECEIVE CARRIAGE BOLTS.
5/16"x2" CADMIUM PLATED LAG BOLTS 2 EA. BRACKET.
LAG BOLT EXPANSION SHIELD. 1 3/4" LONG
2 1/4"
8"
MOUNTING BRACKET
SECTION
3" = 1'-0"

Figure 11.133 *Details for the kiosk in Figure 11.132.*

Bonnell and Associates

WATERFRONT PARK

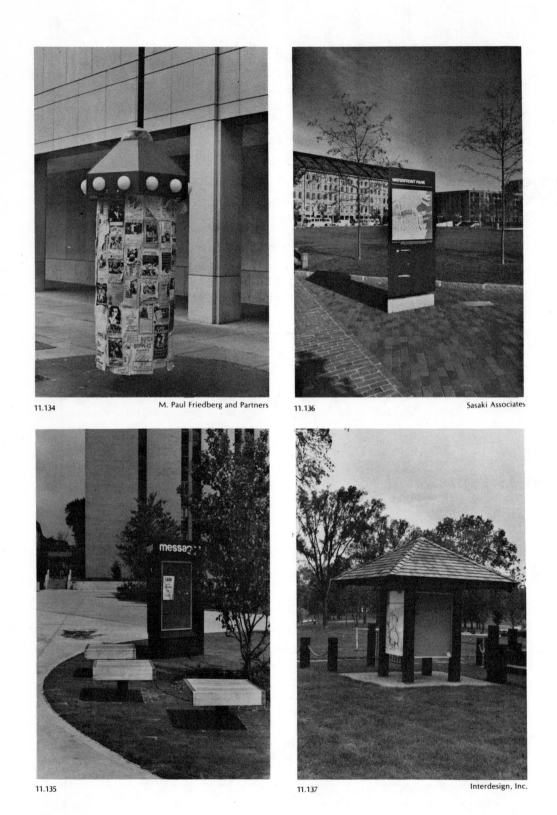

11.134 M. Paul Friedberg and Partners

11.136 Sasaki Associates

11.135

11.137 Interdesign, Inc.

Figures 11.134 - 11.141 *Kiosks in various locations.*

11.138

The Federal Reserve Bank
11.140

11.139

International
West
BARBER SHOP
STYLIST
11.141

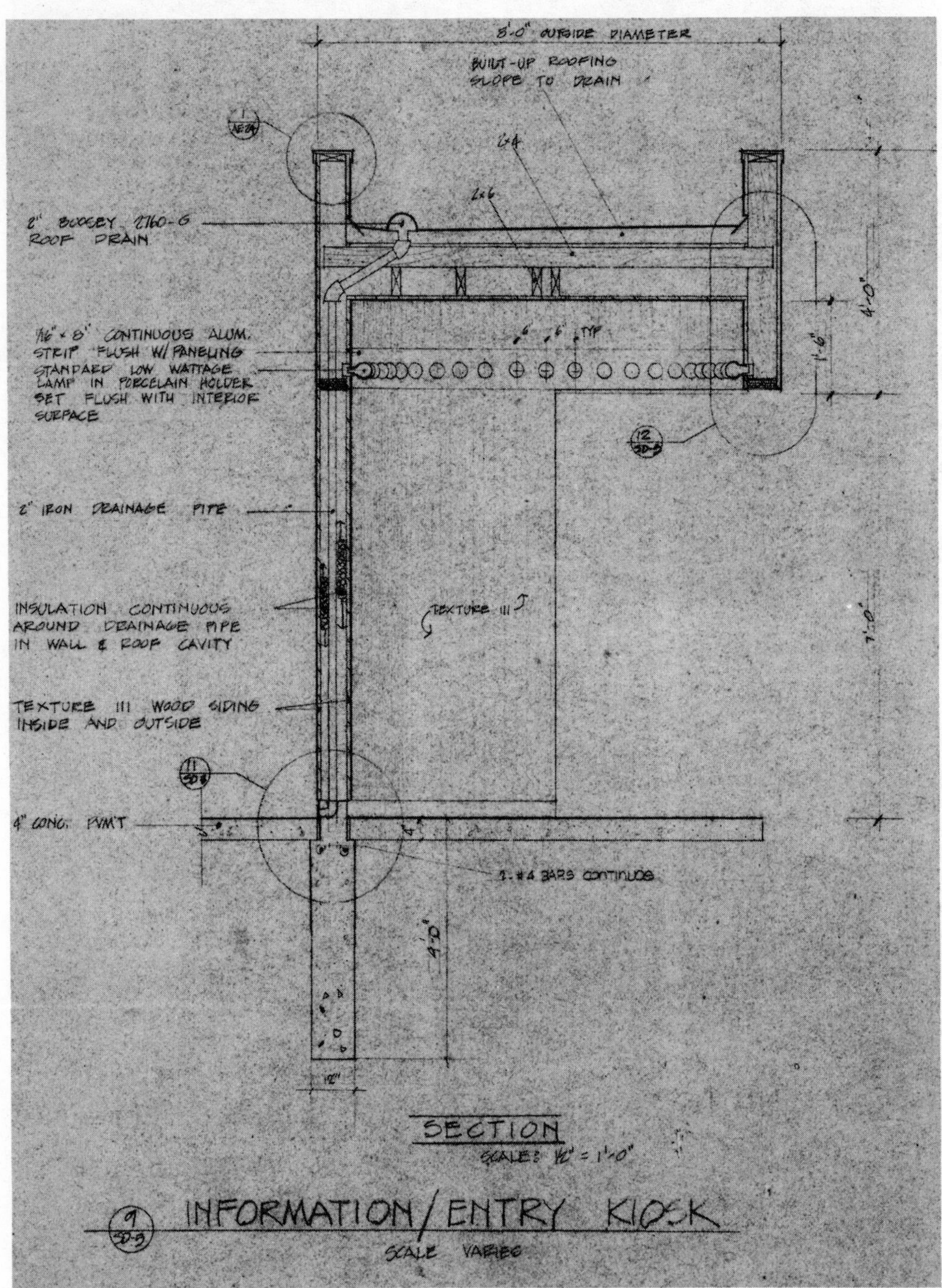
8'-0" OUTSIDE DIAMETER
BUILT-UP ROOFING SLOPE TO DRAIN
2x4
2x6
2" BOOSEY 2760-G ROOF DRAIN
1/16" x 8" CONTINUOUS ALUM. STRIP FLUSH W/ PANELING
STANDARD LOW WATTAGE LAMP IN PORCELAIN HOLDER SET FLUSH WITH INTERIOR SURFACE
6" 6" TYP
4'-0"
1'-6"
7'-0"
2" IRON DRAINAGE PIPE
INSULATION CONTINUOUS AROUND DRAINAGE PIPE IN WALL & ROOF CAVITY
TEXTURE 111
TEXTURE 111 WOOD SIDING INSIDE AND OUTSIDE
4" CONC. PVM'T
2-#4 BARS CONTINUOUS
4'-0"
12"
SECTION
SCALE: 1/2" = 1'-0"
INFORMATION/ENTRY KIOSK
SCALE VARIES

Figure 11.142 *Kiosk details.*

Johnson, Johnson and Roy

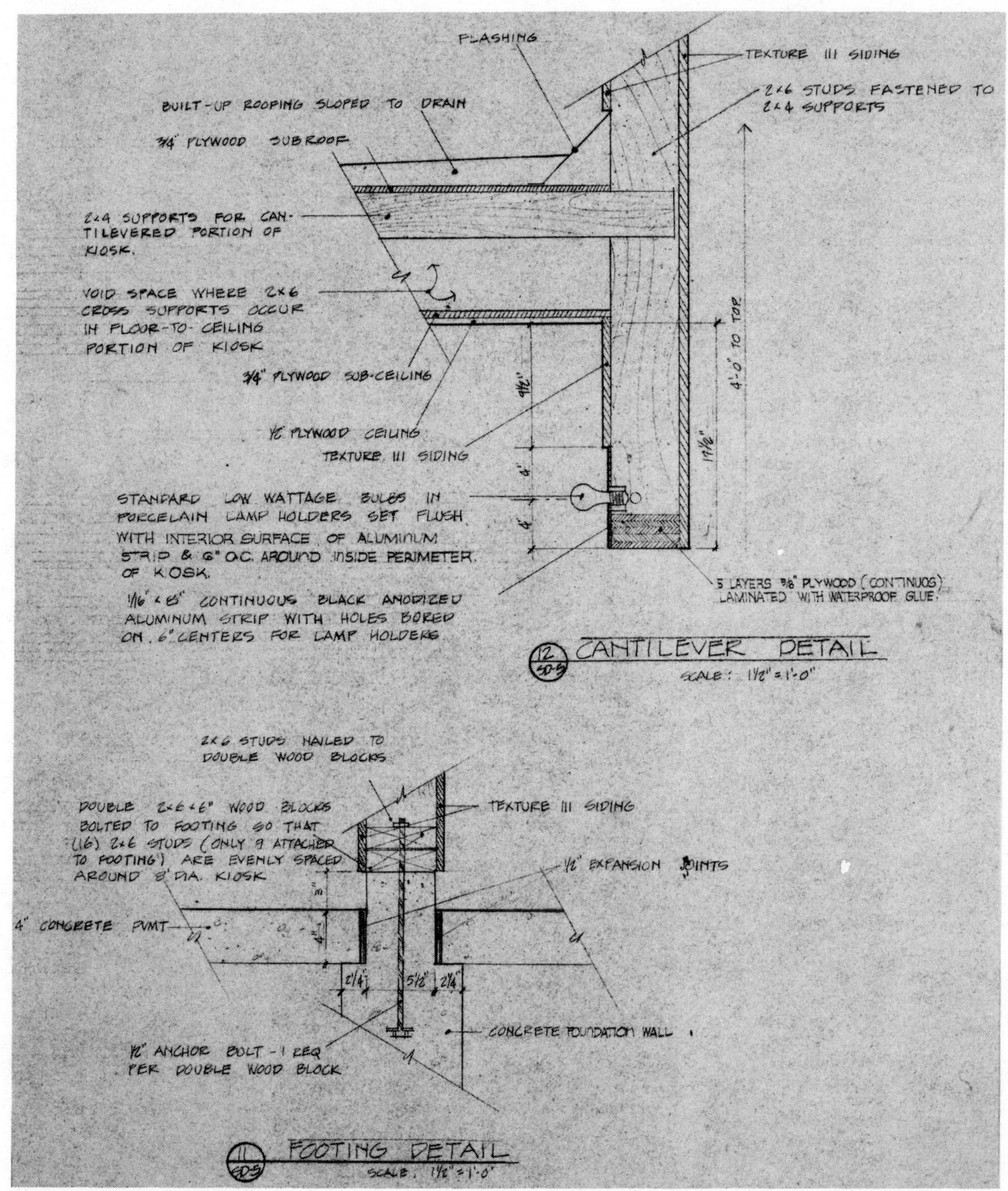
FLASHING
TEXTURE III SIDING
BUILT-UP ROOFING SLOPED TO DRAIN
2x6 STUDS FASTENED TO 2x4 SUPPORTS
3/4" PLYWOOD SUBROOF
2x4 SUPPORTS FOR CANTILEVERED PORTION OF KIOSK.
VOID SPACE WHERE 2x6 CROSS SUPPORTS OCCUR IN FLOOR-TO-CEILING PORTION OF KIOSK
4'-0" TO TOP
3/4" PLYWOOD SUB-CEILING
9½"
½" PLYWOOD CEILING
TEXTURE III SIDING
17½"
4"
STANDARD LOW WATTAGE BULBS IN PORCELAIN LAMP HOLDERS SET FLUSH WITH INTERIOR SURFACE OF ALUMINUM STRIP & 6" O.C. AROUND INSIDE PERIMETER OF KIOSK.
1/16" x 8" CONTINUOUS BLACK ANODIZED ALUMINUM STRIP WITH HOLES BORED ON 6" CENTERS FOR LAMP HOLDERS
5 LAYERS 3/8" PLYWOOD (CONTINUOS) LAMINATED WITH WATERPROOF GLUE.
12 SD-5
CANTILEVER DETAIL
SCALE: 1½" = 1'-0"
2x6 STUDS NAILED TO DOUBLE WOOD BLOCKS
DOUBLE 2x6 x 6" WOOD BLOCKS BOLTED TO FOOTING SO THAT (16) 2x6 STUDS (ONLY 9 ATTACHED TO FOOTING) ARE EVENLY SPACED AROUND 8' DIA. KIOSK
TEXTURE III SIDING
½" EXPANSION JOINTS
4" CONCRETE PVMT
2¼"
5½"
2¼"
½" ANCHOR BOLT - 1 REQ PER DOUBLE WOOD BLOCK
CONCRETE FOUNDATION WALL
11 SD-5
FOOTING DETAIL
SCALE: 1½" = 1'-0"

Figure 11.143 *Kiosk details.*

Johnson, Johnson and Roy

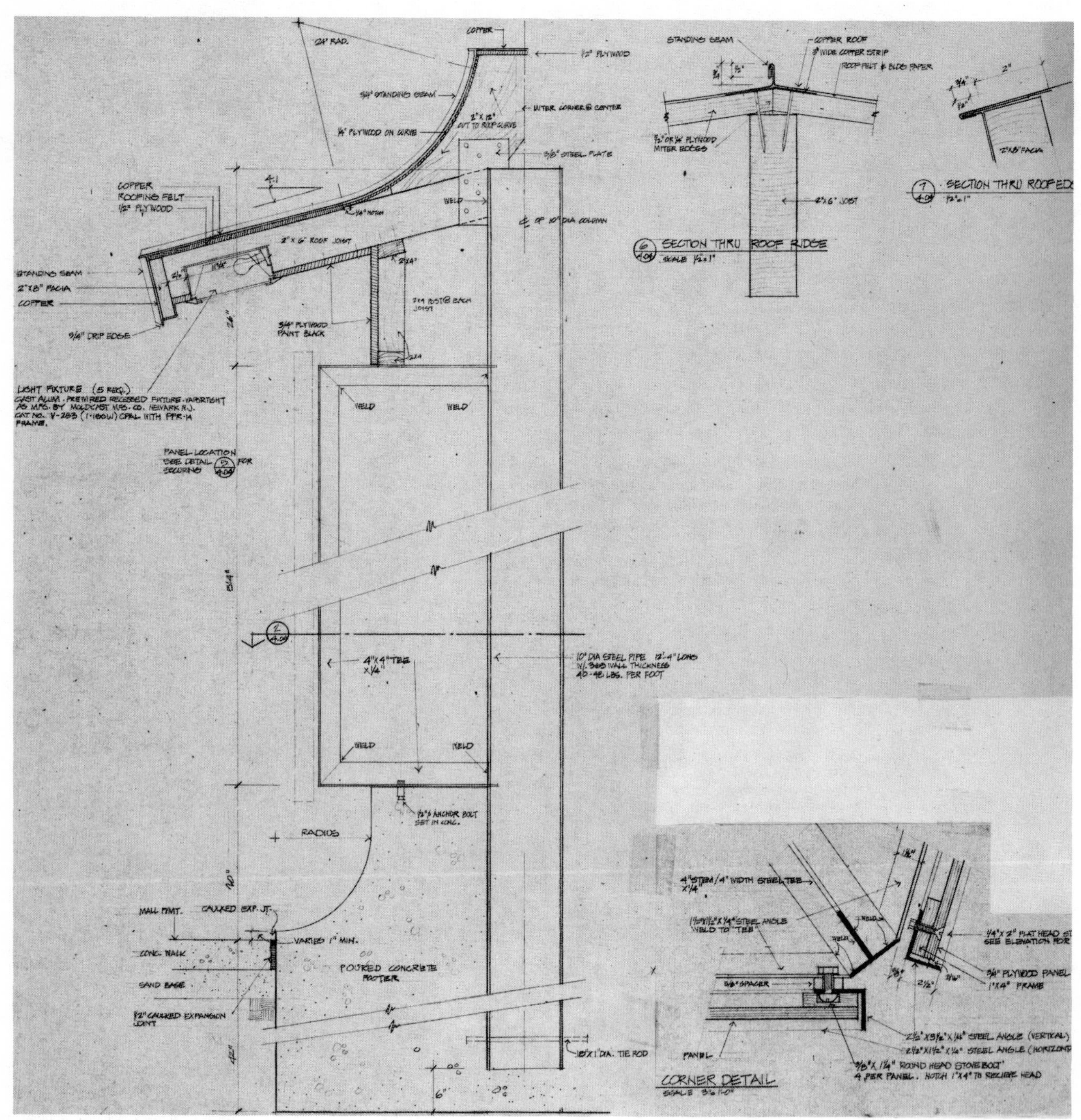

Figure 11.144 *Kiosk details.*

Johnson, Johnson and Roy

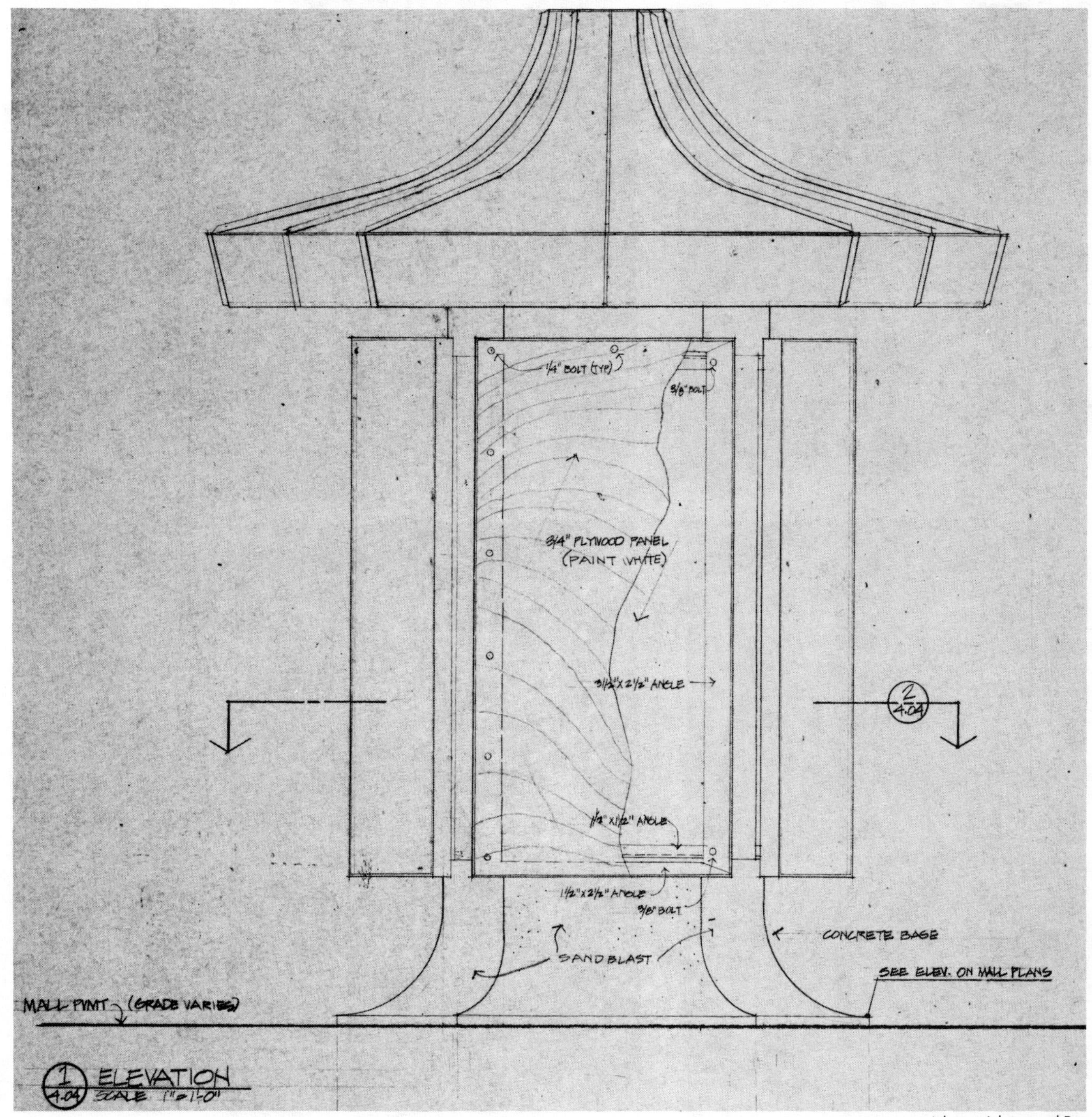
1/4" BOLT (TYP)
3/8" BOLT
3/4" PLYWOOD PANEL
(PAINT WHITE)
3 1/2" X 2 1/2" ANGLE
1/2" X 1 1/2" ANGLE
1 1/2" X 2 1/2" ANGLE
3/8" BOLT
CONCRETE BASE
SANDBLAST
SEE ELEV. ON MALL PLANS
MALL PVMT (GRADE VARIES)
2
4.04
1
4.04
ELEVATION
SCALE 1" = 1'-0"

Johnson, Johnson and Roy

Figure 11.145 *Kiosk details.*

11.146 Environmental Planning and Design

11.148 Environmental Planning and Design

11.147

11.149

Figures 11.146 - 11.148 *Clock towers in urban settings.*

Figure 11.149 *Carillon tower at a western university.*

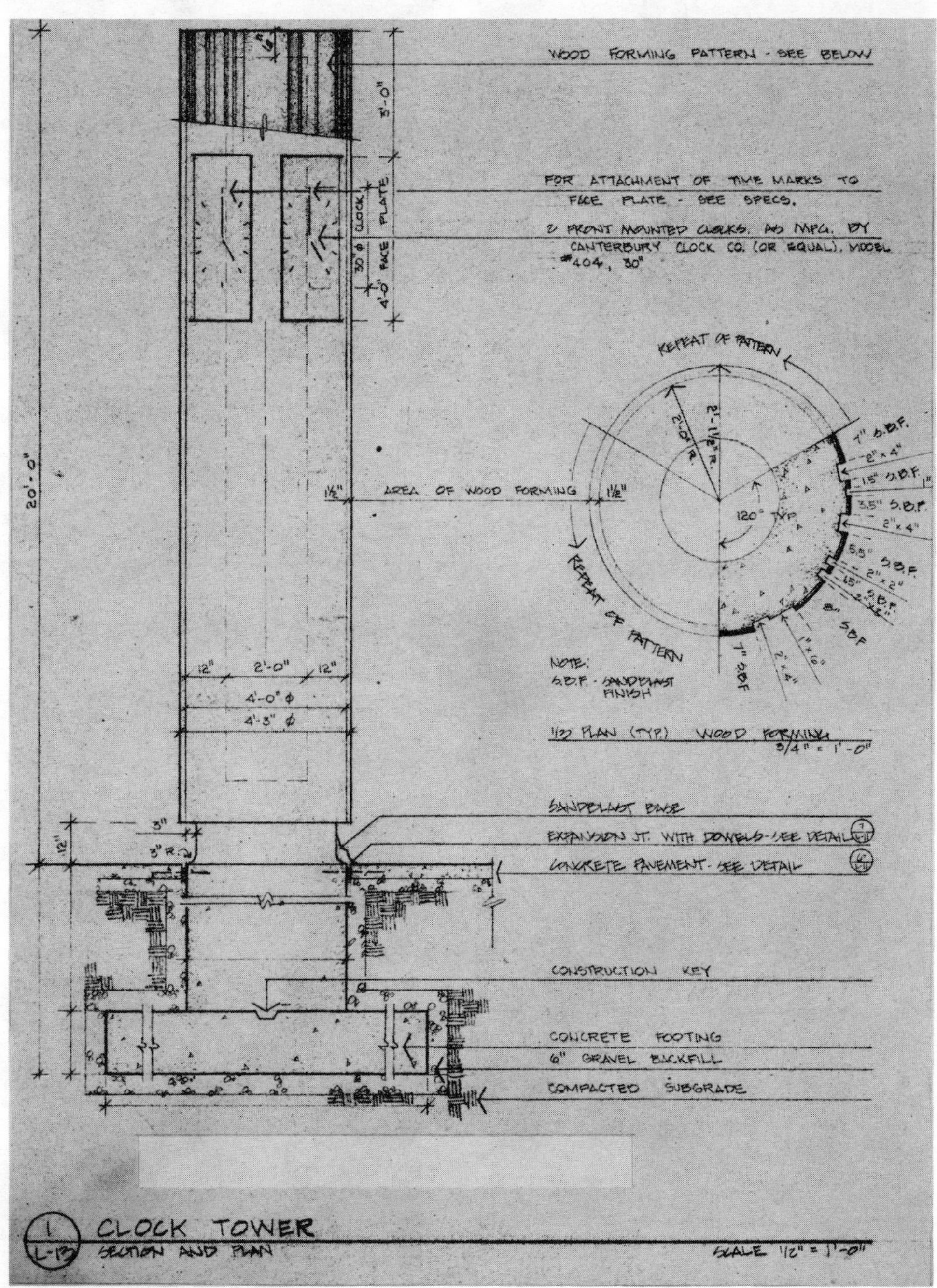
WOOD FORMING PATTERN - SEE BELOW
FOR ATTACHMENT OF TIME MARKS TO FACE PLATE - SEE SPECS.
2 FRONT MOUNTED CLOCKS, AS MFG. BY CANTERBURY CLOCK CO. (OR EQUAL), MODEL #404, 30"
3'-0"
CLOCK PLATE
30" FACE
4'-0"
20'-0"
REPEAT OF PATTERN
REPEAT OF PATTERN
120° TYP.
AREA OF WOOD FORMING
1½"
1½"
12"
2'-0"
12"
4'-0" ϕ
4'-3" ϕ
NOTE:
S.B.F. - SANDBLAST FINISH
PLAN (TYP.) WOOD FORMING
3/4" = 1'-0"
SANDBLAST BASE
EXPANSION JT. WITH DOWELS - SEE DETAIL
CONCRETE PAVEMENT - SEE DETAIL
CONSTRUCTION KEY
CONCRETE FOOTING
6" GRAVEL BACKFILL
COMPACTED SUBGRADE
CLOCK TOWER
SECTION AND PLAN
SCALE 1/2" = 1'-0"

Bonnell and Associates

Figure 11.150 *Clock tower detail.*

11.151 M. Paul Friedberg and Partners

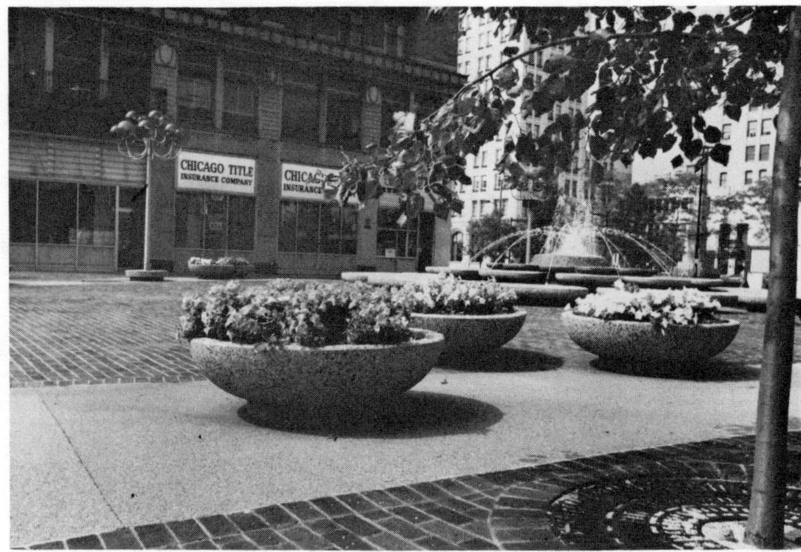
CHICAGO TITLE
INSURANCE COMPANY
11.153 James H. Bassett

11.152

11.154

11.155

Figures 11.151 – 11.157 *Planters of varying sizes, shapes and materials.*

11.156

11.157

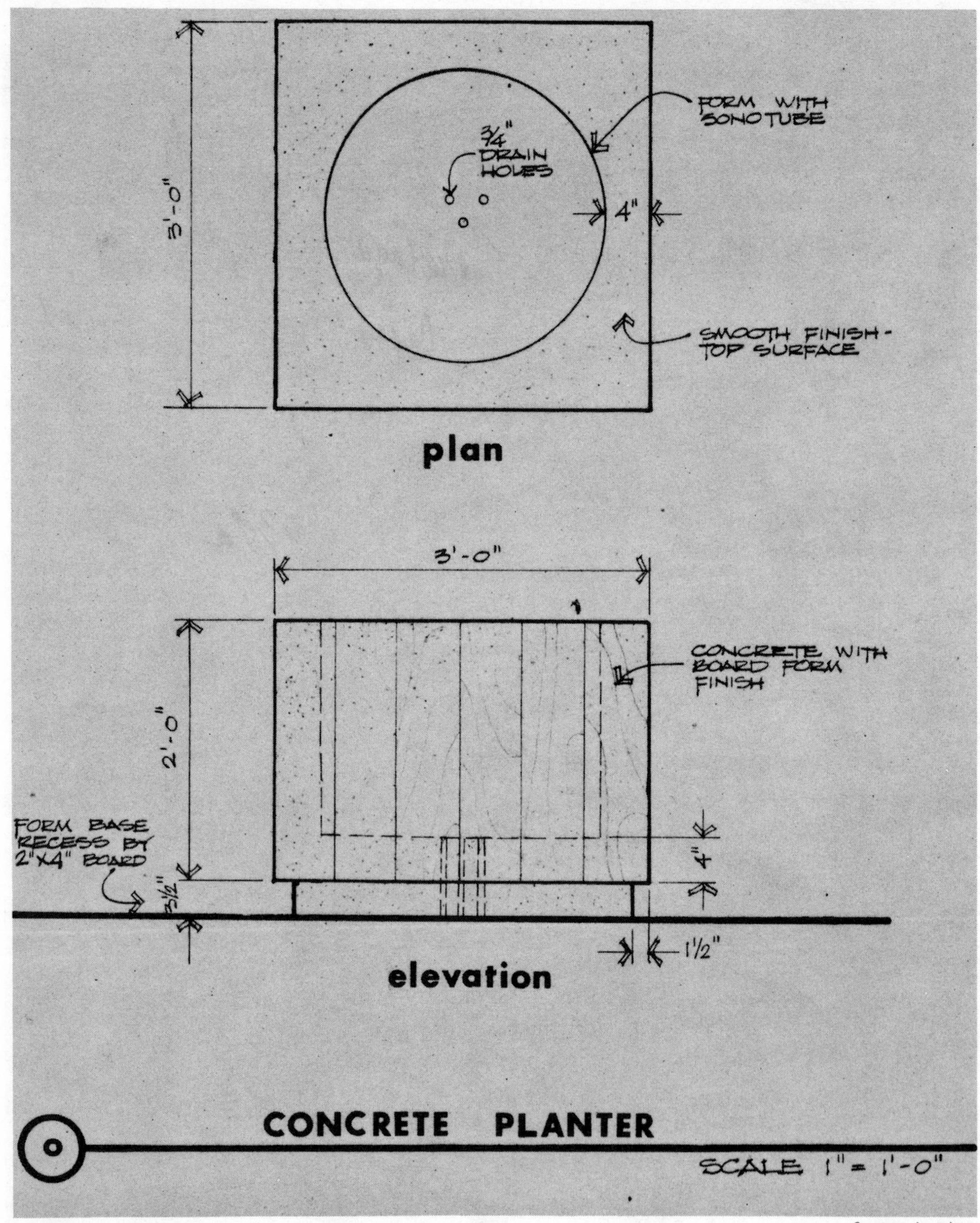
3'-0"
FORM WITH SONOTUBE
3/4" DRAIN HOLES
4"
SMOOTH FINISH - TOP SURFACE
plan
3'-0"
2'-0"
CONCRETE WITH BOARD FORM FINISH
FORM BASE RECESS BY 2"X4" BOARD
3½"
4"
1½"
elevation
CONCRETE PLANTER
SCALE 1" = 1'-0"

Saratoga Associates

Figure 11.158 *Concrete planter detail.*

Figures 11.159 – 11.161 *Planters of different shapes and sizes.*

Figure 11.162 *Planter in a shallow reflecting pool.*

Figure 11.163 *Concrete planters.*

Figure 11.164 *Pre-cast planters, one became a bench with wood insert.*

11.159

11.160

11.161

11.162

11.163 Johnson, Johnson and Roy

11.164 Bailey and Associates

11.165

11.166

11.167

Figures 11.165 – 11.167 *Concrete and wood planters.*

11.168

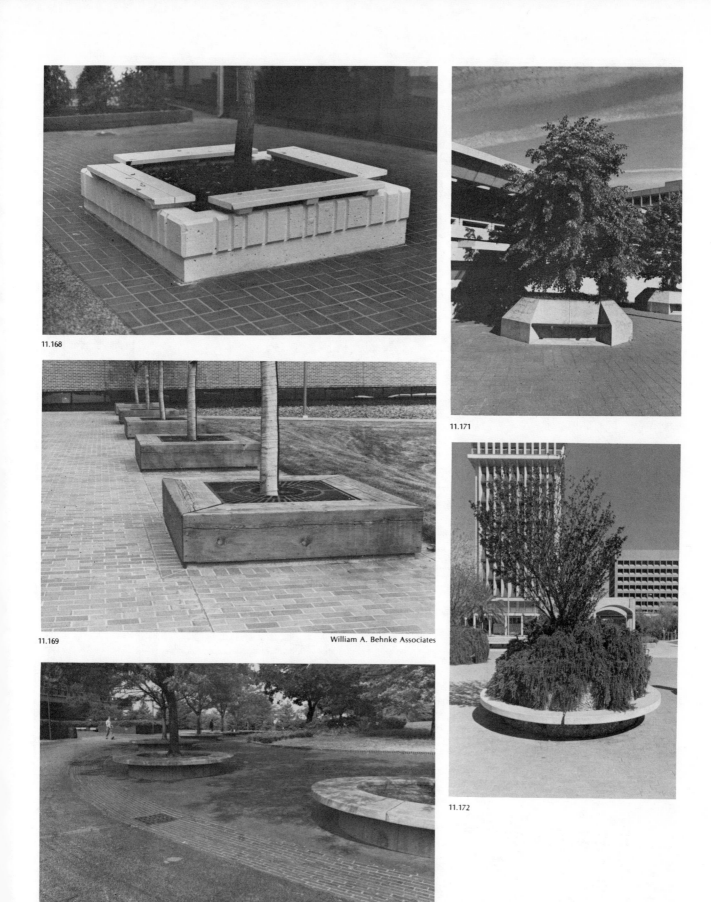

11.169 William A. Behnke Associates

11.170

11.171

11.172

Figures 11.168 – 11.172 *Combination planters and seat walls.*

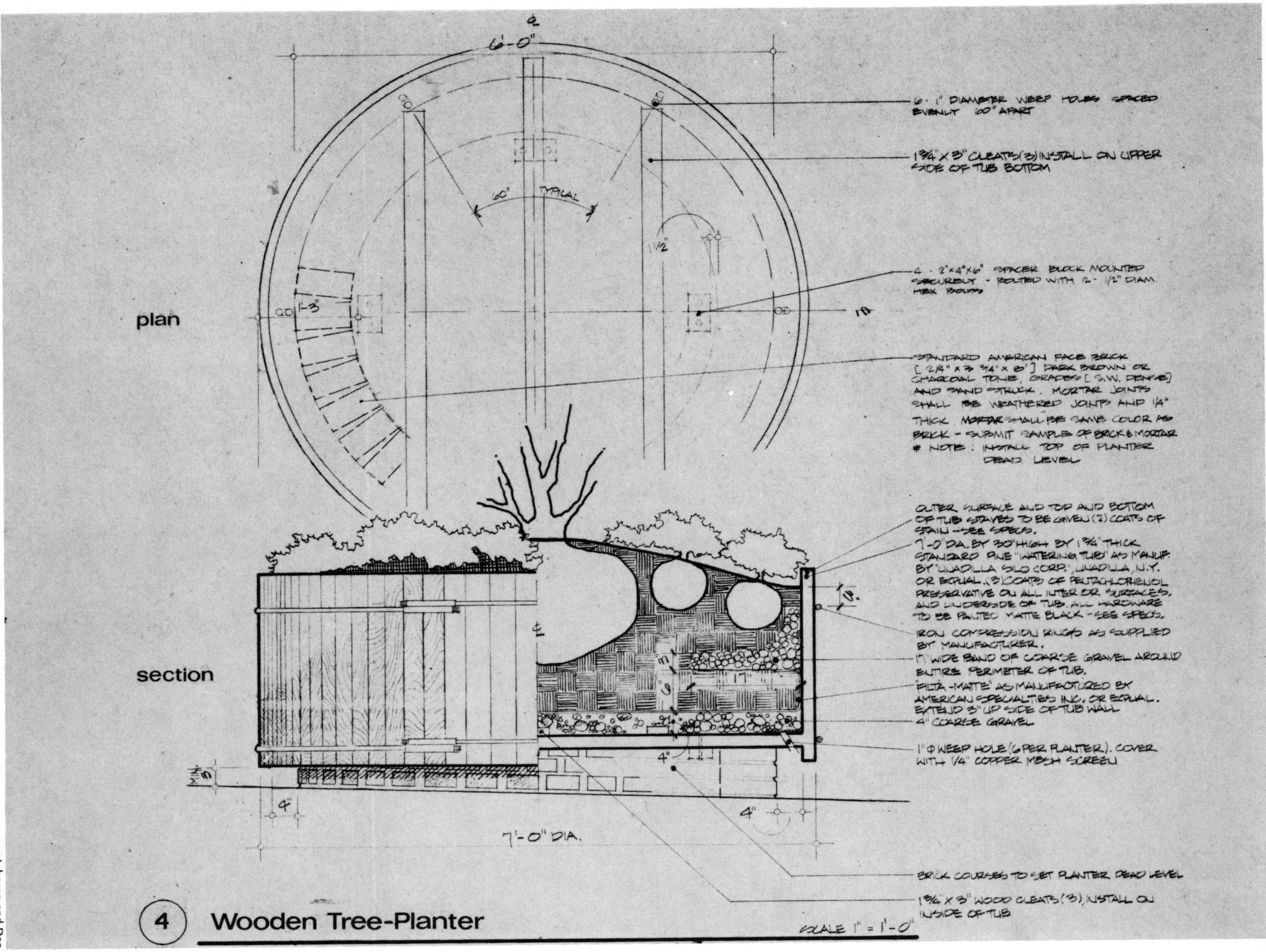

plan
section
6'-0"
60°
TYPICAL
1 1/2"
1'-3"
7'-0" DIA.
4"
6"
6" MIN.
17"
6·1" DIAMETER WEEP HOLES SPACED EVENLY 60° APART
1 3/4" X 3" CLEATS (3) INSTALL ON UPPER SIDE OF TUB BOTTOM
4 · 2"x4"x6" SPACER BLOCK MOUNTED SECURELY - BOLTED WITH 2 - 1/2" DIAM. HEX BOLTS
STANDARD AMERICAN FACE BRICK [2 1/4" x 3 3/4" x 8"] DARK BROWN OR CHARCOAL TONE, GRADES [S.W. DENSE] AND SAND STRUCK. MORTAR JOINTS SHALL BE WEATHERED JOINTS AND 1/4" THICK. MORTAR SHALL BE SAME COLOR AS BRICK - SUBMIT SAMPLE OF BRICK & MORTAR
* NOTE: INSTALL TOP OF PLANTER DEAD LEVEL
OUTER SURFACE AND TOP AND BOTTOM OF TUB STAVES TO BE GIVEN (2) COATS OF STAIN - SEE SPECS.
7'-0" DIA. BY 30" HIGH BY 1 3/4" THICK STANDARD PINE "WATERING TUB" AS MANUF. BY "UNADILLA SILO CORP.", UNADILLA, N.Y. OR EQUAL. (3) COATS OF PENTACHLOROPHENOL PRESERVATIVE ON ALL INTERIOR SURFACES, AND UNDERSIDE OF TUB. ALL HARDWARE TO BE PAINTED MATTE BLACK - SEE SPECS.
IRON COMPRESSION RINGS AS SUPPLIED BY MANUFACTURER.
17" WIDE BAND OF COARSE GRAVEL AROUND ENTIRE PERIMETER OF TUB.
"FILTA-MATTE" AS MANUFACTURED BY AMERICAN SPECIALTIES INC., OR EQUAL. EXTEND 3" UP SIDE OF TUB WALL
4" COARSE GRAVEL
1" Φ WEEP HOLE (6 PER PLANTER). COVER WITH 1/4" COPPER MESH SCREEN
BRICK COURSES TO SET PLANTER DEAD LEVEL
1 3/4" X 3" WOOD CLEATS (3), INSTALL ON INSIDE OF TUB
4 Wooden Tree-Planter
SCALE 1" = 1'-0"

Johnson and Dee

Figure 11.173 *Planter detail.*

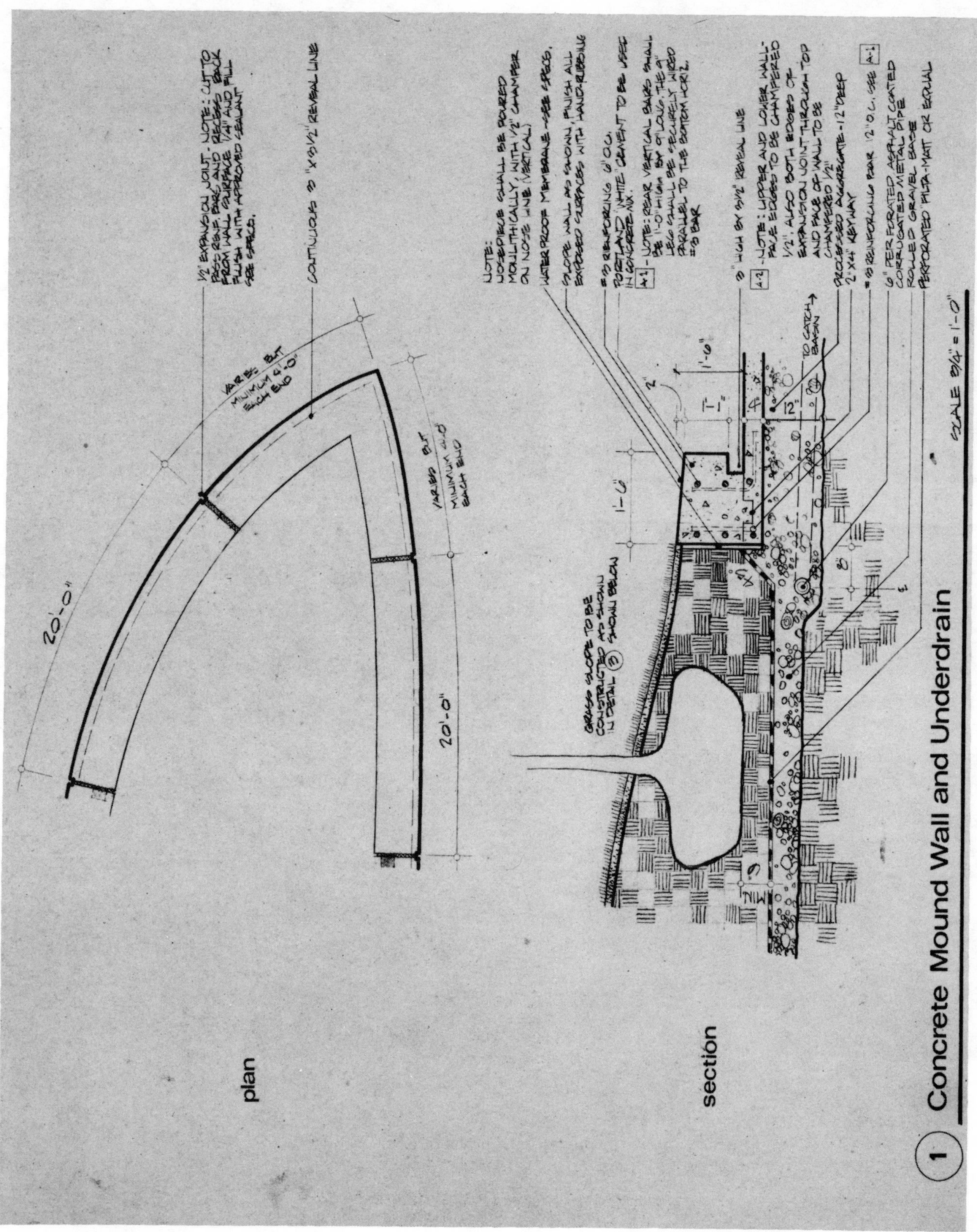
1
Concrete Mound Wall and Underdrain
plan
section
20'-0"
20'-0"
SCALE 3/4" = 1'-0"

Figure 11.174 *Planter-seatwall detail.*

Johnson and Dee

11.175 Photo courtesy of: California Redwood Association

11.177

11.176 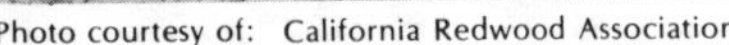 Photo courtesy of: California Redwood Association

11.178

Figures 11.175 – 11.178 *Wood planters.*

11.179

11.180

11.181

11.182

Figures 11.179 – 11.182 *Various designs for tree grates using cast iron, steel and pre-cast concrete.*

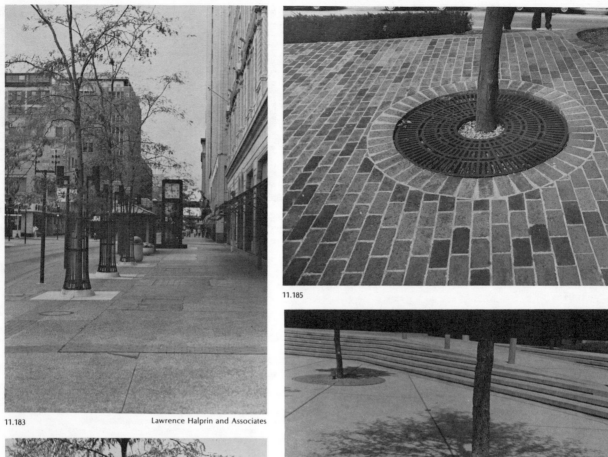

11.183 Lawrence Halprin and Associates

11.184 Sasaki Associates

11.185 James H. E

11.186

Figures 11.183 – 11.186 *Tree guards and grates.*

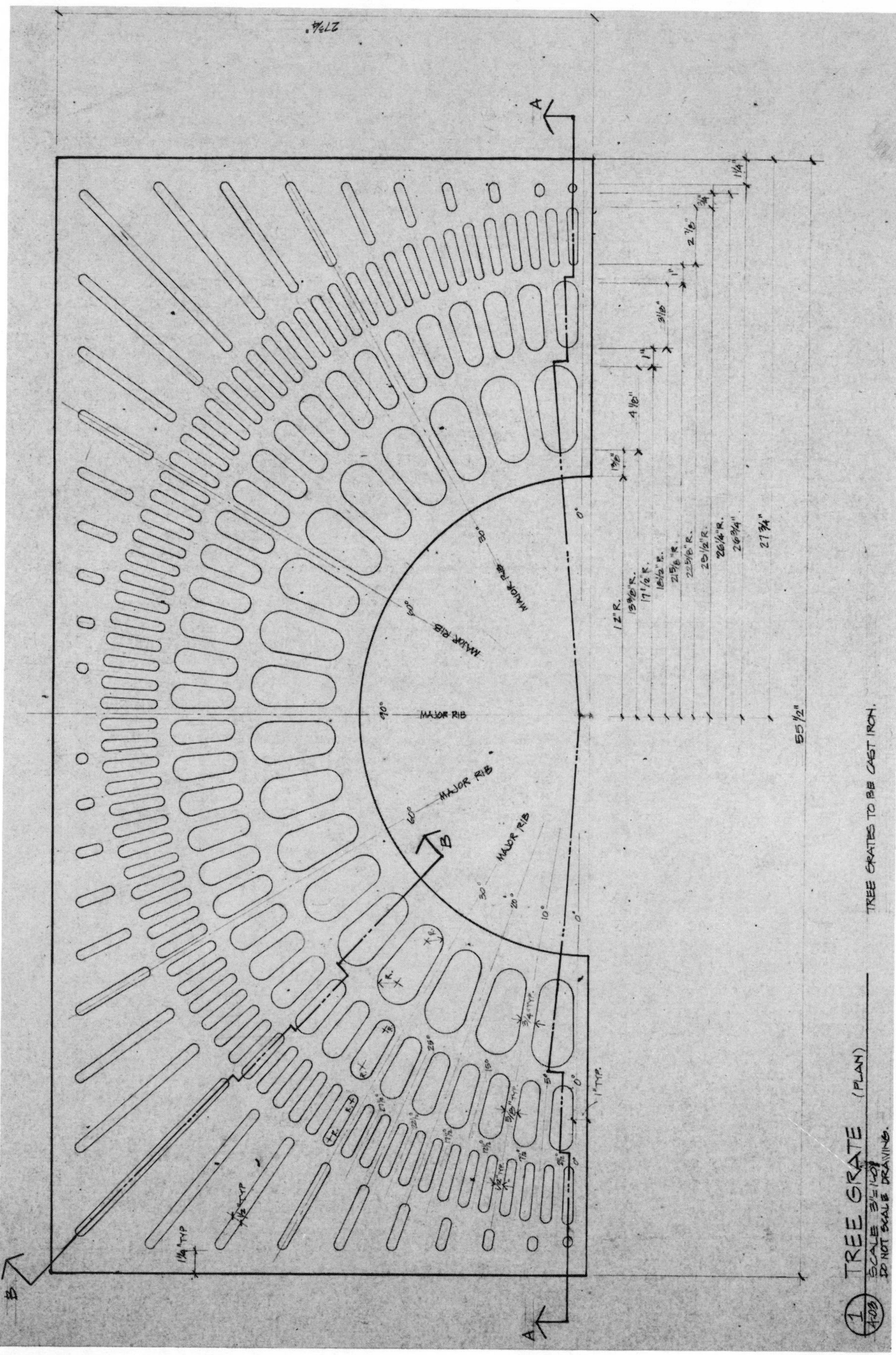
TREE GRATE (PLAN)
DO NOT SCALE DRAWING.
TREE GRATES TO BE CAST IRON.
MAJOR RIB
55 1/2"
27 3/4"

Figure 11.187 *Tree grate detail.*

Johnson, Johnson and Roy

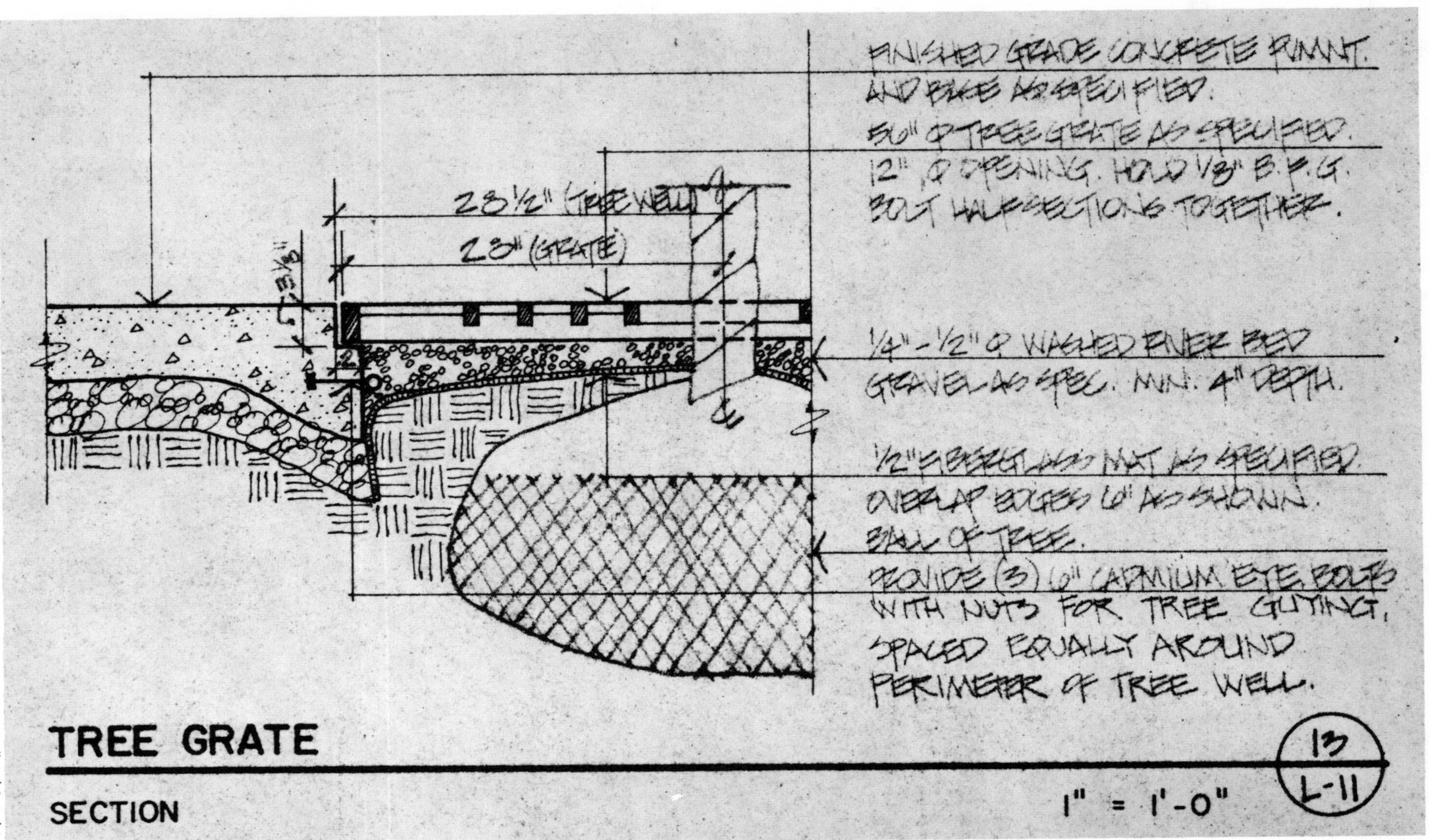

FINISHED GRADE CONCRETE PVMNT.
AND BASE AS SPECIFIED.
50" Ø TREE GRATE AS SPECIFIED.
12" Ø OPENING. HOLD 1/8" B.F.G.
BOLT HALF SECTIONS TOGETHER.
1/4"-1/2" Ø WASHED RIVER BED
GRAVEL AS SPEC. MIN. 4" DEPTH.
1/2" FIBERGLASS MAT AS SPECIFIED.
OVERLAP EDGES 6" AS SHOWN.
BALL OF TREE.
PROVIDE (3) 6" CADMIUM EYE BOLTS
WITH NUTS FOR TREE GUYING,
SPACED EQUALLY AROUND
PERIMETER OF TREE WELL.
28 1/2" (TREE WELL)
23" (GRATE)
TREE GRATE
SECTION
1" = 1'-0"
13
L-11

Bonnell and Associates

Figure 11.188 *Tree grate detail.*

11.189

11.191 Bircher-Bonnell Associates

11.190

11.192

Figures 11.189 – 11.193 *Bicycle racks and parking slots.*

11.193 Browning-Day-Pollak-Associates-Inc.

11.194 Bailey and Associates

11.195 Bailey and Associates

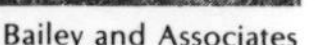

11.196

11.197 Sasaki Associates

11.198 Michael Painter

Figures 11.194 – 11.198 *Bicycle parking design variations.*

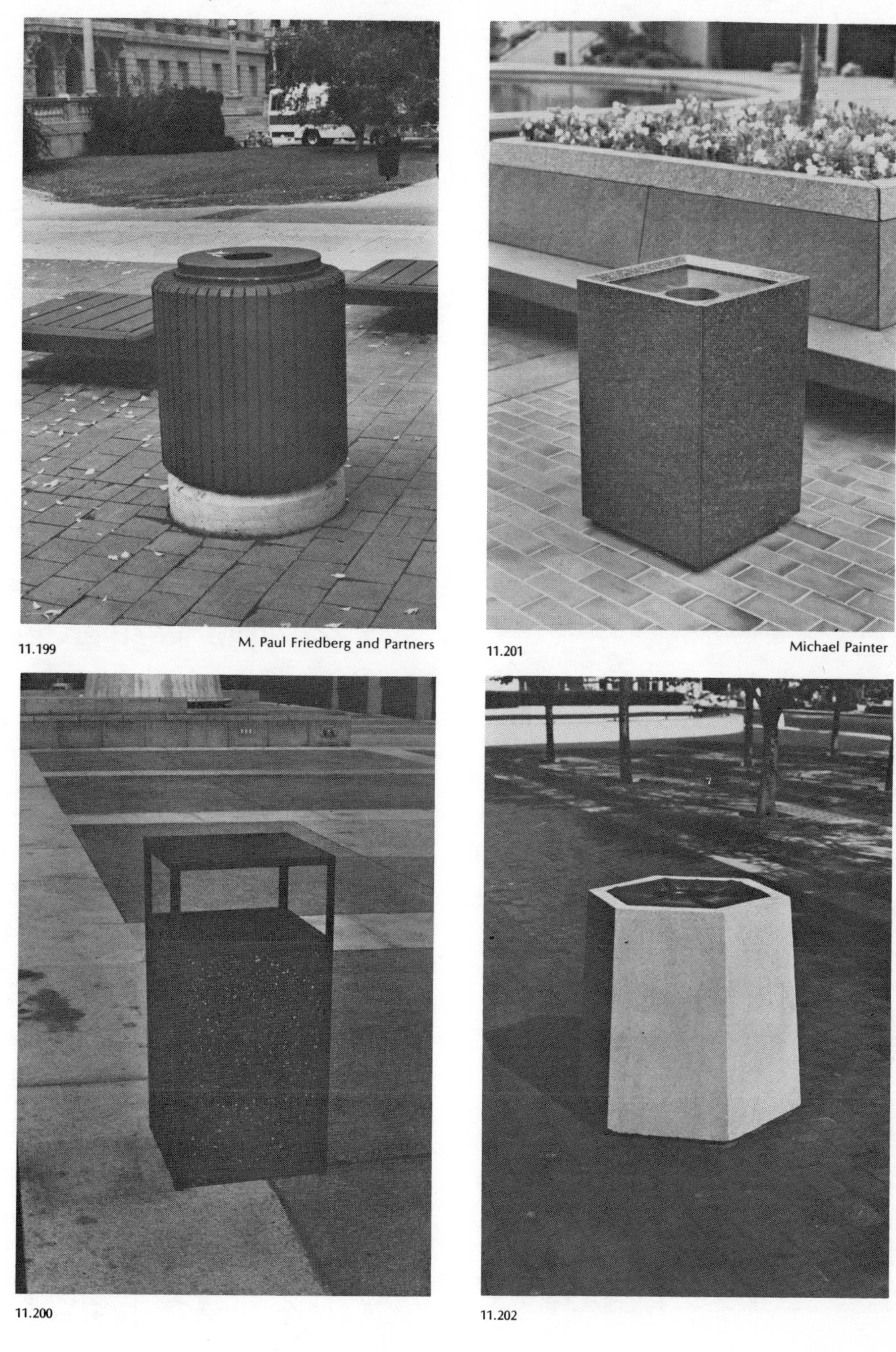

11.199 M. Paul Friedberg and Partners

11.201 Michael Painter

11.200

11.202

Figures 11.199 - 11.202 *Trash containers.*

11.203 James H. Bassett

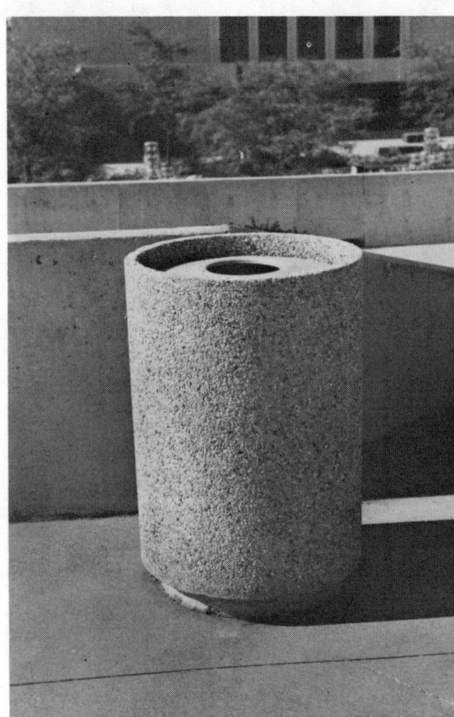

11.204

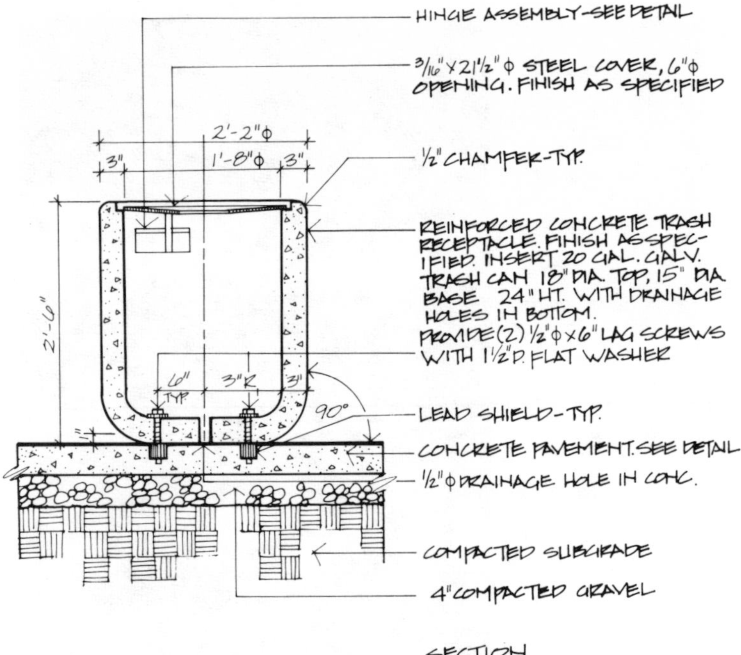

HINGE ASSEMBLY-SEE DETAIL
3/16"×21½"ϕ STEEL COVER, 6"ϕ OPENING. FINISH AS SPECIFIED
2'-2"ϕ
3" 1'-8"ϕ 3"
½" CHAMFER-TYP.
REINFORCED CONCRETE TRASH RECEPTACLE. FINISH AS SPECIFIED. INSERT 20 GAL. GALV. TRASH CAN 18" DIA. TOP, 15" DIA. BASE 24" HT. WITH DRAINAGE HOLES IN BOTTOM.
PROVIDE (2) ½"ϕ×6" LAG SCREWS WITH 1½" D. FLAT WASHER
2'-6"
6" TYP 3"R 3"
90°
LEAD SHIELD-TYP.
CONCRETE PAVEMENT. SEE DETAIL
½"ϕ DRAINAGE HOLE IN CONC.
COMPACTED SUBGRADE
4" COMPACTED GRAVEL
SECTION
CONCRETE TRASH RECEPTACLE

11.205 Bonnell and Associates

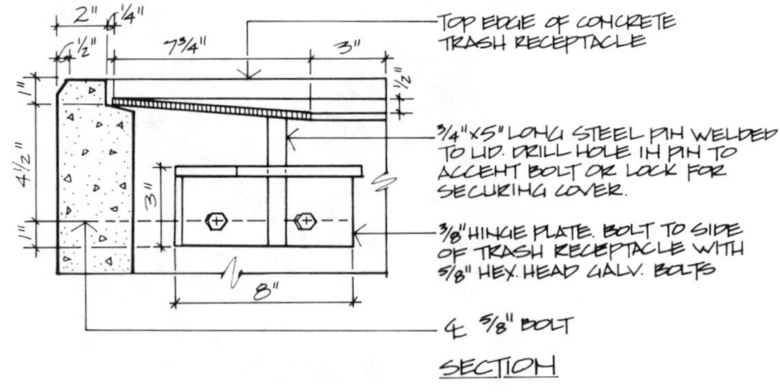

2" ¼"
½" 7¾" 3"
1" ½"
4½" 3" 1"
TOP EDGE OF CONCRETE TRASH RECEPTACLE
¾"×5" LONG STEEL PIN WELDED TO LID. DRILL HOLE IN PIN TO ACCEPT BOLT OR LOCK FOR SECURING COVER.
⅜" HINGE PLATE. BOLT TO SIDE OF TRASH RECEPTACLE WITH ⅝" HEX. HEAD GALV. BOLTS
8"
℄ ⅝" BOLT
SECTION

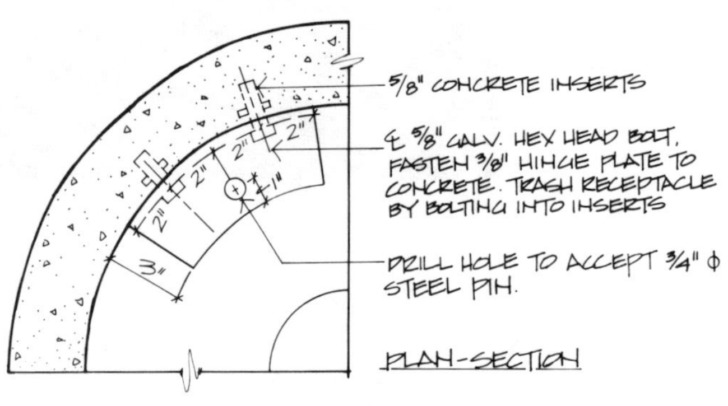

⅝" CONCRETE INSERTS
℄ ⅝" GALV. HEX HEAD BOLT, FASTEN ⅜" HINGE PLATE TO CONCRETE. TRASH RECEPTACLE BY BOLTING INTO INSERTS
2" 2" 2" 2" 1" 3"
DRILL HOLE TO ACCEPT ¾" ϕ STEEL PIN.
PLAN-SECTION
HINGE ASSEMBLY

11.206 Bonnell and Associates

Figures 11.203 – 11.206 *Trash containers with details.*

11.207

11.209

11.208

11.210

William A. Behnke Associates

Figures 11.207 - 11.210 *Trash containers.*

Tamarron

11.211

G STREET MOLE
RESTAURANT
AMERICAN TUNABOAT ASSN.
FISHERMEN'S VILLAGE SEAFOOD

11.212

11.213

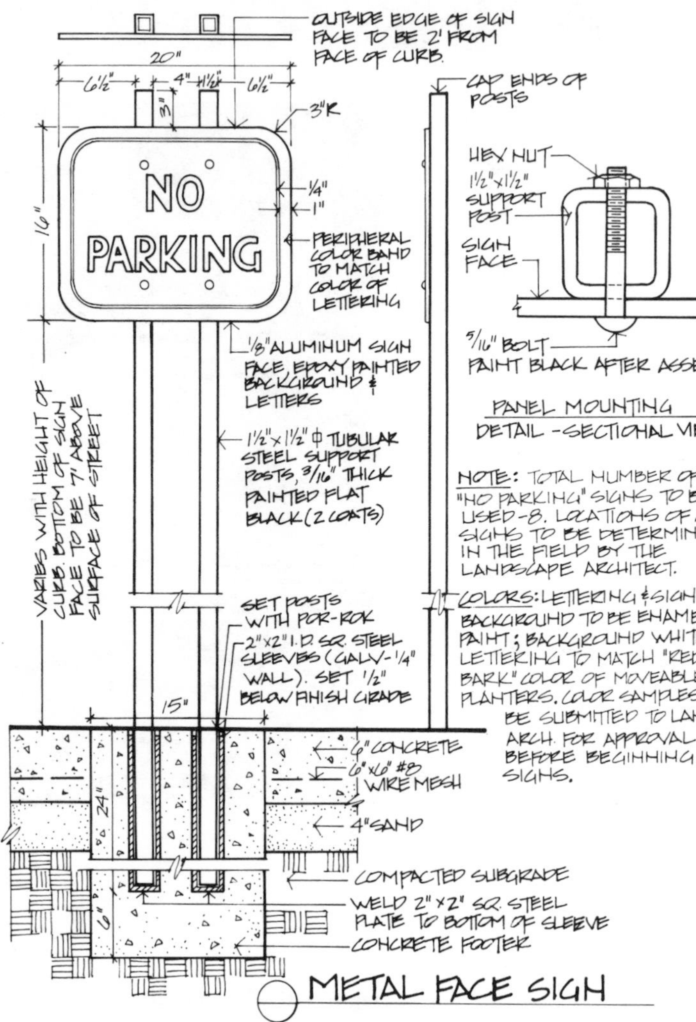
OUTSIDE EDGE OF SIGN FACE TO BE 2' FROM FACE OF CURB.
20"
6½"
4"
1½"
6½"
3"
3"R
CAP ENDS OF POSTS
16"
NO PARKING
¼"
1"
PERIPHERAL COLOR BAND TO MATCH COLOR OF LETTERING
HEX NUT
1½"x1½" SUPPORT POST
SIGN FACE
5/16" BOLT
PAINT BLACK AFTER ASSE
PANEL MOUNTING DETAIL - SECTIONAL VIE
⅛" ALUMINUM SIGN FACE, EPOXY PAINTED BACKGROUND & LETTERS
VARIES WITH HEIGHT OF CURB. BOTTOM OF SIGN FACE TO BE 7' ABOVE SURFACE OF STREET
1½"x1½" ϕ TUBULAR STEEL SUPPORT POSTS, 3/16" THICK PAINTED FLAT BLACK (2 COATS)
NOTE: TOTAL NUMBER OF "NO PARKING" SIGNS TO BE USED - 8. LOCATIONS OF A SIGNS TO BE DETERMINE IN THE FIELD BY THE LANDSCAPE ARCHITECT.
SET POSTS WITH POR-ROK
2"x2" I.D. SQ. STEEL SLEEVES (GALV - ¼" WALL). SET ½" BELOW FINISH GRADE
COLORS: LETTERING & SIGN BACKGROUND TO BE ENAME PAINT; BACKGROUND WHITE LETTERING TO MATCH "RED BARK" COLOR OF MOVEABLE PLANTERS. COLOR SAMPLES BE SUBMITTED TO LAN ARCH. FOR APPROVAL BEFORE BEGINNING SIGNS.
15"
6" CONCRETE
6"x6" #8 WIRE MESH
24"
4" SAND
COMPACTED SUBGRADE
WELD 2"x2" SQ. STEEL PLATE TO BOTTOM OF SLEEVE
6"
CONCRETE FOOTER
METAL FACE SIGN

11.214

Johnson, Johnson and Roy

Figures 11.211 – 11.212 *Design variety in signs.*

Figure 11.213 *This is a bronze scale model of a shopping center with numbers identifying each store.*

Figure 11.214 *Sign detail.*

Village Center

11.215 Bailey and Associates

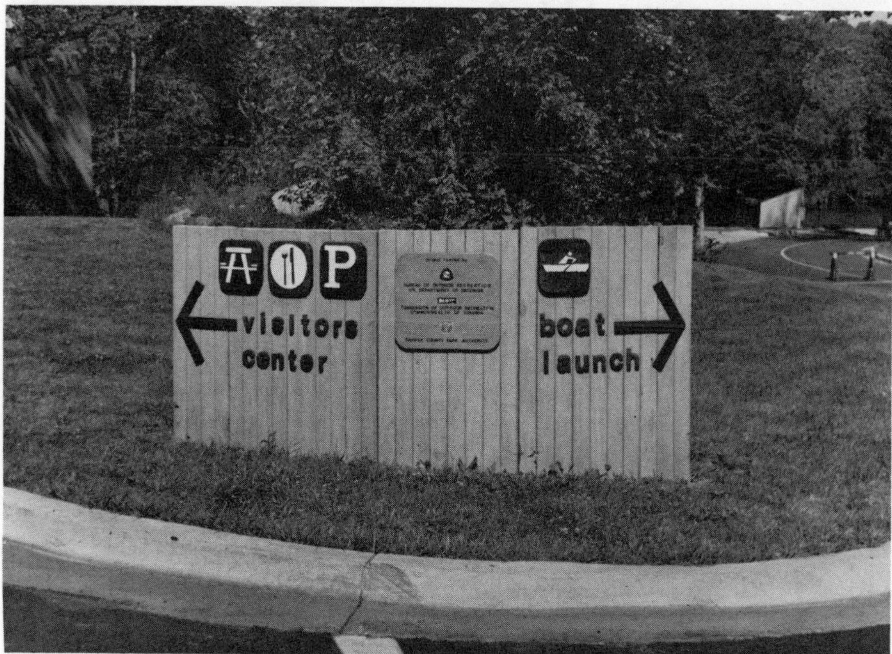
visitors
center
boat
launch

11.216 Fairfax County Parks

Figures 11.215 - 11.216 *Signs made of large vertical timbers.*

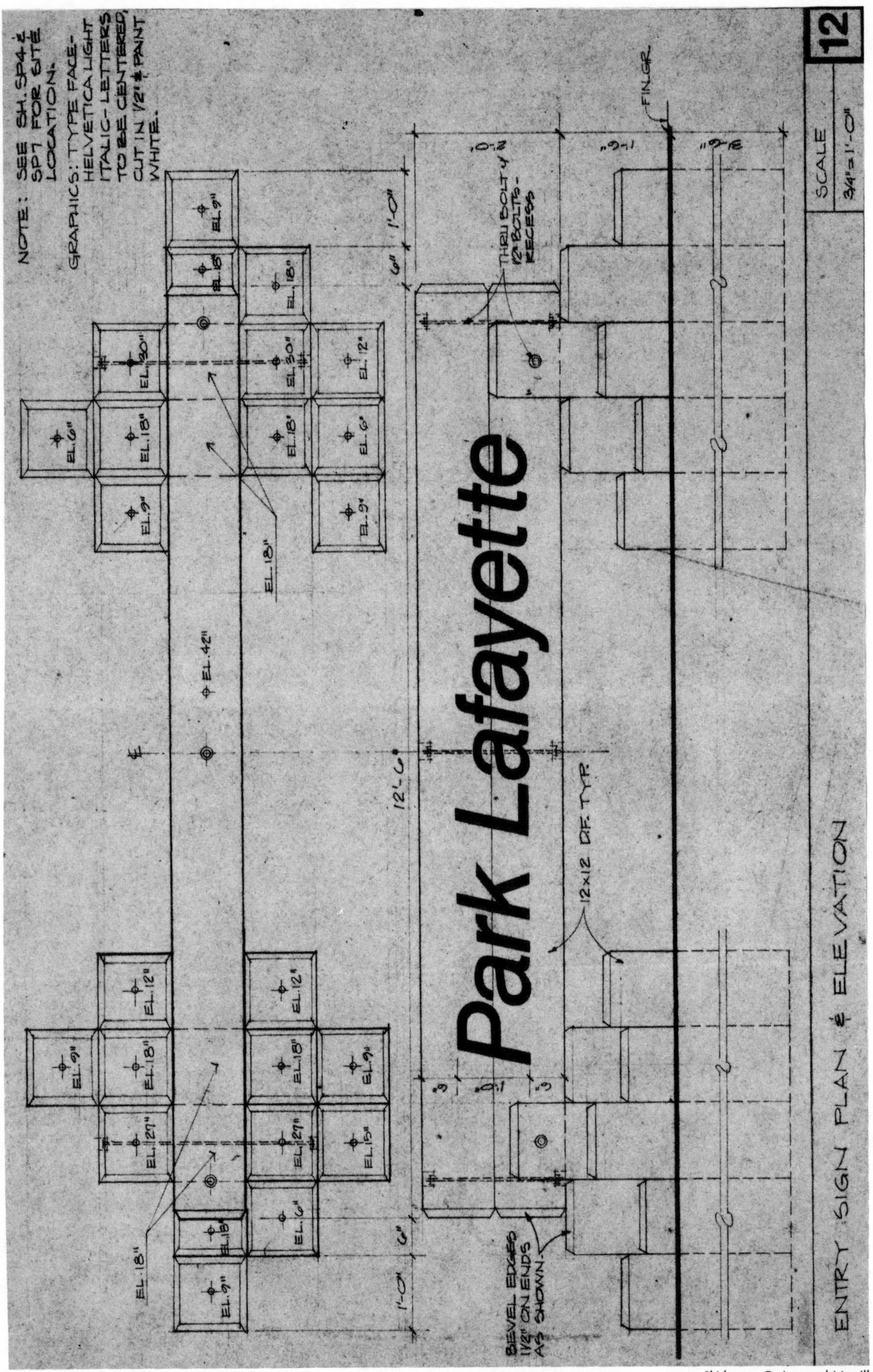
NOTE: SEE SH. SP4 & SP7 FOR SITE LOCATION.
GRAPHICS: TYPE FACE-HELVETICA LIGHT ITALIC- LETTERS TO BE CENTERED, CUT IN 1/2" & PAINT WHITE.
Park Lafayette
12x12 DF. TYP.
BEVEL EDGES 1 1/2" ON ENDS AS SHOWN.
FIN.GR.
12'-6"
ENTRY SIGN PLAN & ELEVATION
SCALE 3/4"=1'-0"
12

Skidmore, Owings and Merrill

Figure 11.217 *Wood sign detail.*

FLAME

11.218

11.219 William A. Behnke Associates

CrosbyPark
Akron Board Of Education And The City Of Akron

11.220 William A. Behnke Associates

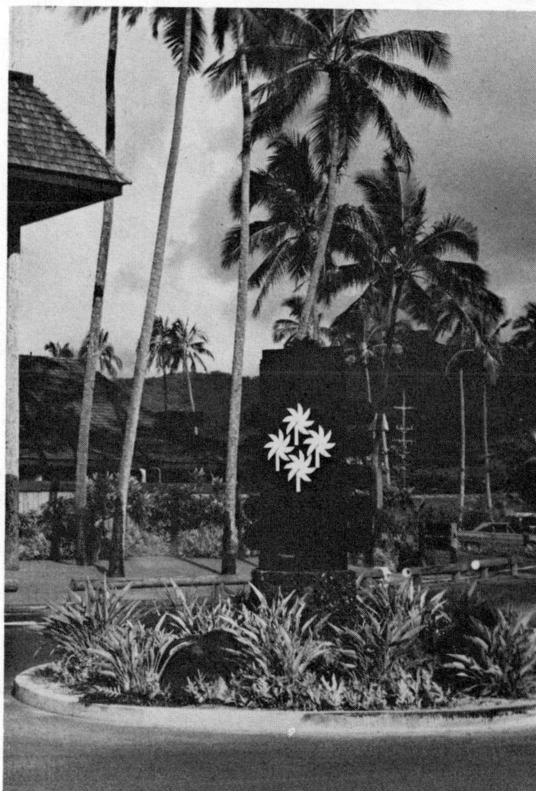

11.221

Figures 11.218 – 11.221 *Wood signs.*

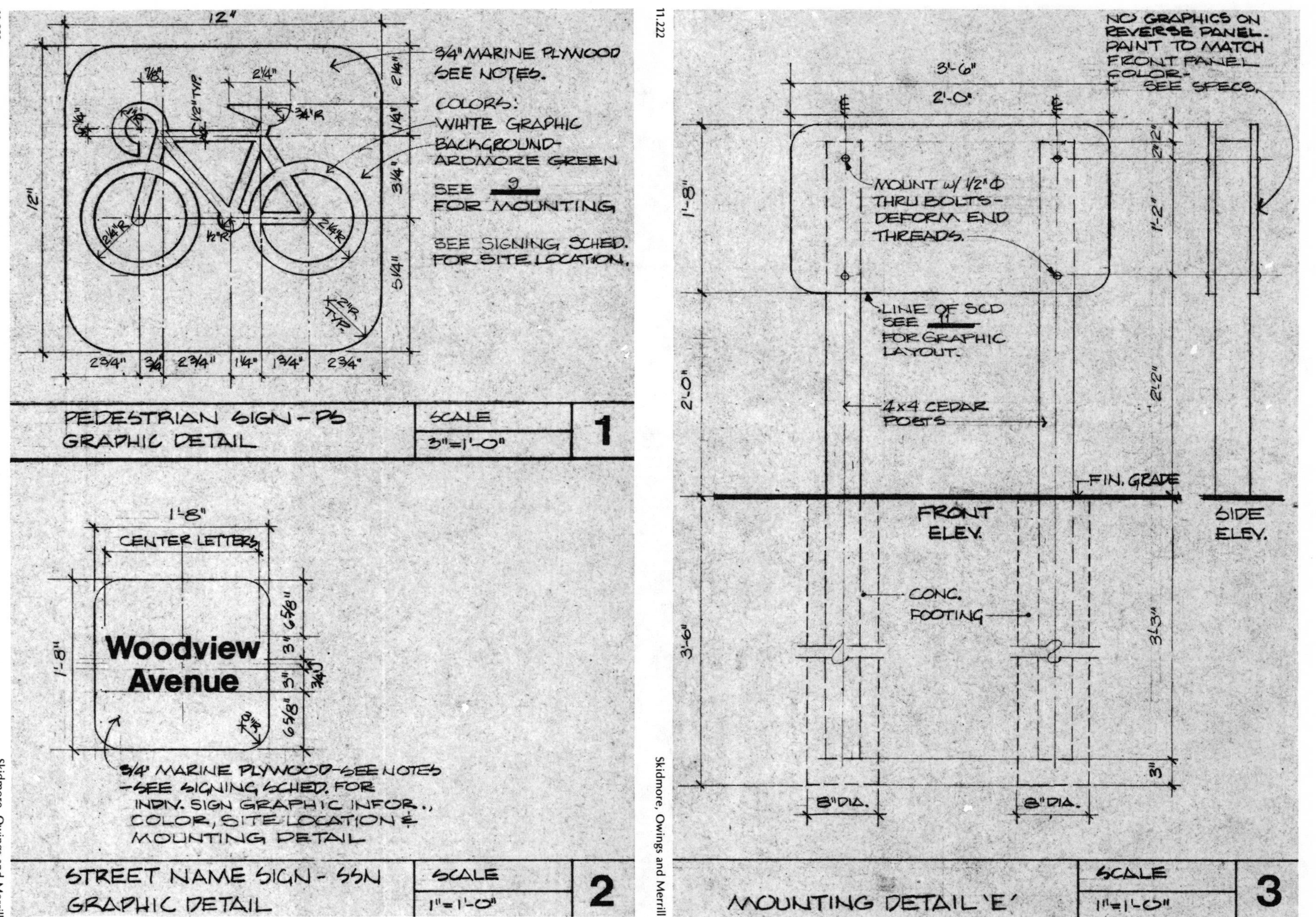
12"
3/4" MARINE PLYWOOD SEE NOTES.
COLORS:
WHITE GRAPHIC
BACKGROUND- ARDMORE GREEN
SEE 3 FOR MOUNTING
SEE SIGNING SCHED. FOR SITE LOCATION.
PEDESTRIAN SIGN - PS
GRAPHIC DETAIL
SCALE
3"=1'-0"
1
1'-8"
CENTER LETTERS
Woodview
Avenue
3/4" MARINE PLYWOOD - SEE NOTES - SEE SIGNING SCHED. FOR INDIV. SIGN GRAPHIC INFOR., COLOR, SITE LOCATION & MOUNTING DETAIL
STREET NAME SIGN - SSN
GRAPHIC DETAIL
SCALE
1"=1'-0"
2
NO GRAPHICS ON REVERSE PANEL. PAINT TO MATCH FRONT PANEL COLOR - SEE SPECS.
3'-6"
2'-0"
MOUNT w/ 1/2"⌀ THRU BOLTS - DEFORM END THREADS.
LINE OF SCD SEE 1 FOR GRAPHIC LAYOUT.
4x4 CEDAR POSTS
FIN. GRADE
FRONT ELEV.
SIDE ELEV.
CONC. FOOTING
8" DIA.
8" DIA.
MOUNTING DETAIL 'E'
SCALE
1"=1'-0"
3

11.223

Skidmore, Owings and Merrill

11.222

Skidmore, Owings and Merrill

Figures 11.222 – 11.223 *Wood sign details.*

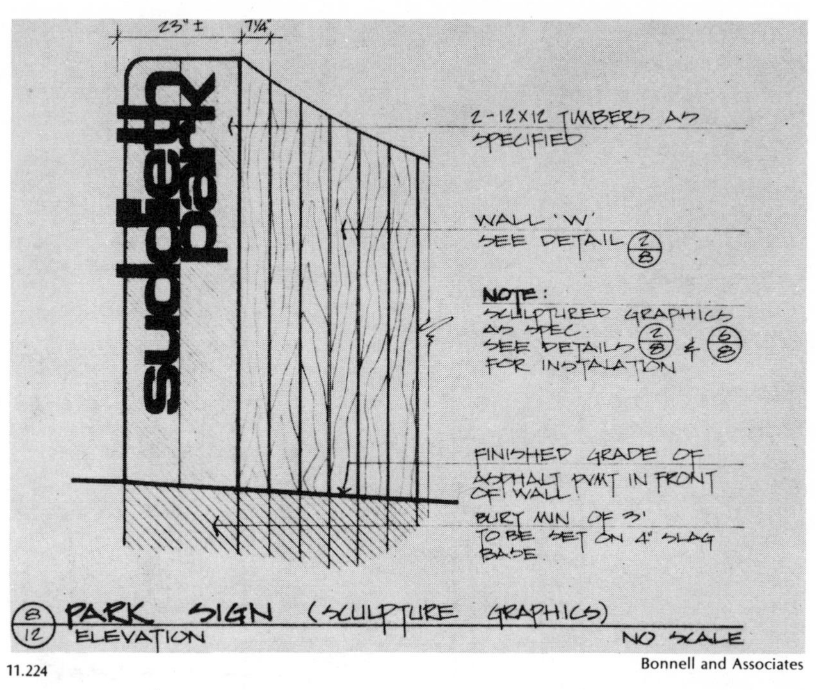

23" ±
7¼"
suddeth
park
2-12X12 TIMBERS AS SPECIFIED
WALL 'W' SEE DETAIL 2/8
NOTE: SCULPTURED GRAPHICS AS SPEC. SEE DETAILS 2/8 & 6/8 FOR INSTALLATION
FINISHED GRADE OF ASPHALT PVMT IN FRONT OF WALL
BURY MIN OF 3' TO BE SET ON 4" SLAG BASE
8/12 PARK SIGN (SCULPTURE GRAPHICS) ELEVATION
NO SCALE

11.224

Bonnell and Associates

Figure 11.224 *Wood sign detail. See page 309 for photo.*

Figures 11.225 – 11.226 *Drinking fountains.*

11.225

11.226

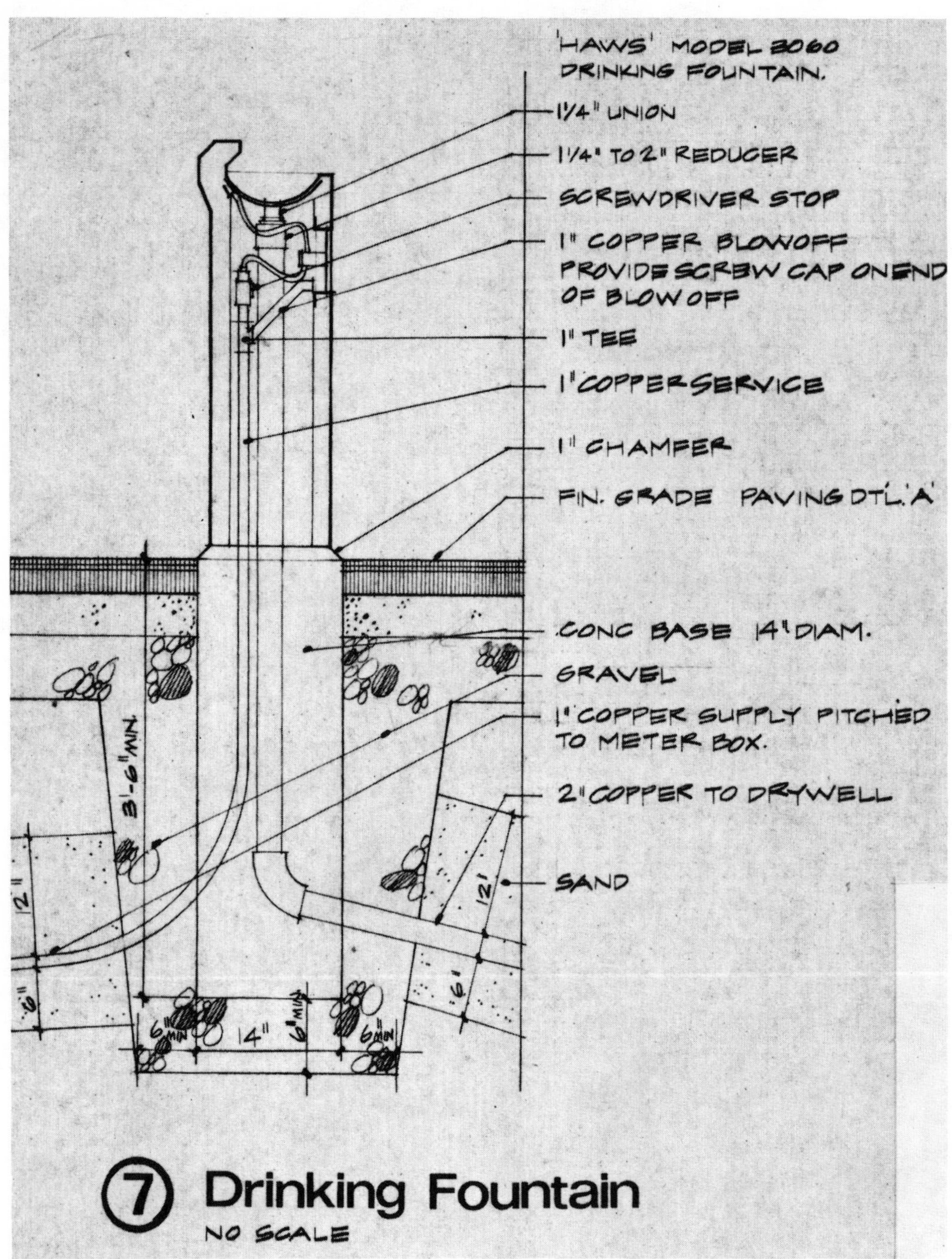
'HAWS' MODEL 3060
DRINKING FOUNTAIN.
1¼" UNION
1¼" TO 2" REDUCER
SCREWDRIVER STOP
1" COPPER BLOWOFF
PROVIDE SCREW CAP ON END
OF BLOWOFF
1" TEE
1" COPPER SERVICE
1" CHAMFER
FIN. GRADE PAVING DTL. 'A'
CONC BASE 14" DIAM.
GRAVEL
1" COPPER SUPPLY PITCHED
TO METER BOX.
2" COPPER TO DRYWELL
SAND
3'-6" MIN.
12"
6"
12"
6"
6" MIN
14"
6" MIN
6" MIN
7 Drinking Fountain
NO SCALE

Figure 11.227 *Drinking fountain detail.*

CR3, inc.

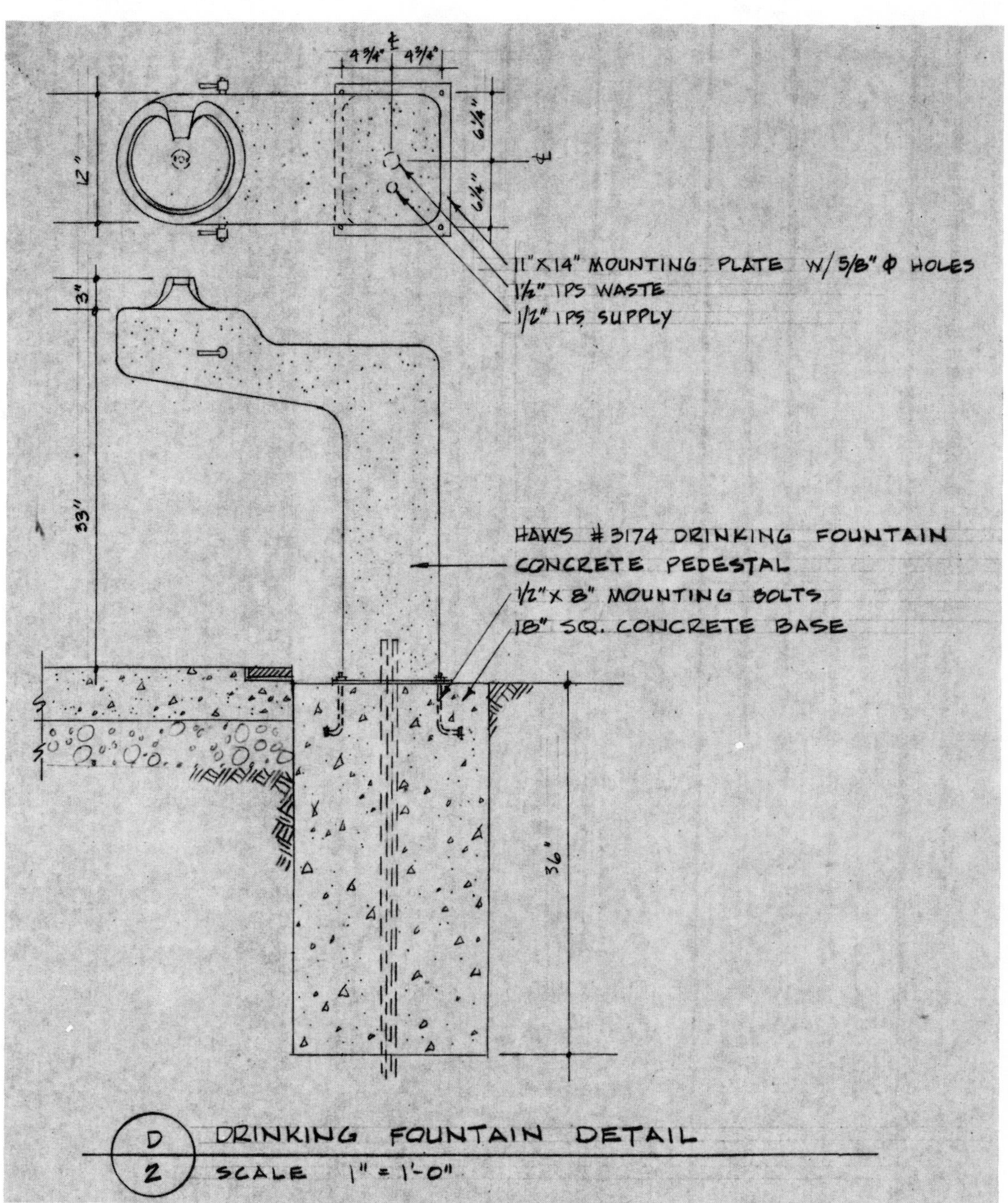
4 3/4"
4 3/4"
℄
12"
6 1/4"
6 1/4"
℄
11"X14" MOUNTING PLATE W/ 5/8" ϕ HOLES
1/2" IPS WASTE
1/2" IPS SUPPLY
3"
33"
HAWS #3174 DRINKING FOUNTAIN
CONCRETE PEDESTAL
1/2"X 8" MOUNTING BOLTS
18" SQ. CONCRETE BASE
36"
D
2
DRINKING FOUNTAIN DETAIL
SCALE 1" = 1'-0"
Walker-Harris-Associates-Inc.

Figure 11.228 *Drinking fountain detail.*

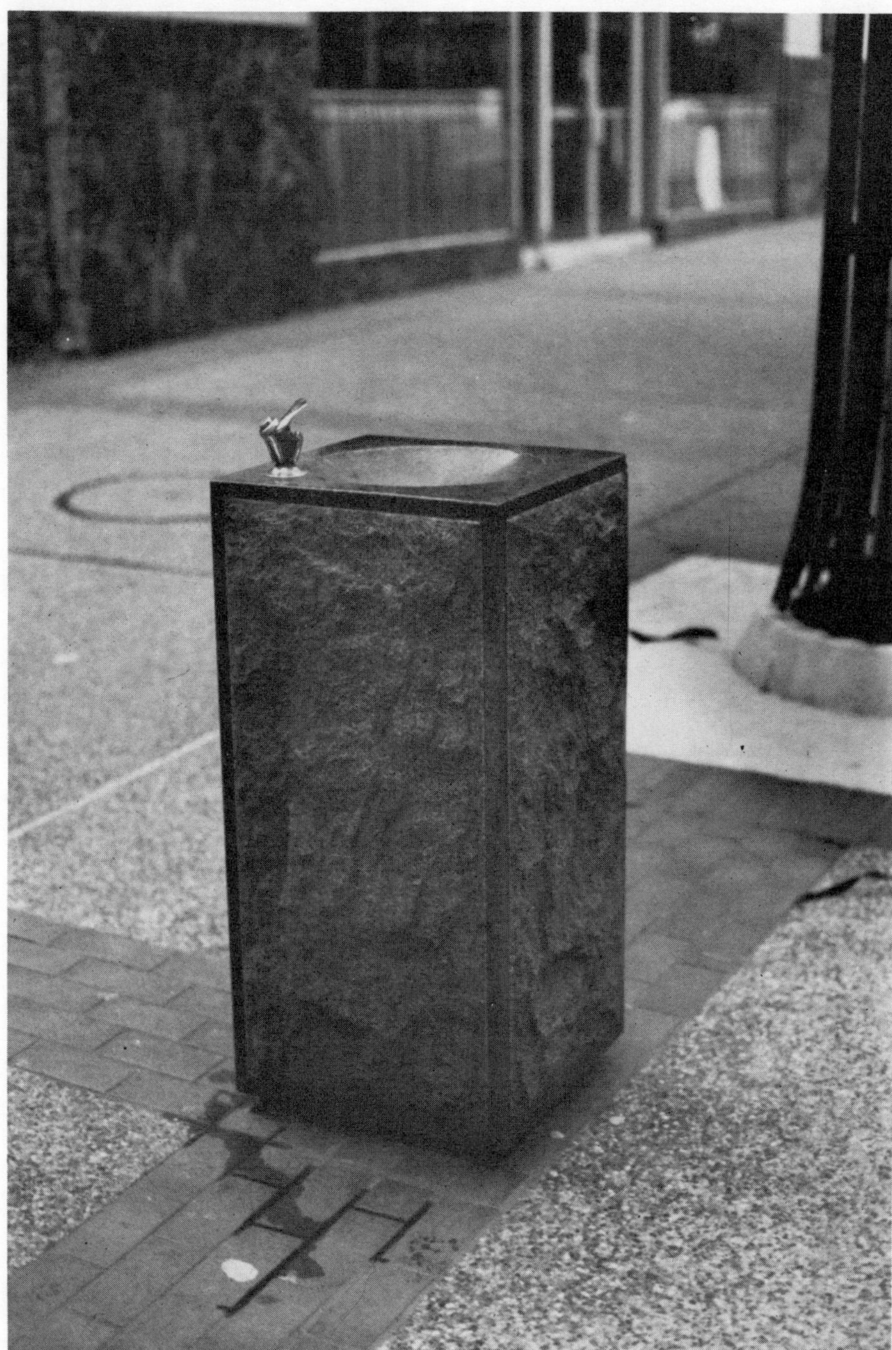

Lawrence Halprin and Associates

Figure 11.229 *Drinking fountain.*

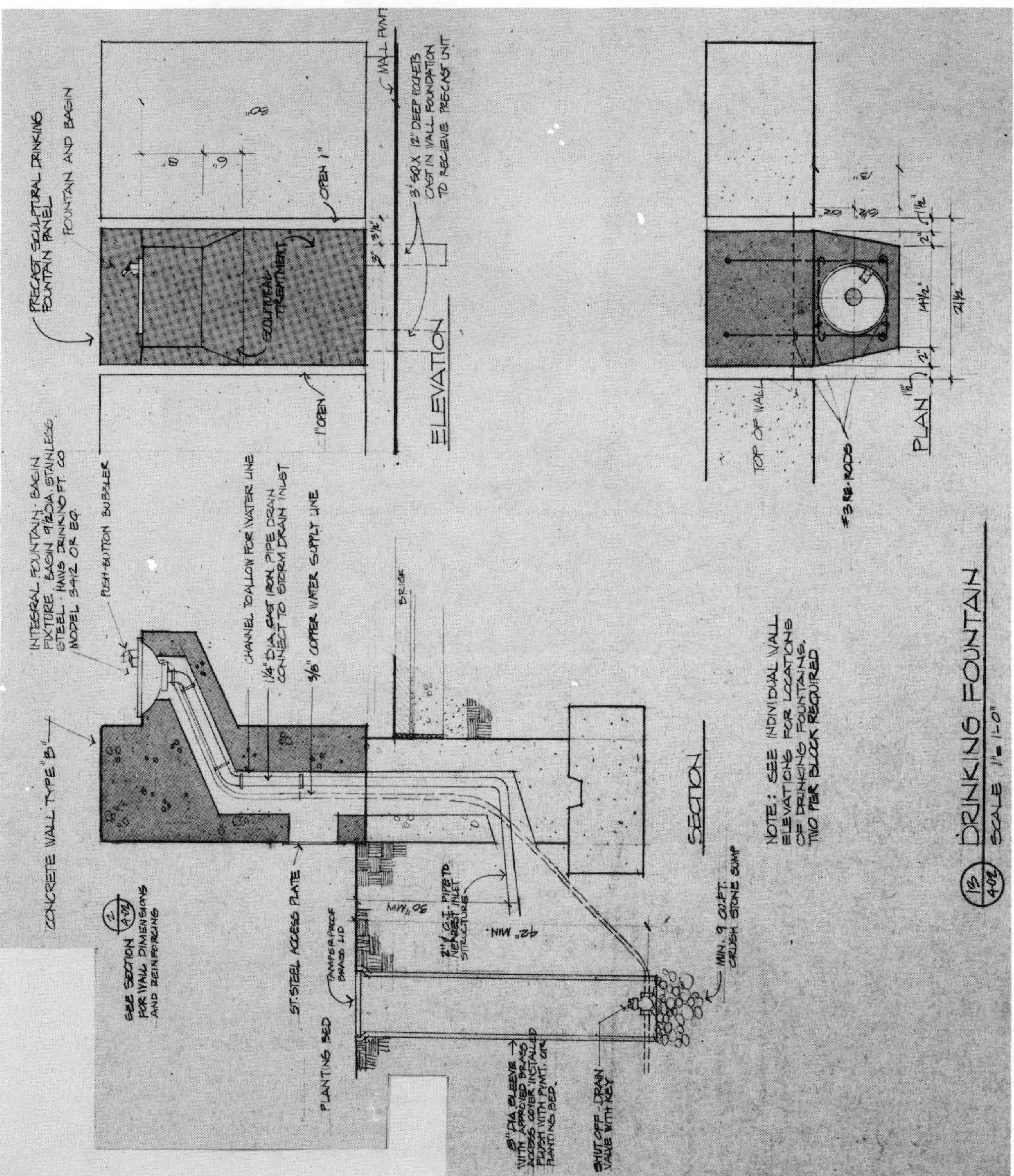
CONCRETE WALL TYPE "B"
INTEGRAL FOUNTAIN: BASIN FIXTURE. BASIN 9 1/2" DIA. STAINLESS STEEL. HAWS DRINKING FT. CO MODEL 3412 OR EQ.
PUSH-BUTTON BUBBLER
CHANNEL TO ALLOW FOR WATER LINE
1 1/4" DIA CAST IRON PIPE DRAIN CONNECT TO STORM DRAIN INLET
3/8" COPPER WATER SUPPLY LINE
BRICK
SEE SECTION FOR WALL DIMENSIONS AND REINFORCING
ST. STEEL ACCESS PLATE
TAMPERPROOF BRASS LID
PLANTING BED
8" DIA SLEEVE WITH APPROVED BRASS ACCESS COVER INSTALLED FLUSH WITH PVMT. OR PLANTING BED.
SHUT OFF - DRAIN VALVE WITH KEY
MIN. 9 CU. FT. CRUSH STONE SUMP
2" Ø C.I. PIPE TO NEAREST INLET STRUCTURE
30" MIN.
42" MIN.
SECTION
PRECAST SCULPTURAL DRINKING FOUNTAIN PANEL
FOUNTAIN AND BASIN
SCULPTURAL TREATMENT
OPEN 1"
1" OPEN
WALL PVMT
3' SQ. X 12" DEEP POCKETS CAST IN WALL FOUNDATION TO RECIEVE PRECAST UNIT
ELEVATION
TOP OF WALL
#3 RE-RODS
PLAN
NOTE: SEE INDIVIDUAL WALL ELEVATIONS FOR LOCATIONS OF DRINKING FOUNTAINS. TWO PER BLOCK REQUIRED
DRINKING FOUNTAIN
SCALE 1" = 1'-0"

Figure 11.230 *Drinking fountain details.*

Johnson, Johnson and Roy

11.231 Maurice Wrangell

11.232

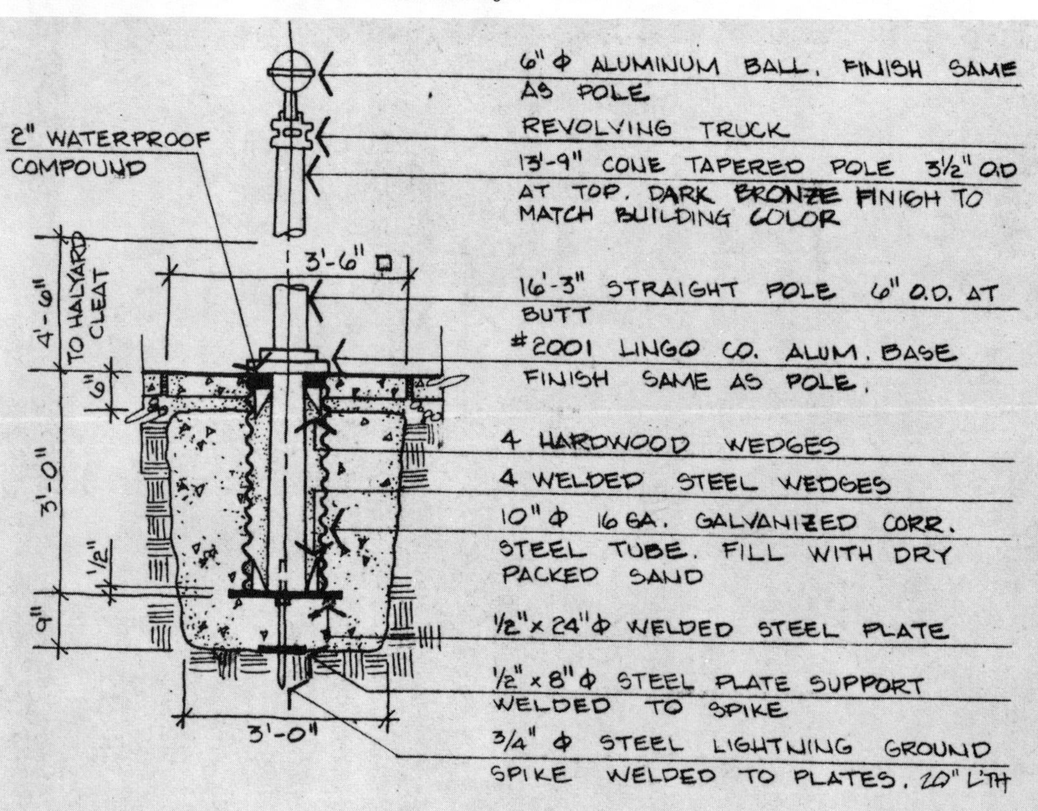

6" Φ ALUMINUM BALL, FINISH SAME AS POLE
REVOLVING TRUCK
13'-9" CONE TAPERED POLE 3½" O.D AT TOP, DARK BRONZE FINISH TO MATCH BUILDING COLOR
2" WATERPROOF COMPOUND
4'-6" TO HALYARD CLEAT
3'-6" □
16'-3" STRAIGHT POLE 6" O.D. AT BUTT
#2001 LINGO CO. ALUM. BASE FINISH SAME AS POLE.
6"
3'-0"
½"
9"
4 HARDWOOD WEDGES
4 WELDED STEEL WEDGES
10" Φ 16 GA. GALVANIZED CORR. STEEL TUBE. FILL WITH DRY PACKED SAND
½" x 24" Φ WELDED STEEL PLATE
½" x 8" Φ STEEL PLATE SUPPORT WELDED TO SPIKE
3'-0"
¾" Φ STEEL LIGHTNING GROUND SPIKE WELDED TO PLATES, 20" L'TH

3
SD·11
FLAGPOLE
SECTION

1/2" = 1'-0"

11.233 Bonnell and Associates

11.234 Bailey and Associates

11.235 H. Jay Harris

Figures 11.231 - 11.233 *Flagpoles and details.*

Figure 11.234 *Mailboxes for a housing development.*

Figure 11.235 *Unique sundial on the campus of a midwestern university.*

11.236 Bailey and Associates

11.238 Sasaki Associa

3-GR5

11.237

11.239

11.240

11.241

11.242
11.244
11.243
11.245

Figures 11.236 - 11.241 *Light shields at the base of buildings and adjacent to pedestrian walkways.*

Figures 11.242 - 11.245 *Light fixtures.*

11.246
11.248
11.247
11.249
CUBE - WHITE OPAQUE WITH BLACK ANODIZED TOP AND BOTTOM.
6" PEG
8'-6"
BLACK ANODIZED POLE - ALL EXPOSED ELEMENTS
FINISH GRADE
#6 GROUND WIRE, BOND TO POLE, BASE & CONDUIT
BUSHING
DIRECT BURIAL CABLE
4½"-1"# ANCHOR RODS, 20" LONG
18" MIN.
3'-0" DEEP CONC. BASE TOP TO BE 2" ABOVE GRADE
4-#9 VERTICAL
#3 TIES @ 12" O.C.
RIGID CONDUIT, SIZE AS REQUIRED
3" MIN. CONCRETE ENVELOPE
3/4"x10' GROUND ROD
KUBE SERIES TYPE LIGHTING FIXTURE
BY STERNER LIGHTING CO.

Figures 11.246 – 11.249 *Light fixtures and detail.*

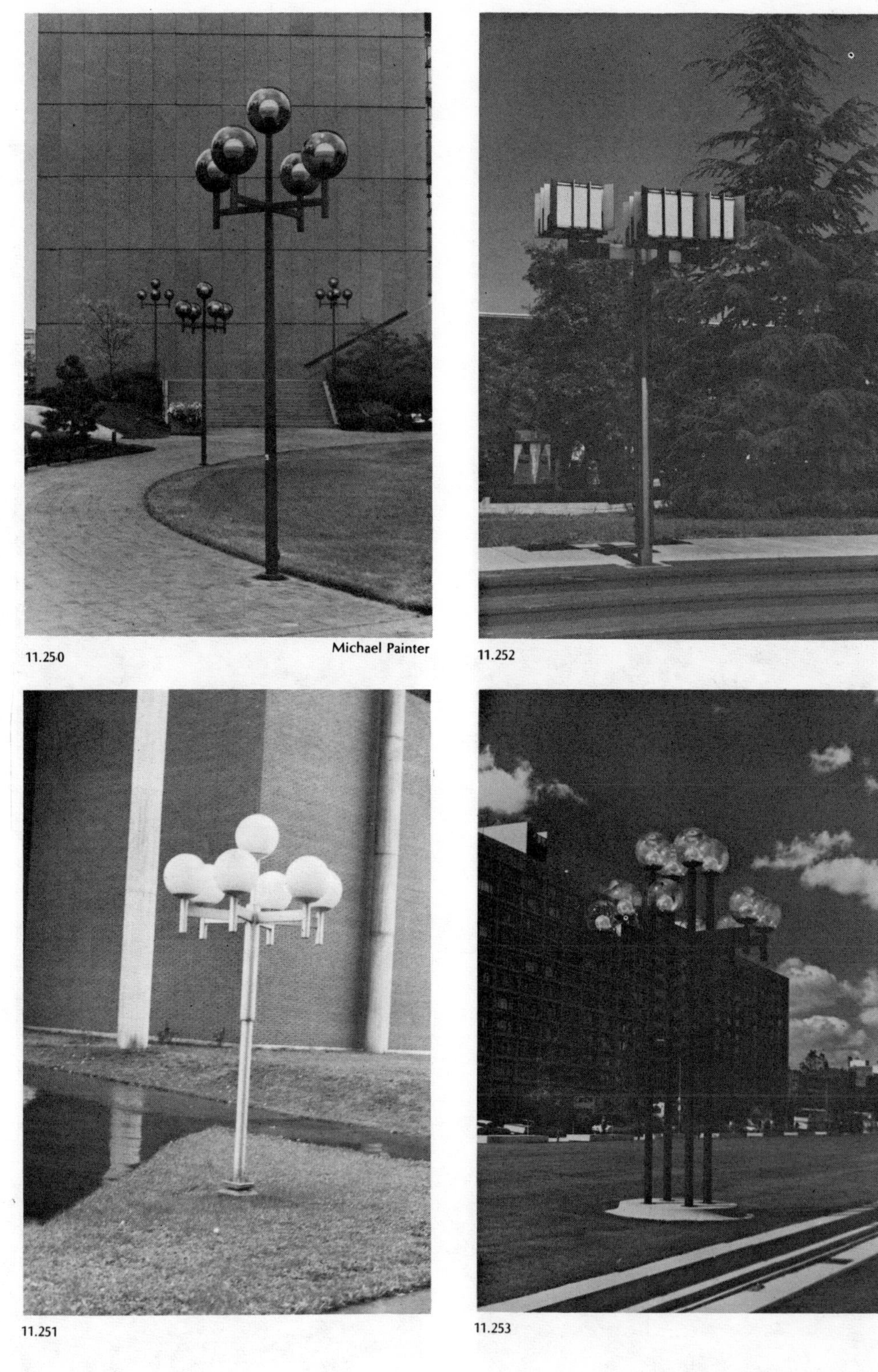
11.250 Michael Painter 11.252
11.251 11.253

Figures 11.250 – 11.253 *A few of the many styles of light fixtures.*

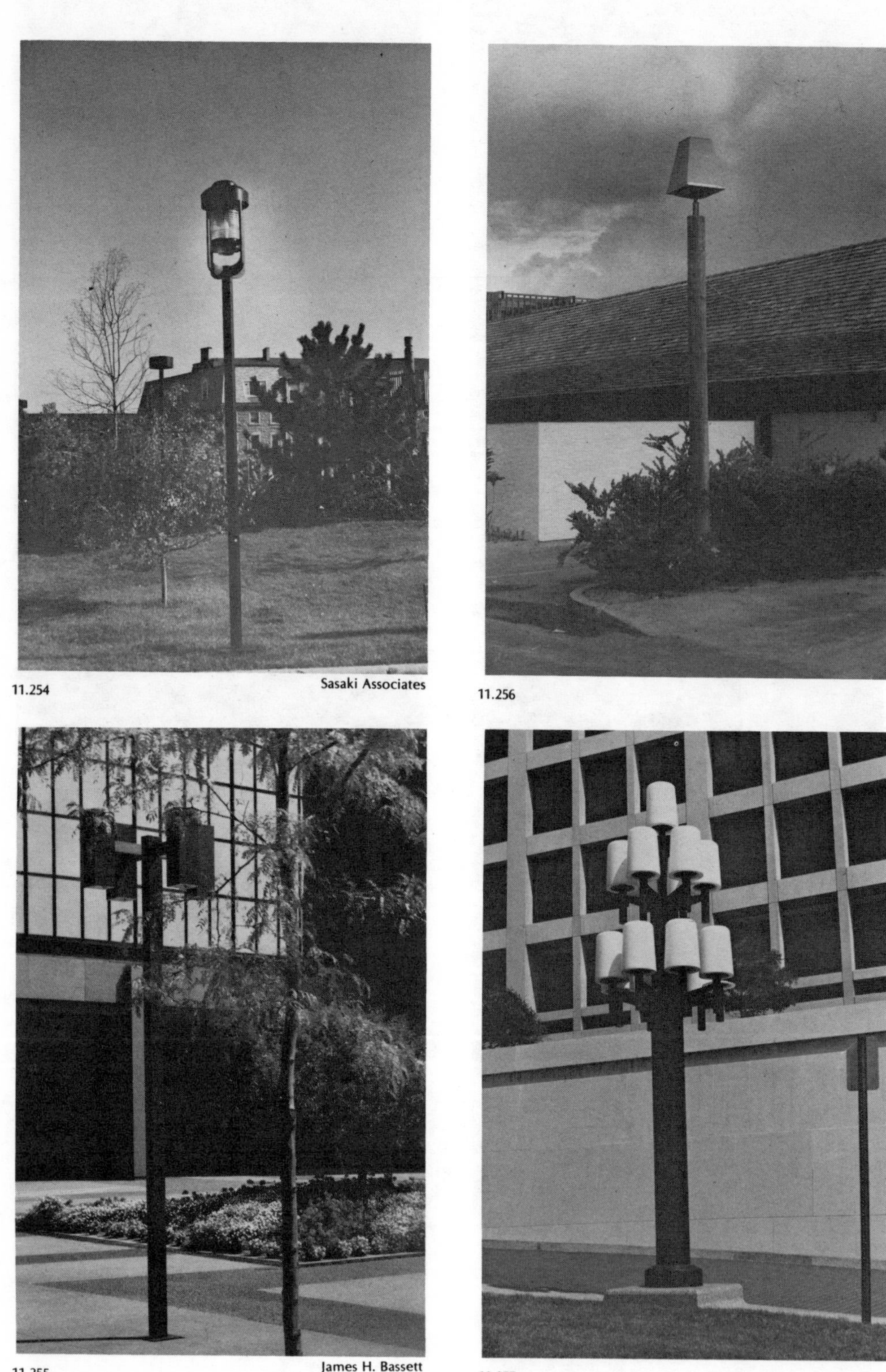
11.254 Sasaki Associates

11.256

11.255 James H. Bassett

11.257

Figures 11.254 – 11.261 *Light fixtures.*

11.258 Lawrence Halprin and Associates

11.260

11.259

11.261 Theodore Brickman Co.

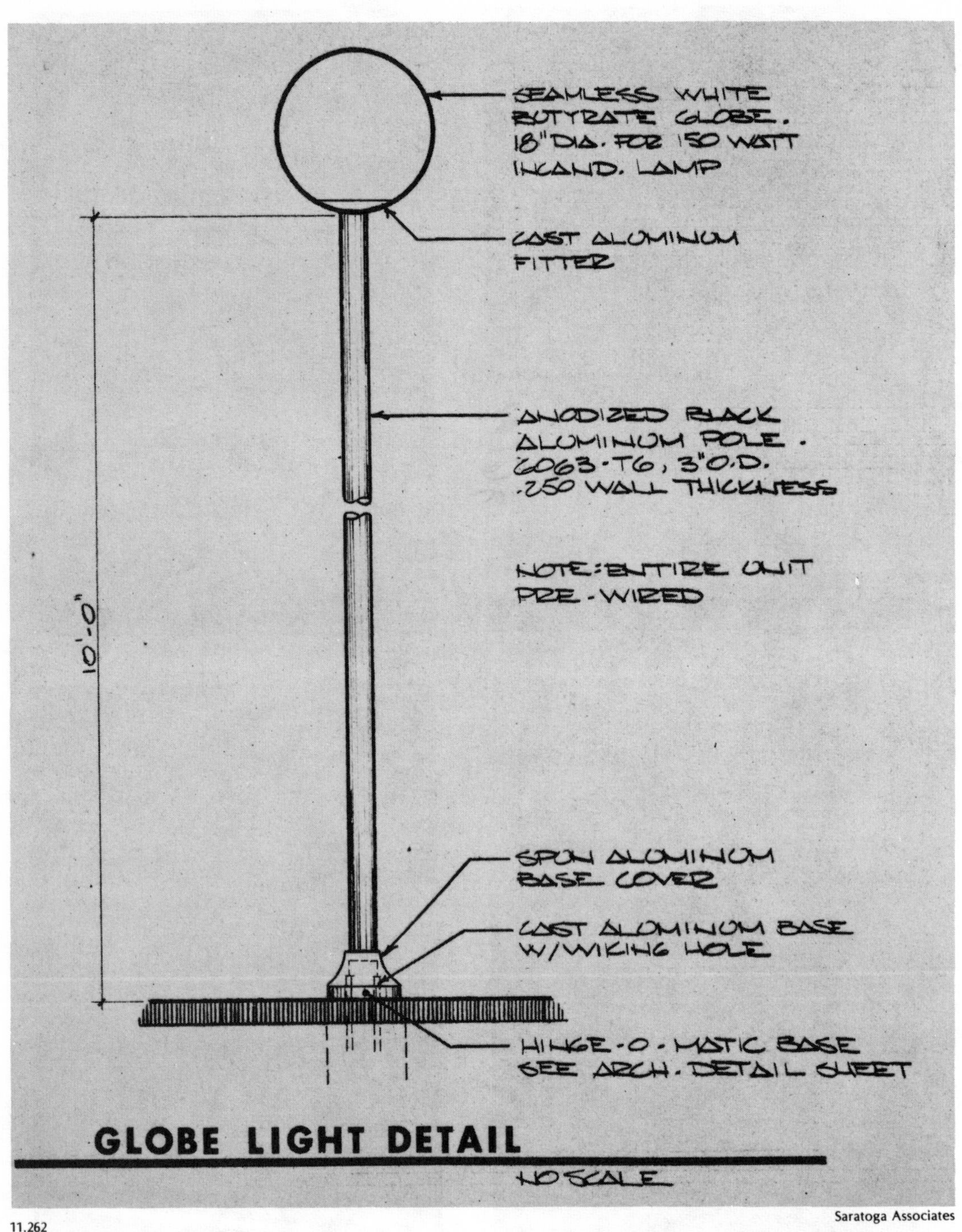
SEAMLESS WHITE BUTYRATE GLOBE. 18" DIA. FOR 150 WATT INCAND. LAMP
CAST ALUMINUM FITTER
ANODIZED BLACK ALUMINUM POLE. 6063-T6, 3" O.D. .250 WALL THICKNESS
NOTE: ENTIRE UNIT PRE-WIRED
10'-0"
SPUN ALUMINUM BASE COVER
CAST ALUMINUM BASE W/WIRING HOLE
HINGE-O-MATIC BASE SEE ARCH. DETAIL SHEET
GLOBE LIGHT DETAIL
NO SCALE

11.262

Saratoga Associates

Figures 11.262 – 11.265 *Light fixture and details.*

Crofter

11.263

11.264

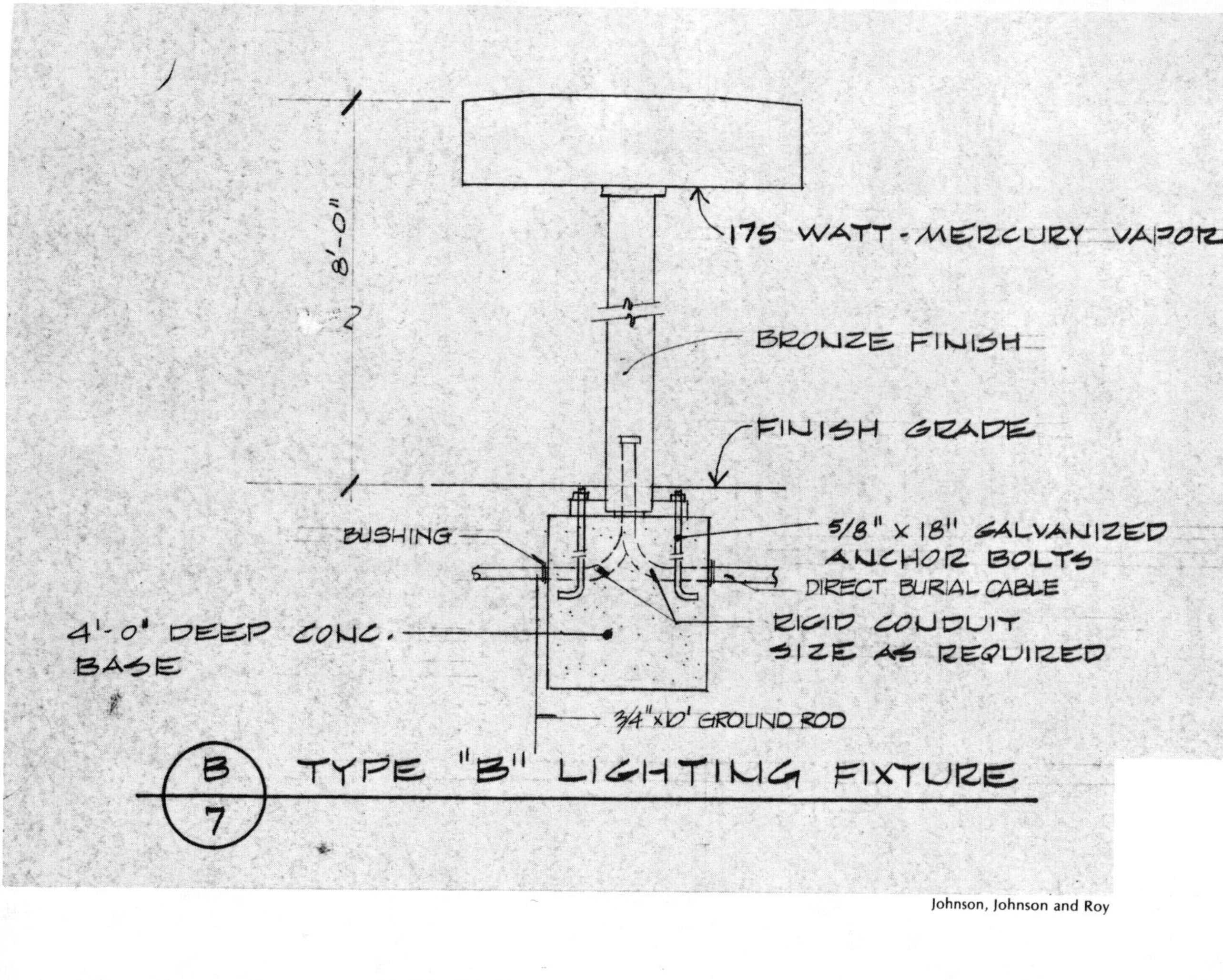

8'-0"

175 WATT-MERCURY VAPOR

BRONZE FINISH

FINISH GRADE

BUSHING

5/8" x 18" GALVANIZED ANCHOR BOLTS

DIRECT BURIAL CABLE

4'-0" DEEP CONC. BASE

RIGID CONDUIT SIZE AS REQUIRED

3/4" x 10' GROUND ROD

B/7 TYPE "B" LIGHTING FIXTURE

Johnson, Johnson and Roy

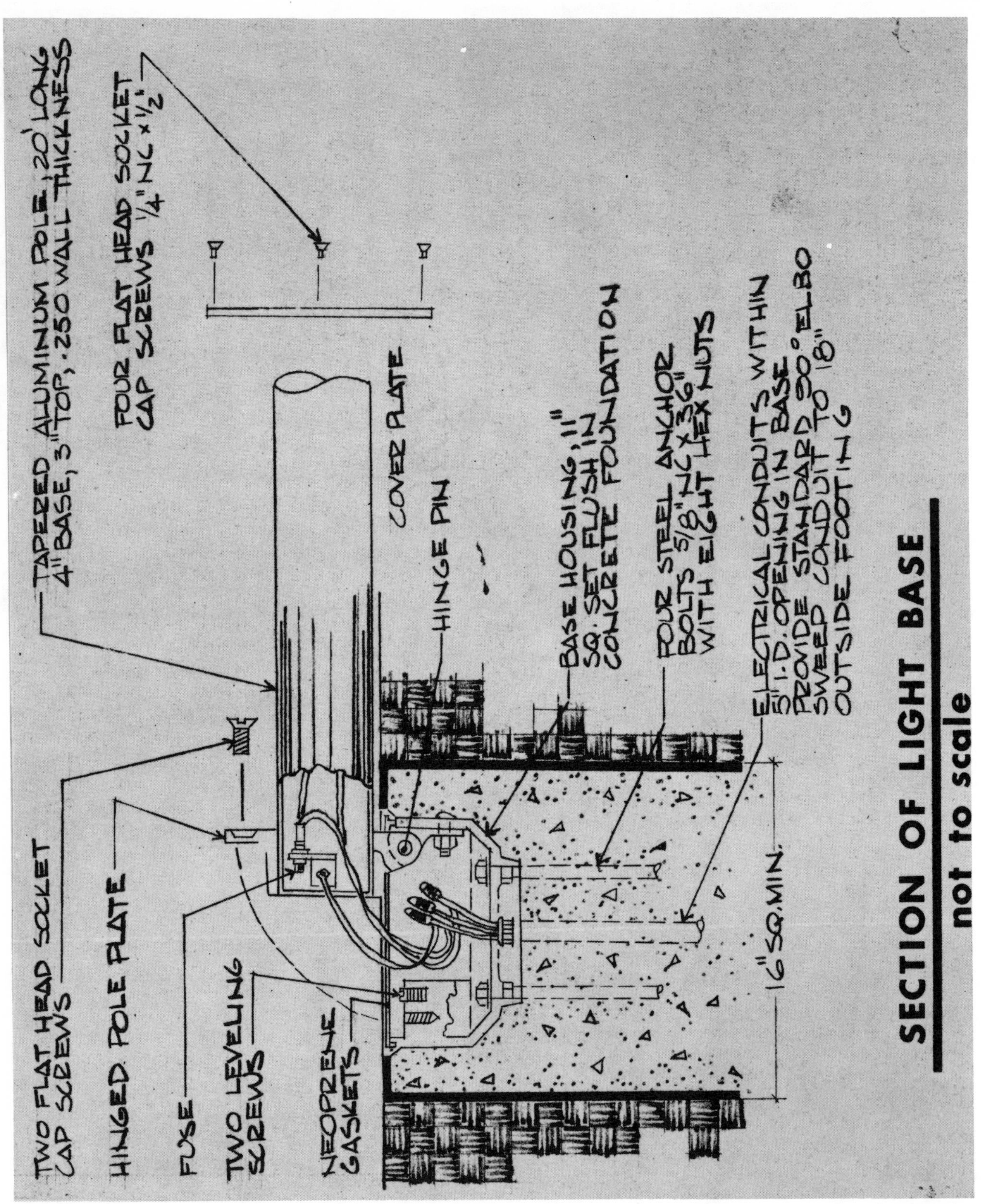
TAPERED ALUMINUM POLE, 20' LONG
4" BASE, 3" TOP, .250 WALL THICKNESS
FOUR FLAT HEAD SOCKET CAP SCREWS 1/4" NC x 1 1/2"
COVER PLATE
HINGE PIN
BASE HOUSING, 11" SQ. SET FLUSH IN CONCRETE FOUNDATION
FOUR STEEL ANCHOR BOLTS 5/8" NC x 36" WITH EIGHT HEX NUTS
ELECTRICAL CONDUITS WITHIN 5" I.D. OPENING IN BASE
PROVIDE STANDARD 90° ELBO SWEEP CONDUIT TO 18" OUTSIDE FOOTING
TWO FLAT HEAD SOCKET CAP SCREWS
HINGED POLE PLATE
FUSE
TWO LEVELING SCREWS
NEOPRENE GASKETS
16" SQ. MIN.
SECTION OF LIGHT BASE
not to scale

Saratoga Associates

Figure 11.266 *Light fixture detail.*

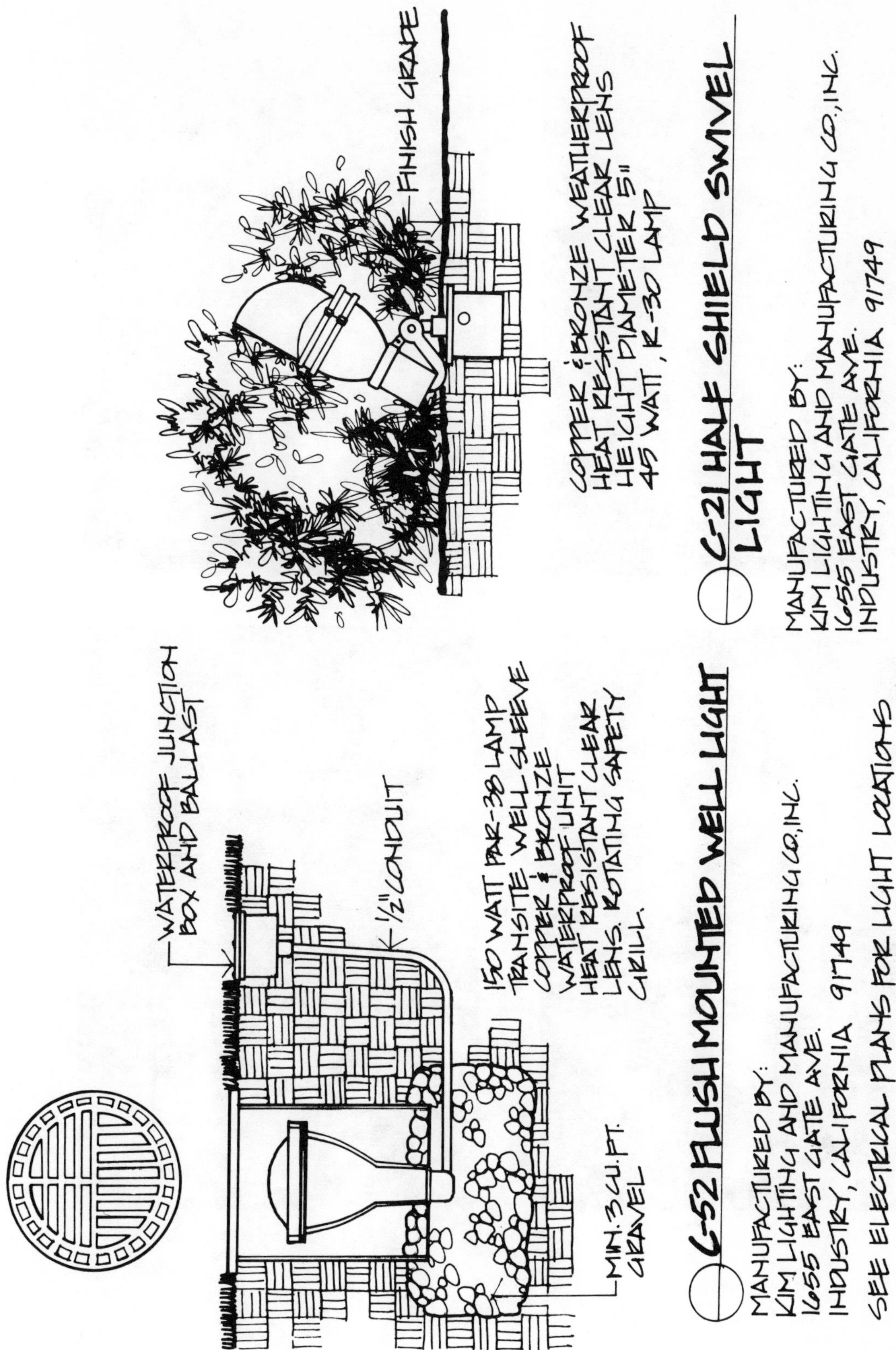
WATERPROOF JUNCTION BOX AND BALLAST
1/2" CONDUIT
150 WATT PAR-38 LAMP
TRANSITE WELL SLEEVE
COPPER & BRONZE
WATERPROOF UNIT
HEAT RESISTANT CLEAR
LENS. ROTATING SAFETY
GRILL.
MIN. 3 CU. FT.
GRAVEL
C-52 FLUSH MOUNTED WELL LIGHT
MANUFACTURED BY:
KIM LIGHTING AND MANUFACTURING CO., INC.
1655 EAST GATE AVE.
INDUSTRY, CALIFORNIA 91749
SEE ELECTRICAL PLANS FOR LIGHT LOCATIONS
FINISH GRADE
COPPER & BRONZE WEATHERPROOF
HEAT RESISTANT CLEAR LENS
HEIGHT DIAMETER 5"
45 WATT, R-30 LAMP
C-21 HALF SHIELD SWIVEL
LIGHT
MANUFACTURED BY:
KIM LIGHTING AND MANUFACTURING CO., INC.
1655 EAST GATE AVE.
INDUSTRY, CALIFORNIA 91749

Figure 11.267 *Light fixture details.*

Johnson, Johnson and Roy

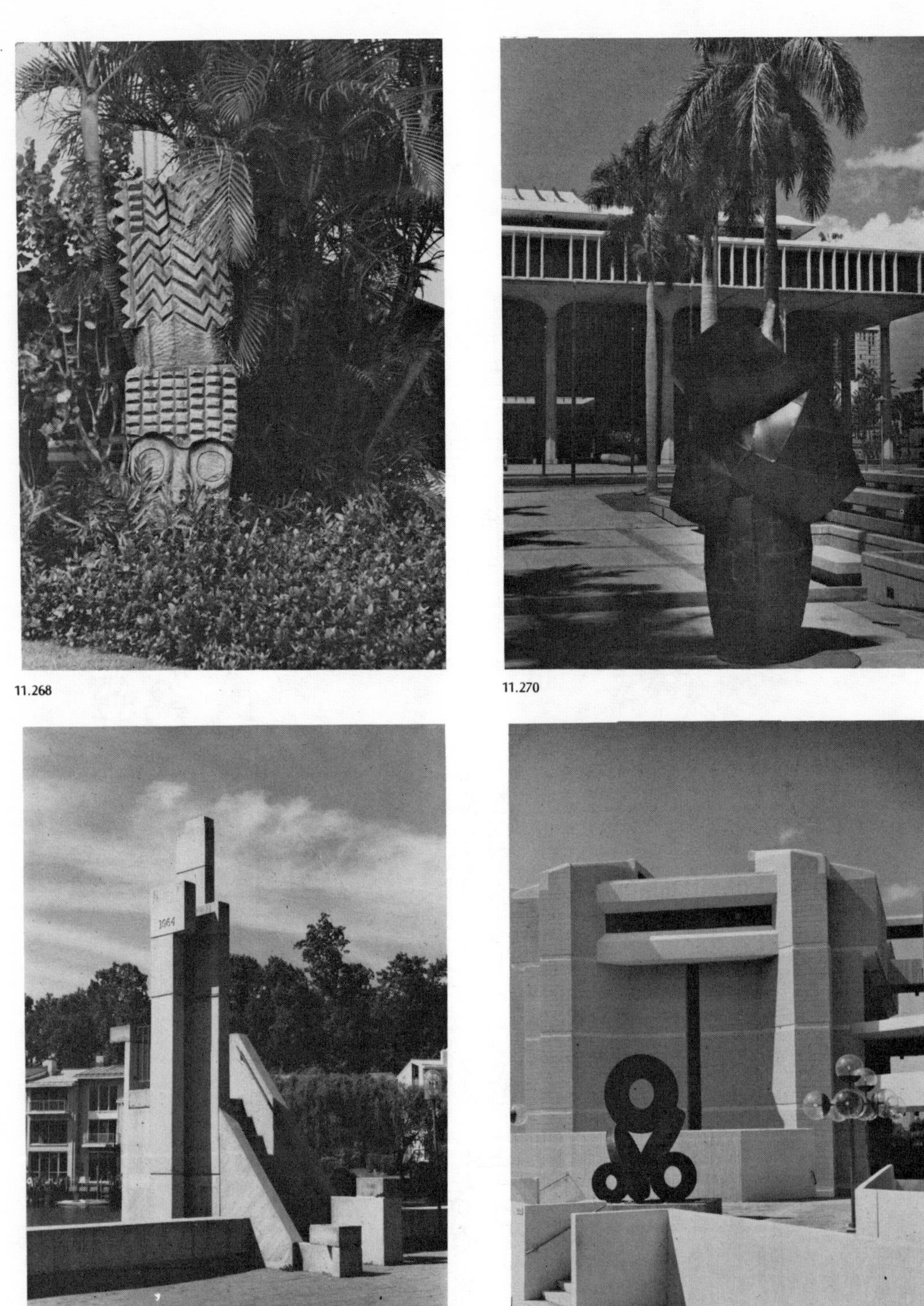
1964
11.268

11.270

11.269

11.271

Figures 11.268 – 11.274 *A sampling of sculptural forms used in site design.*

11.272

11.273

11.274

11.275

11.277

11.276

11.278

Figures 11.275 – 11.276 *Some sculptural forms.*
Figure 11.277 *Cylindrical phone booths.*
Figure 11.278 *Lectern in an amphitheater.*

12

Pools, Ponds, and Fountains

Water has considerable aesthetic appeal. The sight and sound of moving water especially appeals to the senses. Most often it can serve as a focal point within a particular design concept.

Using water, however, in site design is not a simple matter. There are a number of factors which make its use complex and these must be understood before it is incorporated into a design. The use of water not only add to the initial budget cost for installation, but long term maintenance must also be considered. Frequent cleaning of pools and fountains is required to remove dirt, leaves, and debris which accumulate daily. There are also problems encountered with the growth of algae and discoloration from iron and other chemicals which accumulate within the pool or on the fountain structure and equipment. It would be a rare situation where water would be so plentiful that it need not be recirculated. There is a loss, however, through evaporation and this must be replaced.

In those areas of the country where freezing occurs, it is generally desirable that most pools and fountains be drained in the winter time and allowed to remain empty. This leaves the mechanical equipment and other things exposed and can be both a visual and vandalism problem.

In this particular section there will be little discussion concerning swimming pools. This is the most complex water use in design, and because of State Board of Health regulations, competent engineering assistance is a necessity. Engineering assistance may be needed for most other fountain situations except those simple self-contained units which will be discussed later.

In a study of water use, the concerns can be broken down into five different areas: 1) aesthetic, 2) function, 3) structural, 4) mechanical, and 5) electrical.

Aesthetics

In nature, water can be found both quiet and moving. Quiet water is found in lakes, and moving water may be cascading down from waterfalls, shooting out of a geyser, rushing down over rocks in a rugged mountain stream, or slowly meandering in a riverbed.

In design, some of the same effects can be created plus others. The quiet water can be duplicated in reflecting pools, which may be structural in character, e.g. rectangles or natural earthen ponds. Moving water can be in the form of cascades flowing from one level to another, fine sprays, straight streams from simple orifices, or pulsating, aerated, or bubbling water or any combination of these.

By adding programmed timing controls, varied effects can be created within a period of a few minutes to hours and lighting can be added for additional nighttime visual appeal.

Function

Besides the visual appeal and sounds created for aesthetic purposes, there may be

12.1 Theodore Brickman Co. Harr, Hedrich-Blessing

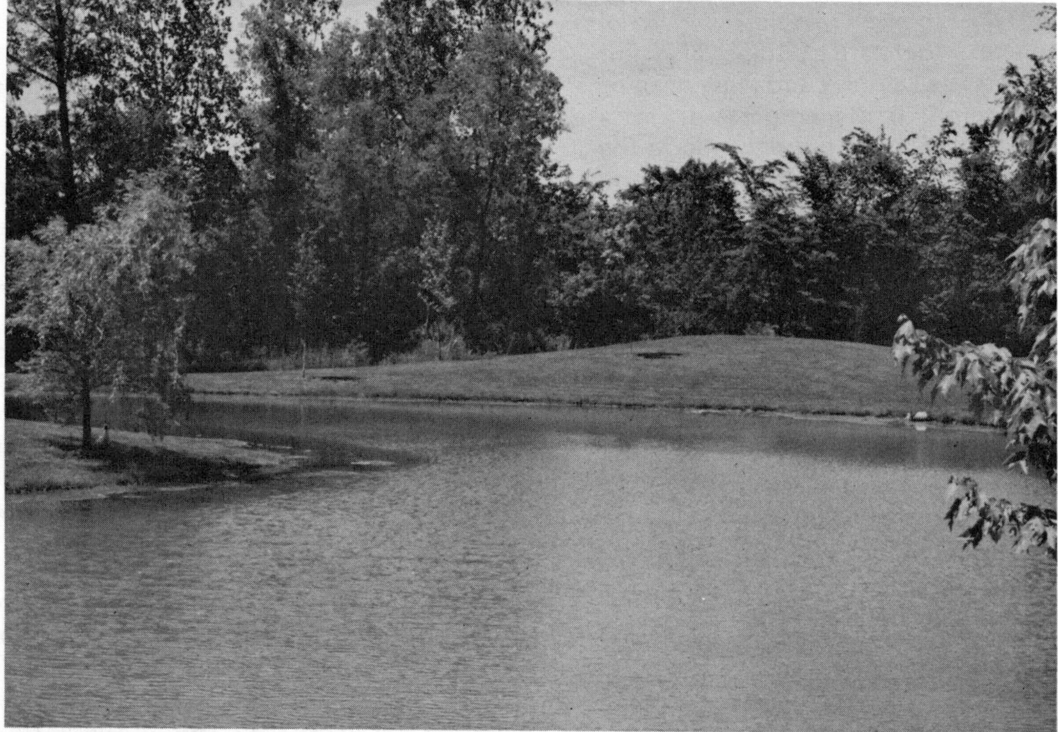

12.2 Walker-Harris-Associates-Inc.

Figure 12.1 *Quiet pond in a housing development.*

Figure 12.2 *Pond in a flood plain with a high water table. Excavated soil was used to create mounding and sculptural effect.*

other functions which pools, ponds, and fountains can serve. In addition to the aesthetics described earlier, the fountain may supplement a piece of sculpture as a focal point. Water may also be used to reflect scenic views, either natural or structural such as buildings. Natural ponds may serve as wildlife and fishing areas or as holding ponds containing water to prevent surges of water to downstream areas after heavy storms. Some water holding ponds may also serve for cooling air conditioning systems.

The sound effects from some water features may be useful in masking adjacent sources of noise that may be irritating if heard without the masking effect of the water.

Water may be useful as a source of recreation for people. Children's and adults' wading pools and play areas (as distinguished from swimming), boating, canoeing, etc., are some examples.

Structural Characteristics

Natural ponds may be constructed in any number of different physical situations. One type can be created by excavating into a natural water table. This is the easiest to construct and maintain because little would have to be done outside of erosion control along the edges. In order to keep the water in a natural pond from stagnating, it is desirable that 50 percent of the surface of the pond be six feet or deeper. If there is some movement of water through the natural water table this would add to the pond's water decreasing stagnation problems. When shallower ponds are used, stagnation can be minimized by using floating jets or other types of forced circulation for the water. Erosion along the edges can be minimized by the use of sod or stone riprap.

When ponds are created in natural drainage ways and they depend upon surface drainage as a water source to fill the pond, other considerations are needed. Depending upon the characteristics of the soil, treatment may be necessary for the bottom of the pond in order to prevent seepage. In clay soils, certain chemicals can be added to bind the soil particles together to prevent water movement through them. Other possibilities include the use of concrete, asphalt, or plastic membranes to seal the bottom of the ponds.

Pools and fountains, other than ponds, will generally be designed as either depressed in character below grade line, flush to grade line, raised, or a combination of any or all three of these. To construct these pools and fountains, reinforced cast-in-place concrete is most commonly used. Concrete is the easiest material to obtain and place into the desired shapes and configurations for design purposes. Less common is the use of metals, carved stone, and plastics. Several other materials are used in combination with concrete, generally as veneers. These include brick, stone, precast concrete, terrazzo, and ceramic tile.

Bare concrete on the inside of pools is not especially attractive particularly when the pool is empty. The addition of a veneer such as a ceramic tile can add much in the way of color and create a surface that is easy to clean. This approach, however, is rather expensive. A less expensive use of color would be to paint the surface. Because concrete is somewhat porous it is ideal to use a material which will seal the concrete against any seepage. Epoxy compounds can perform the function of sealing, at the same time providing color. Black increases the impression of water depth and is very useful for reflection pools. Black, however, becomes readily dirty and begins to look more like gray. Blue is used frequently, especially by non-designers, in an attempt to create an attractive water color, but it is generally too bright and artificial looking and, depending upon individual tastes, may not be that attractive. Smooth river stones can be placed in pool bottoms to stimulate natural effects. They work best when secured in place rather than placed in loosely. The use of a clear epoxy sealer over this kind of a surface may help minimize cleaning problems.

Water which is shot into the air by jets will splash a considerable distance when it comes back into contact with the surface of the pool. To minimize splash beyond the pool, the edge of the pool should be in a one to one relationship with the height of the water. A jet which shoots water ten feet in the air would require a pool 20 feet in diameter as a minimum. This is in a situation with no wind. Where wind is a problem, either the height of the jet needs to be reduced or the size of the pool increased. Aeration of the water apparently helps to reduce some of the splashing problem.

Other complexities involving water include the flow of water over an edge or lip. Water will tend to follow the lip around and down the adjacent wall unless a very positive drip edge is provided forcing the water to fall vertically. Except in the rarest of instances, reinforcing is required in most pour-in-place concrete. The amount of reinforcing depends upon the size and complexity of the structure. In large structures, expansion joints would be needed. In order to prevent water from leaking through these joints, vinyl waterstops can be

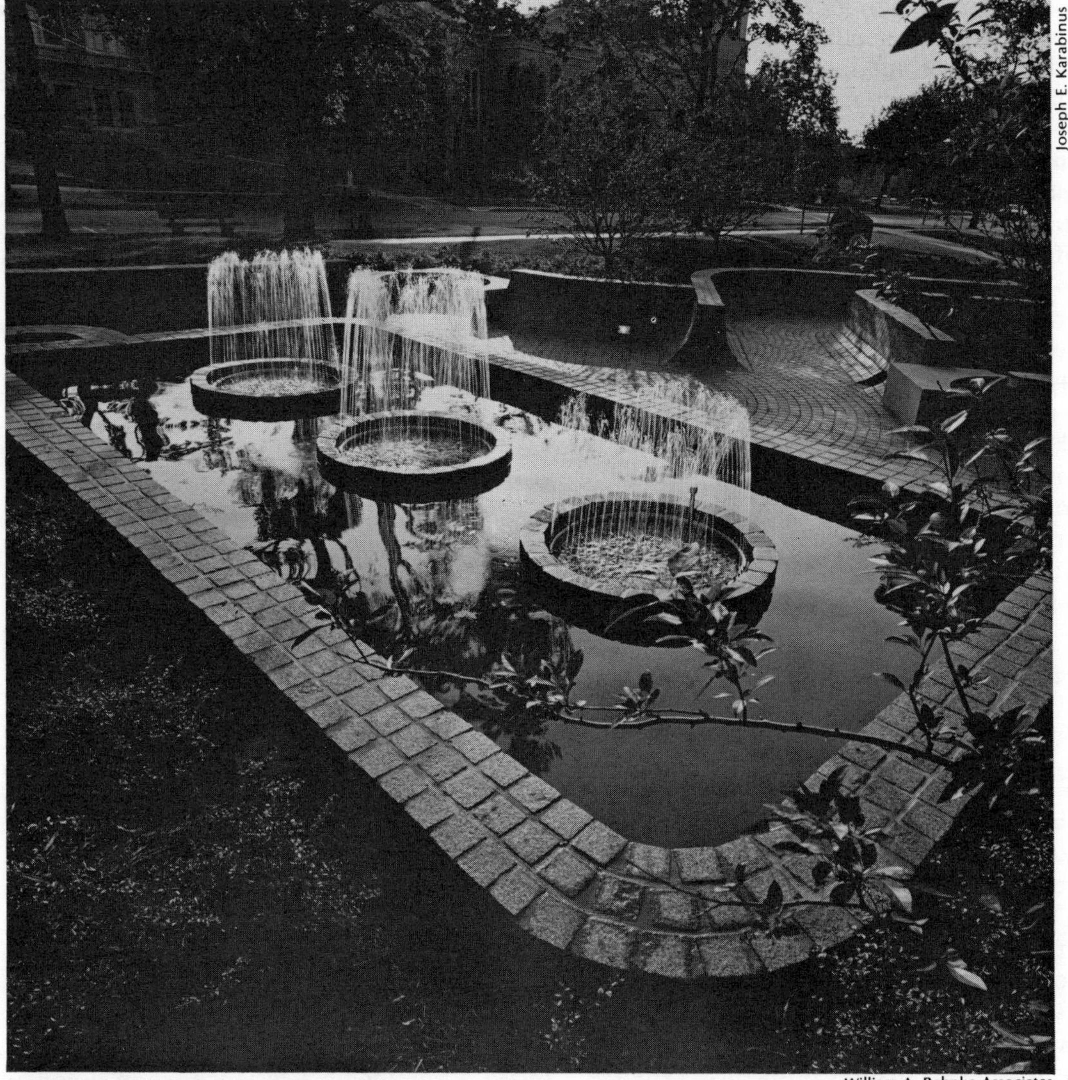
Joseph E. Karabinus

William A. Behnke Associates

Figure 12.3 *Fountain in a small park.*

used with the added assistance of a urethane sealant in the top of the joint.

Water depth may be more of a consideration of safety and equipment needs than other factors. Some pool lights require a minimum water depth of approximately 18 inches in order to provide two inches of water coverage over the lens of the lamp. However, if a water depth of six inches is desired for the design concept, equipment can be placed in a pit with a metal grate at the six-inch depth to cover the equipment. Pools with water which is too deep may be classified as swimming pools and would come under the jurisdiction of the Board of Health. This might not be desirable from a cost and design standpoint.

When plants such as water lilies are to be incorporated into a pool, a water depth of approximately 24 inches is desirable. Most aquatic plants prefer quiet water.

Mechanical Characteristics

Besides the most obvious part of the mechanical system (the jets), there are related piping, pumps, drains, water level controls, overflows, etc., which form the mechanical system. Complex systems may also involve filtration and chlorination.

Several manufacturers sell self-contained fountains equipment which simply requires the placement of the unit within a pool and the connecting of it to an underwater junction box for power. This eliminates the complexity involved in calculating hydraulics and sizing the pump, piping, and control valves. However, the designer would need to consider such things as water inlets and water level controls to add water to compensate for evaporation. A simple floor drain with its accompanying control valve and some method for handling overflow must be considered. The overflow can be either a screened box on the side of the pool or the more commonly used mushroom-type located toward the edge or center of the pool. The mushroom-type cap on the vertical pipe of the overflow prevents leaves and debris from clogging it. Where simplicity is desired, the overflow can double as a drain simply by removing the overflow at its base in the bottom of the pool. In this particular case the overflow needs to be located near the side so that it is readily accessible.

Water level controls are of two kinds. One is a simple float system in a recessed box on the side of the pool which allows water to come in when the floats drop below a certain level. The other type is an electronic level control utilizing probes which activate an electric valve when the water is too low and water is brought into the pool through the regular inlet.

In people participation situations, chlorination and filteration of the water would be needed, if not required. Chlorination would aid in cutting down on the growth of algae; filteration would keep the water cleaner and reduce some of the problems with maintenance. Both of these items, however, add to the initial as well as later maintenance costs.

Electrical Characteristics

In order to move water, electrical power is required. At the very least there will be a pump which will need to be connected into a power source. Most submersible pumps come with a cord to be connected to a waterproof junction box inside the pool. A conduit from the connecting base of the junction box would run to some safe place away from the pool for connection to a control panel. A circuit breaker and ground fault interrupter (GFI) along with any timing devices would be located in this control panel. The GFI prevents accidental electrical shock should the grounding to any electrical device fail. This same electrical control panel could have the controls and timer for any lighting used in the pool, as well as any programmer to be used for alternating the effects of lighting and/or jets. The electronic water level control and wind control connections could also be made in this control panel.

The wind control includes a sensor which is placed in a high position, usually on a light pole. When winds reach a certain speed the sensor senses the movement of the air and sends an electronic pulse which shuts off the pump or activates electronic valves which reduce the height of the water displays to eliminate splash.

Large pools and fountains requiring pumps larger than those available in submersible sizes will need a buried vault to house a dry pump. This vault will also contain all of the pool equipment such as pumps, filters, valves, chlorinator, and electrical control panels. Access to this vault is usually through a manhole cover in the pavement surface above. Most vaults housing pumps and other equipment for pools and fountains will need to have a ventilating system constantly bringing in fresh air to dissipate odors and excess heat.

Underwater lighting is available in a number of different styles and designs. One type is recessed into the concrete and can be installed either in the bottom or the sides of the pool or fountain. Another type is a fixture which sits on the bottom of the pool and generally requires about 18 inches of water in the pool to completely cover the fixture, as water is needed to cool the lamp. Most need at least two inches of water over the lens of the lamp. Lights in this latter style provide the maximum amount of lumens and are best placed directly under the splashing water for maximum upward light movement and effects. Lenses of several colors can be used to create different effects except that excessive variation may create a feeling of too much activity and they may distract rather than create a harmonious whole. Too many colors and too many changes of color in the programming might create a circus effect.

REFERENCES FOR FURTHER READING

Aurand, C.D. *Fountains and Pools: Construction Guidelines and Specifications.* Mesa, Arizona: PDA Publishers, 1985.

Halprin, L. *Cities.* Revised Edition. Cambridge, MA: MIT Press, 1973.

McCulley, E.B. "Water: Pools and Fountains," *Handbook of Landscape Architectural Construction.* Washington, DC: Landscape Architecture Foundation, 1973.

SEA

12.4 Lawrence Halprin and Associates

12.6 Lawrence Halprin and Associates

12.5

12.7 Browning-Day-Pollak-Associates-Inc.

Figures 12.4 – 12.9 *Fountains in a variety of design styles.*

12.8

W. T. GRANT CO.

12.9

Johnson, Johnson and Roy

12.10 Edward D. Stone, Jr. and Associates

12.12

12.11

Figures 12.10 – 12.12 *Fountains.*

12.13 Sasaki Associates

12.15

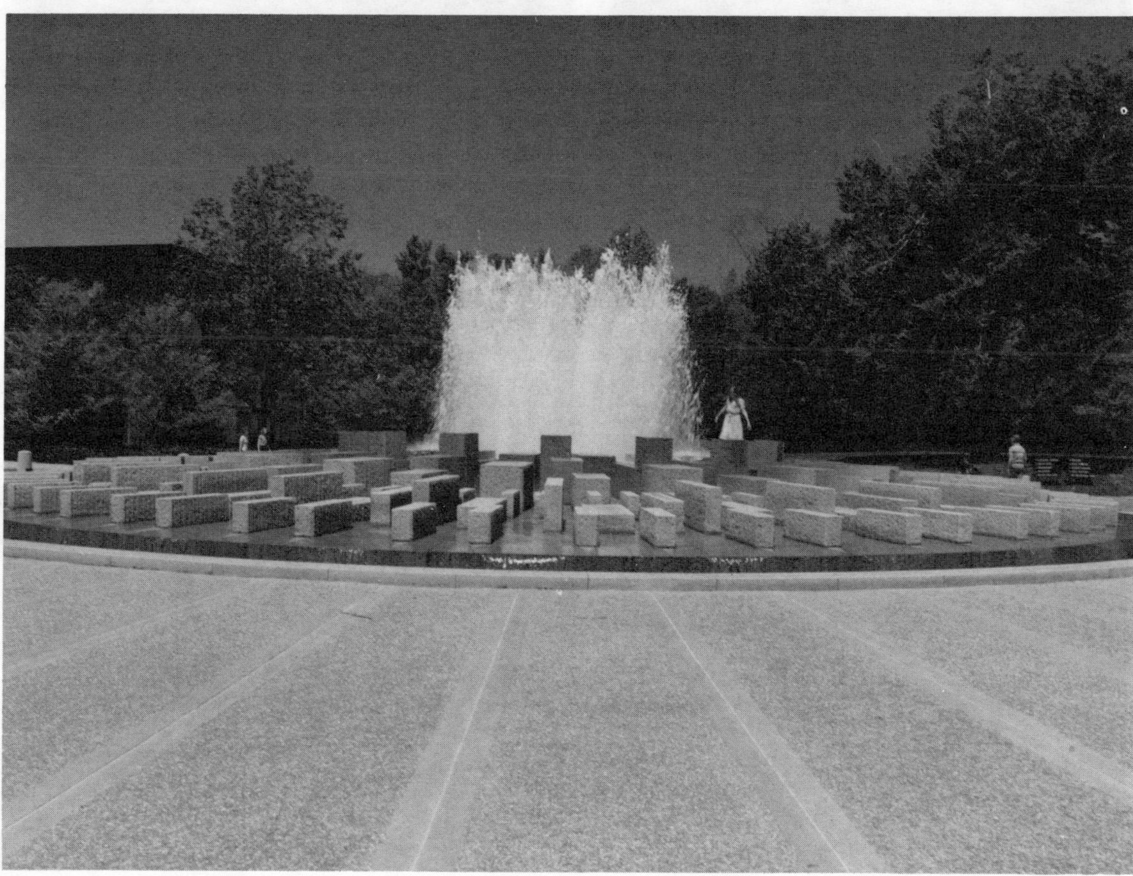

12.14

Figures 12.13 – 12.15 *Fountains at art museums.*

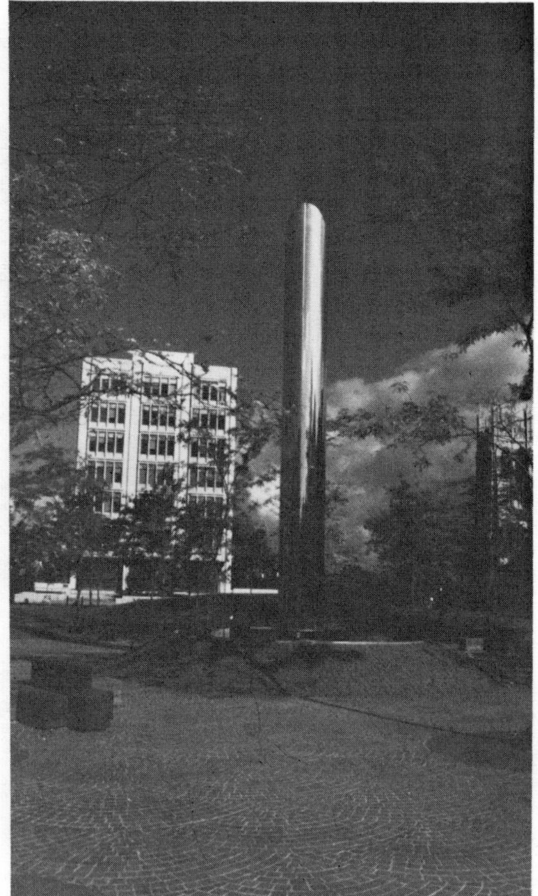
12.16

William A. Behnke Associates

12.17

12.18

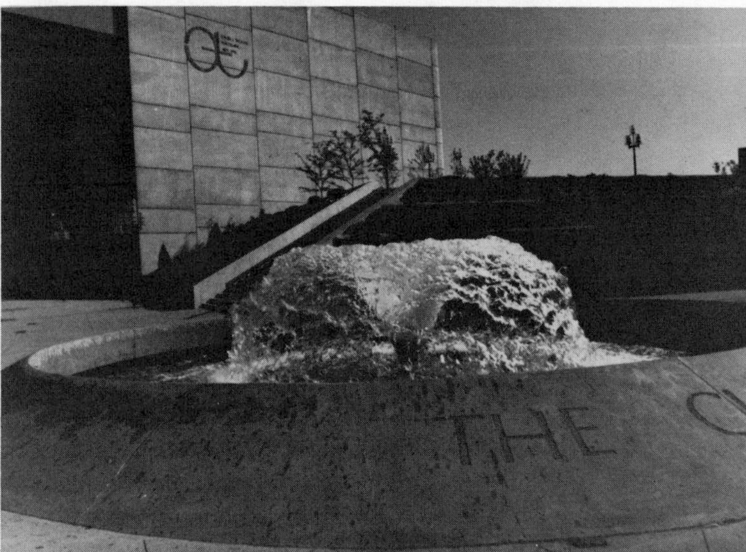
THE
12.19

Figures 12.16 – 12.19 *Fountains in college campus settings.*

Figures 12.20 – 12.21 *Fountains designed flush with the paving. When the water is off, pedestrians can use the area as a plaza.*

Figures 12.22 – 12.24 *Miscellaneous fountains.*

12.20

12.23

12.21

12.24

12.22

12.25

12.26

12.27

12.28

Figures 12.25 - 12.28 *Fountains as a part of new town design and development.*

Figures 12.29, 12.30, 12.32 *Miscellaneous fountains.*

Figure 12.31 *Use of rock and water in a civic center.*

Figure 12.33 *Rock and water in a zoo.*

12.29

12.30 Environmental Planning and Design

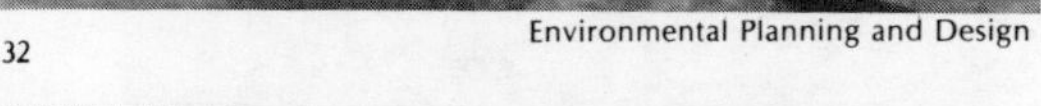

12.32 Environmental Planning and Design

12.31

12.33

12.34

12.35

Figure 12.34 *Oriental scarecrow using water.*

Figures 12.35 – 12.38 *Miscellaneous pools and fountains.*

12.36

12.37

12.38

12.39

12.40

12.41

12.42 Doede, Inc.

12.43

Figure 12.39 *Reflecting pool in a sculpture garden.*

Figures 12.40 - 12.43 *Miscellaneous pools and fountains.*

12.44

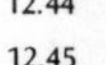

12.45

12.46

12.47

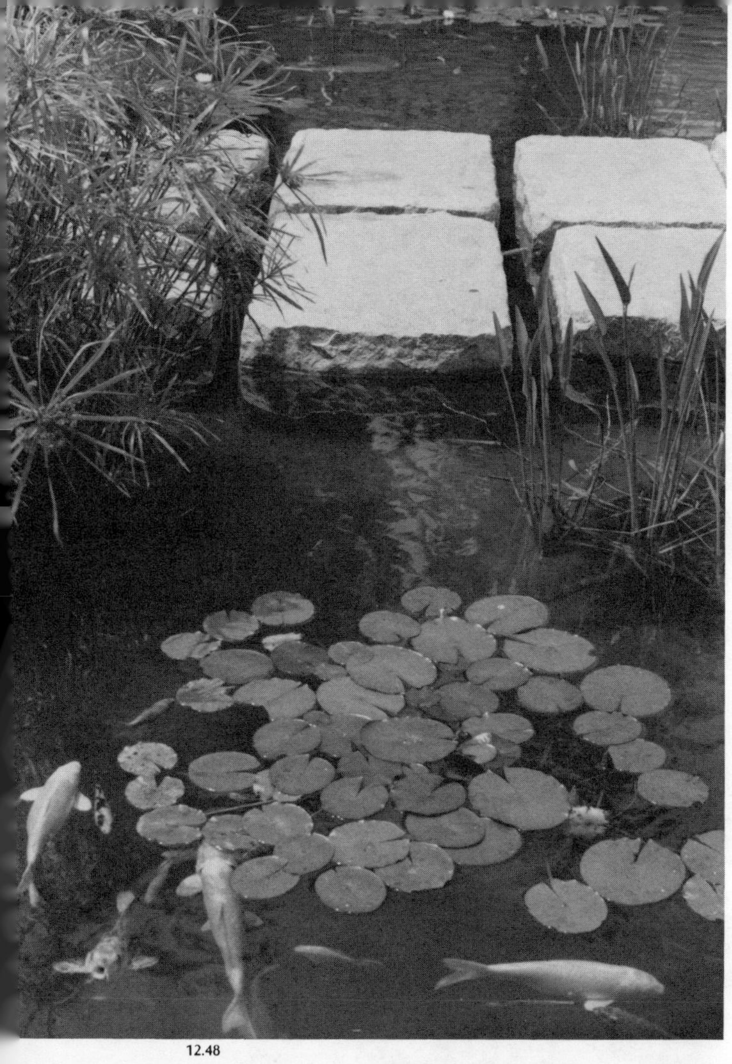

12.48

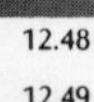

12.49

TRIAD
CENTER

12.50

Figures 12.44 – 12.50 *Fountains and water used in a wide variety of situations.*

12.51 Environmental Planning and Design

12.52

Figures 12.51 – 12.52 *Fountain in a downtown mall. Smooth black pebbles were set in concrete and form the base for water dropping from the jets. Equipment is recessed and a cast ring covers the center pit. The pump, filter, and controls are located in a nearby sub-surface vault accessible through a manhole.*

12.53 Environmental Planning and Design

12.54

Figures 12.53 – 12.54 *Fountain in a downtown mall. Ceramic tile is used to create the pattern in the bottom of this shallow fountain. The deeper equipment pit is covered with a cast grate. Projecting through and above the grate is the central geyser jet encircled by small multi-jet heads, overflow, and electronic water level control. Lights and waterproof junction box are below the grate.*

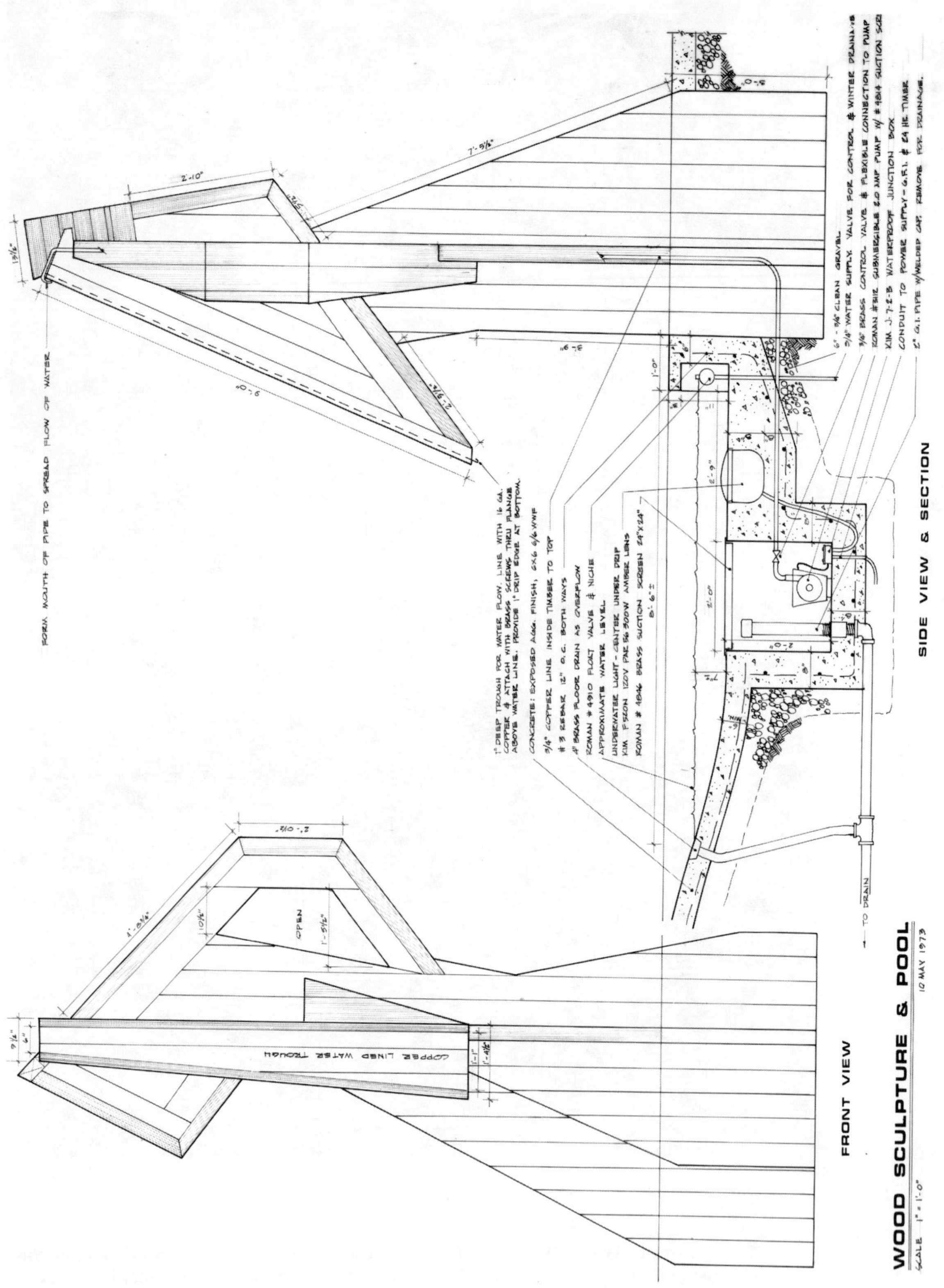
FORM MOUTH OF PIPE TO SPREAD FLOW OF WATER
1" DEEP TROUGH FOR WATER FLOW. LINE WITH 16 GA. COPPER & ATTACH WITH BRASS SCREWS THRU FLANGE ABOVE WATER LINE. PROVIDE 1" DRIP EDGE AT BOTTOM.
CONCRETE: EXPOSED AGG. FINISH, 6X6 6/6 WWF
3/4" COPPER LINE INSIDE TIMBER TO TOP
3 REBAR 12" O.C. BOTH WAYS
4" BRASS FLOOR DRAIN AS OVERFLOW
ROMAN # 4910 FLOAT VALVE & NICHE
APPROXIMATE WATER LEVEL
UNDERWATER LIGHT - CENTER UNDER DRIP
KIM P52ON 120V PAR 56 300W AMBER LENS
ROMAN # 4846 BRASS SUCTION SCREEN 24"X24"
6" - 3/4" CLEAN GRAVEL
3/4" WATER SUPPLY. VALVE FOR CONTROL & WINTER DRAINAGE
3/4" BRASS CONTROL VALVE & FLEXIBLE CONNECTION TO PUMP
ROMAN #812 SUBMERSIBLE 1/2 HP PUMP W/ # 4814 SUCTION SCREEN
KIM J-7-E-B WATERPROOF JUNCTION BOX
CONDUIT TO POWER SUPPLY - G.F.I. & 24 HR TIMER
2" G.I. PIPE W/WELDED CAP. REMOVE FOR DRAINAGE.
SIDE VIEW & SECTION
TO DRAIN
OPEN
COPPER LINED WATER TROUGH
FRONT VIEW
WOOD SCULPTURE & POOL
SCALE 1" = 1'-0"
10 MAY 1973

Figure 12.55 *Fountain details.*

Walker-Harris-Associates-Inc.

Figures 12.56 – 12.58 *Terraced fountains.*

12.56

12.57

12.58

12.59

12.60

Figures 12.59 – 12.60 *Tall fountains, one in a community lake, and the other on a college campus.*

12.61

12.62

12.63

12.64

Figures 12.61 – 12.62 *Waterwalls.*

Figures 12.63 – 12.66 *Miscellaneous fountains in parks and shopping centers.*

Figure 12.67 *Reflecting pool on the roof of a corporate headquarters.*

Figures 12.68 – 12.69 *Fountains in urban settings.*

12.65 Lawrence Halprin and Associates

12.66

12.67 CR3, inc.

Bob Porth, Hedrich-Blessing

12.68 Theodore Brickman Co.

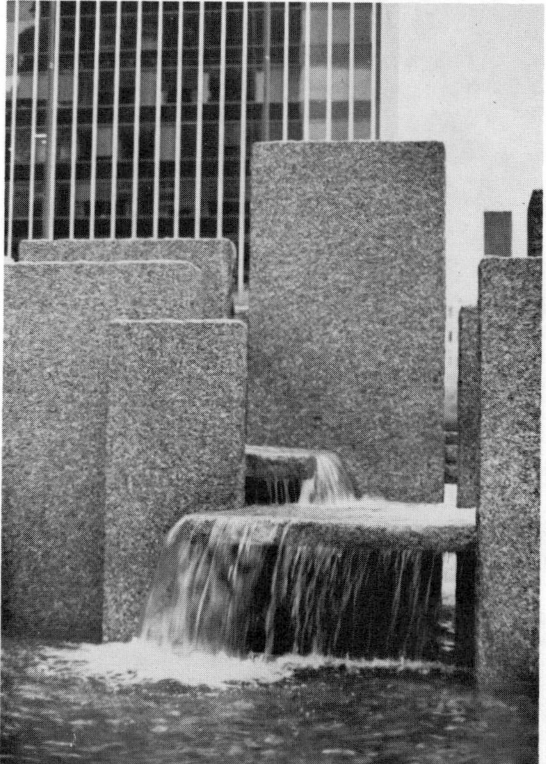
12.69 Sasaki Associates

1943
1918
1917

12.70 Donald Molnar

12.72

P
PEOPLES
BANK

12.71 James H. Bassett

12.73 Environmental Planning and Design

Figure 12.70 *Fountain memorial for war dead.*
Figures 12.71 – 12.73 *Fountains in urban malls.*

Figures 12.74 - 12.75 *Fountain and park in an urban redevelopment project.*

12.74

12.75

Browning-Day-Pollak-Associates-Inc.

12.76

12.77

Walker-Harris-Assoc

Figure 12.76 *Fountain in a civic center plaza.*

Figure 12.77 *Fountain plaza adjacent to a hospital entrance.*

Figure 12.78 *Fountain detail.*

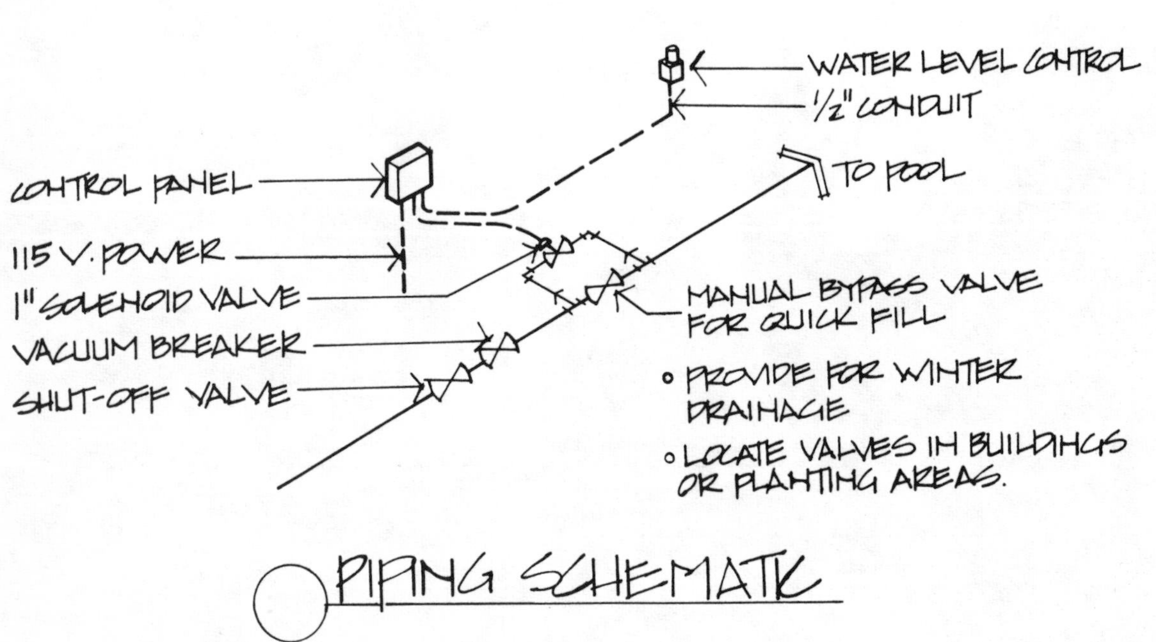
WATER LEVEL CONTROL
1/2" CONDUIT
TO POOL
CONTROL PANEL
115 V. POWER
1" SOLENOID VALVE
VACUUM BREAKER
SHUT-OFF VALVE
MANUAL BYPASS VALVE FOR QUICK FILL
• PROVIDE FOR WINTER DRAINAGE
• LOCATE VALVES IN BUILDINGS OR PLANTING AREAS.
PIPING SCHEMATIC

12.78

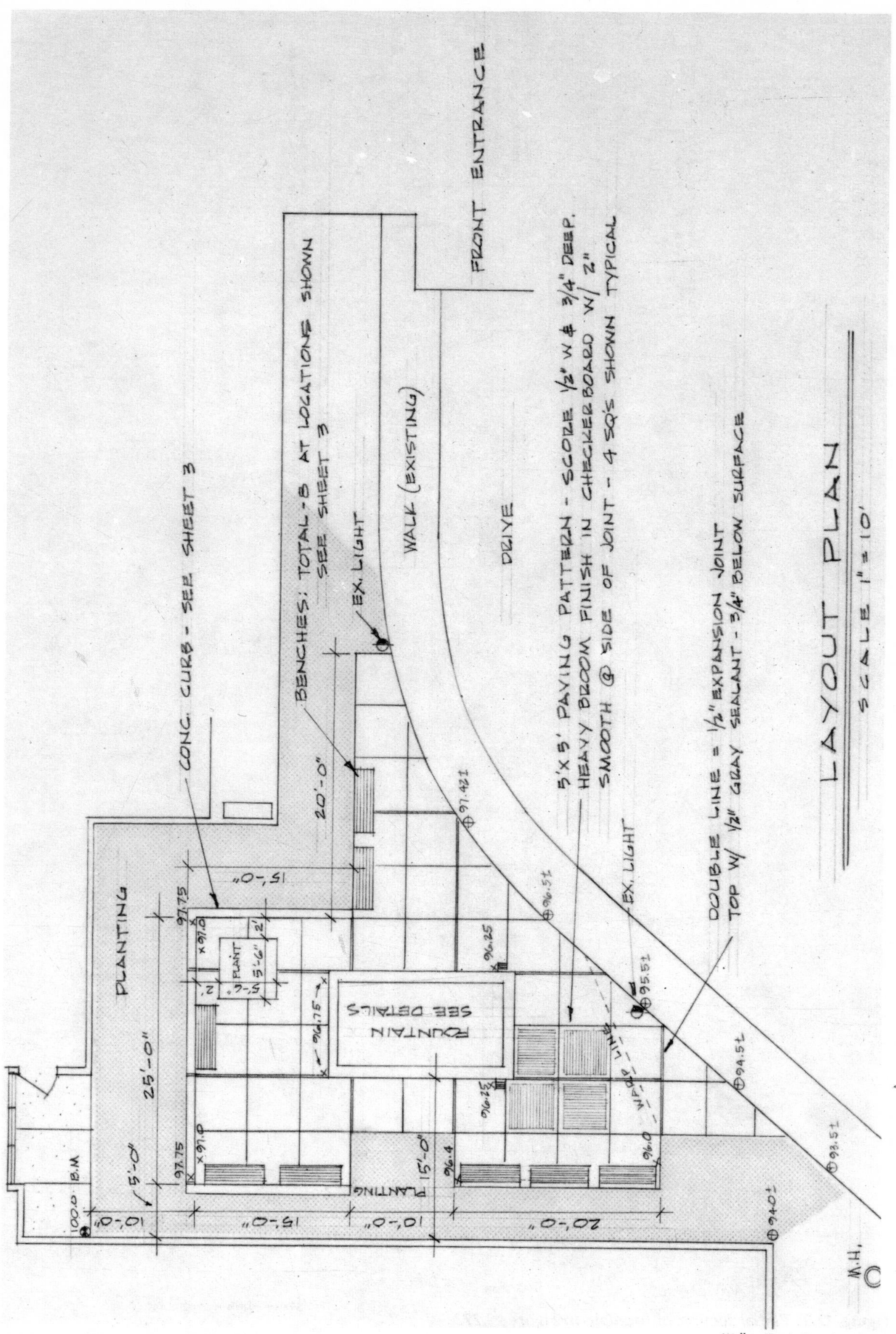

FRONT ENTRANCE
CONC. CURB - SEE SHEET 3
BENCHES; TOTAL - 8 AT LOCATIONS SHOWN
SEE SHEET 3
EX. LIGHT
WALK (EXISTING)
DRIVE
5'x5' PAVING PATTERN - SCORE 1/2" W & 3/4" DEEP.
HEAVY BROOM FINISH IN CHECKERBOARD W/ 2"
SMOOTH @ SIDE OF JOINT - 4 SQ'S SHOWN TYPICAL
DOUBLE LINE = 1/2" EXPANSION JOINT
TOP W/ 1/2" GRAY SEALANT - 3/4" BELOW SURFACE
PLANTING
FOUNTAIN
SEE DETAILS
LAYOUT PLAN
SCALE 1" = 10'

Figure 12.79 *Plan for the fountain in Figure 12.77.*

Walker-Harris-Associates-Inc.

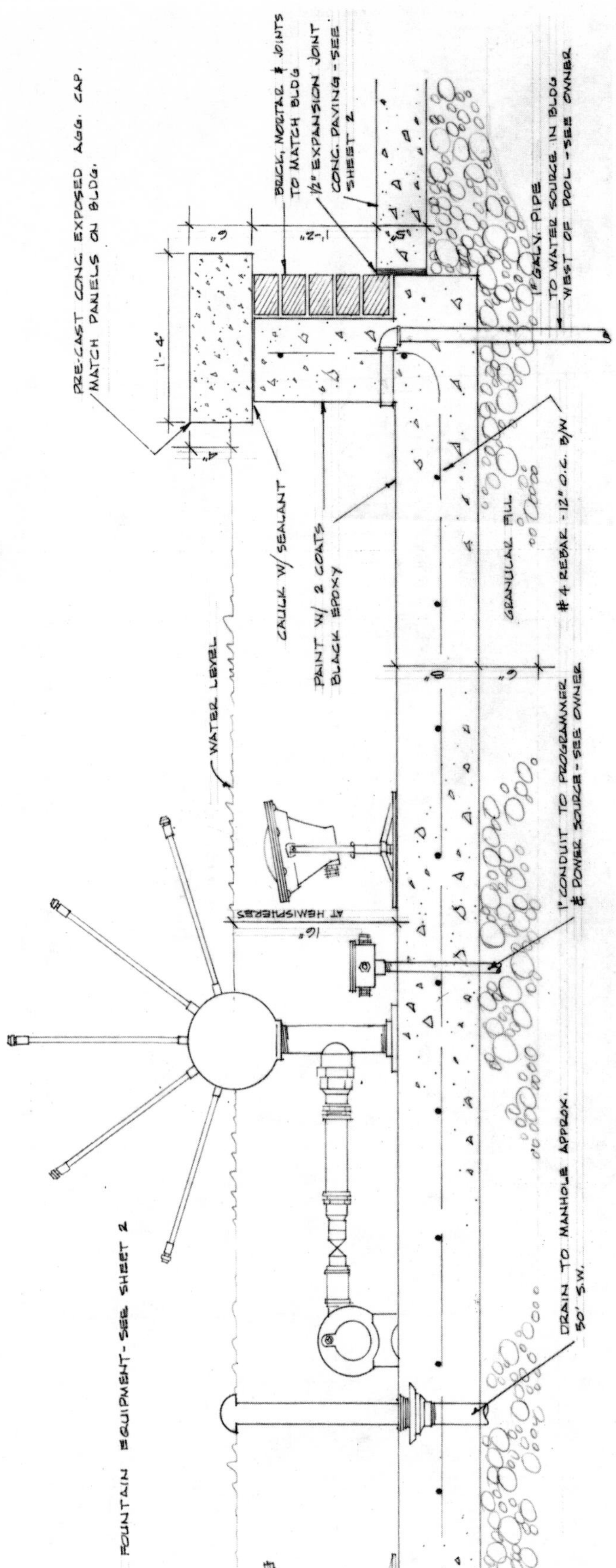
PRE-CAST CONC. EXPOSED AGG. CAP. MATCH PANELS ON BLDG.
1'-4"
BRICK, MORTAR & JOINTS TO MATCH BLDG
½" EXPANSION JOINT
CONC. PAVING - SEE SHEET 2
1" GALV. PIPE
TO WATER SOURCE IN BLDG WEST OF POOL - SEE OWNER
CAULK W/ SEALANT
PAINT W/ 2 COATS BLACK EPOXY
GRANULAR FILL
#4 REBAR - 12" O.C. B/W
WATER LEVEL
1" CONDUIT TO PROGRAMMER & POWER SOURCE - SEE OWNER
16" AT HEMISPHERES
DRAIN TO MANHOLE APPROX. 50' S.W.
FOUNTAIN EQUIPMENT - SEE SHEET 2
Walker-Harris-Associates-Inc.

Figure 12.80 *Partial section of fountain in Figure 12.77.*

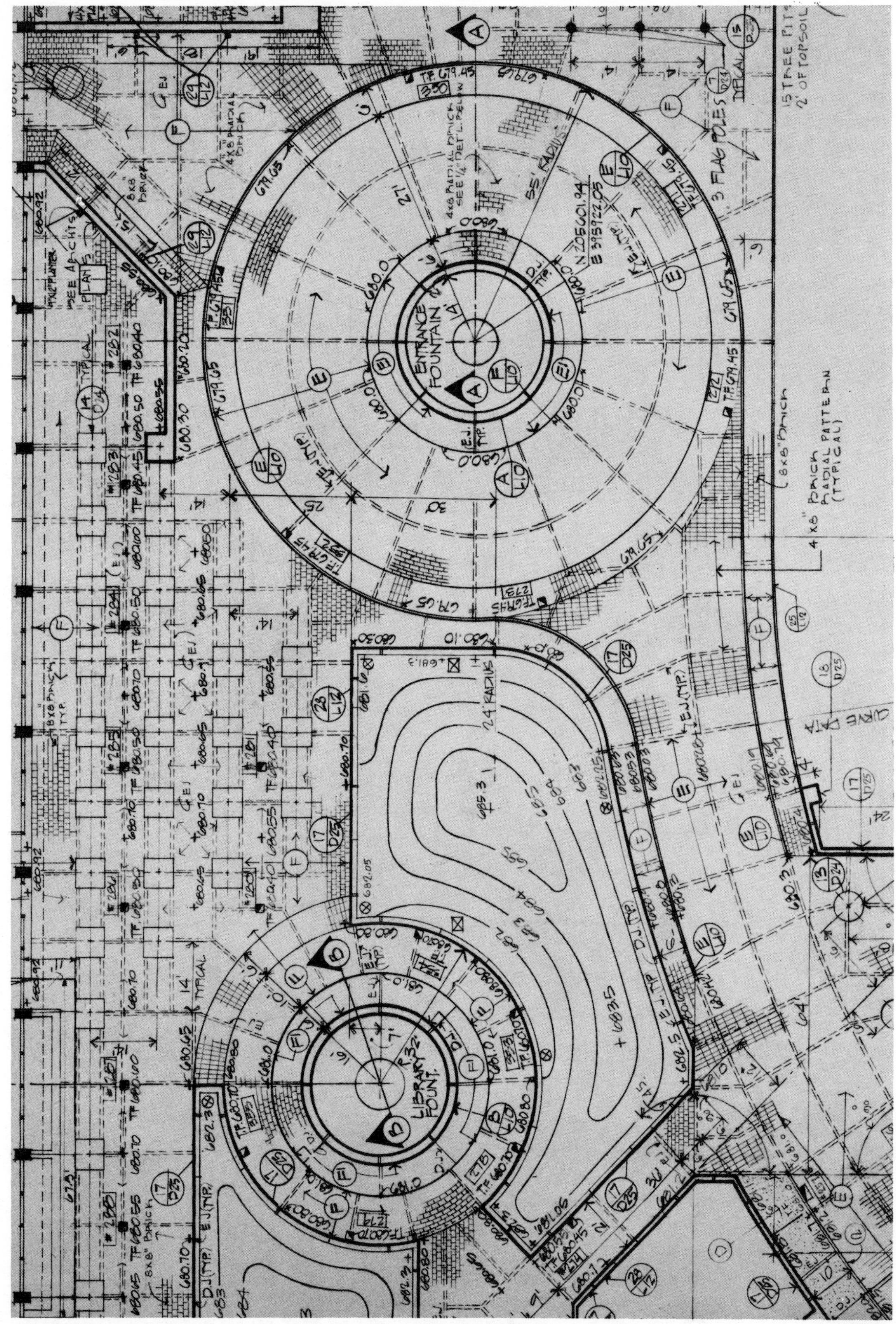

Figure 12.81 *Plan for a fountain – see details on pages 448 to 452.*

CR3, inc.

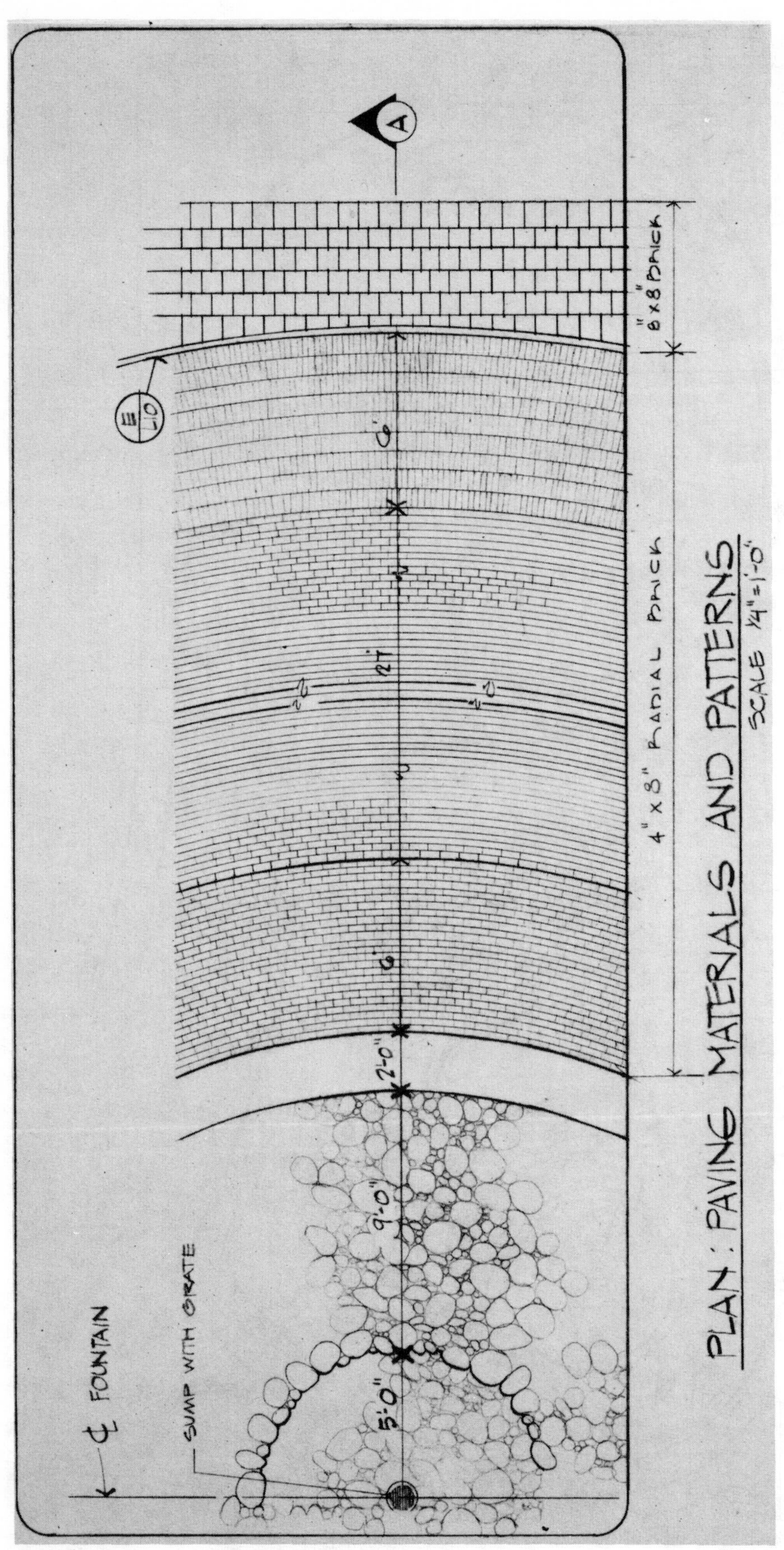

PLAN : PAVING MATERIALS AND PATTERNS
SCALE 1/4" = 1'-0"
4" x 8" RADIAL BRICK
8" x 8" BRICK
SUMP WITH GRATE
℄ FOUNTAIN
A
5'-0"
9'-0"
2'-0"
6'
12'

CR3, inc.

Figure 12.82 *Details for fountain in Figure 12.81.*

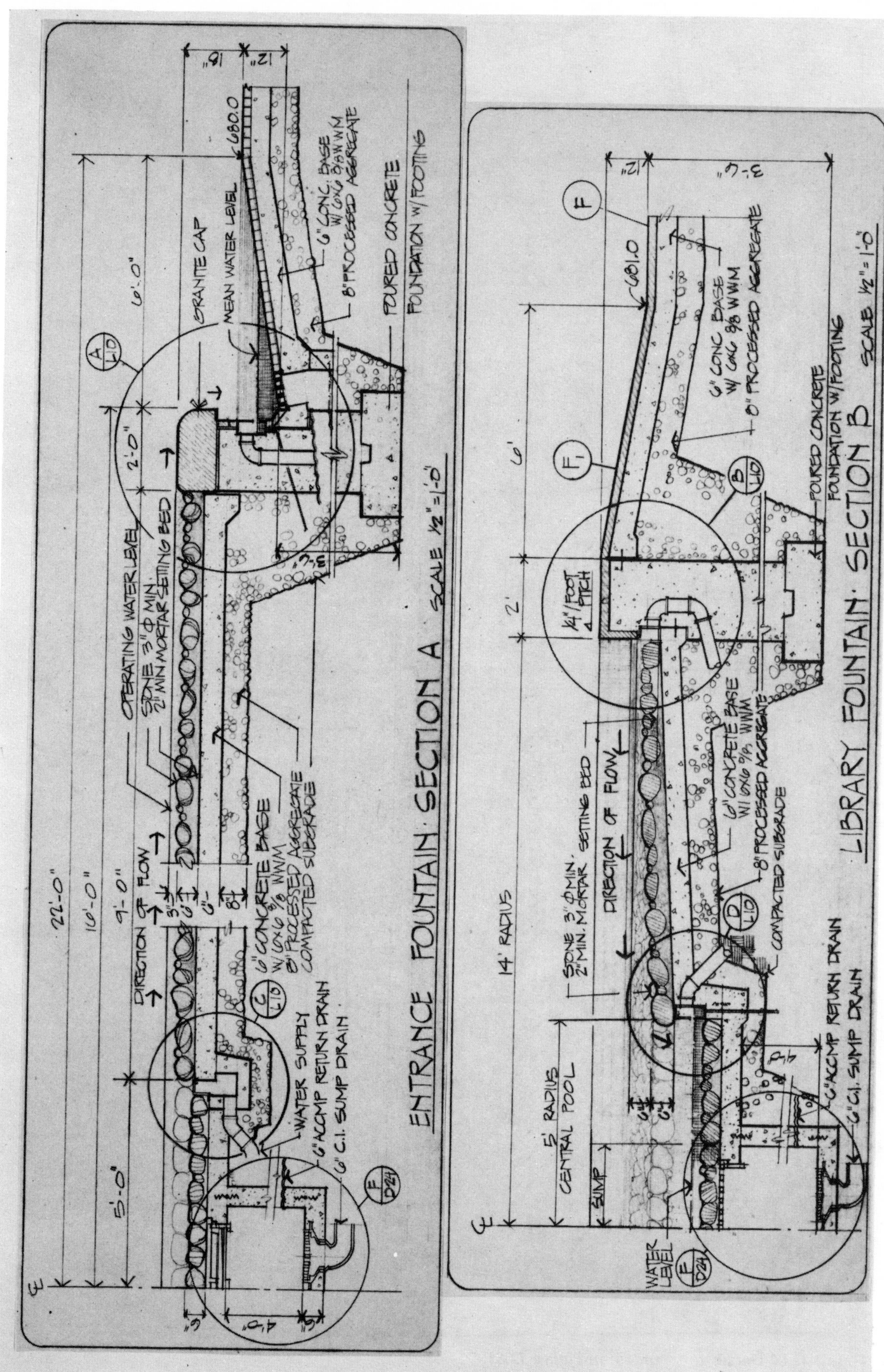
ENTRANCE FOUNTAIN SECTION A
SCALE 1/2"=1'-0"
22'-0"
16'-0"
9'-0"
6'-0"
5'-0"
2'-0"
GRANITE CAP
MEAN WATER LEVEL
680.0
6" CONC. BASE W/ 6X6 8/8 WWM
8" PROCESSED AGGREGATE
POURED CONCRETE FOUNDATION W/FOOTING
OPERATING WATER LEVEL
STONE 3" Φ MIN.
2" MIN MORTAR SETTING BED
DIRECTION OF FLOW
6" CONCRETE BASE W/ 6X6 9/9 WWM
8" PROCESSED AGGREGATE
COMPACTED SUBGRADE
WATER SUPPLY
6" ACCMP RETURN DRAIN
6" C.I. SUMP DRAIN
LIBRARY FOUNTAIN SECTION B
SCALE 1/2"=1'-0"
681.0
1/4"/FOOT PITCH
14' RADIUS
5' RADIUS
CENTRAL POOL
SUMP
WATER LEVEL
STONE 3" Φ MIN.
2" MIN. MORTAR SETTING BED
DIRECTION OF FLOW
6" CONCRETE BASE W/ 6X6 9/9 WWM
8" PROCESSED AGGREGATE
COMPACTED SUBGRADE
6" CONC BASE W/ 6X6 9/8 WWM
8" PROCESSED AGGREGATE
POURED CONCRETE FOUNDATION W/FOOTING
6" ACCMP RETURN DRAIN
6" C.I. SUMP DRAIN

Figure 12.83 *Details for fountain in Figure 12.81.*

CR3, inc.

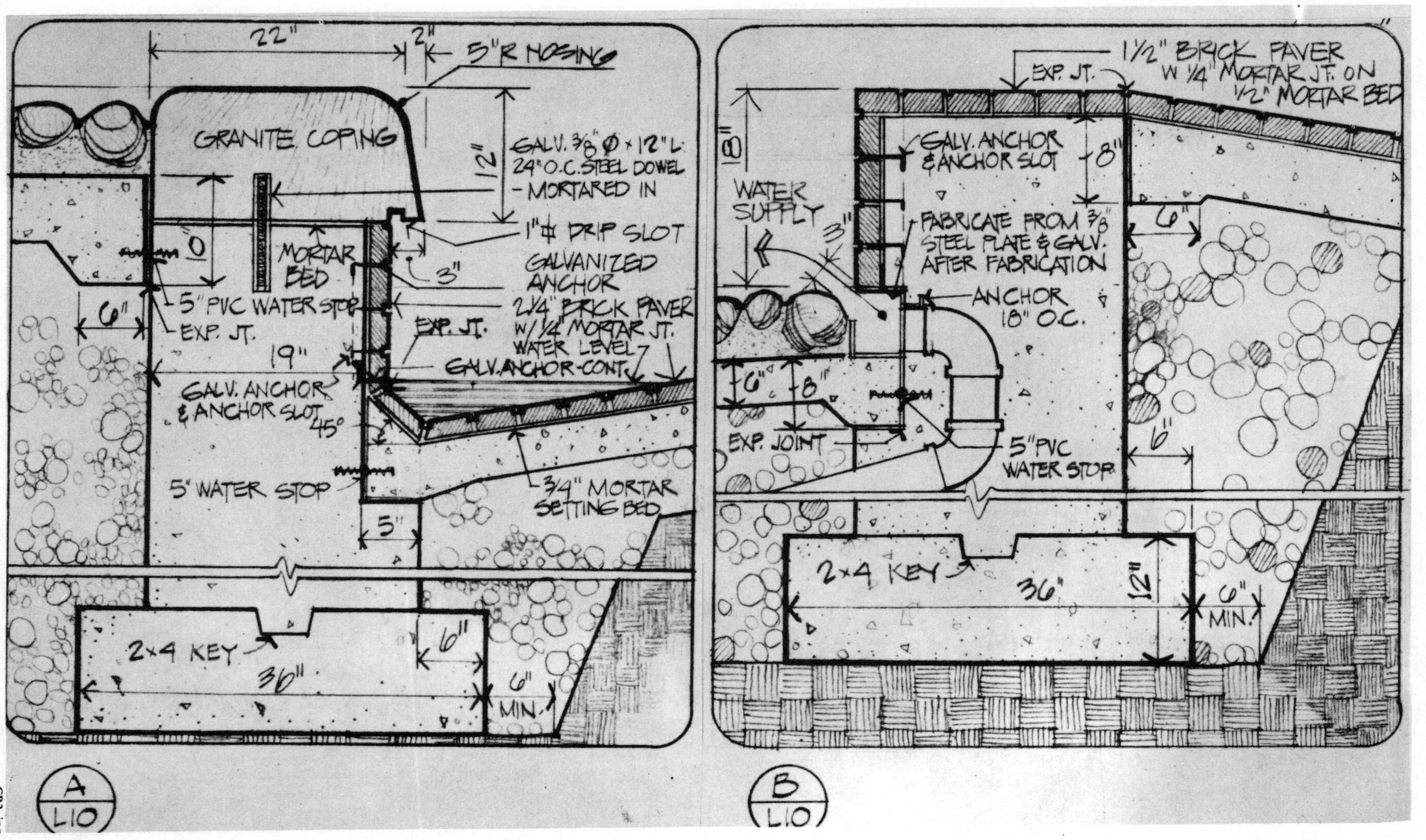
22"
2"
5" R NOSING
GRANITE COPING
12"
GALV. 3/8" Ø × 12" L. 24" O.C. STEEL DOWEL - MORTARED IN
10"
1" Ø DRIP SLOT
MORTAR BED
3"
GALVANIZED ANCHOR
5" PVC WATER STOP
EXP. JT.
2 1/4" BRICK PAVER W/ 1/4" MORTAR JT.
EXP. JT.
WATER LEVEL
6"
19"
GALV. ANCHOR-CONT.
GALV. ANCHOR & ANCHOR SLOT
45°
5" WATER STOP
3/4" MORTAR SETTING BED
5"
2×4 KEY
36"
6"
6" MIN.
A
L10
1 1/2" BRICK PAVER W 1/4" MORTAR JT. ON 1/2" MORTAR BED
EXP. JT.
18"
GALV. ANCHOR & ANCHOR SLOT
8"
WATER SUPPLY
3"
FABRICATE FROM 3/8" STEEL PLATE & GALV. AFTER FABRICATION
6"
ANCHOR 18" O.C.
6"
8"
EXP. JOINT
5" PVC WATER STOP
6"
2×4 KEY
36"
12"
6" MIN.
B
L10

CR3, inc.

Figure 12.84 *Details for fountain in Figure 12.81.*

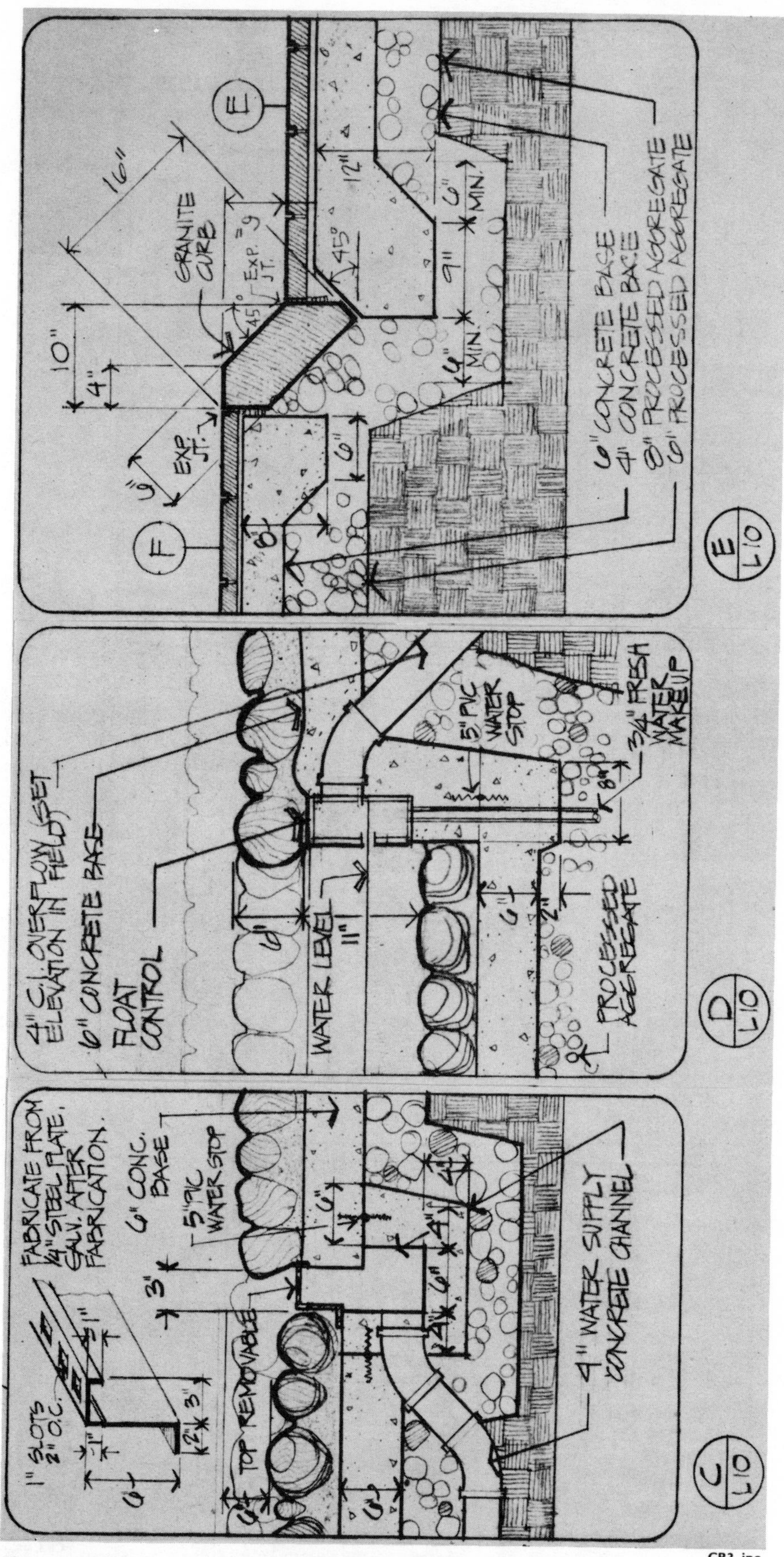

CR3, inc.

Figure 12.85 *Details for fountain in Figure 12.81.*

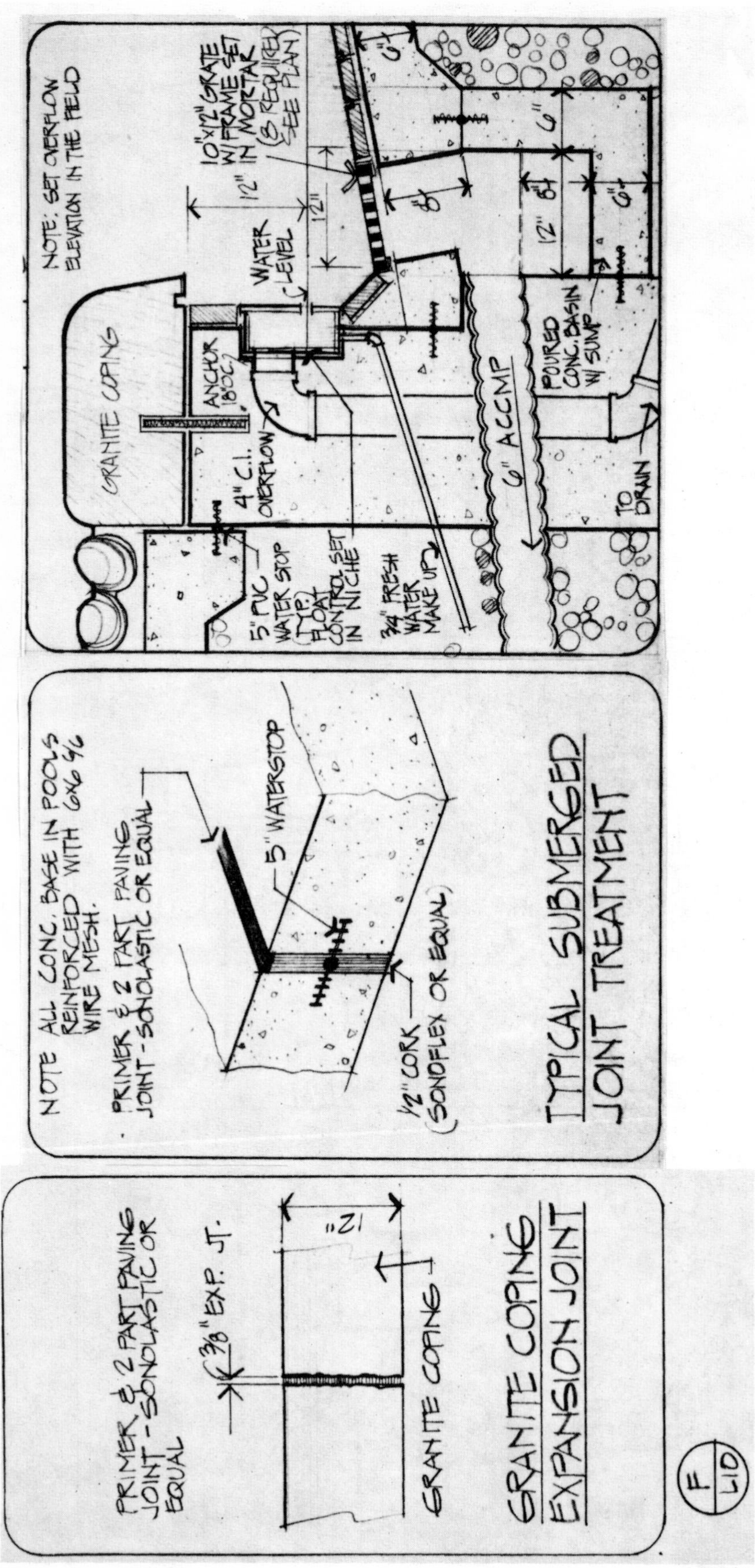

PRIMER & 2 PART PAVING JOINT - SONOLASTIC OR EQUAL
3/8" EXP. JT.
12"
GRANITE COPING
GRANITE COPING EXPANSION JOINT
F
L10
NOTE ALL CONC. BASE IN POOLS REINFORCED WITH 6x6 6/6 WIRE MESH.
PRIMER & 2 PART PAVING JOINT - SONOLASTIC OR EQUAL
5" WATERSTOP
1/2" CORK (SONOFLEX OR EQUAL)
TYPICAL SUBMERGED JOINT TREATMENT
NOTE: SET OVERFLOW ELEVATION IN THE FIELD
GRANITE COPING
ANCHOR 18" O.C.
4" C.I. OVERFLOW
WATER LEVEL
10"x12" GRATE W/ FRAME SET IN MORTAR (3 REQUIRED SEE PLAN)
12"
8"
6"
5" PVC WATER STOP (TYP.)
FLOAT CONTROL SET IN NICHE
3/4" FRESH WATER MAKE UP
6" ACCMP
POURED CONC. BASIN W/ SUMP
TO DRAIN

CR3, inc.

Figure 12.86 *Details for fountain in Figure 12.81.*

Figure 12.87 *In a reverse to most fountains, water leaves the sides and cascades into the center.*

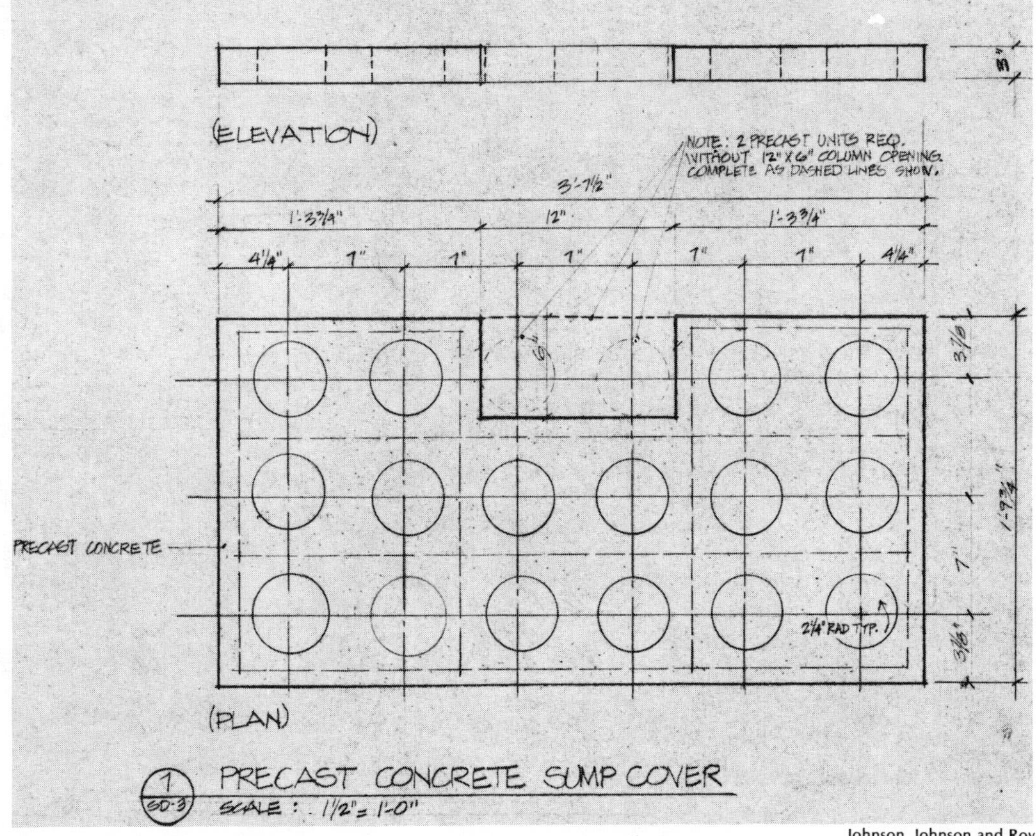
(ELEVATION)
NOTE: 2 PRECAST UNITS REQ. WITHOUT 12" X 6" COLUMN OPENING. COMPLETE AS DASHED LINES SHOW.
3'-7½"
1'-3¾"
12"
1'-3¾"
4¼"
7"
7"
7"
7"
7"
4¼"
3⅜"
1'-9¾"
7"
3⅜"
PRECAST CONCRETE
2¼" RAD TYP.
(PLAN)
1
SD-3
PRECAST CONCRETE SUMP COVER
SCALE : 1½" = 1'-0"

Johnson, Johnson and Roy

Figure 12.88 *Fountain detail.*

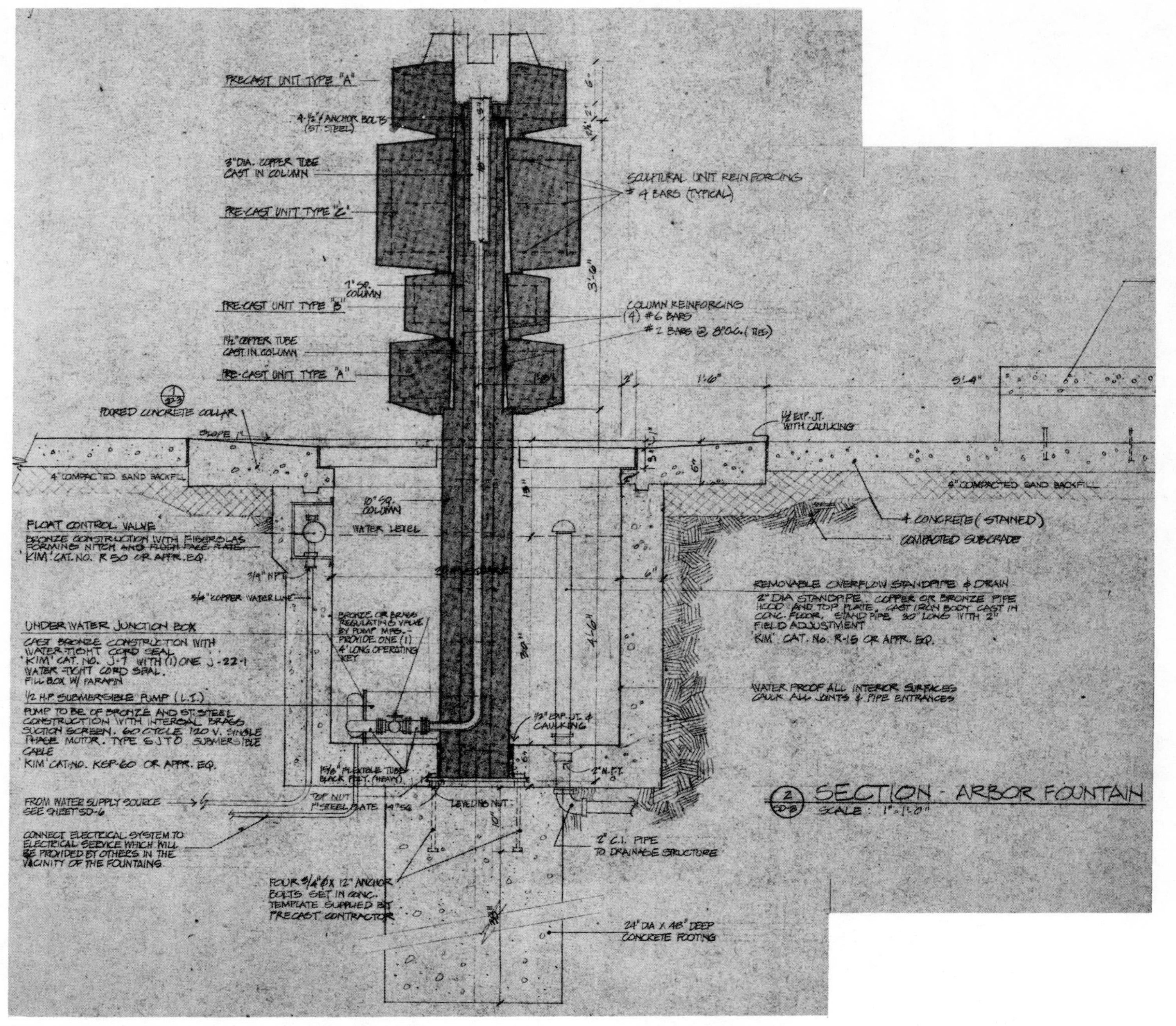

PRECAST UNIT TYPE "A"
4-½" ANCHOR BOLTS (ST. STEEL)
3" DIA. COPPER TUBE CAST IN COLUMN
PRE-CAST UNIT TYPE "C"
SCULPTURAL UNIT REINFORCING #4 BARS (TYPICAL)
7" SQ. COLUMN
PRE-CAST UNIT TYPE "B"
COLUMN REINFORCING (4) #6 BARS #2 BARS @ 8" O.C. (TIES)
1½" COPPER TUBE CAST IN COLUMN
PRE-CAST UNIT TYPE "A"
POURED CONCRETE COLLAR
SLOPE
½" EXP. JT. WITH CAULKING
4" COMPACTED SAND BACKFILL
10" SQ. COLUMN
WATER LEVEL
4" CONCRETE (STAINED)
COMPACTED SUBGRADE
FLOAT CONTROL VALVE
BRONZE CONSTRUCTION WITH FIBERGLAS FORMING NITCH AND FLUSH FACE PLATE. KIM' CAT. NO. R 50 OR APPR. EQ.
3/4" NPT
3/4" COPPER WATER LINE
BRONZE OR BRASS REGULATING VALVE BY PUMP MFG. PROVIDE ONE (1) 4' LONG OPERATING KEY
REMOVABLE OVERFLOW STANDPIPE & DRAIN
2" DIA STANDPIPE. COPPER OR BRONZE PIPE HOOD AND TOP PLATE. CAST IRON BODY CAST IN CONC. FLOOR. STANDPIPE 30" LONG WITH 2" FIELD ADJUSTMENT
KIM' CAT. No. R-15 OR APPR. EQ.
UNDER WATER JUNCTION BOX
CAST BRONZE CONSTRUCTION WITH WATER TIGHT CORD SEAL KIM' CAT. NO. J-7 WITH (1) ONE J-22-1 WATER TIGHT CORD SEAL. FILL BOX W/ PARAFIN
½ H.P. SUBMERSIBLE PUMP (L.I.)
PUMP TO BE OF BRONZE AND ST. STEEL CONSTRUCTION WITH INTERNAL BRASS SUCTION SCREEN. 60 CYCLE 120 V. SINGLE PHASE MOTOR. TYPE SJTO SUBMERSIBLE CABLE
KIM' CAT. NO. KEP-60 OR APPR. EQ.
WATER PROOF ALL INTERIOR SURFACES CAULK ALL JOINTS & PIPE ENTRANCES
½" EXP. JT. & CAULKING
1⅝" FLEXIBLE TUBE BLACK POLY. (HEAVY)
2" N.P.T.
FROM WATER SUPPLY SOURCE SEE SHEET SD-6
TOP NUT
1" STEEL PLATE
LEVELING NUT
SECTION - ARBOR FOUNTAIN
SCALE: 1" = 1'-0"
CONNECT ELECTRICAL SYSTEM TO ELECTRICAL SERVICE WHICH WILL BE PROVIDED BY OTHERS IN THE VICINITY OF THE FOUNTAINS.
2" C.I. PIPE TO DRAINAGE STRUCTURE
FOUR ¾" Ø X 12" ANCHOR BOLTS SET IN CONC. TEMPLATE SUPPLIED BY PRECAST CONTRACTOR
24" DIA X 48" DEEP CONCRETE FOOTING

Figure 12.89 *Fountain details.*

Johnson, Johnson and Roy

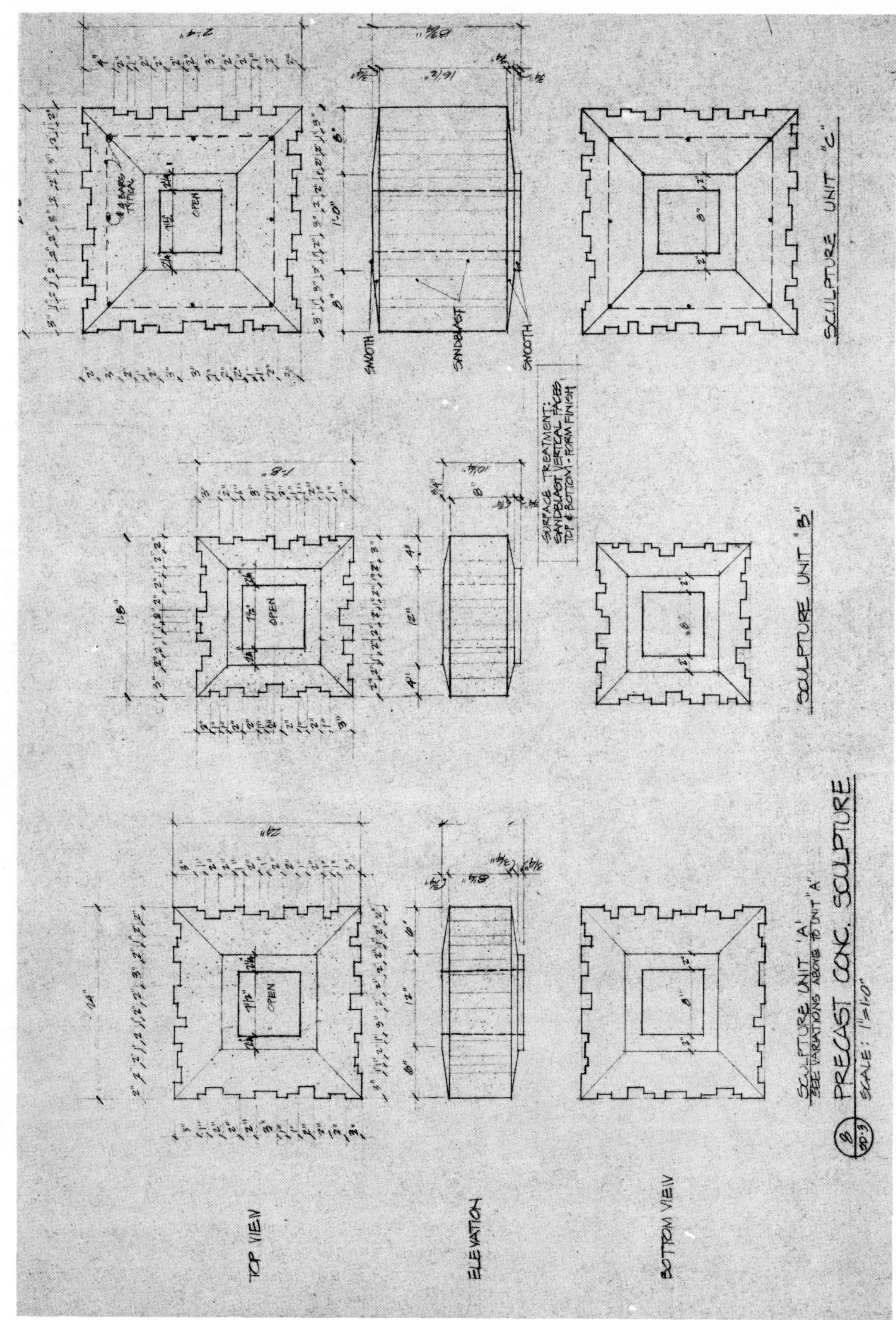
TOP VIEW
ELEVATION
BOTTOM VIEW
OPEN
SMOOTH
SANDBLAST
SMOOTH
SURFACE TREATMENT:
SANDBLAST VERTICAL FACES
TOP & BOTTOM - FORM FINISH
SCULPTURE UNIT 'A'
SEE VARIATIONS ABOVE TO UNIT "A"
PRECAST CONC. SCULPTURE
SCALE: 1"=1'-0"
SCULPTURE UNIT "B"
SCULPTURE UNIT "C"

Figure 12.90 *Details for fountain sculpture in Figure 12.89.*

Johnson, Johnson and Roy

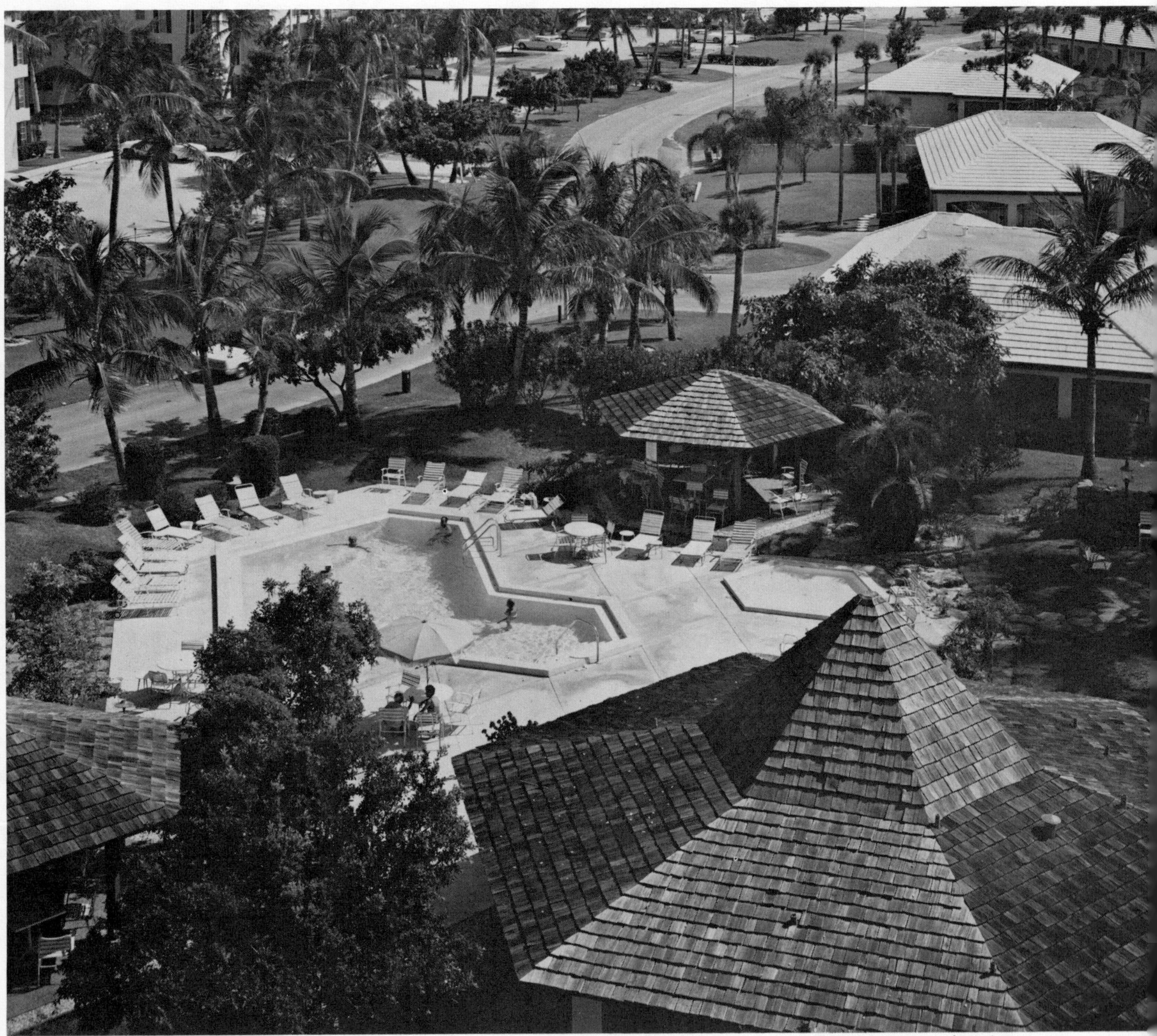

Edward D. Stone, Jr. and Associates

Figure 12.91 *Swimming pool with bathhouse, shelters and sun deck.*

13

Site Utilities

Because most utilities are not to be seen, they may not be as exciting to the site designer as paving, benches, walls, planters, etc. However, their presence is necessary and some could be critical to the successful functioning of a site. Some things, such as manhole covers, can either blend into or detract from the paving design.

This chapter includes such items as drain inlets, catch basins, manholes, trench drains, dry wells, curb hydrants, curb boxes, drinking fountains, telephone booths, and light fixtures. Nearly all of these items, in one form or another, can be obtained as catalog items from manufacturers. It is possible, in nearly every instance, to custom design something new and unique by careful coordination with a manufacturer during the design process. This will ensure that the product can be built and will provide an estimate of cost. A number of manufacturers suggest various installation techniques, and these suggestions can be used by the site designer as he selects a product for his particular project. Illustrated in the chapter are a number of these items as they were incorporated into construction drawings.

Chapter 3 discusses sizes and types of materials for utility pipes and culverts. Telephone and power companies now utilize direct burial cable for many installations except in urban areas where conduit is desirable or required.

REFERENCES FOR FURTHER READING

Irrigation Systems Design Handbook. Glendora, CA: RainBird, 1976.

Munson, A.E. *Construction Design for Landscape Architects*. New York: McGraw-Hill, 1974.

Ramsey, C.G., and Sleeper, H.R. *Architectural Graphics Standards*. 7th Edition. New York: Wiley, 1981.

Sears, B.G. "Surface Drainage," *Handbook of Landscape Architectural Construction*. Washington, DC: Landscape Architecture Foundation, 1973.

13.1 Betonwerk Munderkingen GmbH

13.2 Environmental Planning and Design

Figure 13.1 *No cutting is required to fit round pavers adjacent to a manhole cover.*

Figures 13.2 – 13.3 *Some examples of manhole covers which have been designed to blend with adjacent paving.*

13.3 Environmental Planning and Design

13.4

13.5

13.6

13.7

Figure 13.4 *Trench drain with a slate cover.*

Figure 13.5 *Trench drain with granite grate to match adjacent paving.*

Figure 13.6 *Metal grate outline with interior to match paving.*

Figure 13.7 *Metal grate for trench drain.*

13.8 Browning-Day-Pollak-Associates-Inc.

13.11 M. Paul Friedberg and Partners

13.9

13.12

13.10

Figures 13.8 – 13.9 *Trench drains.*

Figure 13.10 *Drainage slot drops water into intergrally connected corrugated metal pipe.*

Figures 13.11 – 13.12 *Shielded water hydrants.*

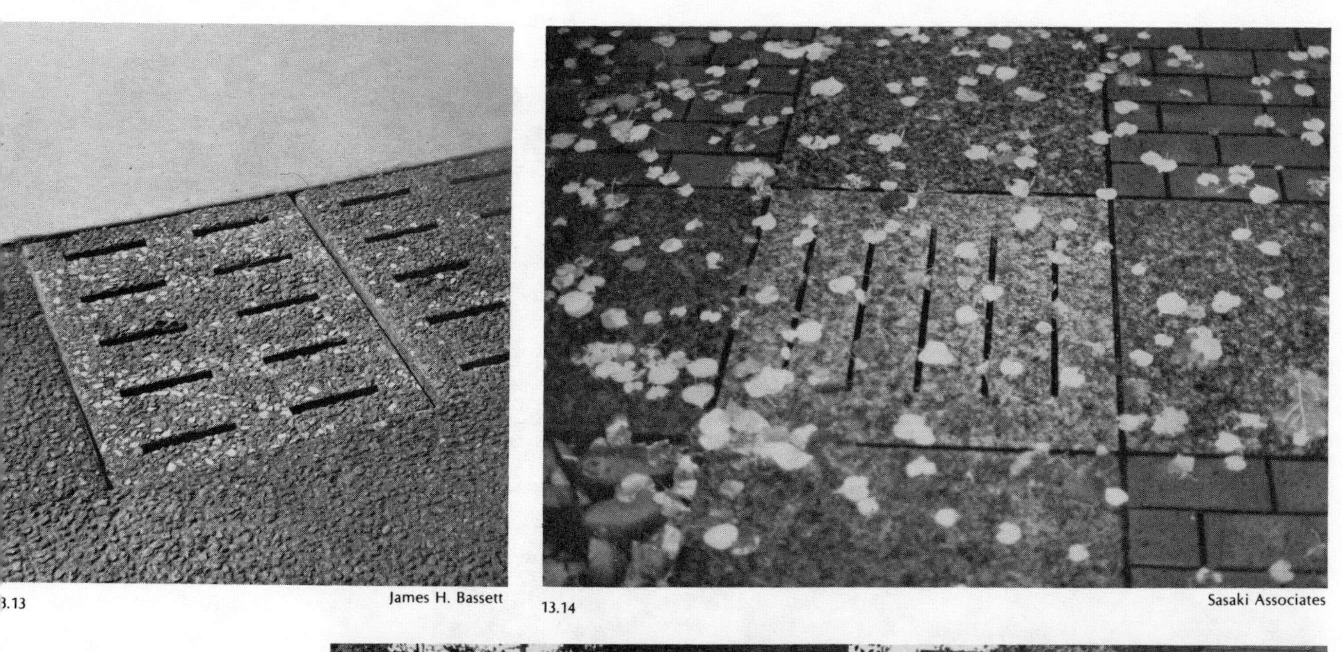

3.13 James H. Bassett

13.14 Sasaki Associates

13.15 James H. Bassett

Figures 13.13 – 13.14 *Pre-cast and cut stone catch basin grates.*

Figure 13.15 *A round pre-cast concrete pad matching the color and texture of the adjacent planter is used to cover an air vent.*

13.16

13.17

James H. Bassett

Figure 13.16 *Pass through drain in a brick wall. May reduce need for catch basins in some situations.*

Figure 13.17 *A slit in the riser catches the drainage water. The manhole cover in the tread provides access to the catch basin below.*

Figures 13.18 – 13.23 *Six different types of drainage grates.*

13.18

13.21 Lawrence Halprin and Associates

13.19

13.22 M. Paul Friedberg and Partners

13.20

13.23

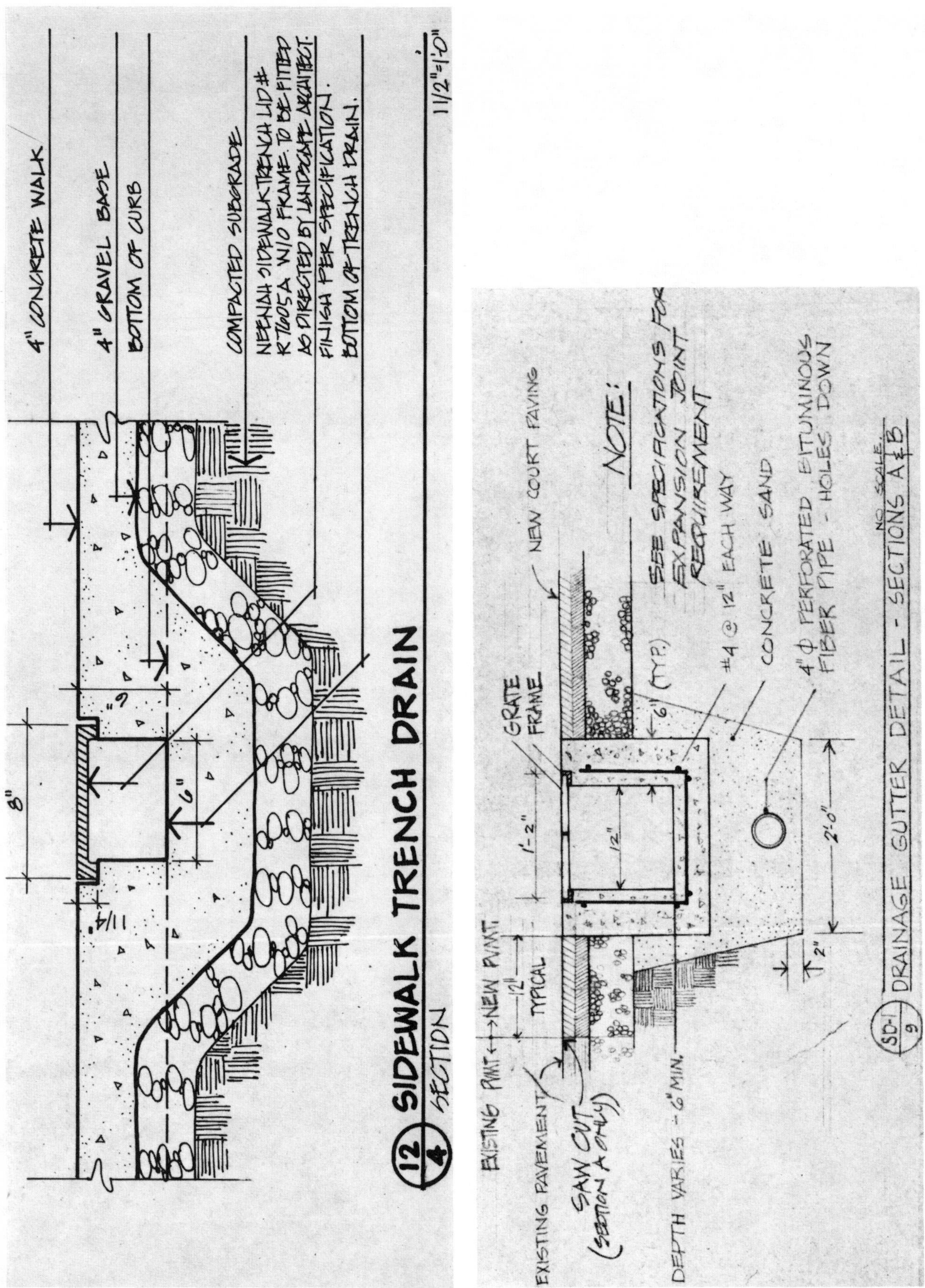
4" CONCRETE WALK
4" GRAVEL BASE
BOTTOM OF CURB
COMPACTED SUBGRADE
NEENAH SIDEWALK TRENCH LID # R-4005A W/O FRAME. TO BE FITTED AS DIRECTED BY LANDSCAPE ARCHITECT.
FINISH PER SPECIFICATION.
BOTTOM OF TRENCH DRAIN.
1 1/2"=1'-0"
8"
6"
6"
1 1/4
12
4
SIDEWALK TRENCH DRAIN
SECTION
EXISTING PVMT. ←→ NEW PVMT.
12"
TYPICAL
EXISTING PAVEMENT
SAW CUT (SECTION A ONLY)
DEPTH VARIES - 6" MIN.
GRATE
FRAME
NEW COURT PAVING
1'-2"
12"
6" (TYP.)
#4 @ 12" EACH WAY
CONCRETE SAND
4" ϕ PERFORATED BITUMINOUS FIBER PIPE - HOLES DOWN
2'-0"
2"
NOTE:
SEE SPECIFICATIONS FOR EXPANSION JOINT REQUIREMENT
SD-1
9
DRAINAGE GUTTER DETAIL - SECTIONS A & B
NO SCALE

Bonnell and Associates

Johnson, Johnson and Roy

Figure 13.24 *Trench drain details.*

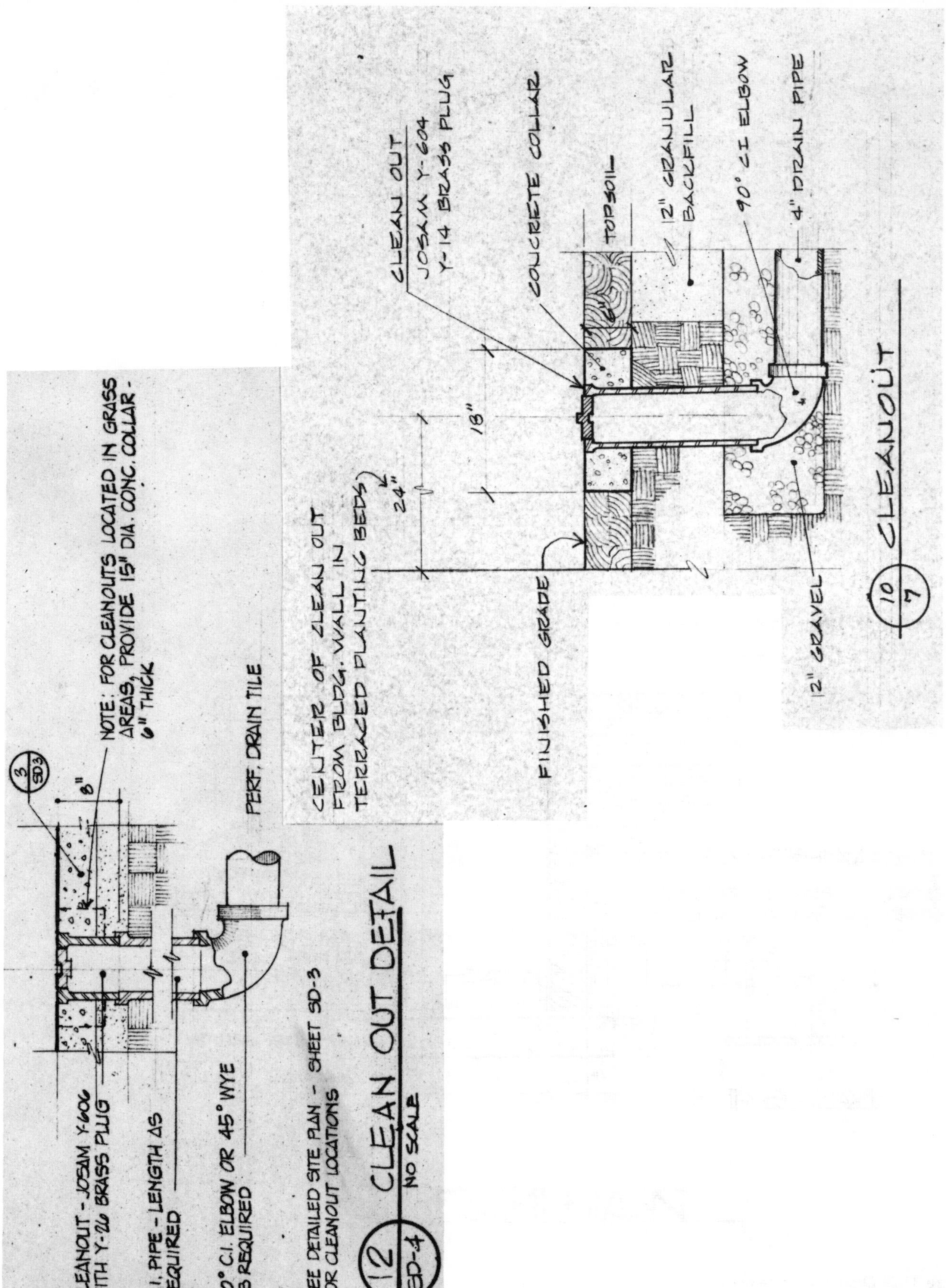
CLEANOUT - JOSAM Y-606 WITH Y-26 BRASS PLUG
C.I. PIPE - LENGTH AS REQUIRED
90° C.I. ELBOW OR 45° WYE AS REQUIRED
SEE DETAILED SITE PLAN - SHEET SD-3 FOR CLEANOUT LOCATIONS
12
SD-4
CLEAN OUT DETAIL
NO SCALE
3
SD3
8"
NOTE: FOR CLEANOUTS LOCATED IN GRASS AREAS, PROVIDE 15" DIA. CONC. COLLAR - 6" THICK
PERF. DRAIN TILE
CENTER OF CLEAN OUT FROM BLDG. WALL IN TERRACED PLANTING BEDS
24"
18"
FINISHED GRADE
CLEAN OUT
JOSAM Y-604
Y-14 BRASS PLUG
CONCRETE COLLAR
TOPSOIL
12" GRANULAR BACKFILL
90° CI ELBOW
4" DRAIN PIPE
12" GRAVEL
10
7
CLEANOUT

Figure 13.25 *Clean-out details.*

Johnson, Johnson and Roy

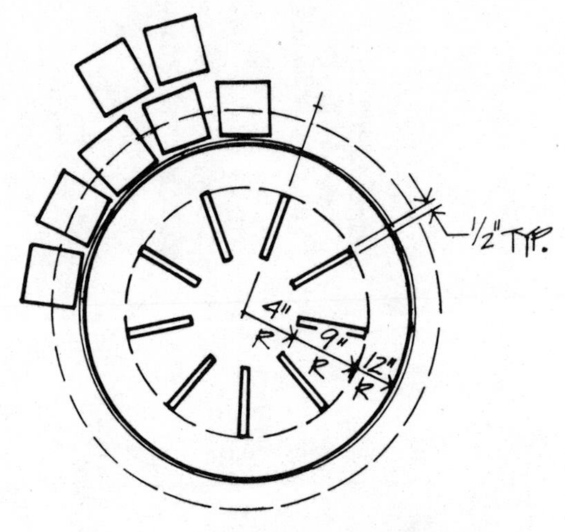
1/2" TYP.
4"
9"
12"
R
R
R
PLAN - GRANITE GRATE

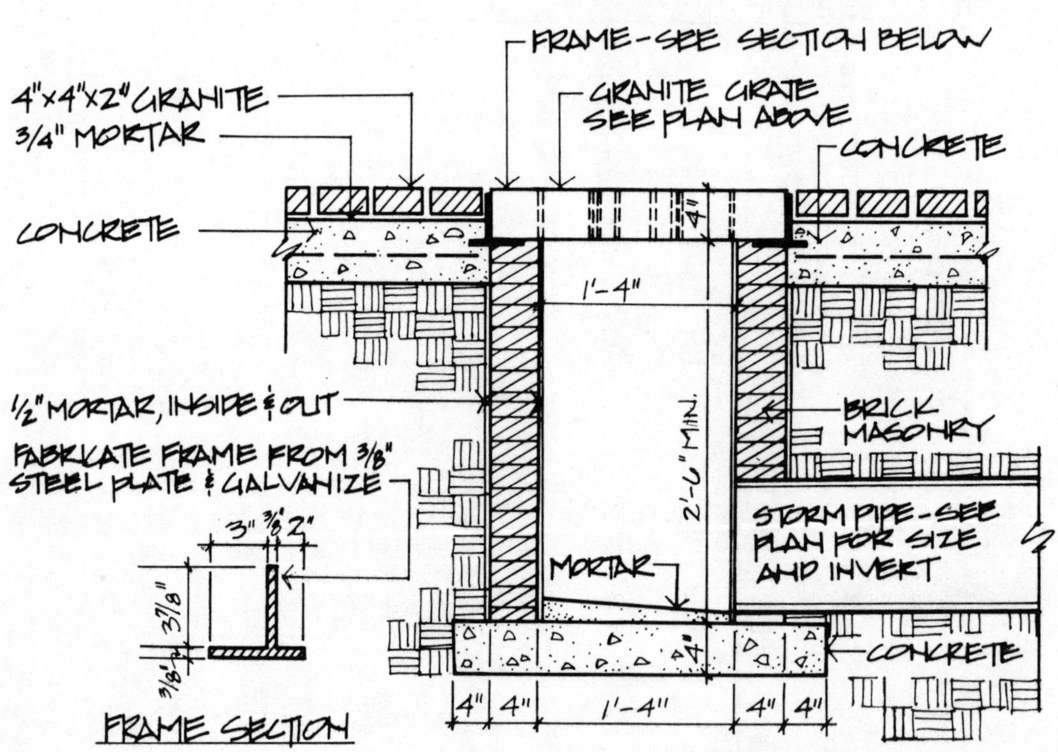
FRAME - SEE SECTION BELOW
4"x4"x2" GRANITE
GRANITE GRATE
SEE PLAN ABOVE
3/4" MORTAR
CONCRETE
CONCRETE
4"
1'-4"
1/2" MORTAR, INSIDE & OUT
BRICK
MASONRY
FABRICATE FRAME FROM 3/8"
STEEL PLATE & GALVANIZE
2'-6" MIN.
STORM PIPE - SEE
PLAN FOR SIZE
AND INVERT
3" 3/8" 2"
3 7/8"
3/8"
MORTAR
4"
CONCRETE
4" 4" 1'-4" 4" 4"
FRAME SECTION

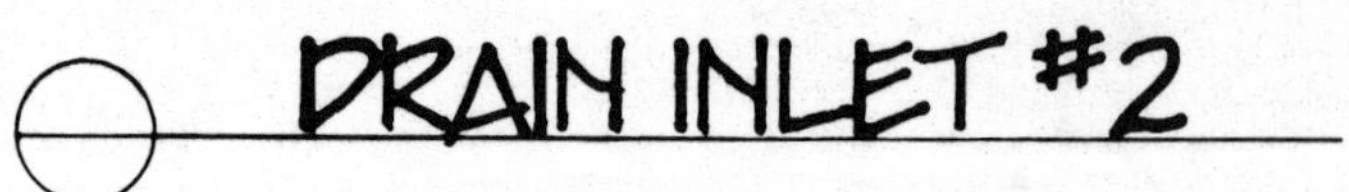
DRAIN INLET #2

Figure 13.26 *Drainage grate details.*

Johnson, Johnson and Roy

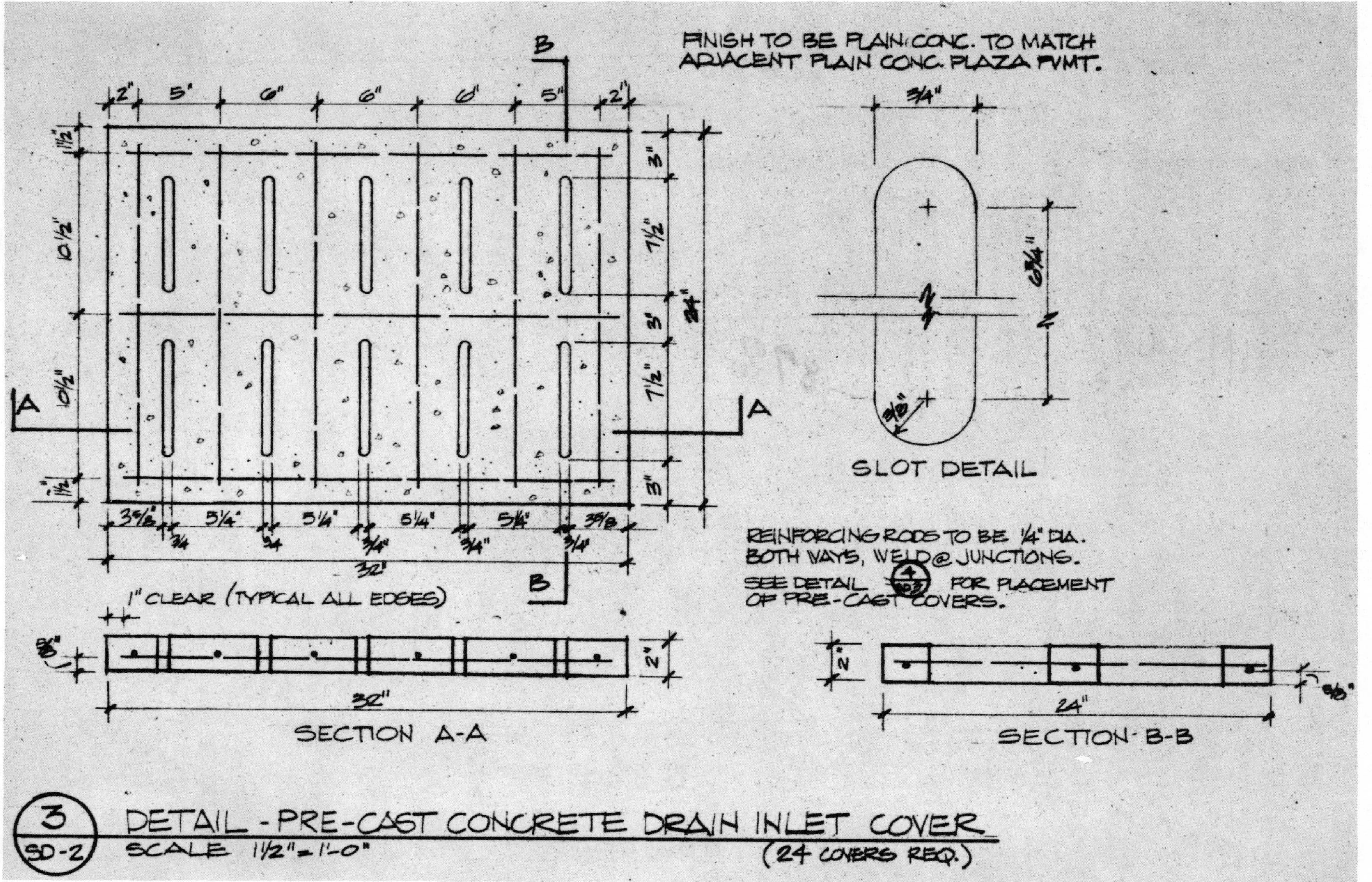
FINISH TO BE PLAIN CONC. TO MATCH ADJACENT PLAIN CONC. PLAZA PVMT.
SLOT DETAIL
REINFORCING RODS TO BE 1/4" DIA. BOTH WAYS, WELD @ JUNCTIONS.
SEE DETAIL FOR PLACEMENT OF PRE-CAST COVERS.
1" CLEAR (TYPICAL ALL EDGES)
SECTION A-A
SECTION B-B
3
SD-2
DETAIL - PRE-CAST CONCRETE DRAIN INLET COVER
SCALE 1 1/2" = 1'-0"
(24 COVERS REQ.)

Figure 13.27 *Drainage grate details.*

Johnson, Johnson and Roy

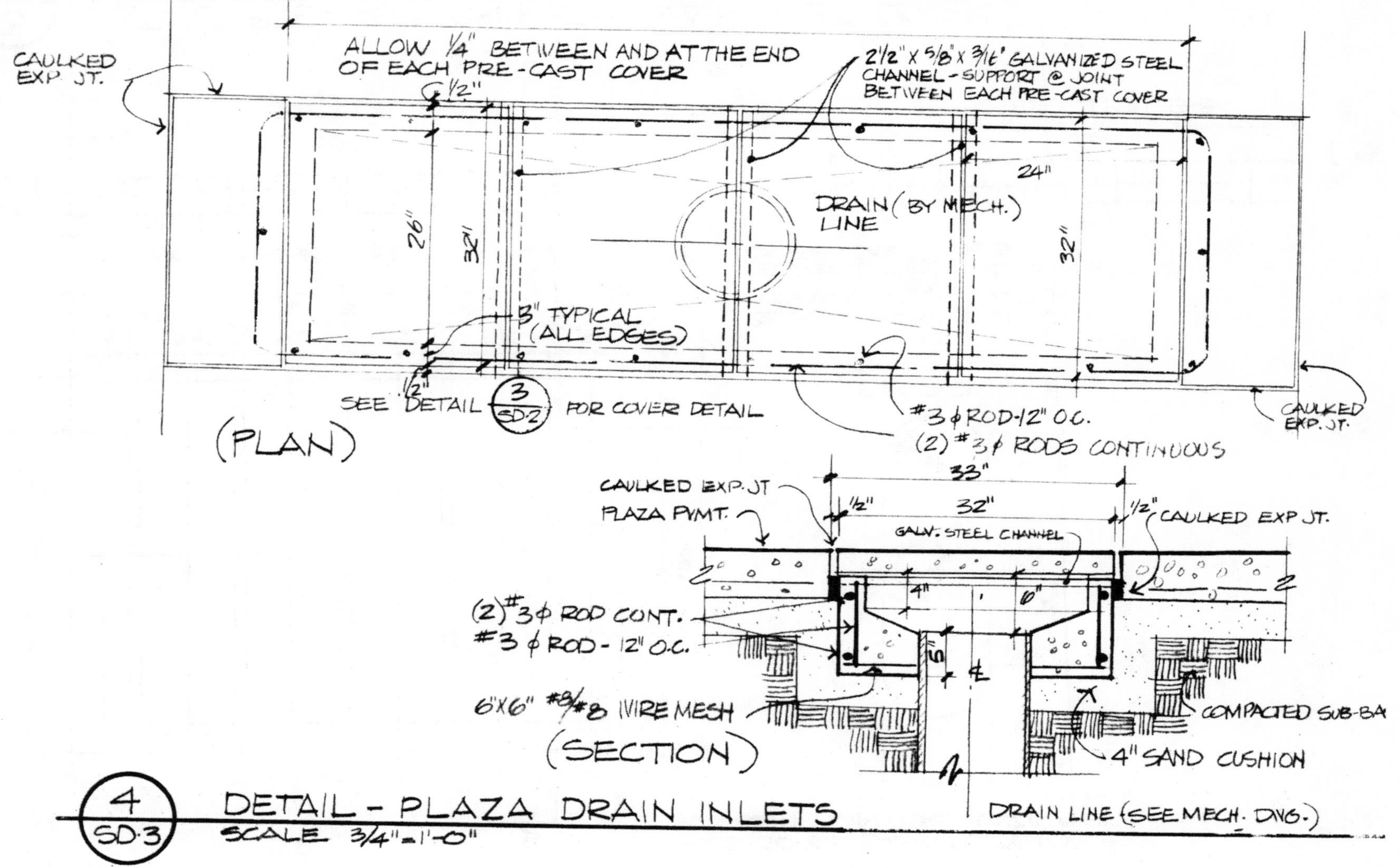
ALLOW 1/4" BETWEEN AND AT THE END OF EACH PRE-CAST COVER
1/2"
2 1/2" x 5/8" x 3/16" GALVANIZED STEEL CHANNEL - SUPPORT @ JOINT BETWEEN EACH PRE-CAST COVER
CAULKED EXP. JT.
24"
DRAIN (BY MECH.) LINE
26"
32"
32"
3" TYPICAL (ALL EDGES)
1/2"
SEE DETAIL 3 SD-2 FOR COVER DETAIL
#3 ϕ ROD-12" O.C.
(2) #3 ϕ RODS CONTINUOUS
CAULKED EXP. JT.
(PLAN)
CAULKED EXP. JT
PLAZA PVMT.
33"
1/2"
32"
1/2" CAULKED EXP JT.
GALV. STEEL CHANNEL
4"
6"
(2) #3 ϕ ROD CONT.
#3 ϕ ROD - 12" O.C.
6"x6" #8/#8 WIRE MESH
COMPACTED SUB-BA
4" SAND CUSHION
(SECTION)
4
SD·3
DETAIL - PLAZA DRAIN INLETS
SCALE 3/4" = 1'-0"
DRAIN LINE (SEE MECH. DWG.)

Figure 13.28 *Drain inlet detail.*

Johnson, Johnson and Roy

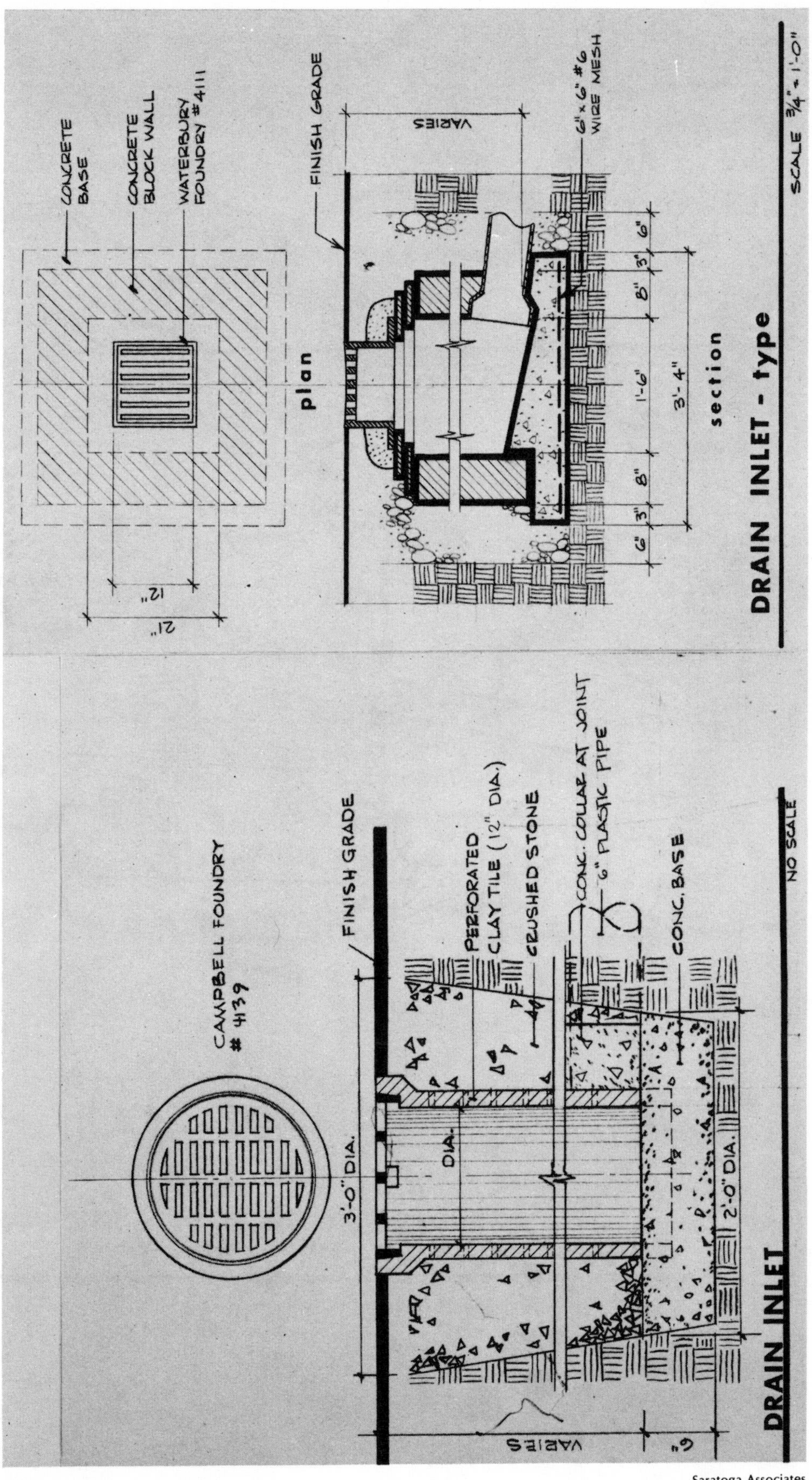
CONCRETE BASE
CONCRETE BLOCK WALL
WATERBURY FOUNDRY #4111
21"
12"
plan
FINISH GRADE
VARIES
6"x 6" #6 WIRE MESH
6" 3" 8" 1'-6" 8" 3" 6"
3'-4"
section
DRAIN INLET - type
SCALE 3/4" = 1'-0"
CAMPBELL FOUNDRY # 4139
3'-0" DIA.
DIA.
FINISH GRADE
PERFORATED CLAY TILE (12" DIA.)
CRUSHED STONE
CONC. COLLAR AT JOINT
6" PLASTIC PIPE
CONC. BASE
2'-0" DIA.
VARIES
6"
DRAIN INLET
NO SCALE

Saratoga Associates

Figure 13.29a *Drain inlet details.*

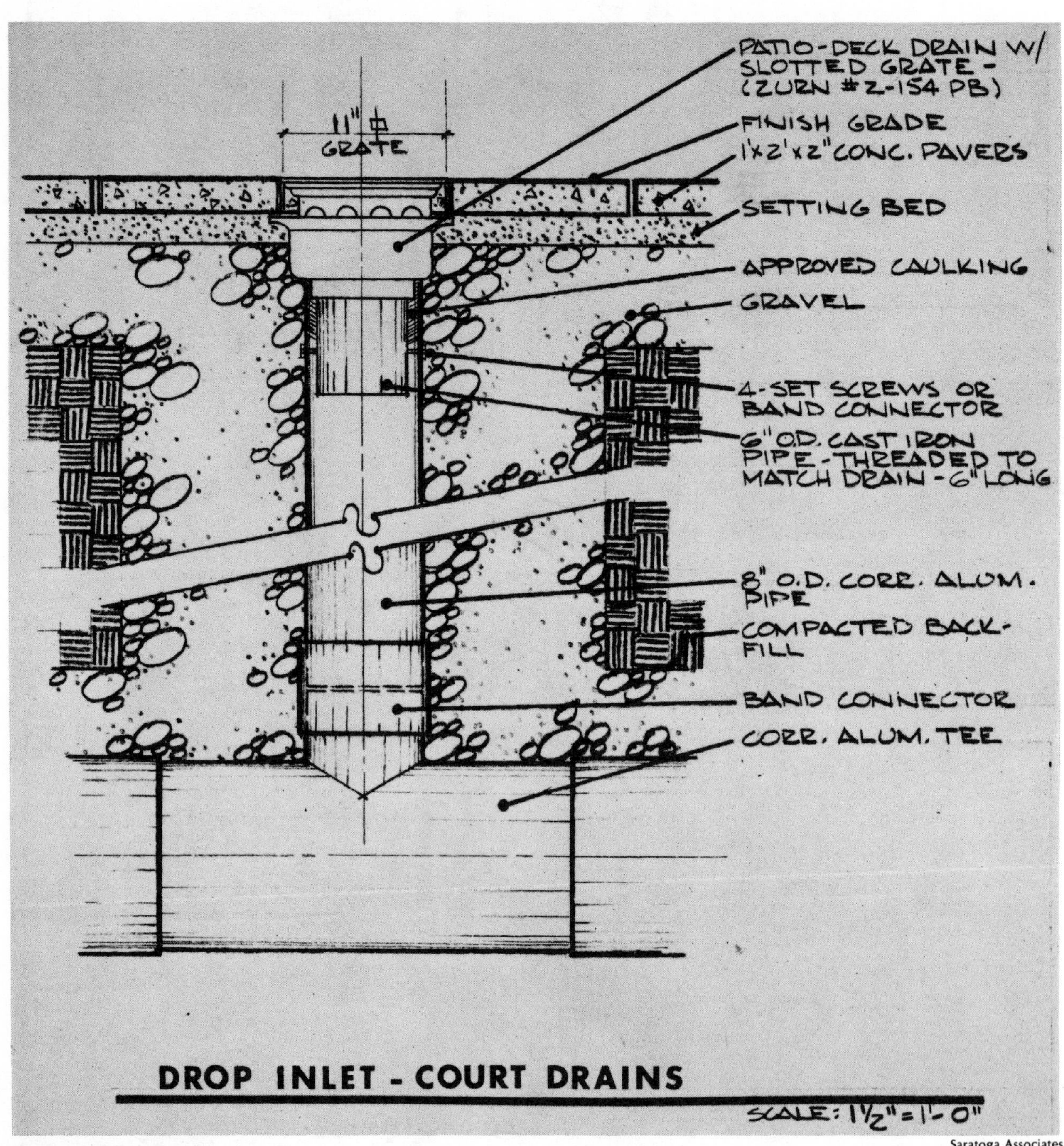
11" ⌀ GRATE
PATIO-DECK DRAIN W/ SLOTTED GRATE - (ZURN #Z-154 PB)
FINISH GRADE
1'x2'x2" CONC. PAVERS
SETTING BED
APPROVED CAULKING
GRAVEL
4-SET SCREWS OR BAND CONNECTOR
6" O.D. CAST IRON PIPE-THREADED TO MATCH DRAIN - 6" LONG
8" O.D. CORR. ALUM. PIPE
COMPACTED BACK-FILL
BAND CONNECTOR
CORR. ALUM. TEE
DROP INLET - COURT DRAINS
SCALE: 1½"=1'-0"

Saratoga Associates

Figure 13.29b *Drop inlet details.*

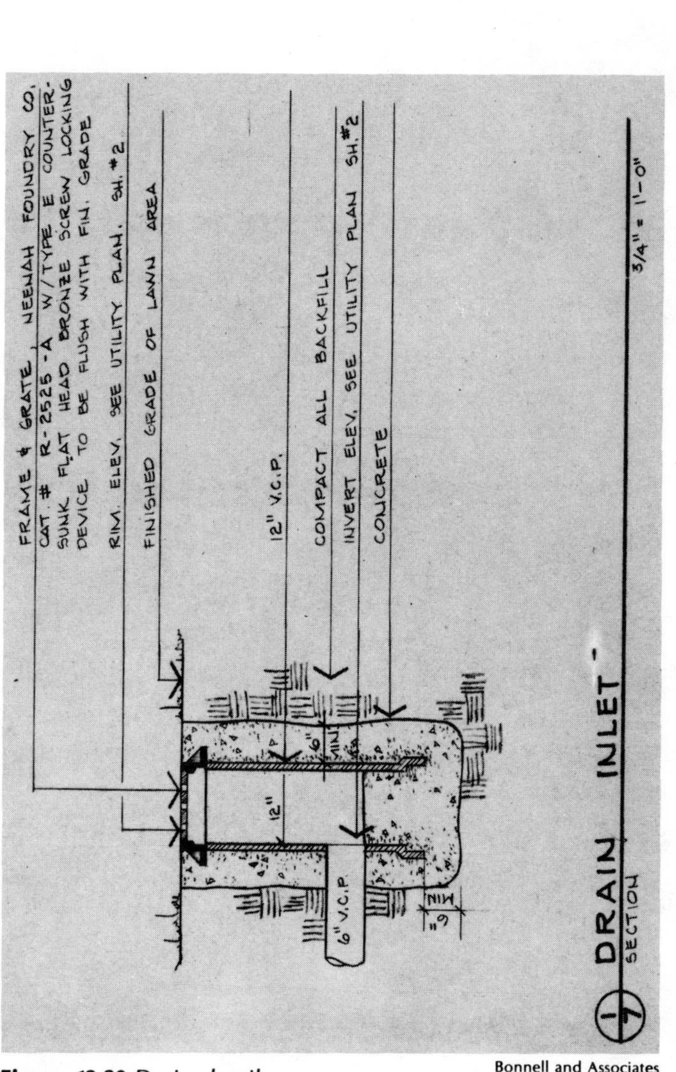
FRAME & GRATE, NEENAH FOUNDRY CO,
CAT. # R-2525-A W/TYPE E COUNTER-
SUNK FLAT HEAD BRONZE SCREW LOCKING
DEVICE TO BE FLUSH WITH FIN. GRADE
RIM. ELEV. SEE UTILITY PLAN. SH. #2
FINISHED GRADE OF LAWN AREA
12" V.C.P.
COMPACT ALL BACKFILL
INVERT ELEV. SEE UTILITY PLAN SH. #2
CONCRETE
12"
6"
6" V.C.P.
DRAIN INLET
SECTION
3/4" = 1'-0"

Bonnell and Associates

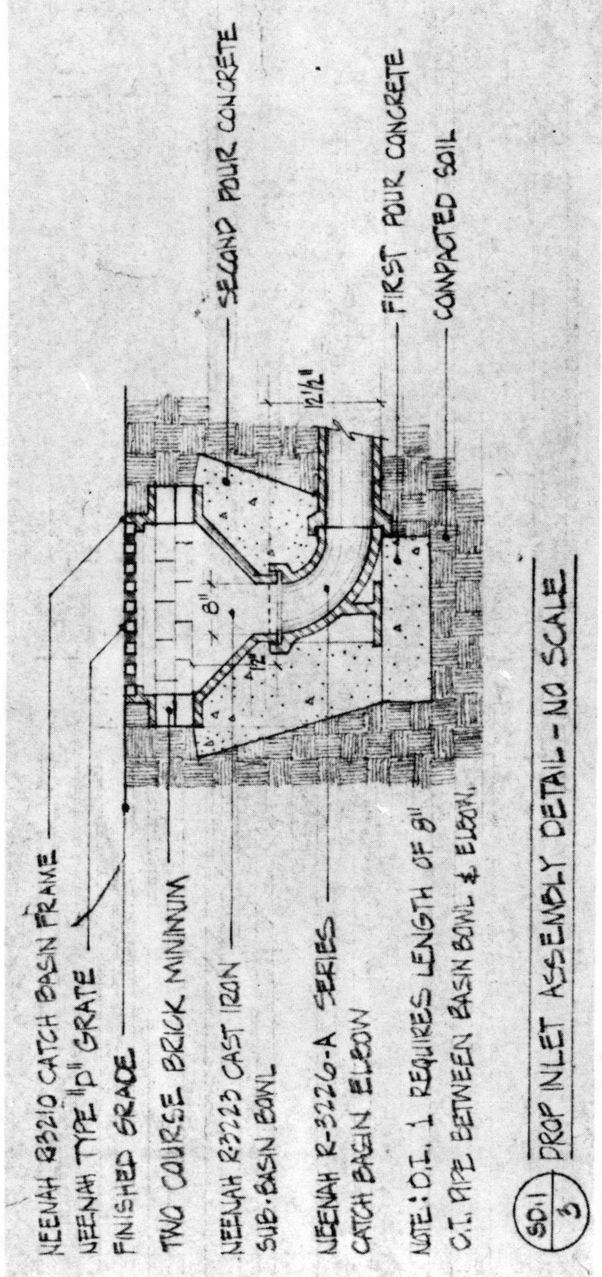
NEENAH R3210 CATCH BASIN FRAME
NEENAH TYPE "D" GRATE
FINISHED GRADE
TWO COURSE BRICK MINIMUM
NEENAH R3223 CAST IRON
SUB-BASIN BOWL
NEENAH R-3226-A SERIES
CATCH BASIN ELBOW
NOTE: D.I. 1 REQUIRES LENGTH OF 8"
C.I. PIPE BETWEEN BASIN BOWL & ELBOW.
SECOND POUR CONCRETE
FIRST POUR CONCRETE
COMPACTED SOIL
12 1/2"
8"
SD.1
3
PROP INLET ASSEMBLY DETAIL - NO SCALE

Johnson, Johnson and Roy

Figure 13.30 *Drain details.*

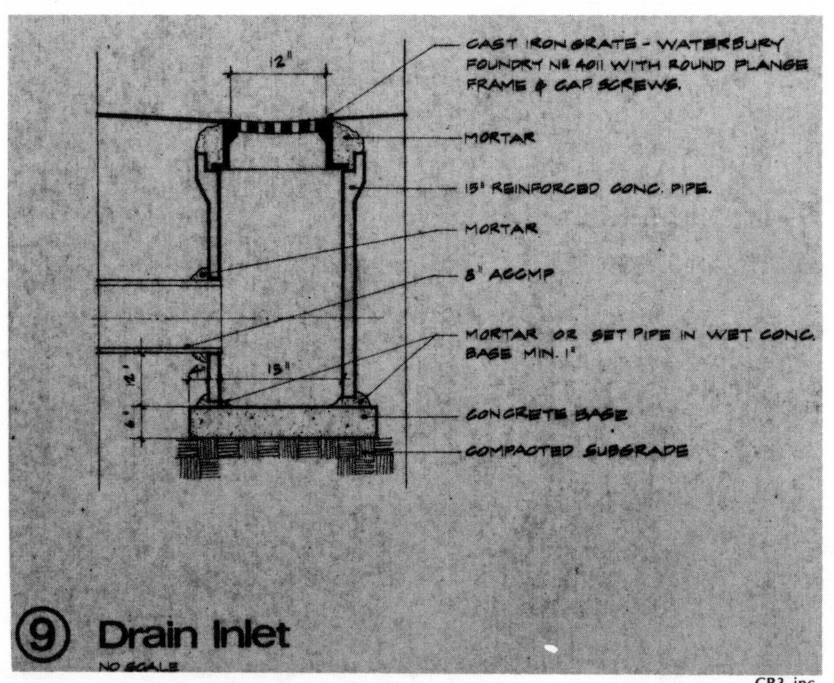
CAST IRON GRATE - WATERBURY FOUNDRY NO 4011 WITH ROUND FLANGE FRAME & CAP SCREWS.
MORTAR
15" REINFORCED CONC. PIPE.
MORTAR
8" ACCMP
MORTAR OR SET PIPE IN WET CONC. BASE MIN. 1"
CONCRETE BASE
COMPACTED SUBGRADE
12"
15"
9 Drain Inlet
NO SCALE

13.31 CR3, inc.

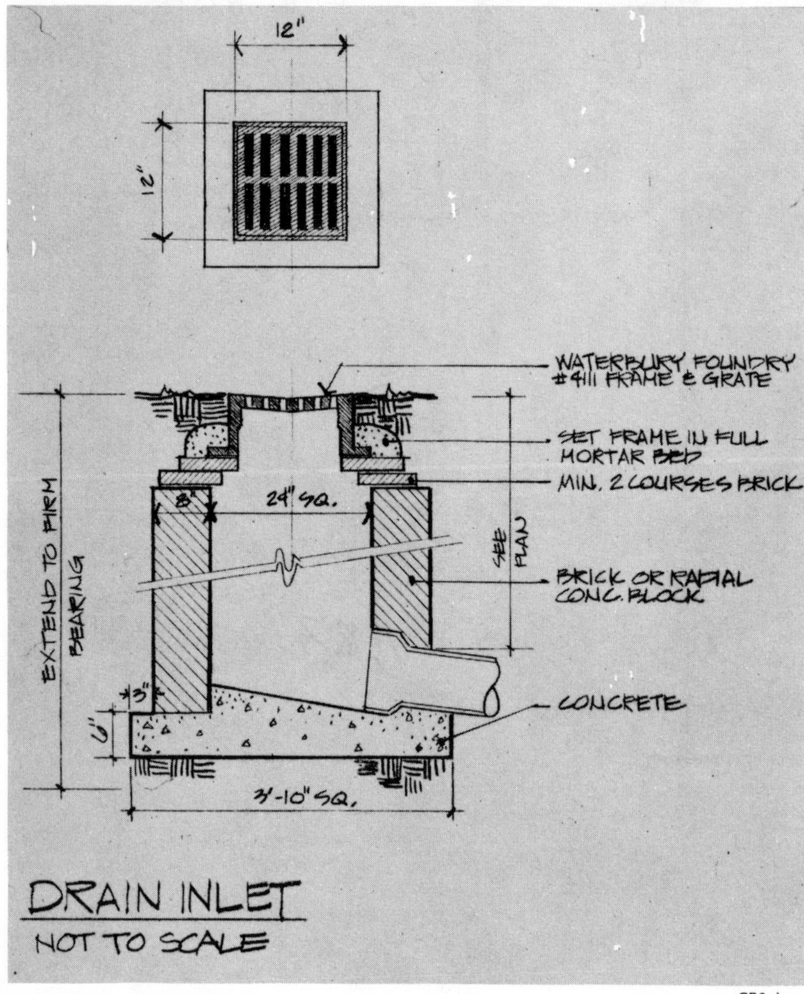
12"
12"
WATERBURY FOUNDRY #4111 FRAME & GRATE
SET FRAME IN FULL MORTAR BED
MIN. 2 COURSES BRICK
24" SQ.
8"
SEE PLAN
BRICK OR RADIAL CONC. BLOCK
EXTEND TO FIRM BEARING
3"
6"
CONCRETE
3'-10" SQ.
DRAIN INLET
NOT TO SCALE

13.32 CR3, inc.

Figures 13.31 – 13.32 *Drain details.*

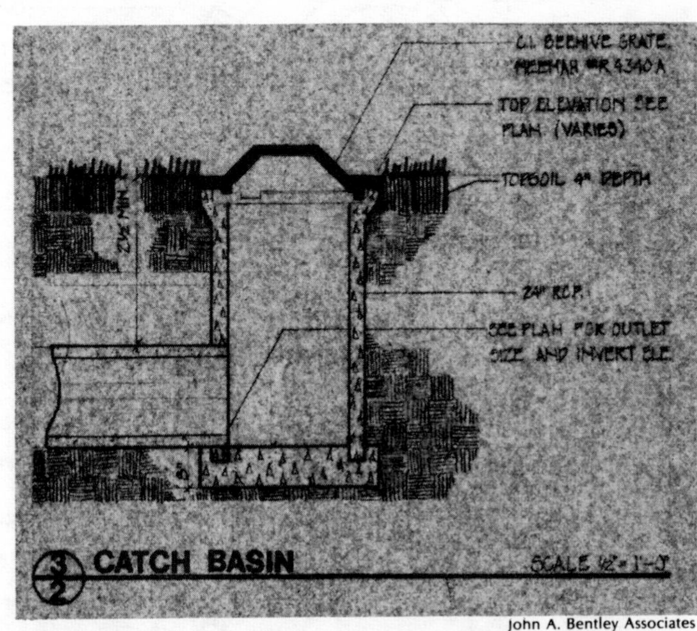
C.I. BEEHIVE GRATE.
NEENAH #R 4340 A
TOP ELEVATION SEE
PLAN (VARIES)
TOPSOIL 4" DEPTH
24" R.C.P.
SEE PLAN FOR OUTLET
SIZE AND INVERT ELE.
CATCH BASIN
SCALE 1/2" = 1'-0"

Figures 13.33 – 13.34 *Drain details.*

13.33

John A. Bentley Associates

FINISH GRADE OF SHREDDED BARK
MULCH
6" SLAG BASE
1" THICK LANDSCAPE FIBERGLASS
MATT TO EXTEND 6" BEYOND C.B.
EX. C.B. GRADE
EXISTING CATCH BASIN
COMPACTED SUBGRADE
C.B. COVERING
SECTION
1/2" = 1'-0"

13.34

Bonnell and Associates

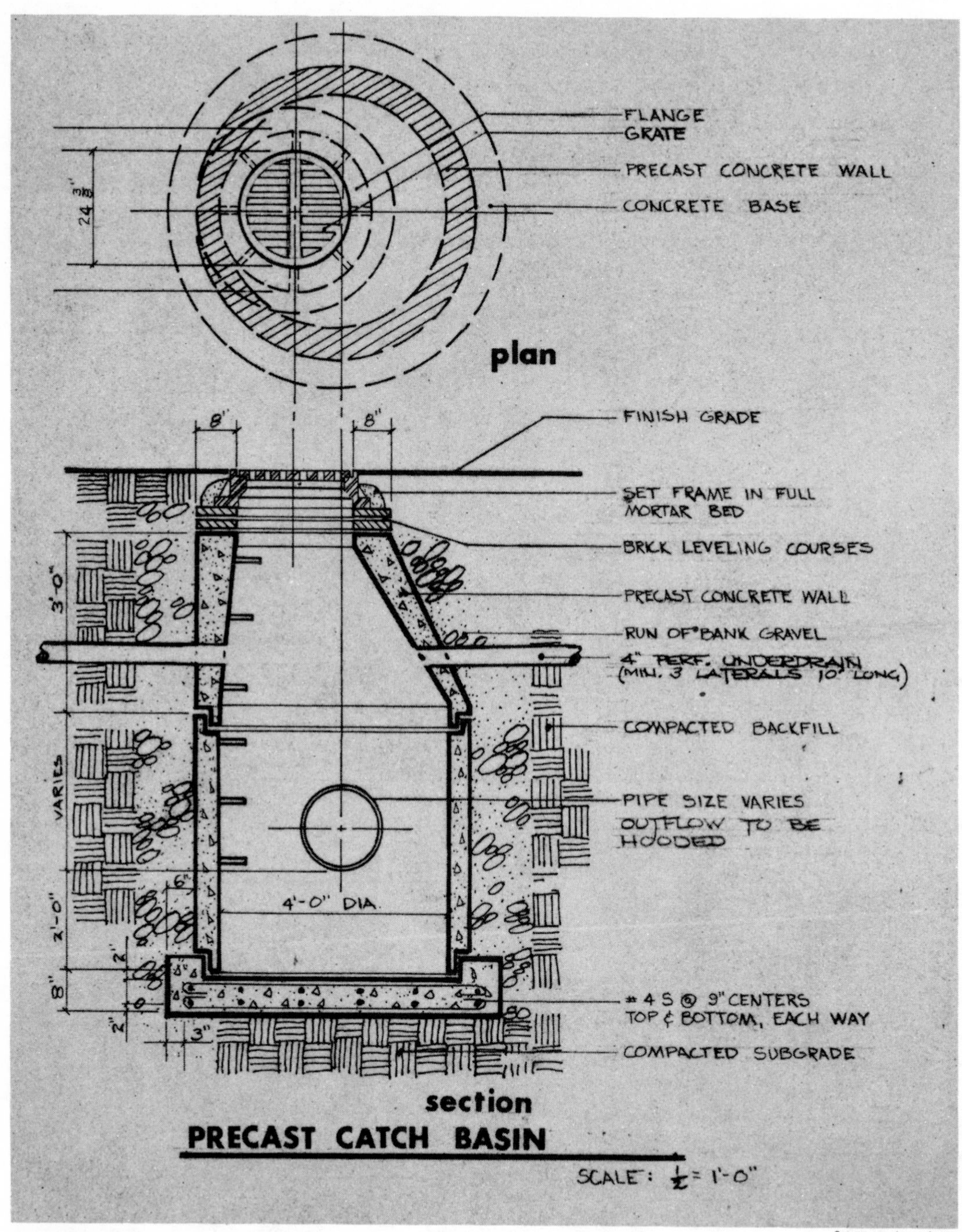
FLANGE
GRATE
PRECAST CONCRETE WALL
CONCRETE BASE
24 3/8"
plan
8"
8"
FINISH GRADE
SET FRAME IN FULL MORTAR BED
BRICK LEVELING COURSES
PRECAST CONCRETE WALL
RUN OF BANK GRAVEL
4" PERF. UNDERDRAIN (MIN. 3 LATERALS 10' LONG)
COMPACTED BACKFILL
PIPE SIZE VARIES
OUTFLOW TO BE HOODED
3'-0"
VARIES
2'-0"
6"
4'-0" DIA.
2"
8"
2"
3"
4 S @ 9" CENTERS TOP & BOTTOM, EACH WAY
COMPACTED SUBGRADE
section
PRECAST CATCH BASIN
SCALE: 1/2" = 1'-0"

Saratoga Associates

Figure 13.35 *Catch basin details.*

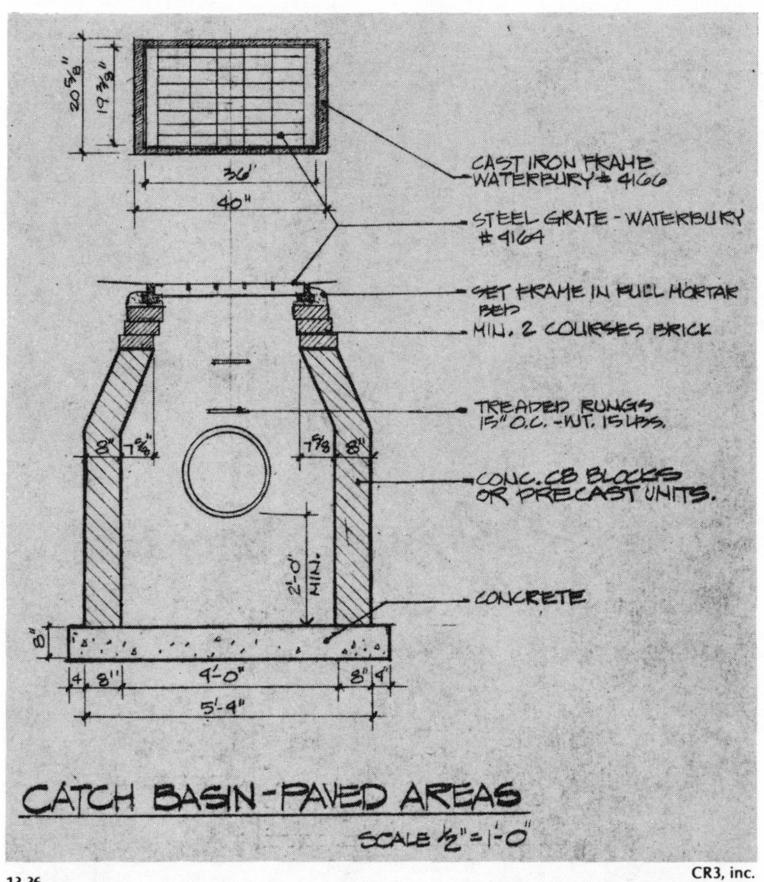
20 5/8"
19 3/8"
36"
40"
CAST IRON FRAME WATERBURY # 4166
STEEL GRATE - WATERBURY # 4164
SET FRAME IN FULL MORTAR BED
MIN. 2 COURSES BRICK
TREADED RUNGS 15" O.C. - WT. 15 LBS.
8"
7 3/8"
7 3/8"
8"
CONC. CB BLOCKS OR PRECAST UNITS.
2'-0" MIN.
CONCRETE
8"
4
8"
4'-0"
8"
4"
5'-4"
CATCH BASIN-PAVED AREAS
SCALE 1/2"=1'-0"

13.36

CR3, inc.

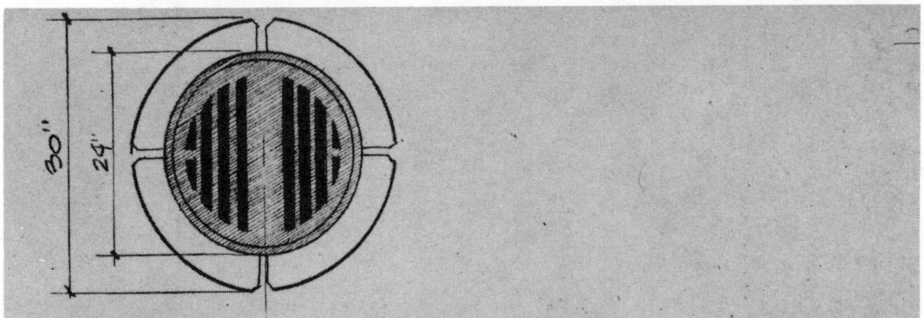

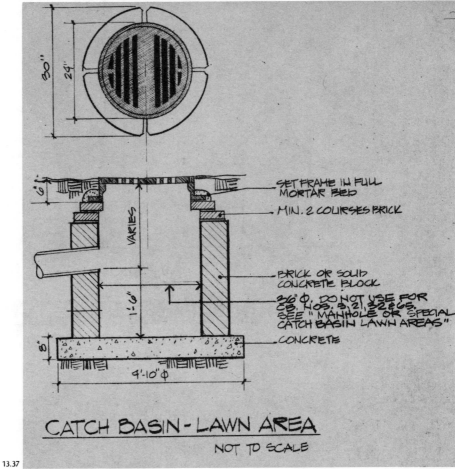

30"
24"
6"
SET FRAME IN FULL MORTAR BED
MIN. 2 COURSES BRICK
VARIES
BRICK OR SOLID CONCRETE BLOCK
1'-6"
36" Φ. DO NOT USE FOR CB. NOS. 3, 21, 32 & 65. SEE "MANHOLE OR SPECIAL CATCH BASIN LAWN AREAS"
8"
CONCRETE
4'-10" Φ
CATCH BASIN - LAWN AREA
NOT TO SCALE

13.37

CR3, inc.

Figures 13.36 – 13.37 *Catch basin details.*

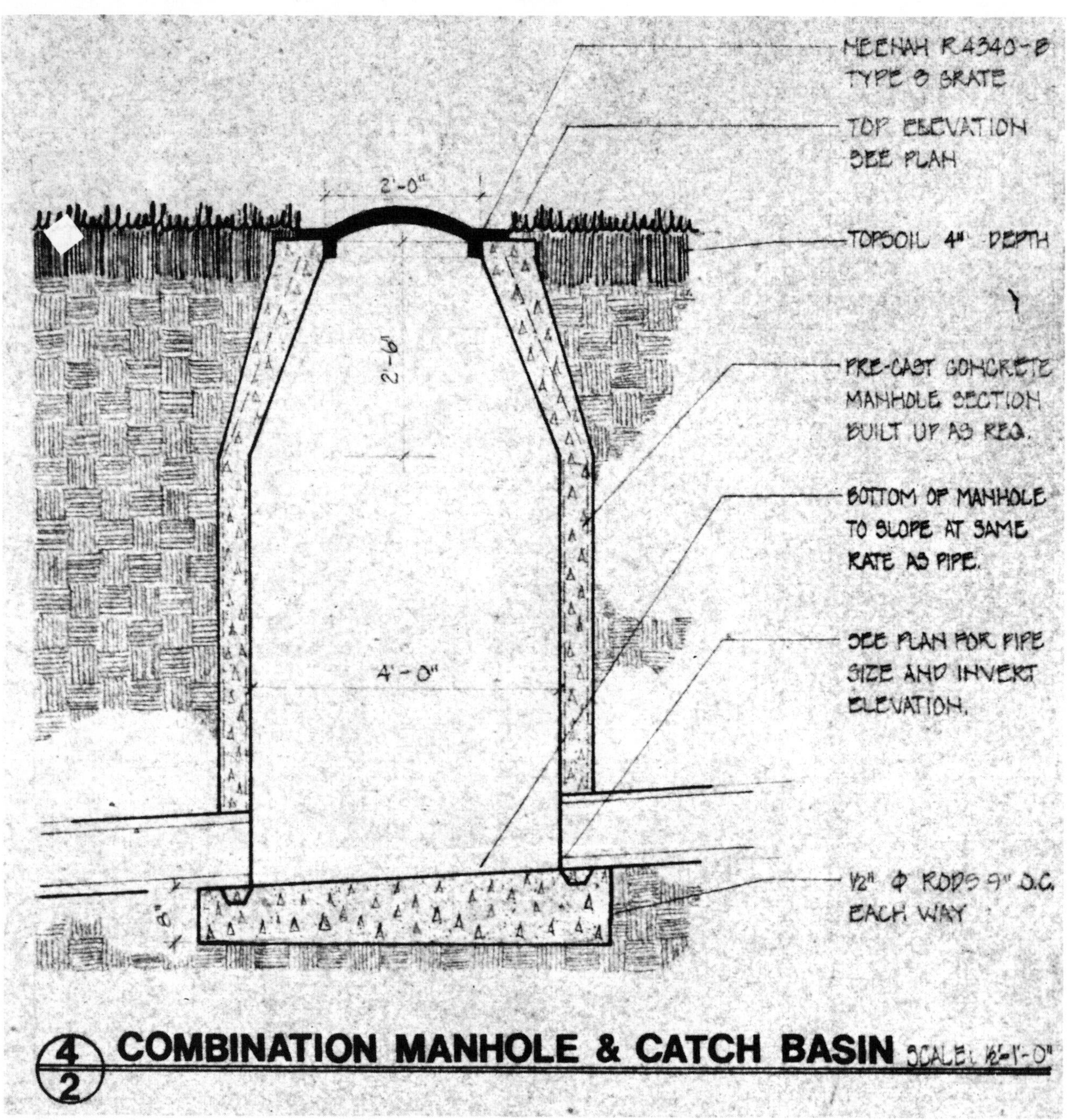
NEENAH R-4340-B TYPE G GRATE
TOP ELEVATION SEE PLAN
TOPSOIL 4" DEPTH
PRE-CAST CONCRETE MANHOLE SECTION BUILT UP AS REQ.
BOTTOM OF MANHOLE TO SLOPE AT SAME RATE AS PIPE.
SEE PLAN FOR PIPE SIZE AND INVERT ELEVATION.
1/2" Φ RODS 9" O.C. EACH WAY
2'-0"
2'-6"
4'-0"
8"
4/2
COMBINATION MANHOLE & CATCH BASIN
SCALE: 1/2"=1'-0"

John A. Bentley Associates

Figure 13.38 *Catch basin – manhole detail.*

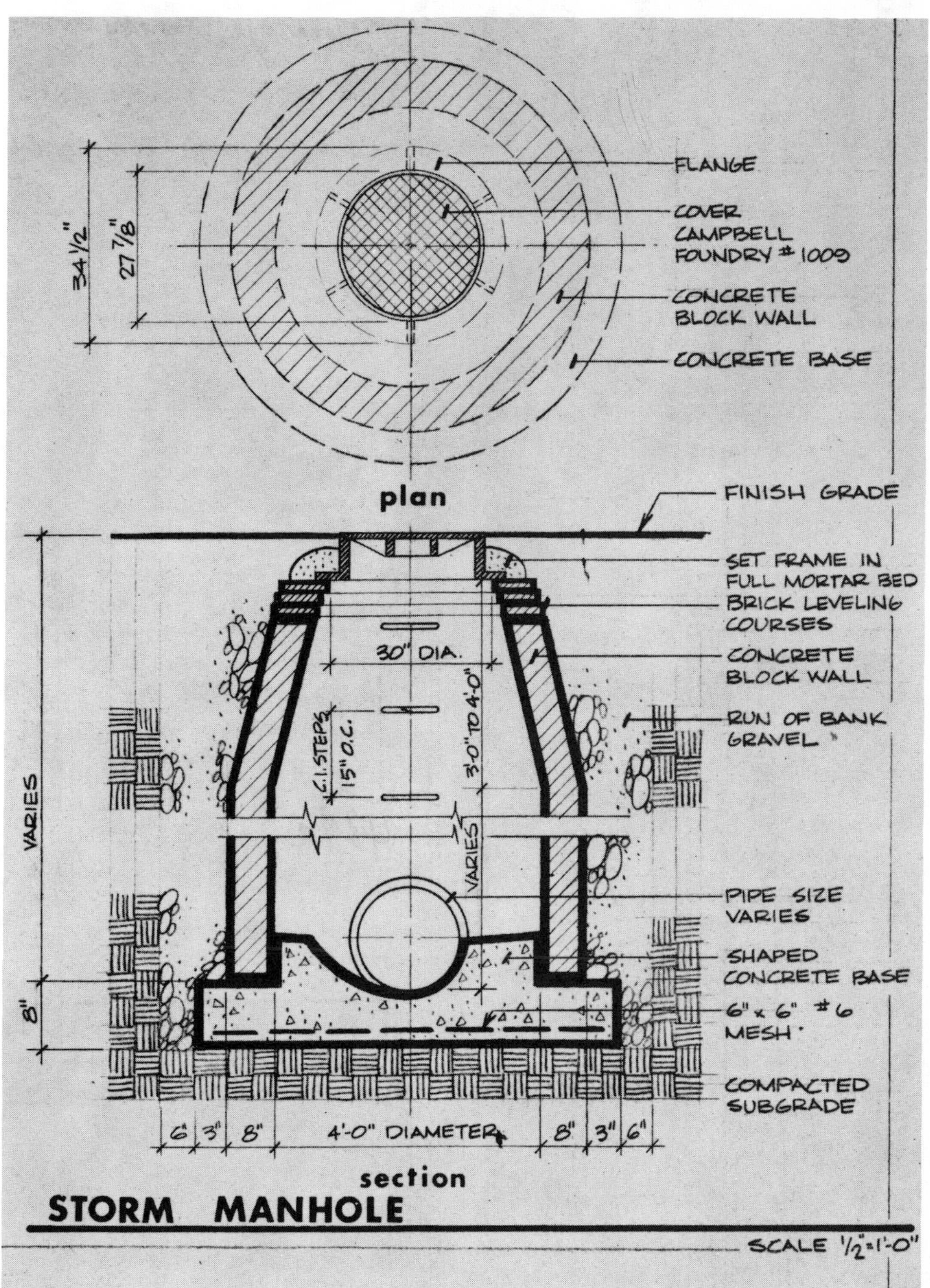
FLANGE
COVER
CAMPBELL
FOUNDRY # 1009
CONCRETE
BLOCK WALL
CONCRETE BASE
34 1/2"
27 7/8
plan
FINISH GRADE
SET FRAME IN
FULL MORTAR BED
BRICK LEVELING
COURSES
CONCRETE
BLOCK WALL
RUN OF BANK
GRAVEL
30" DIA.
C.I. STEPS
15" O.C.
3'-0" TO 4'-0"
VARIES
VARIES
PIPE SIZE
VARIES
SHAPED
CONCRETE BASE
6" x 6" #6
MESH
8"
COMPACTED
SUBGRADE
6" 3" 8" 4'-0" DIAMETER 8" 3" 6"
section
STORM MANHOLE
SCALE 1/2"=1'-0"

Saratoga Associates

Figure 13.39 *Manhole detail.*

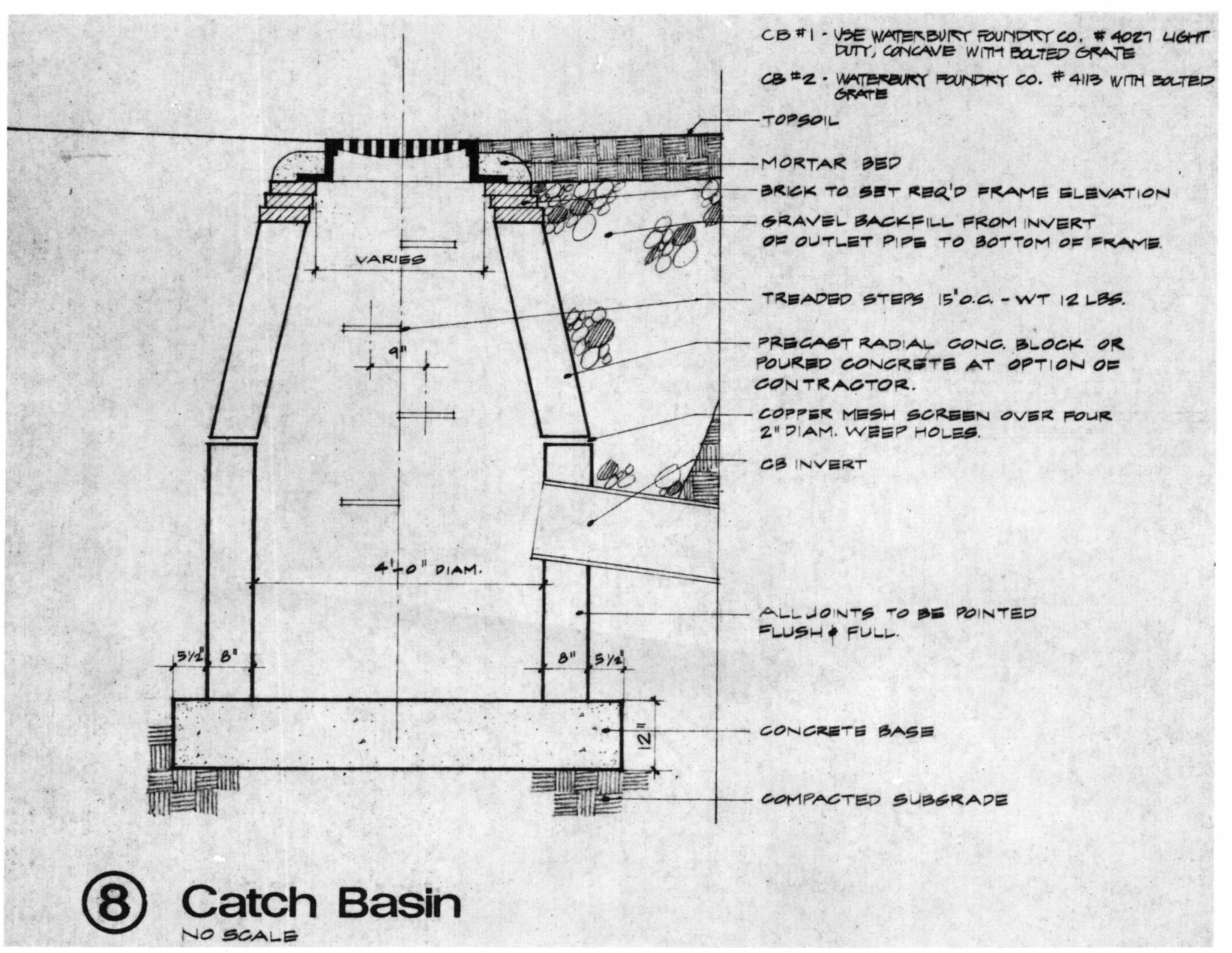
CB #1 - USE WATERBURY FOUNDRY CO. # 4027 LIGHT DUTY, CONCAVE WITH BOLTED GRATE
CB #2 - WATERBURY FOUNDRY CO. # 4113 WITH BOLTED GRATE
TOPSOIL
MORTAR BED
BRICK TO SET REQ'D FRAME ELEVATION
GRAVEL BACKFILL FROM INVERT OF OUTLET PIPE TO BOTTOM OF FRAME.
TREADED STEPS 15" O.C. - WT 12 LBS.
PRECAST RADIAL CONC. BLOCK OR POURED CONCRETE AT OPTION OF CONTRACTOR.
COPPER MESH SCREEN OVER FOUR 2" DIAM. WEEP HOLES.
CB INVERT
ALL JOINTS TO BE POINTED FLUSH & FULL.
CONCRETE BASE
COMPACTED SUBGRADE
VARIES
9"
4'-0" DIAM.
5 1/2"
8"
12"
8
Catch Basin
NO SCALE

CR3, inc.

Figure 13.40 *Catch basin detail.*

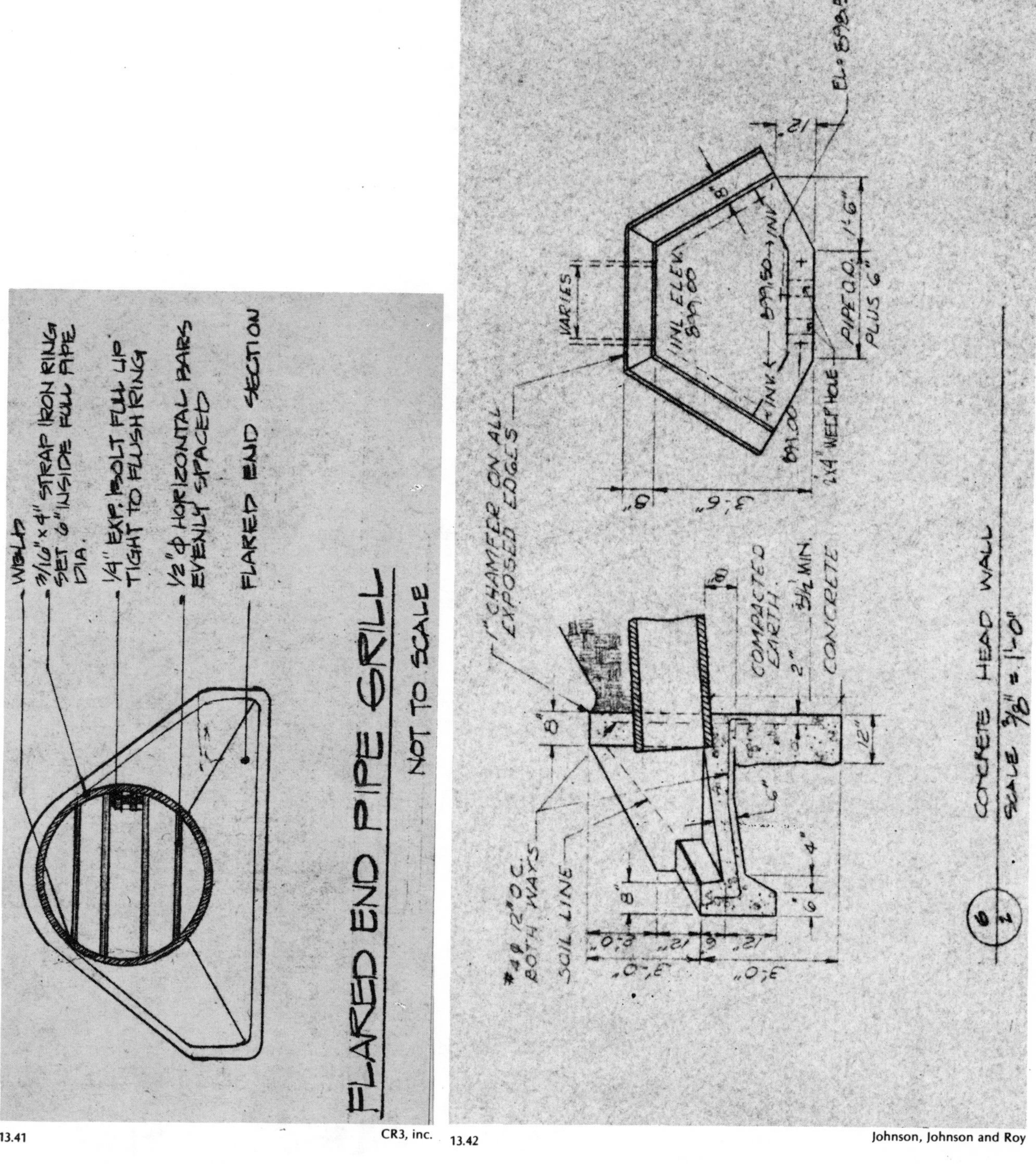
WELD
3/16" x 4" STRAP IRON RING SET 6" INSIDE FULL PIPE DIA.
1/4" EXP. BOLT FULL UP TIGHT TO FLUSH RING
1/2" ϕ HORIZONTAL BARS EVENLY SPACED
FLARED END SECTION
FLARED END PIPE GRILL
NOT TO SCALE
1" CHAMFER ON ALL EXPOSED EDGES
#4 ϕ 12" O.C. BOTH WAYS
SOIL LINE
COMPACTED EARTH
3 1/2" MIN.
CONCRETE
VARIES
INL. ELEV. 899.00
INV.
899.50
2x4" WEEP HOLE
PIPE O.D. PLUS 6"
EL. 898.50
CONCRETE HEAD WALL
SCALE 3/8" = 1'-0"

13.41 CR3, inc.

13.42 Johnson, Johnson and Roy

Figures 13.41 – 13.42 *Headwall details.*

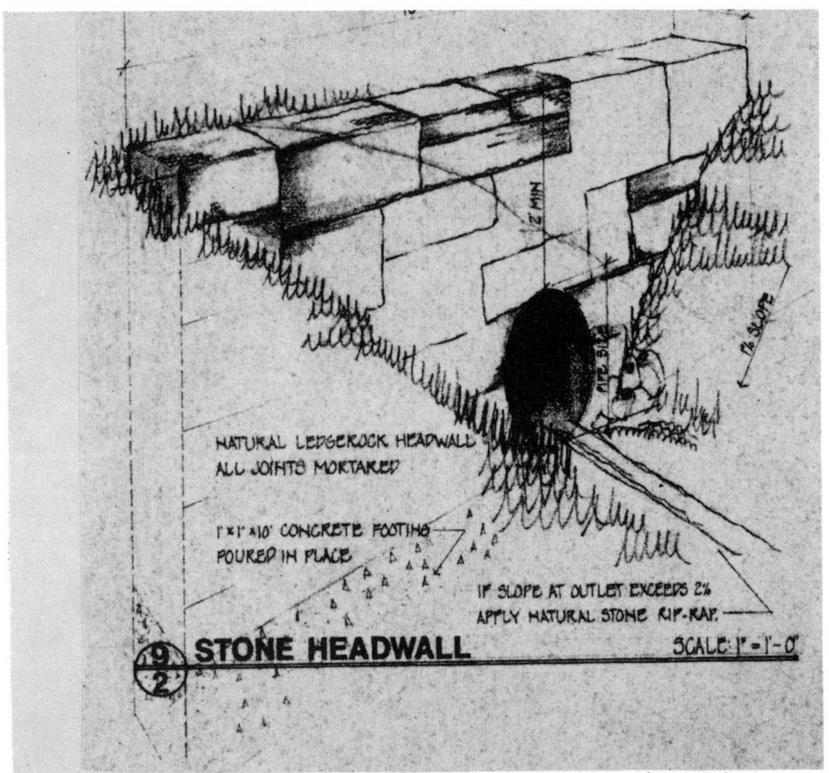
2' MIN
1% SLOPE
PIPE SIZE
NATURAL LEDGEROCK HEADWALL
ALL JOINTS MORTARED
1'x1'x10' CONCRETE FOOTING
POURED IN PLACE
IF SLOPE AT OUTLET EXCEEDS 2%
APPLY NATURAL STONE RIP-RAP.
9/2 STONE HEADWALL
SCALE: 1" = 1'-0"

13.43

John A. Bentley Associates

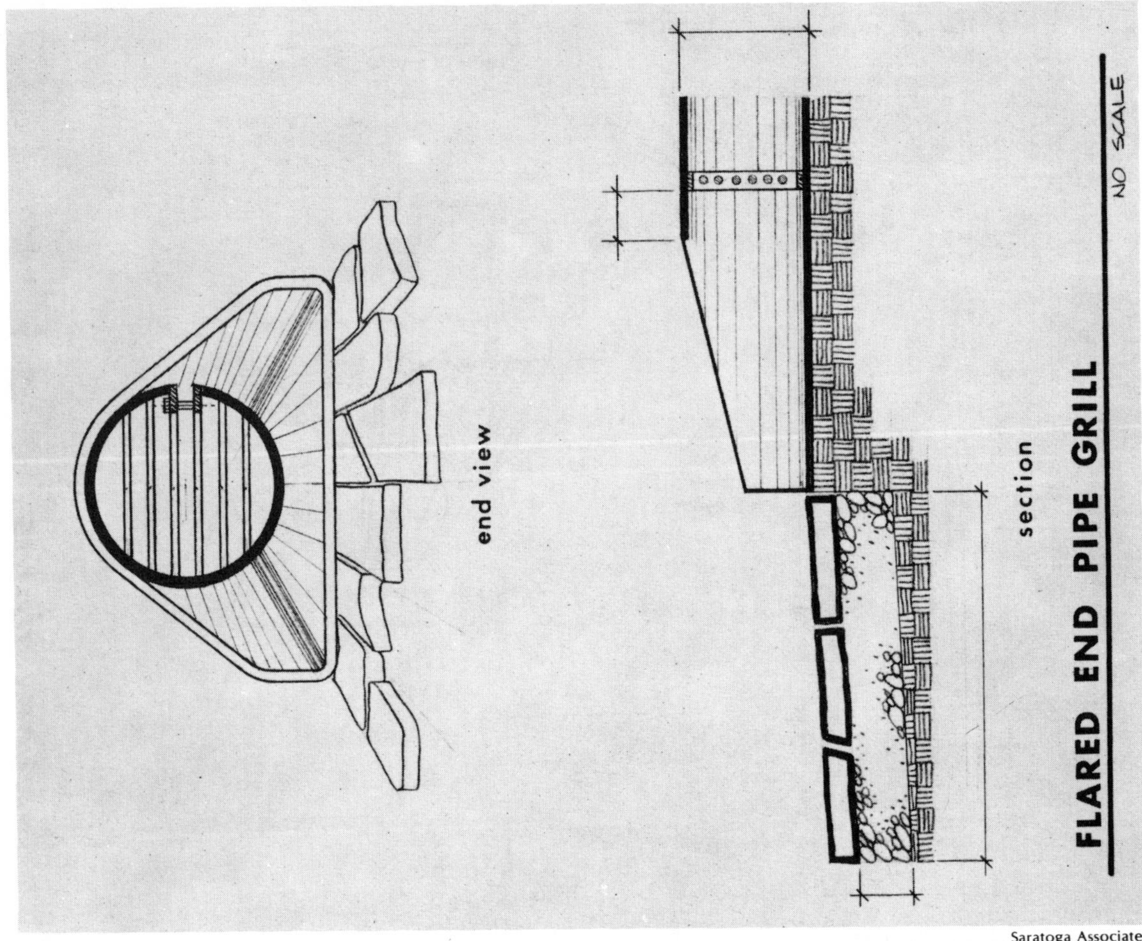
end view
section
FLARED END PIPE GRILL
NO SCALE

13.44

Saratoga Associates

Figures 13.43 – 13.44 *Headwall details.*

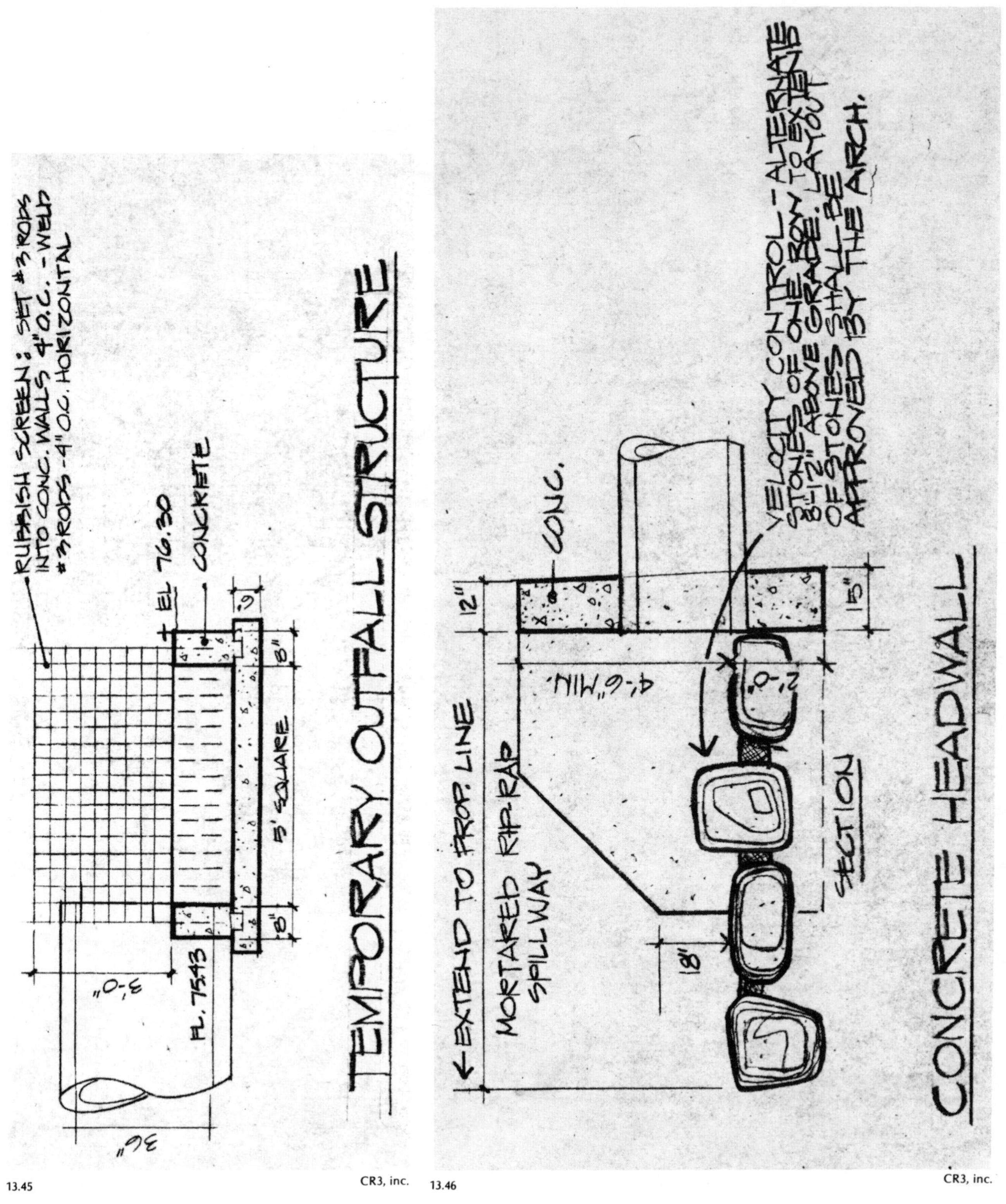
RUBBISH SCREEN: SET #3 RODS INTO CONC. WALLS 4" O.C. -WELD #3 RODS-4" O.C. HORIZONTAL
EL 76.30
CONCRETE
6"
8"
5' SQUARE
8"
FL. 75.43
3'-0"
36"
TEMPORARY OUTFALL STRUCTURE
← EXTEND TO PROP. LINE
MORTARED RIP-RAP SPILLWAY
18"
4'-6" MIN.
2'-0"
12"
CONC.
15"
VELOCITY CONTROL - ALTERNATE STONES OF ONE ROW TO EXTEND 8"-12" ABOVE GRADE. LAYOUT OF STONES SHALL BE APPROVED BY THE ARCH.
SECTION
CONCRETE HEADWALL

13.45 CR3, inc.

13.46 CR3, inc.

Figures 13.45 – 13.46 *Headwall details.*

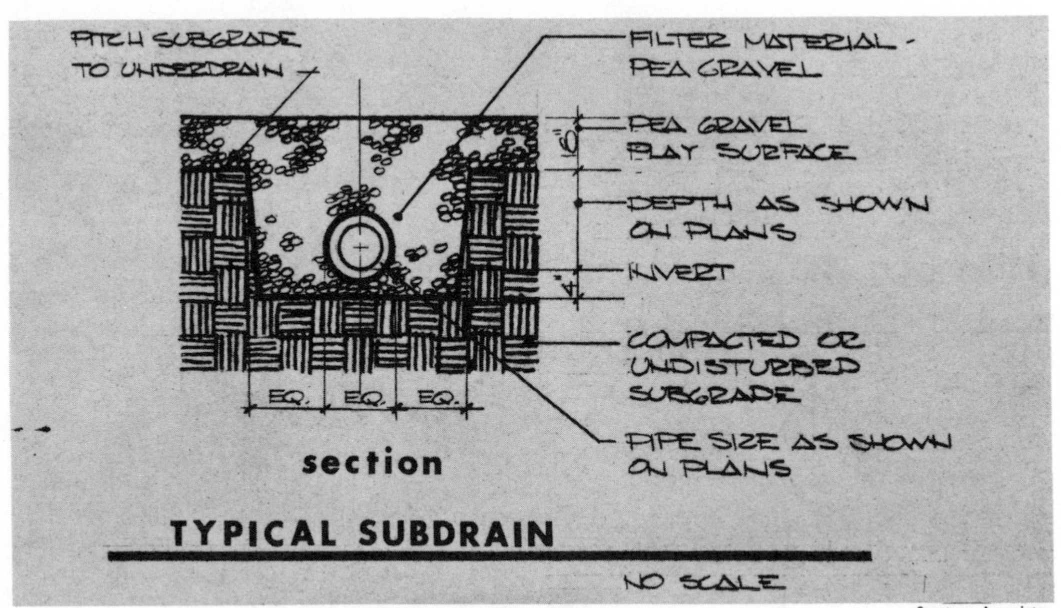
PITCH SUBGRADE
TO UNDERDRAIN
FILTER MATERIAL -
PEA GRAVEL
PEA GRAVEL
PLAY SURFACE
6"
DEPTH AS SHOWN
ON PLANS
INVERT
4"
COMPACTED OR
UNDISTURBED
SUBGRADE
EQ.
EQ.
EQ.
PIPE SIZE AS SHOWN
ON PLANS
section
TYPICAL SUBDRAIN
NO SCALE

13.47

Saratoga Associates

8'-0"
DIAMETER
MIN. 6" SHREDDED BARK
MULCH AS SPECIFIED.
6" BASE AS SPECIFIED.
1/2" FIBERGLASS MAT.
COMPACTED BACKFILL
4'
BACKFILL WITH NO. 4
WASHED GRAVEL.
COMPACTED SUBGRADE
9/11 DRYWELL
SECTION
1/2" = 1'-0"

13.48

Bonnell and Associates

Figures 13.47 – 13.48 *Drywell and subdrain details.*

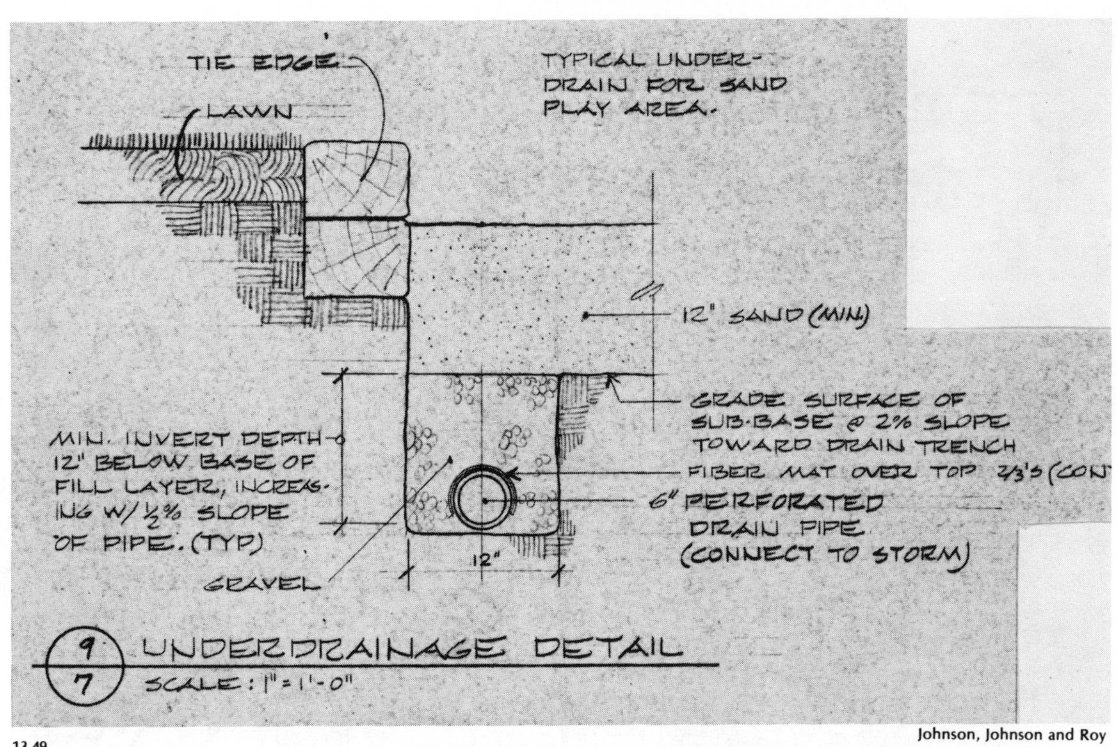
TIE EDGE
LAWN
TYPICAL UNDER-DRAIN FOR SAND PLAY AREA.
12" SAND (MIN.)
GRADE SURFACE OF SUB-BASE @ 2% SLOPE TOWARD DRAIN TRENCH
MIN. INVERT DEPTH 12" BELOW BASE OF FILL LAYER, INCREAS-ING W/ 1/2% SLOPE OF PIPE. (TYP.)
FIBER MAT OVER TOP 2/3'S (CONT
6" PERFORATED DRAIN PIPE (CONNECT TO STORM)
12"
GRAVEL
9
7
UNDERDRAINAGE DETAIL
SCALE: 1" = 1'-0"

13.49

Johnson, Johnson and Roy

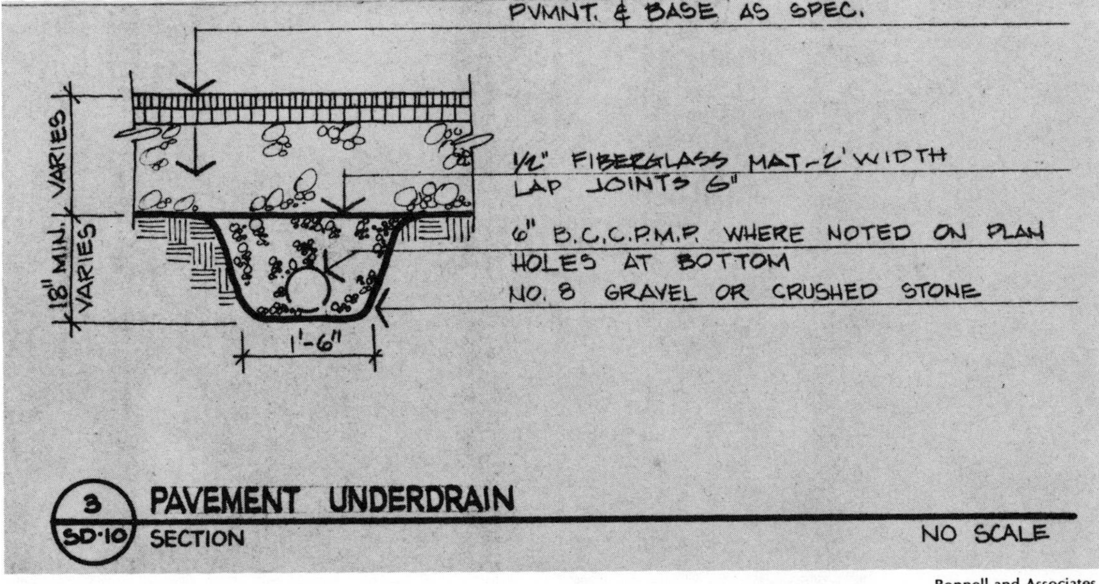
PVMNT. & BASE AS SPEC.
1/2" FIBERGLASS MAT - 2' WIDTH
LAP JOINTS 6"
6" B.C.C.P.M.P. WHERE NOTED ON PLAN
HOLES AT BOTTOM
NO. 8 GRAVEL OR CRUSHED STONE
VARIES
18" MIN. VARIES
1'-6"
3
SD-10
PAVEMENT UNDERDRAIN
SECTION
NO SCALE

13.50

Bonnell and Associates

Figures 13.49 – 13.50 *Underdrain details.*

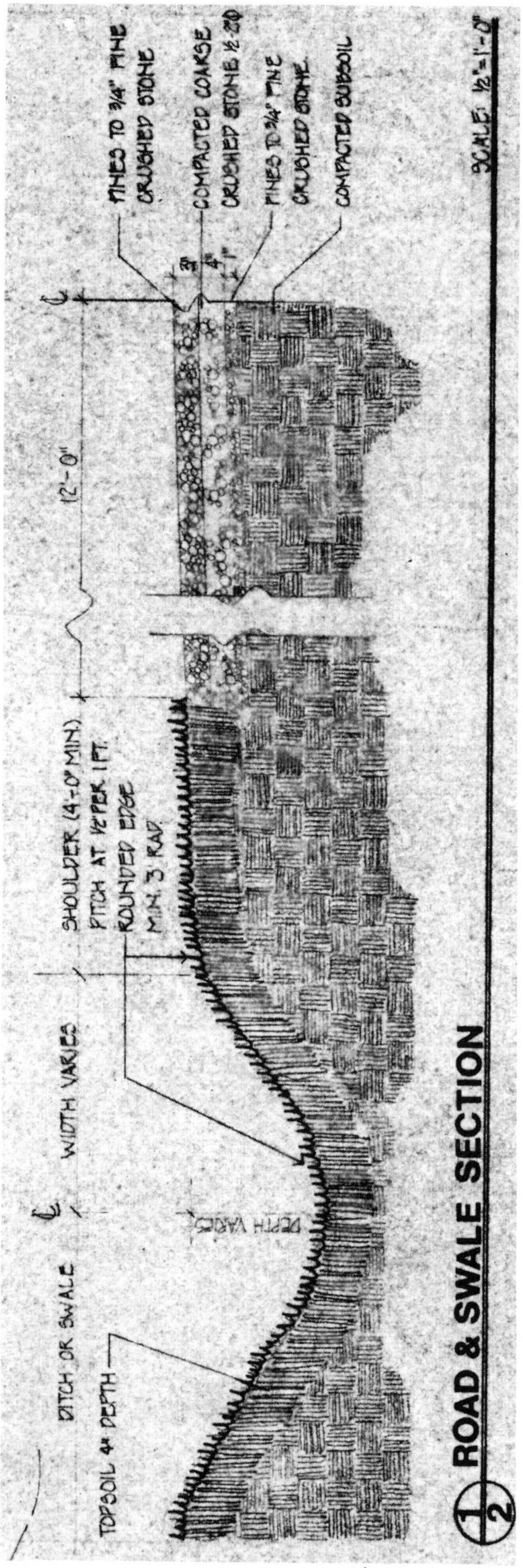

John A. Bentley Associates

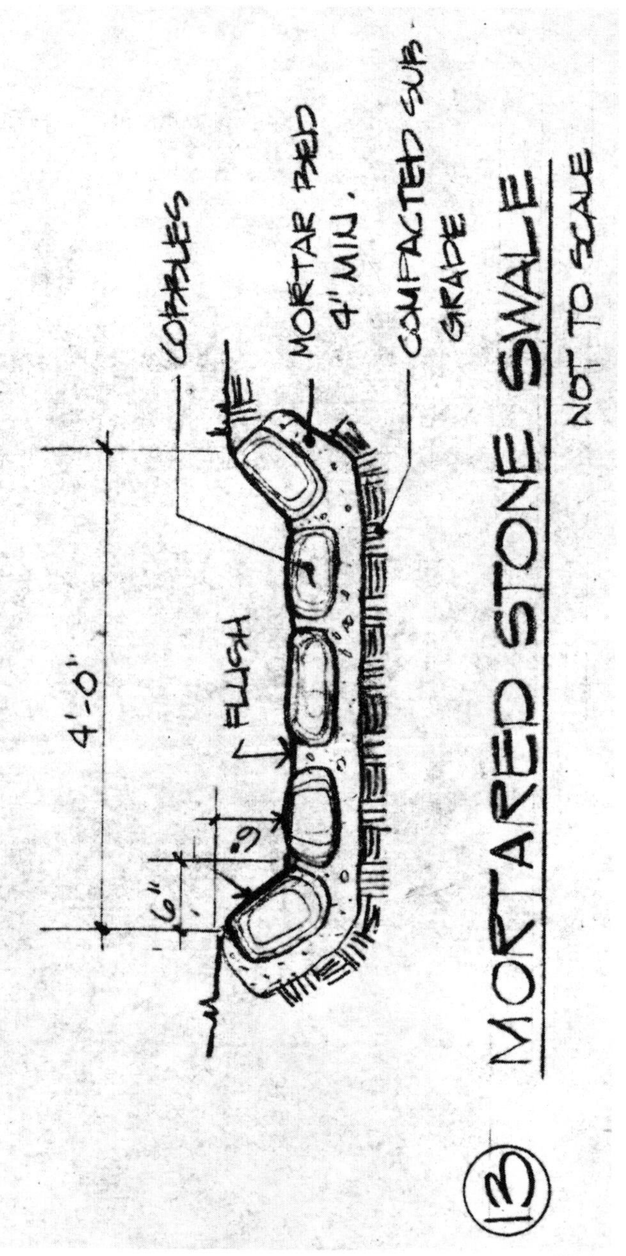

4'-0"
6"
6"
FLUSH
COBBLES
MORTAR BED
4" MIN.
COMPACTED SUB
GRADE
13
MORTARED STONE SWALE
NOT TO SCALE

CR3, inc.

Figure 13.51 *Drainage swale details.*

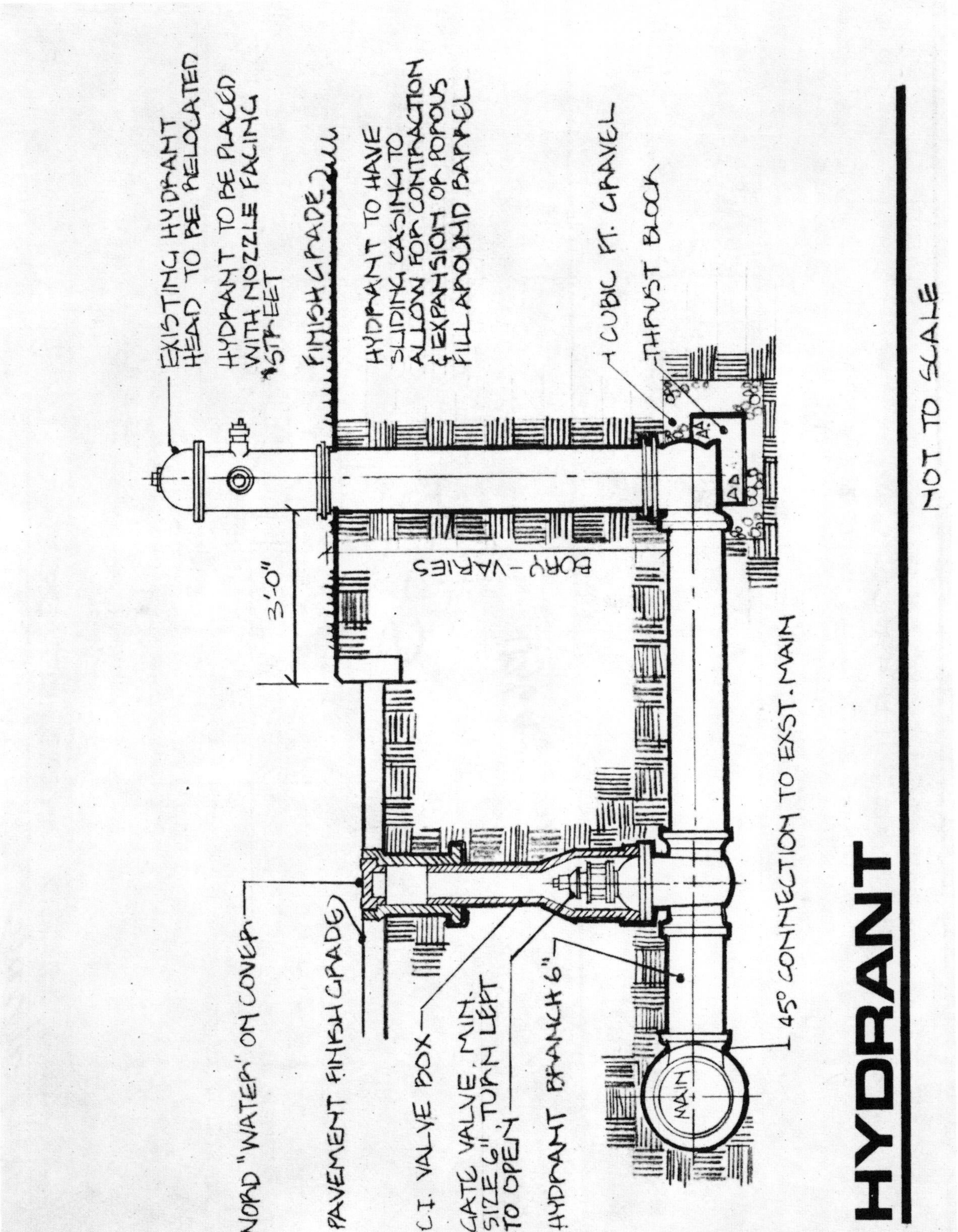

EXISTING HYDRANT HEAD TO BE RELOCATED
HYDRANT TO BE PLACED WITH NOZZLE FACING STREET
FINISH GRADE
HYDRANT TO HAVE SLIDING CASING TO ALLOW FOR CONTRACTION & EXPANSION OR POROUS FILL AROUND BARREL
1 CUBIC FT. GRAVEL
THRUST BLOCK
3'-0"
BDRY-VARIES
WORD "WATER" ON COVER
PAVEMENT FINISH GRADE
C.I. VALVE BOX
GATE VALVE, MIN. SIZE 6", TURN LEFT TO OPEN
HYDRANT BRANCH 6"
MAIN
45° CONNECTION TO EXST. MAIN
HYDRANT
NOT TO SCALE

Saratoga Associates

Figure 13.52 *Fire hydrant detail.*

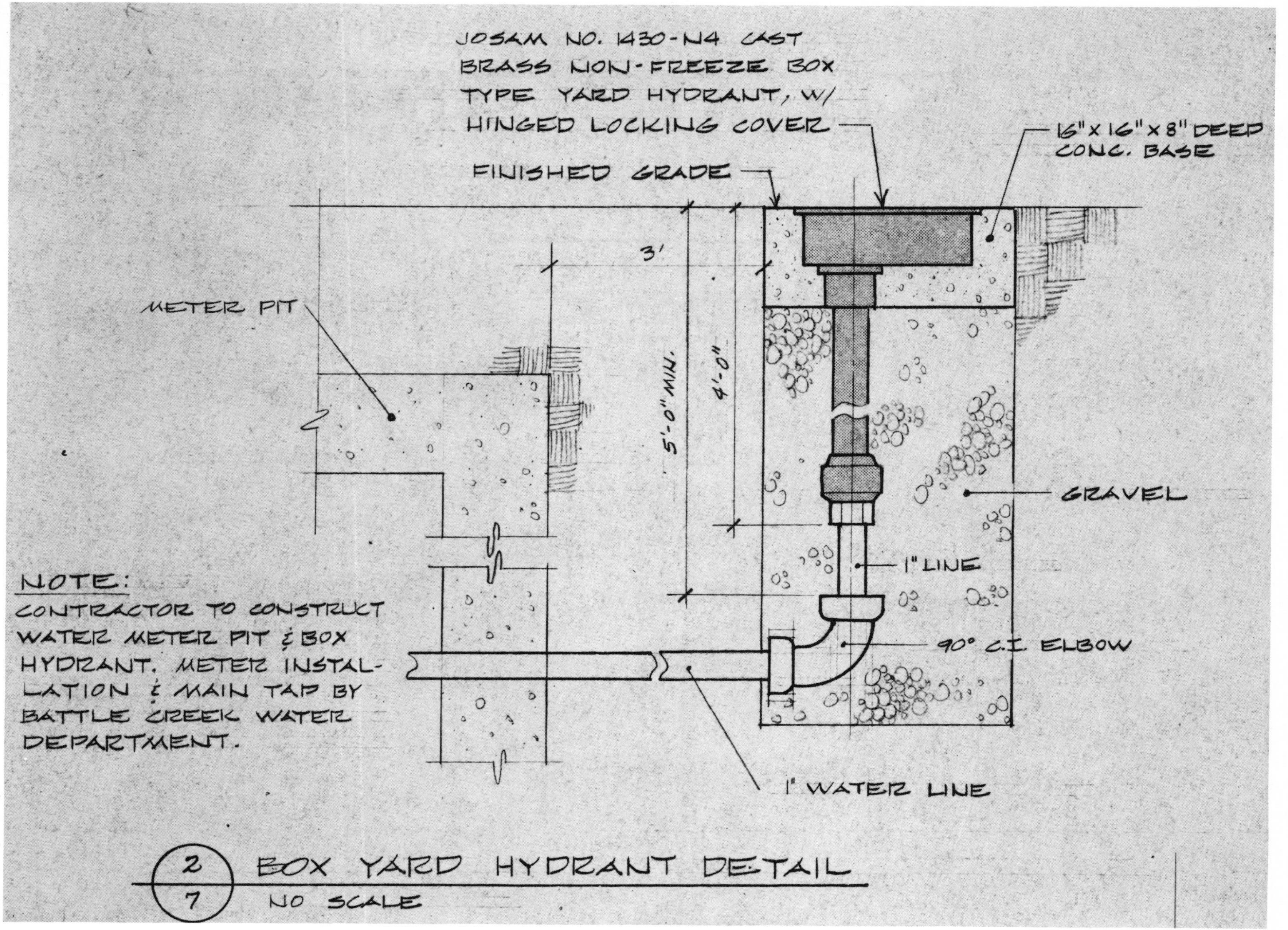
JOSAM NO. 1430-N4 CAST
BRASS NON-FREEZE BOX
TYPE YARD HYDRANT, W/
HINGED LOCKING COVER
16"x16"x8" DEEP
CONC. BASE
FINISHED GRADE
3'
METER PIT
5'-0" MIN.
4'-0"
GRAVEL
1" LINE
90° C.I. ELBOW
NOTE:
CONTRACTOR TO CONSTRUCT
WATER METER PIT & BOX
HYDRANT. METER INSTAL-
LATION & MAIN TAP BY
BATTLE CREEK WATER
DEPARTMENT.
1" WATER LINE
2
7
BOX YARD HYDRANT DETAIL
NO SCALE

Figure 13.53 *Yard hydrant detail.*

Johnson, Johnson and Roy

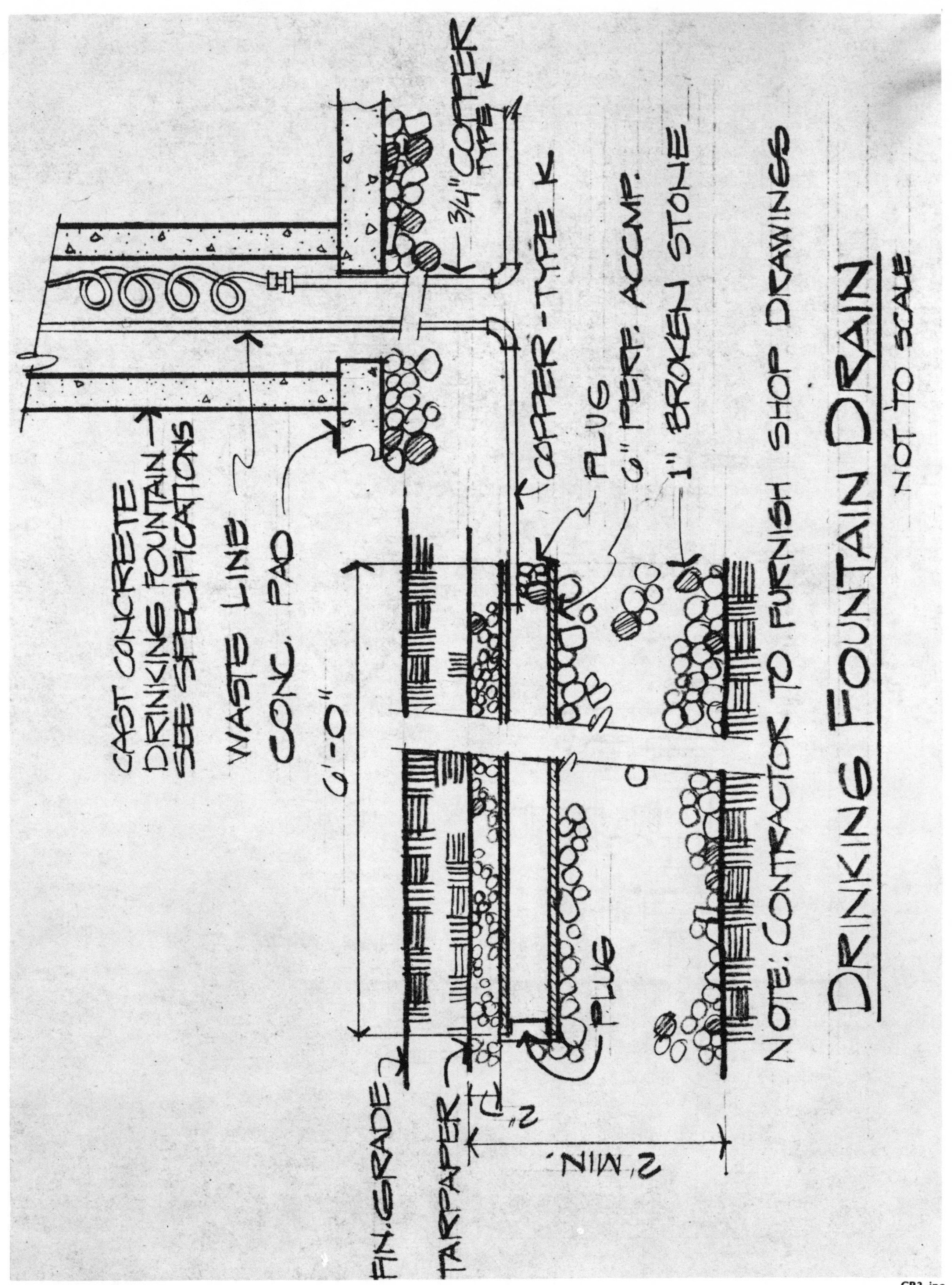

CAST CONCRETE
DRINKING FOUNTAIN
SEE SPECIFICATIONS
WASTE LINE
CONC. PAD
6'-0"
3/4" COPPER
TYPE K
COPPER-TYPE K
PLUG
6" PERF. ACCMP.
1" BROKEN STONE
NOTE: CONTRACTOR TO FURNISH SHOP DRAWINGS
DRINKING FOUNTAIN DRAIN
NOT TO SCALE
FIN. GRADE
TARPAPER
2"
2' MIN.
PLUG

CR3, inc.

Figure 13.54 *Drinking fountain drain.*

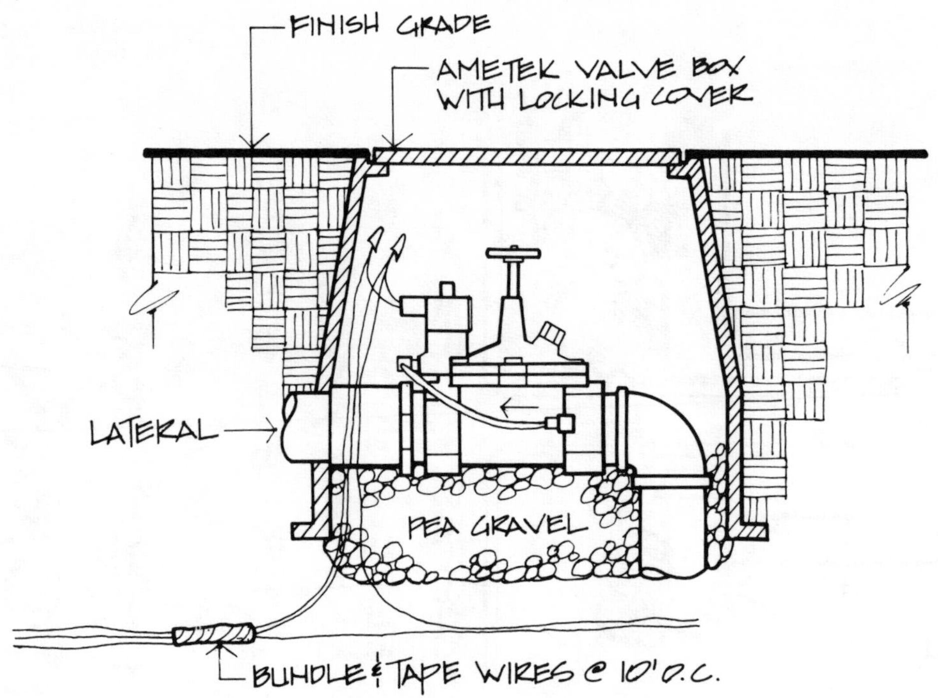
FINISH GRADE
AMETEK VALVE BOX
WITH LOCKING COVER
LATERAL
PEA GRAVEL
BUNDLE & TAPE WIRES @ 10' O.C.
ELECTRIC VALVE DETAIL

13.55

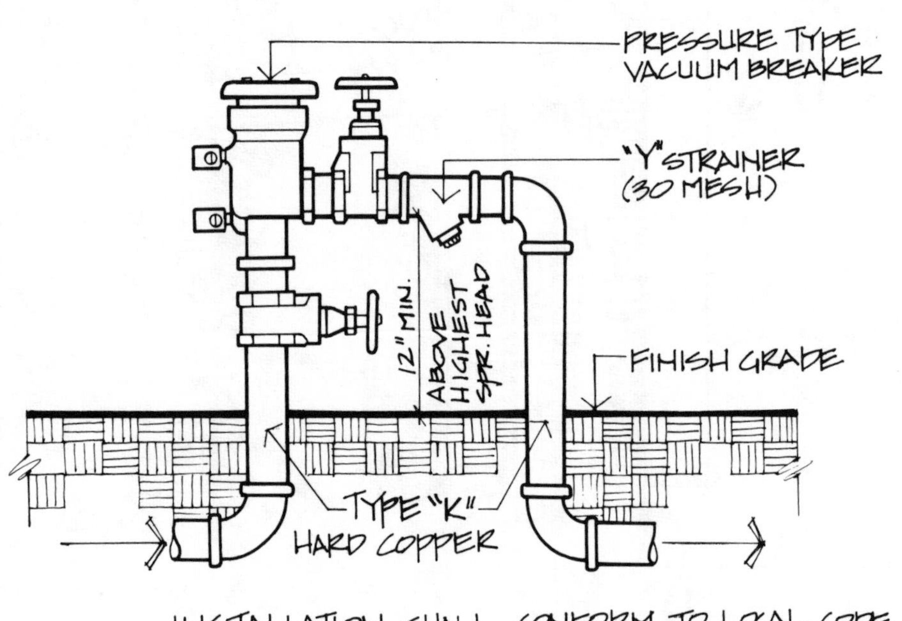
PRESSURE TYPE
VACUUM BREAKER
"Y" STRAINER
(30 MESH)
12" MIN.
ABOVE
HIGHEST
SPR. HEAD
FINISH GRADE
TYPE "K"
HARD COPPER
INSTALLATION SHALL CONFORM TO LOCAL CODE
BACKFLOW PREVENTION DETAIL

13.56

Figures 13.55 – 13.58 *Irrigation system details.*

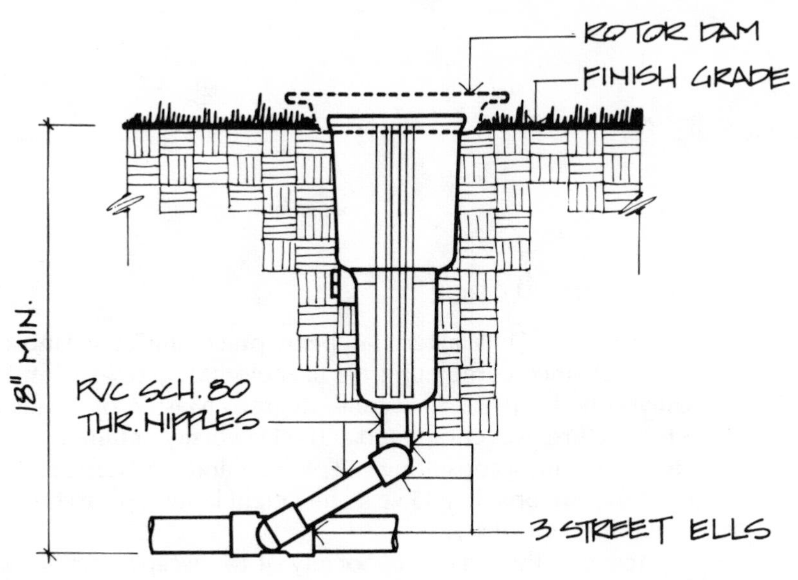
ROTOR DAM
FINISH GRADE
18" MIN.
PVC SCH. 80
THR. NIPPLES
3 STREET ELLS

13.57 POP-UP ROTOR DETAIL

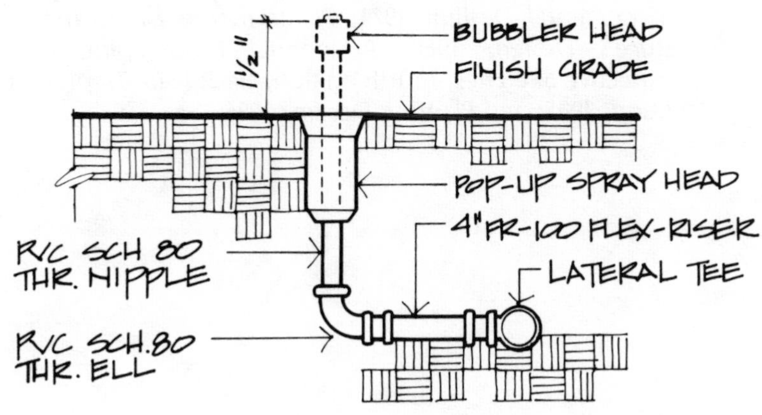
BUBBLER HEAD
1½"
FINISH GRADE
POP-UP SPRAY HEAD
4" FR-100 FLEX-RISER
PVC SCH 80
THR. NIPPLE
LATERAL TEE
PVC SCH. 80
THR. ELL

13.58 SPRAY & BUBBLER DETAIL

ABOUT THE AUTHOR

Theodore D. Walker has been practicing as a landscape architect since completing his Bachelors degree at Utah State University in 1957. A second degree, Master of Landscape Architecture, was completed at the University of Illinois in 1967. He is currently a consulting site planner and landscape architect in Mesa, Arizona. For 15 years he taught landscape architecture at Purdue University.

Active in the American Society of Landscape Architects, he has served in various Chapter offices and six years as a member of the Board of Trustees representing the Indiana Chapter. From 1972 to 1974 he served on the Board of Landscape Architectural Accredition. He is a member of Sigma Lambda Alpha, landscape architecture honor societ, and in 1980 was awarded a Certificate of Special Recognition by the Council of Educators in Landscape Architecture for his outstanding contributions to landscape architecture education. In 1985 Mr. Walker was elected a Fellow of ASLA.

Other books which he has authored include: *Perception and Environmental Design,* 1971; *Plants in the Landscape,* 1975; *Nature's Design,* 1980; *Residential Landscaping I,* 1982; *Perspective Sketches,* fourth edition, 1982; *Plan Graphics,* third edition, 1985; and *Planting Design,* 1985.

Appendix

MAXIMUM FROST PENETRATION (inches)

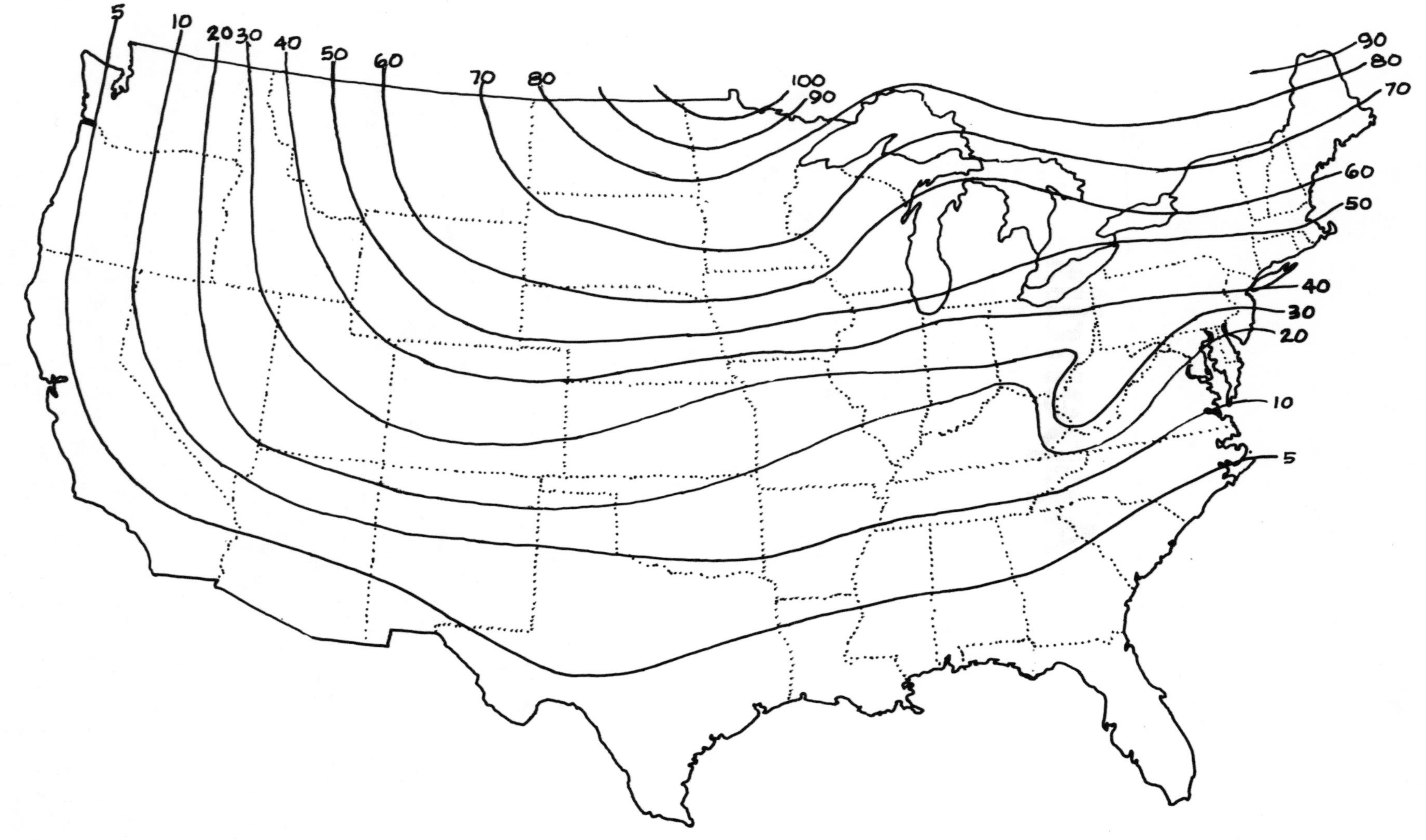
5
10
20
30
40
50
60
70
80
100
90
90
80
70
60
50
40
30
20
10
5

AVERAGE ANNUAL DEPTH OF FROST PENETRATION (inches)

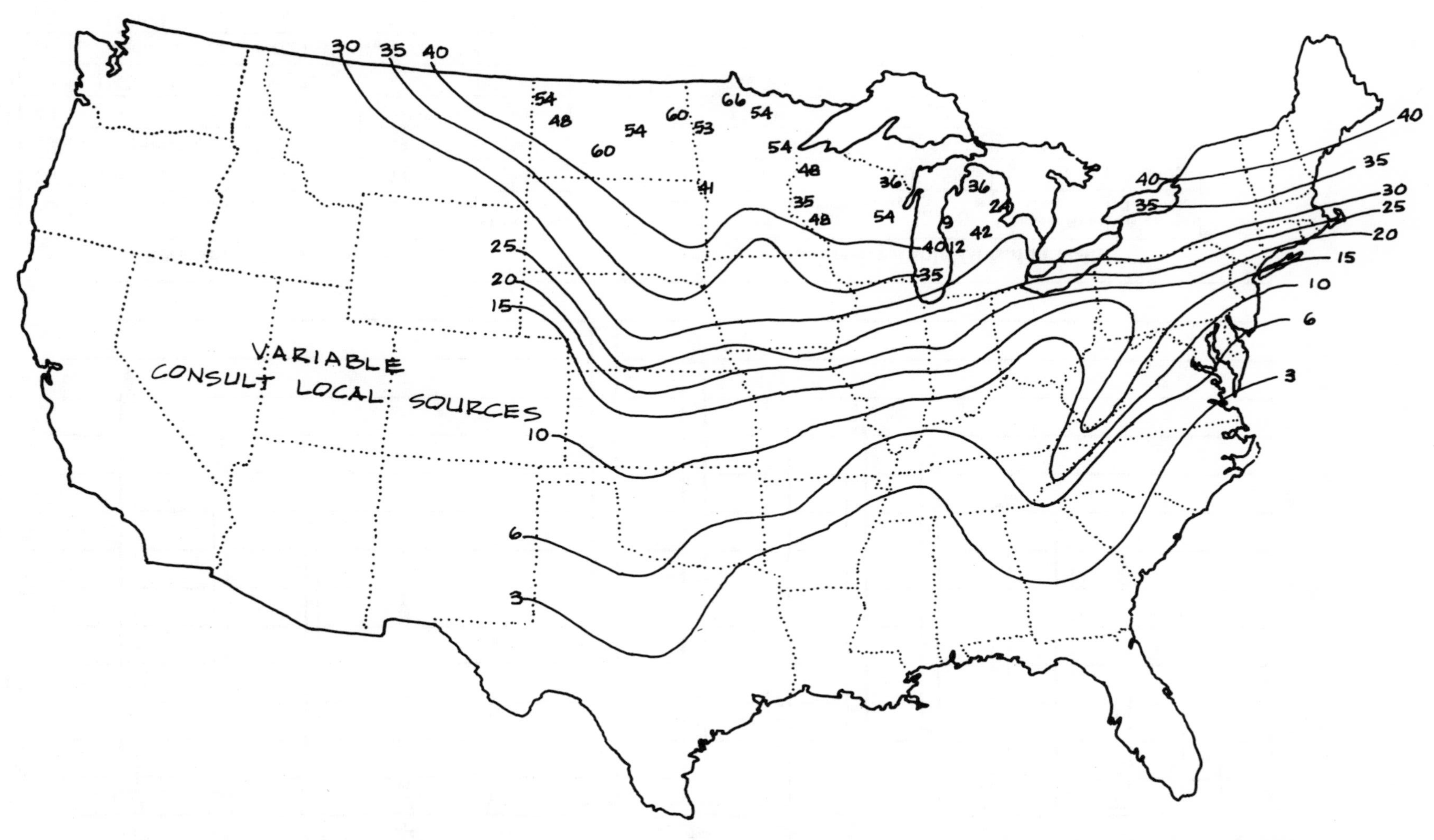
30
35
40
54
48
60
54
60
53
66
54
41
54
48
35
48
36
54
36
24
9
42
40
12
35
25
20
15
VARIABLE
CONSULT LOCAL SOURCES
10
6
3
40
35
30
25
20
15
10
6
3

FAA AC150/5320-6A 9/68

TABLE OF NAIL SIZES

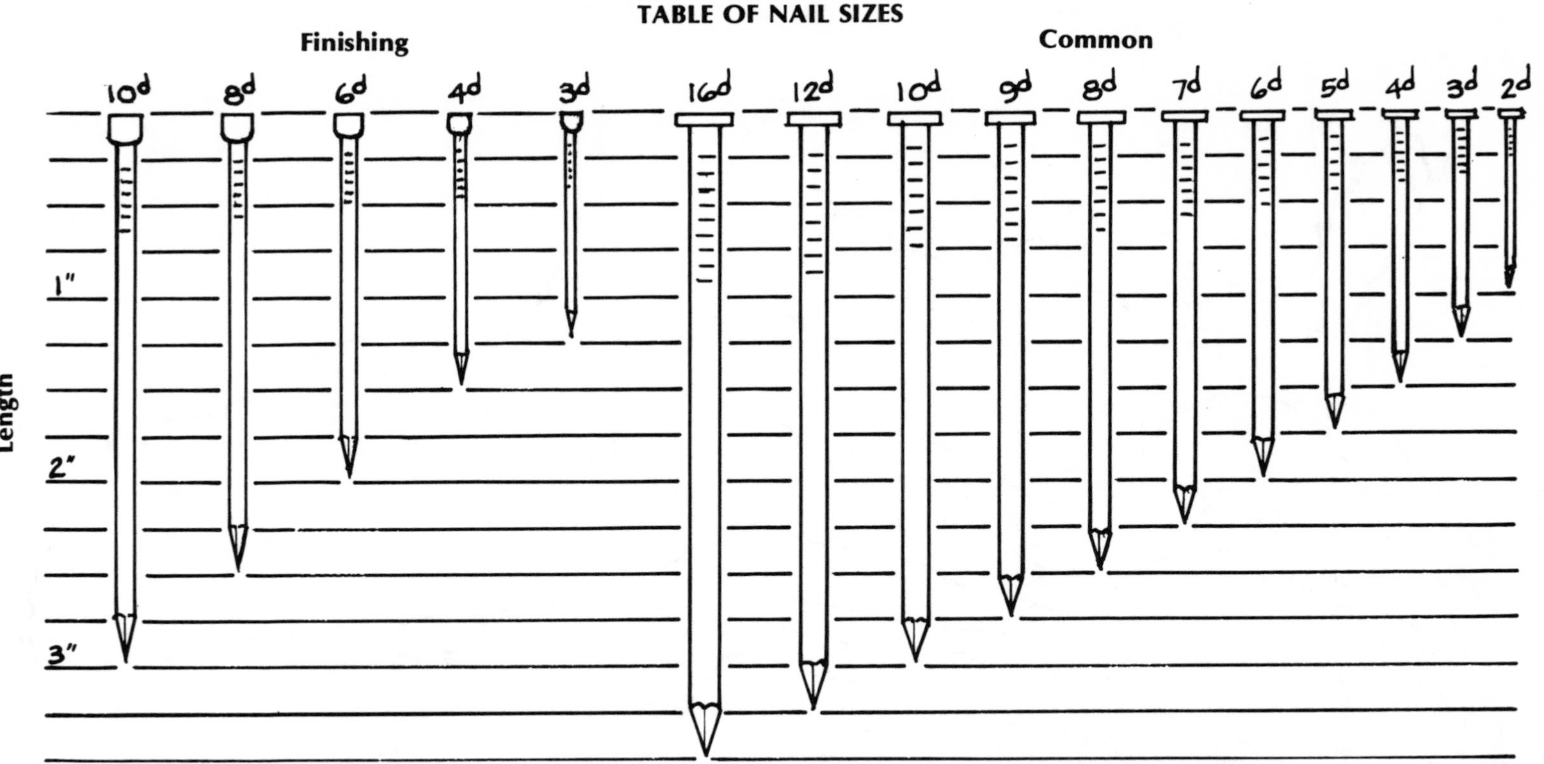
Finishing
Common
10d
8d
6d
4d
3d
16d
12d
10d
9d
8d
7d
6d
5d
4d
3d
2d
Length
1"
2"
3"

Reference Table-Common Nails

Size	Length and Gauge	Diameter Head	Approx. No. To Pound
2d	1 inch ...... No. 15	11/64"	845
3d	1¼ inch ..... No. 14	13/64"	540
4d	1½" .... No. 12½	¼"	290
5d	1¾" inch .... No. 12½	¼"	250
6d	2 inch ...... No. 11½	17/64"	165
7d	2¼ inch ..... No. 11½	17/64"	150
8d	2½ inch ..... No. 10¼	9/32"	100
9d	2¾ inch ..... No. 10¼	9/32"	90
10d	3 inch ...... No. 9	5/16"	65
12d	3¼ inch ..... No. 9	5/16"	60
16d	3½ inch ..... No. 8	11/32"	45

Reference Table-Finishing Nails

Size	Length and Gauge	Diameter Head Gauge	Approx. No. To Pound
3d	1¼ inch ..... No. 15½	12½	880
4d	1½ inch ..... No. 15	12	630
6d	2 inch ...... No. 13	10	290
8d	2½ inch ..... No. 12½	9½	195
10d	3 inch ...... No. 11½	8½	125

The nails shown are those most commonly used.
There are many other types and sizes of nails.
Consult local sources of availability.

TABLE OF WOOD SCREWS

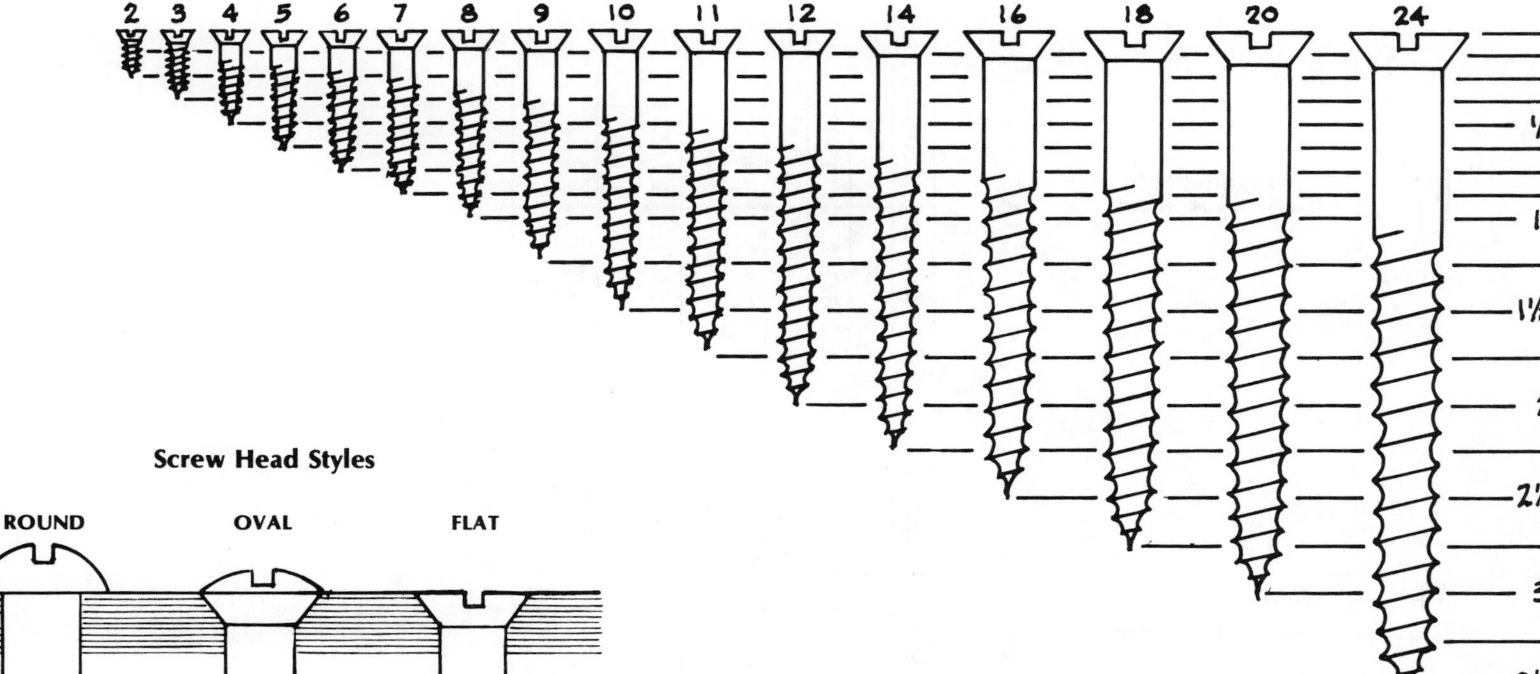
Shank Sizes
2
3
4
5
6
7
8
9
10
11
12
14
16
18
20
24
½"
1"
1½"
2"
2½"
3"
3½"
Screw Head Styles
ROUND
OVAL
FLAT

Wood Screw Length Variables

Gauge	Length
2	¼"-¾"
3	¼"-1"
4	¼"-1½"
5	⅜"-1½"
6	⅜"-2½"
7	⅜"-2½"
8	⅜"-3"
9	½"-3"

Gauge	Length
10	½"-3½"
11	⅝"-3½"
12	⅝"-4"
14	¾"-5"
16	1"-5"
18	1¼"-5"
20	1½"-5"
24	3"-5"

Increment of length =
⅛" increments up to 1",
¼" increments from 1¼" to 3",
½" increments from 3½" to 5".

TABLE OF BOLT SIZES

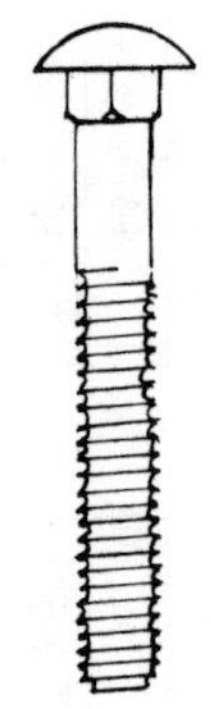
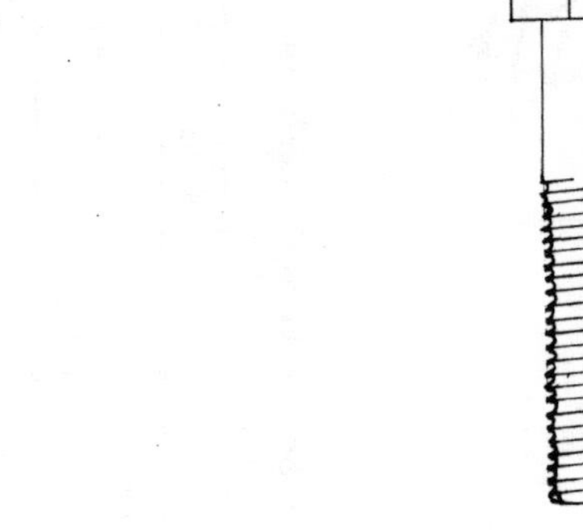
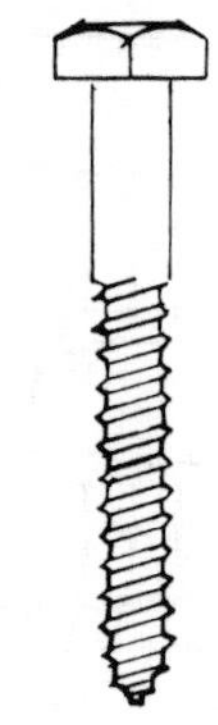

CARRIAGE

Diameter	Length
1/4″	3/4″-8″
5/16″	3/4″-8″
3/8″	3/4″-12″
7/16″	1″-12″
1/2″	1″-20″
9/16″	1″-20″
5/8″	1″-20″
3/4″	1″-20″

MACHINE

Diameter	Length
1/4″	1/2″-8″
5/16″	1/2″-8″
3/8″	3/4″-12″
7/16″	3/4″-12″
1/2″	3/4″-24″
9/16″	1″-30″
5/8″	1″-30″
3/4″	1″-30″
7/8″	1 1/2″-30″
1″	1 1/2″-30″

LAG

Diameter	Length
1/4″	1″-6″
5/16″	1″-10″
3/8″	1″-12″
7/16″	1″-12″
1/2″	1″-12″
5/8″	1 1/2″-16″
3/4″	1 1/2″-16″
7/8″	2″-16″
1″	2″-16″

Increments of length =
¼″ increments up to 6″,
½″ increments up to 8″,
1″ increments over 8″.

APPROXIMATE WEIGHTS OF MATERIALS

Soil, Etc.	lbs. per cu. ft.
Clay, damp	110
Clay, dry	63
Sand or gravel, loose & dry	90-105
Sand or gravel, wet	118-120
Topsoil, loose & dry	76
Topsoil, moist & packed	96

Stone	lbs. per cu. ft.
Granite	175
Limestone & Marble	165
Sandstone & Bluestone	147
Slate	175

Concrete	lbs. per cu. ft
With stone, reinforced	150
With stone, not reinforced	144
With Perlite	35-50
With Vermiculite	25-60

Fluids	lbs. per cu. ft.
Gasoline	75
Water at 4°C.	62.4
Water, ice	56

Metals	lbs. per cu. ft.
Aluminum, cast	165
Bronze, statuary	509
Iron, cast gray	450
Iron, wrought	485
Lead	710
Steel, rolled	490

Wood (12% MC)	lbs per cu. ft
Birch & Red Oak	44
Cedar, western red	23
Douglas Fir	34
Oak, white	47
Pine, southern	29-36
Redwood	28

Masonry (with mortar)	lbs. per sq. ft.
4″ brick	35
4″ stone or gravel	34
6″ concrete block	50
8″ stone, gravel, block	58
12″ stone, gravel, block	90

TABLES OF MEASUREMENT

Weights

English (Avoirdupois)		Metric	
1 ton	= 2,000 pounds	1 ton	= 1,000 Kilograms
1 pound	= 16 ounces	1 kilogram	= 1,000 grams
1 ounce	= 16 drams	1 gram	= 1,000 milligrams
1 dram	= 27.34 grains		

Liquid

1 gallon	= 4 quarts	1 liter	= 1,000 milliliters
1 quart	= 2 pints		
1 pint	= 16 fluid ounces		

Length

1 mile	= 5,280 feet	1 kilometer	= 1,000 meters
1 furlong	= 40 rods	1 meter	= 100 centimeters
1 rod	= 5½ yards	1 centimeter	= 10 millimeters
1 yard	= 3 feet		
1 foot	= 12 inches		

Surface

1 square mile	= 640 acres	1 square kilometer	= 100 hectares
1 acre	= 43,560 square feet	1 hectare	= 10,000 square meters
1 square yard	= 9 square feet		
1 square foot	= 144 square inches		

MEASUREMENT EQUIVALENTS

Length

Meter	= 1.093 yards	Yard	= 0.9144 meter
	= 3.281 feet	Foot	= 0.3048 meter
	= 39.370 inches	Inch	= 0.0254 meter
Kilometer	= 0.621 mile	Mile	= 1.609 kilometers

MEASUREMENT EQUIVALENTS (Continued)

Metric (cont.)		English (cont.)	

Surface

Square meter	= 1.196 square yards	Square yard	= 0.836 square meter
	= 10.764 square feet	Square foot	= 0.092 square meter
Square centimeter	= 0.155 square inch	Square inch	= 6.45 square centimeters
Square kilometer	= 0.386 square mile	Square mile	= 2.590 square kilometers
Hectare	= 2.471 acres	Acre	= 0.405 hectare

Volume

Cubic meter	= 1.308 cubic yards	Cubic yard	= 0.764 cubic meter
	= 35.314 cubic feet	Cubic foot	= 0.028 cubic meter
Cubic centimeter	= 0.061 cubic inch	Cubic inch	= 16.387 cubic centimeters
Stere	= 0.275 cord (wood)	Cord	= 3.624 steres

Capacity

Liter	= 1.056 U.S. liquid quarts	U.S. liquid quart	= 0.946 liter
	or 0.880 English liquid quart	Dry quart	= 1.111 liters
	= 0.908 dry quart	U.S. gallon	= 3.785 liters
	= 0.264 U.S. gallon or	English gallon	= 4.543 liters
	= 0.220 English gallon	U.S. bushel	= 0.352 hectoli
Hectoliter	= 2.837 U.S. bushels or	English bushel	= 0.363 hectoli
	= 2.75 English bushels		

Weight

Gram	= 15.432 grains	Grain	= 0.0648 gram
	= 0.032 troy ounce	Troy ounce	= 31.103 grams
	= 0.0352 avoirdupois ounce	Avoirdupois ounce	= 28.35 grams
Kilogram	= 2.2046 pounds avoirdupois	Pound	= 0.4536 kilogram
Metric ton	= 2204.62 pounds avoirdupois	Short ton	= 0.907 metric
Carat	= 3.08 grains avoirdupois		

CONVERSION FACTORS

When you know:	You can find:	If you multiply by:
Area		
acres	sq. feet	43,560.
acres	sq. meters	4,046.8
sq. centimeters	sq. feet	0.00108
sq. centimeters	sq. inches	0.1550
sq. feet	sq. centimeters	929.03
sq. feet	sq. inches	144.
sq. feet	sq. meters	0.0929
sq. feet	sq. yards	0.1111
sq. inches	sq. centimeters	6.4516
sq. inches	sq. feet	0.00694
sq. inches	sq. meters	0.000645
sq. meters	sq. feet	10.764
sq. meters	sq. yards	1.196
sq. yards	sq. feet	9.
sq. yards	sq. meters	0.8361
Energy and Power		
Btu	foot pounds	778.2
Btu per min.	horsepower	0.02358
foot pounds	Btu	0.001285
foot pounds	kilogram-meters	0.13826
ft-lb per min.	horsepower	0.0000303
horsepower	Btu per min.	42.41
horsepower	ft-lb per min.	33,000.
horsepower	ft-lb per sec.	550.
horsepower	kilowatts	0.7457
kilogram-meters	foot-pounds	7.2330
Flow		
cubic feet per sec.	cubic meters per sec.	0.02832
gallons/minute	cubic meters per sec.	0.0000631
gallons/minute	cubic meters per hr.	0.22716

CONVERSION FACTORS (Continued)

When you know:	You can find:	If you multiply by:
Length		
centimeters	inches	0.3937
centimeters	yards	0.01094
feet	inches	12.0
feet	meters	0.30481
feet	yards	0.333
inches	centimeters	2.540
inches	feet	0.08333
inches	meters	0.02540
inches	millimeters	25.400
inches	yards	0.2778
kilometers	feet	3,281.
kilometers	miles (nautical)	0.5336
kilometers	miles (statute)	0.6214
kilometers	yards	1,094.
meters	feet	3.2809
meters	yards	1.0936
miles (statute)	feet	5,280.
miles (statute)	kilometers	1.6093
miles (statute)	meters	1,609.34
miles (statute)	yards	1,760.
miles (nautical)	feet	6,080.2
miles (nautical)	kilometers	1.8520
miles (nautical)	meters	1,852.0
millimeters	inches	0.03937
rods	meters	5.0292
yards	centimeters	91.44
yards	feet	3.0
yards	inches	36.0
yards	meters	0.9144
Pressure		
grams per cu. cm.	oz. per cu. in.	0.5780
kilograms per sq. cm.	pounds per sq. in.	14.223
kilograms per sq. meter	pounds per sq. ft.	0.2048
kilograms per sq. meter	pounds per sq. yd.	1.8433
kilograms per cu. meter	pounds per cu. ft.	0.06243
ounces per cu. in.	grams per cu. cm.	1.7300
pounds per cu. ft.	kilograms per cu. meter	16.019
pounds per sq. ft.	kilograms per sq. meter	4.8824
pounds per sq. in.	kilograms per sq. cm.	0.0703
pounds per sq. yd.	kilograms per sq. meter	0.5425

CONVERSION FACTORS (Continued)

When you know:	You can find:	If you multiply by:
Velocity		
feet per minute	meters per sec.	0.00508
feet per second	meters per sec.	0.3048
inches per second	meters per sec.	0.0254
kilometers per hour	meters per sec.	0.2778
knots	meters per sec.	0.5144
miles per hour	meters per sec.	0.4470
miles per minute	meters per sec.	26.8224
Volume		
cubic centimeters	cubic inches	0.06102
cubic feet	cubic inches	1,728.0
cubic feet	cubic meters	0.0283
cubic feet	cubic yards	0.0370
cubic feet	gallons	7.481
cubic feet	liters	28.32
cubic feet	quarts	29.9222
cubic inches	cubic centimeters	16.39
cubic inches	cubic feet	0.0005787
cubic inches	cubic meters	0.00001639
cubic inches	liters	0.0164
cubic inches	gallons	0.004329
cubic inches	quarts	0.01732
cubic meters	cubic feet	35.31
cubic meters	cubic inches	61,023.
cubic meters	cubic yards	1.3087
cubic yards	cubic feet	27.0
cubic yards	cubic meters	0.7641
gallons	cubic feet	0.1337
gallons	cubic inches	231.0
gallons	cubic meters	0.003785
gallons	liters	3.785
gallons	quarts	4.0
liters	cubic feet	0.03531
liters	cubic inches	61.017
liters	gallons	0.2642
liters	pints	2.1133
liters	quarts	1.057
liters	cubic meters	0.0010
pints	cubic meters	0.004732
pints	liters	0.4732
pints	quarts	0.50

CONVERSION FACTORS (Continued)

When you know:	You can find:	If you multiply by:
quarts	cubic feet	0.03342
quarts	cubic inches	57.75
quarts	cubic meters	0.0009464
quarts	gallons	0.25
quarts	liters	0.9464
quarts	pints	2.0
Weight		
grams	kilograms	0.001
grams	ounces	0.03527
grams	pounds	0.002205
kilograms	ounces	35.274
kilograms	pounds	2.2046
ounces	grams	28.35
ounces	kilograms	0.02835
ounces	pounds	0.0625
pounds	grams	453.6
pounds	kilograms	0.4536
pounds	ounces	16.0

ACKNOWLEDGMENTS

Many professional firms and individuals contributed to this book and the author is deeply indebted to their generosity. In the case of drawings, credit lines have been provided at the bottom of each. Photographs, unless credited otherwise, are by the author. Many photographs do not contain credit lines for the designer involved due to the inavailability of that information when the photograph was taken. Designers are invited to contact the author at the publisher's address to provide this information for any future revisions. Some of the drawings for the second edition were prepared by Cathy Lambert.

INDEX